LEADING

CONSTITUTIONAL

DECISIONS

SIXTEENTH EDITION

Robert F. Cushman

PRENTICE-HALL, INC., Englewood Cliffs, New Jersey 07632

Library of Congress Cataloging in Publication Data

Cushman, Robert F. (date)
  Leading constitutional decisions.

  1. United States—Constitutional law—
Cases. I. Title.
KF4549.C83 1981   342.73'002643   81-13923
ISBN 0-13-527374-9   347.30202643   AACR2

Editorial production supervision
  and interior design by *Edith Riker*
Cover design by *Jayne Conte*
Manufacturing buyer *Edmund W. Leone*

Printed in the United States of America

10 9 8 7 6 5 4

ISBN 0-13-527374-9

Prentice-Hall International, Inc., *London*
Prentice-Hall of Australia Pty. Limited, *Sydney*
Prentice-Hall of Canada, Ltd., *Toronto*
Prentice-Hall of India Private Limited, *New Delhi*
Prentice-Hall of Japan, Inc., *Tokyo*
Prentice-Hall of Southeast Asia Pte. Ltd., *Singapore*
Whitehall Books Limited, *Wellington, New Zealand*

Contents

Table of Cases

Boldface capitals (with boldface page numbers) indicate the cases reprinted in this text; italic type indicates cases commented on in the notes; roman type indicates cases quoted or discussed in the Court opinions. For convenience, all cases in which the United States is plaintiff are also indexed under the name of the defendant.

Martin v. Hunter's Lessee, 1 Wheat. 304 (1816)   110
Martin v. Mott, 12 Wheat. 19 (1827)   12, 38
Maryland v. Wirtz, 392 U. S. 183 (1968)   104, 105ff.
Massachusetts v. Mellon, 262 U. S. 447 (1923)   10, 261
Massiah v. United States, 377 U. S. 201 (1964)   297
Maxwell v. Dow, 176 U. S. 581 (1900)   138f., 173, 175
Mayer v. Chicago, 404 U. S. 189 (1971)   177
McCabe v. Atchison, T. & S. F. Ry. Co., 235 U. S. 151 (1914)   327
McCardle, Ex parte, 7 Wall. 506 (1869)   22, *120*
McCollum v. Board of Education, 333 U. S. 203 (1948)   269, 270ff.
McCray v. United States, 195 U. S. 27 (1904)   35
McCulloch v. Maryland, 4 Wheat. 316 (1819)   *3,* 53, **59,** *80, 103,* 110
McDaniel v. Barresi, 402 U. S. 39 (1971)   349, 351
McGautha v. California, 402 U. S. 183 (1971)   308f., 312, 319
McGrain v. Daugherty, 273 U. S. 135 (1927)   26f., 30
McLaurin v. Oklahoma State Regents, 339 U. S. 637 (1950)   333f.
Meek v. Pittenger, 421 U. S. 349 (1975)   267
Memoirs v. Massachusetts, 383 U. S. 413 (1966)   221f.
Merryman, Ex parte, 17 Fed. Cas 144 (No. 9487) (1861)   119
Metcalf & Eddy v. Mitchell, 269 U. S. 514 (1926)   105
Metromedia v. San Diego, July 2, 1981   244
Meyer v. Nebraska, 262 U. S. 390 (1923)   164, 196ff.
Michael M. v. Sonoma County, March 23, 1981   See Rostker
Michigan v. De Fillippo, 443 U. S. 31 (1979)   277
Michigan v. Tucker, 417 U. S. 433 (1974)   280
Miller v. California, 413 U. S. 15 (1973)   221f.
Milligan, Ex parte, 4 Wall. 2 (1866)   *23,* **118,** *127, 230*
Milliken v. Bradley, 418 U. S. 717 (1974)   331
Minersville School District v. Gobitis, 310 U. S. 586 (1940)   259
Miranda v. Arizona, 384 U. S. 436 (1966)   290, **295,** 310
Mississippi v. Johnson, 4 Wall. 475 (1867)   49, 120
Missouri ex rel. Gaines v. Canada, 305 U. S. 337 (1938)   327, 333
Missouri v. Lewis, 101 U. S. 22 (1880)   160
Moore v. Dempsey, 261 U. S. 86 (1923)   174, 176
Morehead v. New York ex rel. Tipaldo, 298 U. S. 587 (1936)   151
Mugler v. Kansas, 123 U. S. 623 (1887)   150
Mulford v. Smith, 307 U. S. 38 (1939)   92, 97, 111
Muller v. Oregon, 208 U. S. 412 (1908)   150, 365
Munn v. Illinois, 94 U. S. 113 (1877)   148
Murdock v. Pennsylvania, 319 U. S. 104 (1943)   193
Murray v. Goldstein, 385 U. S. 816 (1966)   261
Murray's Lessee v. Hoboken Land & Improvement Co., 18 How. 272 (1856)   158, 159
Muskrat v. United States, 219 U. S. 346 (1911)   9
Myers v. United States, 272 U. S. 52 (1926)   43
NAACP v. Alabama, 357 U. S. 449 (1958)   192, 243
NAACP v. Alabama, 377 U. S. 288 (1964)   243
NAACP v. Button, 371 U. S. 415 (1963)   243
NLRB v. Jones & Laughlin Steel Corp., 301 U. S. 1 (1937)   92, 96, 111
National League of Cities v. Usery, 426 U. S. 833 (1976)   103
Neagle, In re, 135 U. S. 1 (1890)   39
Near v. Minnesota, 283 U. S. 697 (1931)   *164,* 173, **219,** *244*
Nebbia v. New York, 291 U. S. 502 (1934)   149
Nebraska Press Asso. v. Stuart, 427 U. S. 539 (1976)   232, 234, 236, 239
New Jersey v. Portash, 440 U. S. 450 (1979)   298
New York Times Co. v. United States, 403 U. S. 713 (1971)   229

Preface

No one can understand fully and clearly how our American national government works, or how it came to be the kind of government it is, unless he is familiar with the way in which the Supreme Court of the United States does its work, and with some of its decisions which are milestones in the growth of our American constitutional system. This collection of cases is intended primarily to serve the needs of students of American government and American history.

The Supreme Court does not work in a vacuum. Its decisions upon important constitutional questions can be fully understood only when viewed against the background of history, politics, and economics out of which they grew. The brief introductory notes attempt to reconstruct this background, to suggest the significance of the cases in our constitutional development, and, to a limited extent, to indicate the relationship of the decisions printed to other, and perhaps equally important, ones which could not be included.

In editing the cases and writing the notes the guiding assumptions have, in general, been these: (1) The job of the Supreme Court is to provide reasoned opinions so that lower courts and administrators can apply its rulings intelligently to similar problems; (2) The extent to which the Court supplies such guidance and the skill with which it develops its present reasoning from what has gone before are measures of how well it is doing its job; and (3) students should be encouraged to evaluate this aspect of the Court's work.

For these reasons the emphasis in this edition, as in earlier ones, is on the evolution of the ideas used to explain our Constitution rather than on stating "the law" of any particular moment. And so that students will have ammunition with which to do intellectual battle, some important dissents have been included and a fuller exploration of a few problems has been favored over a more superficial treatment of many.

Loyal and valued users of the earlier edition may, like the author himself, find some favorite subject missing. But the preparation of a new edition inevitably involves parting with old friends and it is only hoped that the new ones will be as useful and as much fun to know. The following cases printed in the 15th edition have been omitted from the 16th, though for the most part they have been summarized in the notes: United States v. Butler; Heart of Atlanta Motel v. United States; United States v. Robel; New York Times Co. v. United States; Paris Adult Theater v. Slaton; United States v. Robinson; Bolling v. Sharpe; Furman v. Georgia; Milliken v. Bradley. In their place have been added: National League of Cities v. Usery; Richmond Newspaper Co. v. Virginia; United States v. Peltier; Gregg v. Georgia; University of California v. Bakke; Geduldig v. Aiello; Rostker vs. Goldberg.

In the interest of an up-to-date book, cases have been added and the notes have been updated through the end of the 1980–1981 term of the Supreme Court.

Robert F. Cushman

The Judicial Branch

MARBURY v. MADISON

1 Cranch 137; 2 L. Ed. 60 (1803)

Although the election in the autumn of 1800 brought to the Federalists a defeat from which they never recovered, President Adams and his Federalist associates did not retire from office until March 1801. The Federalists had been for some time considering plans to reform the federal courts by remodeling the Judiciary Act of 1789, and now in the eleventh hour they boldly set themselves to the task with renewed energy in order, undoubtedly, to insure a fortress for Federalist principles which would not easily be broken down. Accordingly they passed the Judiciary Act of February 13, 1801, which relieved the Supreme Court justices of circuit court duty, reduced the size of the Supreme Court from six to five, and created six new circuit courts with 16 new judgeships. Two weeks later Congress passed an act providing that the President might appoint for the District of Columbia for five-year terms as many justices of the peace as he thought necessary. President Adams proceeded during the last 16 days of his administration to fill these newly created vacancies (58 in all) with loyal Federalists; and the task of signing their commissions occupied him until well into the night before the inauguration of Jefferson on March 4, 1801. Among the judicial appointments made by Adams in the closing weeks of his administration was that of John Marshall, a staunch Federalist, to be Chief Justice of the United States.

The federal courts had already incurred the bitter animosity of the Jeffersonians, largely because of the vigor with which they had enforced the obnoxious Alien and

Sedition Acts of 1798; and the Republicans were enraged beyond measure at what they deemed the effrontery of the Federalists in enacting the Judiciary Act of 1801. The judiciary was caustically referred to by Randolph as a "hospital for decayed politicians," while Jefferson wrote to a friend, "The Federalists have retired into the judiciary as a stronghold . . . and from that battery all the works of republicanism are to be beaten down and erased." One of the first efforts of the Republican administration was to repeal the Judiciary Act of 1801, and after a long and acrimonious debate this was accomplished, March 8, 1802. The repealing act restored the Supreme Court justices to circuit court duty, restored the size of the Supreme Court to six, and abolished the new circuit judgeships which had been created. The Federalists in Congress bitterly assailed the repealing statute as unconstitutional. Marshall himself apparently adhered to that view, and probably would have held the law void if it had come before him immediately in his judicial capacity. In order to prevent this, however, the repealing act had so altered the sessions of the Supreme Court that it did not convene again for 14 months, by which time acquiescence in the act by the judges affected made a decision of unconstitutionality impracticable.

However, when the Court convened in February 1803, the case of Marbury v. Madison was on the docket. Marbury was one of those whom President Adams had appointed to a five-year justiceship of the peace in the District of Columbia. His commission, signed and sealed on March 3, was among four that had not been delivered when Jefferson had taken office on March 4. It was, in fact, Marshall, then serving as Secretary of State as well as Chief Justice, who had sealed but had not delivered Marbury's commission. Jefferson immediately ordered his new Secretary of State, James Madison, to withhold the commission; and Marbury filed suit asking the Supreme Court in the exercise of its original jurisdiction to issue a writ of mandamus to compel Madison to give him his commission. The right to issue such a writ had been conferred upon the Court by a provision of the Judiciary Act of 1789, and jurisdiction thereunder had been exercised by the Court twice before Marshall's accession to the bench. When the case came on for argument, it assumed very largely the aspect of a quarrel between the President and the judiciary. Marbury's own interest in it was small, since Jefferson made it fairly clear that he had no intention of giving Marbury his commission even if the Court ordered him to do so. The Republicans seem to have expected that the Court would issue the mandamus asked for, and there were open threats that Marshall and his colleagues would be impeached if that occurred.

Marshall's decision that the Constitution forbade the Court to issue the writ of mandamus asked for by Marbury might have placated the Republicans had he not in their judgment gratuitously gone beyond the necessities of the case. While holding that the Court could not take jurisdiction and decide the case, inasmuch as the statute authorizing it was unconstitutional, he nonetheless pointed out that Marbury was entitled to his commission; that a writ of mandamus was the proper remedy; and that the executive was properly subject to mandamus if the case were started in the proper court. In addition he scolded the administration for not delivering the commission. In the storm of criticism thereby engendered, the judicial review aspect of the case seems largely to have escaped attack; and when, six months later, a circuit court held unconstitutional another act of Congress abolishing fees granted by an earlier law to justices of the peace in the District of Columbia, it evoked no criticism of any kind. The case, not in any offical report, is noted in Charles Warren's, *The Supreme Court in United States History.**

---

*Charles Warren, *The Supreme Court in United States History,* Vol. 1. (Boston: Little, Brown, 1947), p. 255.

No more vehement argument has ever raged in the field of constitutional law and theory than that over the genesis of the power of judicial review. Did the framers of the Constitution intend to grant the power as part of the checks and balances system in the first three articles? Or did Chief Justice Marshall "usurp" this power for the judiciary in his decision in Marbury v. Madison? Scholars still disagree, and the real intention of the framers will probably never be known. But a number of things are certain. It is certain that this was the first case in which the Supreme Court openly and clearly held unconstitutional an act of Congress. It is equally certain that the idea of judicial review did not originate with Marshall. Most of the arguments which he used in his famous opinion had been presented again and again in the debates in Congress on the Repeal Act of 1802, and the basic theory had been advanced by Hamilton in Number 78 of *The Federalist.* Moreover, the lower federal courts, without exciting opposition, had held invalid the act of Congress making them, in effect, claims commissioners for pension claims (a fact pointed out by Marshall in his opinion); and a number of earlier state cases have been considered as embodying the principle; see Bayard v. Singleton (1787). That Marshall cited no precedents to bolster his interpretation of judicial power is not particularly surprising. As a jurist he relied heavily on deductive reasoning, and in neither Gibbons v. Ogden nor McCulloch v. Maryland, two of his most famous opinions, did he cite a single case as precedent.

There is evidence that public opinion tended to look upon the power of judicial review as one of the normal incidents of judicial power. The Court considered the constitutionality of the carriage tax in Hylton v. United States (1796); and its refusal to declare it unconstitutional, as well as the refusal of the lower federal courts to hold unconstitutional the Alien and Sedition Acts and the United States Bank Charter, was bitterly condemned by the Republicans, who seemed to feel that the courts were neglecting their duty in not sustaining the Constitution against legislative usurpation of power. That Congress itself recognized the power is perhaps evidenced by their alteration of the term of the Supreme Court to prevent the Repeal Act of 1802 from coming to the Court for review for more than a year after its enactment.

The power of the Supreme Court to declare acts of Congress unconstitutional has so long been an integral part of our constitutional system, and Marshall's reasoning in the case of Marbury v. Madison is so impressive, that it is easy to lose sight of the fact that a most cogent argument may be made against the establishment of the power, and that had the Supreme Court never enjoyed it no very calamitous results would have ensued. Jefferson, Marshall's most bitter personal and political adversary, never admitted the paramount authority of the Supreme Court to determine the validity of an act of Congress, but held that each of the three departments of the national government being equal and separate was equally empowered "to decide on the validity of an act according to its own judgement and uncontrolled by the opinions of any other department." This view was shared by many other thoughtful men of the day. In the exercise of its power of judicial review the Court will not pass upon what it terms "political questions," questions the final determination of which has been confided by the Constitution to the discretion of the political departments, that is, the legislative or the executive. According to the view of Jefferson and his followers, all questions involving the constitutionality of acts of Congress which might come before the Court would be "political questions." The statute might conflict with the Constitution, but that fact would not of itself endow the Court with any power to invalidate it; rather it would be the duty of the Court to enforce the statute without questioning its validity. That such a system would not have been followed by any strikingly disastrous results may be inferred from the fact that in most of the constitutional governments of the world the courts do not enjoy the power of judicial review, and that in this country fewer than 150 statutes of

Congress have been held unconstitutional, of which only a very few involved problems of any vital or lasting importance. As Justice Holmes declared, "The United States would not come to an end if we lost our power to declare an act of Congress void." In fact, the power to declare an act of Congress invalid is a power very much less important to the Supreme Court than the power to pass upon the validity of state legislation. This last authority may well be regarded as vital to the preservation of our federal system by providing a necessary method of preventing the state governments from encroaching upon the domain of federal authority or impairing the federal rights and immunities of the individual.

The case of Marbury v. Madison has a certain strategic significance which should not be left out of account. The next case in which an act of Congress was invalidated by the Supreme Court was the famous Dred Scott case, decided in 1857. By that time nearly 70 years had elapsed from the time of the formation of our constitutional system, and the Court was composed of men holding nationalistic views far less strong than those of Marshall and his associates. Moreover, Marbury v. Madison involved the use of judicial power to protect the Court itself against interference by the legislature, a use reasonably easy to justify in view of the separation of powers; while the Dred Scott case involved the use of congressional power in quite another field. Had the power of judicial review not been exercised and the doctrine established in the case of Marbury v. Madison, one may well conjecture whether our constitutional development would have been the same.

The Supreme Court has always had its critics, and following particularly unpopular decisions invalidating acts of Congress the attacks have been exceedingly bitter. Such decisions as the Dred Scott case, the Income Tax Cases, and a whole series of cases prior to 1937 which invalidated social legislation, stirred up opposition which reduced the prestige of the Court and which endured until either a constitutional amendment or the Court itself changed the effect of the ruling. Recognizing the wide latitude left to the judges in interpreting the Constitution, and the manifest political and economic character of many of their decisions, a number of critics have attacked the power of judicial review as an undemocratic instrument of government in an increasingly democratic society, and from time to time some of the justices on the Court itself have appeared to share this view. It was in response to such critics that Justice Roberts, speaking for six members of the Court in United States v. Butler (1936), felt called upon to explain the role of the Court in exercising its power of judicial review. "When an act of Congress is appropriately challenged in the courts as not conforming to the constitutional mandate the judicial branch of the Government has only one duty,—to lay the article of the Constitution which is invoked beside the statute which is challenged and to decide whether the latter squares with the former. All the court does, or can do, is to announce its considered judgment upon the question. The only power it has, if such it may be called, is the power of judgment. This court neither approves nor condemns any legislative policy. Its delicate and difficult office is to ascertain and declare whether the legislation is in accordance with, or in contravention of, the provisions of the Constitution; and, having done that, its duty ends."

Against the background of this conflict it is interesting to note that at no time in our history has the power of judicial review been seriously endangered. Despite attacks on the Court's decisions, on its personnel, and even on the procedures by which review is exercised, no major political party has ever urged the complete abolition of the power of review itself. The resounding defeat in Congress of the so-called "Court Packing Plan," suggested by President Franklin D. Roosevelt at the height of his popularity, indicates that popular dissatisfaction with the use of the power of judicial review does not necessarily imply a feeling that the Court should be dominated by the political branches of the government.

Mr. Chief Justice Marshall delivered the opinion of the Court, saying in part:

In the order in which the court has viewed this subject, the following questions have been considered and decided.

1st. Has the applicant a right to the commission he demands? . . . [The Court finds that he has.]

2d. If he has a right, and that right has been violated, do the laws of his country afford him a remedy? . . . [The Court finds that they do.]

3d. If they do afford him a remedy, is it a mandamus issuing from this court? . . .

This, then, is a plain case for a mandamus, either to deliver the commission, or a copy of it from the record; and it only remains to be inquired,

Whether it can issue from this court.

The act to establish the judicial courts of the United States authorizes the Supreme Court "to issue writs of mandamus in cases warranted by the principles and usages of law, to any courts appointed, or persons holding office, under the authority of the United States."

The Secretary of State, being a person holding an office under the authority of the United States, is precisely within the letter of the description, and if this court is not authorized to issue a writ of mandamus to such an officer, it must be because the law is unconstitutional, and therefore absolutely incapable of conferring the authority, and assigning the duties which its words purport to confer and assign.

The constitution vests the whole judicial power of the United States in one Supreme Court, and such inferior courts as congress shall, from time to time, ordain and establish. . . .

In the distribution of this power it is declared that "the Supreme Court shall have original jurisdiction in all cases affecting ambassadors, other public ministers and consuls, and those in which a state shall be a party. In all other cases, the Supreme Court shall have appellate jurisdiction." . . .

If it had been intended to leave it in the discretion of the legislature to apportion the judicial power between the supreme and inferior courts according to the will of that body, it would certainly have been useless to have proceeded further than to have defined the judicial power, and the tribunals in which it should be vested. The subsequent part of the section is mere surplusage, is entirely without meaning, . . . the distribution of jurisdiction, made in the constitution, is form without substance. . . .

It cannot be presumed that any clause in the constitution is intended to be without effect; and, therefore, such a construction is inadmissible, unless the words require it. . . .

To enable this court, then, to issue a mandamus, it must be shown to be an exercise of appellate jurisdiction, or to be necessary to enable them to exercise appellate jurisdiction. . . .

It is the essential criterion of appellate jurisdiction, that it revises and corrects the proceedings in a cause already instituted, and does not create that cause. Although, therefore, a mandamus may be directed to courts, yet to issue such a writ to an officer for the delivery of a paper, is in effect the same as to sustain an original action for that paper, and, therefore, seems not to belong to appellate, but to original jurisdiction. Neither is it necessary in such a case as this, to enable the court to exercise its appellate jurisdiction.

The authority, therefore, given to the Supreme Court, by the act establishing the judicial courts of the United States, to issue writs of mandamus to public officers, appears not to be warranted by the constitution; and it becomes necessary to inquire whether a jurisdiction so conferred can be exercised.

The question, whether an act, repugnant to the constitution can become the law of the land, is a question deeply interesting to the United States; but, happily, not of an intricacy proportioned to its interest. It seems only necessary to recognize certain principles, supposed to have been long and well established, to decide it.

That the people have an original right to establish, for their future government, such principles, as, in their opinion, shall most conduce to their own happiness is the basis on which the whole American fabric has been erected. The exercise of this original right is a very great exertion; nor can it, nor ought it, to be frequently repeated. The principles, therefore, so established, are deemed fundamental. And as the authority from which they proceed is supreme, and can seldom act, they are designed to be permanent.

This original and supreme will organizes the government, and assigns to different departments their respective powers. It may either stop here, or establish certain limits not to be transcended by those departments.

The government of the United States is of the latter description. The powers of the legislature are defined and limited; and that those limits may not be mistaken, or forgotten, the Constitution is written. To what purpose are powers limited, and to what purpose is that limitation committed to writing, if these limits may, at any time, be passed by those intended to be restrained? The distinction between a government with limited and unlimited powers is abolished, if those limits do not confine the persons on whom they are imposed, and if acts prohibited and acts allowed, are of equal obligation. It is a proposition too plain to be contested, that the constitution controls any legislative act repugnant to it; or, that the legislature may alter the constitution by an ordinary act.

Between these alternatives there is no middle ground. The constitution is either a superior paramount law, unchangeable by ordinary means, or it is on a level with ordinary legislative acts, and, like other acts, is alterable when the legislature shall please to alter it.

If the former part of the alternative be true, then a legislative act contrary to the constitution is not law: if the latter part be true, then written constitutions are absurd attempts, on the part of the people, to limit a power in its own nature illimitable.

Certainly all those who have framed written constitutions contemplate them as forming the fundamental and paramount law of the nation, and, consequently, the theory of every such government must be, that an act of the legislature, repugnant to the constitution, is void.

This theory is essentially attached to a written constitution, and, is consequently, to be considered, by this court, as one of the fundamental principles of our society. It is not therefore to be lost sight of in the further consideration of this subject.

If an act of the legislature, repugnant to the constitution, is void, does it, notwithstanding its invalidity, bind the courts, and oblige them to give it effect? Or, in other words, though it be not law, does it constitute a rule as operative as if it was a law? This would be to overthrow in fact what was established in theory; and would seem, at first view, an absurdity too gross to be insisted on. It shall, however, receive a more attentive consideration.

It is emphatically the province and duty of the judicial department to say what the law is. Those who apply the rule to particular cases, must of necessity expound and interpret that rule. If two laws conflict with each other, the courts must decide on the operation of each.

So if a law be in opposition to the constitution; if both the law and the constitution apply to a particular case, so that the court must either decide that case conformably to the law, disregarding the constitution; or conformably to the constitution, disregarding the law; the court must determine which of these conflicting rules governs the case. This is of the very essence of judicial duty.

If, then, the courts are to regard the constitution, and the constitution is superior to any ordinary act of the legislature, the constitution, and not such ordinary act, must govern the case to which they both apply.

Those, then, who controvert the principle that the constitution is to be considered, in court, as a paramount law, are reduced to the necessity of maintaining that courts must close their eyes on the constitution, and see only the law.

This doctrine would subvert the very foundation of all written constitutions. It would declare that an act which, according to the principles and theory of our government, is entirely void, is yet, in practice, completely obligatory. It would declare that if the legislature shall do what is expressly forbidden, such act, notwithstanding the express prohibition, is in reality effectual. It would be giving to the legislature a practical and real omnipotence, with the same breath which professes to restrict their powers within narrow limits. It is prescribing limits, and declaring that those limits may be passed at pleasure.

That it thus reduces to nothing what we have deemed the greatest improvement on political institutions, a written constitution, would of itself be sufficient, in America, where written constitutions have been viewed with so much reverence, for rejecting the construction. But the peculiar expressions of the constitution of the United States furnish additional arguments in favor of its rejection.

The judicial power of the United States is extended to all cases arising under the constitution.

Could it be the intention of those who gave this power, to say that in using it the constitution should not be looked into? That a case arising under the constitution should be decided without examining the instrument under which it arises?

This is too extravagant to be maintained.

In some cases, then, the constitution must be looked into by the judges. And if they can open it all, what part of it are they forbidden to read or to obey?

There are many other parts of the constitution which serve to illustrate this subject.

It is declared that "no tax or duty shall be laid on articles exported from any state." Suppose a duty on the export of cotton, of tobacco, or of flour; and a suit instituted to recover it. Ought judgment to be rendered in such a case? ought the judges to close their eyes on the constitution, and only see the law?

The constitution declares "that no bill of attainder or ex post facto law shall be passed."

If, however, such a bill should be passed, and a person should be prosecuted under it, must the court condemn to death those victims whom the constitution endeavors to preserve?

"No person," says the constitution, "shall be convicted of treason unless on the testimony of two witnesses to the same overt act, or on confession in open court."

Here the language of the constitution is addressed especially to the courts. It prescribes, directly for them, a rule of evidence not to be departed from. If the legislature should change that rule, and declare one witness, or a confession out of court, sufficient for conviction, must the constitutional principle yield to the legislative act?

From these, and many other selections which might be made, it is apparent, that the framers of the constitution contemplated that instrument as a rule for the government of courts, as well as of the legislature.

Why otherwise does it direct the judges to take an oath to support it? This oath certainly applies in an especial manner, to their conduct in their official character. How immoral to impose it on them, if they were to be used as the instruments, and the knowing instruments, for violating what they swear to support!

The oath of office, too, imposed by the legislature, is completely demonstrative of the legislative opinion on this subject. It is in these words: "I do solemnly swear that I will administer justice without respect to persons, and do equal right to the poor and to the rich; and that I will faithfully and impartially discharge all the duties incumbent on me as———, according to the best of my abilities and understanding agreeably to the constitution and laws of the United States."

Why does a judge swear to discharge his duties agreeably to the constitution of the United States, if that constitution forms no rule for his government? if it is closed upon him, and cannot be inspected by him?

If such be the real state of things, this is worse than solemn mockery. To prescribe, or to take this oath, becomes equally a crime.

It is also not entirely unworthy of observation, that in declaring what shall be the supreme law of the land, the constitution itself is first mentioned; and not the laws of the United States generally, but those only which shall be made in pursuance of the constitution, have that rank.

Thus, the particular phraseology of the constitution of the United States confirms and strengthens the principle, supposed to be essential to all written constitutions, that a law repugnant to the constitution is void; and that courts, as well as other departments, are bound by that instrument.

The rule must be discharged.

BAKER v. CARR

369 U. S. 186; 82 S. Ct. 691; 7 L. Ed. 2d 663
(1962)

In his opinion in Marbury v. Madison (1803) Marshall grounded his constitutional argument for judicial review upon the language of Article III, which extends to the Supreme Court (and inferior courts) judicial power to be exercised in "all cases, in law and equity, arising under this Constitution. . . ." In short, the reason why the Court occasionally declares an act of Congress unconstitutional is that, according to Marshall, it has to do so in deciding the "cases and controversies" coming before it in the exercise of its "judicial power." Thus Marshall permanently tied judicial review to "cases and controversies." This has meant, over the years, that only when one of the parties in an actual "case" relies for his rights upon a statute will the Court undertake to decide whether or not that statute violates the Constitution; furthermore, it will do so only when such a decision is essential to the disposal of the case. Since Article III also extends judicial power to "such inferior courts as the Congress may from time to time ordain and establish," these lower courts also exercise the power of judicial review. Under the statutes, however, such lower court decisions on constitutional questions are subject to review by the Supreme Court, and almost invariably they are so reviewed. The Supreme Court has the last word.

But what is a "case" or "controversy" within the meaning of Article III? An essential requirement is that there be actual litigants with conflicting interests of such a nature that they are subject to judicial determination.

Following the admission to citizenship of the Cherokee Indians, Congress had by law altered the original distribution of tribal property. Since this had the effect of reducing the amount of lands and funds to which certain Indians were entitled, its constitutionality was seriously questioned. To settle the matter Congress passed an act specifically providing that David Muskrat and others might bring suits in the court of claims, with a right of appeal to the Supreme Court, to test the constitutionality of the redistribution statutes. The courts involved were ordered to give preference to these suits; the Attorney General was ordered to defend them; and if Muskrat et al. lost, the government was to pay their attorney's fees. In Muskrat v. United States (1911) the Supreme Court held there was no case or controversy involved and refused jurisdiction. The United States, the Court pointed out, was not claiming Muskrat's land and had no interest adverse to his. "The whole purpose of the law is to determine the constitutional validity of this class of legislation, in a suit not arising between parties concerning a property right necessarily involved in the decision in question, but in a proceeding against the government in its sovereign capacity, and concerning which the only judgment required is to settle the doubtful character of the legislation in question. . . . In a legal sense the judgment could not be executed, and amounts in fact to no more than an expression of opinion upon the validity of the acts in question."

Another critical component of a case or controversy is that the parties have "standing" to sue; that they allege the kind of personal injury that entitles them to judicial relief.

In 1923, in Frothingham v. Mellon, the Court held that the amount an individual taxpayer contributed to the funds of the United States was "comparatively minute and indeterminable": hence, the injury done to the taxpayer when Congress supported programs of which she did not approve was too slight to entitle her to sue to enjoin them.

Frothingham v. Mellon stood as a general bar to federal taxpayer's suits until 1968 when the Court held in Flast v. Cohen that a taxpayer could challenge the use of federal money to support religious schools. The Court distinguished the precision of the prohibition against aiding religion implicit in the First Amendment from the more general limits of the delegation of powers doctrine involved in the Frothingham case.

The importance of these seemingly technical legal questions regarding standing cannot be overemphasized, for it is in the decision of these issues that the Court establishes the role it will play in the governmental process. For example, it is not hard to imagine that the Court could reasonably have found that Mrs. Frothingham had suffered sufficient injury to warrant relief, thus opening up to judicial review all the things the government does with its money. And by deciding in the case below that a person was "injured" by malapportionment and thus had standing to sue, the Court extended to the judiciary control over this long-standing and seemingly insoluble problem. The extent to which the Court should play an "activist" role, moving aggressively into new areas to solve difficult social problems, or exercise "judicial self-restraint" and stay out of them, is a matter on which members of the Court over the years have been sharply and often bitterly divided. The opinions represent on the part of the justices a struggle to develop an intellectually coherent theory to explain and justify their position.

In the years following Flast v. Cohen (1968) the Court dealt with the problem of standing largely in terms of a person's right to complain about the actions of government agencies that affected him adversely. The essential test under Article III was whether the individual had alleged sufficient injury to provide a case or controversy, and in a series of cases the Court found injury in such widely varied allegations as: (1) The Comptroller of the Currency was permitting business competition by letting banks sell data processing services (Data Processing Service v. Camp, 1970); (2) The Secretary of Agriculture had changed the agricultural subsidy rules to make a tenant farmer more dependent on his landlord (Barlow v. Collins, 1970); and (3) The ICC was raising railroad rates, thus discouraging the use of recyclable materials and damaging the environment (United States v. SCRAP, 1973). Only in Sierra Club v. Morton (1972) did the Court fail to find injury. There the well-known nature club had sought to enjoin the building of a ski resort in Mineral King Valley and Sequoia National Park, but unlike the students involved in the SCRAP case, it had failed to claim that it or any of its members used the park and would suffer actual injury as a result of injury to the environment.

In distinguishing the SCRAP case from Sierra, the Court made clear that the only test was the threat of actual personal injury. "Unlike the specific and geographically limited federal action of which the petitioner complained in Sierra Club, the challenged agency action in this case is applicable to substantially all the Nation's railroads, and thus allegedly has an adverse environmental impact on all the natural resources of the country. Rather than a limited group of persons who used a picturesque valley in California, all persons of the country, and indeed all who breathe its air, could claim harm similar to that alleged by the environmental groups here. But we have already made it clear that standing is not to be denied simply because many people suffer the same injury. . . . To deny standing to persons who are in fact injured simply because many others are also injured, would mean that the most injurious and widespread Government actions could be questioned by nobody. We cannot accept that conclusion."

In Schlesinger v. Reservists To Stop the War (1974) members of the group brought a class action on behalf of themselves and all others who wanted to stop the war in

Vietnam by the process of persuading Congress to take action. They pointed out that Article I, §2, Cl. 3, provides that no person "holding office under the United States, shall be a member of either house" of Congress and challenged the membership of congressmen in the military reserves on the ground that they were personally injured by such membership both as citizens and as taxpayers. Such membership in the military, they argued, denied them representatives who could approach the Vietnam War question impartially.

The Court rejected their right to sue as citizens on the ground that they had failed to allege actual injury, since the failure of congressmen to observe the Incompatability Clause "would adversely affect only the generalized interest of all citizens in constitutional governance, and that is an abstract injury. . . . To permit a complainant who has no concrete injury to require a court to rule on important constitutional issues in the abstract would create the potential for abuse of the judicial process, distort the role of the Judiciary in its relationship to the Executive and the Legislature and open the Judiciary to an arguable charge of providing 'government by injunction'." The Court distinguished the Data Processing and SCRAP cases, noting that they provide "the setting for a focused consideration of a concrete injury," while in the present case "it can be only a matter of speculation whether the claimed violation has caused concrete injury to the particular complainant." Nor could they sue as taxpayers, since the Incompatibility Clause was not a limit on the spending power and thus did not meet the test of Flast v. Cohen. On the basis of similar reasoning it held in United States v. Richardson (1974) that a taxpayer had no standing to sue because Congress did not require an accounting from the Central Intelligence Agency despite a constitutional requirement that a "regular statement and account of the receipts and expenditures of all public money shall be published from time to time."

One other important corollary of the Court's refusal to exercise nonjudicial powers is the doctrine of "political questions." Very early in the exercise of its power of judicial review the Court pointed out that certain powers are vested in the legislative or executive departments of the government to be exercised in a purely discretionary manner, and that whether they have been constitutionally exercised or not is a "political question" which the Court will not undertake to decide. One of the early and very striking instances of this type of question was that which was raised in the famous case of Luther v. Borden (1849).

This case arose out of the following facts: The original constitution of Rhode Island, which was merely the colonial charter with a few minor adaptations, provided for a very restricted suffrage based upon the possession of property; and the right to vote continued to be thus limited long after universal manhood suffrage had been rather generally adopted throughout the country. Many efforts were made to have the constitution amended so as to put the franchise upon a more democratic basis, but all such attempts were defeated by the relatively small group of legal voters. In 1841 the popular feeling regarding the situation ran even higher than before; mass meetings were held throughout the state, and without any semblance of constitutional sanction the citizens were directed to choose by universal manhood suffrage, delegates to a constitutional convention. The convention thus formed duly met and drafted a new state constitution which established adult manhood suffrage and made many other changes. A popular referendum was conducted in which all the adult male citizens of the state were permitted to vote, and the new constitution was approved by a majority of the votes cast. The leader of the whole movement was a young lawyer, Thomas W. Dorr, who was elected governor under the new constitution and immediately attempted to put the new government into operation. The regular charter government, of course, did not recognize the validity of any of these acts. It called out the state militia, declared martial law, and finally appealed to President Tyler to send federal troops to aid in putting down the insurrection. The President took steps to comply with this request and the "Dorr Rebellion" collapsed. Dorr himself was captured, tried for treason, and finally sentenced to life imprisonment. He was later pardoned.

Luther had been a supporter of the Dorr movement; and in an effort to arrest him, Borden and others who were enrolled as members of the militia under the charter government broke into Luther's house. This act they justified upon the ground that martial law had been declared and that they were acting under the orders of their superior officers. Luther, however, sued Borden for trespass, claiming that the act of the legislature establishing martial law was void inasmuch as the Dorr government, elected by the people of the state, was the lawful government. (It should be noted that in January 1842, the charter government had called a constitutional convention and drafted a new constitution which was ratified by the people in due form and went into effect in 1843. Thus the Dorr movement did not entirely fail in its purposes.)

By the facts as presented in this case, the Supreme Court was invited to decide which of the two governments struggling for supremacy in Rhode Island in the year 1842 was the lawful one. But this question, replied the Court, was a "political question." The President in exercising the power conferred on him by Congress to send federal troops to aid states in suppressing insurrection had indicated that he regarded the charter government as the lawful government, and this decision was binding upon the Court. The Court intimated that Congress itself would also share the power of deciding between the competing governments by deciding which group of rival senators and representatives it would seat in Congress, but it was not asked to make such a decision. The Court declined to decide whether Rhode Island had a republican form of government within the meaning of the guaranty in the United States Constitution, Article IV, Sec. 4, but held that the enforcement of that guaranty was confided to the political departments of the government.

There are, of course, numerous other questions which have been held by the courts to be "political" in character. Such is the question whether there is a sufficient emergency to justify the President, acting under the authority of an act of Congress, in calling out the militia to repel invasion or to put down insurrection; see Martin v. Mott (1827). Such, also, are many of the questions which arise for determination in the course of conducting foreign relations; as, for instance, the recognition of a foreign government, the acquisition of territory, the determination of boundaries, the existence or termination of a treaty, and the like. The question whether or not a state of the Union has a republican form of government within the meaning of that clause of the Constitution guaranteeing such form of government was squarely raised in 1912 in the case of Pacific States Telephone & Telegraph Co. v. Oregon. In 1902 Oregon had amended the state constitution to establish the initiative and referendum. In 1906 a law was proposed by popular initiative and duly enacted by the people which imposed certain taxes on corporations. The plaintiff corporation resisted the payment of the tax on the ground that the incorporation of the initiative and referendum into the constitutional system of the state destroyed the republican character of its government and thus robbed it of lawful authority. The argument was that republican government means representative government and that representative government is destroyed by the system of direct legislation. The Supreme Court refused to pass on the question whether Oregon had a republican form of government or not, and pointed out that that question was political in character and had been determined by Congress in admitting senators and representatives of the state to their seats in Congress.

In Coleman v. Miller (1939) the Court held that most of the questions relating to the procedure of federal amendment are "political" in nature. The Court was there asked to rule that the Child Labor Amendment could no longer be validly ratified because it had been before the states for ratification for too long a time, and that a state which had once rejected a proposed amendment could not later ratify it. On each point the Court held that the final decision rested with Congress, not with the Court. But in Powell v. McCormack (1969) the Court rejected the contention of the House of Representatives that the question of Adam Clayton Powell Jr.'s right to his House seat was a political one because the Constitution made each house "the judge of the . . . qualifications of its own members." This power, the Court held, was limited to judging the existence of those qualifications for representatives explicitly stated in the Constitution —and only those. Powell, it was conceded, met these formal qualifications.

By far the most important political question in terms of its political impact on our system of government involved the apportionment of legislators, state and federal, among the election districts set within the states. One of the anomalous by-products of our system of representative government is the fact that voters are not equally represented in the legislature. This is true because the districts from which representatives are elected vary in population, with the result that the influence of one voter in electing his representative may be much greater than the influence of another voter in another district. Also the boundaries of legislative districts are drawn by state legislatures; and astute politicians, by the skillful juggling of these district lines, have achieved wonderful feats of inflating or deflating party voting strength by what is called the "gerrymander." Quite as important, however, is the effect of what is known as the "silent gerrymander," the underrepresentation of cities and overrepresentation of rural areas achieved simply by a failure over the years to redraw district lines to keep pace with the movement of the population from the farm to the city.

Both the state and federal legislatures had long felt the oppressive effect of the "silent gerrymander" in Illinois. The Illinois constitution of 1870 provided that the state should be divided into 51 state senatorial districts, from each of which one state senator and three state representatives should be chosen. The legislature, after each census, was to redraw the lines of these districts to meet changes in population. By the turn of the century it was obvious that more than half the population of the state would shortly be concentrated in the metropolitan area of Chicago. Legislators from the down-state rural districts, enjoying a comfortable legislative majority, felt no inclination to yield their political control by reapportioning the state to give the growing metropolis the proportion of the 51 districts to which its population clearly entitled it.

Nor were they any more willing to grant Chicago its fair share of the congressional seats awarded to Illinois after each decennial census. Finally, with one congressional district in Chicago having a population of 914,053, while one in southern Illinois had only 112,116, the Supreme Court was asked in Colegrove v. Green (1946) to enjoin the use of these districts in the impending election. The Court, voting four to three, denied the injunction. Speaking for himself and Justices Reed and Burton, Justice Frankfurter held the matter to be a political question. Since the "times, manner and places" clause of Art. I, Sec. 4, gave Congress power to secure fair representation, it was up to Congress or the states to cure the inequities. "Whether Congress faithfully discharges its duty or not, the subject has been committed to the exclusive control of Congress. An aspect of government from which the judiciary, in view of what is involved, has been excluded by the clear intention of the Constitution cannot be entered by the federal courts because Congress may have been in default in exacting from States obedience to its mandate." This opinion was widely construed as the ruling of the case, although Justice Rutledge concurred on different grounds.

The first break in the Court's attitude came in 1960 in the case of Gomillion v. Lightfoot. There the Court, without passing upon the truth of the alleged discrimination, unanimously rejected the idea that legislative apportionment could never be the subject for judicial review. The issue raised was unique. An Alabama statute of 1957 had redefined the boundaries of the city of Tuskeegee, within which is the well-known

Tuskeegee Institute. The city, which had been square in shape, was transformed "into a strangely irregular twenty-eight sided figure," with the intention and result of removing from the city "all save four or five of its 400 Negro voters while not removing a single white voter or resident." The Negroes thus excluded could not, as a result, vote in municipal elections. The lower federal courts, relying in part upon Colegrove v. Green, had dismissed the complaint attacking the validity of the statute. In an opinion by Justice Frankfurter, eight justices agreed that the plaintiffs had a right to have a court decide whether the weird apportionment denied them the right to vote in violation of the Fifteenth Amendment. Justice Whittaker, denying that the right to vote was involved "inasmuch as no one has the right to vote in . . . an area in which he does not reside," argued that the discrimination violated both the equal protection and due process clauses of the Fourteenth Amendment.

Mr. Justice Brennan delivered the opinion of the Court, saying in part:

This civil action was brought . . . to redress the alleged deprivation of federal constitutional rights. The complaint, alleging that by means of a 1901 statute of Tennessee apportioning the members of the General Assembly among the State's 95 counties, "these plaintiffs and others similarly situated, are denied the equal protection of the laws accorded them by the Fourteenth Amendment to the Constitution of the United States by virtue of the debasement of their votes," was dismissed by a three-judge court. . . . We hold that the dismissal was error, and remand the cause to the District Court for trial and further proceedings consistent with this opinion.

The General Assembly of Tennessee consists of the Senate with 33 members and the House of Representatives with 99 members. The Tennessee Constitution provides in Art. II as follows: . . . [The text of sections 3-6 follows.]

Thus, Tennessee's standard for allocating legislative representation among her counties is the total number of qualified voters resident in the respective counties, subject only to minor qualifications. . . . In 1901 the General Assembly abandoned separate enumeration in favor of reliance upon the Federal Census and passed the Apportionment Act here in controversy. In the more than 60 years since that action, all proposals in both Houses of the General Assembly for reapportionment have failed to pass.

Between 1901 and 1961, Tennessee has experienced substantial growth and redistribution of her population. In 1901 the population was 2,020,616, of whom 487,380 were eligible to vote. The 1960 Federal Census reports the State's population of 3,567,089, of whom 2,092,891 are eligible to vote. The relative standings of the counties in terms of qualified voters have changed significantly. It is primarily the continued application of the 1901 Apportionment Act to this shifted and enlarged voting population which gives rise to the present controversy.

Indeed, the complaint alleges that the 1901 statute, even as of the time of its passage, "made no apportionment of Representatives and Senators in accordance with the constitutional formula . . ., but instead arbitrarily and capriciously apportioned representatives in the Senate and House without reference . . . to any logical or reasonable formula whatever." It is further alleged that "because of the population changes since 1900, and the failure of the Legislature to reapportion itself since 1901," the 1901 statute became "unconstitutional and obsolete." Appellants also argue that, because of the composition of the legislature effected by the 1901 Apportionment Act, redress in the form of a state constitutional amendment to change the entire mechanism for reapportioning, or any other change short of that, is difficult or impossible. The complaint concludes that "these plaintiffs and others similarly situated, are denied the equal protection of the laws accorded them by the Fourteenth Amendment to the Constitution of the United States by virtue of the debasement of their votes." They seek a declaration that the 1901 statute is unconstitutional and an injunction restraining the appellees from acting to conduct any further elections under it. They also pray that unless and until the General Assembly enacts a valid reapportionment, the District Court should either decree a reapportionment by mathematical application of the Tennessee constitutional formulae to the most recent Federal Census figures, or direct the appellees to conduct legislative elections, primary and general, at large. They also pray for such other and further relief as may be appropriate.

I. The District Court's Opinion and Order of Dismissal.
[Here summarized.]

In the light of the District Court's treatment of the case, we hold today only (a) that the court possessed jurisdiction of the subject matter; (b) that a justiciable cause of action is stated upon which appellants would be entitled to appropriate relief; and (c) because appellees raise the issue before this Court, that the appellants have standing to challenge the Tennessee apportionment statutes. Beyond noting that we have no cause at this stage to doubt the District Court will be able to fashion relief if violations of constitutional rights are found, it is improper now to consider what remedy would be most appropriate if appellants prevail at the trial.

II. Jurisdiction of the Subject Matter.

The District Court was uncertain whether our cases withholding federal judicial relief rested upon a lack of federal jurisdiction or upon the inappropriateness of the subject matter for judicial consideration—what we have designated "nonjusticiability." The distinction between the two grounds is significant. In the instance of nonjusticiability, consideration of the cause is not wholly and immediately foreclosed; rather, the Court's inquiry necessarily proceeds to the point of deciding whether the duty asserted can be judicially identified and its breach judicially determined, and whether protection for the right asserted can be judicially molded. In the instance of lack of jurisdiction the cause either does not "arise under" the Federal Constitution, laws or treaties (or fall within one of the other enumerated categories of Art. 3, § 2), or is not a "case or controversy" within the meaning of that section; or the cause is not one described by any jurisdictional statute. Our conclusion that this cause presents no nonjusticiable "political question" settles the only possible doubt that it is a case or controversy. Under the present heading of "Jurisdiction of the Subject Matter" we hold only that the matter set forth in the complaint does arise under the Constitution. . . .

Article 3, § 2, of the Federal Constitution provides that "The Judicial Power shall extend to all Cases, in Law and Equity, arising under this Constitution, the Laws of the United States, and Treaties made, or which shall be made, under their Authority. . . ." It is clear that the cause of action is one which "arises under" the Federal Constitution. The complaint alleges that the 1901 statute effects an apportionment that deprives the appellants of the equal protection of the laws in violation of the Fourteenth Amendment. Dismissal of the complaint upon the ground of lack of jurisdiction of the subject matter would, therefore, be justified only if that claim were "so attenuated and unsubstantial as to be absolutely devoid of merit." . . . Since the District Court obviously and correctly did not deem the asserted federal constitutional claim unsubstantial and frivolous, it should not have dismissed the complaint for want of jurisdiction of the subject matter. And of course no further consideration of the merits of the claim is relevant to a determination of the court's jurisdiction of the subject matter. . . .

An unbroken line of our precedents sustains the federal courts' jurisdiction of the subject matter of federal constitutional claims of this nature. The first cases involved the redistricting of States for the purpose of electing Representatives to the Federal Congress. When the Ohio Supreme Court sustained Ohio legislation against an attack for repugnancy to Art. 1 § 4, of the Federal Constitution, we affirmed on the merits and expressly refused to dismiss for want of jurisdiction "in view . . . of the subject-matter of the controversy and the Federal characteristics which inhere in it. . . ." Ohio ex rel. Davis v. Hildebrant [1916]. When the Minnesota Supreme Court affirmed the dismissal of a suit to enjoin the Secretary of State of Minnesota from acting under Minnesota redistricting legislation, we reviewed the constitutional merits of the legislation and reversed the State Supreme Court. Smiley v. Holm [1932]. . . .

The appellees refer to Colegrove v. Green [1946], as authority that the District Court lacked jurisdiction of the subject matter. Appellees misconceive the holding of that case. The holding was precisely contrary to their reading of it. Seven members of the Court participated in the decision. Unlike many other cases in this field which have assumed without discussion that there was jurisdiction, all three opinions filed in Colegrove discussed the question. Two of the opinions expressing the views of four of the Justices, a majority, flatly held that there was jurisdiction of the subject matter. Mr. Justice Black joined by Mr. Justice Douglas and Mr. Justice Murphy stated: "It is my judgment that the District Court had jurisdiction. . . ." Mr. Justice Rutledge, writing separately, expressed agreement with this conclusion. . . .

We hold that the District Court has jurisdiction of the subject matter of the federal constitutional claim asserted in the complaint.

III. Standing.

A federal court cannot "pronounce any statute, either of a State or of the United States, void, because irreconcilable with the Constitution, except as it is called upon to adjudge the legal rights of litigants in actual controversies." . . . Have the appellants alleged such a personal stake in the outcome of the controversy as to assure that concrete adverseness which sharpens the presentation of issues upon which the court so largely depends for illumination of difficult constitutional questions? This is the gist of the question of standing. It is, of course, a question of federal law. . . .

We hold that the appellants do have standing to maintain this suit. Our decisions plainly support this conclusion. Many of the cases have assumed rather than articulated the premise in deciding the merits of similar claims. And Colegrove v. Green squarely held that voters who allege facts showing disadvantage to themselves as individuals have standing to sue. . . .

These appellants seek relief in order to protect or vindicate an interest of their own, and of those similarly situated. Their constitutional claim is, in substance, that the 1901 statute constitutes arbitrary and capricious state action, offensive to the Fourteenth Amendment in its irrational disregard of the standard of apportionment prescribed by the State's Constitution or of any standard, effecting a gross disproportion of representation to voting population. The injury which appellants assert is that this classification disfavors the voters in the counties in which they reside, placing them in a position of constitutionally unjustifiable inequality vis-à-vis voters in irrationally favored counties. A citizen's right to vote free of arbitrary impairment by state action has been judicially recognized as a right secured by the Constitution, when such impairment resulted from dilution by a false tally, cf. United States v. Classic [1941] or by a refusal to count votes from arbitrarily selected precincts, . . . or by a stuffing of the ballot box, cf. Ex parte Siebold [1880]. . . .

It would not be necessary to decide whether appellants' allegations of impairment of their votes by the 1901 apportionment will, ultimately, entitle them to any relief, in order to hold that they have standing to seek it. If such impairment does produce a legally cognizable injury, they are among those who have sustained it. They are asserting "a plain, direct and adequate interest in maintaining the effectiveness of their votes," . . . not merely a claim of "the right, possessed by every citizen, to require that the Government be administered according to law. . . ." Fairchild v. Hughes [1922]. . . . They are entitled to a hearing and to the District Court's decision on their claims. "The very essence of civil liberty certainly consists in the right of every individual to claim the protection of the laws, whenever he receives an injury."

IV. Justiciability.

In holding that the subject matter of this suit was not justiciable, the District Court relied on Colegrove v. Green, and subsequent per curiam cases. The court stated: "From a review of these decisions there can be no doubt that the federal rule . . . is that the federal courts . . . will not intervene in cases of this type to compel legislative reapportionment." We understand the District Court to have read the cited cases as compelling the conclusion that since the appellants sought to have a legislative apportionment held unconstitutional, their suit presented a "political question" and was therefore nonjusticiable. We hold that this challenge to an apportionment presents no nonjusticiable "political question." The cited cases do not hold the contrary.

Of course the mere fact that the suit seeks protection of a political right does not mean it presents a political question. Such an objection "is little more than a play upon words." . . . Rather, it is argued that apportionment cases, whatever the actual wording of the complaint, can involve no federal constitutional right except one resting on the guaranty of a republican form of government, and that complaints based on that clause have been held to present political questions which are nonjusticiable.

We hold that the claim pleaded here neither rests upon nor implicates the Guaranty Clause and that its justiciability is therefore not foreclosed by our decisions of cases involving that clause. The District Court misinterpreted Colegrove v. Green and other decisions of this Court on which it relied. Appellants' claim that they are being denied equal protection is justiciable, and if "discrimination is sufficiently shown, the right to relief under the equal protection clause is not diminished by the fact that the discrimination relates to political rights." . . . To show why we reject the argument based on the Guaranty Clause, we must examine the authorities under it. But because there appears to be some uncertainty as to why those cases did present political questions, and specifically as to whether this apportionment case is like those cases, we deem it necessary first to consider the contours of the "political question" doctrine.

Our discussion, even at the price of extending this opinion, requires review of a number of political question cases, in order to expose the attributes of the doctrine—attributes which, in various settings, diverge, combine, appear, and disappear in seeming disorderliness. Since that review is undertaken solely to demonstrate that neither singly nor collectively do these cases support a conclusion that this apportionment case is nonjusticiable, we of course do not explore their implications in other contexts. That review reveals that in the Guaranty Clause cases and in the other "political question" cases, it is the relationship between the judiciary and the coordinate branches of the Federal Government, and not the federal judiciary's relationship to the States, which gives rise to the "political question."

We have said that "In determining whether a question falls within [the political question] category, the appropriateness under our system of government of attributing finality to the action of the political departments and also the lack of satisfactory criteria for a judicial determination are dominant considerations." Coleman v. Miller [1939]. The nonjusticiability of a political question is primarily a function of the separation of powers. Much confusion results from the capacity of the "political question" label to obscure the need for case-by-case inquiry. Deciding whether a matter has in any measure been committed by the Constitution to another branch of government, or whether the action of that branch exceeds whatever authority has been committed, is itself a delicate exercise in constitutional interpretation, and is a responsibility of this Court as ultimate interpreter of the Constitution. To demonstrate this requires no less than to analyze representative cases and to infer from them the analytical threads that make up the political question doctrine. We shall then show that none of those threads catches this case. . . .

[Here follows a long summary of cases involving the political question doctrine as they have arisen in the fields of (1) foreign relations, (2) dates of duration of hostilities, (3) validity of enactments, (4) status of Indian tribes, and (5) republican form of government.]

We come, finally, to the ultimate inquiry whether our precedents as to what constitutes a nonjusticiable "political question" bring the case before us under the umbrella of that doctrine. A natural beginning is to note whether any of the common characteristics which we have been able to identify and label descriptively are present. We find none: The question here is the consistency of state action with the Federal Constitution. We have no question decided, or to be decided, by a political branch of government coequal with this Court. Nor do we risk embarrassment of our government abroad, or grave disturbance at home if we take issue with Tennessee as to the constitutionality of her action, here challenged. Nor need the appellants, in order to succeed in this action, ask the Court to enter upon policy determinations for which judicially manageable standards are lacking. Judicial standards under the Equal Protection Clause are well developed and familiar, and it has been open to courts since the enactment of the Fourteenth Amendment to determine, if on the particular facts they must, that a discrimination reflects *no* policy, but simply arbitrary and capricious action. . . .

We conclude that the complaint's allegations of a denial of equal protection present a justiciable constitutional cause of action upon which appellants are entitled to a trial and a decision. The right asserted is within the reach of judicial protection under the Fourteenth Amendment.

The judgment of the District Court is reversed and the cause is remanded for further proceedings consistent with this opinion.

Reversed and remanded.

Mr. Justice Whittaker did not participate in the decision of this case.

Mr. Justice Douglas, concurring, said in part:

While I join the opinion of the Court and, like the Court, do not reach the merits, a word of explanation is necessary. I put to one side the problems of "political" questions involving the distribution of power between this Court, the Congress, and the Chief Executive. We have here a phase of the recurring problem of the relation of the federal courts to state agencies. More particularly, the question is the extent to which a State may weight one person's vote more heavily than it does another's. . . .

I agree with my Brother Clark that if the allegations in the complaint can be sustained a case for relief is established. We are told that a single vote in Moore County, Tennessee, is worth 19 votes in Hamilton County, that one vote in Stewart or in Chester County is worth nearly eight times a single vote in Shelby or Knox County. The opportunity to prove that an "invidious discrimination" exists should therefore be given the appellants. . . .

With the exceptions of Colegrove v. Green, MacDougall v. Green, South v. Peters, and the decisions they spawned, the Court has never thought that protection of voting rights was beyond judicial cognizance. Today's treatment of those cases removes the only impediment to judicial cognizance of the claims stated in the present complaint. . . .

Mr. Justice Clark, concurring, said in part:

One emerging from the rash of opinions with their accompanying clashing of views may well find himself suffering a mental blindness. The Court holds that the appellants have alleged a cause of action. However, it refuses to award relief here—although the facts are undisputed—and fails to give the District Court any guidance whatever. One dissenting opinion, bursting with words that go through so much and conclude with so little, condemns the majority action as "a massive repudiation of the experience of our whole past." Another describes the complaint as merely asserting conclusory allegations that Tennessee's apportionment is "incorrect," "arbitrary," "obsolete," and "unconstitutional." I believe it can be shown that this case is distinguishable from earlier cases dealing with the distribution of political power by a State, that a patent violation of the Equal Protection Clause of the United States Constitution has been shown, and that an appropriate remedy may be formulated.

. . . The widely heralded case of Colegrove v. Green was one not only in which the Court was bobtailed but in which there was no majority opinion. Indeed, even the "political question" point in Mr. Justice Frankfurter's opinion was no more than an alternative ground. Moreover, the appellants did not present an equal protection argument. While it has served as a Mother Hubbard to most of the subsequent cases, I feel it was in that respect ill-cast and for all of these reasons put it to one side. . . .

The controlling facts cannot be disputed. . . .

. . . The frequency and magnitude of the inequalities in the present districting admit of no policy whatever. . . . It leaves but one conclusion, namely that Tennessee's apportionment is a crazy quilt without rational basis. . . .

[Examples are given of the inequalities in apportionment in Tennessee.]

The truth is that—although this case has been here for two years and has had over six hours' argument (three times the ordinary case) and has been most carefully considered over and over again by us in Conference and individually—no one, not even the State nor the dissenters, has come up with any rational basis for "Tennessee's apportionment statute.

. . . Like the District Court, I conclude that appellants have met the burden of showing "Tennessee is guilty of a clear violation of the state constitution and of the [federal] rights of the plaintiffs. . . ."

Although I find the Tennessee apportionment statute offends the Equal Protection Clause, I would not consider intervention by this Court into so delicate a field if there were any other relief available to the people of Tennessee. But the majority of the people of Tennessee have no "practical opportunities for exerting their political weight at the polls" to correct the existing "invidious discrimination." Tennessee has no initiative and referendum. I have searched diligently for other "practical opportunities" present under the law. I find none other than through the federal courts. . . .

As John Rutledge (later Chief Justice) said 175 years ago in the course of the Constitutional Convention, a chief function of the Court is to secure the national rights. Its decision today supports the proposition for which our forebears fought and many died, namely, that to be fully conformable to the principle of right, the form of government must be representative. That is the keystone upon which our government was founded and lacking which no republic can survive. It is well for this Court to practice self-restraint and discipline in constitutional adjudication, but never in its history have those principles received sanction where the national rights of so many have been so clearly infringed for so long a time. National respect for the courts is more enhanced through the forthright enforcement of those rights rather than by rendering them nugatory through the interposition of subterfuges. In my view the ultimate decision today is in the greatest tradition of this Court.

Mr. Justice Stewart wrote a brief concurring opinion.

Mr. Justice Frankfurter, whom Mr. Justice Harlan joins, dissenting, said in part:

The Court today reverses a uniform course of decision established by a dozen cases, including one by which the very claim now sustained was unanimously rejected only five years ago. The impressive body of rulings thus cast aside reflected the equally uniform course of our political history regarding the relationship between population and legislative representation—a wholly different matter from denial of the franchise to individuals because of race, color, religion or sex. Such a massive repudiation of the experience of our whole past in asserting destructively novel judicial power demands a detailed analysis of the role of this Court in our constitutional scheme. Disregard of inherent limits in the effective exercise of the Court's "judicial Power" not only presages the futility of judicial intervention in the essentially political conflict of forces by which the relation between population and representation has time out of mind been and now is determined. It may well impair the Court's position as the ultimate organ of "the supreme Law of the Land" in that vast range of legal problems, often strongly entangled in popular feeling, on which this Court must pronounce. The Court's authority—possessed neither of the purse nor the sword—ultimately rests on sustained public confidence in its moral sanction. Such feeling must be nourished by the Court's complete detachment, in fact and in appearance, from political entanglements and by abstention from injecting itself into the clash of political forces in political settlements. . . .

. . . The Framers carefully and with deliberate forethought refused so to enthrone the judiciary. In this situation, as in others of like nature, appeal for relief does not belong here. Appeal must be to an informed, civically militant electorate. In a democratic society like ours, relief must come through an aroused popular conscience that sears the conscience of the people's representatives. In any event there is nothing judicially more unseemly nor more self-defeating than for this Court to make in terrorem pronouncements, to indulge in merely empty rhetoric, sounding a word of promise to the ear, sure to be disappointing to the hope. . . .

[Mr. Justice Frankfurter continued in a long and heavily documented opinion to support the position he had taken in Colegrove v. Green.]

Mr. Justice Harlan wrote a dissenting opinion in which Mr. Justice Frankfurter joined.

EX PARTE McCARDLE

7 Wallace 506; 19 L. Ed. 264 (1869)

A court, in order to be a court and behave like one, must possess two kinds of authority. The first is jurisdiction, which is the power of the court to bring parties before it for the purpose of deciding the kinds of disputes in which those parties are involved. What the court can do about a dispute properly before it depends upon its possession of *judicial* power. Both jurisdiction and judicial power are provided for the federal courts in Article III of the Constitution.

Article III provides that "the judicial power shall extend to all cases . . ." and then proceeds to enumerate the bases upon which federal jurisdiction may be taken. One class of cases comes to the courts because of the subject matter of the case, and these are cases in which federal questions are raised, i.e., questions of the interpretation of the Constitution, law, or treaties of the United States. A second category is based on the parties to the suit and includes generally cases where impartiality might not be had in the courts of the states. Here are the cases between citizens of different states. Does the phrase "shall extend" mean that any federal court, as soon as it is created by Congress, is fully invested with both kinds of jurisdiction by the Constitution? The answer is no, despite the urging of Federalists who favored a strong independent judiciary. The wording of the Judiciary Act of 1789 creating the courts, and the circumstances surrounding its passage, both indicate a legislative acceptance of the idea that Congress has complete control over the jurisdiction of the lower federal courts; ten years later, in Turner v. Bank of North America (1799), the Supreme Court approved that interpretation. Congress had specifically denied the courts a portion of the jurisdiction based upon diversity of citizenship; and the bank argued that since diversity jurisdiction was given by Article III, Congress had no power to take it away. The Court upheld the congressional limitation and refused to take jurisdiction. Congress has made free use of its power to grant, withhold, or distribute the jurisdiction of the lower federal courts as it has thought wise. Some of the jurisdiction mentioned in Article III, such as diversity jurisdiction in cases involving small sums, has never been conferred on the federal courts at all. It was not until 1875 that the lower federal courts were given jurisdiction over cases involving federal questions.

The Constitution, in providing for the Supreme Court, distinguishes between its *original* jurisdiction to decide cases which start in the Supreme Court and its *appellate* jurisdiction to decide cases which come to it on appeal, or by other procedure, from some other court. Article III provides that "in all cases affecting ambassadors, other public ministers, and consuls, and those in which a State shall be a party, the Supreme Court shall have original jurisdiction. In all the cases before mentioned, the Supreme Court shall have appellate jurisdiction, both as to law and fact, with such exceptions, and under such regulations as the Congress shall make." The Supreme Court held in Marbury v. Madison (1803) that Congress cannot validly enlarge the original jurisdiction of the Court. That portion of the Judiciary Act of 1789 which purported to enlarge the original jurisdiction of the Court to include the power to issue writs of mandamus was held unconstitutional.

But to what extent and by what means may Congress control the appellate jurisdiction of the Supreme Court? The present case was one of a series of attempts by the Southern states to get from the Supreme Court a clear decision on the validity of the military reconstruction program set up by Congress after the Civil War. The behavior of the Court must to some extent be judged in the light of the bitterness which this conflict engendered. McCardle, a Southern newspaper editor, was arrested for sedition and tried and convicted by a federal military commission. When his petition to the circuit court for a writ of habeas corpus was denied, he appealed directly to the Supreme Court under a statute designed, ironically, to protect the rights of Negroes and federal officers in the South. The Court unanimously agreed that the statute gave it jurisdiction in McCardle's case; and in view of its denunciation of military commissions in Ex parte Milligan two years before (1866), there was a widespread expectation that the Court would hold the Reconstruction Acts unconstitutional because of their establishment of military government throughout much of the South. To prevent possible judicial sabotage of its reconstruction program, the House had already passed a bill providing that the Court could invalidate acts of Congress only by a two-thirds vote, but the Senate had not concurred. Then, with argument in the McCardle case already concluded, Congress undertook to block a decision of the Court by repealing the law by which jurisdiction to hear McCardle's appeal had been conferred. Despite impeachment proceedings against him, the President vetoed the act; but it was repassed over his veto. The Court, which had waited to see whether the repealing statute would pass, put off until the following term the question of the effect of this repeal on its jurisdiction in the McCardle case. Justices Grier and Field bitterly excoriated their brethren for what they regarded as a shameful and cowardly delay in deciding the case.

Over 100 years since Ex parte McCardle, the action by Congress in lopping off part of the appellate jurisdiction of the Supreme Court in order to forestall an unwanted decision has been generally regarded as a regrettable legislative assault upon the independence of the Court—a precedent which it was hoped would not be followed.

If Congress finds itself in conflict with the Supreme Court on constitutional issues, it may always seek to employ the direct and orderly process of constitutional amendment to accomplish its ends. It has done this in three cases. Chisholm v. Georgia (1793) was nullified by the Eleventh Amendment; the Dred Scott case (1857), ruling on the nature and source of citizenship, was nullified by the first section of the Fourteenth Amendment; while the Sixteenth Amendment reversed at least part of the Court's ruling in the Income Tax Cases (1895). Such changes are not easy to accomplish, however, and most efforts to alter or nullify controversial Court decisions have been unsuccessful. Moreover, as the history of the Income Tax Amendment makes clear, the meaning of an amendment is subject to the interpretation of the Supreme Court just as was the original constitutional provision.

Mr. Chief Justice Chase delivered the opinion of the Court, saying in part:

. . . The first question necessarily is that of jurisdiction; for, if the Act of March, 1868, takes away the jurisdiction defined by the Act of February, 1867, it is useless, if not improper, to enter into any discussion of other questions.

It is quite true, as was argued by the counsel for the petitioner, that the appellate jurisdiction of this court is not derived from Acts of Congress. It is, strictly speaking, conferred by the Constitution. But it is conferred "with such exceptions and under such regulations as Congress shall make."

It is unnecessary to consider whether, if Congress had made no exceptions and no regulations, this court might not have exercised general appellate jurisdiction under rules prescribed by itself. From among the earliest Acts of the first Congress, at its first session, was the Act of September 24th, 1789, to establish the judicial courts of the United States. That Act provided for the organization of this court, and prescribed regulations for the exercise of its jurisdiction.

The source of that jurisdiction, and the limitations of it by the Constitution and by statute, have been on several occasions subjects of consideration here. In the case of Durousseau v. United States [1910]; Wiscart v. Dauchy [1796], particularly, the whole matter was carefully examined, and the court held, that while "the appellate powers of this court are not given by the Judicial Act, but are given by the Constitution"; they are, nevertheless, "limited and regulated by that Act, and by such other acts as have been passed on the subject." The court said, further, that the Judicial Act was an exercise of the power given by the Constitution to Congress "of making exceptions to the appellate jurisdiction of the Supreme Court."

"They have described affirmatively," said the court, "its jurisdiction, and this affirmative description has been understood to imply a negation of the exercise of such appellate power as is not comprehended within it."

The principle that the affirmation of appellate jurisdiction implies the negation of all such jurisdiction not affirmed having been thus established, it was an almost necessary consequence that Acts of Congress, providing for the exercise of jurisdiction, should come to be spoken of as Acts granting jurisdiction, and not as Acts making exceptions to the constitutional grant of it.

The exception to appellate jurisdiction in the case before us, however, is not an inference from the affirmation of other appellate jurisdiction. It is made in terms. The provision of the Act of 1867, affirming the appellate jurisdiction of this court in cases of habeas corpus, is expressly repealed. It is hardly possible to imagine a plainer instance of positive exception.

We are not at liberty to inquire into the motives of the Legislature. We can only examine into its power under the Constitution; and the power to make exceptions to the appellate jurisdiction of this court is given by express words.

What, then, is the effect of the repealing Act upon the case before us? We cannot doubt as to this. Without jurisdiction the court cannot proceed at all in any cause. Jurisdiction is power to declare the law, and when it ceases to exist, the only function remaining to the court is that of announcing the fact and dismissing the cause. And this is not less clear upon authority than upon principle.

Several cases were cited by the counsel for the petitioner in support of the position that jurisdiction of this case is not affected by the repealing Act. But none of them, in our judgment, afford any support to it. . . .

On the other hand, the general rule, supported by the best elementary writers . . . is, that "when an Act of the Legislature is repealed, it must be considered, except as to transactions past and closed, as if it never existed." And the effect of repealing Acts upon suits under Acts repealed, has been determined by the adjudications of this court. The subject was fully considered in Norris v. Crocker [1852], and more recently in Insurance Company v. Ritchie [1867]. In both of these cases it was held that no judgment could be rendered in a suit after the repeal of the Act under which it was brought and prosecuted.

It is quite clear, therefore, that this court cannot proceed to pronounce judgment in this case, for it has no longer jurisdiction of the appeal; and judicial duty is not less fitly performed by declining ungranted jurisdiction than in exercising firmly that which the Constitution and the laws confer.

Counsel seem to have supposed, if effect be given to the repealing Act in question, that the whole appellate power of the court, in cases of habeas corpus, is denied. But this is in error. The Act of 1868 does not except from that jurisdiction any cases but appeals from circuit courts under the Act of 1867. It does not affect the jurisdiction which was previously exercised. . . .

The appeal of the petitioner in this case must be dismissed for want of jurisdiction.

2

The Legislative Branch

BARENBLATT v. UNITED STATES

360 U. S. 109; 79 S. Ct. 1081; 3 L. Ed. 2nd 1115
(1959)

The legislative power of Congress is the power to pass laws, and the actual process of lawmaking is not subject to judicial control. The extent to which Congress can, by making laws, enlarge or diminish the powers of the judiciary and executive is discussed in connection with those branches. But may Congress, as a means of performing its own delegated functions, borrow the powers of another branch? The power to subpoena witnesses and punish them for contempt by fine and imprisonment if they do not appear and testify is a vital and inherent judicial power. No court is really a court without it. Can a house of Congress borrow this judicial power as a means of performing its own delegated functions without violating the doctrine of the separation of powers?

This question was effectively dealt with in McGrain v. Daugherty (1927). Early in the Harding administration scandals were uncovered in the federal government, with the result that the Senate created a special committee to investigate the Department of Justice and the possible misconduct in office of Attorney General Harry M. Daugherty. In the course of the investigation the committee subpoenaed Mally S. Daugherty, brother of the Attorney General, to appear before it and testify. This he refused to do. The Senate than issued a warrant ordering McGrain, a deputy sergeant-at-arms, to arrest Mally S. Daugherty and bring him before the Senate to testify. Daugherty challenged the Senate's power to compel him to do this.

The Court upheld the Senate action. Its opinion mentioned that in 1792 the House of Representatives had appointed a select committee to inquire into the ill-fated St. Clair expedition against the Indians; and it then reviewed the legislative practice, congressional enactments, and court decisions bearing on the power of Congress to conduct inquiries and to punish for contempt. The Court concluded "that the power of inquiry —with process to enforce it—is an essential and appropriate auxiliary to the legislative function." However, it is a power which may validly be used only "in aid of the legislative function." Daugherty had alleged, and the lower court had agreed, that the committee was not seeking information to help it in legislation, but was in reality putting the Attorney General on trial. The Supreme Court disagreed. It said, "The only legitimate object the Senate could have in ordering the investigation was to aid it in legislating; and we think the subject-matter was such that the presumption should be indulged that this was the object. An express avowal of the object would have been better; but . . . was not indispensable."

The power to investigate and compel the attendance of witnesses may also be used by Congress to facilitate its exercise of nonlegislative congressional powers. In the case of Barry v. United States ex rel. Cunningham (1929) the Court upheld the power of a Senate committee investigating senatorial campaign expenditures in Pennsylvania to punish for contempt a witness who refused to answer relevant questions. There can be no doubt of the similar right of a committee of the House of Representatives to punish recalcitrant witnesses in a hearing on the question of bringing impeachment charges against an officer of the government.

There are two ways in which either house of Congress may exercise its power to punish a stubborn witness for contempt. First, it may pass a resolution holding him in contempt and punishing him summarily. He may be fined, or he may be sent at once to prison. In Anderson v. Dunn (1821) the Supreme Court held that such imprisonment could not, however, extend beyond the adjournment of Congress. While Congress still enjoys this power of direct and summary punishment for contempt, experience early proved it unsatisfactory in a number of ways. Accordingly, in 1857 Congress provided a second method for dealing with the problem. It passed a statute making it a crime for a person to refuse to testify or answer questions before either house of Congress or any congressional committee when subpoenaed to do so. The maximum penalty is a fine of $1000 or a year in prison. The procedure under this statute is as follows: If a witness refuses to testify before a congressional investigating committee, the committee reports this refusal to the House (or Senate), and that body, usually as a matter of routine, passes a resolution declaring the witness to be in contempt of the House or Senate. This resolution is then sent to the United States attorney in the District of Columbia, who presents the matter to a grand jury for indictment under the statute. If thus indicted, the witness is tried in the federal district court, and at the trial presents any legal or constitutional defenses available. Punishment is, of course, imposed by the court.

The opinion of the Court in McGrain v. Daugherty had very reasonably given Congress and its committees a sense of security from judicial inteference with the legislative power to compel testimony. The Court had generously declared that if there was a possible legislative purpose which could be served by a congressional demand for evidence and facts, the Court would presume that that was the purpose of the investigation whether it was or not. What more latitude could Congress and its committees wish? But the McGrain case had not given congressional committees carte blanche. There were two reservations: The investigation must be in aid of a valid congressional duty or power, and the questions asked of witnesses must be relevant to the purpose of the inquiry.

From the time of their origin, congressional committees that were set up to investigate subversive or "un-American" activities were in a number of respects sui generis. They were given by Congress roving commissions to find out what they could about persons, organizations, or movements which were believed to be subversive or unorthodox, and to suggest ways and means of defeating these undermining influences. Very early in the game these committees convinced themselves that their most useful function was the public "exposure" of persons of dubious loyalty. This had been explicitly stated by Congressman Martin Dies when his resolution calling for the creation of the House Committee on Un-American Activities (HUAC) was being debated in the House. He said, "I am not in a position to say whether we can legislate effectively in reference to this matter, but I do know that exposure in a democracy of subversive activities is the most effective weapon that we have in our possession." During the Second World War and the subsequent cold war, House and Senate committees investigating subversion were dominated by this zeal to "expose" persons or groups whose loyalty was open to question, in the well-grounded belief that an aroused public opinion would inflict its own nonlegal punishments or reprisals. The "exposure" of disloyalty or crime came to be generally accepted as the controlling purpose of such legislative investigating committees. The idea that committee investigations were justifiable only if they aided Congress in its wise consideration of legislation was almost wholly forgotten.

When, in 1957, the Supreme Court in Watkins v. United States held void a conviction for contempt of HUAC, it understandably came as a profound and unwelcome shock to those who regarded our congressional committees on subversive activities as the most useful defenders of our national security and as enjoying unrestricted authority in their investigations. Apparently striking at the very core of the committee, the Court made clear that "there is no congressional power to expose for the sake of exposure," and "investigations conducted solely for the personal aggrandizement of the investigators or to 'punish' those investigated are indefensible." Moreover, questions asked of a witness had to be pertinent to the matter under inquiry, and the vagueness of the term "un-American" and the "excessively broad charter" of HUAC, coupled with the failure of the committee itself to define the "question under inquiry," made it impossible for the witness to judge whether or not the committee had the right to insist that he answer. "Fundamental fairness," said the Court, "demands that no witness be compelled to make such a determination with so little guidance."

The decision of the Court in the Watkins case (1957) was widely hailed by critics of HUAC as a long overdue rebuke, and the language of the opinion suggested that the whole concept of un-Americanism was so vague that the investigation of it could in no way serve a proper legislative purpose. This interpretation was apparently shared by the supporters of the Committee as well, and bills were immediately introduced in Congress to curb the jurisdiction of the federal courts to review the Committee's work.

The decision in the Barenblatt case, printed below, came as a shock to those who had welcomed the Watkins decision and as a relief to its critics. Not only did the Court not strike dead the HUAC, but it seemed to back away from Chief Justice Warren's statement in Watkins that the Committee could not "expose for the sake of exposure." But the impression that Barenblatt had in effect overruled Watkins proved to be unwarranted, and in subsequent cases the Supreme Court has both sustained and struck down convictions for contempt of congressional committees. In Braden v. United States and Wilkinson v. United States the Court in 1961 upheld by a five-to-four vote the contempt convictions of the defendants who refused to testify before the HUAC. Although the Committee's investigation was apparently sparked by the opposition these men had expressed to the work of the Committee, the Court held that this did not alter the validity of what, on the basis of Barenblatt, was an otherwise valid investigation. In Deutch v. United States (1961), on the other hand, the Court held that questions regarding Communist activity at Cornell University were not pertinent to an investigation of Communism in the Albany, New York, labor movement.

The decision of the cases just discussed turned on whether the legislative committee was authorized to investigate a particular activity, and if it was, whether the question asked of the witness was pertinent to such investigation. In 1962 the Court added a new dimension to this last problem. In Russell v. United States, it held that a prosecution for contempt was void unless the indictment by which the charge was brought stated explicitly the purpose of the investigation. The indictment in question had listed as a separate count each question the witness had refused to answer, but had stated merely that they were pertinent without stating what the subject of the inquiry was. This, said the Court, not only made it impossible to make an independent judgment of pertinency on appeal but did not sufficiently clearly indicate to the defendant the exact crime for which he was being tried.

For 25 years the Supreme Court has been asked to hold that there was a constitutional "right to silence" flowing from the First Amendment which would justify a person in refusing to testify before a legislative committee. The Court has never conceded such a right, but in 1963 in Gibson v. Florida Investigation Committee it upheld for the first time against a legislative committee the closely related claim of "associational privacy." The Florida committee, in the course of investigating Communist infiltration of the civil rights movement, subpoenaed the membership lists of the Miami chapter of the NAACP. The Court sustained the chapter's refusal to produce them. Conceding the right of the state to inform itself, the Court held that the absence of any tie in, or "nexus," between the NAACP and subversion, there was no showing of a "subordinating interest" sufficient to override the right of association. A similar result was reached in De Gregory v. Attorney General (1966), where the New Hampshire attorney general sought to inquire into De Gregory's Communist activities of a decade earlier. Since the record was "devoid of any evidence that there is any Communist movement in New Hampshire," there was no " 'overriding and compelling state interest' . . . that would warrant intrusion into the realm of political and associational privacy. . . ." Justices Harlan, Stewart, and Clark dissented on the ground that the purpose of the inquiry was to find out if there were such a "movement."

In 1975, in Eastland v. United States Servicemen's Fund, the Court held the speech and debate clause, Article 1, Sec. 6, Cl. 1, forbade judicial interference with a Senate committee investigation. The Senate Internal Security Subcommittee had subpoenaed bank records showing who had contributed to an organization operating on and near military bases which it considered disruptive and possibly foreign-dominated. The bank agreed to turn over the records and the Fund, arguing that the records were the same as membership lists, sought an injunction against the committee on the basis of the Gibson case, above. Eight members of the Supreme Court agreed that the speech and debate clause was absolute and since the subpoena fell within the sphere of legitimate legislative activity the committee could not be made answerable to the courts by injunction.

Mr. Justice Harlan delivered the opinion of the Court, saying in part:

Once more the Court is required to resolve the conflicting constitutional claims of congressional power and of an individual's right to resist its exercise. The congressional power in question concerns the internal process of Congress in moving within its legislative domain; it involves the utilization of its committees to secure "testimony needed to enable it efficiently to exercise a legislative function belonging to it under the Constitution."

McGrain v. Daugherty [1927]. The power of inquiry has been employed by Congress throughout our history, over the whole range of the national interests concerning which Congress might legislate or decide upon due investigation not to legislate; it has similarly been utilized in determining what to appropriate from the national purse, or whether to appropriate. The scope of the power of inquiry, in short, is as penetrating and far-reaching as the potential power to enact and appropriate under the Constitution.

Broad as it is, the power is not, however, without limitations. Since Congress may only investigate into those areas in which it may potentially legislate or appropriate, it cannot inquire into matters which are within the exclusive province of one of the other branches of the Government. Lacking the judicial power given to the Judiciary, it cannot inquire into matters that are exclusively the concern of the Judiciary. Neither can it supplant the Executive in what exclusively belongs to the Executive. And the Congress, in common with all branches of the Government, must exercise its powers subject to the limitations placed by the Constitution on governmental action, more particularly in the context of this case the relevant limitations of the Bill of Rights.

The congressional power of inquiry, its range and scope, and an individual's duty in relation to it, must be viewed in proper perspective. . . . The power and the right of resistance to it are to be judged in the concrete, not on the basis of abstractions. In the present case congressional efforts to learn the extent of a nationwide, indeed world wide, problem have brought one of its investigating committees into the field of education. Of course, broadly viewed, inquiries cannot be made into the teaching that is pursued in any of our educational institutions. When academic teaching-freedom and its corollary learning-freedom, so essential to the well-being of the Nation, are claimed, this Court will always be on the alert against intrusion by Congress into this constitutionally protected domain. But this does not mean that the Congress is precluded from interrogating a witness merely because he is a teacher. An educational institution is not a constitutional sanctuary from inquiry into matters that may otherwise be within the constitutional legislative domain merely for the reason that inquiry is made of someone within its walls.

In the setting of this framework of constitutional history, practice and legal precedents, we turn to the particularities of this case.

We here review petitioner's conviction for contempt of Congress, arising from his refusal to answer certain questions put to him by a Subcommittee of the House Committee on Un-American Activities during the course of an inquiry concerning alleged Communist infiltration into the field of education. . . .

Petitioner's various contentions resolve themselves into three propositions: First, the compelling of testimony by the Subcommittee was neither legislatively authorized nor constitutionally permissible because of the vagueness of Rule XI of the House of Representatives, Eighty-third Congress, the charter of authority of the parent Committee. Second, petitioner was not adequately apprised of the pertinency of the Subcommittee's questions to the subject matter of the inquiry. Third, the questions petitioner refused to answer infringed rights protected by the First Amendment.

Subcommittee's Authority to Compel Testimony.

At the outset it should be noted that Rule XI authorized this Subcommittee to compel testimony within the framework of the investigative authority conferred on the Un-American Activities Committee. Petitioner contends that Watkins v. United States [1957], nevertheless held the grant of this power in all circumstances ineffective because of the vagueness of Rule XI in delineating the Committee jurisdiction to which its exercise was to be appurtenant. This view of Watkins was accepted by two of the dissenting judges below.

The Watkins Case cannot properly be read as standing for such a proposition. A principal contention in Watkins was that the refusals to answer were justified because the requirement of 2 USC § 192 that the questions asked be "pertinent to the question under inquiry" had not been satisfied. This Court reversed the conviction solely on that ground, holding that Watkins had not been adequately apprised of the subject matter of the Subcommittee's investigation or the pertinency thereto of the questions he refused to answer. In so deciding the Court drew upon Rule XI only as one of the facets in the total mise en scène in its search for the "question under inquiry" in that particular investigation. The Court, in other words, was not dealing with Rule XI at large, and indeed in effect stated that no such issue was before it. That the vagueness of Rule XI was not alone determinative is also shown by the Court's further statement that aside from the Rule "the remarks of the chairman or members of the committee, or even the nature of the proceedings themselves, might sometimes make the topic [under inquiry] clear." In short, while Watkins was critical of Rule XI, it did not involve the broad and inflexible holding petitioner now attributes to it.

Petitioner also contends, independently of Watkins, that the vagueness of Rule XI deprived the Subcommittee of the right to compel testimony in this investigation into Communist activity. We cannot agree with this contention, which in its furthest reach would mean that the House Un-American Activities Committee under its existing authority has no right to compel testimony in any circumstances. Granting the vagueness of the Rule, we may not read it in isolation from its long history in the House of Representatives. Just as legislation is often given meaning by the gloss of legislative reports, administrative interpretation, and long usage, so the proper meaning of an authorization to a congressional committee is not to be derived alone from its abstract terms unrelated to the definite content furnished them by the course of congressional actions. The Rule comes to us with a "persuasive gloss of legislative history," which shows beyond doubt that in pursuance of its legislative concerns in the domain of "national security" the House has clothed the Un-American Activities Committee with pervasive authority to investigate Communist activities in this country. . . .

[The Court here summarizes the history of the Committee, showing the wide range of areas in which it had pursued its search for Communists.]

In the context of these unremitting pursuits, the House has steadily continued the life of the Committee at the commencement of each new Congress; it has never narrowed the powers of the Committee, whose authority has remained throughout identical with that contained in Rule XI;

31

and it has continuingly supported the Committee's activities with substantial appropriations. Beyond this, the Committee was raised to the level of a standing committee of the House in 1945, it having been but a special committee prior to that time.

In light of this long and illuminating history it can hardly be seriously argued that the investigation of Communist activities generally, and the attendant use of compulsory process, was beyond the purview of the Committee's intended authority under Rule XI.

We are urged, however, to construe Rule XI so as at least to exclude the field of education from the Committee's compulsory authority. . . .

[The Court finds Congress was aware of and did not disapprove previous investigations in this field.]

In this framework of the Committee's history we must conclude that its legislative authority to conduct the inquiry presently under consideration is unassailable, and that independently of whatever bearing the broad scope of Rule XI may have on the issue of "pertinency" in a given investigation into Communist activities, as in Watkins, the Rule cannot be said to be constitutionally infirm on the score of vagueness. The constitutional permissibility of that authority otherwise is a matter to be discussed later.

Pertinency Claim.

Undeniably a conviction for contempt under 2 USC § 192 cannot stand unless the questions asked are pertinent to the subject matter of the investigation. Watkins v. United States. But the factors which led us to rest decision on this ground in Watkins were very different from those involved here.

In Watkins the petitioner had made specific objection to the Subcommittee's questions on the ground of pertinency; the question under inquiry had not been disclosed in any illuminating manner; and the questions asked the petitioner were not only amorphous on their face, but in some instances clearly foreign to the alleged subject matter of the investigation—"Communism in labor."

In contrast, petitioner in the case before us raised no objections on the ground of pertinency at the time any of the questions were put to him. . . .

We need not, however, rest decision on petitioner's failure to object on this score, for here "pertinency" was made to appear "with undisputable clarity." First of all, it goes without saying that the scope of the Committee's authority was for the House, not a witness, to determine, subject to the ultimate reviewing responsibility of this Court. What we deal with here is whether petitioner was sufficiently apprised of "the topic under inquiry" thus authorized "and the connective reasoning whereby the precise questions asked relate[d] to it." In light of his prepared memorandum of constitutional objections there can be no doubt that this petitioner was well aware of the Subcommittee's authority and purpose to question him as it did. In addition the other sources of this information which we recognized in Watkins leave no room for a "pertinency" objection on this record. The subject matter of the inquiry had been identified at the commencement of the investigation as Communist infiltration into the field of education. Just prior to petitioner's appearance before the Subcommittee, the scope of the day's hearings had been announced as "in the main communism in education and the experiences and background in the party by Francis X. T. Crowley. It will deal with activities in Michigan, Boston, and in some small degree, New York." Petitioner had heard the Subcommittee interrogate the witness Crowley along the same lines as he, petitioner, was evidently to be questioned, and had listened to Crowley's testimony identifying him as a former member of an alleged Communist student organization at the University of Michigan while they both were in attendance there. Further, petitioner had stood mute in the face of the Chairman's statement as to why he had been called as a witness by the Subcommittee. And, lastly, unlike Watkins, petitioner refused to answer questions as to his own Communist Party affiliations, whose pertinency of course was clear beyond doubt.

Petitioner's contentions on this aspect of the case cannot be sustained.

Constitutional Contentions.

Our function, at this point, is purely one of constitutional adjudication in the particular case and upon the particular record before us, not to pass judgment upon the general wisdom or efficacy of the activities of this Committee in a vexing and complicated field.

The precise constitutional issue confronting us is whether the Subcommittee's inquiry into petitioner's past or present membership in the Communist Party transgressed the provisions of the First Amendment, which of course reach and limit congressional investigations. Watkins.

The Court's past cases establish sure guides to decision. Undeniably, the First Amendment in some circumstances protects an individual from being compelled to disclose his associational relationships. However, the protections of the First Amendment, unlike a proper claim of the privilege against self-incrimination under the Fifth Amendment, do not afford a witness the right to resist inquiry in all circumstances. Where First Amendment rights are asserted to bar governmental interrogation resolution of the issue always involves a balancing by the courts of the competing private and public interests at stake in the particular circumstances shown. These principles were recognized in the Watkins Case. . . .

The first question is whether this investigation was related to a valid legislative purpose, for Congress may not constitutionally require an individual to disclose his political relationships or other private affairs except in relation to such a purpose. See Watkins v. United States.

That Congress has wide power to legislate in the field of Communist activity in this Country, and to conduct appropriate investigations in aid thereof, is hardly debatable. The existence of such power has never been questioned by this Court, and it is sufficient to say, without particularization, that Congress has enacted or considered in this field a wide range of legislative measures, not a few of which have stemmed from recommendations of the very Committee whose actions have been drawn in question here. In the last analysis this power rests on the right of self-preservation, "the ultimate value of any society," Dennis v. United States [1951]. Justification for its exercise in turn rests on the long and widely accepted view that the tenets of the Communist Party include the ultimate overthrow of the Government of the United States by force and violence, a view which has been given formal expression by the Congress. . . .

. . . To suggest that because the Communist Party may also sponsor peaceable political reforms the constitutional issues before us should now be judged as if that Party were just an ordinary political party from the standpoint of national security, is to ask this Court to blind itself to world affairs which have determined the whole course of our national policy since the close of World War II, . . . and to the vast burdens which these conditions have entailed for the entire Nation.

We think that investigatory power in this domain is not to be denied Congress solely because the field of education is involved. Nothing in the prevailing opinions in Sweezy v. New Hampshire [1957] stands for a contrary view. The vice existing there was that the questioning of Sweezy, who had not been shown ever to have been connected with the Communist Party, as to the contents of a lecture he had given at the University of New Hampshire, and as to his connections with the Progressive Party, then on the ballot as a normal political party in some 26 States, was too far removed from the premises on which the constitutionality of the State's investigation had to depend to withstand attack under the Fourteenth Amendment. . . . This is a very different thing from inquiring into the extent to which the Communist Party has succeeded in infiltrating into our universities, or elsewhere, persons and groups committed to furthering the objective of overthrow. Indeed we do not understand petitioner here to suggest that Congress in no circumstances may inquire into Communist activity in the field of education. Rather, his position is in effect that this particular investigation was aimed not at the revolutionary aspects but at the theoretical classroom discussion of communism.

In our opinion this position rests on a too constricted view of the nature of the investigatory process, and is not supported by a fair assessment of the record before us. An investigation of advocacy of or preparation for overthrow certainly embraces the right to identify a witness as a member of the Communist Party . . . and to inquire into the various manifestations of the Party's tenets. The strict requirements of a prosecution under the Smith Act, see Dennis v. United States [1951] and Yates v. United States [1957], are not the measure of the permissible scope of a congressional investigation into "overthrow," for of necessity the investigatory process must proceed step by step. Nor can it fairly be concluded that this investigation was directed at controlling what is being taught at our universities rather than at overthrow. The statement of the Subcommittee Chairman at the opening of the investigation evinces no such intention, and so far as this record reveals nothing thereafter transpired which would justify our holding that the thrust of the investigation later changed. The record discloses considerable testimony concerning the foreign domination and revolutionary purposes and efforts of the Communist Party. That there was also testimony on the abstract philosophical level does not detract from the dominant theme of this investigation—Communist infiltration furthering the alleged ultimate purpose of overthrow. And certainly the conclusion would not be justified that the questioning of petitioner would have exceeded permissible bounds had he not shut off the Subcommittee at the threshold.

Nor can we accept the further contention that this investigation should not be deemed to have been in furtherance of a legislative purpose because the true objective of the Committee and of the Congress was purely "exposure." So long as Congress acts in pursuance of its constitutional power, the Judiciary lacks authority to intervene on the basis of the motives which spurred the exercise of that power. . . . "It is, of course, true," as was said in McCray v. United States [1904], "that if there be no authority in the judiciary to restrain a lawful exercise of power by another department of the government, where a wrong motive or purpose has impelled to the exertion of the power, that abuses of a power conferred may be temporarily effectual. The remedy for this, however, lies, not in the abuse by the judicial authority of its functions, but in the people, upon whom, after all, under our institutions, reliance must be placed for the correction of abuses committed in the exercise of a lawful power." These principles of course apply as well to committee investigations into the need for legislation as to the enactments which such investigations may produce. . . . Thus, in stating in the Watkins Case that "there is no congressional power to expose for the sake of exposure," we at the same time declined to inquire into the "motives of committee members," and recognized that their "motives alone would not vitiate an investigation which had been instituted by a House of Congress if that assembly's legislative purpose is being served." Having scrutinized this record we cannot say that the unanimous panel of the Court of Appeals which first considered this case was wrong in concluding that "the primary purposes of the inquiry were in aid of legislative processes." . . . Certainly this is not a case like Kilbourn v. Thompson [1881], where "the House of Representatives not only exceeded the limit of its own authority, but assumed a power which could only be properly exercised by another branch of the government, because it was in its nature clearly judicial." The constitutional legislative power of Congress in this instance is beyond question.

Finally, the record is barren of other factors which in themselves might sometimes lead to the conclusion that the individual interests at stake were not subordinate to those of the state. There is no indication in this record that the Subcommittee was attempting to pillory witnesses. Nor did petitioner's appearance as a witness follow from indiscriminate dragnet procedures, lacking in probable cause for belief that he possessed information which might be helpful to the Subcommittee. And the relevancy of the questions put to him by the Subcommittee is not open to doubt.

We conclude that the balance between the individual and the governmental interests here at stake must be struck in favor of the latter, and that therefore the provisions of the First Amendment have not been offended.

We hold that petitioner's conviction for contempt of Congress discloses no infirmity, and that the judgment of the Court of Appeals must be Affirmed.

[Mr. Justice Black, with whom Chief Justice Warren and Mr. Justice Douglas concurred, dissented on grounds that (1) the term "un-American" was so vague as to make the Committee's mandate void for vagueness under the due process clause; (2) the Court's "balancing test" is not the way to determine the scope of freedom of speech, and if it were, the Court should have balanced the interest of society in "being able to join organizations, advocate causes and make political 'mistakes,' " against the government's limited interest in making laws in the area of free speech—an interest which cannot reasonably be equated with "self-preservation"; (3) the chief aim of the HUAC is to "try witnesses and punish them because they are or have been Communists," which constitutes a bill of attainder.]

Mr. Justice Brennan dissented, saying in part:

I would reverse this conviction. It is sufficient that I state my complete agreement with my Brother Black that no purpose for the investigation of Barenblatt is revealed by the record except exposure purely for the sake of exposure. This is not a purpose to which Barenblatt's rights under the First Amendment can validly be subordinated. An investigation in which the processes of law-making and law-evaluating are submerged entirely in exposure of individual behavior—in adjudication, of a sort, through the exposure process—is outside the constitutional pale of congressional inquiry. Watkins v. United States. . . .

3

The Executive Branch

**YOUNGSTOWN SHEET & TUBE COMPANY
v. SAWYER**

343 U. S. 579; 72 S. Ct. 863; 96 L. Ed. 1153
(1952)

The President exercises the bulk of his policy-making powers under delegations of authority made by Congress. But there are important areas in which he enjoys powers granted not by Congress, but by the Constitution itself. The conduct of foreign affairs has traditionally been the concern of the executive branch of government, and the Constitution of the United States recognizes this fact. The President appoints our foreign ambassadors, ministers, and consuls. He alone receives ambassadors and other public ministers from abroad and thereby "recognizes" the governments by which such officers are sent. It is he who, usually through the Secretary of State, negotiates treaties. But Congress has some power with respect to foreign affairs. Treaties or other agreements which call for the expenditure of money will be ineffective unless Congress appropriates that money by statute. The Senate must consent to the appointments of our diplomatic representatives, and two-thirds of the Senate must give its approval to a treaty. This latter requirement has tended to limit the use of the treaty power to fairly formal and important international agreements, among which have been military alliances, the making of peace, and adherence to international organizations. A substantial proportion of our international agreements take the form of executive agreements concluded between the President and the executive of a foreign nation. Some of these, particularly in the field of foreign trade, are specifically authorized by Congress. Others are made solely on the authority of the President as chief executive.

While the Constitution provides that treaties shall be the law of the land, and executive agreements made with congressional consent would also have the authority of law, there had long been some doubt about the binding nature of an agreement made by the executive alone.

In 1937, in United States v. Belmont, the Court laid this doubt to rest. The case involved the title to money which a Russian company had on deposit in Belmont's bank. The Soviet government had nationalized the company in 1918 and confiscated its assets, including, presumably, the funds in Belmont's bank. Then in 1933 the President, by receiving the Soviet ambassador, recognized the Soviet government as the legitimate government of Russia. A final settlement of the claims and counter claims between the two countries was concluded in the Litvinov Assignments, and the Belmont deposits were assigned to the United States. The assignments were made by an exchange of diplomatic correspondence between the Soviet government and the United States and were not submitted to the Senate in the form of a treaty. The Supreme Court rejected the argument that the assignments were void since confiscation was against the public policy both of New York and the United States. "The recognition, establishment of diplomatic relations, the assignment, and agreements with respect thereto, were all parts of one transaction, resulting in an international compact between the two governments. That the negotiations, acceptance of the assignment and agreements and understandings in respect thereof were within the competence of the President may not be doubted. Governmental power over internal affairs is distributed between the national government and the several states. Governmental power over external affairs is not distributed, but is vested exclusively in the national government. And in respect of what was done here, the Executive had authority to speak as the sole organ of that government. The assignment and the agreements in connection therewith did not, as in the case of treaties, as that term is used in the treaty-making clause of the Constitution (Article II, Sec. 2), require the advice and consent of the Senate."

Another area in which the President receives direct constitutional powers is found in Article II, which makes the President the Commander in Chief of the Army and Navy. This is clearly not a power merely to command the disposition of the armed forces. But if it is more than that, how much more? A democratic distrust of executive power cannot alter the fact that in times of war a near-dictatorship may be necessary to preserve the nation. In such times Congress has wisely delegated vast areas of authority to the President. But where Congress has not done so, and the President has felt that the emergency justified it, he has often acted on his own authority. The fact that Congress usually gives belated approval to such executive acts hardly obscures the fact that the crucial policy decisions are made by the executive.

The Constitution gives Congress the power to declare war; but may the President on his own authority decide that a state of war exists, and on the strength of this decision take action affecting the lives and property of American citizens? Following the firing upon Fort Sumter in 1861, President Lincoln declared the existence of a state of insurrection and called out the militia. Authority to do this had been given him by Congress, and the Court had held in Martin v. Mott (1827) that vesting of this discretion in the President was valid. But a week after Sumter the President, acting wholly on his own authority, declared a naval blockade of the Confederate ports. Pursuant to this proclamation four blockade runners were captured and condemned. The Court sustained this action in the Prize Cases (1863), pointing out that "if a war be made by invasion of a foreign nation, the President is not only authorized but bound to resist force, by force. He does not initiate the war, but is bound to accept the challenge without waiting for any special legislative authority. And whether the hostile party be a foreign invader, or States organized in rebellion, it is none the less a war. . . ." The proclamation of a blockade was held "itself, official and conclusive evidence to the court that a state of war existed which demanded and authorized a recourse to such a measure, under the circumstances peculiar to the case."

Even the most drastic and dictatorial exercises of power by the President acting under his authority as Commander in Chief have usually not resulted in clarifying or determining the actual constitutional scope of pure executive power. This is because Congress in nearly all such cases has hastened to shore up the President's authority by legislative ratification of what he has done. Thus when Congress came into session on July 4, 1861, it underwrote the President's blockade of Southern ports by passing an act "approving, legalizing and making valid all the acts, proclamations, and orders of the President, & c., as if they had been issued and done under the previous express authority and direction of the Congress. . . ." In 1944, following the issue of the executive order creating military districts from which persons of Japanese ancestry were excluded (see the Korematsu case), Congress made it a crime to "enter, remain in, leave, or commit any act in any military area . . . prescribed [by executive order] . . . contrary to the order of the Secretary of War or any such military commander. . . ."

On November 4, 1979 Iranian radicals, demanding the return of the deposed Shah, took hostage 53 members of the American embassy in Tehran. President Carter refused to return the Shah, ordered frozen all Iranian property in the United States, and nullified all claims against such property including those in litigation. Release of the hostages was finally effected 14 months later in exchange for the return of the property to Iran. In Dames & Moore v. Regan (1981) the Court upheld the presidential seizure. It distinguished the Youngstown case, noting that "The inferences to be drawn from the character of the legislation Congress has enacted in the area . . . and from the history of acquiescence in executive claims settlement—we conclude that the President was authorized to suspend pending claims. . . ."

The constitutional grants of power over foreign affairs and as Commander in Chief have always been interpreted as being independent grants to the President to make important policy decisions in these two fields, and whatever power Congress has in these areas can be delegated to the President virtually without limit. In contrast to this his duty to "take care that the laws be faithfully executed" seems a requirement that he carry out the laws of Congress. In the case of In re Neagle (1890), the Court interpreted this clause, too, as a grant of policy-making authority. The laws are not merely the laws of Congress, but include independent acts of the President himself. There is, moreover, a peace of the United States, and the President, as chief executive, is protector of that peace with power to prevent violations.

The case arose out of an extraordinary set of circumstances. A long and bitter legal battle involving title to more than a million dollars had culminated in the United States circuit court in California at a time when Justice Field of the United States Supreme Court was sitting as circuit justice. The disappointed contestant was represented by her husband, a lawyer named Terry who had once been chief justice of the California supreme court. At the close of the case Mrs. Terry accused Justice Field of selling justice, and the United States marshal was ordered to quiet her. A fight ensued and Terry and his wife went to prison for six months for contempt of court. Upon their release they threatened to kill Justice Field if he ever came back to California. Since the law at that time required Supreme Court justices to ride circuit, the matter was laid before the Attorney General; and when Field again returned to California, Neagle, a deputy marshal, was detailed to serve as a bodyguard. Terry, following up his threat, tried to make a murderous attack upon the justice in a railroad restaurant where the justice had stopped while traveling on circuit duty. He was about to draw his knife when Neagle shot and killed him. Neagle was promptly arrested by the local authorities and held for murder. He was released from the custody of the state court upon a writ of habeas corpus by the federal circuit court on the ground that he was held in custody for "an act done in pursuance of a law of the United States" within the meaning of the federal statute providing for the issuance of the writ in such cases.

The most significant feature of the case is that the "law of the United States" in pursuance of which Neagle acted was not an act of Congress, but merely an executive order issued by authority of the President. In sustaining Neagle's release, the Court holds that the President in the exercise of the duty imposed upon him to see that the laws are faithfully executed may, without special statutory authority, appoint an officer to protect the life of a federal judge. It was on the President's power to "take care that the laws be faithfully executed" that Chief Justice Vinson relied in his dissent in the Steel Seizure Case, printed below.

This case climaxed a long dispute between the steel companies and the steel workers. On December 18, 1951, the United Steel Workers of America, CIO, gave notice that it would strike on December 31. The Federal Mediation and Conciliation Service failed to effect a settlement. The Federal Wage Stabilization Board, to which President Truman referred the dispute on December 22, also failed. The President did not invoke the provisions of the Taft-Hartley Act, which would have set up a "period of waiting" before a strike. On April 4, 1952, the union announced that it would call a nationwide strike on April 9. A few hours before the strike was to begin the President directed Secretary of Commerce Sawyer to seize and operate most of the country's steel mills. The Secretary issued the appropriate orders. The President reported the seizure to Congress on April 9, and again on April 21, but Congress took no action. The steel companies complied under protest with the seizure order, but sought a temporary injunction to restrain the government's action. On April 30, the district court of the District of Columbia issued a preliminary injunction, which was stayed on the same day by the court of appeals.

On May 3, the Supreme Court, bypassing the court of appeals, brought the case to its docket by certiorari. It heard argument on May 12, and decided the case on June 2. These dates indicate the celerity with which the Supreme Court can act when the national interest requires speed.

The difficulty and complexity of the case is shown by the fact that the Court divided six to three, and that seven justices wrote separate opinions totaling 128 pages. The Court did not face here the naked question of the President's power to seize the steel plants in the absence of any congressional enactments or expressions of policy. Congress had provided limited powers of seizure in the Selective Service Act of 1948 and in the Defense Production Act of 1950. Furthermore, in its debates on the Taft-Hartley Act of 1947 Congress had considered an amendment authorizing seizure of plants by the President in case of strike, and had rejected it. In fact, over a period of years, Congress had made it clear that the seizure of private property in time of emergency was a problem to be controlled by congressional policy. For a variety of reasons, the majority of the Court found that this legislative occupation of the field made untenable the President's claim of authority to seize the plants as an exercise of inherent executive power or as Commander in Chief. Congress had set up various procedures for the President to follow in such cases, and he had not followed them.

Mr. Justice Black delivered the opinion of the Court, saying in part:

We are asked to decide whether the President was acting within his constitutional power when he issued an order directing the Secretary of Commerce to take possession of and operate most of the Nation's steel mills. The mill owners argue that the President's order amounts to lawmaking, a legislative function which the Constitution has expressly confided to the Congress and not to the President. The Government's position is that the order was made on findings of the President that his action was necessary to avert a national catastrophe which would inevitably result from a stoppage of steel production, and that in meeting this grave emergency the President was acting within the aggregate of his constitutional powers as the Nation's Chief Executive and the Commander in Chief of the Armed Forces of the United States. . . .

The President's power, if any, to issue the order must stem either from an act of Congress or from the Constitution itself. There is no statute that expressly authorizes the President to take possession of property as he did here. Nor is there any act of Congress to which our attention has been directed from which such a power can fairly be implied. Indeed, we do not understand the Government to rely on statutory authorization for this seizure. There are two statutes which do authorize the President to take both personal and real property under certain conditions. [The Selective Service Act of 1948 and the Defense Production Act of 1950.] However, the Government admits that these conditions were not met and that the President's order was not rooted in either of the statutes. The Government refers to the seizure provisions of one of these statutes (§ 201 (b) of the Defense Production Act) as "much too cumbersome, involved, and time-consuming for the crisis which was at hand."

Moreover, the use of the seizure technique to solve labor disputes in order to prevent work stoppages was not only unauthorized by any congressional enactment; prior to this controversy, Congress had refused to adopt that method of settling labor disputes. When the Taft-Hartley Act was under consideration in 1947, Congress rejected an amendment which would have authorized such governmental seizures in cases of emergency. Apparently it was thought that the technique of seizure, like that of compulsory arbitration, would interfere with the process of collective bargaining. Consequently, the plan Congress adopted in that Act did not provide for seizure under any circumstances. Instead, the plan sought to bring about settlements by use of the customary devices of mediation, conciliation, investigation by boards of inquiry, and public reports. In some instances temporary injunctions were authorized to provide cooling-off periods. All this failing, unions were left free to strike after a secret vote by employees as to whether they wished to accept their employers' final settlement offer.

It is clear that if the President had authority to issue the order he did, it must be found in some provision of the Constitution. And it is not claimed that express constitutional language grants this power to the President. The contention is that presidential power should be implied from the aggregate of his powers under the Constitution. Particular reliance is placed on provisions in Article II which say that "The executive Power shall be vested in a President . . ."; that "he shall take Care that the Laws be faithfully executed"; and that he "shall be Commander in Chief of the Army and Navy of the United States."

The order cannot properly be sustained as an exercise of the President's military power as Commander in Chief of the Armed Forces. The Government attempts to do so by citing a number of cases upholding broad powers in military commanders engaged in day-to-day fighting in a theater of war. Such cases need not concern us here. Even though "theater of war" be an expanding concept, we cannot with faithfulness to our constitutional system hold that the Commander in Chief of the Armed Forces has the ultimate power as such to take possession of private property in order to keep labor disputes from stopping production. This is a job for the Nation's lawmakers, not for its military authorities.

Nor can the seizure order be sustained because of the several constitutional provisions that grant executive power to the President. In the framework of our Constitution, the President's power to see that the laws are faithfully executed refutes the idea that he is to be a lawmaker. The Constitution limits his functions in the lawmaking process to the recommending of laws he thinks wise and the vetoing of laws he thinks bad. And the Constitution is neither silent nor equivocal about who shall make laws which the President is to execute. The first section of the first article says that "All legislative Powers herein granted shall be vested in a Congress of the United States." . . .

The President's order does not direct that a congressional policy be executed in a manner prescribed by Congress—it directs that a presidential policy be executed in a manner prescribed by the President. The preamble of the order itself, like that of many statutes, sets out reasons why the President believes certain policies should be adopted, proclaims these policies as rules of conduct to be followed, and again, like a statute, authorizes a government official to promulgate additional rules and regulations consistent with the policy proclaimed and needed to carry that policy into execution. The power of Congress to adopt such public policies as those proclaimed by the order is beyond question. It can authorize the taking of private property for public use. It can make laws regulating the relationships between employers and employees, prescribing rules designed to settle labor disputes, and fixing wages and working conditions in certain fields of our economy. The Constitution does not subject this lawmaking power of Congress to presidential or military supervision or control.

It is said that other Presidents without congressional authority have taken possession of private business enterprises in order to settle labor disputes. But even if this be true, Congress has not thereby lost its exclusive constitutional authority to make laws necessary and proper to carry out the power vested by the Constitution "in the Government of the United States, or any Department or Officer thereof."

The Founders of this Nation entrusted the lawmaking power to the Congress alone in both good and bad times. It would do no good to recall the historical events, the fears of power and the hopes for freedom that lay behind their choice. Such a review would but confirm our holding that this seizure order cannot stand.

The judgment of the District Court is
Affirmed.

Mr. Justice Frankfurter, concurring with the judgment and opinion of the Court, said in part:

Apart from his vast share of responsibility for the conduct of our foreign relations, the embracing function of the President is that "he shall take Care that the Laws be faithfully executed. . . ." Art. 2, § 3. The nature of that authority has for me been comprehensively indicated by Mr. Justice Holmes. "The duty of the President to see that the laws be executed is a duty that does not go beyond the laws or require him to achieve more than Congress sees fit to leave within his powers" Myers v. United States [1926]. The powers of the President are not as particularized as are those of Congress. But unenumerated powers do not mean undefined powers. The separation of powers built into our Constitution gives essential content to undefined provisions in the frame of our government. . . .

A scheme of government like ours no doubt at times feels the lack of power to act with complete, all-embracing, swiftly moving authority. No doubt a government with distributed authority, subject to be challenged in the courts of law, at least long enough to consider and adjudicate the challenge, labors under restrictions from which other governments are free. It has not been our tradition to envy such governments. In any event our government was designed to have such restrictions. The price was deemed not too high in view of the safeguards which these restrictions afforded. . . .

Mr. Justice Douglas, concurring with the judgment and opinion of the Court, said in part:

There can be no doubt that the emergency which caused the President to seize these steel plants was one that bore heavily on the country. But the emergency did not create power; it merely marked an occasion when power should be exercised. And the fact that it was necessary that measures be taken to keep steel in production does not mean that the President, rather than the Congress, had the constitutional authority to act. The Congress, as well as the President, is trustee of the national welfare. The President can act more quickly than the Congress. The President with the armed services at his disposal can move with force as well as with speed. All executive power —from the reign of ancient kings to the rule of modern dictators—has the outward appearance of efficiency.

Legislative power, by contrast, is slower to exercise. There must be delay while the ponderous machinery of committees, hearings, and debates is put into motion. That takes time; and while the Congress slowly moves into action, the emergency may take its toll in wages, consumer goods, war production, the standard of living of the people, and perhaps even lives. Legislative action may indeed often be cumbersome, time-consuming, and apparently inefficient. But as Mr. Justice Brandeis stated in his dissent in Myers v. United States [1926]:

"The doctrine of the separation of powers was adopted by the Convention of 1787, not to promote efficiency but to preclude the exercise of arbitrary power. The purpose was, not to avoid friction, but, by means of the inevitable friction incident to the distribution of the governmental powers among three departments, to save the people from autocracy."

We therefore cannot decide this case by determining which branch of government can deal most expeditiously with the present crisis. The answer must depend on the allocation of powers under the Constitution. That in turn requires an analysis of the conditions giving rise to the seizure and of the seizure itself. . . .

The great office of President is not a weak and powerless one. The President represents the people and is their spokesman in domestic and foreign affairs. The office is respected more than any other in the land. It gives a position of leadership that is unique. The power to formulate policies and mould opinion inheres in the Presidency and conditions our national life. The impact of the man and the philosophy he represents may at times be thwarted by the Congress. Stalemates may occur when emergencies mount and the Nation suffers for lack of harmonious, reciprocal action between the White House and Capitol Hill. That is a risk inherent in our system of separation of powers. The tragedy of such stalemates might be avoided by allowing the President the use of some legislative authority. The Framers with memories of the tyrannies produced by a blending of executive and legislative power rejected that political arrangement. Some future generation may, however, deem it so urgent that the President have legislative authority that the Constitution will be amended. We could not sanction the seizures and condemnations of the steel plants in this case without reading Article 2 as giving the President not only the power to execute the laws but to make some. Such a step would most assuredly alter the pattern of the Constitution.

We pay a price for our system of checks and balances, for the distribution of power among the three branches of government. It is a price that today may seem exorbitant to many. Today a kindly President uses the seizure power to effect a wage increase and to keep the steel furnaces in production. Yet tomorrow another President might use the same power to prevent a wage increase, to curb trade-unionists, to regiment labor as oppressively as industry thinks it has been regimented by this seizure.

Mr. Justice Jackson, concurring in the judgment and opinion of the Court, said in part:

That seems to be the logic of an argument tendered at our bar—that the President having, on his own responsibility, sent American troops abroad derives from that act "affirmative power" to seize the means of producing a supply of steel for them. . . .

I cannot foresee all that it might entail if the Court should indorse this argument. Nothing in our Constitution is plainer than that declaration of a war is entrusted only to Congress. Of course, a state of war may in fact exist without a formal declaration. But no doctrine that the Court could promulgate would seem to me more sinister and alarming than that a President whose conduct of foreign affairs is so largely uncontrolled, and often even is unknown, can vastly enlarge his mastery over the internal affairs of the country by his own commitment of the Nation's armed forces to some foreign venture. . . .

The Solicitor General lastly grounds support of the seizure upon nebulous, inherent powers never expressly granted but said to have accrued to the office from the customs and claims of preceding administrations. The plea is for a resulting power to deal with a crisis or an emergency according to the necessities of the case, the unarticulated assumption being that necessity knows no law.

The appeal, however, that we declare the existence of inherent powers *ex necessitate* to meet an emergency asks us to do what many think would be wise, although it is something the forefathers omitted. They knew what emergencies were, knew the pressures they engender for authoritative action, knew, too, how they afford a ready pretext for usurpation. We may also suspect that they suspected that emergency powers would tend to kindle emergencies. . . .

In the practical working of our Government we already have evolved a technique within the framework of the Constitution by which normal executive powers may be considerably expanded to meet an emergency. Congress may and has granted extraordinary authorities which lie dormant in normal times but may be called into play by the Executive in war or upon proclamation of a national emergency. In 1939, upon congressional request, the Attorney General listed ninety-nine such separate statutory grants by Congress of emergency or war-time executive powers. They were invoked from time to time as need appeared. Under this procedure we retain Government by law—special, temporary law, perhaps, but law nonetheless. The public may know the extent and limitations of the powers that can be asserted, and persons affected may be informed from the statute of their rights and duties.

In view of the ease, expedition and safety with which Congress can grant and has granted large emergency powers, certainly ample to embrace this crisis, I am quite unimpressed with the argument that we should affirm possession of them without statute. Such power either has no beginning or it has no end. If it exists, it need submit to no legal restraint. I am not alarmed that it would plunge us straightway into dictatorship, but it is at least a step in that wrong direction. . . .

But I have no illusion that any decision by this Court can keep power in the hands of Congress if it is not wise and timely in meeting its problems. A crisis that challenges the President equally, or perhaps primarily, challenges Congress. If not good law, there was worldly wisdom in the maxim attributed to Napoleon that "The tools belong to the man who can use them." We may say that power to legislate for emergencies belongs in the hands of Congress, but only Congress itself can prevent power from slipping through its fingers.

The essence of our free Government is "leave to live by no man's leave, underneath the law"—to be governed by those impersonal forces which we call law. Our Government is fashioned to fulfill this concept so far as humanly possible. The Executive, except for recommendation and veto, has no legislative power. The executive action we have here originates in the individual will of the President and represents an exercise of authority without law. No one, perhaps not even the President, knows the limits of the power he may seek to exert in this instance and the parties affected cannot learn the limit of their rights. We do not know today what powers over labor or property would be claimed to flow from Government possession if we should legalize it, what rights to compensation would be claimed or recognized, or on what contingency it would end. With all its defects, delays and inconveniences, men have discovered no technique for long preserving free government except that the Executive be under the law, and that the law be made by parliamentary deliberations.

Such institutions may be destined to pass away. But it is the duty of the Court to be last, not first, to give them up.

Mr. Justice Burton, concurring in the opinion and judgment of the Court, said in part:

. . . In the case before us, Congress authorized a procedure which the President declined to follow. Instead, he followed another procedure which he hoped might eliminate the need for the first. Upon its failure, he issued an executive order to seize the steel properties in the face of the reserved right of Congress to adopt or reject that course as a matter of legislative policy.

This brings us to a further crucial question. Does the President, in such a situation, have inherent constitutional power to seize private property which makes congressional action in relation thereto unnecessary? We find no such power available to him under the present circumstances. The present situation is not comparable to that of an imminent invasion or threatened attack. We do not face the issue of what might be the President's constitutional power to meet such catastrophic situations. Nor is it claimed that the current seizure is in the nature of a military command addressed by the President, as Commander-in-Chief, to a mobilized nation waging, or imminently threatened with, total war.

The controlling fact here is that Congress, within its constitutionally delegated power, has prescribed for the President specific procedures, exclusive of seizure, for his use in meeting the present type of emergency. Congress has reserved to itself the right to determine where and when to authorize the seizure of property in meeting such an emergency. Under these circumstances, the President's order of April 8 invaded the jurisdiction of Congress. It violated the essence of the principle of the separation of governmental powers. Accordingly, the injunction against its effectiveness should be sustained.

Mr. Justice Clark, concurring in the judgment of the Court, said in part:

. . . In my view . . . the Constitution does grant to the President extensive authority in times of grave and imperative national emergency. In fact, to my thinking, such a grant may well be necessary to the very existence of the Constitution itself. As Lincoln aptly said, "[is] it possible to lose the nation and yet preserve the Constitution?" In describing this authority I care not whether one calls it "residual," "inherent," "moral," "implied," "aggregate," "emergency," or otherwise. . . .

I conclude that where Congress has laid down specific procedures to deal with the type of crisis confronting the President, he must follow those procedures in meeting the crisis; but that in the absence of such action by Congress, the President's independent power to act depends upon the gravity of the situation confronting the nation. I cannot sustain the seizure in question because here ... Congress had prescribed methods to be followed by the President in meeting the emergency at hand. ...

... The Government made no effort to comply with the procedures established by the Selective Service Act of 1948, a statute which expressly authorizes seizures when producers fail to supply necessary defense matériel. ...

Mr. Chief Justice Vinson, with whom Justices Reed and Minton joined, dissented, saying in part:

Focusing now on the situation confronting the President on the night of April 8, 1952, we cannot but conclude that the President was performing his duty under the Constitution "to take Care that the Laws be faithfully executed"—a duty described by President Benjamin Harrison as "the central idea of the office."

The President reported to Congress the morning after the seizure that he acted because a work stoppage in steel production would immediately imperil the safety of the Nation by preventing execution of the legislative programs for procurement of military equipment. And, while a shutdown could be averted by granting the price concessions requested by plaintiffs, granting such concessions would disrupt the price stabilization program also enacted by Congress. Rather than fail to execute either legislative program, the President acted to execute both.

Much of the argument in this case has been directed at straw men. We do not now have before us the case of a President acting solely on the basis of his own notions of the public welfare. Nor is there any question of unlimited executive power in this case. The President himself closed the door to any such claim when he sent his Message to Congress stating his purpose to abide by any action of Congress, whether approving or disapproving his seizure action. Here, the President immediately made sure that Congress was fully informed of the temporary action he had taken only to preserve the legislative programs from destruction until Congress could act.

The absence of a specific statute authorizing seizure of the steel mills as a mode of executing the laws—both the military procurement program and the anti-inflation program—has not until today been thought to prevent the President from executing the laws. Unlike an administrative commission confined to the enforcement of the statute under which it was created, or the head of a department when administering a particular statute, the President is a constitutional officer charged with taking care that a "mass of legislation" be executed. Flexibility as to mode of execution to meet critical situations is a matter of practical necesity. ...

As the District Judge stated, this is no time for "timorous" judicial action. But neither is this a time for timorous executive action. Faced with the duty of executing the defense programs which Congress had enacted and the disastrous effects that any stoppage in steel production would have on those programs, the President acted to preserve those programs by seizing the steel mills. There is no question that the possession was other than temporary in character and subject to congressional direction—either approving, disapproving or regulating the manner in which the mills were to be administered and returned to the owners. The President immediately informed Congress of his action and clearly stated his intention to abide by the legislative will. No basis for claims of arbitrary action, unlimited powers or dictatorial usurpation of congressional power appears from the facts of this case. On the contrary, judicial, legislative and executive precedents throughout our history demonstrate that in this case the President acted in full conformity with his duties under the Constitution. Accordingly, we would reverse the order of the District Court.

UNITED STATES v. NIXON

418 U.S. 683; 94 S. Ct. 3090; 41 L. Ed. 2d 1039
(1974)

In setting up a government based on the separation of powers, the framers deliberately devised a form in which authority was divided and policies would necessarily be made as a result of compromise rather than by a single man or body. Given what they viewed as a choice between "liberty" and "tyranny," they opted for liberty, but the decision to sacrifice speed and efficiency for debate and compromise was perhaps easier to make then than it would be now. The image of George III and the teachings of Montesquieu were fresh in their minds, government played a minimal role in people's lives, and the slowness of communications made quick decisions less important than they are today.

Since the turn of the century, and especially in the last 40 years, all this has changed dramatically. The role of government has grown until it is the dominant force in people's lives, the world has shrunk until the most distant part is only a few hours away, the spectre of George III has been relegated to the pages of history, and effective policy-making power has been steadily shifted to the President. With the new pace of the world and our intimate involvement in the affairs of other countries, the frustration and delays imposed by the separation of powers seem scarcely tolerable. Although given virtually dictatorial powers, presidents like Lincoln and Franklin Roosevelt had not betrayed the public trust and that kind of presidency seemed essential to the effectiveness of the United States in that area of world politics upon which our national safety depended. Demands for more government and more effeciency were inexorable and few people saw in them a threat to essential democratic values. The choice made by the framers seemed scarcely relevant.

Against this background it is easy to view Watergate as a turn in destiny—a Gilbert and Sullivan operetta played to awaken us to our danger. For it is hard to imagine a more improbable plot in which to set a crucial test of presidential power. Any competent writer of fiction could do better. On June 17, 1972, seven men were caught breaking into the Democratic National Committee headquarters in the Watergate, a luxury apartment-office complex a few blocks from the White House. (The reasons for the break-in are still obscure.) Instead of immediately admitting White House involvement in the affair with an apology for the enthusiasm of his followers (a course which he could almost certainly have survived politically), the President and his staff undertook the bizarre and dramatically ill-fated "Watergate cover-up." The outcome was the resignation on August 9, 1974, of the President of the United States.

The burglary itself was the culmination of some three years of White House-directed investigation and harassment of political enemies, sparked in part by leaks to the press of the secret bombing of Cambodia and the "Pentagon Papers," and in part by a growing fear that President Nixon might not be reelected in 1972. A successful entry into the Democratic National Committee headquarters the month before had netted nothing of value, and this entry was apparently for the purpose of placing additional electronic bugging equipment.

Five of the "Watergate Seven" pleaded guilty to the burglary and the other two, both members of the Committee to Reelect the President, were convicted. While the upshot of the trial was to suggest that Watergate was merely the work of a few enthusiastic but misguided underlings whose intense loyalty to the President had led them into illegal activities, something about the trial itself belied this conclusion. At its close the presiding judge, John J. Sirica, stated that in his opinion the entire truth had not come out, and on the day of the sentencing he read in court a letter from James W. McCord, Jr., one of those convicted, stating that others involved in the break-in had not been prosecuted, that there had been perjury during the trial, and that pressure had been brought on him and others to plead guilty and keep silent. . . .

A shocked Senate investigating committee heard McCord's story; then called John W. Dean III, a former counsel to the President. Dean testified for a week, explaining how the White House staff, and ultimately the President, had congratulated him on successfully limiting the case to the few who had been tried and discussed with him the question of executive clemency and hush money for some of them. He said the President had known of the White House involvement almost from the beginning and had been actively involved in permitting the cover-up to continue. Implicated by Dean's testimony were former Attorney General John Mitchell and top presidential aides H. R. Haldeman and John Erlichman. White House denials raised the question: Who was telling the truth?

The present constitutional issue appeared with the startling disclosure that presidential conversations for the previous two years had been recorded on tape including, apparently, those crucial conversations with John Dean. Since it seemed the credibility issue could thus be easily resolved, an immediate demand was made for the tapes; but the President, citing the separation of powers and the absolute right of the President to keep his conversations confidential, refused to release them either to the Senate committee or to Archibald Cox, the Special Prosecutor heading the government's investigation of the matter.

There the issue was joined. Judge Sirica, after hearing argument in August of 1973, ordered the President to turn the tapes over to Cox. (He declined to enforce the Senate committee's subpoena for want of jurisdiction.) He conceded that executive privilege did exist, but denied "that it is the Executive that finally determines whether its privilege is properly invoked. . . . Judicial control over the evidence in a case cannot be abdicated to the caprice of executive officers." Nor was he persuaded by the argument based on the separation of powers. Whatever the merits of Mississippi v. Johnson (1867), it would be unrealistic to argue since Youngstown Sheet and Tube Co. v. Sawyer (1952) that compulsory court process cannot touch the White House. "In all candor," he added, "the court fails to perceive any reason for suspending the power of courts to get evidence and rule on questions of privilege in criminal matters simply because it is the President of the United States who holds the evidence." He ordered the tapes turned over to him for in-camera inspection with the understanding that unprivileged portions would be made available to the grand jury. After an abortive effort to get the two parties to compromise, the court of appeals sustained Judge Sirica's order; Nixon v. Sirica, 487 Fed. 2d 700 (1973).

Despite a widespread assumption that the President would seek from the Supreme Court that "definitive decision" by which he had announced he would abide, he instead decided to avoid a "constitutional crisis" by declining to appeal the decision and ordered Cox, as "an employee of the executive branch," not to pursue the matter further. Declining to follow the court's order, he proposed instead to provide White House "summaries" of the tapes. Cox rejected the offer, and on October 20, in what has become known as the "Saturday Night Massacre," the President accepted the resignation of Attorney General Elliot Richardson when he refused to fire Cox, then fired Deputy Attorney General Ruckelshaus when *he* refused to fire Cox, and finally persuaded Solicitor General Robert H. Bork to fire Cox and his staff of 90 investigators.

Three days later, bowing to a "fire storm" of public protest and the start of formal impeachment proceedings in the House of Representatives, the President agreed to turn over the tapes themselves. By the end of the week Leon Jaworski, a former head of the American Bar Association, had been chosen as the new special prosecutor and was assured even more independence than Cox had enjoyed.

Although two of the nine tapes ordered released turned out to be missing, and one had an unexplained 18-minute gap in it, enough was produced to clinch the indictments of seven more conspirators, including Mitchell, Haldeman, and Ehrlichman, on charges of conspiring to obstruct justice. On Jaworski's advice that a sitting president could not be indicted, President Nixon was named merely as an "unindicted co-conspirator." On order of Judge Sirica the grand jury evidence, including the tapes Jaworski had received, was turned over to the House Judiciary Committee for use in its impeachment investigation.

But the constitutional confrontation was not over. The House committee subpoenaed 42 more conversations and Jaworski 64, but the President refused to yield and instead made public some 1200 pages of White House-edited transcripts—some of them were those already released under court order. The public response to this brutally candid glimpse of the workings of the Nixon presidency was one of horrified shock, and demands for his impeachment became overwhelming. If he would release this kind of material, the argument ran, what was he concealing?

In a last-ditch stand the President not only elected to carry Jaworski's subpoena to the Supreme Court, but to protest his being named an unindicted co-conspirator (a point later dismissed by the Court). Over the objection of the President, the Court agreed to by-pass the court of appeals and hear argument in the closing days of its term. The President, in a series of procedural maneuvers, argued that no case or controversy existed, since the dispute between the President and Jaworski was entirely within the executive branch and the President could decide what evidence he wanted to present in prosecuting a case. The Court, in the case below, rejected this argument on the ground that Jaworski had been given freedom to ask for just such information, that the President had promised him complete freedom to pursue in court any interference by the executive, and this was, in fact, "the kind of controversy courts traditionally resolve."

It is important to note that President Nixon did not claim executive privilege from the tapes on the ground that they contained material involving either military or diplomatic matters. He claimed, rather, that all personal presidential conversations with his aides were privileged because without the assurance of such confidentiality the President could not get the uninhibited advice he needed and the presidency would thus be weakened. It was, in effect, a claim that the sanctity of the presidency was the highest constitutional value, and it was this claim that the Court rejected in the present case.

The President's last constitutional crisis came in the wake of the Court's decision. In 1832, following the Supreme Court's decision in Worcester v. Georgia President Andrew Jackson is reputed to have said, "John Marshall has made his decision, now let him enforce it." The realization that the court has no enforcement machinery at its command must make such a response a tempting one, and President Nixon, who alone knew what the tapes contained, reputedly agonized a whole day over the question whether or not to defy the Supreme Court. But wiser counsel prevailed and he agreed to comply with the Court's order.

Within a week of the Court's decision, while arguing whether to wait for the contents of the tapes, the House judiciary committee voted three articles of impeachment against the President. And President Nixon, even as he began complying with the Court order to release the tapes, elected to release transcripts of three of them which showed that he had known about the Watergate break-in from the beginning. With his concession that he had from the outset lied not only to his supporters in Congress, but even to his own lawyer, those on the judiciary committee who had argued that the President should not be impeached changed their minds. Next morning three members of the congressional leadership visited the President to tell him he could count on no more than 10 votes in the House against impeachment and no more than 15 votes in the Senate against removal. That night, in a television broadcast to the nation, President Nixon resigned his office, effective the following noon.

Mr. Chief Justice Burger delivered the opinion of the Court, saying in part:

IV. The Claim of Privilege

A.

Having determined that the requirements of Rule 17(c) were satisfied, we turn to the claim that the subpoena should be quashed because it demands "confidential conversations between a President and his close advisors that it would be inconsistent with the public interest to produce." The first contention is a broad claim that the separation of powers doctrine precludes judicial review of a President's claim of privilege. The second contention is that if he does not prevail on the claim of absolute privilege, the court should hold as a matter of constitutional law that the privilege prevails over the subpoena duces tecum.

In the performance of assigned constitutional duties each branch of the Government must initially interpret the Constitution, and the interpretation of its powers by any branch is due great respect from the others. The President's counsel, as we have noted, reads the Constitution as providing an absolute privilege of confidentiality for all Presidential communications.

Many decisions of this Court, however, have unequivocally reaffirmed the holding of Marbury v. Madison (1803) that "[it] is emphatically the province and duty of the judicial department to say what the law is."

No holding of the Court has defined the scope of judicial power specifically relating to the enforcement of a subpoena for confidential Presidential communications for use in a criminal prosecution, but other exercises of power by the Executive Branch and the Legislative Branch have been found invalid as in conflict with the Constitution. Powell v. McCormack [1969]; Youngstown Sheet & Tube Co. v. Sawyer (1952). In a series of cases, the Court interpreted the explicit immunity conferred by express provisions of the Constitution on Members of the House and Senate by the Speech or Debate Clause, U.S. Const. Art. I §6. Doe v. McMillan (1973); Gravel v. United States (1972). . . . Since this Court has consistently exercised the power to construe and delineate claims arising under express powers, it must follow that the Court has authority to interpret claims with respect to powers alleged to derive from enumerated powers.

Our system of government "requires that federal courts on occasion interpret the Constitution in a manner at variance with the construction given the document by another branch." Powell v. McCormack. And in Baker v. Carr [1962], the Court stated: "Deciding whether a matter has in any measure been committed by the Constitution to another branch of government, or whether the action of that branch exceeds whatever authority has been committed, is itself a delicate exercise in constitutional interpretation, and is a responsibility of this Court as ultimate interpreter of the Constitution." Notwithstanding the deference each branch must accord the others, the "judicial Power of the United States" vested in the federal courts by Art. III, §1, of the Constitution can no more be shared with the Executive Branch than the Chief Executive, for example, can share with the Judiciary the veto power, or the Congress share with the Judiciary the power to override a Presidential veto. Any other conclusion would be contrary to the basic concept of separation of powers and the checks and balances that flow from the scheme of a tripartite government. . . . We therefore reaffirm that it is the province and duty of this Court "to say what the law is" with respect to the claim of privilege presented in this case. Marbury v. Madison.

B.

In support of his claim of absolute privilege, the President's counsel urges two grounds, one of which is common to all governments and one of which is peculiar to our system of separation of powers. The first ground is the valid need for protection of communications between high Government officials and those who advise and assist them in the performance of their manifold duties; the importance of this confidentiality is too plain to require further discussion. Human experience teaches that those who expect public dissemination of their remarks may well temper candor with a concern for appearances and for their own interests to the detriment of the decision making process.* Whatever the nature of the privilege of confidentiality of Presidential communications in the exercise of Art. II powers the privilege can be said to derive from the supremacy of each branch within its own assigned area of constitutional duties. Certain powers and privileges flow from the nature of enumerated powers;† the protection of the confidentiality of Presidential communications has similar constitutional underpinnings.

The second ground asserted by the President's counsel in support of the claim of absolute privilege rests on the doctrine of separation of powers. Here it is argued that the independence of the Executive Branch within its own sphere, Humphrey's Executor v. United States [1935]; Kilbourn v. Thompson (1881), insulates a President from a judicial subpoena in an ongoing criminal prosecution, and thereby protects confidential Presidential communications. However, neither the doctrine of separation of powers, nor the need for confidentiality of high level communications, without more, can sustain an absolute, unqualified Presidential privilege of immunity from judicial process under all circumstances. The President's need for complete candor and objectivity from advisers calls for great deference from the courts. However, when the privilege depends solely on the broad, undifferentiated claim of public interest in the confidentiality of such conversations, a confrontation with other values arises. Absent a claim of need to protect military, diplomatic, or sensitive national security secrets, we find it difficult to accept the argument that even the very important interest in confidentiality of Presidential communications is significantly diminished by production of such material for in camera inspection with all the protection that a district court will be obliged to provide.

The impediment that an absolute, unqualified privilege would place in the way of the primary constitutional duty of the Judicial Branch to do justice in criminal prosecutions would plainly conflict with the function of the courts under Art. III. In designing the structure of our Government and dividing and allocating the sovereign power among three co-equal branches, the Framers of the Constitution sought to provide a comprehensive system, but the separate powers were not intended to operate with absolute independence. "While the Constitution diffuses power the better to secure liberty, it also contemplates that practice will integrate the dis-

---

*There is nothing novel about governmental confidentiality. The meetings of the Constitutional Convention in 1787 were conducted in complete privacy. 1 M. Farrand. The Records of the Federal Convention of 1787, pp. xi–xxv (1911). Moreover, all records of those meetings were sealed for more than 30 years after the Convention. Most of the Framers acknowledged that without secrecy no constitution of the kind that was developed could have been written. C. Warren, The Making of the Constitution, 134–139 (1937).

†The Special Prosecutor argues that there is no provision in the Constitution for a presidential privilege as to the President's communications corresponding to the privilege of Members of Congress under the Speech or Debate Clause. But the silence of the Constitution on this score is not dispositive. "The rule of constitutional interpretation announced in McCulloch v. Maryland [1819] that that which was reasonably appropriate and relevant to the exercise of a granted power was to be considered as accompanying the grant, has been so universally applied that it suffices merely to state it." Marshall v. Gordon (1917).

persed powers into a workable government. It enjoins upon its branches separateness but interdependence, autonomy but reciprocity." Youngstown Sheet & Tube Co. v. Sawyer. (Jackson, J., concurring). To read the Art. II powers of the President as providing an absolute privilege as against a subpoena essential to enforcement of criminal statutes on no more than a generalized claim of the public interest in confidentiality of nonmilitary and nondiplomatic discussions would upset the constitutional balance of "a workable government" and gravely impair the role of the courts under Art. III.

C.

Since we conclude that the legitimate needs of the judicial process may outweigh Presidential privilege, it is necessary to resolve those competing interests in a manner that preserves the essential functions of each branch. The right and indeed the duty to resolve that question does not free the judiciary from according high respect to the representations made on behalf of the President. United States v. Burr, 25 Fed. Cas. 187 (No. 14,694) (1807).

The expectation of a President to the confidentiality of his conversations and correspondence, like the claim of confidentiality of judicial deliberations, for example, has all the values to which we accord deference for the privacy of all citizens and added to those values the necessity for protection of the public interest in candid, objective, and even blunt or harsh opinions in Presidential decision-making. A President and those who assist him must be free to explore alternatives in the process of shaping policies and making decisions and to do so in a way many would be unwilling to express except privately. These are the considerations justifying a presumptive privilege for Presidential communications. The privilege is fundamental to the operation of government and inextricably rooted in the separation of powers under the Constitution. In Nixon v. Sirica, 487 F. 2d 700 (1973), the Court of Appeals held that such Presidential communications are "presumptively privileged," and this position is accepted by both parties in the present litigation. We agree with Mr. Chief Justice Marshall's observation, therefore, that "[in] no case of this kind would a court be required to proceed against the President as against an ordinary individual." United States v. Burr.

But this presumptive privilege must be considered in light of our historic commitment to the rule of law. This is nowhere more profoundly manifest than in our view that "the twofold aim [of criminal justice] is that guilt shall not escape or innocence suffer." Berger v. United States [1935]. We have elected to employ an adversary system of criminal justice in which the parties contest all issues before a court of law. The need to develop all relevant facts in the adversary system is both fundamental and comprehensive. The ends of criminal justice would be defeated if judgments were to be founded on a partial or speculative presentation of the facts. The very integrity of the judicial system and public confidence in the system depend on full disclosure of all the facts, within the framework of the rules of evidence. To ensure that justice is done, it is imperative to the function of courts that compulsory process be available for the production of evidence needed either by the prosecution or by the defense. . . .

In this case the President challenges a subpoena served on him as a third party requiring the production of materials for use in a criminal prosecution; he does so on the claim that he has a privilege against disclosure of confidential communications. He does not place his claim of privilege on the ground they are military or diplomatic secrets. As to these areas of Art. II duties the courts have traditionally shown the utmost deference to Presidential responsibilities. In [Chicago] & S. Air Lines v. Waterman Steamship Corp. (1948), dealing with Presidential authority involving foreign policy considerations, the Court said: "The President, both as Commander-in-Chief and as the Nation's organ for foreign affairs, has available intelligence services whose reports are not and ought not to be published to the world. It would be intolerable that courts, without the relevant information, should review and perhaps nullify actions of the Executive taken on information properly held secret." In United States v. Reynolds (1953), dealing with a claimant's demand for evidence in a damage case against the Government the Court said: "It may be possible to satisfy the court, from all the circumstances of the case, that there is a reasonable danger that compulsion of the evidence will expose military matters which, in the interest of national security, should not be divulged. When this is the case, the occasion for the privilege is appropriate, and the court should not jeopardize the security which the privilege is meant to protect by insisting upon an examination of the evidence, even by the judge alone, in chambers." No case of the Court, however, has extended this high degree of deference to a President's generalized interest in confidentiality. Nowhere in the constitution, as we have noted earlier, is there any explicit reference to a privilege of confidentiality, yet to the extent this interest relates to the effective discharge of a President's powers, it is constitutionally based.

The right to the production of all evidence at a criminal trial similarly has constitutional dimensions. The Sixth Amendment explicitly confers upon every defendant in a criminal trial the right "to be confronted with the witnesses against him" and "to have compulsory process for obtaining witnesses in his favor." Moreover, the Fifth Amendment also guarantees that no person shall be deprived of liberty without due process of law. It is the manifest duty of the courts to vindicate those guarantees, and to accomplish that it is essential that all relevant and admissible evidence be produced.

In this case we must weigh the importance of the general privilege of confidentiality of Presidential communications in performance of his responsibilities against the inroads of such a privilege on the fair administration of criminal justice.* The interest in preserving confidentiality is weighty

---

*We are not here concerned with the balance between the President's generalized interest in confidentiality and the need for relevant evidence in civil litigation, nor with that between the confidentiality interest and congressional demands for information, nor with the President's interest in preserving state secrets. We address only the conflict between the President's assertion of a generalized privilege of confidentiality and the constitutional need for relevant evidence in criminal trials.

indeed and entitled to great respect. However, we cannot conclude that advisers will be moved to temper the candor of their remarks by the infrequent occasions of disclosure because of the possibility that such conversations will be called for in the context of a criminal prosecution.*

On the other hand, the allowance of the privilege to withhold evidence that is demonstrably relevant in a criminal trial would cut deeply into the guarantee of due process of law and gravely impair the basic function of the courts. A President's acknowledged need for confidentiality in the communications of his office is general in nature; whereas the constitutional need for production of relevant evidence in a criminal proceeding is specific and central to the fair adjudication of a particular criminal case in the administration of justice. Without access to specific facts a criminal prosecution may be totally frustrated. The President's broad interest in confidentiality of communications will not be vitiated by disclosure of a limited number of conversations preliminarily shown to have some bearing on the pending criminal cases.

We conclude that when the ground for asserting privilege as to subpoenaed materials sought for use in a criminal trial is based only on the generalized interest in confidentiality, it cannot prevail over the fundamental demands of due process of law in the fair administration of criminal justice. The generalized assertion of privilege must yield to the demonstrated, specific need for evidence in a pending criminal trial.

D.

. . . Here the District Court treated the material as presumptively privileged, proceeded to find that the Special Prosecutor had made sufficient showing to rebut the presumption, and ordered an in camera examination of the subpoenaed material. On the basis of our examination of the record we are unable to conclude that the District Court erred in ordering the inspection. Accordingly we affirm the order of the District Court that subpoenaed materials be transmitted to that court. We now turn to the important question of the District Court's responsibilities in conducting the in camera examination of Presidential materials or communications delivered under the compulsion of the subpoena duces tecum.

---

*Mr. Justice Cardozo made this point in an analogous context. Speaking for a unanimous Court in Clark v. United States (1933), he emphasized the importance of maintaining the secrecy of the deliberations of a petit jury in a criminal case. "Freedom of debate might be stifled and independence of thought checked if jurors were made to feel that their arguments and ballots were to be freely published to the world." Nonetheless, the Court also recognized that isolated inroads on confidentiality designed to serve the paramount need of the criminal law would not vitiate the interests served by secrecy: "A juror of integrity and reasonable firmness will not fear to speak his mind if the confidences of debate are barred to the ears of mere impertinence or malice. He will not expect to be shielded against the disclosure of his conduct in the event that there is evidence reflecting upon his honor. The chance that now and then there may be found some timid soul who will take counsel of his fears and give way to their repressive power is too remote and shadowy to shape the course of justice."

E.

Enforcement of the subpoena duces tecum was stayed pending this Court's resolution of the issues raised by the petitions for certiorari. Those issues now having been disposed of, the matter of implementation will rest with the District Court. "[T]he guard, furnished to [the President] to protect him from being harassed by vexatious and unnecessary subpoenas, is to be looked for in the conduct of a [district] court after the subpoenas have issued; not in any circumstance which is to precede their being issued." United States v. Burr. Statements that meet the test of admissibility and relevance must be isolated; all other material must be excised. At this stage the District Court is not limited to representations of the Special Prosecutor as to the evidence sought by the subpoena; the material will be available to the District Court. It is elementary that in camera inspection of evidence is always a procedure calling for scrupulous protection against any release or publication of material not found by the court, at that stage, probably admissible in evidence and relevant to the issues of the trial for which it is sought. That being true of an ordinary situation, it is obvious that the District Court has a very heavy responsibility to see to it that Presidential conversations, which are either not relevant or not admissible, are accorded that high degree of respect due the President of the United States. Mr. Chief Justice Marshall sitting as a trial judge in the Burr case was extraordinarily careful to point out that "[i]n no case of this kind would a court be required to proceed against the president as against an ordinary individual." Marshall's statement cannot be read to mean in any sense that a President is above the law, but relates to the singularly unique role under Art. II of a President's communications and activities, related to the performance of duties under that Article. Moreover, a President's communications and activities encompass a vastly wider range of sensitive material than would be true of any "ordinary individual." It is therefore necessary* in the public interest to afford Presidential confidentiality the greatest protection consistent with the fair administration of justice. The need for confidentiality even as to idle conversations with associates in which casual reference might be made concerning political leaders within the country or foreign statesmen is too obvious to call for further treatment. We have no doubt that the District Judge will at all times accord to Presidential records that high degree of deference suggested in United States v. Burr and will discharge his responsibility to see to it that until released to the Special Prosecutor no in camera material is revealed to anyone. This burden applies with even greater force to excised material; once the decision is made to excise, the material is restored to its privileged status and should be returned under seal to its lawful custodian.

---

*When the subpoenaed material is delivered to the District Judge in camera questions may arise as to the excising of parts and it lies within the discretion of that court to seek the aid of the Special Prosecutor and the President's counsel for in camera consideration of the validity of particular excisions, whether the basis of excision is relevancy or admissibility or under such cases as Reynolds or Waterman Steamship.

Since this matter came before the Court during the pendency of a criminal prosecution, and on representations that time is of the essence, the mandate shall issue forthwith.

Affirmed.

Mr. Justice Rehnquist took no part in the consideration or decision of these cases.

4

State
and
Federal Powers

McCULLOCH v. MARYLAND

4 Wheaton 316; 4 L. Ed. 579 (1819)

Perhaps the most difficult problem faced by the government of a large nation is the reconciliation of local and national interests. To be strong, a country must have a strong central government. To be strong it must also have the support of its people, and this support will come only if the people are allowed to solve at the local level those problems which they regard as local in nature. The American Revolution stemmed from the failure of George III to allow his American colonies sufficient local autonomy, and the framers of the new Constitution knew that they must find a wiser adjustment of these competing interests and loyalties if the country was to endure as a political unit. The solution they worked out was to delegate in Article I, Sec. 8, certain enumerated powers to the national government. The Tenth Amendment declared that those powers not so delegated were left to the states, or to the people, to be later assigned by constitutional amendments.

One of the axioms of American constitutional law is that Congress has only powers that are delegated to it by the Constitution, or are reasonably implied from those so delegated. The origin and history of this theory of national power is as follows: When Randolph proposed the Virginia Plan in the Constitutional Convention of 1787, it contained the only sound principle by which the powers of nation and state could be divided. It stated: "... the national legislature ought to be empowered ... to legislate in all cases to which the separate states are incompetent, or in which the harmony of the United States may be interrupted by the exercise of individual legislation." This stated a principle rather than a method of allocating powers, and as a principle it was received with approval by the Convention. After two months of debate the Convention created a committee of detail to formulate the text of a constitution and gave it various instructions. The instruction with regard to national powers was that: "The national legislature ought to possess the legislative rights vested in Congress by the Confederation; and, moreover, to legislate in all cases for the general interest of the Union, and also in those to which the states are separately incompetent, or in which the harmony of the United States may be interrupted by individual legislation." Acting upon this instruction the committee of detail reported back to the Convention the specific enumeration of the powers of Congress found in Article I, Sec. 8. The committee, adhering, as did the entire Convention, to the principle of delegated powers, thus gave to the new Congress all of the powers then believed to be described in the article of instruction; and by providing for amendments in Article V, it created the means by which those powers could be increased or altered when it seemed desirable to do so.

In spite of this very conclusive evidence to the contrary, it has sometimes been urged that the framers intended that Congress should have the power to deal with any truly national problem whether that power is delegated to it or not. James Wilson, a member of the Convention of 1787 and later a justice of the Supreme Court, is quoted, not too convincingly, as sponsoring this theory. It remained for President Theodore Roosevelt to publicize the doctrine in his forceful discussions of what he called the New Nationalism. He pointed out the awkward consequences of the fact that business combinations had grown to such proportions that they were beyond the legislative reach of any state or states, and yet could not be effectively controlled by Congress since the power of Congress was limited to the interstate commerce aspects of big business. In one of his better phrases he referred to the "twilight zone" in our constitutional system, a zone lying safely between state and federal authority, to which "malefactors of great wealth" might repair and be safe from punishment and restraint. He urged that "whenever the states cannot act, because the need to be met is not one merely of a single locality, then the national government, representing all the people, should have complete power to act."

The Supreme Court rejected this doctrine out of hand in Kansas v. Colorado (1907), a case in which the United States tried to intervene in a dispute over the control of river water on the ground that the problem of reclaiming arid land was "national," since it was beyond the geographical jurisdiction of any one state. The Court emphasized that ours is a government of "enumerated powers" and pointed out that the Tenth Amendment had been adopted because of a "widespread fear that the national government might, under the pressure of a supposed general welfare, attempt to exercise powers which had not been granted."

Although the Court has never questioned the doctrine that the national government is one of delegated powers, as early as 1819 in McCulloch v. Maryland, printed below, it made clear that the fact that they were delegated did not mean they must be given a narrow or rigid interpretation. When Congress in 1791 chartered the First Bank of the United States, it was only after a most full and bitter argument as to whether it had the power to do so. Hamilton, who had proposed the creation of the bank, had written an elaborate opinion defending it as an exercise of a power reasonably implied from those expressly delegated to Congress. Jefferson and his friends had stoutly maintained that congressional powers must be strictly construed and that the granting of the charter was an act of unwarrantable usurpation. Nevertheless the charter of the First Bank was never attacked in the courts as being unconstitutional, and the institution continued to exist until its charter expired in 1811. The financial conditions ensuing after the War of 1812 made the reestablishment of the bank desirable, and the Second Bank of the United States was accordingly chartered in 1816. Almost immediately it incurred the bitter odium of large sections of the country, especially of the West and South. The bank was largely under the control of the Federalists, who were accused of using it as a political machine and of wielding its great influence for political purposes; its stock was largely held by British capitalists and other foreign investors; and it was accused of being responsible for a period of financial depression which brought ruin to thousands. It is true that the bank had begun operations under corrupt and inefficient management and had encouraged a high degree of inflation of credits. This had resulted in heavy losses to investors; in the state of Maryland the Baltimore branch collapsed with a loss to Maryland investors alone of a sum variously estimated from $1,700,000 to $3,000,000. Wiser counsels prevailed shortly, however, and the bank faced about and embarked upon a financial course as conservative as it had hitherto been headlong. It refused to accept the bank notes of the imprudent state banks and insisted upon the liquidation of its credits. One after another these overinflated state banks failed, and hundreds of reckless speculators were ruined. Money was alsmost unobtainable. While most of this financial disaster was the inevitable result of the orgies of inflation and speculation in which the frontier communities in particular had been indulging, the Bank of the United States was popularly regarded as the cause of the disaster, as the ruthless "money trust" which was ruining the prosperity of the country. A popular demand for legislative control of the bank was set up, and eight states passed either laws or constitutional amendments restricting the activities of the bank or imposing heavy burdens upon it. The law involved in this case, passed by the legislature of Maryland, which was particularly hostile to the bank because of its earlier debacle, is typical of this legislative onslaught.

The Maryland statute forbade all banks not chartered by the state itself to issue bank notes save upon special stamped paper obtainable upon the payment of a very heavy tax. This requirement could be commuted by the payment of an annual tax to the state of $15,000. A penalty of $500 forfeiture was inflicted for each offense, an amount which in the case of the now large and prosperous Baltimore branch of the Bank of the United States would have come possibly to millions of dollars. McCulloch, the cashier of the branch in Baltimore, issued notes without complying with the state law, and this action was brought on behalf of the state of Maryland to recover the penalties.

The case was argued for nine days before the Supreme Court by the greatest lawyers of the day; William Pinkney, Daniel Webster, and William Wirt defended the bank, while Luther Martin, Joseph Hopkinson, and Walter Jones represented the state of Maryland. The opinion of Marshall in the case is commonly regarded as his greatest state paper.

The announcement of the decision was the signal for a veritable storm of abuse directed against the Supreme Court. Judge Roane, of the Virginia court of appeals, published a series of newspaper attacks upon the decision so bitter that Marshall was led to write a reply in his defense. The Virginia legislature passed a resolution urging that the Supreme Court be shorn of its power to pass upon cases to which states were parties. Ohio, which had previously passed a law taxing each branch of the Bank of the United States within its limits $50,000 a year, defied the Supreme Court and proceeded to collect the tax in spite of its decision, a position from which it was later obligated to withdraw; see Osborn v. The Bank of the United States (1824). The attack upon the Court in this case was directed in large part against the failure of that tribunal to invalidate an act of Congress (incorporating the bank) and not against the exercise of the judicial veto. The decision was peculiarly odious to the strict constructionists because it not only sustained the doctrine of the implied powers of Congress but also recognized the binding effect of an implied limitation upon the states preventing them from interfering with the functioning of federal agencies.

The doctrine of implied powers in Congress was not new in this case. Not only had it been ably expounded by Hamilton, as mentioned above, but in the case of United

States v. Fisher (1805), which had been decided 14 years before, Marshall himself had given expression to the doctrine; but as that case did not relate to any such important political issue as did the bank case, the decision at that time had evoked no comment.

While it is clear from Kansas v. Colorado that Congress has no authority in the absence of a delegation of power, are there limits to the way in which Congress can exercise those powers that are clearly delegated? From time to time, and in connection with various powers of Congress, the Court has held that there are. In Ashton v. Cameron County Water Dist. (1936) Congress was held unable to extend the bankruptcy power to a state agency, since to do so would be to "pass laws inconsistent with the idea of sovereignty," and in Hammer v. Dagenhart (1918) the Court held for the first time that the powers reserved to the states by the Tenth Amendment acted as a limit to the use of congressional power. There the Court struck down the use of the commerce power to control child labor. The philosophy underlying this decision is that the powers of Congress cannot be used to achieve ends which have not been delegated to Congress, and hence, according to the Tenth Amendment, are reserved to the states.

Perhaps the most lucid explanation of this doctrine, dubbed "dual federalism" by Professor E. S. Corwin, is that made by Justice Roberts in United States v. Butler (1936): "From the accepted doctrine that the United States is a government of delegated powers, it follows that those not expressly granted, or reasonably to be implied from such as are conferred, are reserved to the states or to the people. To forestall any suggestion to the contrary, the Tenth Amendment was adopted. The same proposition, otherwise stated, is that powers not granted are prohibited. None to regulate agricultural production is given, and therefore legislation by Congress for that purpose is forbidden.

"It is an established principle that the attainment of a prohibited end may not be accomplished under the pretext of the exertion of powers which are granted."

The doctrine of dual federalism, in the form that appears here, was destined to be short-lived. In the Social Security Act Cases in 1937 the Court sustained an almost identical use of the tax power, and in United States v. Darby in 1941 the Court consciously abandoned it, noting that the Tenth Amendment "states but a truism that all is retained which has not been surrendered."

Mr. Chief Justice Marshall delivered the opinion of the Court, saying in part:

In the case now to be determined, the defendant, a sovereign state, denies the obligation of a law enacted by the legislature of the Union, and the plaintiff, on his part, contests the validity of an act which has been passed by the legislature of that state. The constitution of our country, in its most interesting and vital parts, is to be considered; the conflicting powers of the government of the Union and of its members, as marked in that constitution, are to be discussed; and an opinion given, which may essentially influence the great operations of the government. No tribunal can approach such a question without a deep sense of its importance, and of the awful responsibility involved in its decision. But it must be decided peacefully, or remain a source of hostile legislation, perhaps of hostility of a still more serious nature; and if it is to be so decided, by this tribunal alone can the decision be made. On the Supreme Court of the United States has the constitution of our country devolved this important duty.

The first question made in the cause is, has Congress power to incorporate a bank? . . .

In discussing this question, the counsel for the state of Maryland have deemed it of some importance, in the construction of the constitution, to consider that instrument not as emanating from the people, but as the act of sovereign and independent states. The powers of the general government, it has been said, are delegated by the states, who alone are truly sovereign; and must be exercised in subordination to the states, who alone possess supreme dominion.

It would be difficult to sustain this proposition. The convention which framed the constitution was, indeed elected by the state legislatures. But the instrument, when it came from their hands, was a mere proposal, without obligation, or pretensions to it. It was reported to the then existing Congress of the United States, with a request that it might "be submitted to a convention of delegates, chosen in each state by the people thereof, under the recommendation of its legislature, for their assent and ratification." This mode of proceeding was adopted; and by the convention, by Congress, and by the state legislatures, the instrument was submitted to the people. They acted upon it in the only manner in which they can act safely, effectively, and wisely, on such a subject, by assembling in convention. It is true, they assembled in their several states—and where else should they have assembled? No political dreamer was ever wild enough to think of breaking down the lines which separate the state and of compounding the American people into one common mass. Of consequence, when they act, they act in their states. But the measures they adopt do not, on that account, cease to be the measures of the people themselves, or become the measures of the state governments.

From these conventions the constitution derives its whole authority. The government proceeds directly from the people; is "ordained and established" in the name of the people; and is declared to be ordained, "in order to form a more perfect union, establish justice, insure domestic tranquility, and secure the blessings of liberty to themselves and to their posterity." The assent of the states, in their sovereign capacity, is implied in calling a convention, and thus submitting that instrument to the people. But the people were at perfect liberty to accept or reject it; and their act was final. It required not the affirmance, and could not be negatived, by the state governments. The constitution, when thus adopted, was of complete obligation, and bound the state sovereignties.

It has been said that the people had already surrendered all their powers to the state sovereignties, and had nothing more to give. But, surely, the question whether they may resume and modify the powers granted to government does not remain to be settled in this country. Much more might the legitimacy of the general government be doubted, had it been created by the states. The powers delegated to the state sovereignties were to be exercised by themselves, not by a distinct and independent sovereignty, created by themselves. To the formation of a league, such as was the confederation, the state sovereignties were certainly competent. But when, "in order to form a more perfect union," it was deemed necessary to change this alliance into an effective government, possessing great and sovereign powers, and acting directly on the people, the necessity of referring it to the people, and of deriving its powers directly from them, was felt and acknowledged by all.

The government of the Union, then (whatever may be the influence of this fact on the case), is, emphatically, and truly, a government of the people. In form and in substance it emanates from them. Its powers are granted by them, and are to be exercised directly on them, and for their benefit.

This government is acknowledged by all to be one of enumerated powers. The principle, that it can exercise only the powers granted to it, would seem too apparent to have required to be enforced by all those arguments which its enlightened friends, while it was depending before the people, found it necessary to urge. That principle is now universally admitted. But the question respecting the extent of the powers actually granted, is perpetually arising, and will probably continue to arise, as long as our system shall exist.

In discussing these questions, the conflicting powers of the general and state government must be brought into view, and the supremacy of their respective laws, where they are in opposition, must be settled.

If any one proposition could command the universal assent of mankind, we might expect it would be this—that the government of the Union, though limited in its powers, is supreme within its sphere of action. This would seem to result necessarily from its nature. It is the government of all; its powers are delegated by all; it represents all, and acts for all. Though any one state may be willing to control its operations, no state is willing to allow others to control them. The nation, on those subjects on which it can act, must necessarily bind its component parts. But this question is not left to mere reason; the people have, in express terms, decided it by saying, "this constitution, and the laws of the United States, which shall be made in pursuance thereof," "shall be the supreme law of the land," and by requiring that the members of the state legislatures, and the officers of the executive and judicial departments of the states, shall take the oath of fidelity to it.

The government of the United States, then, though limited in its powers, is supreme; and its laws, when made in pursuance of the constitution, form the supreme law of the land, "anything in the constitution or laws of any state to the contrary notwithstanding."

Among the enumerated powers, we do not find that of establishing a bank or creating a corporation. But there is no phrase in the instrument which, like the articles of confederation, excludes incidental or implied powers; and which requires that everything granted shall be expressly and minutely described. Even the 10th amendment, which was framed for the purpose of quieting the excessive jealousies which had been excited, omits the word "expressly," and declares only that the powers "not delegated to the United States, nor prohibited to the states, are reserved to the states or to the people"; thus leaving the question, whether the particular power which may become the subject of contest has been delegated to the one government, or prohibited to the other, to depend on a fair construction of the whole instrument. The men who drew and adopted this amendment had experienced the embarrassments resulting from the insertion of this word in the articles of confederation, and probably omitted it to avoid those embarrassments. A constitution, to contain an accurate detail of all the subdivisions of which its great powers will admit, and of all the means by which they may be carried into execution, would partake of the prolixity of a legal code, and could scarcely be embraced by the human mind. It would probably never be understood by the public. Its nature, therefore, requires, that only its great outlines should be marked, its important objects designated, and the minor ingredients which compose those objects be deduced from the nature of the objects themselves. That this idea was entertained by the framers of the American constitution, is not only to be inferred from the nature of the instrument, but from the language. Why else were some of the limitations, found in the ninth section of the 1st article, introduced? It is also, in some degree, warranted by their having omitted to use any restrictive term which might prevent its receiving a fair and just interpretation. In considering this question, then, we must never forget that it is a constitution we are expounding.

Although, among the enumerated powers of government, we do not find the word "bank" or "incorporation," we find the great powers to lay and collect taxes; to borrow money; to regulate commerce; to declare and conduct a war; and to raise and support armies and navies. The sword and the purse, all the external relations, and no inconsiderable portion of the industry of the nation, are entrusted to its government. It can never be pretended that these vast powers draw after them others of inferior importance, merely because they are inferior. Such an idea can never be advanced. But it may, with great reason, be contended, that a government, entrusted with such ample powers, on the due execution of which the happiness and prosperity of the nation so vitally depends, must also be entrusted with ample means for their execution. The power being given, it is the interest of the nation to facilitate its execution. It can never be their interest, and cannot be presumed to have been their intention, to clog and embarrass its execution by withholding the most appropriate means. Throughout this vast republic, from the St. Croix to the Gulf of Mexico, from the Atlantic to the Pacific, revenue is to be collected and expended, armies are to be marched and supported. The exigencies of the nation may require that the treasure raised in the north should be transported to the south, that raised in the east conveyed to the west, or that this order should be reversed. Is that construction of the constitution to be preferred which would render these operations difficult, hazardous, and expensive? Can we adopt that construction (unless the words imperiously require it) which would impute to the framers of that instrument, when granting these powers for the public good, the intention of impeding their exercise by withholding a choice of means? If, indeed, such be the mandate of the constitution, we have only to obey; but that instrument does not profess to enumerate the means by which the powers it confers may be executed; nor does it prohibit the creation of a corporation, if the existence of such a being be essential to the beneficial exercise of those powers. It is, then, the subject of fair inquiry, how far such means may be employed. It is not denied that the powers given to the government imply the ordinary means of execution. That, for example, of raising revenue, and applying it to national purposes, is admitted to imply the power of conveying money from place to place, as the exigencies of the nation may require, and of employing the usual means of conveyance. But it is denied that the government has its choice of means; or, that it may employ the most convenient means, if, to employ them, it be necessary to erect a corporation.

... The power of creating a corporation, though appertaining to sovereignty, is not, like the power of making war, or levying taxes, or of regulating commerce, a great substantive and independent power, which cannot be implied as incidental to other powers, or used as a means of executing them. It is never the end for which other powers are exercised, but a means by which other objects are accomplished. No contributions are made to charity for the sake of an incorporation, but a corporation is created to administer the charity; no seminary of learning is instituted in order to be incorporated, but the corporate character is conferred to subserve the purposes of education. No city was ever built with the sole object of being incorporated, but is incorporated as affording the best means of being well governed. The power of creating a corporation is never used for its own sake, but for the purpose of effecting something else. No sufficient reason is, therefore, perceived, why it may not pass as incidental to those powers which are expressly given, if it be a direct mode of executing them.

But the Constitution of the United States has not left the right of Congress to employ the necessary means for the execution of the powers conferred on the government to general reasoning. To its enumeration of powers is added that of making "all laws which shall be necessary and proper, for carrying into execution the foregoing powers, and all other powers vested by this constitution, in the government of the United States, or in any department thereof."

The counsel for the State of Maryland have urged various arguments, to prove that this clause, though in terms of grant of power, is not so in effect; but is really restrictive of the general right, which might otherwise be implied, of selecting means for executing the enumerated powers.

In support of this proposition, they have found it necessary to contend, that this clause was inserted for the purpose of conferring on Congress the power of making laws. That, without it, doubts might be entertained whether Congress could exercise its powers in the form of legislation.

But could this be the object of which it was inserted? ... That a legislature, endowed with legislative powers, can legislate, is a proposition too self-evident to have been questioned.

But the argument on which most reliance is placed, is drawn from the peculiar language of this clause. Congress is not empowered by it to make all laws, which may have relation to the powers conferred on the government, but such only as may be "necessary and proper" for carrying them into execution. The word "necessary" is considered as controlling the whole sentence, and as limiting the right to pass laws for the execution of the granted powers, to such as are indispensable, and without which the power would be nugatory. That it excludes the choice of means, and leaves to Congress, in each case, that only which is most direct and simple.

Is it true that this is the sense in which the word "necessary" is always used? Does it always import an absolute physical necessity, so strong that one thing, to which another may be termed necessary, cannot exist without that other? We think it does not. If reference be had to its use, in the common affairs of the world, or in approved authors, we find that it frequently imports no more than that one thing is convenient, or useful, or essential to another. To employ the means necessary to an end, is generally understood as employing any means calculated to produce the end, and not as being confined to those single means, without which the end would be entirely unattainable. Such is the character of human language, that no word conveys to the mind, in all situations, one single definite idea; and nothing is more common than to use words in a figurative sense. Almost all compositions contain words, which, taken in their rigorous sense, would convey a meaning different from that which is obviously intended. It is essential to just construction, that many words which import something excessive should be understood in a more mitigated sense—in that sense which common usage justifies. The word "necessary" is of this description. It has not a fixed character peculiar to itself. It admits of all degrees of comparison; and is often connected with other words, which increase or diminish the impression the mind receives of the urgency it imports. A thing may be necessary, very necessary, absolutely or indispensably necessary. To no mind would the same idea be conveyed by these several phrases. . . . This word, then, like others, is used in various senses; and, in its construction, the subject, the context, the intention of the person using them, are all to be taken into view.

Let this be done in the case under consideration. The subject is the execution of those great powers on which the welfare of a nation essentially depends. It must have been the intention of those who gave these powers, to insure, as far as human prudence could insure, their beneficial execution. This could not be done by confiding the choice of means to such narrow limits as not to leave it in the power of Congress to adopt any which might be appropriate, and which were conducive to the end. This provision is made in a constitution intended to endure for ages to come, and, consequently, to be adapted to the various crises of human affairs. To have prescribed the means by which government should, in all future time, execute its powers, would have been to change, entirely, the character of the instrument, and give it the properties of a legal code. It would have been an unwise attempt to provide, by immutable rules, for exigencies which, if foreseen at all, must have been seen dimly, and which can be best provided for as they occur. To have declared that the best means shall not be used, but those alone without which the power given would be nugatory, would have been to deprive the legislature of the capacity to avail itself of experience, to exercise its reason, and to accommodate its legislation to circumstances. . . .

But the argument which most conclusively demonstrates the error of the construction contended for by the counsel for the state of Maryland, is founded on the intention of the convention, as manifested in the whole clause. To waste time and argument in proving that without it Congress might carry its powers into execution, would be not much less idle than to hold a lighted taper to the sun. As little can it be required to prove, that in the absence of this clause, Congress would have some choice of means. That it might employ those which, in its judgment, would most advantageously effect the object to be accomplished. That any means adapted to the end, any means which tended directly to the execution of the constitutional powers of the government, were in themselves constitutional. This clause, as construed by the state of Maryland, would abridge, and almost annihilate this useful and necessary right of the legislature to select its means. That this could not be intended, is, we should think, had it not been already controverted, too apparent for controversy. We think so for the following reasons:

1st. The clause is placed among the powers of Congress, not among the limitations on those powers.

2d. Its terms purport to enlarge, not to diminish the powers vested in the government. It purports to be an additional power, not a restriction on those already granted. No reason has been, or can be assigned for thus concealing an intention to narrow the discretion of the national legislature under words which purport to enlarge it. The framers of the constitution wished its adoption, and well knew that it would be endangered by its strength, not by its weakness. Had they been capable of using language which would convey to the eye one idea, and, after deep reflection, impress on the mind another, they would rather have disguised the grant of power than its limitation. If, then, their intention had been, by this clause, to restrain the free use of means which might otherwise have been implied, that intention would have been inserted in another place, and would have been expressed in terms resembling these. "In carrying into execution the foregoing powers, and all others," etc., "no laws shall be passed but such as are necessary and proper." Had the intention been to make this clause restrictive, it would unquestionably have been so in form as well as in effect.

The result of the most careful and attentive consideration bestowed upon this clause is, that if it does not enlarge, it cannot be construed to restrain the powers of Congress, or to impair the right of the legislature to exercise its best judgment in the selection of measures to carry into execution the constitutional powers of the government. If no other motive for its insertion can be suggested, a sufficient one is found in the desire to remove all doubts respecting the right to legislate on that vast mass of incidental powers which must be involved in the constitution, if that instrument be not a splendid bauble.

We admit, as all must admit, that the powers of the government are limited, and that its limits are not to be transcended. But we think the sound construction of the constitution must allow to the national legislature that discretion, with respect to the means by which the powers it confers are to be carried into execution, which will enable that body to perform the high duties assigned to it, in the manner most beneficial to the people. Let the end be legitimate, let it be within the scope of the constitution, and all means which are appropriate, which are plainly adapted to that end, which are not prohibited, but consist with the letter and spirit of the constitution, are constitutional. . . .

If a corporation may be employed indiscriminately with other means to carry into execution the powers of the government, no particular reason can be assigned for excluding the use of a bank, if required for its fiscal operations. To use one, must be within the discretion of Congress, if it be an appropriate mode of executing the powers of government. That it is a convenient, a useful, and essential instrument in the prosecution of its fiscal operations, is not now a subject of controversy. All those who have been concerned in the administration of our finances, have concurred in representing the importance and necessity; and so strongly have they been felt, that statesmen of the first class, whose previous opinions against it had been confirmed by every circumstance which can fix the human judgment, have yielded those opinions to the exigencies of the nation. . . .

But, were its necessity less apparent, none can deny its being an appropriate measure; and if it is, the degree of its necessity, as has been very justly observed, is to be discussed in another place. Should Congress, in the execution of its powers, adopt measures which are prohibited by the constitution; or should Congress, under the pretext of executing its powers, pass laws for the accomplishment of objects not entrusted to the government, it would become the painful duty of this tribunal, should a case requiring such a decision come before it, to say that such an act was not the law of the land. But where the law is not prohibited, and is really calculated to effect any of the objects entrusted to the government, to undertake here to inquire into the degree of its necessity, would be to pass the line which circumscribes the judicial department, and to tread on legislative ground. This court disclaims all pretensions to such a power. . . .

After the most deliberate consideration, it is the unanimous and decided opinion of this court that the act to incorporate the bank of the United States is a law made in pursuance of the constitution, and is a part of the supreme law of the land. . . .

It being the opinion of the court that the act incorporating the bank is constitutional, and that the power of establishing a branch in the state of Maryland might be properly exercised by the bank itself, we proceed to inquire:

2. Whether the state of Maryland may, without violating the constitution, tax that branch?

That the power of taxation is one of vital importance; that it is retained by the states; that it is not abridged by the grant of a similar power to the government of the Union; that it is to be concurrently exercised by the two governments: are truths which have never been denied. But, such is the paramount character of the constitution, that its capacity to withdraw any subject from the action of even this power, is admitted. The states are expressly forbidden to lay any duties on imports or exports, except what may be absolutely necessary for executing their inspection laws. If the obligation of this prohibition must be conceded—if it may restrain a state from the exercise of its taxing power on imports and exports—the same paramount character would seem to restrain, as it certainly may restrain, a state from such other exercise of this power, as is in its nature incompatible with, and repugnant to, the constitutional laws of the Union. A law, absolutely repugnant to another, as entirely repeals that other as if express terms of repeal were used.

On this ground the counsel for the bank place its claim to be exempted from the power of a state to tax its operations. There is no express provision for the case, but the claim has been sustained on a principle which so entirely pervades the constitution, is so intermixed with the materials which compose it, so interwoven with its web, so blended with its texture, as to be incapable of being separated from it without rending it into shreds.

This great principle is, that the Constitution and the laws made in pursuance thereof are supreme; that they control the Constitution and laws of the respective States, and cannot be controlled by them. From this, which may be almost termed an axiom, other propositions are deduced as corollaries, on the truth or error of which, and on their application to this case, the cause has been supposed to depend. These are, 1st. That a power to create implies a power to preserve. 2d. That a power to destroy, if wielded by a different hand, is hostile to, and incompatible with these powers to create and preserve. 3d. That where this repugnancy exists, that authority which is supreme must control, not yield to that over which it is supreme. . . .

The power of Congress to create, and of course to continue, the bank, was the subject of the preceding part of this opinion; and is no longer to be considered as questionable.

That the power of taxing it by the states may be exercised so as to destroy it, is too obvious to be denied. But taxation is said to be an absolute power, which acknowledges no other limits than those expressly prescribed in the Constitution, and like sovereign power of every other description, is trusted to the discretion of those who use it. . . .

The argument on the part of the state of Maryland is, not that the states may directly resist a law of Congress, but that they may exercise their acknowledged powers upon it, and that the constitution leaves them this right in the confidence that they will not abuse it. . . .

That the power to tax involves the power to destroy; that the power to destroy may defeat and render useless the power to create; that there is a plain repugnance, in conferring on one government a power to control the constitutional measures of another, which other, with respect to those very measures, is declared to be supreme over that which exerts the control, are propositions not to be denied. But all inconsistencies are to be reconciled by the magic of the word confidence. Taxation, it is said, does not necessarily and unavoidably destroy. To carry it to the excess of destruction would be an abuse, to presume which, would banish that confidence which is essential to all government.

But is this a case of confidence? Would the people of any one state trust those of another with a power to control the most insignificant operations of their state government? We know they would not. Why, then, should we suppose that the people of any one state should be willing to trust those of another with a power to control the operations of a government to which they have confided their most important and most valuable interests? In the legislature of the Union alone, are all represented. The legislature of the

Union alone, therefore, can be trusted by the people with the power of controlling measures which concern all, in the confidence that it will not be abused. This, then, is not a case of confidence, and we must consider it as it really is.

If we apply the principle for which the state of Maryland contends, to the constitution generally, we shall find it capable of changing totally the character of that instrument. We shall find it capable of arresting all the measures of the government, and of prostrating it at the foot of the states. The American people have declared their constitution, and the laws made in pursuance thereof, to be supreme; but this principle would transfer the supremacy, in fact, to the states.

If the states may tax one instrument, employed by the government in the execution of its powers, they may tax any and every other instrument. They may tax the mail; they may tax the mint; they may tax patent-rights; they may tax the papers of the custom-house; they may tax judicial process; they may tax all the means employed by the government, to an excess which would defeat all the ends of government. This was not intended by the American people. [They] did not design to make their government dependent on the states. . . .

It has also been insisted, that, as the power of taxation in the general and State governments is acknowledged to be concurrent, every argument which would sustain the right of the general government to tax banks chartered by the states, will equally sustain the right of the states to tax banks chartered by the general government.

But the two cases are not on the same reason. The people of all the states have created the general government, and have conferred upon it the general power of taxation. The people of all the states, and the states themselves, are represented in Congress, and, by their representatives, exercise this power. When they tax the chartered institutions of the states, they tax their constituents; and these taxes must be uniform. But, when a state taxes the operations of the government of the United States, it acts upon institutions created, not by their own constituents, but by people over whom they claim no control. It acts upon the measures of a government created by others as well as themselves, for the benefit of others in common with themselves. The difference is that which always exists, and always must exist, between the action of the whole on a part, and the action of a part on the whole—between the laws of a government declared to be supreme, and those of a government which, when in opposition to those laws, is not supreme.

But if the full application of this argument could be admitted, it might bring into question the right of Congress to tax the state banks, and could not prove the right of the states to tax the Bank of the United States.

The court has bestowed on this subject its most deliberate consideration. The result is a conviction that the states have no power, by taxation or otherwise, to retard, impede, burden, or in any manner control the operations of the constitutional laws enacted by Congress to carry into execution the powers vested in the general government. This is, we think, the unavoidable consequence of that supremacy which the constitution has declared.

We are unanimously of opinion that the law passed by the legislature of Maryland, imposing a tax on the Bank of the United States, is unconstitutional and void.

This opinion does not deprive the states of any resources which they originally possessed. It does not extend to a tax paid by the real property of the bank, in common with the other real property within the state, nor to a tax imposed on the interest which the citizens of Maryland may hold in this institution, in common with other property of the same description throughout the state. But this is a tax on the operations of the bank, and is, consequently, a tax on the operation of an instrument employed by the government of the Union to carry its powers into execution. Such a tax must be unconstitutional. . . .

COYLE v. SMITH

221 U. S. 559; 31 S. Ct. 688; 55 L. Ed. 853 (1911)

The power which Congress possesses to admit new states into the Union is a purely discretionary power. No territory has any right to claim statehood, but must wait until it seems wise to Congress to confer that status. It is not surprising, therefore, that it should be assumed that Congress in the exercise of an unquestioned power to grant or withhold such a privilege might make the enjoyment of the right contingent upon the meeting of such conditions by the incoming state as might seem to the congressional mind desirable. This seems to have been the theory upon which Congress proceeded with reference to the admission of states; and as early as 1802 we find Ohio compelled, as the price of admission into the Union, to enter into an agreement, irrevocable without the consent of Congress, not to tax for a period of five years lands within the state which were sold by the United States government. The imposing of conditions of various kinds upon the incoming states became a settled policy of Congress, and the stipulations agreed to covered a considerable range of topics. They related to the disposition of public lands, many of them being much more detailed than the Ohio provision; to the use of navigable waters; to the protection of the rights of citizens of the United States; to slavery; to civil and religious liberty; to the right to vote. When Utah came into the Union in 1894 it was obliged to make an irrevocable agreement that there should be perfect religious toleration maintained in the state, that the public schools should be kept free from sectarian control, and that polygamous marriages should be forever prohibited. In 1910 Arizona was authorized by a congressional enabling act to draw up a state constitution preparatory to entering the Union. The constitution framed contained provisions for the popular recall of judges. While Congress somewhat reluctantly passed a resolution admitting Arizona into the Union, President Taft, being bitterly opposed to the recall of judges, vetoed the resolution. A new resolution was then passed providing that Arizona be admitted on condition that the objectionable provision be stricken out of the constitution. This was done and Arizona became a member of the Union. The state thereupon promptly restored the recall of judges by amending the new state constitution, and has retained the provision ever since.

But if Congress can thus impose conditions upon the new states as they assume statehood, the question arises: Are the states equal? Do we actually have states in the Union which do not have the power enjoyed by other states; as, for instance, to decide how judges shall be removed from office, or what shall constitute a lawful marriage? It is a rather curious fact that the question of the binding nature of these restrictions was not brought squarely before the Supreme Court until 1911 in the case of Coyle v. Smith. When the time came to admit Oklahoma as a state, two competing factions presented themselves to Congress, each with its own constitution. The enabling act which resulted was a compromise which provided (1) that the new state should locate its capital at Guthrie, (2) that it should irrevocably agree not to move it from that place before the year 1913, and (3) that it should not appropriate any unnecessary money for public buildings. This agreement was ratified by the voters of the state at the time that the new constitution was adopted; and, thus bound, Oklahoma entered the Union. In 1910 a bill initiated by the people providing that the state capital should forthwith be moved to Oklahoma City and appropriating $600,000 for public buildings was approved by the voters of Oklahoma. This was, of course, in plain violation of the "irrevocable" agreement which the state had made, and a proceeding was instituted to test the validity of the law. In sustaining the right of the state to move its capital at its discretion regardless of its agreement, the Supreme Court enunciated the important doctrine of the political equality of the states.

A distinction, however, should be noted between those conditions imposed upon incoming states which relate to political or governmental authority and which would therefore place the state upon an unequal footing in the Union, and those conditions in the nature of business agreements or contracts which relate to property. Thus, for example, the agreement of a new state to conditions in its Enabling Act that lands given to it by the United States in trust for certain purposes has been held enforceable like any other trust agreement. See Ervien v. United States (1919) in which New Mexico, which was given lands for school purposes, was held properly enjoined from using them for advertising the resources of the state.

It may be said that the vital question whether one of the states of the Union may constitutionally secede was effectively and permanently answered upon the battlefields of the Civil War. Four years after the war had ended, however, the Supreme Court found itself under the necessity of deciding, in the case of Texas v. White (1869), whether the Southern states had at any time during the period of attempting secession been actually out of the Union. Was secession, in point of law, constitutionally possible? The facts in this case were as follows:

In 1850 the United States gave the state of Texas $10,000,000 in 5 percent bonds in settlement of certain boundary claims. Half were held in Washington; half were delivered to the state, and made payable to the state or bearer and redeemable after December 31, 1864. A Texas law was passed providing that the bonds should not be available in the hands of any holder until after their endorsement by the governor. Texas joined the Confederacy at the outbreak of the war, and in 1862 the state legislature repealed the act requiring the endorsement of the bonds by the governor and created a military board to provide for the expenses of the war, empowering the board to use any bonds in the state treasury for this purpose up to $1,000,000. In 1865 this board made a contract with White and others for the transfer of some of the bonds for military supplies. None of the bonds was endorsed by the governor of the state. Immediately upon the close of the war, but while the state was still "unreconstructed" or unrestored to its former normal status as a member of the Union, suit was brought by the governor of the state to get the bonds back and to enjoin White and the other defendants from receiving payment for them from the federal government. The suit was brought by Texas in the Supreme Court of the United States as an original action, and at the very threshold of the case arose the question whether Texas, after efforts at secession, was still a "state" within the meaning of Article III, of the Constitution extending the original jurisdiction of the Supreme Court to those cases "in which a State shall be party."

Texas at this time was still unrepresented in Congress, and the radical Republicans like Stevens claimed that she was out of the Union.

The Court held that secession was constitutionally impossible and that Texas had never ceased to be a state in the Union. Chief Justice Chase said the Articles of Confederation created what was solemnly declared to be a "perpetual Union"; that the Constitution was ordained "to form a more perfect Union"; and he concluded that: "The Constitution, in all of its provisions, looks to an indestructible union, composed of indestructible states." The fact that Texas, by its own efforts at secession, had temporarily given up the rights and privileges of membership in the Union did not alter the fact that it could not sever the constitutional ties which bound it to that Union. The Court accordingly took jurisdiction in the case and decided that Texas was entitled to recover the bonds.

In cases of spectacular importance the Supreme Court faced the issue of who holds title to the land beneath the sea within the so-called "three-mile" limit. The discovery of oil off the coasts of California, Louisiana, and Texas gave this underwater land tremendous value; and the three states, assuming the land was theirs, leased to various oil companies the right to drill for offshore oil. The United States, asserting that it was "the owner in fee simple, or possessed of paramount rights in and powers over" this land, brought suit to enjoin the states from trespassing upon it. The Supreme Court, in United States v. California (1947), invoked the "equal footing" rule to sustain the United States, at least in its claim to "paramount rights." A similar question had reached the Court in 1845 in Pollard v. Hagan. Alabama had been admitted to the Union on an equal footing with the other states, but in the act of admission it had been stipulated that Alabama disclaimed title to waste and unappropriated lands under the navigable waters within the state, and that its navigable waters should remain public highways and free to the citizens of the state and of the United States. On the strength of this the United States claimed title to the submerged lands under the navigable waters within the state of Alabama. The Court found that all the other states had had commonlaw title to these submerged lands when they came into the Union. "Alabama is therefore entitled to the sovereignty and jurisdiction over all the territory within her limits, . . . to the same extent that Georgia possessed it before she ceded it to the United States. To maintain any other doctrine, is to deny that Alabama has been admitted into the Union on an equal footing with the original states. . . . "

The Court decided the claims of Louisiana (United States v. Louisiana, 1950) on the basis of the California decision. But United States v. Texas (1950) presented a slightly different problem. Texas had been an independent state prior to its admission to the Union and had had undoubted title to its offshore lands. The Court applied the Pollard argument in reverse: "The 'equal footing' clause, we hold, works the same way in the converse situation presented by this case. It negatives any implied, special limitation of any of the paramount powers of the United States in favor of a State. . . . When Texas came into the Union, she ceased to be an independent nation. She then became a sister State on an 'equal footing' with all the other States. That act concededly entailed a relinquishment of some of her sovereignty. . . . We hold that as an incident to the transfer of that sovereignty any claim that Texas may have had to the marginal sea was relinquished to the United States."

The "tideland's oil" question became an issue in the 1952 presidential campaign, and the victorious Republican Congress redeemed its campaign pledge to cede to the three states the lands which they claimed. Since the acts ceded title to the land extending to the original boundaries of the states, the Gulf states claimed three leagues (nine nautical miles) of marginal sea. Congress' right to make this cession was upheld in Alabama v. Texas in 1954, but in 1960 the Court held that only Texas and Florida were entitled to three leagues. The fact that this apparently leaves these states sticking out some six miles beyond the boundaries of the United States raises potential problems in international law which the Court declined to answer. "It is sufficient for present purposes to note that there is no question of Congress' power to fix state land and water boundaries as a domestic matter. Such a boundary, fully effective as between Nation and State, undoubtedly circumscribes the extent of navigable inland waters and underlying lands owned by the State under the Pollard rule." See United States v. Louisiana (1960).

In the years since 1937, the substance of the power reserved to the states has diminished steadily as Congress has extended its authority under the taxing and commerce powers to areas once solely under state control. So clear has the trend been, and so unwavering the approval of the Supreme Court, that the future seemed bleak for that "residuum of sovereignty" to which the Court alluded in the case below. In 1976, however, in National League of Cities v. Usery, the Court suddenly appeared to reverse this trend. It quoted Coyle v. Smith with approval and held void the application of federal minimum wage legislation to state employees on the ground that it was an infringement of state sovereignty.

Mr. Justice Lurton delivered the opinion of the Court, saying in part:

... The only question for review by us is whether the provision of the enabling act was a valid limitation upon the power of the state after its admission, which overrides any subsequent state legislation repugnant thereto.

The power to locate its own seat of government, and to determine when and how it shall be changed from one place to another, and to appropriate its own public funds for that purpose, are essentially and peculiarly state powers. That one of the original thirteen states could now be shorn of such powers by an act of Congress would not be for a moment entertained. The question, then, comes to this: Can a state be placed upon a plane of inequality with its sister states in the Union if the Congress chooses to impose conditions which so operate, at the time of its admission? The argument is, that while Congress may not deprive a state of any power which it *possesses,* it may, as a condition to the admission of a new state, constitutionally restrict its authority, to the extent, at least, of suspending its powers for a definite time in respect to the location of its seat of government. This contention is predicated upon the constitutional power of admitting new states to this Union, and the constitutional duty of guaranteeing to "every state in this Union a republican form of government." The position of counsel for the plaintiff in error is substantially this: That the power of Congress to admit new states, and to determine whether or not its fundamental law is republican in form, are political powers, and as such, uncontrollable by the courts. That Congress may, in the exercise of such power, impose terms and conditions upon the admission of the proposed new state, which, if accepted, will be obligatory, although they operate to deprive the state of powers which it would otherwise possess, and, therefore, not admitted upon "an equal footing with the original states."

The power of Congress in respect to the admission of new states is found in the 3d section of the 4th article of the Constitution. That provision is that, "new states may be admitted by the Congress into this Union." The only expressed restriction upon this power is that no new state shall be formed within the jurisdiction of any other state, nor by the junction of two or more states, or parts of states, without the consent of such states, as well as of the Congress.

But what is this power? It is not to admit political organizations which are less or greater, or different in dignity or power, from those political entities which constitute the Union. It is, as strongly put by counsel, a "power to admit states."

The definition of "a state" is found in the powers possessed by the original states which adopted the Constitution,—a definition emphasized by the terms employed in all subsequent acts of Congress admitting new states into the Union. The first two states admitted into the Union were the states of Vermont and Kentucky, one as of March 4, 1791, and the other as of June 1, 1792. No terms or conditions were exacted from either. Each act declares that the state is admitted "as a new and *entire member* of the United States of America." . . . Emphatic and significant as is the phrase admitted as "an entire member," even stronger was the declaration upon the admission in 1796 of Tennessee as the third new state, it being declared to be "one of the United States of America," "on an equal footing with the original states in all respects whatsoever,"—phraseology which has ever since been substantially followed in admission acts, concluding with the Oklahoma act, which declares that Oklahoma shall be admitted "on an equal footing with the original states."

The power is to admit "new states into *this* Union."

"This Union" was and is a union of states, equal in power, dignity, and authority, each competent to exert that residuum of sovereignty not delegated to the United States by the Constitution itself. To maintain otherwise would be to say that the Union, through the power of Congress to admit new states, might come to be a union of states unequal in power, as including states whose powers were restricted only by the Constitution, with others whose powers had been further restricted by an act of Congress accepted as a condition of admission. Thus it would result, first, that the powers of Congress would not be defined by the Constitution alone, but in respect to new states, enlarged or restricted by the conditions imposed upon new states by its own legislation admitting them into the Union; and, second, that such new states might not exercise all of the powers which had not been delegated by the Constitution, but only such as had not been further bargained away as conditions of admission.

The argument that Congress derives from the duty of "guaranteeing to each state in this Union a republican form of government," power to impose restrictions upon a new state which deprive it of equality with other members of the Union, has no merit. It may imply the duty of each new state to provide itself with such state government, and impose upon Congress the duty of seeing that such form is not changed to one anti-republican, . . . but it obviously does not confer power to admit a new state which shall be any less a state than those which compose the Union.

We come now to the question as to whether there is anything in the decisions of this court which sanctions the claim that Congress may, by the imposition of conditions in an enabling act, deprive a new state of any of those attributes essential to its equality in dignity and power with other states. In considering the decisions of this court bearing upon the question, we must distinguish, first, between provisions which are fulfilled by the admission of the state; second, between compacts or affirmative legislation intended to operate in futuro, which are within the scope of the conceded powers of Congress over the subject; and third, compacts or affirmative legislation which operate to restrict the powers of such new states in respect of matters which would otherwise be exclusively within the sphere of state power.

As to requirements in such enabling acts as relate only to the contents of the Constitution for the proposed new state, little need[s] to be said. The constitutional provision concerning the admission of new states is not a mandate, but a power to be exercised with discretion. From this alone it would follow that Congress may require, under penalty of denying admission, that the organic law of a new state at the time of admission shall be such as to meet its approval. A Constitution thus supervised by Congress would, after all, be a Constitution of a state, and as such subject to alteration and amendment by the state after admission. Its force would be that of a state Constitution, and not that of an act of Congress. . . .

So far as this court has found occasion to advert to the effect of enabling acts as affirmative legislation affecting the power of new states after admission, there is to be found no sanction for the contention that any state may be deprived of any of the power constitutionally possessed by other states, as states, by reason of the terms in which the acts admitting them to the Union have been framed. . . . [Here follows discussion of a case involving the construction of the act under which Alabama was admitted to the Union.]

The plain deduction from this case is that when a new state is admitted into the Union, it is so admitted with all of the powers of sovereignty and jurisdiction which pertain to the original states, and that such powers may not be constitutionally diminished, impaired, or shorn away by any conditions, compacts, or stipulations embraced in the act under which the new state came into the Union, which would not be valid and effectual if the subject of congressional legislation after admission. . . .

It may well happen that Congress should embrace in an enactment introducing a new state into the Union legislation intended as a regulation of commerce among the states, or with Indian tribes situated within the limits of such new state, or regulations touching the sole care and disposition of the public lands or reservations therein which might be upheld as legislation within the sphere of the plain power of Congress. But in every such case such legislation would derive its force not from any agreement or compact with the proposed new state, nor by reason of its acceptance of such enactment as a term of admission, but solely because the power of Congress extended to the subject, and therefore would not operate to restrict the state's legislative power in respect of any matter which was not plainly within the regulating power of Congress. . . .

No such question is presented here. The legislation in the Oklahoma enabling act relating to the location of the capital of the state, if construed as forbidding a removal by the state after its admission as a state, is referable to no power granted to Congress over the subject, and if it is to be upheld at all, it must be implied from the power to admit new states. If power to impose such a restriction upon the general and undelegated power of a state be conceded as implied from the power to admit a new state, where is the line to be drawn against restrictions imposed upon new states. . . .

. . . If anything was needed to complete the argument against the assertion that Oklahoma has not been admitted to the Union upon an equality of power, dignity, and sovereignty with Massachusetts or Virginia, it is afforded by the express provision of the act of admission, by which it is declared that when the people of the proposed new state have complied with the terms of the act, that it shall be the duty of the President to issue his proclamation, and that "thereupon the proposed state of Oklahoma shall be deemed admitted by Congress into the Union under and by virtue of this act, *on an equal footing with the original states.*" The proclamation has been issued and the Senators and Representatives from the state admitted to their seats in the Congress.

Has Oklahoma been admitted upon an equal footing with the original states? If she has, she, by virtue of her jurisdictional sovereignty as such a state, may determine for her own people the proper location of the local seat of government. She is not equal in power to them if she cannot. . . .

To this we may add that the constitutional equality of the states is essential to the harmonious operation of the scheme upon which the Republic was organized. When that equality disappears we may remain a free people, but the Union will not be the Union of the Constitution.

Judgment affirmed.

Mr. Justice McKenna and Mr. Justice Holmes dissent.

GIBBONS v. OGDEN

9 Wheaton 1; 6 L. Ed. 23 (1824)

In 1798 Robert R. Livingston secured from the New York legislature an exclusive twenty-year grant to navigate by steam the rivers and other waters of the state, provided that within two years he should build a boat which would make four miles an hour against the current of the Hudson River. The grant was made amidst the ribald jeers of the legislators, who had no faith whatever in the project. The terms of the grant were not met, however, and it was renewed in 1803—this time to Livingston together with his partner, Robert Fulton—and again for two years in 1807. In August, 1807, Fulton's steamboat made its first successful trip from New York to Albany, and steamboat navigation became a reality. The following year the legislature, now fully aware of the practical significance of Fulton's achievement, passed a law providing that for each new boat placed on New York waters by Fulton and Livingston they should be entitled to a five-year extension of their monopoly, which should, however, not exceed 30 years. The monopoly was made effective by further providing that no one should be allowed to navigate New York waters by steam without a license from Fulton and Livingston, and any unlicensed vessel should be forfeited to them. The business of steamboat navigation developed rapidly. Boats were put in operation between New York and Albany and intervening points, and steam ferries ran between Fulton Street, New York City, and points in New Jersey. In 1811 the partners obtained from the Territory of Orleans (later Louisiana) a monopoly of steam navigation on the waters of Louisiana similar to that granted by New York, thus assuring them a pivotal position in the two greatest ports of the land. Naturally the monopolistic nature of the Fulton-Livingston rights worked hardship on their would-be competitors, and neighboring states began to pass retaliatory laws directed against the New York partners. The New Jersey legislature in 1811 authorized the owner of any boat siezed under the forfeiture clause of the Fulton-Livingston charter to capture and hold in retaliation any boat belonging to any New York citizen. Connecticut in 1822 forbade any vessel licensed by Fulton and Livingston to enter the waters of that state, and Ohio passed a somewhat similar law in the same year. Granting such exclusive franchises was a game at which more than one state could play; and such grants were made by Georgia, Massachusetts, Pennsylvania, Tennessee, New Hampshire, and Vermont. With the inevitable increase of feeling created by such policies, retaliatory acts became common. In short, an achievement of science which had seemed destined to enlarge the means of communication and develop the commerce of the nation appeared rather to be embroiling the states in bitter antagonisms and commercial warfare such as prevailed during the dismal period of the Confederation. It is against the background of this intensely acute economic situation that the case of Gibbons v. Ogden must be read.

Odgen had secured a license for steam navigation from Fulton and Livingston. Gibbons had originally been his partner but was now his rival and was operating steamboats between New York and New Jersey under the authority of a coasting license obtained from the United States government. Upon Ogden's petition the New York court had enjoined Gibbons from continuing in business. The great jurist Chancellor James Kent wrote the opinion in this case, upholding the validity of the New York statute establishing the monopoly and repudiating the idea that there was any conflict involved between federal and state authority. An appeal was taken by Gibbons to the Supreme Court of the United States, thus presenting to that tribunal its first case under the commerce clause of the Constitution.

So accustomed are we to the free flow of commerce among the states that it is hard to conceive how the nation might have developed had the arguments in favor of the monopoly prevailed, for it was urged that the powers of state and nation to regulate interstate commerce were concurrent; that in the absence of a conflicting congressional statute the state was free to exercise this concurrent power as it pleased; and that the "commerce" which Congress may regulate was "the transportation and sale of commodities." Had that argument prevailed, the federal coasting license under which Gibbons operated would have given him no protection, since he was carrying passengers, not goods. But the most crucial argument of all was that the New York monopoly law was not a regulation of interstate commerce but was merely a regulation of commerce within the boundaries of the state of New York. "It [the law] does not deny the right of entry into its waters to any vessel navigated by steam; it only forbids such vessel, when within its waters and jurisdiction, to be moved by steam; but that vessel may still navigate by all other means; and it leaves the people of other states, or of New York, in full possession of the right of navigation, by all the means known or used at the time of the passage of the law. [Most early steamboats were also sailboats.] It is, therefore, strictly a regulation of internal trade and navigation, which belongs to the state. This may, indeed, indirectly affect the right of commercial intercourse between the states. But so do all other laws regulating internal trade. . . . ''

Webster's argument against the validity of the steamboat monopoly was perhaps his greatest effort before the Supreme Court, and some writers believe that Marshall's opinion invalidating the New York law is his greatest state paper; others would place it second only to the opinion in McCulloch v. Maryland. It was perhaps the only genuinely popular decision which Marshall ever handed down. It was received with widespread expressions of approval, for it was, as one writer has put it, ''the first great anti-trust decision.'' The economic consequences of it in freeing a developing commerce from the shackles of state monopoly can hardly be overestimated; and it established for all time the supremacy of the national government in all matters affecting interstate and foreign commerce.

Mr. Chief Justice Marshall delivered the opinion of the Court, saying in part:

The appellant contends that this decreee is erroneous, because the laws which purport to give the exclusive privilege it sustains, are repugnant to the constitution and laws of the United States.

They are said to be repugnant:

1st. To that clause in the constitution which authorizes Congress to regulate commerce.

2d. To that which authorizes Congress to promote the progress of science and useful arts. . . .

As preliminary to the very able discussions of the constitution, which we have heard from the bar, and as having some influence on its construction, reference has been made to the political situation of these states, anterior to its formation. It has been said that they were sovereign, were completely independent, and were connected with each other only by a league. This is true. But when these allied sovereigns converted their league into a government, when they converted their Congress of Ambassadors, deputed to deliberate on their common concerns, and to recommend measures of general utility, into a legislature, empowered to enact laws on the most interesting subjects, the whole character in which the states appear, underwent a change, the extent of which must be determined by a fair consideration of the instrument by which that change was effected.

This instrument contains an enumeration of powers expressly granted by the people to their government. It has been said that these powers ought to be construed strictly. But why ought they to be so construed? Is there one sentence in the Constitution which gives countenance to this rule? In the last of the enumerated powers, that which grants, expressly, the means of carrying all others into execution, Congress is authorized "to make all laws which shall be necessary and proper" for the purpose. But this limitation on the means which may be used, is not extended to the powers which are conferred; nor is there one sentence in the constitution, which has been pointed out by the gentlemen of the bar, or which we have been able to discern, that prescribes this rule. We do not, therefore, think ourselves justified in adopting it. What do gentlemen mean by a strict construction? If they contend only against that enlarged construction which would extend words beyond their natural and obvious import, we might question the application of the term, but should not controvert the principle. If they contend for that narrow construction which, in support of some theory not to be found in the constitution, would deny to the government those powers which the words of the grant, as usually understood, import, and which are consistent with the general views and objects of the instrument; for that narrow construction, which would cripple the government and render it unequal to the objects for which it is declared to be instituted, and to which the powers given, as fairly understood, render it competent; then we cannot perceive the propriety of this strict construction, nor adopt it as the rule by which the constitution is to be expounded. As men, whose intentions require no concealment, generally employ the words which most directly and aptly express the ideas they intend to convey, the enlightened patriots who framed our constitution, and the people who adopted it, must be understood to have employed words in their natural sense, and to have intended what they have said. If, from the imperfection of human language, there should be serious doubts respecting the extent of any given power, it is a well-settled rule that the objects for which it was given, especially when those objects are expressed in the instrument itself, should have great influence in the construction. We know of no reason for excluding this rule from the present case. The grant does not convey power which might be beneficial to the grantor, if retained by himself, or which can enure solely to the benefit of the grantee, but is an investment of power for the general advantage, in the hands of agents selected for that purpose; which power can never be exercised by the people themselves, but must be placed in the hands of agents or lie dormant. We know of no rule for construing the extent of such powers, other than is given by the language of the instrument which confers them, taken in connection with the purposes for which they were conferred.

The words are: "Congress shall have power to regulate commerce with foreign nations, and among the several states, and with the Indian tribes."

The subject to be regulated is commerce; and our constitution being, as was aptly said at the bar, one of enumeration, and not of definition, to ascertain the extent of the power it becomes necessary to settle the meaning of the word. The counsel for the appellee would limit it to traffic, to buying and selling, or the interchange of commodities, and do not admit that it comprehends navigation. This would restrict a general term, applicable to many objects, to one of its significations. Commerce, undoubtedly, is traffic, but it is something more; it is intercourse. It describes the commercial intercourse between nations, and parts of nations, in all its branches, and is regulated by prescribing rules for carrying on that intercourse. The mind can scarcely conceive a system for regulating commerce between nations, which shall exclude all laws concerning navigation, which shall be silent on the admission of the vessels of the one nation into the ports of the other, and be confined to prescribing rules for the conduct of individuals, in the actual employment of buying and selling, or of barter.

If commerce does not include navigation, the government of the Union has no direct power over that subject, and can make no law prescribing what shall constitute American vessels, or requiring that they shall be navigated by American seamen. Yet this power has been exercised from the commencement of the government, has been exercised with the consent of all, and has been understood by all to be a commercial regulation. All America understands, and has uniformly understood, the word "commerce" to comprehend navigation. It was so understood, and must have been so understood, when the constitution was framed. The power over commerce, including navigation, was one of the primary objects for which the people of America adopted their government, and must have been contemplated in forming it. The convention must have used the word in that sense, because all have understood it in that sense, and the attempt to restrict it comes too late. . . .

The word used in the constitution, then, comprehends, and has been always understood to comprehend, navigation within its meaning; and a power to regulate navigation is as expressly granted as if that term had been added to the word "commerce."

To what commerce does this power extend? The constitution informs us, to commerce "with foreign nations, and among the several states, and with the Indian tribes."

It has, we believe, been universally admitted that these words comprehend every species of commercial intercourse between the United States and foreign nations. No sort of trade can be carried on between this country and any other, to which this power does not extend. It has been truly said that commerce, as the word is used in the constitution, is a unit, every part of which is indicated by the term.

If this be the admitted meaning of the word, in its application to foreign nations, it must carry the same meaning throughout the sentence, and remain a unit, unless there be some plain intelligible cause which alters it.

The subject to which the power is next applied, is to commerce "among the several states." The word "among" means intermingled with. A thing which is among others, is intermingled with them. Commerce among the states cannot stop at the external boundary line of each state, but may be introduced into the interior.

It is not intended to say that these words comprehend that commerce which is completely internal, which is carried on between man and man in a state, or between different parts of the same state, and which does not extend to or affect other states. Such a power would be inconvenient, and is certainly unnecessary.

Comprehensive as the word "among" is, it may very properly be restricted to that commerce which concerns more states than one. . . . The completely internal commerce of a state, then, may be considered as reserved for the state itself.

But, in regulating commerce with foreign nations, the power of Congress does not stop at the jurisdictional lines of the several states. It would be a very useless power if it could not pass those lines. The commerce of the United States with foreign nations, is that of the whole United States. Every district has a right to participate in it. The deep streams which penetrate our country in every direction, pass through the interior of almost every state in the Union, and furnish the means of exercising this right. If Congress has the power to regulate it, that power must be exercised whenever the subject exists. If it exists within the states, if a foreign voyage may commence or terminate at a port within a state, then the power of Congress may be exercised within a state.

This principle is, if possible, still more clear, when applied to commerce "among the several states." They either join each other, in which case they are separated by a mathematical line, or they are remote from each other, in which case other states lie between them. What is commerce "among" them; and how is it to be conducted? Can a trading expedition between two adjoining states commence and terminate outside of each? And if the trading intercourse be between two states remote from each other, must it not commence in one, terminate in the other, and probably pass through a third? Commerce among the states must, of necessity, be commerce with the states. In the regulation of trade with the Indian tribes, the action of the law, especially when the constitution was made, was chiefly within a state. The power of Congress, then, whatever it may be, must be exercised within the territorial jurisdiction of the several states. . . .

We are now arrived at the inquiry, What is this power?

It is the power to regulate; that is, to prescribe the rule by which commerce is to be governed. This power, like all others vested in Congress, is complete in itself, may be exercised to its utmost extent, and acknowledges no limitations, other than are prescribed in the constitution. These are expressed in plain terms, and do not affect the questions which arise in this case, or which have been discussed at the bar. . . .

The power of Congress, then, comprehends navigation within the limits of every state in the Union; so far as that navigation may be, in any manner, connected with "commerce with foreign nations, or among the several states, or with the Indian tribes." It may, of consequence, pass the jurisdictional line of New York, and act upon the very waters to which the prohibition now under consideration applies.

But it has been urged with great earnestness, that although the power of Congress to regulate commerce with foreign nations, and among the several states, be co-extensive with the subject itself, and have no other limits than are prescribed in the constitution, yet the states may severally exercise the same power within their respective jurisdictions. In support of this argument, it is said that they possessed it as an inseparable attribute of sovereignty, before the formation of the constitution, and still retain it, except so far as they have surrendered it by that instrument; that this principle results from the nature of the government, and is secured by the tenth amendment; that an affirmative grant of power is not exclusive, unless in its own nature it be such that the continued exercise of it by the former possessor is inconsistent with the grant, and that this is not of that description.

The appellant, conceding these postulates, except the last, contends that full power to regulate a particular subject, implies the whole power, and leaves no residuum; that a grant of the whole is incompatible with the existence of a right in another to any part of it. . . .

In discussing the question, whether this power is still in the states, in the case under consideration, we may dismiss from it the inquiry, whether it is surrendered by the mere grant to Congress, or is retained until Congress shall exercise the power. We may dismiss that inquiry, because it has been exercised, and the regulations which Congress deemed it proper to make, are now in full operation. The sole question is, can a state regulate commerce with foreign nations and among the states, while Congress is regulating it? . . .

The act passed in 1803, prohibiting the importation of slaves into any state which shall itself prohibit their importation, implies, it is said, an admission that the states possessed the power to exclude or admit them; from which it is inferred that they possess the same power with respect to other articles.

If this inference were correct; if this power was exercised, not under any particular clause in the constitution, but in virtue of a general right over the subject of commerce, to exist as long as the constitution itself, it might now be exercised. Any state might now import African slaves into its own territory. But it is obvious that the power of the states over this subject, previous to the year 1808, constitutes an exception to the power of Congress to regulate commerce, and the exception is expressed in such words as to manifest clearly the intention to continue the pre-existing right of the states to admit or exclude, for a limited period. The words are: "The migration or importation of such persons as any of the states, now existing, shall think proper to admit, shall not be prohibited by the Congress prior to the year 1808." The whole object of the exception is to preserve the power to those states which might be disposed to exercise it; and its language seems to the court to convey this idea unequivocally. The possession of this particular power, then, during the time limited in the constitution, cannot be admitted to prove the possession of any other similar power.

It has been said that the act of August 7th, 1789, acknowledges a concurrent power in the states to regulate the conduct of pilots, and hence is inferred an admission of their concurrent right with Congress to regulate commerce with foreign nations, and amongst the states. But this inference is not, we think, justified by the fact.

Although Congress cannot enable a state to legislate, Congress may adopt the provisions of a state on any subject. When the government of the Union was brought into existence, it found a system for the regulation of its pilots in full force in every state. The act which has been mentioned, adopts this system, and gives it the same validity as if its provisions had been specially made by Congress. But the act, it may be said, is prospective also, and the adoption of laws to be made in future, presupposes the right in the maker to legislate on the subject.

The act unquestionably manifests an intention to leave this subject entirely to the states, until Congress should think proper to interpose; but the very enactment of such a law indicates an opinion that it was necessary; that the existing system would not be applicable to the new state of things, unless expressly applied to it by Congress. . . .

These acts were cited at the bar for the purpose of showing an opinion in Congress that the states possess, concurrently with the legislature of the Union, the power to regulate commerce with foreign nations and among the states. Upon reviewing them, we think they do not establish the proposition they were intended to prove. They show the opinion that the states retain powers enabling them to pass the laws to which allusion has been made, not that those laws proceed from the particular power which has been delegated to Congress.

It has been contended by the counsel for the appellant, that, as the word "to regulate" implies in its nature, full power over the thing to be regulated, it excludes, necessarily, the action of all others that would perform the same operation on the same thing. That regulation is designed for the entire result, applying to those parts which remain as they were, as well as to those which are altered. It produces a uniform whole, which is as much disturbed and deranged by changing what the regulating power designs to leave untouched, as that on which it has operated.

There is great force in this argument, and the court is not satisfied that it has been refuted.

Since, however, in exercising the power of regulating their own purely internal affairs, whether of trading or police, the states may sometimes enact laws, the validity of which depends on their interfering with, and being contrary to, an act of Congress passed in pursuance of the constitution, the court will enter upon the inquiry, whether the laws of New York, as expounded by the highest tribunal of that state, have, in their application to this case, come into collision with an act of Congress, and deprived a citizen of a right to which that act entitles him. Should this collision exist, it will be immaterial whether those laws were passed in virtue of a concurrent power "to regulate commerce with foreign nations and among the several states," or in virtue of a power to regulate their domestic trade and police. In one case and the other, the acts of New York must yield to the law of Congress; and the decision sustaining the privilege they confer, against a right given by a law of the Union, must be erroneous. . . .

The questions, then, whether the conveyance of passengers be a part of the coasting trade, and whether a vessel can be protected in that occupation by a coasting license, are not, and cannot be, raised in this case. The real and sole question seems to be, whether a steam machine, in actual use, deprives a vessel of the privileges conferred by a license.

In considering this question, the first idea which presents itself, is that the laws of Congress, for the regulation of commerce, do not look to the principle by which vessels are moved. That subject is left entirely to individual discretion; and, in that vast and complex system of legislative enactment concerning it, which embraces everything that the legislature thought it necessary to notice, there is not, we believe, one word respecting the peculiar principle by which vessels are propelled through the water, except what may be found in a single act, granting a particular privilege to steamboats. With this exception, every act, either prescribing duties, or granting privileges, applies to every vessel, whether navigated by the instrumentality of wind or fire, of sails or machinery. The whole weight of proof, then, is thrown upon him who would introduce a distinction to which the words of the law give no countenance.

If a real difference could be admitted to exist between vessels carrying passengers and others, it has already been observed that there is no fact in this case which can bring up that question. And, if the occupation of steamboats be a matter of such general notoriety that the court may be presumed to know it, although not specially informed by the record, then we deny that the transportation of passengers is their exclusive occupation. It is a matter of general history, that, in our western waters, their principal employment is the transportation of merchandise; and all know, that in the waters of the Atlantic they are frequently so employed.

But all inquiry into this subject seems to the court to be put completely at rest by the act already mentioned, entitled, "An act for the enrolling and licensing of steamboats."

This act authorizes a steamboat employed, or intended to be employed, only in a river or bay of the United States, owned wholly or in part by an alien, resident within the United States, to be enrolled and licensed as if the same belonged to a citizen of the United States.

This act demonstrates the opinion of Congress, that steamboats may be enrolled and licensed, in common with vessels using sails. They are, of course, entitled to the same privileges, and can no more be restrained from navigating waters, and entering ports which are free to such vessels, than if they were wafted on their voyage by the winds, instead of being propelled by the agency of fire. The one element may be as legitimately used as the other, for every commercial purpose authorized by the laws of the Union; and the act of a state inhibiting the use of either to any vessel having a license under the act of Congress, comes, we think, in direct collision with that act.

As this decides the cause, it is unnecessary to enter in an examination of that part of the constitution which empowers Congress to promote the progress of science and the useful arts. . . .

UNITED STATES v. DARBY

312 U. S. 100; 61 S. Ct. 451; 85 L. Ed. 609 (1941)

It used to be said that the federal government has no police power. In a narrow sense this is true, for the police power is defined as the general power to pass regulatory laws for the protection of the health, morals, safety, good order, and general welfare of the community. The Constitution grants no such broad power to Congress, and so, by the operation of the Tenth Amendment, it is reserved to the states. Since the turn of the century, however, what may be fairly called a federal police power has come into existence through the use by Congress of certain of its delegated powers to achieve some of the same social objectives which the states achieve through the state police power. Thus Congress has no delegated power to forbid the production of impure food products; but it does have power to forbid the shipping of impure food in interstate commerce. It cannot punish ordinary business swindles; but it may make it a crime to use the mails for purposes of fraud. In this way Congress has been able to use its power to regulate interstate commerce, to operate the postal service, and to tax, as "constitutional pegs" upon which to hang policies for the national welfare which it has no direct authority to promulgate. By this somewhat indirect method Congress has come to exercise control over an ever-increasing number of social and economic problems. By far the largest part of this growing federal police power is based upon the commerce clause.

The use of commerce power as a peg on which to hang social legislation developed in two somewhat different ways. The first of these involved the doctrine, first announced in the Lottery Case (Champion v. Ames, 1903), that Congress could validly bar from interstate commerce commodities which are dangerous or otherwise objectionable. In 1895 Congress forbade the sending of lottery tickets through interstate commerce or the mails. After holding that lottery tickets are articles of commerce, the Court decided that Congress had the power to guard the people of the United States from the "widespread pestilence of lotteries" by keeping lottery tickets out of the channels of interstate commerce over which Congress has undisputed control. Congress was not slow to exercise the kind of power sustained in the Lottery Case. It has excluded from interstate commerce impure or misbranded food and drugs, meat not properly inspected, obscene literature, and prize fight films (later modified in part), and other injurious or fraudulent commodities. Under a federal statute, if fabrics shipped in interstate commerce are marked "all wool" they must be in fact all wool. It may be noted in passing that the power of Congress over the postal system has enabled it to exercise a wide police power by excluding objectionable articles from the mails, and by forbidding the use of the mails for purposes of fraud.

The Court found no difference in principle between barring objectionable articles from interstate commerce and forbidding the use of the facilities of interstate commerce to aid immoral or criminal activities. In Hoke v. United States (1913), it held valid the Mann Act of 1910 which makes it a crime to transport women across a state line for immoral purposes. The act was not aimed at localized prostitution, but at the organized gangs of white slavers who carried on the interstate traffic in girls and women upon which commercialized vice depends. In 1925 Congress made it a crime knowingly to drive a stolen automobile across a state line, and this was upheld in Brooks v. United States (1925). Under later "anti-fence" laws, the same ban was put upon the interstate shipment of stolen goods in general. The so-called Lindbergh Act makes kidnapping a federal crime if the kidnapped person is carried across a state line (held valid in Gooch v. United States, 1936), and it is also a federal crime to use the mails, telephone, telegraph, or any system of interstate communication for purposes of extortion or blackmail. The theory in all these cases is clear and convincing. Congress, which is responsible for interstate commerce, may punish those who use the facilities of that commerce for immoral or criminal purposes.

The federal police power development reviewed thus far had fairly plain sailing constitutionally. All the articles barred from commerce had been "bad" articles, and all the forbidden uses of the facilities of that commerce had been "bad" uses. In 1916, however, Congress pushed the police power theory somewhat further in passing the Child Labor Act of 1916. Congress was well aware that it lacked the power to forbid child labor throughout the country. What it did, therefore, was to forbid the transportation in interstate commerce of the products of mines or factories in which children were employed in violation of the standards set up in this act. In other words, any employer who wished to market his goods through interstate commerce would have to stop employing children. It could not be claimed that the commodities produced in establishments using child labor were "bad" commodities, but merely that the conditions under which they were produced were "bad" conditions. The Supreme Court, split five to four, held the statute invalid in Hammer v. Dagenhart (1918). The majority opinion emphasized that the goods barred from interstate commerce by the act were harmless; that the effect of the act was to regulate, not interstate commerce, but the conditions under which goods entering that commerce were produced, and that it was, therefore, not a bona fide exercise of the commerce power. The Court rejected the argument that Congress could validly prevent those who produce goods under unsatisfactory labor conditions from using the channels of interstate commerce in order to compete with producers in other states who maintain decent labor conditions. It said: "Many causes may cooperate to give one state, by reason of local laws or conditions, an economic advantage over others. The commerce clause was not intended to give Congress a general authority to equalize such conditions." Finally, the act was void under the Tenth Amendment because Congress was using its delegated power over commerce for the purpose of regulating child labor, a power which lies within the range of the powers reserved to the states.

Justice Holmes dissented in Hammer v. Dagenhart in a strong opinion in which he declared that the Child Labor Act was a clear and direct exercise of the commerce power and that it should not be held void because of its indirect effects upon state authority. "It does not matter," he said, "whether the supposed evil precedes or follows the transportation. It is enough that, in the opinion of Congress, the transportation encourages the evil. The notion that prohibition is any less prohibition when applied to things now thought evil I do not understand. But if there is any matter upon which civilized countries have agreed,—far more unanimously than they have with regard to intoxicants and some other matters over which this country is now emotionally aroused, —it is the evil of premature and excessive child labor. I should have thought that if we were to introduce our own moral conceptions where, in my opinion, they do not belong, this was preeminently a case for upholding the exercise of all its powers by the United States. But I had thought that the propriety of the exercise of a power admitted to exist in some cases was for the consideration of Congress alone, and that this Court always had disavowed the right to intrude its judgment upon questions of policy or morals. It is not for this Court to pronounce when prohibition is necessary to regulation if it ever may be necessary—to say that it is permissible as against strong drink, but not against the product of ruined lives. The act does not meddle with anything belonging to the states. They may regulate their internal affairs and their domestic commerce as they like. But when they seek to send their products across the state line they are no longer within their rights."

In the 23 years between Hammer v. Dagenhart (1918) and the Darby case which overruled it, dramatic political changes swept the country. The Great Depression of the 1930's revealed that the laissez-faire economic theory which underlay most judicial thinking was unable to prevent economic disaster, and the state and local governments, upon which most of the burden fell, were unable to cope with the ensuing devastation. The result was a widespread change in attitude toward the role of government, particularly national government, in economic affairs. The election in 1932, and overwhelming reelection in 1936, of President Franklin D. Roosevelt was viewed as a mandate for his New Deal, a program of extensive government intervention in and control over the nation's economy.

Faced with an unsympathetic and intransigent Supreme Court, one of FDR's first moves upon reelection was to introduce in Congress a plan to enlarge the Court by one justice for every justice over the age of 70. Public opposition to the move was immediate and overwhelming and the so-called "court packing plan" was defeated. But from 1937 on, a majority of the Court (which included Justice Roberts who had switched over), without alluding to the political pressures upon them, began holding valid measures very like those they had been finding invalid before.

In 1938 Congress enacted the Fair Labor Standards (Wages and Hours) Act, which provided the first comprehensive regulation of the working standards of persons engaged in interstate commerce or producing goods for that commerce. The act provided (the first year) for a minimum wage of 25 cents an hour and a maximum 44-hour week without overtime pay, and required employers subject to the act to keep records of the hours and pay of their workers. Prohibited, also, was the employment of children under 16 in manufacturing and mining, and under 18 in hazardous occupations. The act not only made it a crime to ship in interstate commerce goods manufactured in violation of these standards but, in addition, made it a crime to employ people in the manufacture of goods for commerce under conditions that did not meet the prescribed standards. Darby, the president of a lumber company, was indicted for violating the wages, hours, and record-keeping provisions of the act.

Mr. Justice Stone delivered the opinion of the Court, saying in part:

The two principal questions raised by the record in this case are, *first,* whether Congress has constitutional power to prohibit the shipment in interstate commerce of lumber manufactured by employees whose wages are less than a prescribed minimum or whose weekly hours of labor at that wage are greater than a prescribed maximum, and, *second,* whether it has power to prohibit the employment of workmen in the production of goods "for interstate commerce" at other than prescribed wages and hours. A subsidiary question is whether in connection with such prohibitions Congress can require the employer subject to them to keep records showing the hours worked each day and week by each of his employees including those engaged "in the production and manufacture of goods to wit, lumber, for 'interstate commerce.' " . . .

The Fair Labor Standards Act set up a comprehensive legislative scheme for preventing the shipment in interstate commerce of certain products and commodities produced in the United States under labor conditions as respects wages and hours which fail to conform to standards set up by the Act. Its purpose, as we judicially know from the declaration of policy in § 2(a) of the Act, and the reports of Congressional committees proposing the legislation, . . . is to exclude from interstate commerce goods produced for the commerce and to prevent their production for interstate commerce, under conditions detrimental to the maintenance of the minimum standards of living necessary for health and general well-being; and to prevent the use of interstate commerce as the means of competition in the distribution of goods so produced, and as the means of spreading and perpetuating such substandard labor conditions among the workers of the several states. The Act also sets up an administrative procedure whereby those standards may from time to time be modified generally as to industries subject to the Act or within an industry in accordance with specified standards, by an administrator acting in collaboration with "Industry Committees" appointed by him. . . .

The indictment charges that appellee is engaged, in the state of Georgia, in the business of acquiring raw materials, which he manufacturers into finished lumber with the intent, when manufactured, to ship it in interstate commerce to customers outside the state, and that he does in fact so ship a large part of the lumber so produced. There are numerous counts charging appellee with the shipment in interstate commerce from Georgia to points outside the state of lumber in the production of which, for interstate commerce, appellee has employed workmen at less than the prescribed minimum wage or more than the prescribed maximum hours without payment to them of any wage for overtime. Other counts charge the employment by appellee of workmen in the production of lumber for interstate commerce at wages [of] less than 25 cents an hour or for more than the maximum hours per week without payment to them of the prescribed overtime wage. Still another count charges appellee with failure to keep records showing the hours worked each day a week by each of his employees as required by § 11(c) and the regulation of the administrator, . . . and also that appellee unlawfully failed to keep such records of employees engaged "in the production and manufacture of goods, to-wit lumber, for interstate commerce." . . .

The case comes here on assignments by the Government that the district court erred in so far as it held that Congress was without constitutional power to penalize the acts set forth in the indictment, and appellee seeks to sustain the decision below on the grounds that the prohibition by Congress of those Acts is unauthorized by the commerce clause and is prohibited by the Fifth Amendment. . . . Hence we . . . confine our decision to the validity and construction of the statute.

The prohibition of shipment of the proscribed goods in interstate commerce. Section 15(a) (1) prohibits, and the indictment charges, the shipment in interstate commerce, of goods produced for interstate commerce by employees whose wages and hours of employment do not conform to the requirements of the Act. Since this section is not violated unless the commodity shipped has been produced under labor conditions prohibited by § 6 and § 7, the only question arising under the commerce clause with respect to such shipments is whether Congress has the constitutional power to prohibit them.

While manufacture is not of itself interstate commerce the shipment of manufactured goods interstate is such commerce and the prohibition of such shipment by Congress is indubitably a regulation of the commerce. The power to regulate commerce is the power "to prescribe the rule by which commerce is governed." Gibbons v. Ogden [1824]. It extends not only to those regulations which aid, foster and protect the commerce, but embraces those which prohibit it. . . . It is conceded that the power of Congress to prohibit transportation in interstate commerce includes noxious articles, Lottery Case (Champion v. Ames) [1903] . . . ; stolen articles, Brooks v. United States [1925]; kidnapped persons, Gooch v. United States [1936] . . . and articles such as intoxicating liquor or convict made goods, traffic in which is forbidden or restricted by the laws of the state of destination. Kentucky Whip & Collar Co. v. Illinois C. R. Co. [1937].

But it is said that the present prohibition falls within the scope of none of these categories; that while the prohibition is nominally a regulation of the commerce its motive or purpose is regulation of wages and hours of persons engaged in manufacture, the control of which has been reserved to the states and upon which Georgia and some of the states of destination have placed no restriction; that the effect of the present statute is not to exclude the prescribed articles from interstate commerce in aid of state regulation as in Kentucky Whip & Collar Co. v. Illinois C. R. Co., but instead, under the guise of a regulation of interstate commerce, it undertakes to regulate wages and hours within the state contrary to the policy of the state which has elected to leave them unregulated.

The power of Congress over interstate commerce "is complete in itself, may be exercised to its utmost extent, and acknowledges no limitations other than are prescribed in the Constitution." Gibbons v. Ogden. That power can neither be enlarged nor diminished by the exercise or nonexercise of state power. . . . Congress, following its own conception of public policy concerning the restrictions which may appropriately be imposed on interstate commerce, is free to exclude from the commerce articles whose use in the states for which they are destined it may conceive to be injurious to the public health, morals or welfare, even though the state has not sought to regulate their use. . . .

Such regulation is not a forbidden invasion of state power merely because either its motive or its consequence is to restrict the use of articles of commerce within the states of destination and is not prohibited unless by other constitutional provisions. It is no objection to the assertion of the power to regulate interstate commerce that its exercise is attended by the same incidents which attend the exercise of the police power of the states. . . .

The motive and purpose of the present regulation are plainly to make effective the Congressional conception of public policy that interstate commerce should not be made the instrument of competition in the distribution of goods produced under substandard labor conditions, which competition is injurious to the commerce and to the states from and to which the commerce flows. The motive and purpose of a regulation of interstate commerce are matters for the legislative judgment upon the exercise of which the Constitution places no restriction and over which the courts are given no control. . . . "The judicial cannot prescribe to the legislative department of the government limitations upon the exercise of its acknowledged power." Veazie Bank v. Fenno [1869]. Whatever their motive and purpose, regulations of commerce which do not infringe some constitutional prohibition are within the plenary power conferred on Congress by the Commerce Clause. Subject only to that limitation, presently to be considered, we conclude that the prohibition of the shipment interstate of goods produced under the forbidden substandard labor conditions is within the constitutional authority of Congress.

In the more than a century which has elapsed since the decision of Gibbons v. Ogden, these principles of constitutional interpretation have been so long and repeatedly recognized by this Court as applicable to the Commerce Clause, that there would be little occasion for repeating them now were it not for the decision of this Court twenty-two years ago in Hammer v. Dagenhart [1918]. In that case it was held by a bare majority of the Court over the powerful and now classic dissent of Mr. Justice Holmes setting forth the fundamental issues involved, that Congress was without power to exclude the products of child labor from interstate commerce. The reasoning and conclusion of the Court's opinion there cannot be reconciled with the conclusion which we have reached, that the power of Congress under the Commerce Clause is plenary to exclude any article from interstate commerce subject only to the specific prohibitions of the Constitution.

Hammer v. Dagenhart has not been followed. The distinction on which the decision was rested that Congressional power to prohibit interstate commerce is limited to articles which in themselves have some harmful or deleterious property—a distinction which was novel when made and unsupported by any provision of the Constitution—has long since been abandoned. Brooks v. United States; Kentucky Whip & Collar Co. v. Illinois C. R. Co.; ... Mulford v. Smith [1939]. The thesis of the opinion that the motive of the prohibition or its effect to control in some measure the use or production within the states of the article thus excluded from the commerce can operate to deprive the regulation of its constitutional authority has long since ceased to have force. ... And finally we have declared "The authority of the federal government over interstate commerce does not differ in extent or character from that retained by the states over intrastate commerce." United States v. Rock Royal Co-operative [1939].

The conclusion is inescapable that Hammer v. Dagenhart was a departure from the principles which have prevailed in the interpretation of the commerce clause both before and since the decision and that such vitality, as a precedent, as it then had has long since been exhausted. It should be and now is overruled.

Validity of the wage and hour requirements. Section 15 (a) (2), and §§ 6 and 7 require employers to conform to the wage and hour provisions with respect to all employees engaged in the production of goods for interstate commerce. As appellee's employees are not alleged to be "engaged in interstate commerce" the validity of the prohibition turns on the question whether the employment, under other than the prescribed labor standards, of employees engaged in the production of goods for interstate commerce is so related to the commerce and so affects it as to be within the reach of the power of Congress to regulate it. ...

... The power of Congress over interstate commerce is not confined to the regulation of commerce among the states. It extends to those activities intrastate which so affect interstate commerce or the exercise of the power of Congress over it as to make regulation of them appropriate means to the attainment of a legitimate end, the exercise of the granted power of Congress to regulate interstate commerce. ...

... A recent example is the National Labor Relations Act for the regulation of employer and employee relations in industries in which strikes, induced by unfair labor practices named in the Act, tend to disturb or obstruct interstate commerce. See National Labor Relations Bd. v. Jones & L. Steel Corp. [1937]. ... But long before the adoption of the National Labor Relations Act this Court had many times held that the power of Congress to regulate interstate commerce extends to the regulation through legislative action of activities intrastate which have a substantial effect on the commerce or the exercise of the Congressional power over it.

In such legislation Congress has sometimes left it to the courts to determine whether the intrastate activities have the prohibited effect on the commerce, as in the Sherman Act. It has sometimes left it to an administrative board or agency to determine whether the activities sought to be regulated or prohibited have such effect, as in the case of the Interstate Commerce Act, and the National Labor Relations Act or whether they come within the statutory definition of the prohibited Act as in the Federal Trade Commission Act. And sometimes Congress itself has said that a particular activity affects the commerce as it did in the present act, the Safety Appliance Act and the Railway Labor Act. In passing on the validity of legislation of the class last mentioned the only function of courts is to determine whether the particular activity regulated or prohibited is within the reach of the federal power. . . .

Congress, having by the present Act adopted the policy of excluding from interstate commerce all goods produced for the commerce which do not conform to the specified labor standards, it may choose the means reasonably adapted to the attainment of the permitted end, even though they involve control of intrastate activites. . . . A familiar like exercise of power is the regulation of intrastate transactions which are so commingled with or related to interstate commerce that all must be regulated if the interstate commerce is to be effectively controlled. Shreveport Case [1914]. . . . Similarly Congress may require inspection and preventive treatment of all cattle in a disease infected area in order to prevent shipment in interstate commerce of some of the cattle without the treatment. . . . It may prohibit the removal, at destination, of labels required by the Pure Food & Drugs Act to be affixed to articles transported in interstate commerce. . . . And we have recently held that Congress in the exercise of its power to require inspection and grading of tobacco shipped in interstate commerce may compel such inspection and grading of all tobacco sold at local auction rooms from which a substantial part but not all of the tobacco sold is shipped in interstate commerce. . . .

We think also that § 15(a) (2) now under consideration, is sustainable independently of § 15(a) (1), which prohibits shipment or transportation of the proscribed goods. As we have said the evils aimed at by the Act are the spread of substandard labor conditions through the use of the facilities of interstate commerce for competition by the goods so produced with those produced under the prescribed or better labor conditions; and the consequent dislocation of the commerce itself caused by the impairment or destruction of local businesses by competition made effective through interstate commerce. The Act is thus directed at the suppression of a method or kind of competition in interstate commerce which it has in effect condemned as "unfair," as the Clayton Act has condemned other "unfair methods of competition" made effective through interstate commerce. . . .

The Sherman Act and the National Labor Relations Act are familiar examples of the exertion of the commerce power to prohibit or control activities wholly intrastate because of their effect on interstate commerce. . . .

The means adopted by § 15(a) (2) for the protection of interstate commerce by the suppression of the production of the condemned goods for interstate commerce is so related to the commerce and so affects it as to be within the reach of the commerce power. . . . Congress, to attain its objective in the suppression of nation-wide competition in interstate commerce by goods produced under substandard labor conditions, has made no distinction as to the volume or amount of shipments in the commerce or of production for commerce by any particular shipper or producer. It recognized that in present day industry, competition by a small part may affect the whole and that the total effect of the competition of many small producers may be great. . . . The legislation aimed at a whole embraces all its parts.

So far as Carter v. Carter Coal Co. [1936] is inconsistent with this conclusion, its doctrine is limited in principle by the decisions under the Sherman Act and the National Labor Relations Act, which we have cited and which we follow. . . .

Our conclusion is unaffected by the Tenth Amendment which provides: "The powers not delegated to the United States by the Constitution nor prohibited by it to the states are reserved to the states respectively or to the people." The amendment states but a truism that all is retained which has not been surrendered. There is nothing in the history of its adoption to suggest that it was more than declaratory of the relationship between the national and state governments as it had been established by the Constitution before the amendment or that its purpose was other than to allay fears that the new national government might seek to exercise powers not granted, and that the states might not be able to exercise fully their reserved powers. . . .

From the beginning and for many years the amendment has been construed as not depriving the national government of authority to resort to all means for the exercise of a granted power which are appropriate and plainly adapted to the permitted end. . . . Whatever doubts may have arisen of the soundness of that conclusion they have been put at rest by the decisions under the Sherman Act and the National Labor Relations Act which we have cited. . . .

Reversed.

KATZENBACH v. McCLUNG

379 U. S. 294; 85 S. Ct. 377; 13 L. Ed. 2d 290
(1964)

In the preceding cases the Court permitted Congress to close the channels of interstate commerce to commodities and for purposes of which it disapproves. The effect is to permit a certain diversity of policy among the states without fear of out-of-state interference, as well as to aid in the capture of local criminals by helping to reduce their avenues of escape.

A quite different use of the commerce power, however, lies in the power of Congress to keep the channels of interstate commerce open and unimpeded. The development of this aspect of the commerce power into an effective weapon of social control came very slowly. For one hundred years prior to 1887, Congress made no attempt to regulate interstate commerce, and the Supreme Court was left to struggle alone with the question whether a particular activity was local, and hence subject to state control, or was interstate commerce and hence subject to no control at all.

With the passage of the Interstate Commerce Act in 1887 and the Sherman Act in 1890, Congress for the first time moved to regulate transportation and forbid monopoly in interstate commerce—only to find itself faced with a Supreme Court whose members showed little sympathy for government economic regulation of any kind. While the Court conceded Congress' right to provide for the safe movement of goods across state lines, it drew a sharp line between the control of things which had a direct effect on such commerce, and those whose effect was merely indirect. Thus, in United States v. E. C. Knight Co. (1895), it denied the use of the Sherman Act to break up the powerful sugar trust which had been formed to control the manufacture and distribution of refined sugar throughout the United States. The Court held the Antitrust Act did not apply to combinations in restraint of manufacturing. "Doubtless the power to control the manufacture of a given thing involves in a certain sense the control of its disposition, but this is a secondary and not the primary sense; and although the exercise of that power may result in bringing the operation of commerce into play, it does not control it, and affects it only incidentally and indirectly. Commerce succeeds to manufacture, and is not a part of it. The power to regulate commerce is the power to prescribe the rule by which commerce shall be governed, and is a power independent of the power to suppress monopoly." In Oliver Iron Mining Co. v. Lord (1923) the Court held that mining, like manufacturing, was not interstate commerce.

Even where an interstate carrier was clearly involved, the regulation was limited to things directly affecting interstate movement. A federal statute outlawing so-called "yellow-dog contracts" (by which workmen were forced to agree not to join labor unions) was held void in Adair v. United States (1908) on the ground, among others, that there is no "possible legal or logical connection . . . between an employee's membership in a labor organization and the carrying on of interstate commerce. . . ."

In 1914, in the Shreveport Case, the Court abandoned this outmoded concept of two mutually exclusive areas of intrastate and interstate commerce, each clearly and safely under the control of state or federal government, and put in its place as a rule for measuring federal authority in the field of commerce, the realistic test of whether commercial or business activities—even though they be local—so impinge upon or affect interstate commerce as to bring them reasonably within the range of federal control. The Court recognized a functional relationship between local and interstate commerce and permitted the ICC to forbid a railroad to set local rates which discriminated against interstate rates which had been found by the commission to be reasonable.

In 1922 the doctrine of the Shreveport Case was extended to cover local businesses other than common carriers. In 1921 Congress had passed the Packers and Stockyards Act in an effort to break up discriminatory practices resulting from control of the stockyards by the "Big Five" meat packers: Swift, Armour, Cudahy, Wilson, and Morris. Livestock was shipped into Chicago from producers throughout the West and most of the meat, either before or after packing, was shipped to eastern markets. The control of the stockyards by the packers resulted in discrimination against the western shipper as well as other buyers. The act provided an elaborate scheme of regulation, including approval by the Secretary of Agriculture of all rates and charges for services and facilities in the stockyards. In Stafford v. Wallace (1922) the Supreme Court sustained this regulation, rejecting the argument that Congress had no authority to control purely local sales of cattle after they had come to rest in the stockyards. "The stockyards," the Court said, "are not a place of rest or final destination. Thousands of head of live stock arrive daily by carloads and trainlaod lots, and must be promptly sold and disposed of and moved out to give place to the constantly flowing traffic that presses behind. The stockyards are but a throat through which the current flows, and the transactions which occur therein are only incident to this current from the West to the East, and from one State to another. Such transactions cannot be separated from the movement to which they contribute, and necessarily take on its character. . . ."

In 1935, the Court made clear that this reasoning did not apply to businesses handling commodities which had ceased their interstate journey and come to rest within a state. In Schechter Poultry Corp. v. United States (1935), the Court struck down the Live Poultry Code promulgated under the National Industrial Recovery Act which attempted to regulate hours, wages, and the conditions of sale of poultry which had moved in interstate commerce. Citing the "well-established distinction between direct and indirect effects," the Court found the business of selling chickens within the state had only an "indirect" effect on interstate commerce. "Where the effect of intrastate transactions upon interstate commerce is merely indirect, such transactions remain within the domain of State power." (At the same time the Court struck down the entire NIRA. on the ground that it invalidly delegated legislative power to the President.)

In July, less than two months after the National Industrial Recovery Act had been held void in the Schechter case, Congress passed the National Labor Relations Act (Wagner Act), the first thoroughgoing and genuinely regulatory federal act to deal with the relations between labor and capital. The act was unique both in scope and in method. Its scope included all labor disputes which burdened or obstructed interstate commerce. Such burden or obstruction might take the form of: (1) impairing the efficiency or safety of the instrumentalities of commerce; (2) restraining the flow of raw materials or manufactured goods through interstate commerce, or controlling the prices thereof; (3) reducing employment and wages sufficiently to reduce substantially the market for goods moving in interstate commerce; (4) or obstructing directly the actual current of commerce. The method employed by the act was that of defining carefully seven or eight "unfair labor practices" that were forbidden, and of creating a new National Labor Relations Board with power upon investigation to issue "cease and desist orders," enforceable in the courts, against those guilty of these practices. This was the technique employed in the Federal Trade Commission Act under which the commission issued "cease and desist orders" against those found to be engaging in unfair competitive trade practices. The NLRB was, therefore, a very powerful body.

The Wagner Act appeared at first to rest upon precarious footing, since its provisions extended to labor relations in the process of manufacturing goods which were to be moved in interstate commerce. Ever since the E. C. Knight case the Court had insisted that manufacturing was antecedent to and clearly separate from the interstate commerce in which the manufactured goods later move; see Hammer v. Dagenhart (1918). While the Shreveport Case and Stafford v. Wallace indicated that the Court's attitude toward this distinction was becoming less rigid, the emphasis in the Schechter case upon "direct" and "indirect" effects which local activities produce on interstate commerce did not give supporters of the Wagner Act much encouragement. Moreover, in Carter v. Carter Coal Co. (1936), which held the Guffey Coal Act void, the Court said that the relations between employers and workmen in the coal industry did not directly affect interstate commerce in coal and could not therefore be regulated by Congress. The Court might very consistently have held the Wagner Act void in its application to labor relations in the field of manufacturing.

The Wagner Act came before the Court in the Jones & Laughlin Steel case. The NLRB had found that the Jones & Laughlin Steel Corporation had discharged some of its men because of their labor union activities. The board ordered the company to reinstate them and to cease such discrimination. The company was the fourth largest producer of steel in the country. It had 19 subsidiaries which comprised an integrated system. It owned mines, ships, railroads, furnaces, and mills. The board found that the plants in which the labor troubles occurred "might be likened to the heart of a self-contained, highly integrated body. They draw in the raw materials from Michigan, Minnesota, West Virginia, Pennsylvania in part through arteries and by means controlled by the respondent; they transform the materials and then pump them out to all parts of the nation through the vast mechanism which the respondent has elaborated."

The Court, with the about-face of March 1937 behind it (see the note to the Darby case), brushed aside arguments that the "stream of commerce" was broken, that this was manufacturing, and that its effect on interstate commerce was only indirect. "In view of respondent's far-flung activities, it is idle to say that the effect would be indirect or remote. It is obvious that it would be immediate and might be catastrophic. We are asked to shut our eyes to the plainest facts of our national life and to deal with the question of direct and indirect effects in an intellectual vacuum. . . . When industries organize themselves on a national scale, making their relation to interstate commerce the dominant factor in their activities, how can it be maintained that their industrial labor relations constitute a forbidden field into which Congress may not enter when it is necessary to protect interstate commerce from the paralyzing consequences of industrial war?"

Perhaps even more striking than the extension of federal control in the field of labor relations has been the development of such control in the field of agriculture. The Agricultural Adjustment Act of 1933, which was held void in United States v. Butler (1936), had relied for its constitutional underpinning upon the delegated powers of Congress to tax and to spend money. The Agricultural Adjustment Act of 1938, which aimed at similar objectives, was based on the commerce power. The act declared that its policy (in part) was: "to regulate interstate and foreign commerce in cotton, wheat, corn, tobacco and rice to the extent necessary to provide an orderly, adequate, and balanced flow of such commodities in interstate and foreign commerce through storage or reserve supplies, loans, marketing quotas, assisting farmers to obtain, in so far as practicable, parity prices for such commodities and parity of income, and assisting consumers to obtain an adequate and steady supply of such commodities at fair prices."

The attack upon the validity of the statute arose under the sections providing for the establishment of marketing quotas for flue-cured tobacco. There were similar sections dealing with cotton, wheat, corn, and rice. The act authorized the Secretary of Agriculture, when he found that the supply of tobacco had increased beyond a certain point, to put into effect a national marketing quota, provided that not more than one-third of the previous year's tobacco growers were opposed. The quotas were allocated in such a way that each grower was given a quota which he must not exceed. If tobacco in excess of the quota for a particular farm was marketed through a warehouse man, the latter paid to the Secretary a penalty equal to 50 percent of the market price of the excess, and might deduct this amount from the prices paid to the producer. In Mulford v. Smith (1939) the Supreme Court held the act valid. It was not, the Court said, a regulation of production but only a regulation of the interstate commerce in tobacco at the "throat where tobacco enters the stream of commerce,—the marketing warehouse." The fact that not all the tobacco was sold interstate was considered immaterial since the "regulation to be effective, must, and therefore may constitutionally, apply to all sales."

A more extreme application of the 1938 statute was upheld in Wickard v. Filburn (1942). Quotas were established for the production of wheat in order to prevent surpluses and maintain prices. Filburn raised 23 acres of wheat, none of which was intended for interstate commerce, and all of which he consumed or fed to his stock. The quota allotted to him, however, was 11.1 acres; and the Court held him validly liable to the statutory penalties on the wheat produced in excess of this quota. His production of this wheat affected interstate commerce "directly" just as much as though he had farmed 23,000 acres instead of 23.

To a person unfamiliar with our institutions and constitutional history, it must seem strange that the national government, in its efforts to abolish race discrimination, should be forced to act under a grant of power to regulate interstate commerce. Of course, if a state government does the discriminating, either through its laws or its officials, the courts can interfere under the equal protection clause of the Fourteenth Amendment. But as early as 1883 in the Civil Rights Cases the Court made clear that private discrimination was not forbidden by the Fourteenth Amendment, and Congress had no "police power" under which it could outlaw it generally.

The passage of the Civil Rights Act of 1964, Title II of which was sustained in the present cases, brought to an all-time high congressional efforts to abolish race discrimination in the United States. The act itself was remarkable for a number of reasons. First, for the first time since the ill-fated Civil Rights Act of 1875, Congress made a sweeping attack on race discrimination. Second, the act commanded overwhelming bipartisan support. After five months of committee hearings, 2800 pages of testimony, and seven months of debates, the measure passed the House 289 to 126. In an unusual move, the Senate did not even send it to committee, but worked out a bill with informal bipartisan conferences. The House adopted the Senate bill without change. Third, for the first time in history the Senate, with the all-out support of both majority and minority leaders, invoked cloture to stop a Southern filibuster on a civil rights measure.

In Heart of Atlanta Motel v. United States (1964), a companion to the present case, the Court held that discrimination against black guests by a motel serving interstate travelers was an impediment to the free movement of blacks among the several states.

Mr. Justice Clark delivered the opinion of the Court, saying in part:

This case was argued with Heart of Atlanta Motel v. United States in which we upheld the constitutional validity of Title II of the Civil Rights Act of 1964 against an attack by hotels, motels, and like establishments. This complaint for injunctive relief against appellants attacks the constitutionality of the Act as applied to a restaurant. . . .

2. The Facts.

Ollie's Barbecue is a family-owned restaurant in Birmingham, Alabama, specializing in barbecued meats and homemade pies, with a seating capacity of 220 customers. It is located on a state highway 11 blocks from an interstate one and a somewhat greater distance from railroad and bus stations. The restaurant caters to a family and white-collar trade with a take-out service for Negroes. It employes 36 persons, two-thirds of whom are Negroes.

In the 12 months preceding the passage of the Act, the restaurant purchased locally approximately $150,000 worth of food, $69,683, or 46% of which was meat that it bought from a local supplier who had procured it from outside the State. The District Court expressly found that a substantial portion of the food served in the restaurant had moved in interstate commerce. The restaurant has refused to serve Negroes in its dining accommodations since its original opening in 1927, and since July 2, 1964, it has been operating in violation of the Act. The court below concluded that if it were required to serve Negroes it would lose a substantial amount of business.

On the merits, the District Court held that the Act could not be applied under the Fourteenth Amendment because it was conceded that the State of Alabama was not involved in the refusal of the restaurant to serve Negroes. . . . As to the Commerce Clause, the court found . . . that the clause was . . . a grant of power "to regulate intrastate activities, but only to the extent that action on its part is necessary or appropriate to the effective execution of its expressly granted power to regulate interstate commerce." There must be, it said, a close and substantial relation between local activities and interstate commerce which requires control of the former in the protection of the latter. The court concluded, however, that the Congress, rather than finding facts sufficient to meet this rule, has legislated a conclusive presumption that a restaurant affects interstate commerce if it serves or offers to serve interstate travelers or if a substantial portion of the food which it serves has moved in commerce. This, the court held, it could not do because there was no demonstrable connection between food purchased in interstate commerce and sold in a restaurant and the conclusion of Congress that discrimination in the restaurant would affect that commerce. . . .

3. The Act As Applied.

Section 201 (a) of Title II commands that all persons shall be entitled to the full and equal enjoyment of the goods and services of any place of public accommodation without discrimination or segregation on the gound of race, color, religion, or national origin; and § 201 (b) defines establishments as places of public accommodation if their operations affect commerce or segregation by them as supported by state action. Sections 201 (b) (2) and (c) place any "restaurant . . . principally engaged in selling food for consumption on the premises" under the Act "if . . . it serves or offers to serve interstate travelers or a substantial portion of the food which it serves . . . has moved in commerce."

Ollie's Barbecue admits that it is covered by these provisions of the Act. The Government makes no contention that the discrimination at the restaurant was supported by the State of Alabama. There is no claim that interstate travelers frequented the restaurant. The sole question, therefore, narrows down to whether Title II, as applied to a restaurant annually receiving about $70,000 worth of food which has moved in commerce, is a valid exercise of the power of Congress. The Government has contended that Congress had ample basis upon which to find that racial discimination at restaurants which receive from out of state a substantial portion of the food served does, in fact, impose commercial burdens of national magnitude upon interstate commerce. The appellees' major argument is directed to this premise. They urge that no such basis existed. It is to that question that we now turn.

4. The Congressional Hearings.

As we noted in Heart of Atlanta Motel both houses of Congress conducted prolonged hearings on the Act. And, as we said there, while no formal findings were made, which of course are not necessary, it is well that we make mention of the testimony at these hearings the better to understand the problem before Congress and determine whether the Act is a reasonable and appropriate means toward its solution. The record is replete with testimony of the burdens placed on interstate commerce by racial discrimination in restaurants. A comparison of per capita spending by Negroes in restaurants, theaters, and like establishments indicated less spending, after discounting income differences, in areas where discrimination is widely practiced. This condition, which was especially aggravated in the South, was attributed in the testimony of the Under Secretary of Commerce to racial segregation. . . . This diminutive spending springing from a refusal to serve Negroes and their total loss as customers has, regardless of the absence of direct evidence, a close connection to interstate commerce. The fewer customers a restaurant enjoys the less food it sells and consequently the less it buys. . . . In addition, the Attorney General testified that this type of discrimination imposed "an artificial restriction on the market" and interfered with the flow of merchandise. . . . In addition, there were many references to discriminatory situations causing wide unrest and having a depressant effect on general business conditions in the respective communities. . . .

Moreover there was an impressive array of testimony that discrimination in restaurants had a direct and highly restrictive effect upon interstate travel by Negroes. This resulted, it was said, because discriminatory practices prevent Negroes from buying prepared food served on the premises while on a trip, except in isolated and unkempt restaurants and under most unsatisfactory and often unpleasant conditions. This obviously discourages travel and obstructs interstate commerce for one can hardly travel without eating. Likewise, it was said, that discrimination deterred professional, as well as skilled, people from moving into areas where such practices occurred and thereby caused industry to be reluctant to establish there. . . .

We believe that this testimony afforded ample basis for the conclusion that established restaurants in such areas sold less interstate goods because of the discrimination, that interstate travel was obstructed directly by it, that business in general suffered and that many new businesses refrained from establishing there as a result of it. Hence the District Court was in error in concluding that there was no connection between discrimination and the movement of interstate commerce. The court's conclusion that such a connection is outside "common experience" flies in the face of stubborn fact.

It goes without saying that, viewed in isolation, the volume of food purchased by Ollie's Barbecue from sources supplied from out of state was insignificant when compared with the total foodstuffs moving in commerce. But, as our late Brother Jackson said for the Court in Wickard v. Filburn (1942):

"That appellee's own contribution to the demand for wheat may be trivial by itself is not enough to remove him from the scope of federal regulation where, as here, his contribution, taken together with that of many others similarly situated, is far from trivial."

We noted in Heart of Atlanta Motel that a number of witnesses attested the fact that racial discrimination was not merely a state or regional problem but was one of nationwide scope. Against this background, we must conclude that while the focus of the legislation was on the individual restaurant's relation to interstate commerce, Congress appropriately considered the importance of that connection with the knowledge that the discrimination was but "representative of many others throughout the country, the total incidence of which if left unchecked may well become far-reaching in its harm to commerce." . . .

With this situation spreading as the record shows, Congress was not required to await the total dislocation of commerce. . . .

5. The Power of Congress to Regulate Local Activities.

Article I, § 8, cl. 3, confers upon Congress the power "[t]o regulate Commerce . . . among the several States" and Clause 18 of the same Article grants it the power "[t]o make all Laws which shall be necessary and proper for carrying into Execution the foregoing Powers . . . ." This grant, as we have pointed out in Heart of Atlanta Motel "extends to those activities intrastate which so affect interstate commerce, or the exertion of the power of Congress over it, as to make regulation of them appropriate means to the attainment of a legitimate end, the effective execution of the granted power to regulate interstate commerce." . . . Much is said about a restaurant business being local but "even if appellee's activity be local and though it may not be regarded as commerce, it may still, whatever its nature, be reached by Congress if it exerts a substantial economic effect on interstate commerce . . . ." . . . The activities that are beyond the reach of Congress are "those which are completely within a particular State, which do not affect other States, and with which it is not necessary to interfere, for the purpose of executing some of the general powers of the government." . . . This rule is as good today as it was when Chief Justice Marshall laid it down almost a century and a half ago. . . .

Nor are the cases holding that interstate commerce ends when goods come to rest in the State of destination apposite here. That line of cases has been applied with reference to state taxation or regulation but not in the field of federal regulation.

The appellees contend that Congress has arbitrarily created a conclusive presumption that all restaurants meeting the criteria set out in the Act "affect commerce." Stated another way, they object to the omission of a provision for a case-by-case determination—judicial or administrative—that racial discrimination in a particular restaurant affects commerce.

But Congress' action in framing this Act was not unprecedented. In United States v. Darby, this Court held constitutional the Fair Labor Standards Act of 1938. There Congress determined that the payment of substandard wages to employees engaged in production of goods for commerce, while not itself commerce, so inhibited it as to be subject to federal regulation. The appellees in that case argued, as do the appellees here, that the Act was invalid because it included no provision for an independent inquiry regarding the effect on commerce of substandard wages in a particular business. . . . But the Court rejected the argument, observing that:

"[S]ometimes Congress itself has said that a particular activity affects the commerce, as it did in the present Act, the Safety Appliance Act and the Railway Labor Act. In passing on the validity of legislation of the class last mentioned the only function of courts is to determine whether the particular activity regulated or prohibited is within the reach of the federal power."

Here, as there, Congress has determined for itself that refusals of service to Negroes have imposed burdens both upon the interstate flow of food and upon the movement of products generally. Of course, the mere fact that Congress has said when particular activity shall be deemed to affect commerce does not preclude further examination by this Court. But where we find that the legislators, in light of the facts and testimony before them, have a rational basis for finding a chosen regulatory scheme necessary to the protection of commerce, our investigation is at an end. The only remaining question—one answered in the affirmative by the court below—is whether the particular restaurant either serves or offers to serve interstate travelers or serves food a substantial portion of which has moved in interstate commerce. . . .

Confronted as we are with the facts laid before Congress, we must conclude that it had a rational basis for finding that racial discrimination in restaurants have a direct and adverse effect on the free flow of interstate commerce. Insofar as the sections of the Act here relevant are concerned, §§ 201(b) (2) and (c), Congress prohibited discrimination only in those establishments having a close tie to interstate commerce, i.e., those, like the McClungs', serving food that has come from out of the State. We think in so doing that Congress acted well within its power to protect and foster commerce in extending the coverage of Title II only to those restaurants offering to serve interstate travelers or serving food, a substantial portion of which has moved in interstate commerce.

The absence of direct evidence connecting discriminatory restaurant service with the flow of interstate food, a factor on which the appellees place much reliance, is not, given the evidence as to the effect of such practices on other aspects of commerce, a crucial matter.

The power of Congress in this field is broad and sweeping; where it keeps within its sphere and violates no express constitutional limitation it has been the rule of this Court, going back almost to the founding days of the Republic, not to interfere. The Civil Rights Act of 1964, as here applied, we find to be plainly appropriate in the resolution of what the Congress found to be a national commercial problem of the first magnitude. We find it in no violation of any express limitations of the Constitution and we therefore declare it valid.

The judgment is therefore

Reversed.

Justices Black, Douglas, and Goldberg wrote concurring opinions.

NATIONAL LEAGUE OF CITIES v. USERY

426 U. S. 833; 96 S. Ct. 2465; 49 L. Ed. 2d 245 (1976)

With the judicial turnabout of 1937 went the long-standing doctrine of "dual federalism" (see the note to United States v. Butler, 1936) under which the reserved powers of the states were held to check the delegated powers of Congress. But while important powers have accrued to Congress from the increased use of interstate commerce facilities, Congress has not ordinarily sought to use this new authority to injure the states or subvert their authority. Congress, after all, represents the people of the states as well as the people of the nation. Most uses of this growing federal power have resulted from the inability of the states to cope with problems which have spread beyond their jurisdiction. Where states have local policies they wish to preserve, Congress has frequently used its power over commerce to help them. The practical effect of the Darby decision, for example, is that a state may now outlaw child labor and other substandard labor conditions without subjecting their own manufacturers to competition from goods made by such labor in other states. Even more helpful from the standpoint of state policy are the so-called "divesting statutes" which forbid certain shipments into a state if that state wishes to keep them out; see Clark Distilling Co. v. Western Maryland Ry. Co. (1917). Legislation, similar in purpose, is the Federal Black Bass Act of 1926, which makes it illegal to ship fish out of the state if it violates the law of the state to do so; see United States v. Howard (1957).

The doctrine of dual federalism dealt with the right of a state to exercise the police power which was reserved to it under the Tenth Amendment. But there was another area in which the states asserted their independence from the national government and that was in the area of intergovernmental tax immunity. What was at stake here was not the state's power to control public policy, but rather its right to continued existence, unimpeded by the "power to destroy" implicit in the federal tax power.

Chief Justice Marshall had suggested in McCulloch v. Maryland (1819) that while the states could not tax the federal government, there was no similar bar to the federal government taxing the states. In Collector v. Day (1871), however, the Court held void the application of a federal income tax statute to the income of a state judge. The judge, the Court held, was the embodiment of the state's judicial system, and to permit the national government to tax him would be to permit it to cripple or destroy an instrumentality of the state. The immunity of the state from such a destructive attack, it found, lay in the implicit assumption in the Constitution of the existence of the states and the indispensibility of them to the very existence of the national government. "Without them, the general government itself would disappear from the family of nations."

The result of the decision was the proliferation over the years of the things that were considered instrumentalities. All employees, property, earnings from oil leases, and the income from bonds issued by either government were immune from taxation by the other. Even patents and copyrights were considered federal instrumentalities and royalities earned under them were free from state taxation.

In one area the Court refused to extend immunity. When a state engaged in what was commonly thought of as a private business, as South Carolina did when it went into the liquor business, it had to pay federal taxes on the business like everyone else. The state could not deprive the federal government of its sources of revenue by taking over businesses on which that revenue depended. See South Carolina v. United States (1905).

The Court eventually came to the realization that the true beneficiaries of all this immunity were not the governments involved but a select group of favored individuals, and in the 1930s began retracting the doctrine. Finally, in Graves v. New York ex rel. O'Keefe (1939), it held that government employees were not the embodiment of an essential instrumentality and a tax upon them was not a tax on the government for which they worked. Collector v. Day was overruled.

The withdrawal of constitutional immunity tipped the scales in favor of the federal government which could, of course, always protect its own instrumentalities under the supremacy clause. While the Court continued to pay lip-service to the immunity doctrine, when the shrinking was complete there were few who doubted that, should Congress elect to tax the income from municipal bonds (the only important tangible vestige of the immunity left) the Court would find the tax constitutional. Clearly, the theories on which the immunity had rested has long been abandoned by the Court.

Oddly enough, only the tax power had ever been held limited by the sovereign immunity of the states. In University of Illinois v. United States (1933), the Court had upheld a tax on the importation of scientific equipment by the state on the ground that in taxing imports Congress was really exercising the *commerce* power and not the *tax* power. And in United States v. California (1936), it held valid the federal regulation of a railroad owned by a state. While it might have done this on the ground that the railroad was not an essential government activity, the Court made clear that it was "unimportant to say whether the state conducted its railroad in its 'sovereign' or in its 'private' capacity. . . . The sovereign power of the state is necessarily diminshed to the extent of grants of power to the federal government in the Constitution. . . . California, by engaging in interstate commerce by rail, has subjected itself to the commerce power . . . ."

As recently as 1968, in Maryland v. Wirtz, the Court reaffirmed United States v. California and held valid the extension of the federal minimum wage laws to the employees of state schools and hospitals on the ground that they were major users of interstate goods. In 1975, in Fry v. United States, the Court upheld on the same ground the application of the wage freeze to state employees under the Economic Stabilization Act of 1970.

It is against this background of the undisturbed 30-year accretion of federal power that one must view the Usery case, printed below. In 1974, Congress amended the Fair Labor Standards Act to extend its protection to all public employees, federal, state, or local, who are "engaged in commerce, or in the production of goods for commerce, or employees handling, selling, or otherwise working on goods or materials that have been moved in or produced for commerce." Since the effect was to impose federal minimum wage and maximum hours regulations upon all government agencies, a number of states and cities and their representative organizations challenged the validity of the amendments.

Mr. Justice Rehnquist delivered the opinion of the Court, saying in part:

II.

It is established beyond peradventure that the Commerce Clause of Art. I of the Constitution is a grant of plenary authority to Congress. That authority is, in the words of Mr. Chief Justice Marshall in Gibbons v. Ogden (1824), "the power to regulate; that is, to prescribe the rule by which commerce is to be governed."

When considering the validity of asserted applications of this power to wholly private activity, the Court has made it clear that "[e]ven activity that is purely intrastate in character may be regulated by Congress, where the activity, combined with like conduct by others similarly situated, affects commerce among the States or with foreign nations." Fry v. United States (1975). . . .

Appellants in no way challenge these decisions establishing the breadth of authority granted Congress under the commerce power. Their contention, on the contrary, is that when Congress seeks to regulate directly the activities of States as public employers, it transgresses an affirmative limitation on the exercise of its power akin to other commerce power affirmative limitations contained in the Constitution. Congressional enactments which may be fully within the grant of legislative authority contained in the Commerce Clause may nonetheless be invalid because found to offend against the right to trial by jury . . . .

This Court has never doubted that there are limits upon the power of Congress to override state sovereignty, even when exercising its otherwise plenary powers to tax or to regulate commerce which are conferred by Art. I of the Constitution. In [Maryland v. Wirtz (1968)], for example, the Court took care to assure the appellants that it had "ample power to prevent . . . 'the utter destruction of the State as a sovereign political entity,' " which they feared. . . . In Fry, supra, the Court recognized that an express declaration of this limitation is found in the Tenth Amendment: "While the Tenth Amendment has been characterized as a 'truism,' stating merely that 'all is retained which has not been surrendered,' United States v. Darby (1941), it is not without significance. The Amendment expressly declares the constitutional policy that Congress may not exercise power in a fashion that impairs the States' integrity of their ability to function effectively in a federal system." . . .

In Metcalf & Eddy v. Mitchell (1926), the Court likewise observed that "neither government may destroy the other nor curtail in any substantial manner the exercise of its powers."

Appellee Secretary argues that the cases in which this Court has upheld sweeping exercises of authority by Congress, even though those exercises pre-empted state regulation of the private sector, have already curtailed the sovereignty of the States quite as much as the 1974 amendments to the Fair Labor Standards Act. We do not agree. It is one thing to recognize the authority of Congress to enact laws regulating individual business necessarily subject to the dual sovereignty of the government of the Nation and of the State in which they reside. It is quite another to uphold a similar exercise of congressional authority directed, not to private citizens, but to the States as States. We have repeatedly recognized that there are attributes of sovereignty attaching to every state government which may not be impaired by Congress, not because Congress may lack an affirmative grant of legislative authority to reach the matter, but because the Constitution prohibits it from exercising the authority in that manner. In Coyle v. Oklahoma [Smith] (1911), the Court gave this example of such an attribute:

"The power to locate its own seat of government and to determine when and how it shall be changed from one place to another, and to appropriate its own public funds for that purpose, are essentially and peculiarly state powers. That one of the original thirteen States could now be shorn of such powers by an act of Congress would not be for a moment entertained."

One undoubted attribute of state sovereignty is the States' power to determine the wages which shall be paid to those whom they employ in order to carry out their governmental functions, what hours those persons will work, and what compensation will be provided where these employees may be called upon to work overtime. The question we must resolve here, then, is whether these determinations are " 'functions essential to separate and independent existence,' " so that Congress may not abrogate the States' otherwise plenary authority to make them.

In their complaint appellants advanced estimates of substantial costs which will be imposed upon them by the 1974 amendments. . . .

Judged solely in terms of increased costs in dollars, these allegations show a significant impact on the functioning of the governmental bodies involved. The Metropolitan Government of Nashville and Davidson County, Tenn., for example, asserted that the Act will increase its costs of providing essential police and fire protection, without any increase in service or in current salary levels, by $938,000 per year. . . .

Increased costs are not, of course, the only adverse effects which compliance with the Act will visit upon state and local governments, and in turn upon the citizens who depend upon those governments. In its complaint in intervention, for example, California asserted that it could not comply with the overtime costs (approximately $750,000 per year) which the Act required to be paid to California Highway Patrol cadets during their academy training program. California reported that it had thus been forced to reduce its academy training program from 2,080 hours to only 960 hours, a compromise undoubtedly of substantial importance to those whose safety and welfare may depend upon the preparedness of the California Highway Patrol. . . .

Quite apart from the substantial costs imposed upon the States and their political subdivisions, the Act displaces state policies regarding the manner in which they will structure delivery of those governmental services which their citizens require. The Act, speaking directly to the States qua States, requires that they shall pay all but an extremely limited minority of their employees the minimum wage rates currently chosen by Congress. It may well be that as a matter of economic policy it would be desirable that States, just as private employers, comply with these minimum wage requirements. But it cannot be gainsaid that the federal requirement directly supplants the considered policy choices of the States' elected officials and administrators as to how they wish to structure pay scales in state employment. . . .

Our examination of the effect of the 1974 amendments, as sought to be extended to the States and their political subdivisions, satisfies us that both the minimum wage and the maximum hour provisions will impermissibly interfere with the integral governmental functions of these bodies. We earlier noted some disagreement between the parties regarding the precise effect the amendments will have in application. We do not believe particularized assessments of actual impact are crucial to resolution of the issue presented, however. For even if we accept appellee's assessments concerning the impact of the amendments, their application will nonetheless significantly alter or displace the States' abilities to structure employer-employee relationships in such areas as fire prevention, police protection, sanitation, public health, and parks and recreation. These activities are typical of those performed by state and local governments in discharging their dual functions of administering the public law and furnishing public services. Indeed, it is functions such as these which governments are created to provide, services such as these which the States have traditionally afforded their citizens. If Congress may withdraw from the States the authority to make those fundamental employment decisions upon which their systems for performance of these functions must rest, we think there would be little left of the States' " 'separate and independent existence.' " Coyle. Thus, even if appellants may have overestimated the effect which the Act will have upon their current levels and patterns of governmental activity, the dispositive factor is that Congress has attempted to exercise its Commerce Clause authority to prescribe minimum wages and maximum hours to be paid by the States in their capacities as sovereign governments. In so doing, Congress has sought to wield its power in a fashion that would impair the States' "ability to function effectively in a federal system," Fry. This exercise of congressional authority does not comport with the federal system of government embodied in the Constitution. We hold that insofar as the challenged amendments operate to directly displace the States' freedom to structure integral operations in areas of traditional governmental functions, they are not within the authority granted Congress by Art. I, § 8, cl. 3.

III.

One final matter requires our attention. Appellee has vigorously urged that we cannot, consistently with the Court's decisions in Maryland v. Wirtz (1968), and Fry, supra, rule against him here. It is important to examine this contention so that it will be clear what we hold today, and what we do not. . . .

We think our holding today quite consistent with Fry. The enactment at issue there was occasioned by an extremely serious problem which endangered the well-being of all the component parts of our federal system and which only collective action by the National Government might forestall. The means selected were carefully drafted so as not to interfere with the

States' freedom beyond a very limited, specific period of time. The effect of the across-the-board freeze authorized by that Act, moreover, displaced no state choices as to how governmental operations should be structured, nor did it force the States to remake such choices themselves. Instead, it merely required that the wage scales and employment relationships which the States themselves had chosen be maintained during the period of the emergency. Finally, the Economic Stabilization Act operated to reduce the pressures upon state budgets rather than increase them. These factors distinguish the statute in Fry from the provisions at issue here. The limits imposed upon the commerce power when Congress seeks to apply it to the States are not so inflexible as to preclude temporary enactments tailored to combat a national emergency. . . .

With respect to the Court's decision in Wirtz, we reach a different conclusion. . . . There are undoubtedly factual distinctions between the two situations, but in view of the conclusions expressed earlier in this opinion we do not believe the reasoning in Wirtz may any longer be regarded as authoritative.

Wirtz relied heavily on the Court's decision in United States v. California (1936). The opinion quotes the following language from that case: " '[We] look to the activities in which the states have traditionally engaged as marking the boundary of the restriction upon the federal taxing power. But there is no such limitation upon the plenary power to regulate commerce. The state can no more deny the power if its exercise has been authorized by Congress than can an individual.' "

But we have reaffirmed today that the States as States stand on a quite different footing from an individual or a corporation when challenging the exercise of Congress' power to regulate commerce. We think the dicta* from United States v. California, simply wrong.† Congress may not exercise that power so as to force directly upon the States its choices as to how essential decisions regarding the conduct of integral governmental functions are to be made. . . .

While there are obvious differences between the schools and hospitals involved in Wirtz, and the fire and police departments affected here, each provides an integral portion of those governmental services which the States and their political subdivisions have traditionally afforded their citizens. We are therefore persuaded that Wirtz must be overruled. . . .

---

*The holding of United States v. California, as opposed to the language quoted in the texts, is quite consistent with our holding today. There California's activity to which the congressional command was directed was not in an area that the States have regarded as integral parts of their governmental activities. It was, on the contrary, the operation of a railroad engaged in "common carriage by rail in interstate commerce . . . ."

†Mr. Justice Brennan's dissent leaves no doubt from its discussion that in its view Congress may under its commerce power deal with the States as States just as they might deal with private individuals. We venture to say that it is this conclusion, rather than the one we reach, which is in the words of the dissent a "startling restructuring of our federal system. . . . " Even the appellee Secretary, defending the 1974 amendments in this Court, does not take so extreme a position.

Mr. Justice Blackmun, concurring, said in part:

I may misinterpret the Court's opinion, but it seems to me that it adopts a balancing approach, and does not outlaw federal power in areas such as environmental protection, where the federal interest is demonstrably greater and where state facility compliance with imposed standards would be essential. With this understanding on my part of the Court's opinion, I join it.

Mr. Justice Brennan, with whom Mr. Justice White and Mr. Justice Marshall join, dissenting, said in part:

The Court concedes, as of course it must, that Congress enacted the 1974 amendments pursuant to its exclusive power under Art. I, § 8, cl. 3, of the Constitution "[t]o regulate Commerce . . . among the several States." It must therefore be surprising that my Brethren should choose this bicentennial year of our independence to repudiate principles governing judicial interpretation of our Constitution settled since the time of Mr. Chief Justice John Marshall, discarding his postulate that the Constitution comtemplates that restraints upon exercise by Congress of its plenary commerce power lie in the political process and not in the judicial process. For 152 years ago Mr. Chief Justice Marshall enunciated that principle to which, until today, his successors on this Court have been faithful.

"[T]he power over commerce . . . is vested in Congress as absolutely as it would be in a single government, having in its constitution the same restrictions on the exercise of the power as are found in the constitution of the United States. *The wisdom and the discretion of Congress, their identity with the people, and the influence which their constituents possess at elections, are . . . the sole restraints on which they have relied, to secure them from its abuse. They are the restraints on which the people must often rely solely, in all representative governments.*" Gibbons v. Odgen (1824) [emphasis added].

My Brethren do not successfully obscure today's patent usurpation of the role reserved for the political process by their purported discovery in the Constitution of a restraint derived from sovereignty of the States on Congress' exercise of the commerce power. Mr. Chief Justice Marshall recognized that limitations "prescribed in the constitution," Gibbons v. Ogden, supra, restrain Congress' exercise of the power . . . . Thus laws within the commerce power may not infringe individual liberties protected by the First Amendment . . . or the Sixth Amendment . . . . But there is no restraint based on state sovereignty requiring or permitting judicial enforcement anywhere expressed in the Constitution; our decisions over the last century and a half have explicitly rejected the existence of any such restraint on the commerce power.

We said in United States v. California (1936), for example: "The sovereign power of the states is necessarily diminished to the extent of the grants of power to the federal government in the Constitution. . . . [T]he power of the state is subordinate to the consitutional exercise of the granted federal power." . . . "[It] is not a controversy between equals" when the Federal

Government "is asserting its sovereign power to regulate commerce . . . . [T]he interests of the nation are more important than those of any State." Sanitary District v. United States (1925). . . .

My Brethren thus have today manufactured an abstraction without substance, founded neither in the words of the Constitution nor on precedent. An abstraction having such profoundly pernicious consequences is not made less so by characterizing the 1974 amendments as legislation directed against the "States qua States." Of course, regulations that this Court can say are not regulations of "commerce" cannot stand, . . . and in this sense "[t]he Court has ample power to prevent . . . 'the utter destruction of the State as a sovereign political entity.'" Maryland v. Wirtz (1968). But my Brethren make no claim that the 1974 amendments are not regulations of "commerce"; rather they overrule Wirtz in disagreement with historic principles that United States v. California reaffirmed: "[W]hile the commerce power has limits, valid general regulations of commerce do not cease to be regulations of commerce because a State is involved. If a state is engaging in economic activities that are validly regulated by the Federal Government when engaged in by private persons, the State too may be forced to conform its activities to federal regulation." Wirtz. . . .

The reliance of my Brethren upon the Tenth Amendment as "an express declaration of [a state sovereignty] limitation."* not only suggests that they overrule governing decisions of this Court that address this question but must astound scholars of the Constitution. For not only early decisions, Gibbons v. Ogden, McCulloch v. Maryland, and Martin v. Hunter's Lessee, (1816), hold that nothing in the Tenth Amendment constitutes a limitation on congressional exercise of powers delegated by the Constitution to Congress. . . . Rather, as the Tenth Amendment's significance was more recently summarized:

The amendment states but a truism that all is retained which has not been surrendered. *There is nothing in the history of its adoption to suggest that it was more than declaratory of the realtionship between the national and state governments as it had been established by the Constitution before the amendment* or that its purpose was other than to allay fears that the new national government might seek to exercise powers not granted, and that the states might not be able to exercise fully their reserved powers. . . . " . . . United States v. Darby (emphasis added). . . .

[The Court here discusses the rejection in Case v. Bowles (1946) of the idea that the war power was limited by state sovereignty. Among the cases relied on there was United States v. California.]

. . . Even more significant for our purposes is the Court's citation of United States v. California, a case concerned with Congress' power to regu-

---

*The Court relies on Fry v. United States, . . . (1975), but I cannot subscribe to reading Fry as departing, without analysis, from a principle that has remained unquestioned for over 150 years. Although the Tenth Amendment "is not without significance," its meaning is clear: it declares that our Federal Government is one of delegated powers. And it is because of this constraint, rather than the state-sovereignty doctrine discovered today by the Court, "that Congress may not exercise power in a fashion that impairs the States' integrity or their ability to function effectively in a federal system." . . .

late commerce, as supporting the rejection of the State's contention that state sovereignty is a limitation on Congress' war power. California directly presented the question whether any state sovereignty restraint precluded application of the Federal Safety Appliance Act to a state-owned and - operated railroad. The State argued "that as the state is operating the railroad without profit, for the purpose of facilitating the commerce of the port, and is using the net proceeds of operation for harbor improvement, . . . it is engaged in performing a public function in its sovereign capacity and for that reason cannot constitutionally be subjected to the provisions of the federal Act." Mr. Justice Stone rejected the contention in an opinion for a unanimous Court. His rationale is a complete refutation of today's holding: "That in operating its railroad [the State] is acting within a power reserved to the states cannot be doubted. . . . The only question we need consider is whether the exercise of that power, in whatever capacity, must be in subordination to the power to regulate interstate commerce, which has been granted specifically to the national government. The sovereign power of the states is necessarily diminished to the extent of the grants of power to the federal government in the Constitution. . . .

"The analogy of the constitutional immunity of state instrumentalities from federal taxation, on which [California] relies, is not illuminating. That immunity is implied from the nature of our federal system and the relationship within it of state and national governments, and is equally a restriction on taxation by either of the instrumentalities of the other. Its nature requires that it be so construed as to allow to each government reasonable scope for its taxing power . . . which would be unduly curtailed if either by extending its activities could withdraw from the taxing power of the other subjects of taxation traditionally within it. . . . Hence we look to the activities in which the states have traditionally engaged as marking the boundary of the restriction upon the federal taxing power. *But there is no such limitation upon the plenary power to regulate commerce. The state can no more deny the power if its exercise has been authorized by Congress than can an individual.*" [emphasis added].

Today's repudiation of this unbroken line of precedents that firmly reject my Brethren's ill-conceived abstraction can only be regarded as a transparent cover for invalidating a congressional judgment with which they disagree. The only analysis even remotely resembling that adopted today is found in a line of opinions dealing with the Commerce Clause and the Tenth Amendment that ultimately provoked a constitutional crisis for the Court in the 1930's. E.g. Carter v. Carter Coal Co. (1936); United States v. Butler (1936); Hammer v. Dagenhart (1918). . . . It may have been the eventual abandonment of the overly restrictive construction of the commerce power that spelled defeat for the Court-packing plan, and preserved the integrity of this institution, see, e.g., United States v. Darby (1941); Mulford v. Smith (1939); NLRB v. Jones & Laughlin Steel Corp. (1937), but my Brethren today are transparently trying to cut back on that recognition of the scope of the commerce power. My Brethren's approach to this case is not far different from the dissenting opinions in the cases that averted the crisis. . . .

. . . I cannot recall another instance in the Court's history when the reasoning of so many decisions covering so long a span of time has been discarded in such a roughshod manner. That this is done without any justification not already often advanced and consistently rejected, clearly renders today's decisions an ipse dixit reflecting nothing but displeasure with a congressional judgment. . . .

My Brethren do more than turn aside longstanding constitutional jurisprudence that emphatically rejects today's conclusion. More alarming is the startling restructuring of our federal system, and the role they create therein for the federal judiciary. This Court is simply not at liberty to erect a mirror of its own conception of a desirable governmental structure. If the 1974 amendments have any "vice," my Brother Stevens is surely right that it represents "merely . . . a policy issue which has been firmly resolved by the branches of government having power to decide such question." . . .

It is unacceptable that the judicial process should be thought superior to the political process in this area. Under the Constitution the Judiciary has no role to play beyond finding that Congress has not made an unreasonable legislative judgement respecting what is "commerce." My Brother Blackmun suggests that controlling judicial supervision of the relationship between the States and our National Government by use of a balancing approach diminishes the ominous implications of today's decision. Such an approach, however, is a thinly veiled rationalization for judicial supervision of a policy judgment that our system of government reserves to Congress.

Judicial restraint in this area merely recognizes that the political branches of our Government are structured to protect the interests of the States, as well as the Nation as a whole, and that the States are fully able to protect their own interests in the premises. Congress is constituted of representatives in both the Senate and House elected from the States. . . .

A sense of the enormous impact of States' political power is gained by brief reference to the federal budget. The largest estimate by any of the appellants of the cost impact of the 1974 amendments—$1 billion—pales in comparison with the financial assistance the States receive from the Federal Government. In fiscal 1977 the President's proposed budget recommends $60.5 billion in federal assistance to the States, exclusive of loans. . . . Appellants complain of the impact of the amended FLSA on police and fire departments, but the 1977 budget contemplates outlays for law enforcement assistance of $716 million. Concern is also expressed about the diminished ability to hire students in the summer if States must pay them a minimum wage, but the Federal Government's "summer youth program" provides $400 million for 670,000 jobs. Given this demonstrated ability to obtain funds from the Federal Government for needed state services, there is little doubt that the States' influence in the political process is adequate to safeguard their sovereignty.

Mr. Justice Stevens, dissenting, said in part:

I agree that it is unwise for the Federal Government to exercise its power in the ways described in the Court's opinion. For the proposition that regulation of the minimum price of a commodity—even labor—will increase the quantity consumed is not one that I can readily understand. That concern, however, applies with even greater force to the private sector of the economy where the exclusion of the marginally employable does the greatest harm and, in all events, merely reflects my views on a policy issue which has been firmly resolved by the branches of government having power to decide such questions.

UNITED STATES v. CURTISS-WRIGHT EXPORT CORPORATION

299 U. S. 304; 56 S. Ct. 216; 81 L. Ed. 255 (1936)

The theory that the national government has only delegated powers is categorically true only in the realm of domestic affairs. In many decisions the Supreme Court has held that in conducting its relations with foreign nations the United States is a sovereign nation which possesses all the powers that other sovereign nations enjoy, and these powers are not limited to those which are delegated by the clauses of the Constitution. Thus, while the Constitution mentioned none of these powers, Congress has been held to have the power to punish the counterfeiting in this country of foreign money or securities, to annex unoccupied territory, to set up judicial tribunals in foreign countries, and to exclude, deport, or regulate the admission of aliens.

This broad power of Congress in the field of foreign relations was upheld in the case of Fong Yue Ting v. United States (1893), upholding the power of Congress to exclude or deport aliens. Fong Yue Ting was born in China and came to the United States prior to 1879, during a period when the United States and China had a treaty according the rights of domicile in this country to Chinese. In 1892 Congress passed a statute prohibiting further Chinese immigration and providing that all Chinese laborers who were entitled to remain in the country should apply to the proper authorities for a certificate of residence; if they failed to do this they were to be deemed unlawfully in the country and deported. Fong Yue Ting's failure to comply with the statute resulted in deportation proceedings against him, and in resisting such action he set up the unconstitutionality of the statute. The opinion of the Court sustaining the act is a clear exposition of the doctrine of the sovereign authority of Congress with respect to international affairs. The theory as laid down forms the constitutional basis of all our immigration legislation not resting upon treaty provisions.

In the case printed below the Court reexamines and reaffirmd the Fong Yue Ting doctrine. In 1934 Congress passed a joint resolution providing that if the President finds that an embargo on the sale of arms and munitions in the United States to countries at war in the Chaco (Bolivia and Paraguay) "may contribute to the reestablishment of peace between those countries," he may, after consultation with other American republics, establish such an embargo by proclamation. Violation of such an embargo was made a crime. The joint resolution did not restrict or direct the President's discretion in setting up the embargo. It clearly delegated legislative power without any of the standards which the Court in the Schechter case (1935) had held to be vital if the delegation were to be held valid. The President proclaimed the embargo and the defendant company, convicted of selling guns to Bolivia, challenged the constitutionality of the resolution.

Mr. Justice Sutherland delivered the opinion of the Court, saying in part:

On January 27, 1936, an indictment was returned in the court below, the first count of which charges that appellees, beginning with the 29th day of May, 1934, conspired to sell in the United States certain arms of war, namely fifteen machine guns, to Bolivia, a country then engaged in armed conflict in the Chaco, in violation of the Joint Resolution of Congress approved May 28, 1934, and the provisions of a proclamation issued on the same day by the President of the United States pursuant to authority conferred by § 1 of the resolution. In pursuance of the conspiracy, the commission of certain overt acts was alleged, details of which need not be stated. The Joint Resolution follows:

"*Resolved by the Senate and House of Representatives of the United States of America in Congress assembled,* That if the President finds that the prohibition of the sale of arms and munitions of war in the United States to those countries now engaged in armed conflict in the Chaco may contribute to the reestablishment of peace between those countries, and if after consultation with the governments of other American Republics and with their cooperation, as well as that of such other governments as he may deem necessary, he makes proclamation to that effect, it shall be unlawful to sell, except under such limitations and exceptions as the President prescribes, any arms or munitions of war in any place in the United States to the countries now engaged in that armed conflict, or to any person, company, or association acting in the interest of either country, until otherwise ordered by the President or by Congress.

"Sec. 2. Whoever sells any arms or munitions of war in violation of section 1 shall, on conviction, be punished by a fine not exceeding $10,000 or by imprisonment not exceeding two years, or both." . . .

Appellees severally demurred to the first count of the indictment on the grounds (1) that it did not charge facts sufficient to show the commission by appellees of any offense against any law of the United States; . . . The points urged in support of the demurrers were, first, that the joint resolution effects an invalid delegation of legislative power to the Executive . . . .

The court below sustained the demurrers upon the first point. . . . The government appealed to this court under the provisions of the Criminal Appeals Act of March 2, 1907. . . . That act authorizes the United States to appeal from a district court direct to this court in criminal cases where, among other things, the decision sustaining a demurrer to the indictment or any count thereof is based upon the invalidity or construction of the statute upon which the indictment is founded.

First. It is contended that by the Joint Resolution, the going into effect and continued operation of the resolution was conditioned (a) upon the President's judgment as to its beneficial effect upon the reestablishment of peace between the countries engaged in armed conflict in the Chaco; (b) upon the making of a proclamation, which was left to his unfettered discretion, thus constituting an attempted substitution of the President's will for that of Congress; (c) upon the making of a proclamation putting an end to the operation of the resolution, which again was left to the President's unfettered discretion; and (d) further, that the extent of its operation in particular cases was subject to limitations and exception by the President, controlled by no standard. In each of these particulars, appellees urge that Congress abdicated its essential functions and delegated them to the Executive.

Whether, if the Joint Resolution had related solely to internal affairs it would be open to the challenge that it constituted an unlawful delegation of legislative power to the Executive, we find it unnecessary to determine. The whole aim of the resolution is to affect a situation entirely external to the United States, and falling within the category of foreign affairs. The determination which we are called to make, therefore, is whether the Joint Resolution, as applied to that situation, is vulnerable to attack under the rule that forbids a delegation of the law-making power. In other words, assuming (but not deciding) that the challenged delegation, if it were confined to internal affairs, would be invalid, may it nevertheless be sustained on the ground that its exclusive aim is to afford a remedy for a hurtful condition within foreign territory?

It will contribute to the elucidation of the question if we first consider the differences between the powers of the Federal government in respect of foregn or external affairs and those in respect of domestic or internal affairs. That there are differences between them, and that these differences are fundamental, may not be doubted.

The two classes of powers are different, both in respect of their origin and their nature. The broad statement that the Federal government can exercise no powers except those specifically enumerated in the Constitution, and such implied powers as are necessary and proper to carry into effect the enumerated powers, is categorically true only in respect of our internal affairs. In that field, the primary purpose of the constitution was to carve from the general mass of legislation powers *then possessed by the states* such portions as it was thought desirable to vest in the Federal government, leaving those not included in the enumeration still in the states. Carter v. Carter Coal Co. [1936]. That this doctrine applies only to powers which the states had is self-evident. And since the states severally never possessed international powers, such powers could not have been carved from the mass of state powers but obviously were transmitted to the United States from some other source. During the colonial period, those powers were possessed exclusively by and were entirely under the control of the Crown. By the Declaration of Independence, "the Representatives of the United States of America" declared the United [not the several] Colonies to be free and independent states, and as such to have "full Power to levy War, conclude Peace, contract Alliances, establish Commerce and to do all other Acts and Things which Independent States may of right do."

As a result of the separation from Great Britain by the colonies, acting as a unit, the powers of external sovereignty passed from the Crown not to the colonies severally, but to the colonies in their collective and corporate capacity as the United States of America. Even before the Declaration, the colonies were a unit in foreign affairs, acting through a common agency—

namely the Continental Congress, composed of delegates from the thirteen colonies. That agency exercised the power of war and peace, raised an army, created a navy, and finally adopted the Declaration of Independence. Rulers come and go; governments end and forms of government change; but sovereignty survives. A political society cannot endure without a supreme will somewhere. Sovereignty is never held in suspense. When, therefore, the external sovereignty of Great Britain in respect of the colonies ceased, it immediately passed to the Union. . . . That fact was given practical application almost at once. The treaty of peace, made on September 3, 1783, was concluded between his Britannic Majesty and the "United States of America." . . .

The Union existed before the Constitution, which was ordained and established among other things to form "a more perfect Union." Prior to that event, it is clear that the Union, declared by the Articles of Confederation to be "perpetual," was the sole possessor of external sovereignty, and in the Union it remained without change save in so far as the Constitution in express terms qualified its exercise. . . .

It results that the investment of the Federal government with the powers of external sovereignty did not depend upon the affirmative grants of the Constitution. The powers to declare and wage war, to conclude peace, to make treaties, to maintain diplomatic relations with other sovereignties, if they had never been mentioned in the Constitution, would have vested in the Federal government as necessary concomitants of nationality. Neither the Constitution nor the laws passed in pursuance of it have any force in foreign territory unless in respect to our own citizens . . . ; and operations of the nation in such territory must be governed by treaties, international understandings and compacts, and the principles of international law. As a member of the family of nations, the right and power of the United States in that field are equal to the right and power of the other members of the international family. Otherwise, the United States is not completely sovereign. The power to acquire territory by discovery and occupation (Jones v. United States [1890]), the power to expel undesirable aliens (Fong Yue Ting v. United States [1893]), the power to make such international agreements as do not constitute treaties in the constitutional sense (Altman & Co. v. United States [1912] . . .), none of which is expressly affirmed by the Constitution, nevertheless exist as inherently inseparable from the conception of nationality. This the court recognized, and in each of the cases cited found the warrant for its conclusions not in the provisions of the Constitution, but in the law of nations. . . .

Not only, as we have shown, is the Federal power over external affairs in origin and essential character different from that over internal affairs, but participation in the exercise of the power is significantly limited. In this vast external realm, with its important, complicated, delicate and manifold problems, the President alone has the power to speak or listen as a representative of the nation. He *makes* treaties with the advice and consent of the Senate; but he alone negotiates. Into the field of negotiation the Senate cannot intrude; and Congress itself is powerless to invade it. . . .

It is important to bear in mind that we are here dealing not alone with an authority vested in the President by an exertion of legislative power, but with such an authority plus the very delicate, plenary and exclusive power of the President as the sole organ of the Federal government in the field of international relations—a power which does not require as a basis for its exercise an act of Congress, but which, of course, like every other governmental power, must be exercised in subordination to the applicable provisions of the Constitution. It is quite apparent that if, in the maintenance of our international relations, embarrassment—perhaps serious embarrassment—is to be avoided and success for our aims achieved, congressional legislation which is to be made effective through negotiation and inquiry within the international field must often accord to the President a degree of discretion and freedom from statutory restriction which would not be admissible were domestic affairs alone involved. Moreover, he, not Congress, has the better opportunity of knowing the conditions which prevail in foreign countries, and especially is this true in time of war. He has his confidential sources of information. He has his agents in the form of diplomatic, consular and other officials. Secrecy in respect of information gathered by them may be highly necessary, and the premature disclosure of it productive of harmful results. . . .

In the light of the foregoing observations, it is evident that this court should not be in haste to apply a general rule which will have the effect of condemning legislation like that under review as constituting an unlawful delegation of legislative power. The principles which justify such legislation find overwhelming support in the unbroken legislative practice which has prevailed almost from the inception of the national government to the present day. . . .

Practically every volume of the United States Statutes contains one or more acts or joint resolutions of Congress authorizing action by the President in respect to subjects affecting foreign relations, which either leave the exercise of the power to his unrestricted judgment, or provide a standard far more general than that which has always been considered requisite with regard to domestic affairs. . . .

. . . A legislative practice such as we have here, evidenced not by only occasional instances, but marked by the movement of a steady stream for a century and a half of time, goes a long way in the direction of proving the presence of unassailable ground for the constitutionality of the practice, to be found in the origin and history of the power involved, or in its nature, or in both combined. . . .

We deem it unnecessary to consider, seriatim, the several clauses which are said to evidence the unconstitutionality of the Joint Resolution as involving an unlawful delegation of legislative power. It is enough to summarize by saying that, both upon principle and in accordance with precedent, we conclude there is sufficient warrant for the broad discretion vested in the President to determine whether the enforcement of the statute will have a beneficial effect upon the reestablishment of peace in the affected countries; whether he shall make proclamation to bring the resolution into operation; whether and when the resolution shall cease to operate and to make proclamation accordingly; and to prescribe limitations and exceptions to which the enforcement of the resolution shall be subject. . . .

The judgment of the court below must be reversed and the cause remanded for further proceedings in accordance with the foregoing opinion.

Reversed.

Mr. Justice McReynolds does not agree. He is of opinion that the court below reached the right conclusion and its judgment ought to be affirmed.

Mr. Justice Stone took no part in the consideration or decision of this case.

EX PARTE MILLIGAN

4 Wallace 2; 18 L. Ed. 281 (1866)

The Constitution gives Congress the power to declare war and to raise and support armies. The war power which has developed from these simple grants staggers the imagination by its scope and variety. This is because, as Chief Justice Hughes put it in Home Building & Loan Ass'n. v. Blaisdell (1934), "the war power of the Federal Government . . . is a power to wage war successfully." In short, what is necessary to win the war Congress may do, and the Supreme Court has shown no inclination to hold void new and drastic war measures. In World War II the war power was invoked to fix price ceilings, to ration food and fuel, to commandeer factories, and to direct the production, distribution, and consumption of commodities. Our entire economy was mobilized for the war effort. A number of specific war powers exercised by Congress have been challenged in the courts, but in every case unsuccessfully.

The power of Congress to draft men into the armed services was attacked during World War I, although the draft had been resorted to sporadically and inefficiently during the Civil War. In 1917 Congress passed the Selective Draft Act, which made all male citizens between the ages of 21 and 30 subject to national military service. Public officers, ministers of religion, and theological students were exempt from the draft, while conscientious objectors who were affiliated with a "well recognized" pacifist religious sect were permitted to engage in noncombatant duty. In Selective Draft Law Cases (Arver v. United States, 1918) the Supreme Court unanimously held the act valid. The power to compel men to serve in the armed forces is reasonably implied from the power to raise and support armies, for a grant of power with no compulsion behind it is no power at all. The exemption of ministers and theological students is not an "establishment of religion" forbidden by the First Amendment; nor does compulsory military service constitute "involuntary servitude" forbidden by the Thirteenth Amendment.

In the Selective Training and Service Act of 1940, Congress, changed the exemption rule, making it unnecessary to belong to a pacifist sect if a person's conscientious objection were based on "religious training and belief." The meaning of this phrase was spelled out in more detail in the Selective Service Act of 1948 (renamed in 1951 the Universal Military Training and Service Act): "Religious training and belief," according to the act, was to be defined as "an individual's belief in a relation to a Supreme Being involving duties superior to those arising from any human relation, but [not including] essentially political, sociological, or philosophical views or a merely personal moral code." In United States v. Seeger (1965), the Supreme Court held that this belief in a Supreme Being was not confined to a belief in God, in the traditional sense, but included any "sincere and meaningful belief which occupies in the life of its possessor a place parallel to that filled by the God of those admittedly qualifying for the exemption. . . . " In 1967, following continued bitter and sometimes violent demonstrations against the draft, General Lewis B. Hershey, then head of the selective service system, recommended to the country's draft boards that persons engaged in illegal demonstrations be reclassified if necessary and inducted promptly into the armed service. In 1968 over 500 students who returned their draft cards as a protest against the Vietnam War had their student deferment cancelled and were inducted into the army. The Supreme Court, in Gutknecht v. United States (1970), held that the Selective Service System was not authorized by law to use "immediate induction as a disciplinary or vindictive measure."

Congress, following the Seeger decision, amended the draft act to make explicit that only religiously motivated CO's could be exempted from service, and in United States v. Sisson (297 Fed. Supp. 902, 1969), district judge Charles E. Wyzanski, Jr. of Boston upset the conviction of a nonreligious objector to the Vietnam War both on the ground that the act amounted to an establishment of religion, and that the government's interest in fighting in Vietnam was insufficient to outweigh Sisson's individual rights. The Supreme Court held that Sisson had in effect been ordered acquitted and refused to review the case.

It is apparent from the challenges to the draft laws, mentioned above, that one of the evils of war seems frequently to be a certain incompatibility between the demands of military necessity and a punctilious regard for the civil rights of the individual. Certainly in war emergencies the citizen finds liberty curtailed and rights abridged in ways that in times of peace would seem intolerable. There is plenty of evidence that President Lincoln, largely supported by public opinion, definitely proceeded during the Civil War upon the theory that questions of constitutional power were to be dealt with in the light of the great objective of preserving the Union. No President has ever invaded private constitutional rights more flagrantly, or from worthier motives, than he. This may be illustrated by the famous case of Ex parte Merryman (1861). Merryman was a Southern agitator residing in Maryland who persisted during the early days of the war in conduct and utterances which, in the judgment of the military authorities, hindered the success of the Northern cause. He was thereupon arrested and locked up in the military prison at Fort McHenry. Merryman promptly petitioned Chief Justice Taney for a writ of habeas corpus. Taney issued the writ, directed to the general in command of the fort. The general did not honor the writ, replying that he was authorized by the President to suspend the writ of habeas corpus, but would seek further instructions; and he declined to obey the writ further. Taney thereupon issued a writ of contempt against the general and sent the United States marshal to serve it. The marshal reported that he had not been allowed to enter the outer gate of the fort, although he had sent in his card, and that he had not been able to serve the writ. Taney, while protesting that the marshal had a perfect right to summon a posse comitatus and storm the fort, excused him from that duty. Rather, he contented himself with writing a full account of the entire case which he addressed to President Lincoln and which concluded with the observation that it now remained for the President, acting in fulfillment of his solemn oath of office, to enforce the laws, execute the judgment of the court, and release the prisoner. Lincoln made no answer whatever to this document, but Merryman was later released from military confinement and turned over to the civil authorities.

No case of this kind came to the Supreme Court while the war was in progress, although in 1864 an attempt was made to bring before that tribunal on a writ of habeas corpus the validity of the arrest of the notorious agitator, Vallandigham. The Court held that it was without jurisdiction and dismissed the case; see Ex parte Vallandigham (1864). It is interesting to speculate what the results might have been had the Supreme Court locked horns with the President in such a case; if, for example, the Milligan case had come up for decision during the early part of the war instead of in 1866.

The facts in the Milligan case were as follows: Milligan, a civilian, was arrested by order of General Hovey, who commanded the military district of Indiana; was tried in October, 1864, by a military commission that had been established under presidential authority; was found guilty of initiating insurrection and of various treasonable and disloyal practices; and was sentenced to be hanged on May 19, 1865. This sentence was approved by President Johnson. On May 10, 1865, Milligan sued out a writ of habeas corpus to the United States circuit court in Indiana, alleging the unconstitutional character of the proceedings under which he had been convicted and claiming the right of trial by jury as guaranteed by the Constitution. Thus, for the first time, the Supreme Court faced the question of the right of the President to suspend the writ of habeas corpus and to substitute trial by military authority for trial in the ordinary civil courts in districts outside the actual field of military operations.

The Supreme Court itself found difficulty in agreeing upon the important questions presented. They all held that a military commission set up by the President under such circumstances and without special authority from Congress was unlawful and without any power whatsoever. Five of the judges took the view that neither Congress nor the President had the power to set up military tribunals except in the actual theater of war where the civil courts were no longer functioning. Four judges, while denying such power to the President, held that it could be exercised by Congress. The Court decided, however, that Milligan had been unlawfully convicted and he was released.

The subsequent story of the case is not without interest. Milligan's sentence had been commuted to life imprisonment by the President in June, 1865, and he had been imprisoned by General Hovey in the Ohio penitentiary until his final release on April 10, 1866, as a result of the decision of the Supreme Court. On March 13, 1868, he brought an action of damages against General Hovey for unlawful imprisonment. The case was tried in the federal circuit court and the jury rendered a verdict for Milligan, but awarded only nominal damages inasmuch as the two-year statute of limitations allowed him to recover damages only for his imprisonment between March 13 and April 10, 1866.

The fact that the decision in the Milligan case set up a powerful judicial protection against military and executive invasion of individual constitutional rights was not sufficient to distract contemporary attention from the vital political consequences of the rule regarding congressional power which was laid down. Congress was in the midst of the important work of reconstruction. The radical leaders of the Republican party were committed to a policy of reconstruction which should keep the Southern states under the control of federal military forces until conditions seemed to warrant the adoption of a less drastic policy. But the doctrine of the Milligan case, by condemning military government in peaceful sections where the civil courts were open, was obviously incompatible with any such form of military reconstruction. It looked as though the Court was trying to prevent the carrying out of the congressional policy, and the decision was received with an outburst of anger by the congressional leaders. There was some talk of impeaching the judges; Congress went forward with its plans for military government in the South in contemptuous disregard for the decision, and utterances from prominent men were not lacking to the effect that the Court would come off the loser in any combat over the validity of the reconstruction plan adopted. It is an interesting fact that the constitutionality of these reconstruction acts was never passed upon by the Supreme Court. See the cases of Mississippi v. Johnson (1867), and Ex parte McCardle (1869)

Mr. Justice Davis delivered the opinion of the Court, saying in part:

The importance of the main question presented by this record cannot be overstated, for it involves the very framework of the government and the fundamental principles of American liberty.

During the late wicked Rebellion, the temper of the times did not allow that calmness in deliberation and discussion so necessary to a correct conclusion of a purely judicial question. Then, considerations of safety were mingled with the excerise of power, and feelings and interests prevailed which are happily terminated. Now that the public safety is assured, this question, as well as all others, can be discussed and decided without passion or the admixture of any element not required to form a legal judgment. We approach the investigation of this case fully sensible of the magnitude of the inquiry and the necessity of full and cautious deliberation. . . .

The controlling question in the case is this: Upon the facts stated in Milligan's petition, and the exhibits filed, had the Military Commission mentioned in it jurisdiction, legally, to try and sentence him? Milligan, not a resident of one of the rebellious states, or a prisoner of war, but a citizen of Indiana for twenty years past, and never in the military or naval service, is, while at his home, arrested by the military power of the United States, imprisoned and, on certain criminal charges preferred against him, tried, convicted, and sentenced to be hanged by a military commission, organized under the direction of the military commander of the military district of Indiana. Had this tribunal the legal power and authority to try and punish this man?

No graver question was ever considered by this court, nor one which more nearly concerns the rights of the whole people; for it is the brithright of every American citizen when charged with crime, to be tried and punished according to law. The power of punishment is alone through the means which the laws have provided for that purpose, and if they are ineffectual, there is an immunity from punishment, no matter how great an offender the individual may be, or how much his crimes may have shocked the sense of justice of the country, or endangered its safety. By the protection of the law human rights are secured; withdraw that protection, and they are at the mercy of wicked rulers, or the clamor of an excited people. If there was law to justify this military trial, it is not our province to interfere; if there was not, it is our duty to declare the nullity of the whole proceedings. The decision of this question does not depend on argument or judicial precedents, numerous and highly illustrative as they are. These precedents inform us of the extent of the struggle to preserve liberty and to relieve those in civil life from military trials. The founders of our government were familiar with the history of that struggle; and secured in a written Constitution every right which the people had wrested from power during a contest of ages. By that Constitution and the laws authorized by it, this question must be determined. The provisions of that instrument on the administration of criminal justice are too plain and direct to leave room for misconstruction or doubt of their true meaning. Those applicable to this case are found in that clause of the original Constitution which says "that the trial of all crimes, except in case of impeachment, shall be by jury;" and in the fourth, fifth, and sixth articles of the amendments. . . .

Time has proven the discernment of our ancestors; for even these provisions, expressed in such plain English words, that it would seem the ingenuity of man could not evade them, are now, after the lapse of more than seventy years, sought to be avoided. Those great and good men foresaw that troublous times would arise, when rulers and people would become restive under restraint, and seek by sharp and decisive measures to accomplish ends deemed just and proper; and that the principles of constitutional liberty would be in peril, unless established by irrepealable law. The history of the world had taught them that what was done in the past might be attempted in the future. The Constitution of the United States is a law for rulers and people, equally in war and in peace, and covers with the shield of its protection all classes of men, at all times, and under all circumstances. No doctrine involving more pernicious consequences, was ever invented by the wit of man than that any of its provisions can be suspended during any of the great exigencies of government. Such a doctrine leads directly to anarchy or despotism, but the theory of necessity on which it is based is false; for the government, within the Constitution, has all the powers granted to it which are necessary to preserve its existence, as has been happily proved by the result of the great effort to throw off its just authority.

Have any of the rights guaranteed by the Constitution been violated in the case of Milligan? and if so, what are they?

Every trial involves the exercise of judicial power; and from what source did the Military Commission that tried him derive their authority? Certainly no part of the judicial power of the country was conferred on them; because the Constitution expressly vests it "in one Supreme Court and such inferior courts as the Congress may from time to time ordain and establish," and it is not pretended that the commission was a court ordained and established by Congress. They cannot justify on the mandate of the President; because he is controlled by law, and has his appropriate sphere of duty, which is to execute, not to make, the laws; and there is "no unwritten criminal code to which resort can be had as a source of jurisdiction."

But it is said that the jurisdiction is complete under the "laws and usages of war."

It can serve no useful purpose to inquire what those laws and usages are, whence they originated, where found, and on whom they operate; they can never be applied to citizens in states which have upheld the authority of the government, and where the courts are open and their process unobstructed. This court has judicial knowledge that in Indiana the Federal authority was always unopposed, and its courts always open to hear criminal accusations and redress grievances; and no usage of war could sanction a military trial there for any offense whatever of a citizen in civil life, in nowise connected with the military service. Congress could grant no such power; and to the honor of our national legislature be it said, it had never been provoked by the state of the country even to attempt its exercise. One of the plainest constitutional provisions was, therefore, infringed when Milligan was tried by a court not ordained and established by Congress, and not composed of judges appointed during good behavior.

Why was he not delivered to the circuit court of Indiana to be proceeded against according to law? No reason of necessity could be urged against it; because Congress had declared penalties against the offenses charged, provided for their punishment, and directed that court to hear and determine them. And soon after this military tribunal was ended, the circuit court met, peacefully transacted its business, and adjourned. It needed no bayonets to protect it, and required no military aid to execute its judgments. It was held in a state, eminently distinguished for patriotism, by judges commissioned during the Rebellion who were provided with juries, upright, intelligent, and selected by a marshal appointed by the President. The government had no right to conclude that Milligan, if guilty, would not receive in that court merited punishment; for its records disclose that it was constantly engaged in the trial of similar offenses, and was never interrupted in its administration of criminal justice. If it was dangerous, in the distracted condition of affairs, to leave Milligan unrestrained of his liberty, because he "conspired against the government, afforded aid and comfort to rebels, and incited the people to insurrection," the law said arrest him, confine him closely, render him powerless to do further mischief; and then present his case to the grand jury of the district, with proofs of his guilt and, if indicted, try him according to the course of the common law. If this had been done, the Constitution would have been vindicated, the law of 1863 enforced, and the securities for personal liberty preserved and defended.

Another guarantee of freedom was broken when Milligan was denied a trial by jury. The great minds of the country have differed on the correct interpretation to be given to various provisions of the Federal Constitution; and judicial decision has been often invoked to settle their true meaning; but until recently no one ever doubted that the right of trial by jury was fortified in the organic law against the power of attack. It is now assailed; but if ideas can be expressed in words, and language has any meaning, this right—one of the most valuable in a free country—is preserved to every one accused of a crime who is not attached to the Army, or Navy, or Militia in actual service. The sixth amendment affirms that "in all criminal prosecutions the accused shall enjoy the right to a speedy and public trial by an impartial jury," language broad enough to embrace all persons and cases; but the fifth, recognizing the necessity of an indictment, or presentment, before any one can be held to answer for high crimes, "except cases arising in the land or naval forces, or in the militia, when in actual service, in time of war or public danger"; and the framers of the Constitution, doubtless, meant to limit the right to trial by jury, in the Sixth Amendment, to those persons who were subject to indictment or presentment in the Fifth.

The discipline necessary to the efficiency of the army and navy, required other and swifter modes of trial than are furnished by the common law courts; and, in pursuance of the power conferred by the Constitution, Congress has declared the kinds of trial and the manner in which they shall be conducted, for offenses committed while the party is in the military or naval service. Every one connected with these branches of public service is amenable to the jurisdiction which Congress has created for their government, and, while thus serving, surrenders his right to be tried by the civil courts.

All other persons, citizens of states where the courts are open, if charged with crime, are guaranteed the inestimable privilege of trial by jury. . . .

It is claimed that martial law covers with its broad mantle the proceedings of this Military Commission. The proposition is this: That in a time of war the commander of an armed force (if in his opinion the exigencies of the country demand it, and of which he is to judge) has the power, within the lines of his military district, to suspend all civil rights and their remedies, and subject citizens as well as soldiers to the rule of his will; and in the exercise of his lawful authority cannot be restrained, except by his superior officer or the President of the United States.

If this position is sound to the extent claimed, then when war exists, foreign or domestic, and the country is subdivided into military departments for mere convenience, the commander of one of them can, if he chooses, within the limits, on the plea of necessity, with the approval of the Executive, substitute military force for and [to] the exclusion of the laws, and punish all persons, as he thinks right and proper, without fixed or certain rules.

The statement of this proposition shows its importance; for, if true, republican government is a failure, and there is an end of liberty regulated by law. Martial law, established on such a basis, destroys every guarantee of the Constitution, and effectually renders the "military independent of and superior to the civil power"—the attempt to do which by the King of Great Britain was deemed by our fathers such an offense, that they assigned it to the world as one of the causes which impelled them to declare their independence. Civil liberty and this kind of martial law cannot endure together; the antagonism is irreconcilable and, in the conflict, one or the other must perish.

This nation, as experience has proved, cannot always remain at peace, and has no right to expect that it will always have wise and humane rulers, sincerely attached to the principles of the Constitution. Wicked men, ambitious of power, with hatred of liberty and contempt of law, may fill the place once occupied by Washington and Lincoln; and it this right is conceded, and the calamities of war again befall us, the dangers to human liberty are frightful to contemplate. If our fathers had failed to provide for just such a contingency, they would have been false to the trust reposed in them. They knew—the history of the world told them—the nation they were founding, be its existence short or long, would be involved in war; how often or how long continued, human foresight could not tell; and that unlimited power, wherever lodged at such a time, was especially hazardous to freemen. For this, and other equally weighty reasons, they secured the inheritance they had fought to maintain, by incorporating in a written Constitution the safeguards which time had proved were essential to its preservaion. Not one of these safeguards can the President or Congress or the Judiciary disturb, except the one concerning the writ of habeas corpus.

It is essential to the safety of every government that, in a great crisis, like the one we have just passed through, there should be a power somewhere of suspending the writ of habeas corpus. In every war, there are men of previously good character, wicked enough to counsel their fellow citizens to resist the measures deemed necessary by a good government to sustain its just authority and overthrow its enemies; and their influence may lead to dangerous combinations. In the emergency of the times, an immediate public investigation according to law may not be possible; and yet, the peril to the country may be too imminent to suffer such persons to go at large. Unquestionably, there is then an exigency which demands that the government, if it should see fit, in the exercise of a proper discretion, to make arrests, should not be required to produce the person arrested in answer to a writ of habeas corpus. The Constitution goes no further. It does not say after a writ of habeas corpus is denied a citizen, that he shall be tried otherwise than by the course of common law. If it had intended this result, it was easy by the use of direct words to have accomplished it. The illustrious men who framed that instrument were guarding the foundations of civil liberty against the abuses of unlimited power; they were full of wisdom, and the lessons of history informed them that a trial by an established court, assisted by an impartial jury, was the only sure way of protecting the citizen against oppression and wrong. Knowing this, they limited the suspension to one great right, and left the rest to remain forever inviolable. But, it is insisted that the safety of the country in time of war demands that this broad claim for martial law shall be sustained. If this were true, it could be well said that a country, preserved at the sacrifice of all the cardinal principles of liberty, is not worth the cost of preservation. Happily, it is not so.

It will be borne in mind that this is not a question of the power to proclaim martial law, when war exists in a community and the courts and civil authorities are overthrown. Nor is it a question what rule a military commander, at the head of his army, can impose on States in rebellion to cripple their resources and quell the insurrection. The jurisdiction claimed is much more extensive. The necessities of the service, during the late Rebellion, required that the loyal states should be placed within the limits of certain military districts and commanders appointed in them; and, it is urged, that this, in a military sense, constituted them the theatre of military operations; and, as in this case, Indiana had been and was again threatened with invasion by the enemy, the occasion was furnished to establish martial law. The conclusion does not follow from the premises. If armies were collected in Indiana, they were to be employed in another locality, where the laws were obstructed and the national authority disputed. On her soil there was no hostile foot; if once invaded, that invasion was at an end, and with it all pretext for martial law. Martial law cannot arise from a threatened invasion. The necessity must be actual and present; the invasion real, such as effectually closes the courts and deposes the civil administration.

It is difficult to see how the safety of the country required martial law in Indiana. If any of her citizens were plotting treason, the power of arrest could secure them, until the government was prepared for their trial, when the courts were open and ready to try them. It was as easy to protect witnesses before a civil as a military tribunal; and as there could be no wish to convict, except on sufficient legal evidence, surely an ordained and established court were better able to judge of this than a military tribunal composed of gentlemen not trained to the profession of the law.

It follows, from what has been said on this subject, that there are occasions when martial rule can be properly applied. If, in foreign invasion or civil war, the courts are actually closed, and it is impossible to administer criminal justice according to law, then, on the theatre of actual military operations, where war really prevails, there is a necessity to furnish a substitute for the civil authority, thus overthrown, to preserve the safety of the army and society; and as no power is left but the military, it is allowed to govern by martial rule until the laws can have their free course. As necessity creates the rule, so it limits its duration; for, if this government is continued after the courts are reinstated, it is a gross usurpation of power. Martial rule can never exist where the courts are open, and in the proper and unobstructed exercise of their jurisdiction. It is also confined to the locality of actual war. Because, during the late Rebellion it could have been enforced in Virginia, where the national authority was overturned and the courts driven out, it does not follow that it should obtain in Indiana, where that authority was never disputed, and justice was always administered. And so in the case of a foreign invasion, martial rule may become a necessity, in one state, when, in another, it would be "mere lawless violence." . . .

The two remaining questions in this case must be answered in the affirmative. The suspension of the privilege of the writ of habeas corpus does not suspend the writ itself. The writ issues as a matter of course; and on the return made to it the court decides whether the party applying is denied the right of proceeding any further with it.

If the military trial of Milligan was contrary to law, then he was entitled, on the facts stated in his petition, to be discharged from custody by the terms of the act of Congress of March 3d, 1863. The provisions of this law having been considered in a previous part of this opinion, we will not restate the views there presented. Milligan avers he was a citizen of Indiana, not in the military or naval service, and was detained in close confinement, by order of the President, from the 5th day of October, 1864, until the 2d day of January, 1865, when the circuit court for the district of Indiana, with a grand jury, convened in session at Indianapolis; and afterwards, on the 27th day of the same month, adjourned without finding an indictment or presentment against him. If these averments were true (and their truth is conceded for the purposes of this case), the court was required to liberate him on taking certain oaths prescribed by the law, and entering into recognizance for his good behavior.

But it is insisted that Milligan was a prisoner of war, and, therefore, excluded from the privileges of the statute. It is not easy to see how he can be treated as a prisoner of war, when he lived in Indiana for the past twenty years, was arrested there, and had not been, during the late troubles, a resident of any of the states in rebellion. If in Indiana he conspired with bad men to assist the enemy, he is punishable for it in the courts of Indiana; but, when tried for the offense, he cannot plead the rights of war; for he was not engaged in legal acts of hostility against the government, and only such persons, when captured, are prisoners of war. If he cannot enjoy the immunities attaching to the character of a prisoner of war, how can he be subject to their pains and penalties? . . .

Mr. Chief Justice Chase, for himself and Mr. Justice Wayne, Mr. Justice Swayne, and Mr. Justice Miller, delivered an opinion in which he differed from the Court in several important points, but concurred in the judgment in the case.

KOREMATSU v. UNITED STATES

323 U. S. 214; 65 S. Ct. 193; 89 L. Ed. 194 (1944)

World War I was fought in Europe, brought no serious menace to our domestic national security, and produced no significant clashes between military and civil authority. With World War II, however, the story was very different. This was in every sense a "total" war; its successful outcome was by no means assured, and danger of external attack and internal treachery was at times very real. Military leaders faced unprecedented situations and met them by resort to unprecedented extensions of military authority. Congress, in turn, reinforced these military judgments in cases where such support was needed.

The spectacular case of the Nazi saboteurs, Ex parte Quirin (1942), appeared at first to reopen the major issue settled by the Milligan case. In June, 1942, eight saboteurs landed in this country from a German submarine. They brought with them explosives, incendiaries, fuses, detonators, timing devices, and acids. They had about $175,000 in American money for expenses and bribes, and they carried elaborate lists of American factories, railroad centers, bridges, power plants, and other key war facilities. They were all born in Germany, had previously lived in this country, and had, upon returning to Germany, been trained in a special school for saboteurs. About ten days after they landed, they were arrested by the FBI. Thereupon President Roosevelt issued two proclamations. The first denied to enemies who enter this country to commit sabotage or other hostile acts the right of access to the civil courts and directed that they be tried by military tribunals in accordance with the law of war. The second created a military commission of eight army officers to try the saboteurs, ordered the Attorney General and the Judge Advocate General to prosecute them, and designated two army officers to act as defense counsel. Four charges were filed against the saboteurs, all stating offenses under the law of war. At the outset of the trial, defense counsel attacked the constitutionality of the President's proclamation and the jurisdiction of the military commission, but the trial proceeded. Late in July the country was startled by the announcement that the Supreme Court (then in summer recess) would reconvene in two days to permit the filing of petitions for writs of habeas corpus on behalf of the prisoners. After proceedings that lasted two days, the Court denied the petitions and adjourned. The trial continued and the saboteurs were convicted. Six were executed and two imprisoned. In October, the Court handed down its opinion in the case. It held that the President had the authority to establish the military commission by virtue of statutes passed by Congress, and that the offenses charged were offenses against the law of war. It held that the grand jury indictment and the jury trial provisions of the Fifth and Sixth Amendments are not applicable to trials before military tribunals for crimes against the law of war. The Court then commented upon the Milligan case; it pointed out that Milligan was a citizen and resident of Indiana, had never lived in a rebellious state, was not an enemy belligerent, and was therefore not subject to the law of war. The Court said: "We construe the Court's statement as to the applicability of the law of war to Milligan's case as having particular reference to the facts before it." The most important point about the case is that the Supreme Court did examine the right of the military authorities to try the saboteurs. It upheld the military tribunal, but not until it satisfied itself that the tribunal had jurisdiction and was proceeding according to law.

In December, 1945, the Court scrutinized the authority of an American military commission in the Philippines to try Japanese General Yamashita for offenses against the law of war comprising his failure to restrain his troops from committing atrocities against Americans and Filipinos; see In re Yamashita (1946). Again the Court recognized the right to challenge the military proceedings by a petition for a writ of habeas corpus. It held that the military commission had been properly set up in accordance with federal statutes which provided for trial, by such commissions, of enemy combatants charged with violating the law of war. It found the authority of the military is not ended by the cessation of hostilities but only by the formal establishment of peace by the political departments of the government through proclamation or treaty. It held, further, that the offenses charged against General Yamashita constituted violations of the law of war. It declared that the procedure and rules of evidence employed by the military commission are not subject to judicial scrutiny but are reviewable only by higher military authorities. This meant that the use by the prosecution against General Yamashita of depositions (written testimony) and hearsay evidence (neither of which could validly be introduced in a trial in a civil court) did not violate the due process clause of the Fifth Amendment. A military commission does not have to observe due process of law in trying an enemy combatant. The ruling on this last point elicited vigorous dissents by Justices Murphy and Rutledge.

The present case involved perhaps the most alarming use of executive military authority in our nation's history. Following the bombing of Pearl Harbor in December, 1941, the anti-Japanese sentiment on the West Coast brought the residents of that area to a state of near hysteria; and in February, 1942, President Roosevelt issued an executive order authorizing the creation of military areas from which any or all persons might be excluded as the military authorities might decide. On March 2, the entire West Coast to a depth of about 40 miles was designated by the commanding general as Military Area No. 1, and he thereupon proclaimed a curfew in that area for all persons of Japanese ancestry. Later he ordered the compulsory evacuation from the area of all persons of Japanese ancestry, and by the middle of the summer most of these people had been moved inland to "war relocation centers," the American equivalent of concentration camps. Congress subsequently made it a crime to violate these military orders. Of the 112,000 persons of Japanese ancestry involved, about 70,000 were native-born Americans citizens, none of whom had been specifically accused of disloyalty. Three cases were brought to the Supreme Court challenging the right of the government to override in this manner the customary civil rights of these citizens. In Hirabayashi v. United States (1943) the Court upheld the curfew regulations as a valid military measure to prevent espionage and sabotage. "Whatever views we may entertain regarding the loyalty to this country of the citizens of Japanese ancestry, we cannot reject as unfounded the judgment of the military authorities and of Congress that there were disloyal members of that population, whose number and strength could not be precisely and quickly ascertained. We cannot say that the war-making branches of the Government did not have ground for believing that in a critical hour such persons could not readily be isolated and separately dealt with, and constituted a menace to the national defense and safety. . . ." While emphasizing that distinctions based on ancestry were "by their very nature odious to a free people" the Court nonetheless felt "that in time of war residents having ethnic affiliations with an invading enemy may be a greater source of danger than those of a different ancestry."

While the Court held valid the discriminatory mass evacuation of all persons of Japanese descent, it also held in Ex parte Endo (1944), that an American citizen of Japanese ancestry whose loyalty to this country had been established could not constitutionally be held in a War Relocation Center but must be unconditionally released. The government had allowed persons to leave the Relocation Centers under conditions and restrictions which aimed to guarantee that there should not be "a dangerously disorderly migration of unwanted people to unprepared communities." Permission to leave was granted only if the applicant had the assurance of a job and a place to live, and wanted to go to a place "approved" by the War Relocation Authority. The Court held that the sole purpose of the evacuation and detention program was to protect the war effort against sabotage and espionage. "A person who is concededly loyal presents no problem of espionage or sabotage. . . . He who is loyal is by definition not a spy or a saboteur." It therefore follows that the authority to detain a citizen of Japanese ancestry ends when his loyalty is established. To hold otherwise would be to justify his detention not on grounds of military necessity but purely on grounds of race.

Although no case reached the Court squarely challenging the right of the government to incarcerate citizens of Japanese ancestry pending a determination of their loyalty, the tenor of the opinions leaves little doubt that such action would have been sustained. The present case involved only the right of the military to evacuate such persons from the West Coast. Justice Murphy, one of three dissenters, attacked the qualifications of the military to make sociological judgments about the effects of ancestry, and pointed out that the time consumed in evacuating these persons (11 months) was ample for making an orderly inquiry into their individual loyalty.

Mr. Justice Black delivered the opinion of the Court, saying in part:

The petitioner, an American citizen of Japanese descent, was convicted in a Federal district court for remaining in San Leandro, California, a "Military Area," contrary to Civilian Exclusion Order No. 34 of the Commanding General of the Western Command, U.S. Army, which directed that after May 9, 1942, all persons of Japanese ancestry should be excluded from that area. No question was raised as to petitioner's loyalty to the United States. The Circuit Court of Appeals affirmed, and the importance of the constitutional question involved caused us to grant certiorari.

It should be noted, to begin with, that all legal restrictions which curtail the civil rights of a single racial group are immediately suspect. That is not to say that all such restrictions are unconstitutional. It is to say that courts must subject them to the most rigid scrutiny. Pressing public necessity may sometimes justify the existence of such restrictions; racial antagomism never can.

In the instant case prosecution of the petitioner was begun by information charging violation of an Act of Congress, of March 21, 1942, which provides that ". . . whoever shall enter, remain in, leave, or commit any act in any military area or military zone prescribed, under the authority of an Executive order of the President, by the Secretary of War, or by any military commander designated by the Secretary of War, contrary to the restrictions applicable to any such area or zone or contrary to the order of the Secretary of War or any such military commander, shall, if it appears that he knew or should have known of the existence and extent of the restrictions or order and that his act was in violation thereof, be guilty of a misdemeanor and upon conviction shall be liable to a fine of not to exceed $5,000 or to imprisonment for not more than one year, or both, for each offense."

Exclusion Order No. 34, which the petitioner knowingly and admittedly violated was one of the number of military orders and proclamations, all of which were substantially based upon Executive Order No. 9066. That order, issued after we were at war with Japan, declared that "the successful prosecution of the war requires every possible protection against espionage and against sabotage to national-defense material, national-defense premises, and national-defense utilities. . . ."

One of the series of orders and proclamations, a curfew order, which like the exclusion order here was promulgated pursuant to Executive Order 9066, subjected all persons of Japanese ancestry in prescribed West Coast military areas to remain in their residences from 8 P.M. to 6 A.M. As is the case with the exclusion order here, that prior curfew order was designed as a "protection against espionage and against sabotage." In Hirabayashi v. United States [1943], we sustained a conviction obtained for violation of the curfew order. The Hirabayashi conviction and this one thus rest on the same 1942 Congressional Act and the same basic executive and military orders, all of which orders were aimed at the twin dangers of espionage and sabotage.

The 1942 Act was attacked in the Hirabayashi Case as an unconstitutional delegation of power; it was contended that the curfew order and other orders on which it rested were beyond the war powers of the Congress, the military authorities and of the President, as Commander in Chief of the Army; and finally that to apply the curfew order against none but citizens of Japanese ancestry amounted to a constitutionally prohibited discrimination solely on account of race. To these questions, we gave the serious consideration which their importance justified. We upheld the curfew order as an exercise of the power of the government to take steps necessary to prevent espionage and sabotage in an area threatened by Japanese attack.

In the light of the principles we announced in the Hirabayashi Case, we are unable to conclude that it was beyond the war power of Congress and the Executive to exclude those of Japanese ancestry from the West Coast war area at the time they did. True, exclusion from the area in which one's home is located is a far greater deprivation than constant confinement to the home from 8 P.M. to 6 A.M. Nothing short of apprehension by the proper military authorities of the gravest imminent danger to the public safety can constitutionally justify either. But exclusion from a threatened area, no less than curfew, has a definite and close relationship to the prevention of espionage and sabotage. The military authorities, charged with the primary responsibility of defending our shores, concluded that curfew provided inadequate protection and ordered exclusion. They did so, as pointed out in our Hirabayashi opinion, in accordance with Congressional authority to the military to say who should, and who should not, remain in the threatened areas.

In this case the petitioner challenges the assumptions upon which we rested our conclusions in the Hirabayashi Case. He also urges that by May 1942, when Order No. 34 was promulgated, all danger of Japanese invasion of the West Coast had disappeared. After careful consideration of these contentions we are compelled to reject them.

Here, as in the Hirabayashi Case, "we cannot reject as unfounded the judgment of the military authorities and of Congress that there were disloyal members of that population, whose number and strength could not be precisely and quickly ascertained. We cannot say that the war-making branches of the Government did not have ground for believing that in a critical hour such persons could not readily be isolated and separately dealt with, and constituted a menace to the national defense and safety, which demanded that prompt and adequate measures be taken to guard against it."

Like curfew, exclusion of those of Japanese origin was deemed necessary because of the presence of an unascertained number of disloyal members of the group, most of whom we have no doubt were loyal to this country. It was because we could not reject the finding of the military authorities that it was impossible to bring about an immediate segregation of the disloyal from the loyal that we sustained the validity of the curfew order as applying to the whole group. In the instant case, temporary exclusion of the entire group was rested by the military on the same ground. The judgment that exclusion of the whole group was for the same reason a military imperative answers the contention that the exclusion was in the nature of group punishment based on antagonism of those of Japanese origin. That there were members of the group who retained loyalties to Japan has been confirmed by investigations made subsequent to the exclusion. Approximately five thousand American citizens of Japanese ancestry refused to swear unqualified allegiance to the United States and to renounce allegiance to the Japanese Emperor, and several thousand evacuees requested repatriation to Japan.

We uphold the exclusion order as of the time it was made and when the petitioner violated it. . . . In doing so, we are not unmindful of the hardships imposed by it upon a large group of American citizens. . . . But hardships are part of war, and war is an aggregation of hardships. All citizens alike, both in and out of uniform, feel the impact of war in greater or lesser measure. Citizenship has its responsibilities as well as its privileges, and in time of war the burden is always heavier. Compulsory exclusion of large groups of citizens from their homes, except under circumstances of direst emergency and peril, is inconsistent with our basic governmental institution. But when under conditions of modern warfare our shores are threatened by hostile forces, the power to protect must be commensurate with the threatened danger. . . .

[The Court dealt at some length with a technical complication which arose in the case. On May 30, the date on which Korematsu was charged with remaining unlawfully in the prohibited area, there were two conflicting military orders outstanding, one forbidding him to remain in the area, the other forbidding him to leave but ordering him to report to an assembly center. Thus, he alleged, he was punished for doing what it was made a crime to fail to do. The Court held the orders not to be contradictory, since the requirement to report to the assembly center was merely a step in an orderly program of compulsory evacuation from the area.]

It is said that we are dealing here with the case of imprisonment of a citizen in a concentration camp solely because of his ancestry, without evidence or inquiry concerning his loyalty and good disposition towards the United States. Our task would be simple, our duty clear, were this a case involving the imprisonment of a loyal citizen in a concentration camp because of racial prejudice. Regardless of the true nature of the assembly and relocation centers—and we deem it unjustifiable to call them concentration camps with all the ugly connotations that term implies—we are dealing specifically with nothing but an exclusion order. To cast this case into outlines of racial prejudice, without reference to the real military dangers which were presented, merely confuses the issue. Korematsu was not excluded from the Military Area because of hostility to him or his race. He *was* excluded because we are at war with the Japanese Empire, because the properly constituted military authorities feared an invasion of our West Coast and felt constrained to take proper security measures, because they decided that the military urgency of the situation demanded that all citizens of Japanese ancestry be segregated from the West Coast temporarily, and finally, because Congress, reposing its confidence in this time of war in our military leaders—as inevitably it must—determined that they should have the power to do just this. There was evidence of disloyalty on the part of some, the military authorities considered that the need for action was great, and time was short. We cannot—by availing ourselves of the calm perspective of hindsight—now say that at that time these actions were unjustified.

Affirmed.

Mr. Justice Frankfurter wrote a concurring opinion. Justices Roberts, Murphy, and Jackson each wrote a dissenting opinion.

5

The Nationalization of the Bill of Rights

BARRON v. BALTIMORE

7 Peters 243; 8 L. Ed. 672 (1833)

One of the bitter criticisms urged against our federal Constitution as it came from the hands of the Convention was that it contained no bill of rights. It was feared that without specific guarantees the civil rights and liberties of the people and the states would be at the mercy of the proposed national government. Ratification was secured, but with a tacit understanding that a bill of rights should promptly be added which should restrict the national government in behalf of individual liberty. That the early statesmen thought of a federal bill of rights only in terms of restriction on national power is emphasized by Hamilton's ingenious argument in *The Federalist* (No. 84) that since the proposed central government was one which possessed only the powers delegated to it, it would be not only unnecessary but unwise to prohibit it from doing things which were clearly outside the scope of its delegated authority.

When the First Congress convened, the House of Representatives proposed seventeen amendments in the nature of a bill of rights. One of these, the fourteenth, provided that "no state should infringe the right of trial by jury in criminal cases, nor the rights of conscience, nor the freedom of speech or of the press." This amendment, which was the only one restricting the powers of the states, was rejected by the Senate. The substance of the others was consolidated into twelve amendments, ten of which were finally ratified by the states.

The First Amendment indicates by its own language that it is directed only against the federal government, for it begins, "Congress shall make no law. . . ." The other amendments are couched in terms of general prohibition; and in spite of the perfectly clear historical evidence as to the intention of those who framed them, it came to be argued that these guarantees of civil liberty ought to be construed as restrictions upon state and federal governments alike. Whether this view is correct is the issue involved in Barron v. Baltimore, the last constitutional decision in which Chief Justice Marshall participated.

While paving its streets, the city of Baltimore had diverted from their natural courses certain streams, with the result that sand and gravel were deposited near Barron's wharf. The wharf, which had previously enjoyed the deepest water in the harbor, was rendered practically useless, for the deposits prevented the approach of vessels. A verdict of $4500 for Barron had been reversed by the state court of appeals, and a writ of error was taken to the Supreme Court of the United States. It was alleged by Barron that this action upon the part of the city constituted a violation of that clause of the Fifth Amendment which forbids taking private property for public use without just compensation. He insisted that this amendment, being a guarantee in behalf of individual liberty, ought to be construed to restrain the states as well as the national government.

The decision in Barron v. Baltimore has left an indelible impression on the development of civil rights in this country. While today Barron would have brought his case under the due process clause of the Fourteenth Amendment (which does restrict the states), the process of change by which parts of the Bill of Rights have come to be applicable to the states has been slow, uncertain, and confusing. While most rights in the Bill of Rights now do apply to the states, they do so only because they are essential to due process of law. The ruling in the present case that the Bill of Rights does not apply *directly* to the states has never been overruled.

Mr. Chief Justice Marshall delivered the opinion of the court:

The judgment brought up by this writ of error having been rendered by the court of a State, this tribunal can exercise no jurisdiction over it unless it be shown to come within the provisions of the twenty-fifth section of the Judicial Act.

The plaintiff in error contends that it comes within that clause in the fifth amendment to the Constitution which inhibits the taking of private property for public use without just compensation. He insists that this amendment, being in favor of the liberty of the citizen, ought to be so construed as to restrain the legislative power of a State, as well as that of the United States. If this proposition be untrue, the court can take no jurisdiction of the cause.

The question thus presented is, we think, of great importance, but not of much difficulty.

The Constitution was ordained and established by the people of the United States for themselves, for their own government, and not for the government of the individual States. Each State established a constitution for itself, and in that constitution provided such limitations and restrictions on the powers of its particular government as its judgment dictated. The people of the United States framed such a government for the United States as they supposed best adapted to their situation, and best calculated to promote their interests. The powers they conferred on this government were to be exercised by itself; and the limitations on power, if expressed in general terms, are naturally, and, we think, necessarily applicable to the government created by the instrument. They are limitations of power granted in the instrument itself; not of distinct governments, framed by different persons and for different purposes.

If these propositions be correct, the fifth amendment must be understood as restraining the power of the general government, not as applicable to the States. In their several constitutions they have imposed such restrictions on their respective governments as their own wisdom suggested; such as they deemed most proper for themselves. It is a subject on which they judge exclusively, and with which others interfere no farther than they are supposed to have a common interest.

The counsel for the plaintiff in error insists that the Constitution was intended to secure the people of the several States against the undue exercise of power by their respective State governments; as well as against that which might be attempted by their general government. In support of this argument he relies on the inhibitions contained in the tenth section of the first article.

We think that section affords a strong if not a conclusive argument in support of the opinion already indicated by the court.

The preceding section contains restrictions which are obviously intended for the exclusive purpose of restraining the exercise of power by the departments of the general government. Some of them use language applicable only to Congress, others are expressed in general terms. The third clause, for example, declares that "no bill of attainder or ex post facto law shall be passed." No language can be more general; yet the demonstration is complete that it applies solely to the government of the United States. In addition to the general arguments furnished by the instrument itself, some of which have been already suggested, the succeeding section, the avowed purpose of which is to restrain State legislation, contains in terms the very prohibition. It declares that "no State shall pass any bill of attainder or ex post facto law." This provision, then, of the ninth section, however comprehensive its language, contains no restriction on State legislation.

The ninth section having enumerated, in the nature of a bill of rights, the limitations intended to be imposed on the powers of the general government, the tenth proceeds to enumerate those which were to operate on the State legislatures. These restrictions are brought together in the same section, and are by express words applied to the States. "No State shall enter into any treaty," etc. Perceiving that in a Constitution framed by the people of the United States for the government of all, no limitation of the action of government on the people would apply to the State government unless expressed in terms; the restrictions contained in the tenth section are in direct words so applied to the States.

It is worthy of remark, too, that these inhibitions generally restrain State legislation on subjects intrusted to the general government, or in which the people of all the States feel an interest.

A State is forbidden to enter into any treaty, alliance or confederation. If these compacts are with foreign nations, they interfere with the treaty-making power which is conferred entirely on the general government; if with each other, for political purposes, they can scarcely fail to interfere with the general purpose and intent of the Constitution. To grant letters of marque and reprisal would lead directly to war, the power of declaring which is expressly given to Congress. To coin money is also the exercise of a power conferred on Congress. It would be tedious to recapitulate the several limitations on the powers of the States which are contained in this section. They will be found, generally, to restrain State legislation on subjects intrusted to the government of the Union, in which the citizens of all the States are interested. In these alone were the whole people concerned. The question of their application to States is not left to construction. It is averred in positive words.

If the original Constitution, in the ninth and tenth sections of the first article, draws this plain and marked line of discrimination between the limitations it imposes on the powers of the general government and on those of the States; if in every inhibition intended to act on State power, words are employed which directly express that intent, some strong reason must be assigned for departing from this safe and judicious course in framing the amendments, before that departure can be assumed.

We search in vain for that reason.

Had the people of the several States, or any of them, required changes in their constitutions; had they required additional safeguards to liberty from the apprehended encroachments of their particular governments, the remedy was in their own hands, and would have been applied by themselves. A convention would have been assembled by the discontented State, and the required improvements would have been made by itself. The unwieldy and cumbrous machinery of procuring a recommendation from two-thirds of Congress and the assent of three-fourths of their sister States, could never have occurred to any human being as a mode of doing that which might be effected by the State itself. Had the framers of these amendments intended them to be limitations on the powers of the State governments they would have imitated the framers of the original Constitution, and have expressed that intention. Had Congress engaged in the extraordinary occupation of improving the constitutions of the several States by affording the people additional protection from the exercise of power by their own governments in matters which concerned themselves alone, they would have declared this purpose in plain and intelligible language.

But it is universally understood, it is a part of the history of the day, that the great revolution which established the Constitution of the United States was not effected without immense opposition. Serious fears were extensively entertained that those powers which the patriot statesmen who then watched over the interests of our country, deemed essential to union, and to the attainment of those invaluable objects for which union was sought, might be exercised in a manner dangerous to liberty. In almost every convention by which the Constitution was adopted, amendments to guard against the abuse of power were recommended. These amendments demanded security against the apprehended encroachments of the general government—not against those of the local government.

In compliance with a sentiment thus generally expressed, to quiet fears thus extensively entertained, amendments were proposed by the required majority in Congress, and adopted by the States. These amendments contain no expression indicating an intention to apply them to the State governments. This court cannot so apply them.

We are of opinion that the provision in the fifth amendment to the Constitution, declaring that private property shall not be taken for public use without just compensation, is intended solely as a limitation on the exercise of power by the government of the United States, and is not applicable to the legislation of the States. We are therefore of opinion that there is no repugnancy between the several acts of the General Assembly of Maryland, given in evidence by the defendants at the trial of this cause in the court of that State, and the Constitution of the United States.

This court, therefore, has no jurisdiction of the cause, and [it] is dismissed.

THE SLAUGHTER-HOUSE CASES

16 Wallace 36; 21 L. Ed. 394 (1873)

In the years prior to the Civil war the individual relied almost entirely on the constitution of his state for the protection of his rights and liberties. The Supreme Court had ruled in Barron v. Baltimore (1833) that the Bill of Rights limited only the national government, and with the exception of the Alien and Sedition Acts, Congress had passed no law which anyone seriously believed had violated these limitations. The ordinary citizen looked to the state legislature to protect his person and property from private interference, and to the state bill of rights for protection against injury by his state government. Certainly he did not, and could not, expect the national government to step in and protect him either from his neighbor or from his state government.

At the close of the Civil War it seemed clear that without the intervention of the federal government the Southern states would by legislative restrictions strip the newly freed Negro of most of the ordinary rights and immunities of free citizens. To place the civil rights of the Negro upon a firm basis Congress proposed the Fourteenth Amendment authorizing the national government to step in and protect the Negro against actions by his own state government. The states were forbidden to take life, liberty, or property without due process of law, or to deny anyone the equal protection of the laws. The amendment defined United States citizenship in terms which included the Negro, and the states were forbidden to make laws abridging the privileges and immunities of that citizenship.

Exactly what the framers of the amendment intended to include in the phrase "privileges and immunities of citizens of the United States" is not altogether clear, and there is evidence to indicate that it was not clear even to the framers. Some apparently believed that the clause would include within its protection those basic rights enjoyed by all persons—such as the right to marry, to own property, to do business, and to move about freely. Others thought that it would include all or part of the protections listed in the federal Bill of Rights. In the Slaughter-House Cases the Court held that the privileges and immunities clause protected none of these rights, and from this decision the Court has never retreated.

The Slaughter-House Cases were the first cases brought under the Fourteenth Amendment, and they had nothing whatever to do with the rights of freedmen. The case arose on the following facts: The Reconstruction or "carpetbag" government in Louisiana, unquestionably under corrupt influence, had granted a monopoly of the slaughterhouse business to a single concern, thus preventing over one thousand other persons and firms from continuing in that business. The validity of the law was attacked under the Fourteenth Amendment. The case was argued before the Supreme Court twice and was decided by a majority of five to four.

The importance of the case can hardly be overestimated. By distinguishing between state citizenship and national citizenship, and by emphasizing that the rights and privileges of federal citizenship do not include the protection of ordinary civil liberties such as freedom of speech and press, religion, etc., but only the privileges which one enjoys by virtue of his federal citizenship, the Court averted, for the time being at least, the revolution in our constitutional system apparently intended by the framers of the amendment and reserved to the states the responsibility for protecting civil rights generally. Nor has the Court been willing to expand the scope of the privileges and immunities clause beyond this early, limited interpretation. Five years before the Slaughter-House Cases the Supreme Court had held void, in Crandall v. Nevada (1868), a state tax on transporting persons out of the state, on the ground that such a tax would obstruct the citizen in his inherent federal right to come to the seat of his government. Two members of the Court, while concurring in the judgment, held the tax to be a violation of the commerce clause. In his opinion in the Slaughter-House Cases, Justice Miller cites this freedom of movement as an example of the privileges and immunities of United States citizens, and in 1941 in Edwards v. California, four members of the Court strongly urged that the California "anti-Okie" law should be held invalid on this ground. The majority had rested their decision, as had the minority in the Crandall case, upon the commerce power.

The Slaughter-House Cases held that the privileges and immunities of United States citizenship did not include the right to engage in a business of one's choice since such a privilege did not owe its existence to the national Constitution or laws. But it did not deal with the question whether such privileges include the rights listed in the Bill of Rights—rights which were certainly extended by the Constitution to United States citizens. The Court in the case of Maxwell v. Dow (1900), held that they did not, reasoning that such privileges were those enjoyed only by citizens, and since all persons enjoyed the protection of the Bill of Rights, its guarantees could not be considered privileges and immunities of that citizenship.

There have long been judges and legal scholars who have disputed the soundness of this ruling, and who continue to urge that the framers of the Fourteenth Amendment intended that the privileges and immunities of national citizenship should include all of the protections found in the Bill of Rights. In O'Neil v. Vermont (1892) Justices Field and Harlan both argued that the Eighth Amendment protection against cruel and unusual punishments was a privilege of United States citizenship, and in Twining v. New Jersey (1908) Justice Harlan again dissented when the Court held that such privileges did not include the Fifth Amendment's protection against self-incrimination. In 1947 in Adamson v. California, the question was again presented to the Court; and in a five-to-four decision the Twining v. New Jersey decision was reaffirmed. Justice Black, with the concurrence of Justices Douglas, Murphy, and Rutledge, dissented on the ground that Twining v. New Jersey was wrongly decided; in his elaborate opinion Black assembles material to show that the framers of the Fourteenth Amendment intended to make the Bill of Rights in its entirety applicable to the states. Professor Charles Fairman, in a critique of the Adamson case in the *Stanford Law Review,* December 1949, reexamines the historical material and concludes that Justice Black's position is not supported by the available data.

It looked for a time (1935–1940) as though the Court might also broaden the scope and applicability of the privileges and immunities clause of the Fourteenth Amendment.

In Colgate v. Harvey (1935) the Court held void a provision of a Vermont income tax law which taxed income from money loaned outside the state at a higher rate than that loaned inside the state. Besides denying the equal protection of the laws, this act was held to abridge the privileges and immunities of citizens of the United States. The right to carry on business freely across state lines was declared to be a privilege or immunity of federal citizenship, a doctrine sharply differing from the rule of the Slaughter-House Cases. The case was overruled five years later in Madden v. Kentucky (1940), a case involving a similar set of facts, and the Court returned to the time-worn narrow construction of the privileges and immunities clause embodied in the Slaughter-House Cases.

It is not possible to list with certainty the rights protected by the privileges and immunities clause, since, except in Colgate v. Harvey, the Supreme Court has never held the clause to be violated. The Court's interpretation indicates, however, that a privilege or immunity of federal citizenship must meet two tests. First, it must be a right which the federal government itself confers by its Constitution or its laws. Second, as indicated in Maxwell v. Dow, it must be a right which is enjoyed solely because one is a citizen, and is not enjoyed, as a matter of constitutional right, by those who are not citizens. This would include such things as the right to become a citizen of a state (guaranteed by the Fourteenth Amendment itself), the right to settle a homestead on federal land, and the right to take a United States Civil Service examination. It also includes the right to vote in a federal election, which owes its existence to the federal government (see Ex parte Yarbrough, 1884), although the states under their authority to establish suffrage qualifications could extend the right to aliens, and in the past have done so. The federal voter must meet, however, the valid voting qualifications of the state.

Mr. Justice Miller delivered the opinion of the Court, saying in part:

The plaintiffs in error accepting this issue, allege that the statute is a violation of the Constitution of the United States in these several particulars:

That it creates an involuntary servitude forbidden by the 13th article of amendment;

That it abridges the privileges and immunities of citizens of the United States;

That it denies to the plaintiffs the equal protection of the laws; and,

That it deprives them of their property without due process of law; contrary to the provisions of the 1st section of the 14th article of amendment.

This court is thus called upon for the first time to give construction to these articles. . . .

Twelve articles of amendment were added to the Federal Constitution soon after the original organization of the government under it in 1789. Of these all but the last were adopted so soon afterwards as to justify the statement that they were practically contemporaneous with the adoption of the original; and the twelfth, adopted in eighteen hundred and three, was so nearly so as to have become, like the others, historical and of another age. But within the last eight years three other articles of amendment of vast importance have been added, by the voice of the people, to that now venerable instrument.

The most cursory glance at these articles discloses a unity of purpose, when taken in connection with the history of the times, which cannot fail to have an important bearing on any question of doubt concerning their true meaning. . . . Fortunately that history is fresh within the memory of us all, and its leading features, as they bear upon the matter before us, free from doubt. . . . [Here follows a discussion of the Thirteenth and Fifteenth Amendments.]

The 1st section of the 14th article, to which our attention is more specially invited, opens with a definition of citizenship—not only citizenship of the United States, but citizenship of the states. No such definition was previously found in the Constitution, nor had any attempt been made to define it by act of Congress. It had been the occasion of much discussion in the courts, by the executive departments and in the public journals. It had been said by eminent judges that no man was a citizen of the United States except as he was a citizen of one of the states composing the Union. Those, therefore, who had been born and resided always in the District of Columbia or in the territories, though within the United States, were not citizens. Whether this proposition was sound or not had never been judicially decided. But it had been held by this court, in the celebrated Dred Scott Case, only a few years before the outbreak of the Civil War, that a man of African descent, whether a slave or not, was not and could not be a citizen of a state or of the United States. This decision, while it met the condemnation of some of the ablest statesmen and constitutional lawyers of the country, had never been overruled; and, if it was to be accepted as a constitutional limitation of the right of citizenship, then all the negro race who had recently been made freemen were still, not only not citizens, but were incapable of becoming so by anything short of an amendment to the Constitution.

To remove this difficulty primarily, and to establish a clear and comprehensive definition of citizenship which should declare what should constitute citizenship of the United States and also citizenship of a state, the 1st clause of the 1st section was framed:

"All persons born or naturalized in the United States and subject to the jurisdiction thereof are citizens of the United States and of the state wherein they reside."

The first observation we have to make on this clause is that it puts at rest both the questions which we stated to have been the subject of differences of opinion. It declares that persons may be citizens of the United States without regard to their citizenship of a particular state, and it overturns the Dred Scott decision by making all persons born within the United States and subject to its jurisdiction citizens of the United States. That its main purpose was to establish the citizenship of the negro can admit of no doubt. The phrase "subject to its jurisdiction" was intended to exclude from its operation children of ministers, consuls and citizens or subjects of foreign states born within the United States.

The next observation is more important in view of the arguments of counsel in the present case. It is that the distinction between citizenship of the United States and citizenship of a state is clearly recognized and established. Not only may a man be a citizen of the United States without being a citizen of a state, but an important element is necessary to convert the former into the latter. He must reside within the state to make him a citizen of it, but it is only necessary that he should be born or naturalized in the United States to be a citizen of the Union.

It is quite clear, then, that there is a citizenship of the United States and a citizenship of a state, which are distinct from each other and which depend upon different characteristics or circumstances in the individual.

We think this distinction and its explicit recognition in this Amendment of great weight in this argument, because the next paragraph of this same section, which is the one mainly relied on by the plaintiffs in error, speaks only of privileges and immunities of citizens of the United States, and does not speak of those of citizens of the several states. The argument, however, in favor of the plaintiffs, rests wholly on the assumption that the citizenship is the same and the privileges and immunities guaranteed by the clause are the same.

The language is: "No state shall make or enforce any law which shall abridge the privileges or immunities of citizens of the United States." It is a little remarkable, if this clause was intended as a protection to the citizen of a state against the legislative power of his own state, that the words "citizen of the state" should be left out when it is so carefully used, and used in contradistinction to "citizens of the United States" in the very sentence which precedes it. It is too clear for argument that the change in phraseology was adopted understandingly and with a purpose.

Of the privileges and immunities of the citizens of the United States, and of the privileges and immunities of the citizen of the state, and what they respectively are, we will presently consider; but we wish to state here that it is only the former which are placed by this clause under the protection of the Federal Constitution, and that the latter, whatever they may be, are not intended to have any additional protection by this paragraph of Amendment.

If, then, there is a difference between the privileges and immunities belonging to a citizen of the United States as such, and those belonging to the citizen of the state as such, the latter must rest for their security and protection where they have heretofore rested; for they are not embraced by this paragraph of the Amendment.

The first occurence of the words "privilege and immunities" in our constitutional history is to be found in the fourth of the Articles of the old Confederation.

It declares "That, the better to secure and perpetuate mutual friendship and intercourse among the people of the different states in this Union, the free inhabitants of each of these states, paupers, vagabonds, and fugitives from justice excepted, shall be entitled to all the privileges and immunities of free citizens in the several states; and the people of each state shall have free ingress and regress to and from any other state, and shall enjoy therein all the privileges of trade and commerce, subject to the same duties, impositions, and restrictions as the inhabitants thereof respectively."

In the Constitution of the United States, which superseded the Articles of Confederation, the corresponding provision is found in section two of the

4th article, in the following words: The citizens of each state shall be entitled to all the privileges and immunities of citizens of the several states.

There can be but little question that the purpose of both these provisions is the same, and that the privileges and immunities intended are the same in each. In the Article[s] of the Confederation we have some of these specifically mentioned, and enough perhaps to give some general idea of the class of civil rights meant by the phrase.

Fortunately we are not without judicial construction of this clause of the Constitution. The first and the leading case on the subject is that of Corfield v. Coryell, decided by Mr. Justice Washington in the circuit court for the district of Pennsylvania in 1823.

"The inquiry," he says, "is, what are the privileges and immunities of citizens of the several states? We feel no hesitation in confining these expressions to those privileges and immunities which are fundamental; which belong of right to the citizens of all free governments, and which have at all times been enjoyed by citizens of the several states which compose this Union, from the time of their becoming free, independent, and sovereign. What these fundamental principles are, it would be more tedious than difficult to enumerate." "They may all, however, be comprehended under the following general heads: protection by the government, with the right to acquire and possess property of every kind, and to pursue and obtain happiness and safety, subject, nevertheless, to such restraints as the government may prescribe for the general good of the whole."

This definition of the privileges and immunities of citizens of the states is adopted in the main by this court in the recent case of Ward v. Maryland [1871], while it declines to undertake an authoritative definition beyond what was necessary to that decision. The description, when taken to include others not named, but which are of the same general character, embraces nearly every civil right for the establishment and protection of which organized government is instituted. They are, in the language of Judge Washington, those rights which are fundamental. Throughout his opinion, they are spoken of as rights belonging to the individual as a citizen of a state. They are so spoken of in the constitutional provision which he was construing. And they have always been held to be the class of rights which the state governments were created to establish and secure. . . .

The constitutional provision there alluded to did not create those rights, which it called privileges and immunities of citizens of the states. It threw around them in that clause no security for the citizen of the state in which they were claimed or exercised. Nor did it profess to control the power of the state governments over the rights of its own citizens.

Its sole purpose was to declare to the several states, that whatever those rights, as you grant or establish them to your own citizens, or as you limit or qualify, or impose restrictions on their exercise, the same, neither more nor less, shall be the measure of the rights of citizens of other states within your jurisdiction.

It would be the vainest show of learning to attempt to prove by citations of authority, that up to the adoption of the recent Amendments, no claim or pretense was set up that those rights depended on the Federal government for their existence or protection, beyond the very few express limitations which the Federal Constitution imposed upon the states—such, for instance, as the prohibition against ex post facto laws, bills of attainder, and laws impairing the obligation of contracts. But with the exception of these and a few other restrictions, the entire domain of the privileges and immunities of citizens of the states, as above defined, lay within the constitutional and legislative power of the states, and without that of the Federal government. Was it the purpose of the 14th Amendment, by the simple declaration that no state should make or enforce any law which shall abridge the privileges and immunities of citizens of the United States, to transfer the security and protection of all the civil rights which we have mentioned, from the states to the Federal government? And where it is declared that Congress shall have the power to enforce that article, was it intended to bring within the power of Congress the entire domain of civil rights heretofore belonging exclusively to states?

All this and more must follow, if the proposition of the plaintiffs in error be sound. For not only are these rights subject to the control of Congress whenever in its discretion any of them are supposed to be abridged by state legislation, but that body may also pass laws in advance, limiting and restricting the exercise of legislative power by the states, in their most ordinary and usual functions, as in its judgment it may think proper on all such subjects. And still further, such a construction followed by the reversal of the judgments of the supreme court of Louisiana in these cases would constitute this court a perpetual censor upon all legislation of the states, on the civil rights of their own citizens, with authority to nullify such as it did not approve as consistent with those rights, as they existed at the time of the adoption of this Amendment. The argument, we admit, is not always the most conclusive which is drawn from the consequences urged against the adoption of a particular construction of an instrument. But when, as in the case before us, these consequences are so serious, so far reaching and pervading, so great a departure from the structure and spirit of our institutions; when the effect is to fetter and degrade the state governments by subjecting them to the control of Congress, in the exercise of powers heretofore universally conceded to them of the most ordinary and fundamental character; when in fact it radically changes the whole theory of the relations of the state and Federal governments to each other and of both these governments to the people; the argument has a force that is irresistible, in the absence of language which expresses such a purpose too clearly to admit of doubt.

We are convinced that no such results were intended by the Congress which proposed these amendments, nor by the legislatures of the states, which ratified them.

Having shown that the privileges and immunities relied on in the argument are those which belong to citizens of the states as such, and that they are left to the state governments for security and protection, and not by this article placed under the special care of the Federal government, we may hold ourselves excused from defining the privileges and immunities of citizens of the United States which no state can abridge, until some case involving those privileges may make it necessary to do so.

But lest it should be said that no such privileges and immunities are to be found if those we have been considering are excluded, we venture to suggest some which owe their existence to the Federal government, its national character, its Constitution, or its laws.

One of these is well described in the case of Crandall v. Nevada [1868]. It is said to be the right of the citizen of this great country, protected by implied guarantees of its Constitution, "to come to the seat of government to assert any claim he may have upon that government, to transact any business he may have with it, to seek its protection, to share its offices, to engage in administering its functions. He has the right of free access to its seaports, through which all operations of foreign commerce are conducted, to the subtreasuries, land-offices, and courts of justice in the several states." . . .

Another privilege of a citizen of the United States is to demand the care and protection of the Federal government over his life, liberty, and property when on the high seas or within the jurisdiction of a foreign government. Of this there can be no doubt, nor that the right depends upon his character as a citizen of the United States. The right to peaceably assemble and petition for redress of grievances, the privilege of the writ of habeas corpus, are rights of the citizen guaranteed by the Federal Constitution. The right to use the navigable waters of the United States, however they may penetrate the territory of the several states, and all rights secured to our citizens by treaties with foreign nations, are dependent upon citizenship of the United States, and not citizenship of a state. One of these privileges is conferred by the very article under consideration. It is that a citizen of the United States can, of his own volition, become a citizen of any state of the Union by a bona fide residence therein, with the same rights as other citizens of that state. To these may be added the rights secured by the 13th and 15th articles of Amendment, and by the other clause of the Fourteenth, next to be considered.

But it is useless to pursue this branch of the inquiry, since we are of opinion that the rights claimed by these plaintiffs in error, if they have any existence, are not privileges and immunities of citizens of the United States within the meaning of the clause of the 14th Amendment under consideration.

"All persons born or naturalized in the United States, and subject to the jurisdiction thereof, are citizens of the United States and of the state, wherein they reside. No state shall make or enforce any law which shall abridge the privileges or immunities of citizens of the United States; nor shall any state deprive any person of life, liberty or property without due process of law, nor deny to any person within its jurisdiction the equal protection of its laws."

The argument has not been much pressed in these cases that the defendant's charter deprives the plaintiffs of their property without due process of law, or that it denies to them the equal protection of the law. The first of these paragraphs has been in the Constitution since the adoption of the 5th

Amendment, as a restraint upon the Federal power. It is also to be found in some form of expression in the constitutions of nearly all the states, as a restraint upon the power of the states. This law, then, has practically been the same as it now is during the existence of the government, except so far as the present Amendment may place the restraining power over the states in this matter in the hands of the Federal government.

We are not without judicial interpretation, therefore, both state and national, of the meaning of this clause. And it is sufficient to say that under no construction of that provision that we have ever seen, or any that we deem admissible, can the restraint imposed by the state of Louisiana upon the exercise of their trade by the butchers of New Orleans be held to be a deprivation of property within the meaning of that provision.

"Nor shall any state deny to any person within its jurisdiction the equal protection of the laws."

In the light of the history of these amendments, and the pervading purpose of them, which we have already discussed, it is not difficult to give a meaning to this clause. The existence of laws in the states where the newly emancipated negroes resided, which discriminated with gross injustice and hardship against them as a class, was the evil to be remedied by this clause, and by it such laws are forbidden.

If, however, the states did not conform their laws to its requirements, then by the 5th section of the article of amendment Congress was authorized to enforce it by suitable legislation. We doubt very much whether any action of a state not directed by way of discrimination against the negroes as a class, or on account of their race, will ever be held to come within the purview of this provision. It is so clearly a provision for that race and that emergency, that a strong case would be necessary for its application to any other. But as it is a state that is to be dealt with, and not alone the validity of its laws, we may safely leave that matter until Congress shall have exercised its power, or some case of state oppression, by denial of equal justice in its courts, shall have claimed a decision at our hands. We find no such case in the one before us, and we do not deem it necessary to go over the argument again, as it may have relation to this particular clause of the Amendment. . . .

The judgments of the Supreme Court of Louisiana in these cases are affirmed.

Mr. Justice Field, with whom Mr. Chief Justice Chase, Mr. Justice Swayne, and Mr. Justice Bradley concurred, dissented, saying in part:

The Amendment does not attempt to confer any new privileges or immunities upon citizens or to enumerate or define those already existing. It assumes that there are such privileges and immunities which belong of right to citizens as such, and ordains that they shall not be abridged by state legislation. If this inhibition has no reference to privileges and immunities of this character, but only refers, as held by the majority of the court in their opinion, to such privileges and immunities as were before its adoption specially designated in the Constitution or necessarily implied as belonging to citizens of the United States, it was a vain and idle enactment, which accomplished nothing, and most unnecessarily excited Congress and the people on its passage. With privileges and immunities thus designated no state could ever have interfered by its laws, and no new constitutional provision was required to inhibit such interference. The supremacy of the Constitution and the laws of the United States always controlled any state legislation of that character. But if the Amendment refers to the natural and inalienable rights which belong to all citizens, the inhibition has a profound significance and consequence. . . .

Mr. Justice Swayne and Mr. Justice Bradley filed separate dissenting opinions.

LOCHNER v. NEW YORK

198 U. S. 45; 25 S. Ct. 539; 49 L. Ed. 937 (1905)

At the time the Fourteenth Amendment was adopted the due process clause of the Fifth Amendment had been in effect against the federal government for three-quarters of a century. During that entire period the Supreme Court had decided only four or five cases interpreting the clause, but from Coke and Blackstone the ancient lineage and narrow meaning of the clause were abundantly clear. The clause traces its beginning to the guarantee embodied in Magna Charta that "no freeman shall be taken or imprisoned or deprived of his freehold or his liberties or free customs, or outlawed or exiled, or in any manner destroyed, nor shall we come upon him or send against him, except by a legal judgment of his peers or by the law of the land." With the reaffirmation of these guarantees in the Statute of Westminster (1354) Ed. III, "per legem terrae" became "due process of the law," although at the time of the adoption of the Bill of Rights the eight state constitutions providing such protection used the term "law of the land." Whichever words were used, the guarantee involved was the same: The government was forbidden to limit in any way the individual's personal or property rights unless it did so through proper procedures. In short, it was a check not on what the government could do but on the process it had to follow in order to do it.

This "procedural" due process was the only kind of due process there was until after the middle of the nineteenth century, when pressure from important property interests for a "substantive" content to the due process clause began to make itself felt. Among the leading purposes for which the United States Constitution had been framed was the protection of private property from the irresponsible attacks of the "too popular" state governments. Hence those with vested property rights looked from the beginning to the judicially enforceable Constitution to protect them from legislation, particularly state legislation. They turned first to the protection against bills of attainder and ex post facto laws, but in Calder v. Bull (1798) the Supreme Court held that the ex post facto clause applied only to criminal legislation. Better luck was had with the contract clause, and in such cases as Fletcher v. Peck (1810) and the Dartmouth College Case (1819) the Court held that a vested right implied a contract not to divest it or interfere with its exercise. But with the passing of Chief Justice Marshall the strength of even this doctrine began to wane. In Charles River Bridge v. Warren Bridge (1837) the Court under Taney made clear that henceforth contracts would be strictly construed in favor of the people and against the vested interests; and much later, in

Stone v. Mississippi (1880), the Court held that the police power to legislate in the public interest could not be limited by the contract clause.

So it was natural that pressure should mount to persuade the courts that the guarantee of due process of law should provide constitutional protection to the vested interests. In 1856 in Wynhammer v. New York a state court finally struck down a provision of a state prohibition statute as a denial of due process of law because the law provided for the confiscation of stocks of liquor in possession when the law took effect. The court's basic premise was that liquor was property which could not be transformed into a nuisance merely by the whim of the legislature; hence a statute providing for its confiscation was void, even though the procedures by which the confiscation took place followed "the forms which belong to due process of law." The court said, "The act . . . itself pronounces the sentence of condemnation, and the judicial machinery, such as it is, which it provides are agencies merely to insure the execution of the sentence."

This theory that the substance of a law itself could be held void for want of due process made its way slowly into the Supreme Court. In 1857, Chief Justice Taney in the Dred Scott case, after holding the Missouri Compromise Act void on a number of grounds, added that "an act of Congress which deprives a citizen of the United States of his liberty or property merely because he came himself or brought his property into a particular territory of the United States and who had committed no offense against the laws could hardly be dignified with the name of due process of law." But the Court was not yet ready to receive the doctrine. Justice Miller rejected it in the Slaughter-House Cases (1873); and in 1875 in Loan Association v. Topeka, the Court, completely ignoring the due process clause, held bad the expenditure of public money for a private purpose on the ground that this was a violation of those limits on governmental power "which grow out of the essential nature of all free governments; implied reservations of individual rights, without which the social compact could not exist. . . ." Again in 1878 in Davidson v. New Orleans, the Court made clear its attitude toward due process, going so far as to scold the bar for pressing upon them this new concept of due process. "There is here abundant evidence that there exists some strange misconception of the scope of this provision as found in the Fourteenth Amendment. In fact, it would seem, from the character of many of the cases before us, and the arguments made in them, that the clause under consideration is looked upon as a means of bringing to the test of the decision of this court the abstract opinions of every unsuccessful litigant in a State court of the justice of the decision against him, and of the merits of the legislation on which such a decision may be founded."

In 1877 there came before the Supreme Court a group of cases known as the "Granger Cases," in which the Court faced for the first time the right of a state legislature to regulate private business. The close of the Civil War ushered in a period of rapid railroad expansion. In the East, where industrial development tended to keep pace with the multiplication of transportation facilities, railroad building proved satisfactorily profitable. In the West, however, where new country was being opened up and population was sparse, the railroads had difficulty in paying dividends and frequently yielded to the temptation to indulge in stock-watering, questionable manipulation of credits, and doubtful practices in respect to grants of lands; to rebating and discrimination; and to other objectionable practices. Pitted against the desperate efforts of the railroads to make profits was the Western farmer, who wished to enjoy adequate railraod facilities at reasonable rates in order to facilitate the movement of crops in sparsely settled communities and who resented the unfair or dishonest methods of which some of the roads were known to be guilty. Out of this conflict of interests grew the Granger Movement, an organized effort on the part of the Western farmers which finally culminated in state legislation designed to cure the worst abuses. Starting in

Illinois in 1871, the movement spread to other states; and soon railroads and warehousemen in Minnesota, Iowa, and Wisconsin found themselves subject to severe regulation with respect to rates and services. It was these laws which were challenged in the Granger Cases.

The first of these cases, Munn v. Illinois (1877), did not relate to railroad rate legislation but dealt rather with the question of the validity of an Illinois statute providing for the fixing of maximum charges for the storage of grain, in Chicago and other places having not less than one hundred thousand population, in warehouses "in which grain is stored in bulk, and in which the grain of different owners is mixed together, or in which grain is stored in such a manner that the identity of different lots or parcels cannot be accurately preserved." Here, as in the Slaughter-House Cases, an attempt was made to convince the Court that the legislation in question was in violation of the Fourteenth Amendment. It was urged that it involved a deprivation of property without due process of law and a denial of the equal protection of the laws. The Court again rejected the substantive due process argument, at least as applied to the regulatory measure before it. It held that terminal grain elevators were businesses sufficiently affected with a public interest to enable the legislature to regulate the charges which they made. It then went on to point out that the Fourteenth Amendment provided no restriction upon burdensome or confiscatory rates; in cases where the legislature could regulate rates at all the degree of regulation was a matter of legislative discretion, and "for protection against abuses by legislatures the people must resort to the polls, not to the courts."

The acceptance by the Supreme Court of this "substantive" due process, in addition to the earlier exclusively "procedural" due process, took place gradually over a period of nearly 20 years as cases involving the validity of state laws came before it. The change came first in the area of rate controls. Within a decade after the Munn case the Court started to backtrack from Chief Justice Waite's dictum in that case—that the only appeal from an unjust rate was to elect a new legislature to enact a just one. In the Railroad Commission Cases (Stone v. Farmers' Loan & Trust Co., 1886) the Court, while confirming the legislature's power to regulate rates, added that "this power to regulate is not a power to destroy, and limitation is not the equivalent of confiscation. Under pretense of regulating fares and freights, the State cannot require a railroad corporation to carry persons or property without reward; neither can it do that which in law amounts to taking of private property for public use without just compensation, or without due process of law." Thus the legislature is apparently forbidden by due process to enact a regulatory measure which in substance is unreasonable. In Chicago, M & St. P. R. Co. v. Minnesota (1890), the Court, abandoning the dictum of the Munn case, held that only by providing judicial review of the reasonableness of a rate, in contrast to an appeal to the legislature, could the requirement of due process of law be met.

For over 40 years the Supreme Court supervised with jealous care the rate regulation, whether by regulatory commission or by the legislature itself, of the nation's public utilities. Any rate which did not produce a fair return on a fair evaluation of the property was a denial of due process of law, and both the evaluation and the fairness of the return were subject, ultimately, to judicial review. It was not until 1944 in Federal Power Commission v. Hope Natural Gas Co. that the Court, noting that the value of a company depends on the rates it is allowed to charge, indicated that henceforth it would look to the overall reasonableness of the rate in terms of its general effect on the business, and leave to the proper agency the method by which the rate was to be set.

In Munn v. Illinois and the cases which followed it, the Court established the doctrine that the government could regulate prices and control terms of service (within limits) only of businesses which were "affected with a public interest." To impose these regulations upon a business not affected with a public interest was to deprive it of its liberty and property without due process of law. This doctrine seemed fair on its face and comported with the tradition of American individualism. But what is a business "affected with a public interest"? The Court found it difficult to answer this question because as cases involving it arose, it became obvious that there was no single characteristic by which a business so affected with a public interest could invariably be identified. Furthermore, even those businesses so affected could not necessarily be regulated in their entirety, but only in those aspects demanded by the need to protect the public interest. Thus, in the years in which the Court applied this elusive and difficult doctrine, it held void efforts to control wages in the meat packing business, the resale price of theater tickets, the price of gasoline, the rates charged by an employment agency, and the licensing of ice dealers. When, during the financial depression of the 1930s, New York undertook to improve the lot of the dairy industry by setting a minimum price for milk, it was generally expected the Court would hold the price-fixing statute void. By none of the definitions in use could the milk industry be described as "affected with a public interest." and hence subject to price controls.

In Nebbia v. New York (1934), the Court held the New York statute valid. "The phrase 'affected with a public interest' can," said the Court, "in the nature of things, mean no more than that an industry, for adequate reason, is subject to control for the public good." Many facets of the milk industry were already subject to state regulation, and the Court saw no reason why prices should be "peculiarly sacrosanct." "So far as the requirement of due process is concerned, and in the absence of other constitutional restriction, a state is free to adopt whatever economic policy may reasonably be deemed to promote public welfare, and to enforce that policy by legislation adapted to its purpose. The courts are without authority either to declare such policy, or, when it is declared by the legislature, to override it. . . ."

What persuaded the Supreme Court, toward the end of the nineteenth century, to assert a supervisory power over the substance of state legislation which they had so carefully rejected in the Slaughter-House Cases is not difficult to surmise. During the two decades involved, the entire personnel of the Court, with the exception of Justice Field, had changed; and Field, who had dissented in the Slaughter-House Cases, had always been an apostle of the new faith. The new members coming on the Court tended to reflect the social and economic pressures of the post-Civil War period: the tremendous expansion of the railroads and industry, the brawling struggle between management and labor with the growth of the trade union movement, and the increasing use of political power by the workingman to secure the enactment of protective labor legislation. Naturally, organized industry looked upon legislative efforts to ameliorate factory conditions and hours of labor as intolerable interferences with the employer's private affairs and a deprivation of his liberty and property. A generation of judges steeped in the individualism of the common law tended to share this view. Due process of law came to seem the completely appropriate and adequate constitutional weapon with which to combat the onward march of the new social control—the new police power.

This individualistic interpretation by the courts of due process of law found finally a definite basis in the development during the 1880s of the doctrine of "liberty of contract." The first case turning upon this doctrine was decided by the supreme court of Pennsylvania in 1886, Godcharles v. Wigeman, but the theory was ultimately incorporated into the doctrine of due process of law as applied by both state and federal courts. The concept of "liberty of contract" was both plausible and alluring. It asserted in substance that when two parties, neither of whom was under any legal disability, came together to make a contract which was not contrary to public policy, the legislature had no right to interfere and dictate the terms of the agreement. The application of this doctrine to the problem of protective labor legislation produced, however, some very startling results, due in large measure to the naïve assumption by the courts that the individual employee of a great industrial corporation possessed full liberty of contract and could dicker with his employer upon equal terms. Naturally, as time went on the courts found frequently that this vaunted liberty of contract was infringed by the laws regulating hours of labor, method and time of wage payment, employer's liability, factory conditions, and similar matters.

Sir Henry Maine's statement that "the movement of the progressive societies has hitherto been a movement from status to contract" marked this as a liberal doctrine which emancipated the individual, especially the laborer, from governmental controls and allowed him to bargain freely about his affairs. Hence it was only natural that it should receive a preferred place in the constitutional scheme. The normal presumption that a state statute is constitutional gradually gave way, and the burden of proof was placed upon those who would sustain a law alleged to limit such liberty of contract. The Court's insistence in Mugler v. Kansas (1887) that a state statute purporting to protect the public health, safety, and morals must bear a "real or substantial relation to those objects" meant that the Court had to be shown that such was the case before the act could be upheld.

The difficulty came in showing that such a relationship did in fact exist. In the Mugler case the Court had taken judicial notice of the evils of drink and had upheld the validity of a state prohibition statute; but the judges themselves had no knowledge of the social and economic conditions which led to the passage of laws regulating the hours of labor and working conditions. Nor was the bar, if it had such knowledge, in a position to transmit it to the bench, since the traditional method of arguing cases was to cite case precedents and attempt to show by rational analysis how the case at bar was similar. Thus the protagonists of protective labor laws found themselves with a strong presumption against the validity of the laws and no effective way to rebut the presumption.

If the burden of proof on those defending labor and social welfare legislation was unusually heavy, it was ultimately assumed in a novel and telling way. When Muller v. Oregon (1908), involving the validity of the Oregon ten-hour law for women, was argued in the Supreme Court, the justices had before them the first of the famous "Brandeis briefs." This brief, prepared by Louis D. Brandeis (later Justice Brandeis) set out very little in the way of strictly legal argument, but at great length presented documentary evidence of the social and economic facts and conditions which had led the legislature to pass the law. The Court was impressed, and while insisting that constitutional questions "are not settled by even a consensus of present public opinion . . .," held that "at the same time, when a question of fact is debated and debatable, and the extent to which a special constitutional limitation goes is affected by the truth in respect to that fact, a widespread and long continued belief concerning it is worthy of consideration. We take judicial cognizance of all matters of general knowledge." The Court unanimously sustained the act.

A second break in the doctrine of the Lochner case came in 1917 in the case of Bunting v. Oregon, a case involving an Oregon statute providing a ten-hour day for all industrial workers. In a five-to-three decision the Court sustained the act and in doing so made it plain that the burden of proof had shifted to those who attacked its validity. "But we need not cast about for reasons for the legislative judgment. We are not required to be sure of the precise reasons for its exercise, or be convinced of the wisdom of its exercise. . . . It is enough for our decision if the legislation under review was passed in the exercise of an admitted power of government . . . . There is a contention made that the law . . . is not either necessary or useful 'for preservation of the health of employees . . . .' The record contains no facts to support the contention, and against it is the judgment of the legislature and the supreme court . . . ." The same day the Court divided four to four to sustain the Oregon minimum wage law in Stettler

v. O'Hara (1917). Justice Brandeis took no part in the decision of either of these cases. He had been counsel in the cases in the beginning, and with his appointment to the Supreme Court his place on the briefs had been taken by Felix Frankfurter, a professor in the Harvard Law School.

While the Court decided the Bunting case without any mention of the Lochner decision, it was widely assumed that the Lochner doctrine had been permanently abandoned. But in 1922 George Sutherland and Pierce Butler were appointed to the Court, and the following year the minimum wage statute of the District of Columbia was held void as a denial of due process of law. This was the case of Adkins v. Children's Hospital (1923). The Court divided five to three. Again Justice Brandeis did not sit, this time because his daughter was a member of the minimum wage commission. The majority opinion of Justice Sutherland reads like the opinion of the Court in the Lochner case, from which it quotes at length with approval. It held that there is no such connection between the wages women receive and their health, morals, or welfare as to justify destroying by law the freedom of contract of employers and the women who work for them. Furthermore, the Court said, the act does not guarantee that the minimum wage fixed shall not exceed the fair value of the service for which it is paid. Thus the Court returned to the old presumption of the invalidity of the statute and announced that while the materials in Professor Frankfurter's brief were useful enough to the legislature in passing the law, "they reflect no legitimate light upon the question of its validity." In 1925 and in 1927 the Court without opinion ruled that the Adkins case rendered invalid the state minimum wage laws of Arizona and Arkansas respectively.

In 1933 New York passed a minimum wage law for women and children. Its framers sought to escape the ban of the Adkins decision by providing that the wages fixed should be based on the fair value of the labor paid for. The attempt failed. In Morehead v. New York ex rel. Tipaldo (1936) the Supreme Court in a five-to-four decision held the New York statute invalid. In the majority opinion, Justice Butler stated that the statute was like the one held void in the Adkins case, but further said in substance that any minimum wage law, regardless of its provisions, would be invalid as a denial of due process of law. In a dissenting opinion Justice Stone observed: "It is difficult to imagine any grounds, other than our own personal economic predilections, for saying that the contract of employment is any the less an appropriate subject of legislation than are scores of others, in dealing with which this Court has held that legislatures may curtail individual freedom in the public interest."

Public disenchantment with the Tipaldo decision was almost universal. Even the Republican Party repudiated it as it organized for the 1936 presidential campaign, and President Roosevelt, following his overwhelming reelection that November, immediately began laying plans for an attack on a Supreme Court he was convinced would ultimately strike down his entire New Deal program. On February 5, with his national prestige at an all-time high, he sent to Congress his ill-fated court-packing plan calling for the addition of a new justice to the Court for every justice over the age of 70 (of which there were six). While it presented no technical constitutional problems, since Congress sets the size of the Supreme Court, it aroused almost as much public antagonism as had the Tipaldo decision before it. A public which badly wanted New Deal legislation declared constitutional was clearly unprepared to sacrifice the independence of the Supreme Court to get it.

During all this time a Washington minimum wage statute passed in 1913 had been in force, and the case of West Coast Hotel Co. v. Parrish challenging its validity was on the docket at the time the Tipaldo case was decided. At the opening of the new term in October, 1936, the Court refused to rehear the Tipaldo case, and the West Coast Hotel case was argued in December. On March 29, 1937, with the court-packing battle in full swing, Justice Roberts switched his vote: The Court overruled Adkins and Tipaldo and sustained the Washington statute. Justices Sutherland, Van Devanter, McReynolds, and Butler dissented. To the chant of "a switch in time saves nine," the country watched with relief as one New Deal statute after another was held valid. The Supreme Court, in a philosophical about-face, had returned to the political branches of government the power to regulate the nation's economy.

The Lochner case is presented here because it is, in a sense, a museum piece. The archaic opinion of Justice Peckham for the majority expresses with accuracy the dominant judicial doctrine of that period, with its reliance upon the concept of "liberty of contract," a doctrine which was widely believed to be essential to stability and good order in our economic and social life. The classic dissenting opinion of Justice Holmes, however, laid down the challenge which was to revolutionize judicial thinking with respect to the state's power to legislate in behalf of the economic and social welfare of its citizens.

Lochner was convicted of violating a New York statute called the Labor Law, which provided that no employee should be "required or permitted to work in a biscuit, bread or cake bakery, or confectionery establishment more than sixty hours in any one week, or more than ten hours in any one day unless for the purpose of making a shorter day on the last day of the week." The legislature had proceeded upon the assumption that the conditions in the baking industry were such as to demand the intervention of the state in behalf of the employees. The majority of the Supreme Court did not agree that such protection was reasonably necessary and accordingly held that there was no adequate justification for this infringement of the private rights of the employer. Four justices dissented on the ground that there was sufficient support for the view of the legislature to make it a debatable question whether the law was arbitrary or not and that when such was the case, the courts should not override the legislative judgment. The dissenting opinion of Justice Holmes has become almost a classic as a statement of the more liberal judicial attitude toward the question of the validity of social and economic legislation under the Fourteenth Amendment.

Mr. Justice Peckham delivered the opinion of the Court, saying in part:

The statute necessarily interferes with the right of contract between the employer and employees, concerning the number of hours in which the latter may labor in the bakery of the employer. The general right to make a contract in relation to his business is part of the liberty of the individual protected by the 14th Amendment of the Federal Constitution. . . . Under that provision no state can deprive any person of life, liberty, or property without due process of law. The right to purchase or to sell labor is part of the liberty protected by this amendment, unless there are circumstances which exclude the right. There are, however, certain powers, existing in the sovereignty of each state in the Union, somewhat vaguely termed police powers, the exact description and limitation of which have not been attempted by the courts. Those powers, broadly stated, and without, at present, any attempt at a more specific limitation, relate to the safety, health, morals, and general welfare of the public. Both property and liberty are held on such reasonable conditions as may be imposed by the governing power of the state in the exercise of those powers, and with such conditions the 14th Amendment was not designed to interfere. . . .

The state, therefore, has power to prevent the individual from making certain kinds of contracts, and in regard to them the Federal Constitution offers no protection. If the contract be one which the state, in the legitimate exercise of its police power, has the right to prohibit, it is not prevented from prohibiting it by the 14th Amendment. Contracts in violation of a statute, either of the Federal or state government, or a contract to let one's property for immoral purposes, or to do any other unlawful act, could obtain no protection from the Federal Constitution, as coming under the liberty of person or of free contract. Therefore, when the state, by its legislature, in the assumed exercise of its police powers, has passed an act which seriously limits the right to labor or the right of contract in regard to their means of livelihood between persons who are sui juris (both employer and employee), it becomes of great importance to determine which shall prevail,—the right of the individual to labor for such time as he may choose, or the right of the state to prevent the individual from laboring, or from entering into any contract to labor, beyond a certain time prescribed by the state. . . .

It must, of course, be conceded that there is a limit to the valid exercise of the police power by the state. There is no dispute concerning this general proposition. Otherwise the 14th Amendment would have no efficacy and the legislatures of the states would have unbounded power, and it would be enough to say that any piece of legislation was enacted to conserve the morals, the health, or the safety of the people; such legislation would be valid, no matter how absolutely without foundation the claim might be. The claim of the police power would be a mere pretext,—become another and delusive name for the supreme sovereignty of the state to be exercised free from constitutional restraint. This is not contended for. In every case that comes before this court, therefore, where legislation of this character is concerned, and where the protection of the Federal Constitution is sought, the question necessarily arises: Is this a fair, reasonable, and appropriate exercise of the police power of the state, or is it an unreasonable, unnecessary, and arbitrary interference with the right of the individual to his personal liberty, or to enter into those contracts in relation to labor which may seem to him appropriate or necessary for the support of himself and his family? Of course the liberty of contract relating to labor includes both parties to it. The one has as much right to purchase as the other to sell labor.

This is not a question of substituting the judgment of the court for that of the legislature. If the act be within the power of the state it is valid, although the judgment of the court might be totally opposed to the enactment of such a law. But the question would still remain: Is it within the police power of the state? and that question must be answered by the court.

The question whether this act is valid as a labor law, pure and simple, may be dismissed in a few words. There is no reasonable ground for interfering with the liberty of person or the right of free contract, by determining the hours of labor, in the occupation of a baker. There is no contention that bakers as a class are not equal in intelligence and capacity to men in other trades or manual occupations, or that they are not able to assert their rights and care for themselves without the protecting arm of the state, interfering with their independence of judgment and of action. They are in no sense wards of the state. Viewed in the light of a purely labor law, with no reference whatever to the question of health, we think that a law like the one before us involves neither the safety, the morals, nor the welfare, of the public, and that the interest of the public is not in the slightest degree affected by such an act. The law must be upheld, if at all, as a law pertaining to the health of the individual engaged in the occupation of a baker. It does not affect any other portion of the public than those who are engaged in that occupation. Clean and wholesome bread does not depend upon whether the baker works but ten hours per day or only sixty hours a week. The limitation of the hours of labor does not come within the police power on that ground.

It is a question of which of two powers or rights shall prevail,—the power of the state to legislate or the right of the individual to liberty of person and freedom of contract. The mere assertion that the subject relates, though but in a remote degree, to the public health, does not necessarily render the enactment valid. The act must have a more direct relation, as a means to an end, and the end itself must be appropriate and legitimate, before an act can be held to be valid which interferes with the general right of an individual to be free in his person and in his power to contract in relation to his own labor. . . .

We think the limit of the police power has been reached and passed in this case. There is, in our judgment, no reasonable foundation for holding this to be necessary or appropriate as a health law to safeguard the public health, or the health of the individuals who are following the trade of a baker. If this statute be valid, and if, therefore, a proper case is made out in which to deny the right of an individual, sui juris, as employer or employee, to make contracts for the labor of the latter under the protection of the provisions of the Federal Constitution, there would seem to be no length to which legislation of this nature might not go. . . .

We think that there can be no fair doubt that the trade of a baker, in and of itself, is not an unhealthy one to that degree which would authorize the legislature to interfere with the right to labor, and with the right of free contract on the part of the individual, either as employer or employee. In looking through statistics regarding all trades and occupations, it may be true that the trade of a baker does not appear to be as healthy as some other trades, and is also vastly more healthy than still others. To the common understanding the trade of a baker has never been regarded as an unhealthy one. Very likely physicians would not recommend the exercise of that or of any other trade as a remedy for ill health. Some occupations are more healthy than others, but we think there are none which might not come under the power of the legislature to supervise and control the hours of working therein, if the mere fact that the occupation is not absolutely and perfectly healthy is to confer that right upon the legislative department of the government. It might be safely affirmed that almost all occupations more or less affect the health. There must be more than the mere fact of the possible existence of some small amount of unhealthiness to warrant legislative interference with liberty. It is unfortunately true that labor, even in any department, may possibly carry with it the seeds of unhealthiness. But are we all, on that account, at the mercy of legislative majorities? A printer, a tinsmith, a locksmith, a carpenter, a cabinetmaker, a dry goods clerk, a bank's, a lawyer's, or a physician's clerk, or a clerk in almost any kind of business, would all come under the power of the legislature, on this assumption. No trade, no occupation, no mode of earning one's living, could escape this all-pervading power, and the acts of the legislature in limiting the hours of labor in all employments would be valid, although such limitation might seriously cripple the ability of the laborer to support himself and his family. In our large cities there are many buildings into which the sun penetrates for but a short time in each day, and these buildings are occupied by people carrying on the business of bankers, brokers, lawyers, real estate, and many other kinds of business, aided by many clerks, messengers, and other employees. Upon the assumption of the validity of this act under review, it is not possible to say that an act, prohibiting lawyers' or bank clerks, or others, from contracting to labor for their employers more than eight hours a day would be invalid. It might be said that it is unhealthy to work more than that number of hours in an apartment lighted by artificial light during the working hours of the day; that the occupation of the bank clerk, the lawyer's clerk, the real-estate clerk, or the broker's clerk, in such offices is therefore unhealthy, and the legislature, in its paternal wisdom, must, therefore, have the right to legislate on the subject of and to limit, the hours for such labor; and, if it exercises that power, and its validity be questioned, it is sufficient to say, it has reference to the public health; it has reference to the health of the employees condemned to labor day after day in buildings where the sun never shines; it is a health law, and therefore it is valid, and cannot be questioned by the courts.

It is also urged, pursuing the same line of argument, that it is to the interest of the state that its population should be strong and robust, and therefore any legislation which may be said to tend to make people healthy must be valid as health laws, enacted under the police power. If this be a valid argument and a justification for this kind of legislation, it follows that the protection of the Federal Constitution from undue interference with liberty of person and freedom of contract is visionary, wherever the law is sought to be justified as a valid exercise of the police power. Scarcely any law but might find shelter under such assumptions, and conduct, properly so called, as well as contract, would come under the restrictive sway of the legislature. Not only the hours of employees, but the hours of employers, could be regulated, and doctors, lawyers, scientists, all professional men, as well as athletes and artisans, could be forbidden to fatigue their brains and bodies by prolonged hours of exercise, lest the fighting strength of the state be impaired. We mention these extreme cases because the contention is extreme. We do not believe in the soundness of the views which uphold this law. On the contrary, we think that such a law as this, although passed in the assumed exercise of the police power, and as relating to the public health, or the health of the employees named, is not within that power, and is invalid. The act is not, within any fair meaning of the term, a health law, but is an illegal interference with the rights of individuals, both employers and employees, to make contracts regarding labor upon such terms as they may think best, or which they may agree upon with the other parties to such contracts. Statutes of the nature of that under review, limiting the hours in which grown and intelligent men may labor to earn their living, are mere meddlesome interferences with the rights of the individual, and they are not saved from condemnation by the claim that they are passed in the exercise of the police power and upon the subject of the health of the individual whose rights are interfered with, unless there be some fair ground, reasonable in and of itself, to say that there is material danger to the public health, or to the health of the employees, if the hours of labor are not curtailed. . . .

It was further urged on the argument that restricting the hours of labor in the case of bakers was valid because it tended to cleanliness on the part of the workers, as a man was more apt to be cleanly when not overworked, and if cleanly then his "output" was also more likely to be so. . . . The connection, if any exists, is too shadowy and thin to build any argument for the interference of the legislature. If the man works ten hours a day it is all right, but if ten and a half or eleven his health is in danger and his bread may be unhealthy, and, therefore, he shall not be permitted to do it. This, we think, is unreasonable and entirely arbitrary. . . .

. . . It seems to us that the real object and purpose were simply to regulate the hours of labor between the master and his employees (all being men, sui juris), in a private business, not dangerous in any degree to morals, or in any real and substantial degree to the health of the employees. Under such circumstances the freedom of master and employee to contract with each other in relation to their employment, and in defining the same, cannot be prohibited or interfered with, without violating the Federal Constitution.

The judgment . . . must be reversed. . . .

Mr. Justice Harlan, with whom Mr. Justice White and Mr. Justice Day concurred, wrote a dissenting opinion.

Mr. Justice Holmes dissenting:

I regret sincerely that I am unable to agree with the judgment in this case, and I think it my duty to express my dissent.

This case is decided upon an economic theory which a large part of the country does not entertain. If it were a question whether I agreed with that theory, I should desire to study it further and long before making up my mind. But I do not conceive that to be my duty, because I strongly believe that my agreement or disagreement has nothing to do with the right of a majority to embody their opinions in law. It is settled by various decisions of this court that state constitutions and state laws may regulate life in many ways which we as legislators might think as injudicious, or if you like as tyrannical, as this, and which, equally with this, interfere with the liberty to contract. Sunday laws and usury laws are ancient examples. A more modern one is the prohibition of lotteries. The liberty of the citizen to do as he likes so long as he does not interfere with the liberty of others to do the same, which has been a shibboleth for some well-known writers, is interfered with by school laws, by the Postoffice, by every state or municipal institution which takes his money for purposes thought desirable, whether he likes it or not. The 14th Amendment does not enact Mr. Herbert Spencer's Social Statics. The other day we sustained the Massachusetts vaccination law. Jacobson v. Massachusetts [1905]. United States and state statutes and decisions cutting down the liberty to contract by way of combination are familiar to this court. Northern Securities Co. v. United States [1904]. Two years ago we upheld the prohibition of sales on margins, or for future delivery, in the Constitution of California. . . . The decision sustaining an eight-hour law for miners is still recent. Holden v. Hardy [1898]. Some of these laws embody convictions or prejudices which judges are likely to share. Some may not. But a Constitution is not intended to embody a particular economic theory, whether of paternalism and the organic relation of the citizen to the state or of laissez faire. It is made for people of fundamentally differing views, and the accident of our finding certain opinions natural and familiar, or novel, and even shocking, ought not to conclude our judgment upon the question whether statutes embodying them conflict with the Constitution of the United States.

General propositions do not decide concrete cases. The decision will depend on a judgment or intuition more subtle than any articulate major premise. But I think that the proposition just stated, if it is accepted, will carry us far toward the end. Every opinion tends to become a law. I think that the word "liberty" in the 14th Amendment, is perverted when it is held to prevent the natural outcome of a dominant opinion, unless it can be said that a rational and fair man necessarily would admit that the statute proposed would infringe fundamental principles as they have been understood by the traditions of our people and our law. It does not need research to show that no such sweeping condemnation can be passed upon the statute before us. A reasonable man might think it a proper measure on the score of health. Men whom I certainly could not pronounce unreasonable would uphold it as a first installment of a general regulation of the hours of work. Whether in the latter aspect it would be open to the charge of inequality I think it unnecessary to discuss.

HURTADO v. CALIFORNIA

110 U. S. 516; 4 S. Ct. 111; 28 L. Ed. 232 (1884)

While the due process clauses of the Fifth and Fourteenth Amendments came to be restrictions by which the validity of the substance of legislation was tested in the courts, it should not be forgotten that originally due process was construed only as a limitation on governmental procedure. Whatever the government did, it had to do in accordance with the "process" which was "due" under the law of the land. But what, concretely, did such process include? To the layman, thinking in terms of criminal procedure, it undoubtedly included the common-law procedures with which he was familiar—procedures spelled out in detail in the Bill of Rights. The Supreme Court, however, rejected the idea that due process required adherence to a fixed list of prescribed procedures, and in Davidson v. New Orleans (1878) it explained that the meaning of the clause would be determined "by the gradual process of judicial inclusion and exclusion, as the cases presented for decision shall require, with the reasoning on which such decisions may be founded."

The Court had already decided, in the case of Murray's Lessee v. Hoboken Land and Improvement Co. (1856), that "due" process did not always mean "judicial" process; and an administrative agency could employ procedures which had the sanction of long-established custom. In this case an administrative warrant authorizing the seizure of a man's property to satisfy a debt to the government was found to be a well-established procedure and hence due process of law.

But if old established procedures were due process of law, then surely those common-law procedures listed in the Bill of Rights were due process of law. And if this were the case, why were they not guaranteed by the Fourteenth Amendment in state criminal cases? This was the argument of Hurtado in the present case. He had been convicted of murder by the state of California and sentenced to be hanged. He claimed a denial of due process because instead of a grand jury indictment, to which he would have been entitled under the common law, he had been charged by an information prepared by the prosecuting attorney—a form of charge authorized by the state of California, but limited at common law to misdemeanors.

Mr. Justice Matthews delivered the opinion of the Court, saying in part:

. . . The proposition of law we are asked to affirm is, that an indictment or presentment by a grand jury, as known to the common law of England, is essential to that "due process of law," when applied to prosecutions for felonies, which is secured and guaranteed by this provision of the Constitution of the United States, and which accordingly it is forbidden to the States respectively to dispense with in the administration of criminal law.

. . . It is maintained on behalf of the plaintiff in error that the phrase "due process of law" is equivalent to "law of the land," as found in the [thirty-]-ninth chapter of Magna Charta; that, by immemorial usage, it has acquired a fixed, definite and technical meaning; that it refers to and includes, not only the general principles of public liberty and private right, which lie at the foundation of all free government, but the very institutions which, venerable by time and custom, have been tried by experience and found fit and necessary for the preservation of those principles, and which, having been the birthright and inheritance of every English subject, crossed the Atlantic with the colonists and were transplanted and established in the fundamental laws of the State; that, having been originally introduced into the Constitution of the United States as a limitation upon the powers of the government, brought into being by that instrument, it has now been added as an additional security to the individual against oppression by the States themselves; that one of these institutions is that of the grand jury, an indictment or presentment by which against the accused in cases of alleged felonies is an essential part of due process of law, in order that he may not be harassed or destroyed by prosecutions founded only upon private malice or popular fury. . . .

It is urged upon us, however, in argument, that the claim made in behalf of the plaintiff in error is supported by the decision of this court in Murray's Lessee v. Hoboken Land & Improvement Company [1856]. There, Mr. Justice Curtis delivering the opinion of the court, after showing that due process of law must mean something more than the actual existing law of the land, for otherwise it would be no restraint upon legislative power, proceeds as follows: "To what principle, then, are we to resort to ascertain whether this process, enacted by Congress, is due process? To this the answer must be twofold. We must examine the Constitution itself to see whether this process be in conflict with any of its provisions. If not found to be so, we must look to those settled usages and modes of proceeding existing in the common and statue law of England before the emigration of our ancestors, and which are shown not to have been unsuited to their civil and political condition by having been acted on by them after the settlement of this country."

This, it is argued, furnishes an indispensable test of what constitutes "due process of law"; that any proceeding otherwise authorized by law, which is not thus sanctioned by usage, or which supersedes and displaces one that is, cannot be regarded as due process of law.

But this inference is unwarranted. The real syllabus of the passage quoted is, that a process of law, which is not otherwise forbidden, must be taken to be due process of law, if it can show the sanction of settled usage both in England and in this country; but it by no means follows, that nothing else can be due process of law. The point in the case cited arose in reference to a summary proceeding, questioned on that account, as not due process of law. The answer was: however exceptional it may be, as tested by definitions and principles of ordinary procedure, nevertheless, this, in substance, has been immemorially the actual law of the land, and, therefore, is due process of law. But to hold that such a characteristic is essential to due process of law, would be to deny every quality of the law but its age, and to render it incapable of progress or improvement. It would be to stamp upon our jurisprudence the unchangeableness attributed to the laws of the Medes and Persians.

This would be all the more singular and surprising, in this quick and active age, when we consider that, owing to the progressive development of legal ideas and instituions in England, the words of Magna Charta stood for very different things at the time of the separation of the American Colonies from what they represented originally. . . .

The Constitution of the United States was ordained, it is true, by descendants of Englishmen, who inherited the traditions of English law and history; but it was made for an undefined and expanding future, and for a people gathered and to be gathered from many Nations and of many tongues. And while we take just pride in the principles and institutions of the common law, we are not to forget that in lands where other systems of jurisprudence prevail, the ideas and processes of civil justice are also not unknown. Due process of law, in spite of the absolutism of continental governments, is not alien to that Code which survived the Roman Empire as the foundation of modern civilization in Europe, and which has given us that fundamental maxim of distributive justice, *Suum cuique tribuere.* There is nothing in Magna Charta, rightly construed as a broad charter of public right and law, which ought to exclude the best ideas of all systems and of every age; and as it was the characteristic principle of the common law to draw its inspiration from every fountain of justice, we are not to assume that the sources of its supply have been exhausted. On the contrary, we should expect that the new and various experiences of our own situation and system will mold and shape it into new and not less useful forms. . . .

We are to construe this phrase in the 14th Amendment by the *usus loquendi* of the Constitution itself. The same words are contained in the 5th Amendment. That article makes specific and express provision for perpetuating the institution of the grand jury, so far as relates to prosecutions, for the more aggravated crimes under the laws of the United States. It declares that "No person shall be held to answer for a capital or otherwise infamous crime, unless on a presentment or indictment of a grand jury, except in cases arising in the land or naval forces, or in the militia when in actual service in time of war or public danger; nor shall any person be subject for the same offense to be twice put in jeopardy of life or limb; nor shall he be compelled in any criminal case to be a witness against himself." It then immediately adds: "nor be deprived of life, liberty or property, without due process of law." According to a recognized canon of interpretation, especially applicable to formal and solemn instruments of constitutional law, we are forbidden to assume, without clear reason to the contrary, that any part of this most important Amendment is superfluous. The natural and obvious inference is, that in the sense of the Constitution, "due process of law" was not meant or intended to include, *ex vi termini*, the institution and procedure of a grand jury in any case. The conclusion is equally irresistible, that when the same phrase was employed in the 14th Amendment to restrain the action of the States, it was used in the same sense and with no greater extent; and that if in the adoption of that Amendment it had been part of its purpose to perpetuate the institution of the grand jury in all the States, it would have embodied, as did the 5th Amendment, express declarations to that effect. Due process of law in the latter refers to that law of the land, which derives its authority from the legislative powers conferred upon Congress by the Constitution of the United States, exercised within the limits therein prescribed, and interpreted according to the principles of the common law. In the 14th Amendment, by parity of reason, it refers to that law of the land in each State, which derives its authority from the inherent and reserved powers of the State, exerted within the limits of those fundamental principles of liberty and justice which lie at the base of all our civil and political institutions, and the greatest security for which resides in the right of the people to make their own laws, and alter them at their pleasure. "The 14th Amendment," as was said by Mr. Justice Bradley in Mo. v. Lewis [1880], "does not profess to secure to all persons in the United States the benefit of the same laws and the same remedies. Great diversities in these respects may exist in two States separated only by an imaginary line. On one side of this line there may be a right of trial by jury, and on the other side no such right. Each State prescribes its own modes of judicial proceeding."

But it is not to be supposed that these legislative powers are absolute and despotic, and that the Amendment prescribing due process of law is too vague and indefinite to operate as a practical restraint. It is not every Act, legislative in form, that is law. Law is something more than mere will exerted as an act of power. . . . Arbitrary power, enforcing its edicts to the injury of the persons and property of its subjects, is not law, whether manifested as the decree of a personal monarch or of an impersonal multitude. And the limitations imposed by our constitutional law upon the action of the governments, both state and national, are essential to the preservation of public and private rights, notwithstanding the representative character of our political institutions. . . .

It follows that any legal proceeding enforced by public authority, whether sanctioned by age and custom, or newly devised in the discretion of the legislative power, in furtherance of the general public good, which regards and preserves these principles of liberty and justice, must be held to be due process of law. . . .

Tried by these principles, we are unable to say that the substitution for a presentment or indictment by a grand jury of the proceeding by information, after examination and commitment by a magistrate, certifying to the probable guilt of the defendant, with the right on his part to the aid of counsel, and to the cross-examination of the witnesses produced for the prosecution, is not due process of law. It is, as we have seen, an ancient proceeding at common law, which might include every case of an offense of less grade than a felony, except misprision of treason; and in every circumstance of its administration, as authorized by the Statute of California, it carefully considers and guards the substantial interest of the prisoner. It is merely a preliminary proceeding, and can result in no final judgment, except as the consequence of a regular judicial trial, conducted precisely as in cases of indictments. . . .

For these reasons, finding no error therein, the judgment of the Supreme Court of California is affirmed.

Mr. Justice Harlan, dissenting, said in part:

. . . I cannot agree that the State may, consistently with due process of law, require a person to answer for a capital offense, except upon the presentment or indictment of a grand jury. . . .

. . . To what principles are we to resort to ascertain whether this process . . . is due process? To this the answer must be twofold. We must examine the Constitution itself to see whether this process be in conflict with any of its provisions. If not found to be so, we must look *"to those settled usages and modes of proceeding existing in the common and statute law of England before the emigration of our ancestors, and which are shown not to have been unsuited to their civil and political condition by having been acted on by them after the settlement of this country."* . . .

. . . Let us inquire (and no other inquiry is at all pertinent) whether according to the settled usages and modes of proceeding to which, this court has said, reference must be had, an information for a capital offense was, prior to the adoption of our Constitution, regarded as due process of law. [Justice Harlan here reviews the authorities and finds it was not.]

My brethren concede that there are principles of liberty and justice, lying at the foundation of our civil and political institutions, which no State can violate consistently with that due process of law required by the 14th Amendment in proceedings involving life, liberty or property. Some of these principles are enumerated in the opinion of the court. But, for reasons which do not impress my mind as satisfactory, they exclude from that enumeration the exemption from prosecution, by information, for a public offense involving life. By what authority is that exclusion made? Is it justified by the settled usages and modes of procedure, existing under the common and statute law of England at the emigration of our ancestors or at the foundation of our government? Does not the fact that the people of the original States required an amendment of the National Constitution, securing exemption from prosecution, for a capital offense, except upon the indictment or presentment of a grand jury, prove that, in their judgment, such an exemption was essential to protection against accusation and unfounded prosecution and, therefore, was a fundamental principle in liberty and justice? . . .

But it is said that the framers of the Constitution did not suppose that due process of law necessarily required for a capital offense the institution and procedure of a grand jury, else they would not in the same amendment prohibiting the deprivation of life, liberty or property without due process of law, have made specific and express provision for a grand jury where the crime is capital or otherwise infamous; therefore, it is argued, the requirement by the 14th Amendment, of due process of law in all proceedings involving life, liberty and property, without specific reference to grand juries in any case whatever, was not intended as a restriction upon the power which it is claimed the States previously had, so far as the express restrictions of the National Constitution are concerned, to dispense altogether with grand juries.

This line of argument, it seems to me, would lead to results which are inconsistent with the vital principles of republican government. If the presence in the 5th Amendment of a specific provision for grand juries in capital cases, alongside the provision for due process of law in proceedings involving life, liberty or property, is held to prove that due process of law did not, in the judgment of the framers of the Constitution, necessarily require a grand jury in capital cases, inexorable logic would require it to be, likewise, held that the right not to be put twice in jeopardy of life and limb for the same offense, nor compelled in a criminal case to testify against one's self (rights and immunities also specifically recognized in the 5th Amendment) were not protected by that due process of law required by the settled usages and proceedings existing under the common and statute law of England at the settlement of this country. More than that, other Amendments of the Constitution proposed at the same time, expressly recognize the right of persons to just compensation for private property taken for public use; their right, when accused of crime, to be informed of the nature and cause of the accusation against them, and to a speedy and public trial, by an impartial jury of the State and district wherein the crime was committed; to be confronted by the witnesses against them; and to have compulsory process for obtaining witnesses in their favor. Will it be claimed that these rights were not secured by the "law of the land" or by "due process of law," as declared and established at the foundation of our government? Are they to be excluded from the enumeration of the fundamental principles of liberty and justice and, therefore, not embraced by "due process of law?" . . .

It seems to me that too much stress is put upon the fact that the framers of the Constitution made express provision for the security of those rights which at common law were protected by the requirement of due process of law and, in addition, declared, generally, that no person shall "be deprived of life, liberty or property without due process of law." The rights, for the security of which these express provisions were made, were of a character so essential to the safety of the people that it was deemed wise to avoid the possibility that Congress, in regulating the processes of law, would impair or destroy them. Hence their specific enumeration in the earlier Amendments of the Constitution. . . .

POWELL v. ALABAMA

287 U. S. 45; 53 S. Ct. 55; 77 L. Ed. 158 (1932)

The Court in the Hurtado case not only rejected the idea that the protections listed in the Bill of Rights are included in due process, but the reasoning on which the decision was based seemed to make impossible such inclusion in the future. In 1897, however, with the advent of the concept of substantive due process, the Court held that due process forbade a state to seize private property without just compensation; see Chicago, B. & Q. R. Co. v. Chicago. Justice Harlan, who had dissented in Hurtado, wrote the opinion of the Court without alluding to that case or calling attention to the fact that the right was one listed in the Bill of Rights. He held, simply, that the right to compensation was a right "founded in natural equity" and "laid down as a principle of universal law. Indeed, in a free government almost all other rights would become worthless if the government possessed an uncontrollable power over the private fortune of every citizen." He emphasized that "in determining what is due process of law regard must be had to substance, not to form," and pointed out that while "the legislature may prescribe a form of procedure to be observed in the taking of private property for public use, . . . it is not due process of law if provision be not made for compensation."

The C. B. & Q. decision had not overruled Hurtado, but since the two cases were in some ways incompatible, it seemed plausible to suppose that some of the Bill of Rights guarantees for persons accused of crime might also be found essential to due process. In the case of Twining v. New Jersey (1908), the Court refused to apply any such notion to the right against compulsory self-incrimination. The Court conceded that it was "possible that some of the personal rights safeguarded by the first eight Amendments against national action may also be safeguarded against state action, because a denial of them would be a denial of due process of law. Chicago, B. & Q. R. Co. v. Chicago. If this is so, it is not because those rights are enumerated in the first eight Amendments, but because they are of such a nature that they are included in the conception of due process of law. . . ." It reviewed the historical development of the protection against self-incrimination and concluded it was not really thought of as an "immutable principle of justice," but merely as a "just and useful principle of law." Certainly it did not rank "with the right to hearing before condemnation, the immunity from arbitrary power not acting by general laws, and the inviolability of private property." The Court noted further that, with the exception of requiring jurisdiction, notice, and hearing, it had uniformly "sustained all state laws, statutory or judicially declared regulating procedure, evidence, and methods of trial, and held them to be consistent with due process of law. . . ." The decision stands in sharp contrast to the decisions in Lochner v. New York (1905) and Adkins v. Children's Hospital (1923). Clearly, the rights protected by due process were property rights—not rights involving criminal procedure. It was not until 1964, in Malloy v. Hogan, that the Court overruled Twining and held the protection against self-incrimination essential to due process.

With the rise of the doctrine of substantive due process it was increasingly urged on the Court that the "liberty" protected by the due process clause of the Fourteenth Amendment should include, at the very least, the freedom of speech and press mentioned in the First Amendment. The pressure was not only from members of the bar, but from the Court itself. In 1907 Justice Harlan, in a dissenting opinion in Patterson v. Colorado, declared "I go further and hold that the privileges of free speech and a free press, belonging to every citizen of the United States, constitute essential parts of every man's liberty, and are protected against violation by that clause of the Fourteenth Amendment forbidding a state to deprive any person of his liberty without due process of law." Essentially the same view was expressed by Justice Brandeis in his dissenting opinion in Gilbert v. Minnesota (1920), a case in which the Court assumed for the sake of argument that freedom of speech was "a natural and inherent" right but held that it had not been violated. Although in Prudential Insurance Co. v. Cheek (1922) the Court insisted that "neither the Fourteenth Amendment nor any other provision of the Constitution of the United States imposes upon the states any restrictions about 'freedom of speech,' " the following year it began to show signs of conversion to a broader conception of the term "liberty." In Meyer v. Nebraska (1923) Justice McReynolds, in an opinion holding invalid a Nebraska statute forbidding the teaching of any subject in any language but English in any private, parochial, or public school, defined the "liberty" protected by the due process clauses as follows: "Without doubt, it denotes not merely freedom from bodily restraint, but also the right of the individual to contract, to engage in any of the common occupations of life, to acquire useful knowledge, to marry, establish a home and bring up children, to worship God according to the dictates of his own conscience, and, generally, to enjoy those privileges long recognized at common law as essential to the orderly pursuit of happiness by free men."

Two years later, in what was in fact a constitutional revolution, the Court, in Gitlow v. New York (1925), reversed its stand. Gitlow had challenged a state statute as violating his freedom of speech and thereby denying him due process; the Supreme Court took jurisdiction under the due process clause, declaring that "For present purposes we may and do assume that freedom of speech and of the press—which are protected by the First Amendment from abridgment by Congress—are among the fundamental personal rights and 'liberties' protected by the due process clause of the Fourteenth Amendment from impairment by the states." In Gitlow's case the Court held the state statute valid and upheld Gitlow's conviction; but in 1931, in Near v. Minnesota, the Court held a state statute void on the ground that it denied due process by unreasonably restricting freedom of speech and press. With these two cases these important liberties became effectively "nationalized," and the states came under federal judicial scrutiny and discipline in dealing with freedom of speech and press.

The other liberties mentioned in the First Amendment followed in due course. In Hamilton v. Board of Regents of the University of California (1934) freedom of religion was held to be protected by the Fourteenth Amendment, although the Court held that Hamilton's religious liberty was not abridged by making him take military drill as a condition of attending the state university. In De Jonge v. Oregon (1937) freedom of assembly was added to the list. The assimilation of the First Amendment into the Fourteenth was completed in Everson v. Board of Education (1947). The preceding cases were decided on the theory that the due process clause protects "liberty" and that "liberty" includes freedom of speech, press, religion, and assembly. The Everson case, however, which involved state aid to parochial school pupils, raised no question of "freedom" of religion but the question whether the state action amounted to an "establishment" of religion. It could be argued that a state-supported religion does not abridge freedom of religion and hence is not an abridgment of "liberty" protected by due process of law, but the Supreme Court in the Everson case did not argue the point; it simply declared that "the First Amendment, as made applicable to the states by the Fourteenth . . . commands that a state 'shall make no law respecting an establishment of religion. . . .' "

With the incorporation of First Amendment rights into the due process clause of the Fourteenth, pressure was again brought on the Court to reconsider its stand in Hurtado and Twining, to find other rights in the Bill of Rights to be "essential to due process" and hence applicable to the states. The present case, one of the famous Scottsboro Cases, raises the question whether the right to counsel, guaranteed against federal infringement by the Sixth Amendment, is applicable to the states through the Fourteenth.

Mr. Justice Sutherland delivered the opinion of the Court, saying in part:

The petitioners, hereinafter referred to as defendants, are negroes charged with the crime of rape, committed upon the persons of two white girls. The crime is said to have been committed on March 25, 1931. The indictment was returned in a state court of first instance on March 31, and the record recites that on the same day the defendants were arrained and entered pleas of not guilty. There is a further recital to the effect that upon the arraignment they were represented by counsel. But no counsel had been employed, and aside from a statement made by the trial judge several days later during a colloquy immediately preceding the trial, the record does not disclose when, or under what circumstances, an appointment of counsel was made, or who was appointed. During the colloquy referred to, the trial judge, in response to a question, said that he had appointed all the members of the bar for the purpose of arraigning the defendants and then of course anticipated that the members of the bar would continue to help the defendants if no counsel appeared. Upon the argument here both sides accepted that as a correct statement of the facts concerning the matter.

There was a severance upon the request of the state, and the defendants were tried in three several groups, as indicated above. As each of the three cases was called for trial, each defendant was arraigned, and, having the indictment read to him, entered a plea of not guilty. Whether the original arraignment and pleas were regarded as ineffective is not shown. Each of the three trials was completed within a single day. Under the Alabama statute the punishment for rape is to be fixed by the jury, and in its discretion may be from ten years' imprisonment to death. The juries found defendants guilty and imposed the death penalty upon all. The trial court overruled motions for new trials and sentenced the defendants in accordance with the verdicts. The judgments were affirmed by the state supreme court. Chief Justice Anderson thought the defendants had not been accorded a fair trial and strongly dissented.

In this court the judgments are assailed upon the grounds that the defendants, and each of them, were denied due process of law and the equal protection of the laws, in contravention of the Fourteenth Amendment, specifically as follows: (1) They were not given a fair, impartial and deliberate trial; (2) they were denied the right of counsel, with the accustomed incidents of consultation and opportunity of preparation for trial; and (3) they were tried before juries from which qualified members of their own race were systematically excluded. These questions were properly raised and saved in the courts below.

The only one of the assignments which we shall consider is the second, in respect of the denial of counsel; and it becomes unnecessary to discuss the facts of the case or the circumstances surrounding the prosecution except in so far as they reflect light upon that question.

The record shows that on the day when the offense is said to have been committed, these defendants, together with a number of other negroes, were upon a freight train on its way through Alabama. On the same train were seven white boys and two white girls. A fight took place between the negroes and the white boys, in the course of which the white boys, with the exception of one named Gilley, were thrown off the train. A message was sent ahead, reporting the fight and asking that every negro be gotten off the train. The participants in the fight, and the two girls, were in an open gondola car. The two girls testified that each of them was assaulted by six different negroes in turn, and they identified the seven defendants as having been among the number. None of the white boys was called to testify, with the exception of Gilley, who was called in rebuttal.

Before the train reached Scottsboro, Alabama, a sheriff's posse seized the defendants and two other negroes. Both girls and the negroes then were taken to Scottsboro, the county seat. Word of their coming and of the alleged assault had preceded them, and they were met at Scottsboro by a large crowd. It does not sufficiently appear that the defendants were seriously threatened with, or that they were actually in danger of, mob violence; but it does appear that the attitude of the community was one of great hostility. The sheriff thought it necessary to call for the militia to assist in safeguarding the prisoners. Chief Justice Anderson pointed out in his opinion that every step taken from the arrest and arraignment to the sentence was accompanied by the military. Soldiers took the defendants to Gadsden for safekeeping, brought them back to Scottsboro for arraignment, returned them to Gadsden for safekeeping while awaiting trial, escorted them to Scottsboro for trial a few days later, and guarded the courthouse and grounds at every stage of the proceedings. It is perfectly apparent that the proceedings, from beginning to end, took place in an atmosphere of tense, hostile and excited public sentiment. During the entire time, the defendants were closely confined or were under military guard. The record does not disclose their ages, except that one of them was nineteen; but the record clearly indicates that most, if not all, of them were youthful, and they are constantly referred to as "the boys." They were ignorant and illiterate. All of them were residents of other states, where alone members of their families or friends resided.

However guilty defendants, upon due inquiry, might prove to have been, they were, until convicted, presumed to be innocent. It was the duty of the court having their cases in charge to see that they were denied no necessary incident of a fair trial. With any error of the state court involving alleged contravention of the state statutes or constitution we, of course, have nothing to do. The sole inquiry which we are permitted to make is whether the federal Constitution was contravened . . . and as to that, we confine ourselves, as already suggested to the inquiry whether the defendants were in substance denied the right of counsel, and if so, whether such denial infringes the due process clause of the Fourteenth Amendment.

First. The record shows that immediately upon the return of the indictment defendants were arraigned and pleaded not guilty. Apparently they were not asked whether they had, or were able to employ counsel, or wished to have counsel appointed; or whether they had friends or relatives who might assist in that regard if communicated with. That it would not have been an idle ceremony to have given the defendants reasonable opportunity to communicate with their families and endeavor to obtain counsel is demonstrated by the fact that very soon after conviction able counsel appeared in their behalf. . . .

It is hardly necessary to say that the right to counsel being conceded, a defendant should be afforded a fair opportunity to secure counsel of his own choice. Not only was that not done here, but such designation of counsel as was attempted was either so indefinite or so close upon the trial as to amount to a denial of effective and substantial aid in that regard. This will be amply demonstrated by a brief review of the record.

April 6, six days after indictment, the trials began. When the first case was called, the court inquired whether the parties were ready for trial. The state's attorney replied that he was ready to proceed. No one answered for the defendants or appeared to represent or defend them. Mr. Roddy, a Tennessee lawyer not a member of the local bar, addressed the court, saying that he had not been employed, but that people who were interested had spoken to him about the case. He was asked by the court whether he intended to appear for the defendants, and answered that he would like to appear along with counsel that the court might appoint. . . .

It thus will be seen that until the very morning of the trial no lawyer had been named or definitely designated to represent the defendants. Prior to that time, the trial judge had "appointed all the members of the bar" for the limited "purpose of arraigning the defendants." Whether they would represent the defendants thereafter if no counsel appeared in their behalf, was a matter of speculation only, or, as the judge indicated, of mere anticipation on the part of the court. Such a designation, even if made for all purposes, would, in our opinion, have fallen far short of meeting, in any proper sense, a requirement for the appointment of counsel. How many lawyers were members of the bar does not appear; but, in the very nature of things, whether many or few, they would not, thus collectively named, have been given that clear appreciation of responsibility or impressed with that individual sense of duty which should and naturally would accompany the appointment of a selected member of the bar, specifically named and assigned. . . .

. . . In any event, the circumstance lends emphasis to the conclusion that during perhaps the most critical period of the proceedings against these defendants, that is to say, from the time of their arraignment until the beginning of their trial, when consultation, thorough-going investigation and preparation were vitally important, the defendants did not have the aid of counsel in any real sense, although they were as much entitled to such aid during that period as at the trial itself. . . .

Second. The Constitution of Alabama provides that in all criminal prosecutions the accused shall enjoy the right to have the assistance of counsel; and a state statute requires the court in a capital case, where the defendant is unable to employ counsel, to appoint counsel for him. The state supreme court held that these provisions had not been infringed, and with that holding we are powerless to interfere. The question, however, which it is our duty, and within our power, to decide, is whether the denial of the assistance of counsel contravenes the due process clause of the Fourteenth Amendment to the federal Constitution. . . .

One test which has been applied to determine whether due process of law has been accorded in given instances is to ascertain what were the settled usages and modes of proceeding under the common and statute law of England before the Declaration of Independence, subject, however, to the qualification that they be shown not to have been unsuited to the civil and political conditions of our ancestors by having been followed in this country after it became a nation. . . . Plainly, as appears from the foregoing, this test, as thus qualified, has not been met in the present case.

We do not overlook the case of Hurtado v. California [1884], where this court determined that due process of law does not require an indictment by a grand jury as a prerequisite to prosecution by a state for murder. In support of that conclusion the court referred to the fact that the Fifth Amendment, in addition to containing the due process of law clause, provides in explicit terms that "No person shall be held to answer for a capital, or otherwise infamous crime, unless on a presentment or indictment of a grand jury," and said that since no part of this important amendment could be regarded as superfluous, the obvious inference is that in the sense of the Constitution due process of law was not intended to include, ex vi termini, the institution and procedure of a grand jury in any case; and that the same phrase, employed in the Fourteenth Amendment to restrain the action of the states, was to be interpreted as having been used in the same sense and with no greater extent; and that if it had been the purpose of that Amendment to perpetuate the institution of the grand jury in the states, it would have embodied, as did the Fifth Amendment, an express declaration to that effect.

The Sixth Amendment, in terms, provides that in all criminal prosecutions the accused shall enjoy the right "to have the assistance of counsel for his defense." In the face of the reasoning of the Hurtado Case, if it stood alone, it would be difficult to justify the conclusion that the right to counsel, being thus specifically granted by the Sixth Amendment, was also within the intendment of the due process of law clause. But the Hurtado Case does not stand alone. In the later case of Chicago, B. & Q. R. Co. v. Chicago [1897], this court held that a judgment of a state court, even though authorized by statute, by which private property was taken for public use without just compensation, was in violation of the due process of law required by the Fourteenth Amendment, notwithstanding that the Fifth Amendment explicitly declares that private property shall not be taken for public use without just compensation. . . .

Likewise, this court has considered that freedom of speech and of the press are rights protected by the due process clause of the Fourteenth Amendment, although in the First Amendment, Congress is prohibited in specific terms from abridging the right. Gitlow v. New York [1925]. . . .

These later cases establish that notwithstanding the sweeping character of the language in the Hurtado Case, the rule laid down is not without exceptions. The rule is an aid to construction, and in some instances may be conclusive; but it must yield to more compelling considerations whenever such considerations exist. The fact that the right involved is of such a character that it cannot be denied without violating those "fundamental principles of liberty and justice which lie at the base of all our civil and political institutions" (Hebert v. Louisiana, [1926]), is obviously one of those compelling considerations which must prevail in determining whether it is embraced within the due process clause of the Fourteenth Amendment, although it be specifically dealt with in another part of the federal Constitution. Evidently this court, in the later cases enumerated, regarded the rights there under consideration as of this fundamental character. That some such distinction must be observed is foreshadowed in Twining v. New Jersey [1908], where Mr. Justice Moody, speaking for the court, said that ". . . it is possible that some of the personal rights safeguarded by the first eight Amendments against national action may also be safeguarded against state action, because a denial of them would be a denial of due process of law. Chicago, B. & Q. R. Co. v. Chicago [1897]. If this is so, it is not because those rights are enumerated in the first eight Amendments, but because they are of such a nature that they are included in the conception of due process of law." While the question has never been categorically determined by this court, a consideration of the nature of the right and a review of the expressions of this and other courts, make it clear that the right to the aid of counsel is of this fundamental character.

It never has been doubted by this court, or any other so far as we know, that notice and hearing are preliminary steps essential to the passing of an enforceable judgment, and that they, together with a legally competent tribunal having jurisdiction of the case, constitute basic elements of the constitutional requirement of due process of law. . . .

What, then, does a hearing include? Historically and in practice, in our own country at least, it has always included the right to the aid of counsel when desired and provided by the party asserting the right. The right to be heard would be, in many cases, of little avail if it did not comprehend the right to be heard by counsel. Even the intelligent and educated layman has small and sometimes no skill in the science of law. If charged with crime, he is incapable, generally, of determining for himself whether the indictment is good or bad. He is unfamiliar with the rules of evidence. Left without the aid of counsel he may be put on trial without a proper charge, and convicted upon incompetent evidence, or evidence irrelevant to the issue or otherwise inadmissible. He lacks both the skill and knowledge adequately to prepare his defense, even though he have a perfect one. He requires the guiding hand of counsel at every step in the proceedings against him. Without it, though he be not guilty, he faces the danger of conviction because he does not know how to establish his innocence. If that be true of men of intelligence, how much more true is it of the ignorant and illiterate, or those of feeble intellect. If in any case, civil or criminal, a state or federal court were arbitrarily to refuse to hear a party by counsel, employed by and appearing for him, it reasonably may not be doubted that such a refusal would be a denial of a hearing, and, therefore, of due process in the constitutional sense.

The decisions all point to that conclusion. . . . In Ex parte Chin Loy You (D.C.) 223 Fed. 833 [1915], also a deportation case, the district judge held that under the particular circumstances of the case the prisoner, having seasonably made demand, was entitled to confer with and have the aid of counsel. Pointing to the fact that the right to counsel as secured by the Sixth Amendment relates only to criminal prosecutions, the judge said, "But it is equally true that the provision was inserted in the Constitution because the assistance of counsel was recognized as essential to any fair trial of a case against a prisoner." . . .

In the light of the facts outlined in the forepart of this opinion—the ignorance and illiteracy of the defendants, their youth, the circumstances of public hostility, the imprisonment and the close surveillance of the defendants by the military forces, the fact that their friends and families were all in other states and communication with them necessarily difficult, and above all that they stood in deadly peril of their lives—we think the failure of the trial court to give them reasonable time and opportunity to secure counsel was a clear denial of due process.

But passing that, and assuming their inability, even if opportunity had been given, to employ counsel, as the trial court evidently did assume, we are of opinion that, under the circumstances just stated, the necessity of counsel was so vital and imperative that the failure of the trial court to make an effective appointment of counsel was likewise a denial of due process within the meaning of the Fourteenth Amendment. Whether this would be so in other criminal prosecutions, or under other circumstances, we need not determine. All that it is necessary now to decide, as we do decide, is that in a capital case, where the defendant is unable to employ counsel, and is incapable adequately of making his own defense because of ignorance, feeblemindedness, illiteracy, or the like, it is the duty of the court, whether requested or not, to assign counsel for him as a necessary requisite of due process of law; and that duty is not discharged by an assignment at such a time or under such circumstances as to preclude the giving of effective aid in the preparation and trial of the case. To hold otherwise would be to ignore the fundamental postulate, already adverted to, "that there are certain immutable principles of justice which inhere in the very idea of free government which no member of the Union may disregard." . . . In a case such as this, whatever may be the rule in other cases, the right to have counsel appointed, when necessary, is a logical corollary from the constitutional right to be heard by counsel. . . .

The United States by statute and every state in the Union by express provision of law, or by the determination of its courts, make it the duty of the trial judge, where the accused is unable to employ counsel, to appoint counsel for him. In most states the rule applies broadly to all criminal prosecutions, in others it is limited to the more serious crimes, and in a very limited number, to capital cases. A rule adopted with such unanimous accord reflects, if it does not establish the inherent right to have counsel appointed at least in cases like the present, and lends convincing support to the conclusion we have reached as to the fundamental nature of that right.

The judgments must be reversed and the causes remanded for further proceedings not inconsistent with this opinion.

Judgments reversed.

Mr. Justice Butler wrote a dissenting opinion in which Mr. Justice McReynolds concurred.

PALKO v. CONNECTICUT

302 U. S. 319; 58 S. Ct. 149; 82 L. Ed. 288 (1937)

With the decision in Powell v. Alabama it appeared that the long struggle to nationalize the Bill of Rights might at last be bearing fruit. The Court had acknowledged that it no longer felt bound by the Hurtado reasoning; the application to the states of the Fifth Amendment right to just compensation and the First Amendment rights of free speech, press, religion, and assembly showed that some of the Bill of Rights guarantees could be applied to the states through due process of law. And now, in Powell, the Court for the first time had found one of the rights of persons accused of crime to be essential to due process.

The Palko case, printed below, made clear that the Court was not prepared to abandon earlier decisions such as Hurtado and Twining. Instead, it undertook to explain why some rights, such as the rights to counsel and free speech, are absorbed into due process; and why others, like jury trial and grand jury indictment, are not. It should be emphasized that the cases "absorbing" rights into the Fourteenth Amendment do not overrule Barron v. Baltimore (1833). The provisions of the federal Bill of Rights still limit directly only the federal government; it is the Fourteenth Amendment which limits the states. What the Court has done is to reverse the practical effect of the rule in Barron v. Baltimore with respect to part, but not all, of the Bill of Rights. Some of these rights are still not considered by the Court to be so fundamental as to be required by due process of law. The Court in case after case has been classifying the provisions of the Bill of Rights into those which are essential to due process of law and thus bind the states through the operation of the Fourteenth Amendment and those which are not essential to due process and by which the states are not bound. In effect, the Court has established an "honor roll" of superior rights which bind both state and national governments. The opinion in the present case is important since it gives an official summary of this classification up to 1937 and states clearly the principles upon which the classification rests.

One question which the Palko case failed to answer satisfactorily was what was meant by "absorption" or "incorporation" of a Bill of Rights guarantee into due process. Did it mean that the right, as listed in the Bill of Rights and interpreted by the Supreme Court in federal cases, was made applicable to the states? Or was the right as applied to the states a more general right, less clearly defined and permitting more leeway and discretion on the part of the states? Clearly, incorporation of the First Amendment has meant its application to the states exactly as it is applied to the national government. Justices Brandeis and Holmes, in their dissent in the Gitlow case, suggested that the free speech applicable to the states perhaps "may be accepted with a somewhat larger latitude of interpretation than is allowed to Congress by the sweeping language that governs or ought to govern the laws of the United States." The Court, however, has never acknowledged such a distinction, and the same rules for deciding such cases are applied to the state and the nation alike. With the gradual extension of due process to include other rights, however, an important controversy developed as to how these rights would apply to the states.

Mr. Justice Cardozo delivered the opinion of the Court, saying in part:

. . . Appellant was indicted . . . for the crime of murder in the first degree. A jury found him guilty of murder in the second degree, and he was sentenced to confinement in the state prison for life. Thereafter the state of Connecticut, with the permission of the judge presiding at the trial, gave notice of appeal to the Supreme Court of Errors. This it did pursuant to an act adopted in 1886 which is printed in the margin.*. . . Upon such appeal, the Supreme Court of Errors reversed the judgment and ordered a new trial. . . . It found that there had been error of law to the prejudice of the state. . . .

. . . [The] defendant was brought to trial again. Before a jury was impaneled and also at later stages of the case he made the objection that the effect of the new trial was to place him twice in jeopardy for the same offense, and in so doing to violate the Fourteenth Amendment of the Constitution of the United States. Upon the overruling of the objection the trial proceeded. The jury returned a verdict of murder in the first degree, and the court sentenced the defendant to the punishment of death. . . . The case is here upon appeal.

1. The execution of the sentence will not deprive appellant of his life without the process of law assured to him by the Fourteenth Amendment of the Federal Constitution.

---

*"Sec. 6494. *Appeals by the state in criminal cases.* Appeals from the rulings and decisions of the superior court or of any criminal court of common pleas, upon all questions of law arising on the trial of criminal cases, may be taken by the state, with the permission of the presiding judge, to the supreme court of errors, in the same manner and to the same effect as if made by the accused." . . .

The argument for appellant is that whatever is forbidden by the Fifth Amendment is forbidden by the Fourteenth also. The Fifth Amendment, which is not directed to the states, but solely to the federal government, creates immunity from double jeopardy. No person shall be "subject for the same offense to be twice put in jeopardy of life or limb." The Fourteenth Amendment ordains, "nor shall any state deprive any person of life, liberty, or property, without due process of law." To retry a defendant, though under one indictment and only one, subjects him, it is said, to double jeopardy in violation of the Fifth Amendment, if the prosecution is one on behalf of the United States. From this the consequence is said to follow that there is a denial of life or liberty without due process of law, if the prosecution is one on behalf of the People of a State. . . .

We have said that in appellant's view the Fourteenth Amendment is to be taken as embodying the prohibitions of the Fifth. His thesis is even broader. Whatever would be a violation of the original bill of rights (Amendments 1 to 8) if done by the federal government is now equally unlawful by force of the Fourteenth Amendment if done by a state. There is no such general rule.

The Fifth Amendment provides, among other things, that no person shall be held to answer for a capital or otherwise infamous crime unless on presentment or indictment of a grand jury. This court has held that, in prosecutions by a state, presentment or indictment by a grand jury may give way to informations at the instance of a public officer. Hurtado v. California [1884]. . . . The Fifth Amendment provides also that no person shall be compelled in any criminal case to be a witness against himself. This court has said that, in prosecutions by a state, the exemption will fail if the state elects to end it. Twining v. New Jersey [1908]. . . . The Sixth Amendment calls for a jury trial in criminal cases and the Seventh for a jury trial in civil cases at common law where the value in controversy shall exceed twenty dollars. This court has ruled that consistently with those amendments trial by jury may be modified by a state or abolished altogether. Walker v. Sauvinet [1876]; Maxwell v. Dow [1900]. . . . As to the Fourth Amendment, one should refer to Weeks v. United States [1914] and as to other provisions of the Sixth, to West v. Louisiana [1904].

On the other hand, the due process clause of the Fourteenth Amendment may make it unlawful for a state to abridge by its statutes the freedom of speech which the First Amendment safeguards against encroachment by the Congress (De Jonge v. Oregon [1937]) or the like freedom of the press (Near v. Minnesota [1931]), or the free exercise of religion (Hamilton v. University of California [1934] . . .), or the right of peaceable assembly, without which speech would be unduly trammeled (De Jonge v. Oregon), or the right of one accused of crime to the benefit of counsel (Powell v. Alabama [1932]). In these and other situations immunities that are valid as against the federal government by force of the specific pledges of particular amendments have been found to be implicit in the concept of ordered liberty, and thus, through the Fourteenth Amendment, become valid as against the states.

The line of division may seem to be wavering and broken if there is a hasty catalogue of the cases on the one side and the other. Reflection and analysis will induce a different view. There emerges the perception of a rationalizing principle which gives to discrete instances a proper order and coherence. The right to trial by jury and the immunity from prosecution except as the result of an indictment may have value and importance. Even so, they are not of the very essence of a scheme of ordered liberty. To abolish them is not to violate a "principle of justice so rooted in the traditions and conscience of our people as to be ranked as fundamental." . . . Few would be so narrow or provincial as to maintain that a fair and enlightened system of justice would be impossible without them. What is true of jury trials and indictments is true also, as the cases show, of the immunity from compulsory self-incrimination. Twining v. New Jersey. This too might be lost, and justice still be done. Indeed, today as in the past there are students of our penal system who look upon the immunity as a mischief rather than a benefit, and who would limit its scope or destroy it altogether. . . . The exclusion of these immunities and privileges from the privileges and immunities protected against the action of the states has not been arbitrary or casual. It has been dictated by a study and appreciation of the meaning, the essential implications, of liberty itself.

We reach a different plane of social and moral values when we pass to the privileges and immunities that have been taken over from the earlier articles of the federal bill of rights and brought within the Fourteenth Amendment by a process of absorption. These in their origin were effective against the federal government alone. If the Fourteenth Amendment has absorbed them, the process of absorption has had its source in the belief that neither liberty nor justice would exist if they were sacrificed. Twining v. New Jersey. This is true, for illustration, of freedom of thought and speech. Of that freedom one may say that it is the matrix, the indispensable condition, of nearly every other form of freedom. With rare aberrations a pervasive recognition of that truth can be traced in our history, political and legal. So it has come about that the domain of liberty, withdrawn by the Fourteenth Amendment from encroachment by the states, has been enlarged by latter-day judgments to include liberty of the mind as well as liberty of action. . . . Fundamental too in the concept of due process, and so in that of liberty, is the thought that condemnation shall be rendered only after trial. . . . The hearing, moreover, must be a real one, not a sham or a pretense. Moore v. Dempsey [1923]. . . . For that reason, ignorant defendants in a capital case were held to have been condemned unlawfully when in truth, though not in form, they were refused the aid of counsel. Powell v. Alabama. The decision did not turn upon the fact that the benefit of counsel would have been guaranteed to the defendants by the provisions of the Sixth Amendment if they had been prosecuted in a federal court. The decision turned upon the fact that in the particular situation laid before us in the evidence the benefit of counsel was essential to the substance of a hearing.

Our survey of the cases serves, we think, to justify the statement that the dividing line between them, if not unfaltering throughout its course, has been true for the most part to a unifying principle. On which side of the line the case made out by the appellant has appropriate location must be the next inquiry and the final one. Is that kind of double jeopardy to which the statute has subjected him a hardship so acute and shocking that our polity will not endure it? Does it violate those "fundamental principles of liberty and justice which lie at the base of all our civil and political institutions?" . . . The answer surely must be "no." What the answer would have to be if the state were permitted after a trial free from error to try the accused over again or to bring another case against him, we have no occasion to consider. We deal with the statute before us and no other. The state is not attempting to wear the accused out by a multitude of cases with accumulated trials. It asks no more than this, that the case against him shall go on until there shall be a trial free from the corrosion of substantial legal error. . . . This is not cruelty at all, nor even vexation in any immoderate degree. If the trial had been infected with error adverse to the accused, there might have been review at his instance, and as often as necessary to purge the vicious taint. A reciprocal privilege, subject at all times to the discretion of the presiding judge . . ., has now been granted to the state. There is here no seismic innovation. The edifice of justice stands, in its symmetry, to many, greater than before.

2. The conviction of appellant is not in derogation of any privileges or immunities that belong to him as a citizen of the United States. . . .

Maxwell v. Dow [1900], gives all the answer that is necessary.

The judgment is affirmed.

Mr. Justice Butler dissents.

ROCHIN v. CALIFORNIA

342 U. S. 165; 72 S. Ct. 205; 96 L. Ed. 183 (1952)

Despite its obivous reluctance to incorporate the specific guarantees of the Bill of Rights, the Court did take increasing interest in state procedures and machinery, and grew more watchful lest they not meet the requirements of fundamental fairness. Such insistence on fundamental fairness, especially for persons accused of crime, was bound to bring before the Court the widest variety of state activities. In 1927, for instance, the Court in Tumey v. Ohio reversed the conviction of a bootlegger who had been tried before the mayor of a small town. An ordinance provided that the mayor should retain the court costs as payment for his judicial work, but no costs were paid if the defendant were acquitted. Tumey had been fined $100, and the costs involved were $12. The Supreme Court held it to be a denial of due process to "subject his liberty or property to the judgment of a court, the judge of which has a direct, personal, substantial pecuniary interest in reaching a conclusion against him in his case. . . . There are doubtless mayors," the Court conceded, "who would not allow such a consideration as $12 costs in each case to affect their judgment in it, but the require-ment of due process of law in judicial procedure is not satisfied by the argument that men of the highest honor and the greatest self-sacrifice could carry it on without danger of injustice. Every procedure which would offer a possible temptation to the average man as a judge to forget the burden of proof required to convict the defendant, or which might lead him not to hold the balance nice, clear and true between the state and the accused denies the latter due process of law."

The doctrine of Tumey was reaffirmed as recently as 1977 when the Court in Connally v. Georgia held void a search warrant issued by a justice of the peace. The justice received $5.00 if he issued the warrant but nothing if he didn't.

Nor are jurymen expected to be persons of unrestrained self-sacrifice, and a trial conducted in an atmosphere of mob violence is inherently unfair. In Moore v. Dempsey (1923) five Negroes were convicted in an Arkansas court of the murder of a white man and sentenced to death. The Court described the trial in these words: "The court and the neighborhood were thronged with an adverse crowd that threatened the most dangerous consequences to any one interfering with the desired result. The counsel did not venture to demand delay or a change of venue, to challenge a juryman, or to ask for separate trials. He had had no preliminary consultation with the accused, called no witness for the defense, although they could have been produced, and did not put the defendants on the stand. The trial lasted about three quarters of an hour, and in less than five minutes the jury brought in a verdict of murder in the first degree. According to the allegations and affidavits there never was a chance for the petitioners to be acquitted; no juryman could have voted for an acquittal and continued to live in Phillips County, and if any prisoner, by any chance, had been aquitted by a jury, he could not have escaped the mob." Under these conditions no trial in the true sense was possible and the defendants were denied due process of law.

The Supreme Court has made it clear that due process is denied by an attempt to punish a person for a crime which is not clearly defined. In Winters v. New York (1948) it held void for vagueness a statute making it a crime to issue a publication which so masses stories of bloodshed and lust "as to become vehicles for inciting violent and depraved crimes against the person." The Court conceded the "impossibility of defining the precise line between permissible uncertainty in statutes caused by describing crimes by words well understood through long use in the criminal law—obscene, lewd, lascivious, filthy, indecent or disgusting—and the unconstitutional vagueness that leaves a person uncertain as to the kind of prohibited conduct—massing stories to incite crime . . ." but concluded that "an honest distributor of publications could [not] know when he might be held to have ignored such a prohibition. Collections of tales of war horrors, otherwise unexceptionable, might well be found to be 'massed' so as to become 'vehicles for exciting violent and depraved crimes.' Where a statute is so vague as to make criminal an innocent act, a conviction under it cannot be sustained. . . ."

In 1972 the Supreme Court struck down a Jacksonville vagrancy ordinance which, in the archaic language of the Elizabethan Poor Law, defines as vagrants (among others) "rogues and vagabonds, or dissolute persons who go about begging, . . . common night walkers, . . . common railers and brawlers, persons wandering or strolling around from place to place without any lawful purpose or object, habitual loafers, [and] . . . persons able to work but habitually living upon the earnings of their wives or minor children. . . ." Two white girls and their black dates were arrested on the main thoroughfare in Jacksonville and convicted of "prowling by auto." In Papachristou v. Jacksonville (1972) a unanimous Court found the ordinance void for vagueness both in the sense that it " 'fails to give a person of ordinary intelligence fair notice that his contemplated conduct is forbidden by the statute,' . . . and because it encourages arbitrary arrests and convictions." Not only does it make "criminal activities which by modern standards are normally innocent," but it puts "unfettered discretion . . . in the hands of the Jacksonville police." "Those generally implicated by the imprecise terms of the ordinance—poor people, nonconformists, dissenters, idlers—may be required to comport themselves according to the lifestyle deemed appropriate by the Jacksonville police and the courts. Where, as here, there are no standards governing the exercise of the discretion granted by the ordinance, the scheme permits and encourages an arbitrary and discriminatory enforcement of the law. . . . It results in a regime in which the poor and unpopular are permitted to 'stand on a public sidewalk . . . only at the whim of any police officer.' Shuttlesworth v. Birmingham [1969]."

Nor can a state through its criminal procedure favor the wealthy over the poor. In order to carry an appeal to the supreme court of Illinois in a criminal case it is necessary to have a stenographic transcript of the trial proceedings. Only an indigent defendant who had been sentenced to death was provided with a free transcript; all other defendants had to buy it. As a result, a poor man convicted of a noncapital crime and therefore not entitled to a free transcript would be deprived of the right to appeal his case because of his poverty—a right easily available to the well-to-do convict. In Griffin v. Illinois (1956) the Supreme Court held this to be a violation of due process and equal protection of the laws. "In criminal trials," the Court said, "a State can no more discriminate on account of poverty than on account of religion, race, or color. Plainly the ability to pay costs in advance bears no rational relationship to a defendant's guilt or innocence and could not be used as an excuse to deprive a defendant of a fair trial.

. . . There is no meaningful distinction between a rule which would deny the poor the right to defend themselves in a trial court and one which effectively denies the poor an adequate appellate review accorded to all who have money enough to pay the costs in advance." In Mayer v. Chicago (1972) the Court extended the rule to include persons charged with a misdemeanor and liable only to a fine. "Griffin," it emphasized, ". . . is a flat protection against pricing indigent defendants out of as effective an appeal as would be available to others able to pay their own way."

One of the major problems inherent in applying a concept of "fundamental fairness" is that fairness, like reasonableness, is a subjective value on which people may differ widely. Conduct that may seem fair to a policeman hired to protect community persons and property may seem grossly unfair to an individual upon whom the conduct falls. Should a Court deciding an issue between the two apply its own concept of what is fair, or should it enforce detailed rules of conduct which spell out what a person can and cannot do? Justice Frankfurter's opinion in the case below is a classic argument for the former view.

Mr. Justice Frankfurter delivered the opinion of the Court, saying in part:

Having "some information that [the petitioner here] was selling narcotics," three deputy sheriffs of the County of Los Angeles, on the morning of July 1, 1949, made for the two-story dwelling house in which Rochin lived with his mother, common-law wife, brothers and sisters. Finding the outside door open, they entered and then forced open the door to Rochin's room on the second floor. Inside they found petitioner sitting partly dressed on the side of the bed, upon which his wife was lying. On a "night stand" beside the bed the deputies spied two capsules. When asked "Whose stuff is this?" Rochin seized the capsules and put them in his mouth. A struggle ensued, in the course of which the three officers "jumped upon him" and attempted to extract the capsules. The force they applied proved unavailing against Rochin's resistance. He was handcuffed and taken to a hospital. At the direction of one of the officers a doctor forced an emetic solution through a tube into Rochin's stomach against his will. This "stomach pumping" produced vomiting. In the vomited matter were found two capsules which proved to contain morphine.

Rochin was brought to trial before a California Superior Court, sitting without a jury, on the charge of possessing "a preparation of morphine" in violation of the California Health and Safety Code. Rochin was convicted and sentenced to sixty days' imprisonment. The chief evidence against him was the two capsules. They were admitted over petitioner's objection, although the means of obtaining them was frankly set forth in the testimony by one of the deputies, substantially as here narrated. . . .

. . . Regard for the requirements of the Due Process Clause "inescapably imposes upon this Court an exercise of judgment upon the whole course of the proceedings [resulting in a conviction] in order to ascertain whether they offend those canons of decency and fairness which express the notions of justice of English-speaking people even toward those charged with the most heinous offenses." Malinski v. New York [1945]. These standards of justice are not authoritatively formulated anywhere as though they were specifics. Due process of law is a summarized constitutional guarantee of respect for those personal immunities which, as Mr. Justice Cardozo twice wrote for the Court, are "so rooted in the traditions and conscience of our people as to be ranked as fundamental," Snyder v. Massachusetts [1934], or are "implicit in the concept of ordered liberty." Palko v. Connecticut [1937].

The Court's function in the observance of this settled conception of the Due Process Clause does not leave us without adequate guides in subjecting State criminal procedures to constitutional judgment. In dealing not with the machinery of government but with human rights, the absence of formal exactitude, or want of fixity of meaning, is not an unusual or even regrettable attribute of constitutional provisions. Words being symbols do not speak without a gloss. On the one hand the gloss may be the deposit of history, whereby a term gains technical content. Thus the requirements of the Sixth and Seventh Amendments for trial by jury in the Federal courts have a rigid meaning. No changes or chances can alter the content of the verbal symbol of "jury"—a body of twelve men who must reach a unanimous conclusion if the verdict is to go against the defendant. On the other hand, the gloss of some of the verbal symbols of the Constitution does not give them a fixed technical content. It exacts a continuing process of application.

When the gloss has thus not been fixed but is a function of the process of judgment, the judgment is bound to fall differently at different times and differently at the same time through different judges. Even more specific provisions, such as the guaranty of freedom of speech and the detailed protection against unreasonable searches and seizures, have inevitably evoked as sharp divisions in this Court as the least specific and most comprehensive protection of liberties, the Due Process Clause.

The vague contours of the Due Process Clause do not leave judges at large. We may not draw on our merely personal and private notions and disregard the limits that bind judges in their judicial function. Even though the concept of due process of law is not final and fixed, these limits are derived from considerations that are fused in the whole nature of our judicial process. See Cardozo, The Nature of the Judicial Process; The Growth of the Law; The Paradoxes of Legal Science. These are considerations deeply rooted in reason and in the compelling traditions of the legal profession. The Due Process Clause places upon this Court the duty of exercising a judgment, within the narrow confines of judicial power in reviewing State convictions, upon interests of society pushing in opposite directions.

Due process of law thus conceived is not to be derided as resort to a revival of "natural law." To believe that this judicial exercise of judgment could be avoided by freezing "due process of law" at some fixed stage of time or thought is to suggest that the most important aspect of constitutional adjudication is a function for inanimate machines and not for judges, for whom the independence safeguarded by Article 3 of the Constitution was designed and who are presumably guided by established standards of judicial behavior. Even cybernetics has not yet made that haughty claim. To practice the requisite detachment and to achieve sufficient objectivity no doubt demands of judges the habit of self-discipline and self-criticism, incertitude that one's own views are incontestable and alert tolerance toward views not shared. But these are precisely the presuppositions of our judicial process. They are precisely the qualities society has a right to expect from those entrusted with ultimate judicial power.

Restraints on our jurisdiction are self-imposed only in the sense that there is from our decisions no immediate appeal short of impeachment or constitutional amendment. But that does not make due process of law a matter of judicial caprice. The faculties of the Due Process Clause may be indefinite and vague, but the mode of their ascertainment is not self-willed. In each case "due process of law" requires an evaluation based on a disinterested inquiry pursued in the spirit of science, on a balanced order of facts exactly and fairly stated, on the detached consideration of conflicting claims, . . . on a judgment not ad hoc and episodic but duly mindful of reconciling the needs both of continuity and of change in a progressive society.

Applying these general considerations to the circumstances of the present case, we are compelled to conclude that the proceedings by which this conviction was obtained do more than offend some fastidious squeamishness or private sentimentalism about combatting crime too energetically. This is conduct that shocks the conscience. Illegally breaking into the privacy of the petitioner, the struggle to open his mouth and remove what was there, the forcible extraction of his stomach's contents—this course of proceeding by agents of government to obtain evidence is bound to offend even hardened sensibilities. They are methods too close to the rack and the screw to permit of constitutional differentiation.

It has long since ceased to be true that due process of law is heedless of the means by which otherwise relevant and credible evidence is obtained.

This was not true even before the series of recent cases enforced the constitutional principle that the States may not base convictions upon confessions, however much verified, obtained by coercion. These decisions are not arbitrary exceptions to the comprehensive right of States to fashion their own rules of evidence for criminal trials. They are not sports in our constitutional law but applications of a general principle. They are only instances of the general requirement that States in their prosecutions respect certain decencies of civilized conduct. Due process of law, as a historic and generative principle, precludes defining, and thereby confining, these standards of conduct more precisely than to say that convictions cannot be brought about by methods that offend "a sense of justice." See Mr. Chief Justice Hughes, speaking for a unanimous Court in Brown v. Mississippi [1936]. It would be a stultification of the responsibility which the course of constitutional history has cast upon this Court to hold that in order to convict a man the police cannot extract by force what is in his mind but can extract what is in his stomach.

To attempt in this case to distinguish what lawyers call "real evidence" from verbal evidence is to ignore the reasons for excluding coerced confessions. Use of involuntary verbal confessions in State criminal trials is constitutionally obnoxious not only because of their unreliability. They are inadmissible under the Due Process Clause even though statements contained in them may be independently established as true. Coerced confessions offend the community's sense of fair play and decency. So here, to sanction the brutal conduct which naturally enough was condemned by the court whose judgment is before us, would be to afford brutality the cloak of law. Nothing would be more calculated to discredit law and thereby to brutalize the temper of a society. . . .

On the facts of this case the conviction of the petitioner has been obtained by methods that offend the Due Process Clause. The judgment below must be

Reversed.

Mr. Justice Minton took no part in the consideration or decision of this case.

Mr. Justice Black, concurring, said in part:

Adamson v. California [1947] sets out reasons for my belief that state as well as federal courts and law enforcement officers must obey the Fifth Amendment's command that "No person . . . shall be compelled in any criminal case to be a witness against himself." I think a person is compelled to be a witness against himself not only when he is compelled to testify, but also when as here, incriminating evidence is forcibly taken from him by a contrivance of modern science. . . .

Mr. Justice Douglas wrote a concurring opinion.

IRVINE v. CALIFORNIA

347 U. S. 128; 74 S. Ct. 381; 98 L. Ed. 561 (1954)

While it is clear that rights not mentioned in the Bill of Rights must be protected, if at all, through the "fundamental fairness" concept implicit in due process of law, what of those rights listed in the Bill of Rights which are not (as are the First Amendment rights) incorporated into due process? The decision in Powell v. Alabama (1932) was widely regarded as incorporating the Sixth Amendment right to counsel into due process, and this assumption was bolstered by its inclusion in Palko in the list of rights "that have been taken over from the earlier articles of the federal Bill of Rights and brought within the Fourteenth Amendment by a process of absorption." In 1942, however, the Supreme Court made it clear that this was not the case. In Betts v. Brady, it emphasized that "the due process clause of the Fourteenth Amendment does not incorporate, as such, the specific guarantees found in the Sixth Amendment although a denial by a state of rights or privileges specifically embodied in that and others of the first eight amendments may, in certain circumstances, or in connection with other elements, operate, in a given case, to deprive a litigant of due process of law. . . . That which may, in one setting, constitute a denial of fundamental fairness, shocking to the universal sense of justice, may, in other circumstances, and in the light of other considerations, fall short of such denial."

There thus appeared a sharp distinction between the two kinds of rights. Rights like those in the First Amendment were apparently "incorporated" or "absorbed" into due process so that they were applied against the states exactly as they were against the federal government, and state and federal cases served interchangeably as precedent. Rights not so incorporated were protected by the more flexible "fundamental fairness" rule that any state conduct which is grossly unfair denies due process of law.

Important as the distinction was, however, disagreement on the Court both over the implications of incorporation and what language was needed to accomplish it, made it difficult to tell when a right had, in fact, been incorporated. In Louisiana ex rel. Francis v. Resweber (1947), for instance, the Court held it was not a cruel and unusual punishment to try a second time to electrocute a person after the first attempt had failed to kill him. But while four members of the majority stated somewhat ambiguously that the "Fourteenth [Amendment] would prohibit by its due process clause execution by a state in a cruel manner," Justice Frankfurter wrote a concurring opinion to explain that in his view "the penology of a state is not to be tested by the scope of the Eighth Amendment."

In 1949 the Court appeared to incorporate into due process the protection in the Fourth Amendment against unreasonable searches and seizures. In Wolf v. Colorado (1949) it held that "The security of one's privacy against arbitrary intrusion by the police —which is at the core of the Fourth Amendment—is basic to a free society. It is therefore implicit in 'the concept of ordered liberty' and as such enforceable against the States through the Due Process Clause." Despite Justice Frankfurter's later protestation that this did not result in incorporation, it was clear that at least four members of the Court assumed it did. Whatever the merits of this, the Court in Wolf effectively nullified such protection as it had extended by refusing to apply a rule, developed years before in Weeks v. United States (1914), that forbade the admission in court of evidence gotten by unreasonable searches and seizures. This rule, concededly the only real deterrent to unlawful police searches, was held to be merely a rule of evidence, and not a requirement of the Fourth Amendment.

While the Court was being equivocal about the question of incorporation, it continued to be plagued by the theoretical and practical difficulties attendant on the fundamental fairness or "shock the conscience" doctrine, as it came to be known after the Rochin case. Despite Justice Frankfurter's masterful plea for a virtually unfettered judicial discretion, the Court responded to the need of the police and lower courts for guidelines spelling out what kinds of conduct were prohibited.

In the present case the California police had broken into the home of a suspected bookmaker and placed a microphone in several rooms of the house, including the bedroom. For over a month police officers eavesdropped in this way, and on the basis of information thus obtained, Irvine was tried and convicted. Justice Jackson, speaking for four members of the Court, conceded that "few police measures have come to our attention that more flagrantly, deliberately, and persistently violated the fundamental principle declared by the Fourth Amendment," but the Court refused to declare the evidence inadmissible although two members of the majority urged the Attorney General of the United States to determine whether the state officials might not be prosecuted under Section 242 of the Criminal Code for violating rights guaranteed by the Constitution.

Mr. Justice Jackson announced the judgment of the Court and an opinion in which The Chief Justice [Warren], Mr. Justice Reed, and Mr. Justice Minton join, saying in part:

. . . The decision in Wolf v. Colorado [1949], for the first time established that "[t]he security of one's privacy against arbitrary intrusion by the police" is embodied in the concept of due process found in the Fourteenth Amendment.

But Wolf, for reasons set forth therein, declined to make the subsidiary procedural and evidentiary doctrines developed by the federal courts limitations on the states. On the contrary, it declared, "We hold, therefore, that in a prosecution in a State court for a State crime the Fourteenth Amendment does not forbid the admission of evidence obtained by an unreasonable search and seizure." . . . That holding would seem to control here.

An effort is made, however, to bring this case under the sway of Rochin v. California [1952]. That case involved, among other things, an illegal search of the defendant's person. But it also presented an element totally lacking here—coercion . . . applied by a physical assault upon his person to compel submission to the use of a stomach pump. This was the feature which led to a result in Rochin contrary to that in Wolf. Although Rochin raised the search-and-seizure question, this Court studiously avoided it and never once mentioned the Wolf Case. Obviously, it thought that illegal search and seizure alone did not call for reversal. However obnoxious are the facts in the case before us, they do not involve coercion, violence or brutality to the person, but rather a trespass to property, plus eavesdropping.

It is suggested, however, that although we affirmed the conviction in Wolf, we should reverse here because this invasion of privacy is more shocking, more offensive, than the one involved there. The opinions in Wolf were written entirely in the abstract and did not disclose the details of the constitutional violation. Actually, the search was offensive to the law in the same respect, if not the same degree, as here. A deputy sheriff and others went to a doctor's office without a warrant and seized his appointment book, searched through it to learn the names of all his patients, looked up and interrogated certain of them, and filed an information against the doctor on the information that the District Attorney had obtained from the books. The books also were introduced in evidence against the doctor at his trial.

We are urged to make inroads upon Wolf by holding that it applies only to searches and seizures which produce on our minds a mild shock, while if the shock is more serious, the states must exclude the evidence or we will reverse the conviction. We think that the Wolf decision should not be overruled, for the reasons so persuasively stated therein. We think, too, that a distinction of the kind urged would leave the rule so indefinite that no state court could know what it should rule in order to keep its processes on solid constitutional ground. . . .

Judgment affirmed.

Mr. Justice Clark, concurring.

Had I been here in 1949 when Wolf was decided, I would have applied the doctrine of Weeks v. United States [1914] to the states. But the Court refused to do so then, and it still refuses today. Thus Wolf remains the law and, as such, is entitled to the respect of this Court's membership.

Of course, we could sterilize the rule announced in Wolf by adopting a case-by-case approach to due process in which inchoate notions of propriety concerning local police conduct guide our decisions. But this makes for such uncertainty and unpredictability that it would be impossible to foretell—other than by guesswork—just how brazen the invasion of the intimate privacies of one's home must be in order to shock itself into the protective arms of the Constitution. In truth, the practical result of this ad hoc approach is simply that when five Justices are sufficiently revolted by local police action, a conviction is overturned and a guilty man may go free. Rochin bears witness to this. We may thus vindicate the abstract principle of due process, but we do not shape the conduct of local police one whit; unpredictable reversals on dissimilar fact situations are not likely to curb the zeal of those police and prosecutors who may be intent on racking up a high percentage of successful prosecutions. I do not believe that the extension of such a vacillating course beyond the clear cases of physical coercion and brutality, such as Rochin, would serve a useful purpose.

In light of the "incredible" activity of the police here, it is with great reluctance that I follow Wolf. Perhaps strict adherence to the tenor of that decision may produce needed converts for its extinction. Thus I merely concur in the judgment of affirmance.

Mr. Justice Black, with whom Mr. Justice Douglas concurs, wrote a dissenting opinion.

Mr. Justice Frankfurter, whom Mr. Justice Burton joins, dissenting, said in part:

In the Wolf Case, the Court rejected one absolute. In Rochin, it rejected another. . . .

Rochin decided that the Due Process Clause of the Fourteenth Amendment does not leave States free in their prosecutions for crime. The Clause puts limits on the wide discretion of a State in the process of enforcing its criminal law. The holding of the case is that a State cannot resort to methods that offend civilized standards of decency and fairness. The conviction in the Rochin Case was found to offend due process not because evidence had been obtained through an unauthorized search and seizure or was the fruit of compulsory self-incrimination. Neither of these concepts, relevant to federal prosecutions, was invoked by the Court in Rochin, so of course the Wolf Case was not mentioned. While there is in the case before us as there was in Rochin, an element of unreasonable search and seizure, what is decisive here, as in Rochin, is additional aggravating conduct which the Court finds repulsive. . . .

There was lacking here physical violence, even to the restricted extent employed in Rochin. We have here, however, a more powerful and offensive control over the Irvines' life than a single, limited physical trespass. Certainly the conduct of the police here went far beyond a bare search and seizure. The police devised means to hear every word that was said in the Irvine household for more than a month. Those affirming the conviction find that this conduct, in its entirety, is "almost incredible if it were not admitted." Surely the Court does not propose to announce a new absolute, namely, that even the most reprehensible means for securing a conviction will not taint a verdict so long as the body of the accused was not touched by State officials. . . .

Since due process is not a mechanical yardstick it does not afford mechanical answers. In applying the Due Process Clause judicial judgment is involved in an empiric process in the sense that results are not predetermined or mechanically ascertainable. But that is a very different thing from conceiving the results as ad hoc decisions in the opprobrious sense of ad hoc. Empiricism implies judgment upon variant situations by the wisdom of experience. Ad hocness in adjudication means treating a particular case by itself and not in relation to the meaning of a course of decisions and the guides they serve for the future. There is all the difference in the world between disposing of a case as though it were a discrete instance and recognizing it as part of the process of judgment, taking its place in relation to what went before and further cutting a channel for what is to come.

The effort to imprison due process within tidy categories misconceives its nature and is a futile endeavor to save the judicial function from the pains of judicial judgment. It is pertinent to recall how the Court dealt with this craving for unattainable certainty in the Rochin Case:

"The vague contours of the Due Process Clause do not leave judges at large. We may not draw on our merely personal and private notions and disregard the limits that bind judges in their judicial function. Even though the concept of due process of law is not final and fixed, these limits are derived from considerations that are fused in the whole nature of our judicial process. See Cardozo, The Nature of the Judicial Process; The Growth of the Law; The Paradoxes of Legal Science. These are considerations deeply rooted in reason and in the compelling traditions of the legal profession. The Due Process Clause places upon this Court the duty of exercising a judgment, within the narrow confines of judicial power in reviewing State convictions, upon interests of society pushing in opposite directions." . . .

GIDEON v. WAINWRIGHT

372 U. S. 335; 83 S. Ct. 792; 9 L. Ed. 2d 799
(1963)

The attitude of judicial self-restraint under which the states had been shaping their own standards of fair criminal procedure came to an abrupt halt in 1961. In Mapp v. Ohio, the Court overruled Wolf v. Colorado (1949) and clearly made the Fourth Amendment, together with its exclusionary rule, applicable to the states. Then in 1962 it removed all doubt about the "incorporation" of cruel and unusual punishments when it used the formula, made familiar by First Amendment cases, that the state had violated the "Eighth and Fourteenth Amendments"; see Robinson v. California. The following year any lingering doubts about the meaning of "incorporation" were dispelled when eight members of the Court in Ker v. California (1963) agreed that federal constitutional standards of reasonableness of searches "is the same under the Fourth and Fourteenth Amendments." Only Justice Harlan clung to the view that "the more flexible concept of 'fundamental fairness' " should apply to the states.

The incorporation of other rights came rapidly. In 1964 following the decision in the present case, the Court in Malloy v. Hogan incorporated the Fifth Amendment privilege against self-incrimination. This was followed in 1965 by the right to confront one's accusers (Pointer v. Texas), in 1966 by an impartial jury (Parker v. Gladden), and in 1967 by speedy trial (Klopfer v. North Carolina), and the right to subpoena witnesses (Washington v. Texas). In 1968 the Court added the Sixth Amendment right to a jury trial in a criminal case (Duncan v. Louisiana) and in 1969, in Benton v. Maryland, it finally overruled Palko v. Connecticut (1937) and incorporated the protection against double jeopardy. "Palko's roots," the Court explained, "had been cut away years ago. We today only recognize the inevitable."

The decision in Duncan v. Louisiana inaugurated an unforseen development in the doctrine of incorporation. Incorporation had long been viewed as a way of forcing the states to adhere to a higher standard of conduct than was required by mere "fundamental fairness," and was hence a step in the civilizing process of treating more fairly those who were accused of crime. But following the Duncan case two decisions by the Supreme Court began reducing the requirements traditionally thought of as part of the jury trial. In Williams v. Florida (1970) the Court held a six-man jury met the requirements of the Sixth Amendment, and in Apodaca v. Oregon (1972) it held the Amendment did not require a unanimous verdict. The decisions were reached by reviewing the history of the Amendment's adoption, but while eight justices agreed that it had been incorporated into the Fourteenth and therefore applied to the states, four of them dissented on the ground that it required 12 men and a unanimous verdict.

Justice Powell, who had replaced Justice Harlan in 1971, agreed with Justices White, Burger, Blackmun and Rehnquist that "a defendant in a state court may constitutionally be convicted by less than a unanimous verdict." He agreed with his predecessor, however, that not "all of the elements of jury trial within the meaning of the Sixth Amendment are necessarily embodied in or incorporated into the Due Process Clause of the Fourteenth Amendment," and added "that unanimity is one of the indispensible features of *federal* jury trial." Thus, while eight members agreed that the Sixth Amendment requires the same standards of both state and nation, Justice Powell's position threatened to "disincorporate" the Amendment by applying a different standard to each. The threat, however, was short-lived. Justice Brennan switched over, and in 1973, speaking for a five-man majority, held the Seventh Amendment requirement of a civil jury did not preclude a six-person federal jury; see Colegrove v. Battin (1973).

Five years later, in Ballew v. Georgia (1978), the Court held void a five-person jury, and a year later in Burch v. Louisiana (1979) it held void a six-person jury which required only a vote of five to convict. The Court agreed unanimously in both cases that the smaller size defeated the purpose of the jury, but Justices Burger and Rehnquist joined Justice Powell in rejecting the idea that the Sixth Amendment was "incorporated" into the Fourteenth.

Following the reversal of his conviction in the present case, Gideon was retried by the state of Florida in the same courtroom, before the same judge, with the same witnesses, but with a lawyer appointed by the court at Gideon's request. This time he was acquitted.

Mr. Justice Black delivered the opinion of the Court, saying in part:

Petitioner was charged in a Florida state court with having broken and entered a poolroom with intent to commit a misdemeanor. This offense is a felony under Florida law. Appearing in court without funds and without a lawyer, petitioner asked the court to appoint counsel for him, whereupon the following colloquy took place:

"The Court: Mr. Gideon, I am sorry, but I cannot appoint Counsel to represent you in this case. Under the laws of the State of Florida, the only time the Court can appoint Counsel to represent a defendant is when that person is charged with a capital offense. I am sorry, but I will have to deny your request to appoint Counsel to defend you in this case.

"The Defendant: The United States Supreme Court says I am entitled to be represented by Counsel."

Put to trial before a jury, Gideon conducted his defense about as well as could be expected from a layman. He made an opening statement to the jury, cross-examined the State's witnesses, presented witnesses in his own defense, declined to testify himself, and made a short argument "emphasizing his innocence to the charge contained in the Information filed in this case." The jury returned a verdict of guilty, and petitioner was sentenced to serve five years in the state prison. . . . Since 1942, when Betts v. Brady was decided by a divided Court, the problem of a defendant's federal constitutional right to counsel in a state court has been a continuing source of controversy and litigation in both state and federal courts. To give this problem another review here, we granted certiorari. Since Gideon was proceeding in forma pauperis, we appointed counsel to represent him and requested both sides to discuss in their briefs and oral arguments the following: "Should this Court's holding in Betts v. Brady be reconsidered?"

I.

The facts upon which Betts claimed that he had been unconstitutionally denied the right to have counsel appointed to assist him are strikingly like the facts upon which Gideon here bases his federal constitutional claim. Betts was indicted for robbery in a Maryland state court. On arraignment, he told the trial judge of his lack of funds to hire a lawyer and asked the court to appoint one for him. Betts was advised that it was not the practice in that county to appoint counsel for indigent defendants except in murder and rape cases. He then pleaded not guilty, had witnesses summoned, cross-examined the State's witnesses, examined his own, and chose not to testify himself. He was found guilty by the judge, sitting without a jury, and sentenced to eight years in prison. Like Gideon, Betts sought release by habeas corpus, alleging that he had been denied the right to assistance of counsel in violation of the Fourteenth Amendment. Betts was denied any relief, and on review this Court affirmed. It was held that a refusal to appoint counsel for an indigent defendant charged with a felony did not necessarily violate the Due Process Clause of the Fourteenth Amendment, which for reasons given the Court deemed to be the only applicable federal constitutional provision. The Court said:

"Asserted denial [of due process] is to be tested by an appraisal of the totality of facts in a given case. That which may, in one setting, constitute a denial of fundamental fairness, shocking to the universal sense of justice, may, in other circumstances, and in the light of other considerations, fall short of such denial."

Treating due process as "a concept less rigid and more fluid than those envisaged in other specific and particular provisions of the Bill of Rights," the Court held that refusal to appoint counsel under the particular facts and circumstances in the Betts Case was not so "offensive to the common and fundamental ideas of fairness" as to amount to a denial of due process. Since the facts and circumstances of the two cases are so nearly indistinguishable, we think the Betts v. Brady holding if left standing would require us to reject Gideon's claim that the Constitution guarantees him the assistance of counsel. Upon full reconsideration we conclude that Betts v. Brady should be overruled.

II.

The Sixth Amendment provides, "In all criminal prosecutions, the accused shall enjoy the right . . . to have the Assistance of Counsel for his defense." We have construed this to mean that in federal courts counsel must be provided for defendants unable to employ counsel unless the right is competently and intelligently waived. Betts argued that this right is extended to indigent defendants in state courts by the Fourteenth Amendment. In response the Court stated that, while the Sixth Amendment laid down "no rule for the conduct of the States, the question recurs whether the constraint laid by the Amendment upon the national courts expresses a rule so fundamental and essential to a fair trial, and so, to due process of law, that it is made obligatory upon the States by the Fourteenth Amendment." In order to decide whether the Sixth Amendment's guarantee of counsel is of this fundamental nature, the Court in Betts set out and considered "[r]elevant data on the subject . . . afforded by constitutional and statutory provisions subsisting in the colonies and the States prior to the inclusion of the Bill of Rights in the national Constitution, and in the constitutional, legislative, and judicial history of the States to the present date." On the basis of this historical data the Court concluded that "appointment of counsel is not a fundamental right, essential to a fair trial." It was for this reason the Betts Court refused to accept the contention that the Sixth Amendment's guarantee of counsel for indigent federal defendants was extended to or, in the words of that Court, "made obligatory upon the States by the Fourteen Amendment." Plainly, had the Court concluded that appointment of counsel for an indigent criminal defendant was "a fundamental right, essential to a fair trial," it would have held that the Fourteenth Amendment requires appointment of counsel in a state court, just as the Sixth Amendment requires in a federal court.

We think the Court in Betts had ample precedent for acknowledging that those guarantees of the Bill of Rights which are fundamental safeguards of liberty immune from federal abridgment are equally protected against state invasion by the Due Process Clause of the Fourteenth Amendment. This same principle was recognized, explained and applied in Powell v. Alabama (1932), a case upholding the right of counsel, where the Court held that despite sweeping language to the contrary in Hurtado v. California (1884), the Fourteenth Amendment "embraced" those " 'fundamental principles of liberty and justice which lie at the base of all our civil and political institutions,' " even though they had been "specifically dealt with in another part of the federal Constitution." In many cases other than Powell and Betts, this Court has looked to the fundamental nature of original Bill of Rights guarantees to decide whether the Fourteenth Amendment makes them obligatory on the States. Explicitly recognized to be of this "fundamental nature" and therefore made immune from state invasion by the Fourteenth, or some part of it, are the First Amendment's freedoms of speech, press, religion, assembly, association, and petition for redress of grievances. For the same reason, though not always in precisely the same terminology, the Court has made obligatory on the States the Fifth Amendment's command that private property shall not be taken for public use without just compensation, the Fourth Amendment's prohibition of unreasonable searches and seizures, and the Eighth's ban on cruel and unusual punishment. On the other hand, this Court in Palko v. Connecticut (1937), refused to hold that the Fourteenth Amendment made the double jeopardy provision of the Fifth

Amendment obligatory on the States. In so refusing, however, the Court, speaking through Mr. Justice Cardozo, was careful to emphasize that "immunities that are valid as against the federal government by force of the specific pledges of particular amendments have been found to be implicit in the concept of ordered liberty, and thus, through the Fourteenth Amendment, become valid as against the states" and that guarantees "in their origin . . . effective against the federal government alone" had by prior cases "been taken over from the earlier articles of the federal bill of rights and brought within the Fourteenth Amendment by a process of absorption."

We accept Betts v. Brady's assumption, based as it was on our prior cases, that a provision of the Bill of Rights which is "fundamental and essential to a fair trial" is made obligatory upon the States by the Fourteenth Amendment. We think the Court in Betts was wrong, however, in concluding that the Sixth Amendment's guarantee of counsel is not one of these fundamental rights. Ten years before Betts v. Brady, this Court, after full consideration of all the historical data examined in Betts, had unequivocally declared that "the right to the aid of counsel is of this fundamental character." . . . While the court at the close of its Powell opinion did by its language, as this Court frequently does, limit its holding to the particular facts and circumstances of that case, its conclusions about the fundamental nature of the right to counsel are unmistakable. Several years later, in 1936, the Court reemphasized what it had said about the fundamental nature of the right to counsel in this language:

"We concluded that certain fundamental rights, safeguarded by the first eight amendments against federal action, were also safeguarded against state action by the due process of law clause of the Fourteenth Amendment, and among them the fundamental right of the accused to the aid of counsel in a criminal prosecution." Grosjean v. American Press Co. (1936).

And again in 1938 this Court said:

"[The assistance of counsel] is one of the safeguards of the Sixth Amendment deemed necessary to insure fundamental human rights of life and liberty. . . . The Sixth Amendment stands as a constant admonition that if the constitutional safeguards it provides be lost, justice will not 'still be done.'" Johnson v. Zerbst (1938). . . .

In light of these and many other prior decisions of this Court, it is not surprising that the Betts Court, when faced with the contention that "one charged with crime, who is unable to obtain counsel, must be furnished counsel by the State," conceded that "[e]xpressions in the opinions of this court lend color to the argument. . . ." The fact is that in deciding as it did —that "appointment of counsel is not a fundamental right, essential to a fair trial"—the Court in Betts v. Brady made an abrupt break with its own well-considered precedents. In returning to these old precedents, sounder we believe than the new, we but restore constitutional principles established to achieve a fair system of justice. Not only these precedents but also reason and reflection require us to recognize that in our adversary system of criminal justice, any person haled into court, who is too poor to hire a lawyer, cannot be assured a fair trial unless counsel is provided for him. This seems to us to be an obvious truth. Governments, both state and federal, quite properly spend vast sums of money to establish machinery to try defendants accused of crime. Lawyers to prosecute are everywhere deemed essential to protect the public's interest in an orderly society. Similarly, there are few defendants charged with crime, few indeed, who fail to hire the best lawyers they can get to prepare and present their defenses. That government hires lawyers to prosecute and defendants who have the money hire lawyers to defend are the strongest indications of the widespread belief that lawyers in criminal courts are necessities, not luxuries. The right of one charged with crime to counsel may not be deemed fundamental and essential to fair trials in some countries, but it is in ours. From the very beginning, our state and national constitutions and laws have laid great emphasis on procedural and substantive safeguards designed to assure fair trials before impartial tribunals in which every defendant stands equal before the law. This noble ideal cannot be realized if the poor man charged with crime has to face his accusers without a lawyer to assist him. A defendant's need for a lawyer is nowhere better stated than in the moving words of Mr. Justice Sutherland in Powell v. Alabama:

"The right to be heard would be, in many cases, of little avail if it did not comprehend the right to be heard by counsel. Even the intelligent and educated layman has small and sometimes no skill in the science of law. If charged with crime, he is incapable, generally, of determining for himself whether the indictment is good or bad. He is unfamiliar with the rules of evidence. Left without the aid of counsel he may be put on trial without a proper charge, and convicted upon incompetent evidence, or evidence irrelevant to the issue or otherwise inadmissible. He lacks both the skill and knowledge adequately to prepare his defense, even though he have a perfect one. He requires the guiding hand of counsel at every step in the proceedings against him. Without it, though he be not guilty, he faces the danger of conviction because he does not know how to establish his innocence."

The Court in Betts v. Brady departed from the sound wisdom upon which the Court's holding in Powell v. Alabama rested. Florida, supported by two other States, has asked that Betts v. Brady be left intact. Twenty-two States, as friends of the Court, argue that Betts was "an anachronism when handed down" and that it should now be overruled. We agree.

The judgment is reversed and the cause is remanded to the Supreme Court of Florida for further action not inconsistent with this opinion.

Reversed.

Mr. Justice Douglas, while joining the opinion of the Court, wrote a separate opinion, saying in part:

My Brother Harlan is of the view that a guarantee of the Bill of Rights that is made applicable to the States by reason of the Fourteenth Amendment is a lesser version of that same guarantee as applied to the Federal Government. Mr. Justice Jackson shared that view. But that view has not prevailed and rights protected against state invasion by the Due Process Clause of the Fourteenth Amendment are not watered-down versions of what the Bill of Rights guarantees.

Mr. Justice Clark, concurring in the result, wrote a separate opinion.

Mr. Justice Harlan, concurring, said in part:

I agree that Betts v. Brady should be overruled, but consider it entitled to a more respectful burial than has been accorded, at least on the part of those of us who were not on the Court when that case was decided.

I cannot subscribe to the view that Betts v. Brady represented "an abrupt break with its own well-considered precedents." In 1932, in Powell v. Alabama, a capital case, this Court declared that under the particular facts there presented—"the ignorance and illiteracy of the defendants, their youth, the circumstances of public hostility . . . and above all that they stood in deadly peril of their lives"—the state court had a duty to assign counsel for the trial as a necessary requisite of due process of law. It is evident that these limiting facts were not added to the opinion as an afterthought; they were repeatedly emphasized, and were clearly regarded as important to the result.

Thus when this Court, a decade later, decided Betts v. Brady, it did no more than to admit of the possible existence of special circumstances in noncapital as well as capital trials, while at the same time insisting that such circumstances be shown in order to establish a denial of due process. The right to appointed counsel had been recognized as being considerably broader in federal prosecutions, see Johnson v. Zerbst [1938], but to have imposed these requirements on the States would indeed have been "an abrupt break" with the almost immediate past. The declaration that the right appointed counsel in state prosecutions, as established in Powell v. Alabama, was not limited to capital cases was in truth not a departure from, but an extension of, existing precedent. . . .

[Mr. Justice Harlan here notes the "troubled journey" of the Powell and Betts doctrines and concedes that since 1950 no "special circumstances" have been found to justify the absence of counsel.]

. . . The Court has come to recognize, in other words, that the mere existence of a serious criminal charge constituted in itself special circumstances requiring the services of counsel at trial. In truth the Betts v. Brady rule is no longer a reality.

This evolution, however, appears not to have been fully recognized by many state courts, in this instance charged with the front-line responsibility for the enforcement of constitutional rights. To continue a rule which is honored by this Court only with lip service is not a healthy thing and in the long run will do disservice to the federal system. . . .

In agreeing with the Court that the right to counsel in a case such as this should now be expressly recognized as a fundamental right embraced in the Fourteenth Amendment, I wish to make a further observation. When we hold a right or immunity, valid against the Federal Government, to be "implicit in the concept of ordered liberty" and thus valid against the States, I do not read our past decisions to suggest that by so holding, we automatically carry over an entire body of federal law and apply it in full sweep to the States. Any such concept would disregard the frequently wide disparity between the legitimate interests of the States and of the Federal Government, the divergent problems that they face, and the significantly different consequences of their actions. . . . In what is done today I do not understand the Court to depart from the principles laid down in Palko v. Connecticut, or to embrace the concept that the Fourteenth Amendment "incorporates" the Sixth Amendment as such.

On these premises I join in the judgment of the Court.

ROE v. WADE

410 U. S. 113; 93 S. Ct. 705; 35 L. Ed. 2d 147 (1973)

While the Constitution prescribes certain limits on governmental power, these limits are in a continual state of change. As the Court engages in the endless process of interpreting the constitutional guarantees, certain protections are withdrawn and others are added. Ordinarily this process occurs so slowly and subtly that only a careful observer can detect that a real change is actually taking place. While apparently applying the same principles to a new set of facts, the Court is in reality altering the principle by an almost indistinguishable increment. Now and again the Court will find this process incapable of producing the results that it wants; a former interpretation of principle no longer fills what the Court sees as the needs of society, so that principle must be rejected and another put in its place. On such occasions the Court will overrule its previous interpretation of the Constitution and substitute another interpretation—usually one which has been long clamoring for acceptance. This is what the Court did when, starting in the early 1960s, it began in a serious way to incorporate Bill of Rights guarantees into the due process clause of the Fourteenth Amendment.

On very rare occasions, when what seems to the Court to be an important right cannot be brought comfortably under any existing constitutional guarantee, the Court is forced to draw upon what it conceives to be the general or fundamental principles of the Constitution to supply the necessary protection. In the early days little effort was made to tie such protection to specific parts of the document: In Loan Association v. Topeka (1875), for example, the Court forbade spending tax money for private purposes on the ground that it violated limits on governmental power that "grow out of the essential nature of all free governments." With the evolution of the due process clause, this right and the celebrated "liberty of contract" became elements of due process of law. See the note to Lochner v. New York (1905).

In Griswold v. Connecticut (1965), the Supreme Court raised the right of privacy to constitutional status by drawing on a "penumbra" cast by a number of constitutional provisions. "Privacy in one's association" had been protected in NAACP v. Alabama (1958), and the Third, Fourth and Fifth Amendments had all created a zone of privacy which the government might not violate. This newly created right, the Court held, included a right of marital privacy with an attendant right to use contraceptives and receive birth-control information. In Eisenstadt v. Baird (1972) the Court held that equal protection required that unmarried women, too, be allowed birth control information and articles.

"The Court today does *not* pick out particular human activities, characterize them as 'fundamental,' and give them added protection. . . . To the contrary, the Court simply recognizes, as it must, an established constitutional right, and gives to that right no less protection than the Constitution itself demands." Although this quotation from Justice Stewart by the Court in San Antonio v. Rodriguez (1973) states the orthodox view of the Court's role, few scholars today would subscribe to it. While in theory all rights in the Constitution are of equal value (the Constitution nowhere suggests that some rights are more important than others), over the years the Court has always cherished certain rights which it considered more important than other rights and hence entitled to greater constitutional protection. The rights so honored have changed from time to time as the Court perceived changes in basic social values. In the early days private property was given special consideration, and later this came to include the rights of businessmen and "liberty of contract." Then in the 1930s and 1940s, while the economic rights fell from grace, the rights listed in the First Amendment rose to favor. In recent years the rights of privacy, the right to vote, and the right to move freely among the states have joined the ranks of the elite.

Since the ranking of these rights is a matter of value judgment, it has been condemned by those who disapproved the particular ranking as "judicial legislation," "substituting judicial values for those of the community," a "violation of the democratic process," and a "lack of proper judicial restraint." While such attacks seem to challenge the role of the Court in this area, in fact few justices have rejected philosophically the idea that some rights are better than others. The classic example is Justice Holmes, who condemned the judicial favoritism shown to economic rights (see Lochner v. New York, 1905) while insisting that speech could be curtailed only if it presented a "clear and present danger," (see his dissent in Gitlow v. New York, 1925).

Perhaps the easiest method of giving added protection to a right, once it is identified, is to clothe it in language that nullifies the normal presumption in favor of legislative acts and forces the government to show that its laws are reasonable and necessary. Such language abounds in the areas of the First Amendment: the "clear and present danger" test, the statement that First Amendment rights are in a "preferred position" (see Murdock v. Pennsylvania, 1943) and the rule (since modified) that publications cannot be condemned as obscene unless they are utterly without redeeming social value all serve to tip the scales in favor of the right and against the government wishing to suppress or regulate it.

In 1960 in Bates v. Little Rock a new phrase made its appearance. The Court held bad the demand of the city of Little Rock for the publication of the membership lists of the NAACP on the ground that it would destroy the group's organizational privacy and impair its operations. "Where there is a significant encroachment upon personal liberty, the State may prevail only upon showing a subordinating interest which is compelling." This "compelling state interest" phrase appeared again in several cases in 1963 (see Gibson v. Florida Investigating Committee), where its impact was to make the state produce evidence that it had a compelling interest which could be met only by infringing a claimed right of association. In none of the cases was sufficient interest shown.

In 1969 the "compelling state interest" doctrine was applied to the equal protection clause. The Court in this area had long granted favored status to certain bases of classification, such as race and religion, holding that legislative distinctions based on them were, if not "invidious," at least "inherently suspect." But with Shapiro v. Thompson and Kramer v. U.S.F.D. (1969) the Court looked not at the bases of classification alone, but at the aims sought to be achieved by these bases. In striking down the requirement of a year's residence to receive welfare and the requirement of taxpayer (or parental) status to vote in school board elections, the Court found that where a classification limits the right to move freely across state lines or the right to vote, it could only be justified by a compelling state interest.

In the case below, the phrase is moved again—this time into the area of privacy protected by the Constitution. Here the Court not only upholds the right of a mother to decide, in consultation with her doctor, whether or not to have an abortion, but spells out the "compelling points" at which the state's "compelling interest" permits it to undertake regulation of abortions.

Mr. Justice Blackmun delivered the opinion of the Court, saying in part:

V.

The principal thrust of appellant's attack on the Texas statutes is that they improperly invade a right, said to be possessed by the pregnant woman, to choose to terminate her pregnancy. Appellant would discover this right in the concept of personal "liberty" embodied in the Fourteenth Amendment's Due Process Clause; or in personal, marital, familial, and sexual privacy said to be protected by the Bill of Rights or its penumbras, see Griswold v. Connecticut (1965); Eisenstadt v. Baird (1972); (White, J., concurring in result); or among those rights reserved to the people by the Ninth Amendment, Griswold v. Connecticut (Goldberg, J., concurring). Before addressing this claim, we feel it desirable briefly to survey, in several aspects, the history of abortion, for such insight as that history may afford us, and then to examine the state purposes and interests behind the criminal abortion laws.

VI.

It perhaps is not generally appreciated that the restrictive criminal abortion laws in effect in a majority of States today are of relatively recent vintage. Those laws, generally proscribing abortion or its attempt at any time during pregnancy except when necessary to preserve the pregnant woman's life, are not of ancient or even of common-law origin. Instead, they derive from statutory changes effected, for the most part, in the latter half of the 19th century. . . .

[The Court here reviews the history of attitudes toward abortion and abortion laws since ancient times.]

VII.

Three reasons have been advanced to explain historically the enactment of criminal abortion laws in the 19th century and to justify their continued existence.

It has been argued occasionally that these laws were the product of a Victorian social concern to discourage illicit sexual conduct. Texas, however, does not advance this justification in the present case, and it appears that no court or commentator has taken the argument seriously. The appellants and amici contend, moreover, that this is not a proper state purpose at all and suggest that, if it were, the Texas statutes are overbroad in protecting it since the law fails to distinguish between married and unwed mothers.

A second reason is concerned with abortion as a medical procedure. When most criminal abortion laws were first enacted, the procedure was a hazardous one for the woman. This was particuarly true prior to the development of antisepsis. Antiseptic techniques, of course, were based on discoveries by Lister, Pasteur, and others first announced in 1867, but were not generally accepted and employed until about the turn of the century. Abortion mortality was high. Even after 1900, and perhaps until as late as the development of antibiotics in the 1940's, standard modern techniques such as dilation and curettage were not nearly so safe as they are today. Thus, it has been argued that a State's real concern in enacting a criminal abortion law was to protect the pregnant woman, that is, to restrain her from submitting to a procedure that placed her life in serious jeopardy.

Modern medical techniques have altered this situation. Appellants and various amici refer to medical data indicating that abortion in early pregnancy, that is, prior to the end of first trimester, although not without its risk, is now relatively safe. Mortality rates for women undergoing early abortions, where the procedure is legal, appear to be as low as or lower than the rates for normal childbirth. Consequently, any interest of the State in protecting the woman from an inherently hazardous procedure, except when it would be equally dangerous for her to forego it, has largely disappeared. Of course, important state interests in the area of health and medical standards do remain.

The State has a legitimate interest in seeing to it that abortion, like any other medical procedure, is performed under circumstances that insure maximum safety for the patient. This interest obviously extends at least to the performing physician and his staff, to the facilities involved, to the availability of after-care, and to adequate provision for any complication or emergency that might arise. The prevalence of high mortality rates at illegal "abortion mills" strengthens, rather than weakens, the State's interest in regulating the conditions under which abortions are performed. Moreover, the risk to the woman increases as her pregnancy continues. Thus, the State retains a definite interest in protecting the woman's own health and safety when an abortion is proposed at a late stage of pregnancy.

The third reason is the State's interest—some phrase it in terms of duty —in protecting prenatal life. Some of the argument for this justification rests on the theory that a new human life is present from the moment of conception. The State's interest and general obligation to protect life then extends, it is argued, to prenatal life. Only when the life of the pregnant mother herself is at stake, balanced against the life she carries within her, should the interest of the embryo or fetus not prevail. Logically, of course, a legitimate state interest in this area need not stand or fall on acceptance of the belief that life begins at conception or at some other point prior to live birth. In assessing the State's interest, recognition may be given to the less rigid claim that as long as at least *potential* life is involved, the State may assert interests beyond the protection of the pregnant woman alone. . . .

It is with these interests, and the weight to be attached to them, that this case is concerned.

VIII.

The Constitution does not explicitly mention any right of privacy. In a line of decisions, however, going back perhaps as far as Union Pacific R. Co. v. Botsford (1891), the Court has recognized that a right of personal privacy, or a guarantee of certain areas or zones of privacy, does exist under the Constitition. In varying contexts the Court or individual Justices have, indeed, found at least the roots of that right in the First Amendment, Stanley v. Georgia (1969); in the Fourth and Fifth Amendments, Terry v. Ohio (1968), Katz v. United States (1967) . . .; in the penumbras of the Bill of Rights, Griswold v. Connecticut (1965); in the Ninth Amendment; or in the concept of liberty guaranteed by the first section of the Fourteenth Amendment, see Meyer v. Nebraska (1923). These decisions make it clear that only personal rights that can be deemed "fundamental" or "implicit in the concept of ordered liberty," Palko v. Connecticut (1937), are included in this guarantee of personal privacy. They also make it clear that the right has some extension to activities relating to marriage, Loving v. Virginia (1967); procreation, Skinner v. Oklahoma (1942); contraception, Eisenstadt v. Baird (1972) . . . .

This right of privacy, whether it be founded in the Fourteenth Amendment's concept of personal liberty and restrictions upon state action, as we feel it is, or, as the District Court determined, in the Ninth Amendment's reservation of rights to the people, is broad enough to encompass a woman's decision whether or not to terminate her pregnancy. The detriment that the State would impose upon the pregnant woman by denying this choice altogether is apparent. Specific and direct harm medically diagnosable even in early pregnancy may be involved. Maternity, or additional offspring, may force upon the woman a distressful life and future. Psychological harm may be imminent. Mental and physical health may be taxed by child care. There is also the distress, for all concerned, associated with the unwanted child, and there is the problem of bringing a child into a family already unable, psychologically and otherwise, to care for it. In other cases, as in this one, the additional difficulties and continuing stigma of unwed motherhood may be involved. All these are factors the woman and her responsible physician necessarily will consider in consultation.

On the basis of elements such as these, appellant and some amici argue that the woman's right is absolute and that she is entitled to terminate her pregnancy at whatever time, in whatever way, and for whatever reason she alone chooses. With this we do not agree. Appellant's arguments that Texas either has no valid interest at all in regulating the abortion decision, or no interest strong enough to support any limitation upon the woman's sole determination, is unpersuasive. The Court's decisions recognizing a right of privacy also acknowledge that some state regulation in areas protected by that right is appropriate. As noted above, a State may properly assert important interests in safeguarding health, in maintaining medical standards, and in protecting potential life. At some point in pregnancy, these respective interests become sufficiently compelling to sustain regulation of the factors that govern the abortion decision. The privacy right involved, therefore, cannot be said to be absolute. In fact, it is not clear to us that the claim asserted by some amici that one has an unlimited right to do with one's body as one pleases bears a close relationship to the right of privacy previously articulated in the Court's decisions. The Court has refused to recognize an unlimited right of this kind in the past. Jacobson v. Massachusetts (1905) (vaccination); Buck v. Bell (1927) (sterilization).

We therefore conclude that the right of personal privacy includes the abortion decision, but that this right is not unqualified and must be considered against important state interests in regulation. . . .

Where certain "fundamental rights" are involved, the Court has held that regulation limiting these rights may be justified only by a "compelling state interest," Kramer v. Union Free School District (1969); Shapiro v. Thompson (1969); . . . and that legislative enactments must be narrowly drawn to express only the legitimate state interests at stake. Griswold v. Connecticut (1965). . . .

IX.

The District Court held that the appellee failed to meet his burden of demonstrating that the Texas statute's infringement upon Roe's rights was necessary to support a compelling state interest. . . . Appelle argues that the State's determination to recognize and protect prenatal life from and after conception constitutes a compelling state interest. As noted above, we do not agree fully with either formulation.

A. The appellee and certain amici argue that the fetus is a "person" within the language and meaning of the Fourteenth Amendment. In support of this, they outline at length and in detail the well-known facts of fetal development. If this suggestion of personhood is established, the appellant's case, of course, collapses, for the fetus' right to life is then guaranteed specifically by the Amendment. The appellant conceded as much on reargument. On the other hand, the appellee conceded on reargument that no case could be cited that holds that a fetus is a person within the meaning of the Fourteenth Amendment.

The Constitution does not define "person" in so many words. Section 1 of the Fourteenth Amendment contains three references to "person." The first, in defining "citizens," speaks of "persons born or naturalized in the United States." The word also appears both in the Due Process Clause and in the Equal Protection Clause. "Person" is used in other places in the Constitution. . . . But in nearly all these instances, the use of the word is such that it has application only postnatally. None indicates, with any assurance, that it has any possible prenatal application.*

All this, together with our observation, that throughout the major portion of the 19th century prevailing legal abortion practices were far freer than they are today, persuades us that the word "person," as used in the Fourteenth Amendment, does not include the unborn. . . .

B. The pregnant woman cannot be isolated in her privacy. She carries an embryo and, later, a fetus, if one accepts the medical definitions of the developing young in the human uterus. . . . The situation therefore is inherently different from marital intimacy, or bedroom possession of obscene material, or marriage, or procreation, or education, with which Eisenstadt, Griswold, Stanley, Loving, Skinner, Pierce, and Meyer were respectively concerned. As we have intimated above, it is reasonable and appropriate for a State to decide that at some point in time another interest, that of health of the mother or that of potential human life, becomes significantly involved. The woman's privacy is no longer sole and any right of privacy she possesses must be measured accordingly.

Texas urges that, apart from the Fourteenth Amendment, life begins at conception and is present throughout pregnancy, and that, therefore, the State has a compelling interest in protecting that life from and after conception. We need not resolve the difficult question of when life begins. When those trained in the respective disciplines of medicine, philosophy, and theology are unable to arrive at any consensus, the judiciary, at this point in the development of man's knowledge, is not in a position to speculate as to the answer.

It should be sufficient to note briefly the wide divergence of thinking on this most sensitive and difficult question. . . .

X.

In view of all this, we do not agree that, by adopting one theory of life, Texas may override the rights of the pregnant woman that are at stake. We repeat, however, that the State does have an important and legitimate interest in preserving and protecting the health of the pregnant woman, whether she be a resident of the State or a nonresident who seeks medical consultation and treatment there, and that it has still *another* important and legitimate interest in protecting the potentiality of human life. These interests are separate and distinct. Each grows in substantiality as the woman approaches term and, at a point during pregnancy, each becomes "compelling."

---

*When Texas urges that a fetus is entitled to Fourteenth Amendment protection as a person, it faces a dilemma. Neither in Texas nor in any other State are all abortions prohibited. Despite broad proscription, an exception always exists. The exception contained in Art. 1196, for an abortion procured or attempted by medical advice for the purpose of saving the life of the mother, is typical. But if the fetus is a person who is not to be deprived of life without due process of law, and if the mother's condition is the sole determinant, does not the Texas exception appear to be out of line with the Amendment's command? . . .

With respect to the State's important and legitimate interest in the health of the mother, the "compelling" point, in the light of present medical knowledge, is at approximately the end of the first trimester. This is so because of the now established medical fact, referred to above . . . that until the end of the first trimester mortality in abortion may be less than mortality in normal childbirth. It follows that, from and after this point, a State may regulate the abortion procedure to the extent that the regulation reasonably relates to the preservation and protection of maternal health. Examples of permissible state regulation in this area are requirements as to the qualifications of the person who is to perform the abortion; as to the licensure of that person; as to the facility in which the procedure is to be performed, that is, whether it must be a hospital or may be a clinic or some other place of less-than-hospital status; as to the licensing of the facility; and the like.

This means, on the other hand, that, for the period of pregnancy prior to this "compelling" point, the attending physician, in consultation with his patient, is free to determine, without regulation by the State, that in his medical judgment the patient's pregnancy should be terminated. If that decision is reached, the judgment may be effectuated by an abortion free of interference by the State.

With respect to the State's important and legitimate interest in potential life, the "compelling" point is at viability. This is so because the fetus then presumably has the capability of meaningful life outside the mother's womb. State regulation protective of fetal life after viability thus has both logical and biological justifications. If the State is interested in protecting fetal life after viability, it may go so far as to proscribe abortion during that period except when it is necessary to preserve the life or health of the mother.

Measured against these standards, the Texas Penal Code, in restricting legal abortions to those "procured or attempted by medical advice for the purpose of saving the life of the mother," sweeps too broadly. The statute makes no distinction between abortions performed early in pregnancy and those performed later, and it limits to a single reason, "saving" the mother's life, the legal justification for the procedure. The statute, therefore, cannot survive the constitutional attack made upon it here. . . .

Mr. Chief Justice Burger concurred.

Mr. Justice Douglas concurred.

Mr. Justice Stewart, concurring said in part:

In 1963, this Court, in Ferguson v. Skrupa, purported to sound the death knell for the doctrine of substantive due process, a doctrine under which many state laws had in the past been held to violate the Fourteenth Amendment. As Mr. Justice Black's opinion for the Court in Skrupa put it: "We have returned to the original constitutional proposition that courts do not substitute their social and economic beliefs for the judgment of legislative bodies, who are elected to pass laws."

Barely two years later, in Griswold v. Connecticut, the Court held a Connecticut birth control law unconstitutional. In view of what had been so recently said in Skrupa, the Court's opinion in Griswold understandably did its best to avoid reliance on the Due Process Clause of the Fourteenth Amendment as the ground for decision. Yet, the Connecticut law did not violate any provision of the Bill of Rights, nor any other specific provision of the Constitution. So it was clear to me then, and it is equally clear to me now, that the Griswold decision can be rationally understood only as a holding that the Connecticut statute substantively invaded the "liberty" that is protected by the Due Process Clause of the Fourteenth Amendment. As so understood, Griswold stands as one in a long line of pre-Skrupa cases decided under the doctrine of substantive due process, and I now accept it as such.

"In a Constitution for a free people, there can be no doubt that the meaning of "liberty' must be broad indeed." . . . The Constitution nowhere mentions a specific right of personal choice in matters of marriage and family life, but the "liberty" protected by the Due Process Clause of the Fourteenth Amendment covers more than those freedoms explicitly named in the Bill of Rights. . . .

Several decisions of this Court make clear that freedom of personal choice in matters of marriage and family life is one of the liberties protected by the Due Process Clause of the Fourteenth Amendment. Loving v. Virginia, Griswold v. Connecticut . . . . That right necessarily includes the right of a woman to decide whether or not to terminate her pregnancy. "Certainly the interests of a woman in giving of her physical and emotional self during pregnancy and the interests that will be affected throughout her life by the birth and raising of a child are of a far greater degree of significance and personal intimacy than the right to send a child to private school protected in Pierce v. Society of Sisters (1925), or the right to teach a foreign language protected in Meyer v. Nebraska (1923)." . . .

Mr. Justice Rehnquist, dissenting, said in part:

. . . I have difficulty in concluding, as the Court does, that the right of "privacy" is involved in this case. Texas, by the statute here challenged, bars the performance of a medical abortion by a licensed physician on a plaintiff such as Roe. A transaction resulting in an operation such as this is not "private" in the ordinary usage of that word. . . .

If the Court means by the term "privacy" no more than that the claim of a person to be free from unwanted state regulation of consensual transactions may be a form of "liberty" protected by the Fourteenth Amendment, there is no doubt that similar claims have been upheld in our earlier decisions on the basis of that liberty. I agree with the statement of Mr. Justice Stewart in his concurring opinion that the "liberty," against deprivation of which without due process the Fourteenth Amendment protects, embraces more than the rights found in the Bill of Rights. But that liberty is not guaranteed absolutely against deprivation, but only against deprivation without due process of law. The test traditionally applied in the area of social and economic legislation is whether or not a law such as that challenged has a rational relation to a valid state objective. . . . But the Court's sweeping invalidation of any restrictions on abortion during the first trimester is impossible to justify under that standard, and the conscious weighing of competing factors that the Court's opinion apparently substitutes for the established test is far more appropriate to a legislative judgment than to a judicial one.

The Court eschews the history of the Fourteenth Amendment in its reliance on the "compelling state interest" test. . . . But the Court adds a new wrinkle to this test by transposing it from the legal considerations associated with the Equal Protection Clause of the Fourteenth Amendment to this case arising under the Due Process Clause of the Fourteenth Amendment. Unless I misapprehend the consequences of this transplanting of the "compelling state interest test," the Court's opinion will accomplish the seemingly impossible feat of leaving this area of the law more confused than it found it.

While the Court's opinion quotes from the dissent of Mr. Justice Holmes in Lochner v. New York (1905), the result it reaches is more closely attuned to the majority opinion of Mr. Justice Peckham in that case. As in Lochner and similar cases applying substantive due process standards to economic and social welfare legislation, the adoption of the compelling state interest standard will inevitably require this Court to examine the legislative policies and pass on the wisdom of these policies in the very process of deciding whether a particular state interest put forward may or may not be "compelling." . . .

The fact that a majority of the States reflecting, after all, the majority sentiment in those States, have had restrictions on abortions for at least a century is a strong indication, it seems to me, that the asserted right to an abortion is not "so rooted in the traditions and conscience of our people as to be ranked as fundamental," Snyder v. Massachusetts (1934). . . .

Mr. Justice White, with whom Mr. Justice Rehnquist joins, dissented.

6

First
Amendment
Rights

GITLOW v. NEW YORK

268 U. S. 652; 45 S. Ct. 625; 69 L. Ed. 1138 (1925)

Freedom of speech and press are not absolute rights and were never intended to be so. They are relative, in the sense that they are limited by the coexisting rights of others (as in the matter of libel) and by the demands of national security and public decency. As Justice Holmes put it in the Schenck case (below), "The most stringent protection of free speech would not protect a man in falsely shouting fire in a theatre and causing a panic." Free speech and press cases present to the courts difficult questions of degree: questions involved in drawing the line that separates the speech and publication that government must suppress in order to be safe and decent from that which it must allow and protect in order to be free and democratic.

What was perhaps the most conspicuous and interesting instance of interference with freedom of expression in our history never came before the Supreme Court of the United States. The Sedition Act of 1798 provided among other things for the severe punishment of false, scandalous, and malicious writings against the government, either house of Congress, or the President if published with intent to defame any of them, or to excite against them the hatred of the people, or to stir up sedition. It was limited in operation to two years. Ten persons were convicted under it, and many others were indicted but not tried. Its enactment and enforcement called forth great popular indignation, and President Jefferson upon assuming office pardoned all persons still imprisoned under its provisions. Many years later Congress refunded with interest the fines which had been imposed.

The relative character of the right of free speech and press becomes particularly obvious in time of war. Where is the line to be drawn between legitimate and salutary freedom of discussion and utterances which, by reason of their disloyal or seditious character, must be deemed incompatible with the public safety? This is a delicate and important question. During the Civil War such interferences with freedom of speech and press as occurred were perpetrated by military officers under the sanction of martial law, and no question of the validity of these acts of repression ever came squarely before the Supreme Court. World War I brought forth a large grist of restrictive legislation, both state and federal, and numerous judicial questions arose as to the validity of these acts and their application to specific cases. Most conspicuous of these laws were the Espionage Act of 1917—that penalized any circulation of false statements made with intent to interfere with military success, as well as any attempt to cause disloyalty in the Army or Navy or to obstruct recruiting—and the Sedition Act of 1918 —that made it a crime to say or do anything that could obstruct the sale of government bonds, or to utter or publish words intended to bring into contempt or disrepute the form of government of the United States, the Constitution, flag, uniform, etc., or to incite resistance to the government or promote the cause of its enemies. Nearly a thousand persons were convicted under these two acts. Their validity was sustained in six cases coming to the Supreme Court after the close of the war. Schenck v. United States (1919) was the first of these cases, and in it Justice Holmes announced the now famous "clear and present danger" test: "The question in every case is whether the words used are used in such circumstances and are of such a nature as to create a clear and present danger that they will bring about the substantive evils that Congress has a right to prevent. It is a question of proximity and degree." Schenck had been convicted of circulating pamphlets urging resistance to the draft, and the Court found that they presented a clear and present danger of achieving this result. A week later the Court decided two more cases, Frohwerk v. United States (1919), involving a pro-German newspaper man, and Debs v. United States (1919), involving the famous Socialist leader. Holmes wrote the opinions sustaining the convictions of the two men on the grounds that their writings and speeches met the test of clear and present danger.

The Espionage Act of 1917 forbade certain kinds of action, such as causing or attempting to cause insubordination or obstructing the draft. It did not expressly limit freedom of speech; it limited it only when speech amounted to the kind of action forbidden by the statute. In order to determine when a particular speech became "action" and thus punishable under the statute, the Court resorted to two tests, the "bad tendency" test and the "clear and present danger" test.

The "bad tendency" test was designed, as Professor Chafee put it, "to kill the serpent in the egg" by preventing all speech which had a tendency, however remote, to bring about acts in violation of the law. It had its roots in the doctrine of constructive treason, so infamous in English history, under which criticism of the government was construed as an attempt to accomplish the overthrow of that government and was punished as treason. The "clear and present danger" test, devised by Justice Holmes in the Schenck case, held that speech becomes punishable as action only when there is a danger, clear and present, that it will bring the action about. If there is no clear and present danger the speech does not amount to action, and the statute forbidding the action has not been violated. Holmes's doctrine was not intended as a test of the validity of the statute itself, since presumably the "action" which the statute forbids is, like obstructing the draft, something Congress could legitimately prohibit.

The clear and present danger test is not simple to apply. It is, for instance, difficult to apply to a statute which, by its language, forbids certain kinds of speech. If a person makes the kind of speech thus forbidden, then he has violated the statute; in other words, once the legislature has decided for itself what kind of speech is dangerous and forbidden it, the courts can hold the statute unconstitutional but they cannot say it has not been violated. Holmes and Brandeis apparently felt that statutes of this kind could not constitutionally be applied to cases in which there was no clear and present danger of serious substantive evil. See their concurring opinion in Whitney v. California (1927).

In the present case Benjamin Gitlow was prosecuted under the New York Criminal Anarchy Act of 1902 for distributing a document similar to the Communist Manifesto of Marx and Engels (1848). This statute, which formed the model for the federal Smith Act, punishes certain kinds of speech and publication regardless of the intent of the speaker or publisher.

Mr. Justice Sanford delivered the opinion of the Court, saying in part:

Benjamin Gitlow was indicted in the supreme court of New York, with three others, for the statutory crime of criminal anarchy. . . .

The contention here is that the statute, by its terms and as applied in this case, is repugnant to the due process clause of the 14th Amendment. Its material provisions are:

"§ 160. Criminal anarchy defined.—Criminal anarchy is the doctrine that organized government should be overthrown by force or violence, or by assassination of the executive head or of any of the executive officials of government, or by any unlawful means. The advocacy of such doctrine either by word of mouth or writing is a felony.

"§ 161. Advocacy of criminal anarchy.—Any person who:

"1. By word of mouth or writing advocates, advises or teaches the duty, necessity or propriety of overthrowing or overturning organized government by force or violence, or by assassination of the executive head or of any of the executive officials of government, or by any unlawful means; or,

"2. Prints, publishes, edits, issues or knowingly circulates, sells, distributes or publicly displays any book, paper, document, or written or printed matter in any form, containing or advocating, advising or teaching the doctrine that organized government should be overthrown by force, violence or any unlawful means . . .,

"Is guilty of a felony and punishable" by imprisonment or fine, or both.

The indictment was in two counts. The first charged that the defendant had advocated, advised, and taught the duty, necessity, and propriety of overthrowing and overturning organized government by force, violence, and unlawful means, by certain writings therein set forth, entitled, "The Left Wing Manifesto"; the second, that he had printed, published, and knowingly circulated and distributed a certain paper called "The Revolutionary Age," containing the writings set forth in the first count, advocating, advising, and teaching the doctrine that organized government should be overthrown by force, violence, and unlawful means.

. . . It was admitted that the defendant signed a card subscribing to the Manifesto and Program of the Left Wing, which all applicants were required to sign before being admitted to membership; that he went to different parts of the state to speak to branches of the Socialist party about the principles of the Left Wing, and advocated their adoption; and that he was responsible [as business manager] for the Manifesto as it appeared, that "he knew of the publication, in a general way, and he knew of its publication afterwards, and is responsible for its circulation."

There was no evidence of any effect resulting from the publication and circulation of the Manifesto.

No witnesses were offered in behalf of the defendant.

Extracts from the Manifesto are set forth in the margin. Coupled with a review of the rise of Socialism, it condemned the dominant "moderate Socialism" for its recognition of the necessity of the democratic parliamentary state; repudiated its policy of introducing Socialism by legislative measures; and advocated, in plain and unequivocal language, the necessity of accomplishing the "Communist Revolution" by a militant and "revolutionary Socialism," based on "the class struggle" and mobilizing the "power of the proletariat in action," through mass industrial revolts developing into mass political strikes and "revolutionary mass action" for the purpose of conquering and destroying the parliamentary state and establishing in its place, through a "revolutionary dictatorship of the proletariat," the system of Communist Socialism. The then recent strikes in Seattle and Winnipeg were cited as instances of a development already verging on revolutionary action and suggestive of proletarian dictatorship, in which the strike workers were "trying to ursurp the functions of municipal government"; and Revolutionary Socialism, it was urged, must use these mass industrial revolts to broaden the strike, make it general and militant, and develop it into mass political strikes and revolutionary mass action for the annihilation of the parliamentary state.

. . . The sole contention here is, essentially, that, as there was no evidence of any concrete result flowing from the publication of the Manifesto, or of circumstances showing the likelihood of such result, the statute as construed and applied by the trial court penalizes the mere utterance, as such, of "doctrine" having no quality of incitement, without regard either to the circumstances of its utterance or to the likelihood of unlawful sequences; and that, as the exercise of the right of free expression with relation to government is only punishable "in circumstances involving likelihood of substantive evil," the statute contravenes the due process clause of the 14th Amendement. The argument in support of this contention rests primarily upon the following propositions: 1st, that the "liberty" protected by the 14th Amendment includes the liberty of speech and of the press; and 2d, that while liberty of expression "is not absolute," it may be restrained "only in circumstances where its exercise bears a causal relation with some substantive evil, consummated, attempted, or likely"; and as the statute "takes no account of circumstances," it unduly restrains this liberty, and is therefore unconstitutional.

The precise question presented, and the only question which we can consider under this writ of error, then, is whether the statute, as construed and applied in this case by the state courts, deprived the defendant of his liberty of expression, in violation of the due process clause of the 14th Amendment.

The statute does not penalize the utterance or publication of abstract "doctrine" or academic dicussion having no quality of incitement to any concrete action. It is not aimed against mere historical or philosophical essays. It does not restrain the advocacy of changes in the form of government by constitutional and lawful means. What it prohibits is language advocating, advising, or teaching the overthrow of organized government by unlawful means. These words imply urging to action. Advocacy is defined in the Century Dictionary as: "1. The act of pleading for, supporting, or recommending; active espousal." It is not the abstract "doctrine" of overthrowing organized government by unlawful means which is denounced by the statute, but the advocacy of action for the accomplishment of that purpose. . . .

The Manifesto, plainly, is neither the statement of abstract doctrine nor, as suggested by counsel, mere prediction that industrial disturbances and revolutionary mass strikes will result spontaneously in an inevitable process of evolution in the economic system. It advocates and urges in fervent language mass action which shall progressively foment industrial disturbances, and, through political mass strikes and revolutionary mass action, overthrow and destroy organized parliamentary government. It concludes with a call to action in these words: "The proletariat revolution and the Communist reconstruction of society—*the struggle for these*—is now indispensable. . . . The Communist International calls the proletariat of the world to the final struggle!" This is not the expression of philosophical abstraction, the mere prediction of future events: it is the language of direct incitement.

The means advocated for bringing about destruction of organized parliamentary government, namely, mass industrial revolts usurping the functions of municipal government, political mass strikes directed against the parliamentary state, and revolutionary mass action for its final destruction, necessarily imply the use of force and violence, and in their essential nature are inherently unlawful in a constitutional government of law and order. That the jury were warranted in finding that the Manifesto advocated not merely the abstract doctrine of overwhelming organized government by force, violence, and unlawful means, but action to that end, is clear.

For present purposes we may and do assume that freedom of speech and of the press—which are protected by the 1st Amendment from abridgment by Congress—are among the fundamental personal rights and "liberties" protected by the due process clause of the 14th Amendment from impairment by the states. . . .

It is a fundamental principle, long established, that the freedom of speech and of the press which is secured by the Constitution does not confer an absolute right to speak or publish, without responsibility, whatever one may choose, or an unrestricted and unbridled license that gives immunity for every possible use of language, and prevents the punishment of those who abuse this freedom. 2 Story, Const. 5th ed. § 1580, p. 634 . . . . Reasonably limited, it was said by Story in the passage cited, this freedom is an inestimable privilege in a free government; without such limitation, it might become the scourge of the Republic.

That a state, in the exercise of its police power, may punish those who abuse this freedom by utterances inimical to the public welfare, tending to corrupt public morals, incite to crime, or disturb the public peace, is not open to question. . . . Thus it was held by this court in the Fox Case, that a state may punish publications advocating and encouraging a breach of its criminal laws; and, in the Gilbert Case, that a state may punish utterances teaching or advocating that its citizens should not assist the United States in prosecuting or carrying on war with its public enemies.

And, for yet more imperative reasons, a state may punish utterances endangering the foundations of organized government and threatening its overthrow by unlawful means. These imperil its own existence as a constitutional state. Freedom of speech and press, said Story (supra), does not protect disturbances of the public peace or the attempt to subvert the government. It does not protect publications or teachings which tend to subvert or imperil the government or to impede or hinder it in the performance of its governmental duties. . . . It does not protect publications prompting the overthrow of government by force; the punishment of those who publish articles which tend to destroy organized society being essential to the security of freedom and stability of the state. . . . And a state may penalize utterances which openly advocate the overthrow of the representative and constitutional form of government of the United States and the several states, by violence or other unlawful means. . . . In short, this freedom does not deprive a state of the primary and essential right of self-preservation, which, so long as human governments endure, they cannot be denied. . . .

By enacting the present statute the state had determined, through its legislative body, that utterances advocating the overthrow of organized government by force, violence, and unlawful means, are so inimical to the general welfare, and involve such danger of substantive evil, that they may be penalized in the exercise of its police power. That determination must be given great weight. Every presumption is to be indulged in favor of the validity of the statute. . . . That utterances inciting to the overthrow of organized government by unlawful means present a sufficient danger of substantive evil to bring their punishment within the range of legislative discretion is clear. Such utterances, by their very nature, involve danger to the public peace and to the security of the state. They threaten breaches of the peace and ultimate revolution. And the immediate danger is none the less real and substantial because the effect of a given utterance cannot be accurately foreseen. The state cannot reasonably be required to measure the danger from every such utterance in the nice balance of a jeweler's scale. A single revolutionary spark may kindle a fire that, smoldering for a time, may burst into a sweeping and destructive conflagration. It cannot be said that the state is acting arbitrarily or unreasonably when, in the exercise of its judgment as to the measures necessary to protect the public peace and safety, it seeks to extinguish the spark without waiting until it has enkindled the flame or blazed into the conflagration. It cannot reasonably be required to defer the adoption of measures for its own peace and safety until the revolutionary utterances lead to actual disturbances of the public peace or imminent and immediate danger of its own destruction; but it may, in the exercise of its judgment, suppress the threatened danger in its incipiency. . . .

We cannot hold that the present statute is an arbitrary or unreasonable exercise of the police power of the state, unwarrantably infringing the freedom of speech or press; and we must and do sustain its constitutionality.

This being so it may be applied to every utterance—not too trivial to be beneath the notice of the law—which is of such a character and used with such intent and purpose as to bring it within the prohibition of the statute. . . . In other words, when the legislative body has determined generally, in the constitutional exercise of its discretion, that utterances of a certain kind involve such danger of substantive evil that they may be punished, the question whether any specific utterance coming within the prohibited class is likely, in and of itself, to bring about the substantive evil, is not open to consideration. It is sufficient that the statute itself be constitutional, and that the use of the language comes within its prohibition.

It is clear that the question in such cases is entirely different from that involved in those cases where the statute merely prohibits certain acts involving the danger of substantive evil, without any reference to language itself, and it is sought to apply its provisions to language used by the defendant for the purpose of bringing about the prohibted results. There, if it be contended that the statute cannot be applied to the language used by the defendant because of its protection by the freedom of speech or press, it must necessarily be found, as an original question, without any previous determination by the legislative body, whether the specific language used involved such likelihood of bringing about the substantive evil as to deprive it of the constitutional protection. In such cases it has been held that the general provisions of the statute may be constitutionally applied to the specific utterance of the defendant if its natural tendency and probable effect were to bring about the substantive evil which the legislative body might prevent. Schenck v. United States [1919]; Debs v. United States [1919]. And the general statement in the Schenck Case that the "question in every case is whether the words are used in such circumstances and are of such a nature as to create a clear and present danger that they will bring about the substantive evils,"—upon which great reliance is placed in the defendant's argument,—was manifestly intended, as shown by the context, to apply only in cases of this class, and has no application to those like the present, where the legislative body itself has previously determined the danger of substantive evil arising from utterances of a specified character. . . .

And finding, for the reasons stated, that the statute is not in itself unconstitutional, and that it has not been applied in the present case in derogation of any constitutional right, the judgment of the Court of Appeals is affirmed.

Mr. Justice Holmes dissented:

Mr. Justice Brandeis and I are of opinion that this judgment should be reversed. The general principle of free speech, it seems to me, must be taken to be included in the 14th Amendment, in view of the scope that has been given to the word "liberty" as there used, although perhaps it may be accepted with a somewhat larger latitude of interpretation than is allowed to Congress by the sweeping language that governs, or ought to govern, the laws of the United States. If I am right, then I think that the criterion sanctioned by the full court in Schenck v. United States, applies: "The question in every case is whether the words used are used in such circumstances and are of such a nature as to create a clear and present danger that they will bring about the substantive evils that [the state] has a right to prevent." It is true that in my opinion this criterion was departed from in Abrams v. United States [1919] but the convictions that I expressed in that case are too deep for it to be possible for me as yet to believe that it and Schaefer v. United States [1920] have settled the law. If what I think the correct test is applied, it is manifest that there was no present danger of an attempt to overthrow the government by force on the part of the admittedly small minority who shared the defendant's views. It is said that this Manifesto was more than a theory, that it was an incitement. Every idea is an incitement. It offers itself for belief, and, if believed, it is acted on unless some other belief outweighs it, or some failure of energy stifles the movement at its birth. The only difference between the expression of an opinion and an incitement in the narrower sense is the speaker's enthusiasm for the result. Eloquence may set fire to reason. But whatever may be thought of the redundant discourse before us, it had no chance of starting a present conflagration. If, in the long run, the beliefs expressed in proletarian dictatorship are destined to be accepted by the dominant forces of the community, the only meaning of free speech is that they should be given their chance and have their way.

If the publication of this document had been laid as an attempt to induce an uprising against government at once, and not at some indefinite time in the future, it would have presented a different question. The object would have been one with which the law might deal, subject to the doubt whether there was any danger that the publication could produce any result; or, in other words, whether it was not futile and too remote from possible consequences. But the indictment alleges the publication and nothing more.

DENNIS v. UNITED STATES

341 U. S. 494; 71 S. Ct. 857; 95 L. Ed. 1137 (1951)

The Smith Act of 1940, which in 1948 became Section 2385 of Title 18 of the United States Code, directs a five-pronged attack against subversion. First, it punishes anyone who "knowingly or willfully advocates . . . or teaches the duty . . . or propriety of overthrowing . . . the government of the United States . . . by force or violence. . . . Second, it punishes the dissemination of literature advocating such overthrow "with intent to cause such overthrow." Third, it punishes anyone who "organizes . . . any society, group or assembly of persons to teach, advocate or encourage" such overthrow. Fourth, it punishes anyone who "becomes or is a member of . . . any such society, group or assembly . . . knowing the purposes thereof." Finally, it makes it a separate offense to conspire to do any of the above things.

The validity of the act was considered by the Supreme Court for the first time in the Dennis case below. In 1948, the 11 top leaders of the American Communist party were indicted under the act for willfully and knowingly conspiring to teach and advocate the overthrow of government by force and violence, and to organize the Communist party for the purpose of so doing. The trial in District Judge Medina's court in New York ran from January 20 to September 23, 1949, and resulted in conviction. Judge Medina's charge to the jury included two important interpretations of the law. First, he ruled out the possibility that "teaching" or "conspiring to teach" alone would violate the statute. "You must be satisfied from the evidence beyond a reasonable doubt that the defendants had an intent to cause the overthrow or destruction of the Government of the United States by force and violence, and that it was with this intent and for the purpose of furthering that objective that they conspired both (1) to organize the Communist Party . . . and (2) to teach and advocate . . . ." Second, should the jury find that the statute as so construed had been violated, it was their duty to find the defendants guilty. "I find as a matter of law that there is sufficient danger of a substantive evil that the Congress has a right to prevent to justify the application of the statute under the First Amendment. . . ."

Both the conviction and this charge to the jury were upheld by the Court of Appeals in an opinion by Judge Learned Hand. The Supreme Court limited the scope of its review to the constitutional questions raised, chief of which was the First Amendment question of free speech. It did not review the sufficiency of the evidence to support the verdict.

In the five opinions written in the Dennis case, there are four interpretations of the clear and present danger test. Chief Justice Vinson, speaking for four members of the Court, paid allegiance to Holmes's statement and application of the test, but in reality adopted in its place Judge Hand's test of "clear and probable danger." The danger need not be imminent; It is enough that there is a group willing to attempt the overthrow of government if and when possible. The Chief Justice read the time element out of clear and present danger.

Justice Frankfurter had always rejected the idea that a law which on its face invades free speech must be presumed to be unconstitutional, or that the First Amendment occupies any "preferred position." See Thomas v. Collins (1945). He felt that free speech cases call for the weighing of competing interests, and that the legislative judgment embodied in the Smith Act, that the Communist threat to the security of the country justifies punitive action, is amply supported by evidence.

In an incisive concurring opinion Justice Jackson bluntly declared that the test of clear and present danger has no applicability to a criminal conspiracy such as that carried on by the Communist party. It was never intended to be applied in a case like this, and should be reserved for cases involving restrictions upon speeches and publications.

Justices Black and Douglas, dissenting, felt that the clear and present danger test had been destoyed. Justice Douglas emphasized that the defendants were charged with no overt acts, only with speeches and publications. He also felt that the question of clear and present danger should be decided by the jury and not by the court.

The decision in the Dennis case provided for the first time a legal basis for the idea that the Communist party is a criminal conspiracy dedicated to overthrowing the government of the United States by force and violence. It therefore seemed logical to suppose that any official of the party, and probably any member who was familiar with the aims of the party, could be convicted for his part in the conspiracy. Acting upon this assumption the government moved against 14 second-string Communist leaders, and in Yates v. United States (1957) the Supreme Court reversed their convictions, acquitting five of them outright and remanding the other nine for retrial. The district court, it explained, had failed to charge the jury that in order to convict it must find the defendants guilty of advocating "action" in the "language of incitement." "The essense of the Dennis holding," the Court said, "was that indocrination of a group in preparation for future violent action, as well as exhortation to immediate action, by advocacy found to be directed to 'action for the accomplishment' of forcible overthrow, to violence 'as a rule or principle of action,' and employing 'language of incitement,' is not constitutionally protected when the group is of sufficient size and cohesiveness, is sufficiently oriented towards action, and other circumstances are such as reasonably to justify apprehension that action will occur. This is quite a different thing from the view of the District Court here that mere doctrinal justification of forcible overthrow, if engaged in with the intent to accomplish overthrow, is punishable per se under the Smith Act. That sort of advocacy, even though uttered with the hope that it may ultimately lead to violent revolution, is too remote from concrete action to be regarded as the kind of indoctrination preparatory to action which was condemned in Dennis."

Although Justice Harlan stresses that he is merely applying the doctine of the Dennis case, it seems apparent that in insisting in Yates that advocacy amount to incitement to action, he is, without actually using the well-known phrase, moving back toward the clear and present danger rule of Holmes and Brandeis. The Dennis case was widely believed to have modified and weakened that rule.

Four years later, in Scales v. United States (1961), the Supreme Court passed on the validity of the membership section for the first time, and in a five-to-four decision held it valid as applied to Scales. It stated that this was not mere "guilt by association." The guilt was personal and punishable under the act if it was "active membership in an organization [in this case the Communist party] engaged in illegal advocacy by one having guilty knowledge and intent." Scales had been convicted first in 1955, and after a second trial and two full arguments before the Court his case was finally heard and considered in conjunction with Communist Party v. Subversive Activities Control Board (1961). Scales argued that the membership section of the Smith Act had been repealed by the section of the Subversive Activities Control Act of 1950 (requiring registration of Communists), which provides that: "Neither the holding of office nor membership in any Communist organization by any person shall constitute per se a violation of subsection (a) or subsection (c) of this section or any other criminal statute." Justice Harlan's opinion for the majority held that the section quoted from the act of 1950 clarified, rather than repealed, the membership section of the Smith Act; and he emphasized the difference between punishing a man for membership per se and punishing him for membership with guilty knowledge and with intent to aid in the violent overthrow of government. In the dissenting opinions it was urged that the act of 1950 had repealed the Smith Act provision and that the membership section violated the First Amendment.

In Brandenberg v. Ohio (1969), the Supreme Court held void Ohio's criminal syndicalism act—an act passed in the 1920s and patterned after that of California which had been held valid in Whitney v. California (1927). Without actually using the words "clear and present danger," the Court held the act void as forbidding mere advocacy of violence or sabotage, whether or not it would incite the hearers to lawless action. The Court overruled Whitney v. California.

The clear and present danger test was described by Justice Brandeis as a "rule of reason" (Schaefer v. United States, 1920), and it is used by the Court to determine that point at which speech becomes so entwined with action, or so likely to bring about action, as to be punishable under a statute which forbids such action. It was for this reason that the Court refused to apply it in the Gitlow case, where the statute forbade speech, rather than action.

But some social interests are relatively of such slight value that the right of free speech apparently outweighs them even though there is a clear and present danger, and in Schneider v. Irvington (1939) the Court said that keeping the streets clean was such a value. "We are of opinion that the purpose to keep the streets clean and of good appearance is insufficient to justify an ordinance which prohibits a person rightfully on a public street from handing literature to one willing to receive it." The Court assumed there was a clear and present danger the streets would be littered. Thus the Court not only must find a speech presents a clear and present danger, but under what has come to be known as the "balancing of interests" doctrine, must weigh the social value of the restriction against the seriousness of the threat to free speech.

One of the difficulties involved in applying the "balancing of interests" doctrine is the determination of exactly what interests are at stake. When the Supreme Court decides a case arising under the First Amendment, it is deciding between the right of the government to protect some social value from attack, and the right of an individual to attack it. It is easy to argue, is such circumstances, that the interest of the one should yield to the interests of the many—overlooking the fact that there is a vital social value in the right of the individual to make his challenge. Such an argument is especially persuasive where the social value involved is, or can be made to appear to be, the very security of the nation itself. In this situation the individual interest is bound to yield.

To avoid this almost inevitable result in cases where both the public and individual interests are important ones, the Court has devised a new approach which, for the sake of convenience, we will call the "minimum infringement" doctrine. Under this doctrine the government has an obligation to achieve its social goals with the least possible infringement of First Amendment rights, and where it appears to the Court that this standard has not been met, the statute will be held void.

Following a wave of draft-card burning episodes by antiwar demonstrators, an outraged Congress in 1965 made it a crime to "knowingly destroy" a draft card. The following year a Boston University philosophy student publicly burned his draft card as part of a "demonstration against the war and against the draft." In United States v. O'Brien (1968) the Supreme Court sustained his conviction under the act. While it rejected the idea that "an apparently limitless variety of conduct can be labeled 'speech' whenever the person engaging in the conduct intends thereby to express an idea," it proceeded to decide the case "on the assumption that the alleged communicative element in O'Brien's conduct is sufficient to bring into play the First Amendment." The Court applied the balancing of interests and minimum infringement doctrines phrased in these terms: " . . . We think it clear that a government regulation is sufficiently justified if it is within the constitutional power of the government; if it furthers an important or substantial governmental interest; if the governmental interest is unrelated to the suppression of free expression; and if the incidental restriction on alleged First Amendment freedom is no greater than is essential to the furtherance of that interest." Judged by these standards, "the many functions performed by the Selective Service certificates establish beyond doubt that Congress has a legitimate and substantial interest in preventing their wanton and unrestrained destruction." Unlike the "red flag" law held void in Stromberg v. California (1931), which was aimed at suppressing communication, the thrust of the present law was to prevent the destruction of draft cards. "We perceive no alternative means that would more precisely and narrowly assure the continuing availability of issued Selective Service certificates than a law which prohibits their wilful mutilation or destruction. . . . The governmental interest and the scope of the 1956 Amendment are limited to preventing a harm to the smooth and efficient functioning of the Selective Service System."

In United States v. Robel (1967), the Court upheld the right of Robel, an avowed though passive Communist, to work in a shipyard despite a federal statute forbidding such employment to a member of the Communist Party. The Court declined to read the statute as applying only to "active" membership and refused to apply the "balancing of interests" test. Instead it held the statute void on its face because it "casts its net across a broad range of associational activities, indiscriminately trapping membership which can be constitutionally punished and membership which cannot be so proscribed." While Congress is clearly entitled to protect sensitive activities from spies and saboteurs, it "must achieve its goal by means of which have a 'less drastic' impact on the continued vitality of First Amendment freedoms."

Mr. Chief Justice Vinson announced the judgment of the Court and an opinion in which Mr. Justice Reed, Mr. Justice Burton, and Mr. Justice Minton joined, saying in part:

I.

It will be helpful in clarifying the issues to treat next the contention that the trial judge improperly interpreted the statute by charging that the statute required an unlawful intent before the jury could convict. . . .

. . . The structure and purpose of the statute demand the inclusion of intent as an element of the crime. Congress was concerned with those who advocate and organize for the overthrow of the Government. Certainly those who recruit and combine for the purpose of advocating overthrow intend to bring about that overthrow. We hold that the statute requires as an essential element of the crime proof of the intent of those who are charged with its violation to overthrow the Government by force and violence. . . .

II.

The obvious purpose of the statute is to protect existing Government, not from change by peaceable, lawful and constitutional means, but from change by violence, revolution and terrorism. That it is within the *power* of the Congress to protect the Government of the United States from armed rebellion is a proposition which requires little discussion. Whatever theoretical merit there may be to the argument that there is a "right" to rebellion against dictatorial governments is without force where the existing structure of the government provides for peaceful and orderly change. We reject any principal of governmental helplessness in the face of preparation for revolution, which principle, carried to its logical conclusion, must lead to anarchy. No one could conceive that it is not within the power of Congress to prohibit acts intended to overthrow the Government by force and violence. The question with which we are concerned here is not whether Congress has such *power,* but whether the *means* which it has employed conflict with the First and Fifth Amendments to the Constitution.

One of the bases for the contention that the means which Congress has employed are invalid takes the form of an attack on the face of the statute on the grounds that by its terms it prohibits academic discussion of the merits of Marxism-Leninism, that it stifles ideas and is contrary to all concepts of a free speech and a free press. Although we do not agree that the language itself has that significance, we must bear in mind that it is the duty of the federal courts to interpret federal legislation in a manner not inconsistent with the demands of the Constitution. . . . This is a federal statute which we must interpret as well as judge. . . .

The very language of the Smith Act negates the interpretation which petitioners would have us impose on that Act. It is directed at advocacy, not discussion. Thus, the trial judge properly charged the jury that they could not convict if they found that petitioners did "no more than pursue peaceful studies and discussions or teaching and advocacy in the realm of ideas." He further charged that it was not unlawful "to conduct in an American college and university a course explaining the philosophical theories set forth in the books which have been placed in evidence." Such a charge is in strict accord with the statutory language, and illustrates the meaning to be placed on those words. Congress did not intend to eradicate the free discussion of political theories, to destroy the traditional rights of Americans to discuss and evaluate ideas without fear of governmental sanction. Rather Congress was concerned with the very kind of activity in which the evidence showed these petitioners engaged.

III.

But although the statute is not directed at the hypothetical cases which petitioners have conjured, its application in this case has resulted in convictions for the teaching and advocacy of the overthrow of the Government by force and violence, which, even though coupled with the intent to accomplish that overthrow, contains an element of speech. For this reason, we must pay special heed to the demands of the First Amendment marking out the boundaries of speech.

We pointed out in [American Communications Ass'n v. Douds, 1950] that the basis of the First Amendment is the hypothesis that speech can rebut speech, propaganda will answer propaganda, free debate of ideas will result in the wisest governmental policies. It is for this reason that this Court has recognized the inherent value of free discourse. An analysis of the leading cases in this Court which have involved direct limitations on speech, however, will demonstrate that both the majority of the Court and the dissenters in particular cases have recognized that this is not an unlimited, unqualified right, but that the societal value of speech must, on occasion, be subordinated to other values and considerations.

No important case involving free speech was decided by this Court prior to Schenck v. United States (1919). . . . Writing for a unanimous Court,

Justice Holmes stated that the "question in every case is whether the words used are used in such circumstances and are of such a nature as to create a clear and present danger that they will bring about the substantive evils that Congress has a right to prevent." . . . The fact is inescapable, too, that the phrase bore no connotation that the danger was to be any threat to the safety of the Republic. The charge was causing and attempting to cause insubordination in the military forces and obstruct recruiting. The objectionable document denounced conscription and its most inciting sentence was, "You must do your share to maintain, support and uphold the rights of the people of this country." Fifteen thousand copies were printed and some circulated. This insubstantial gesture toward insubordination in 1917 during war was held to be a clear and present danger of bringing about the evil of military insubordination.

In several later cases involving convictions under the Criminal Espionage Act, the nub of the evidence the Court held sufficient to meet the "clear and present danger" test enunciated in Schenck was as follows: [Five cases, 1919–1920, are here discussed.] . . .

The rule we deduce from these cases is that where an offense is specified by a statute in nonspeech or nonpress terms, a conviction relying upon speech or press as evidence of violation may be sustained only when the speech or publication created a "clear and present danger" of attempting or accomplishing the prohibited crime, e.g., interference with enlistment. The dissents, we repeat, in emphasizing the value of speech, were addressed to the argument of the sufficiency of the evidence.

The next important case before the Court in which free speech was the crux of the conflict was Gitlow v. New York (1925). There New York had made it a crime to "advocate . . . the necessity or propriety of overthrowing . . . the government by force. . . ." The evidence of violation of the statute was that the defendant had published a Manifesto attacking the Government and capitalism. The convictions were sustained, Justices Holmes and Brandeis dissenting. The majority refused to apply the "clear and present danger" test to the specific utterance. Its reasoning was as follows: The "clear and present danger" test was applied to the utterance itself in Schenck because the question was merely one of sufficiency of evidence under an admittedly constitutional statute. Gitlow, however, presented a different question. There a legislature had found that a certain kind of speech was, itself, harmful and unlawful. The constitutionality of such a state statute had to be adjudged by this Court just as it determined the constitutionality of any state statute, namely, whether the statute was "reasonable." Since it was entirely reasonable for a state to attempt to protect itself from violent overthrow, the statute was perforce reasonable. The only question remaining in the case became whether there was evidence to support the conviction, a question which gave the majority no difficulty. Justices Holmes and Brandeis refused to accept this approach, but insisted that wherever speech was the evidence of the violation, it was necessary to show that the speech created the "clear and present danger" of the substantive evil which the legislature had the right to prevent. Justices Holmes and Brandeis, then, made no distinction between a federal statute which made certain acts unlawful, the evidence to support the conviction being speech, and a statute which made speech itself the crime. This approach was emphasized in Whitney v. California (1927), where the Court was confronted with a conviction under the California Criminal Syndicalist statute. The Court sustained the conviction, Justices Brandeis and Holmes concurring in the result. In their concurrence they repeated that even though the legislature had designated certain speech as criminal, this could not prevent the defendant from showing that there was no danger that the substantive evil would be brought about.

Although no case subsequent to Whitney and Gitlow has expressly overruled the majority opinions in those cases, there is little doubt that subsequent opinions have inclined toward the Holmes-Brandeis rationale. And in American Communications Ass'n v. Douds, supra . . . we pointed out that Congress did not intend to punish belief, but rather intended to regulate the conduct of union affairs. We therefore held that any indirect sanction on speech which might arise from the oath requirement did not present a proper case for the "clear and present danger" test, for the regulation was aimed at conduct rather than speech. In discussing the proper measure of evaluation of this kind of legislation, we suggested that the Holmes-Brandeis philosophy insisted that where there was a direct restriction upon speech, a "clear and present danger" that the substantive evil would be caused was necessary before the statute in question could be constitutionally applied. And we stated, "[The First] Amendment requires that one be permitted to believe what he will. It requires that one be permitted to advocate what he will unless there is a clear and present danger that a substantial public evil will result therefrom." But we further suggested that neither Justice Holmes nor Justice Brandeis ever envisioned that a shorthand phrase should be crystallized into a rigid rule to be applied inflexibly without regard to the circumstances of each case. Speech is not an absolute, above and beyond control by the legislature when its judgment, subject to review here, is that certain kinds of speech are so undesirable as to warrant criminal sanction. Nothing is more certain in modern society than the principal that there are no absolutes, that a name, a phrase, a standard has meaning only when associated with the considerations which gave birth to the nonmenclature. . . . To those who would paralyze our Government in the face of impending threat by encasing it in a semantic straitjacket we must reply that all concepts are relative.

In this case we are squarely presented with the application of the "clear and present danger" test, and must decide what that phrase imports. We first note that many of the cases in which this Court has reversed convictions by use of this or similar tests have been based on the fact that the interest which the State was attempting to protect was itself too insubstantial to warrant restriction of speech. . . . Overthrow of the Government by force and violence is certainly a substantial enough interest for the Government to limit speech. Indeed, this is the ultimate value of any society, for if a society cannot protect its very structure from armed internal attack, it must follow that no subordinate value can be protected. If, then, this interest may be protected, the literal problem which is presented is what has been meant by the use of the phrase "clear and present danger" of the utterances bringing about the evil within the power of Congress to punish.

Obviously, the words cannot mean that before the Government may act, it must wait until the putsch is about to be executed, the plans have been laid and the signal is awaited. If Government is aware that a group aiming at its overthrow is attempting to indoctrinate its members and to commit them to a course whereby they will strike when the leaders feel the circumstances permit, action by the Government is required. The argument that there is no need for Government to concern itself, for Government is strong, it possesses ample powers to put down a rebellion, it may defeat the revolution with ease needs no answer. For that is not the question. Certainly an attempt to overthrow the Government by force, even though doomed from the outset because of inadequate numbers or power of the revolutionists, is a sufficient evil for Congress to prevent. The damage which such attempts create both physically and politically to a nation makes it impossible to measure the validity in terms of the probability of success, or the immediacy of a successful attempt. In the instant case the trial judge charged the jury that they could not convict unless they found that petitioners intended to overthrow the Government "as speedily as circumstances would permit." This does not mean, and could not properly mean, that they would not strike until there was certainty of success. What was meant was that the revolutionists would strike when they thought the time was ripe. We must therefore reject the contention that success or probability of success is the criterion.

The situation with which Justices Holmes and Brandeis were concerned in Gitlow was a comparatively isolated event, bearing little relation in their minds to any substantial threat to the safety of the community. . . . They were not confronted with any situation comparable to the instant one—the development of an apparatus designed and dedicated to the overthrow of the Government, in the context of world crisis after crisis.

Chief Judge Learned Hand, writing for the majority below, interpreted the phrase as follows: "In each case [courts] must ask whether the gravity of the 'evil,' discounted by its improbability, justifies such invasion of free speech as is necessary to avoid the danger." We adopt this statement of the rule. As articulated by Chief Judge Hand, it is as succinct and inclusive as any other we might devise at this time. It takes into consideration those factors which we deem relevant, and relates their significances. More we cannot expect from words.

Likewise, we are in accord with the court below, which affirmed the trial court's finding that the requisite danger existed. The mere fact that from the period 1945 to 1948 petitioners' activities did not result in an attempt to overthrow the Government by force and violence is of course no answer to the fact that there was a group that was ready to make the attempt. The formation by petitioners of such a highly organized conspiracy, with rigidly disciplined members subject to call when the leaders, these petitioners, felt that the time had come for action, coupled with the inflammable nature of world conditions, similar uprisings in other countries, and the touch-and-go nature of our relations with countries with whom petitioners were in the very least ideologically attuned, convince us that their convictions were justified on this score. And this analysis disposes of the contention that a conspiracy to advocate, as distinguished from the advocacy itself, cannot be constitutionally restrained, because it comprises only the preparation. It is the existence of the conspiracy which creates the danger. . . . If the ingredients of the reaction are present, we cannot bind the Government to wait until the catalyst is added.

IV.

[The Court here considers whether the trial court was correct in not submitting to the jury the question of the existence of clear and present danger.]

. . . The argument that the action of the trial court is erroneous, in declaring as a matter of law that such violation shows sufficient danger to justify the punishment despite the First Amendment, rests on the theory that a jury must decide a question of the application of the First Amendment. We do not agree.

When facts are found that establish the violation of a statute, the protection against conviction afforded by the First Amendment is a matter of law. The doctrine that there must be a clear and present danger of a substantive evil that Congress has a right to prevent is a judicial rule to be applied as a matter of law by the courts. The guilt is established by proof of facts. Whether the First Amendment protects the activity which constitutes the violation of the statute must depend upon a judicial determination of the scope of the First Amendment applied to the circumstances of the case. . . .

V.

There remains to be discussed the question of vagueness—whether the statute as we have interpreted it is too vague, not sufficiently advising those who speak of the limitations upon their activity. . . .

We hold that §§ 2(a)(1), (2)(a)(3) and 3 of the Smith Act, do not inherently, or as construed or applied in the instant case, violate the First Amendment and other provisions of the Bill of Rights, or the First and Fifth Amendments because of indefiniteness. Petitioners intended to overthrow the Government of the United States as speedily as the circumstances would permit. Their conspiracy to organize the Communist Party and to teach and advocate the overthrow of the Government of the United States by force and violence created a "clear and present danger" of an attempt to overthrow the Government by force and violence. They were properly and constitutionally convicted for violation of the Smith Act. The judgments of conviction are

Affirmed.

Mr. Justice Clark took no part in this case.

Mr. Justice Frankfurter wrote a concurring opinion.

Mr. Justice Jackson wrote a concurring opinion.

Mr. Justice Black wrote a dissenting opinion.

Mr. Justice Douglas wrote a dissenting opinion.

NEAR v. MINNESOTA

283 U. S. 697; 51 S. Ct. 625; 75 L. Ed. 1357 (1931)

The struggle to achieve freedom of the press has been long and difficult. Once the invention of the printing press made possible the dissemination of information to the people generally, it became painfully clear to the monarchs of Europe that here lay a serious threat to their absolute powers. Their first reaction was to outlaw and destroy this new engine of seditious propaganda. Failing in this, they resorted to a system of licensing under which all publications, before being released to the public, had to be submitted to the King's Licenser. Serious penalties were meted out to those whose publications did not bear the official "imprimatur." Obviously no criticism of the sovereign or government, whether just or unjust, could be published under such a system; and the long fight against the official licenser was a major part of the fight to establish democratic institutions.

It is against this background that the case of Near v. Minnesota must be read. The law involved had been dubbed the "Minnesota gag law." It provided for the "padlocking," by injunctive process, of a newspaper for printing matter which was scandalous, malicious, defamatory or obscene. Such a "padlock" injunction, enforceable by the customary process of summary punishment for contempt of court, could be lifted only by convincing the judge who issued it that the publication would, in the future, be unobjectionable. This, in the judgment of the majority of the Court, amounted to previous censorship of publication and a violation of long-established canons of free speech and press.

The present case represents the climax of a striking evolution in our constitutional law whereby freedom of speech and press was at last effectively "nationalized" or confided to the protection of the federal courts against both national and state impairment. The steps in that evolution are traced in the note to Powell v. Alabama. The case of Near v. Minnesota was the first case in which a state law was held unconstitutional as violating that freedom of press protected by the due process of clause of the Fourteenth Amendment.

In contrast to the experience in Europe where books and periodicals had been the subject of censorship, the only focus of overt and systematic censorship in the United States was the motion picture. Early movies were largely thought of as entertainment subject to the same police control as stage shows and a number of cities and states censored them for anti-social content. It was not until 1952 that the Supreme Court finally held them to be part of the press of the of the country protected by the First Amendment, and even then it refused to outlaw their censorship entirely. In Burstyn v. Wilson (1952) it held void New York's censorship of *The Miracle* for being sacrilegious, and while it made clear that "the state has no legitimate interest in protecting any or all religions from views distasteful to them," it also emphasized that "it does not follow that the Constitution requires absolute freedom to exhibit every motion picture of every kind at all times and places."

For nearly a decade after Burstyn the Court held void all challenged exercises of censorship without forbidding censorship in theory but without saying what kind of censorship would be upheld. Although the Court had insisted as early as Near v. Minnesota (1931) that "the protection even as to previous restraint is not absolutely unlimited," no scheme of previous censorship had ever been found valid and the Court had never undertaken to explain just what this dictum meant. It had spoken of "exceptional" circumstances that might justify such censorship, but it had defined them, not in terms of when or how the state could censor, but in terms of the kinds of ideas that could be suppressed. But how, without resorting to a general scheme of censorship and licensing, were these suppressible ideas to be located? How was a state to identify and suppress "utterances creating a hindrance to the . . . war effort," or which offended "the primary requirements of decency," without examining all utterances before they were published? Since it was this very "examining" before publication that the Court had held void in the Near case, the theory underlying the dictum seemed incompatible with the holding of the case.

Doubts arose as to whether *any* censorship would be approved, until finally a case came to the Court where the film was not submitted to the censor and a direct challenge was made to the censorship as censorship. In Times Film Corp. v. Chicago (1961) the Court held the censorship valid. A five-man majority pointed out that "one of the exceptional cases" mentioned in Near v. Minnesota (1931) where prior censorship might be permitted included " 'the primary requirements of decency [that] may be enforced against obscene publications,' " and refused to hold, under "petitioner's broadside attack," that "the State is stripped of all constitutional power to prevent, in the most effective fashion, the utterance of this class of speech." The dissenting justices complained that the Court was abandoning the restraints on prior censorship "without requiring any demonstration that this is an exceptional case, whatever that might be, and without any indication that Chicago has sustained the 'heavy burden' which was supposed to have been placed upon it. Clearly, this is neither an exceptional case nor has Chicago sustained any burden. . . ." By holding valid previous censorship in the Times Film case while citing this incompatible dictum in Near as authority, the Court raised serious doubts whether or not the basic holding of the Near case had been abandoned.

Closely allied to the problem of movie censorship is the problem presented by the publication of obscene material generally, and the constitutional theories involved are closely intertwined. Although a state may not resort to prior censorship of the press, it does have authority to punish the publication of matter offensive to public morals and decency. While it had long been assumed that clearly obscene publications could validly be punished, the question was never squarely decided by the Supreme Court until 1957 in the case of Roth v. United States involving the prosecution of Roth by the federal government for sending obscene matter through the mails. On historical grounds the Court decided that the First Amendment was not intended to protect obscenity, and therefore the question whether an obscene publication presented a clear and present danger of "antisocial conduct" was entirely irrelevant.

In Kingsley Books v. Brown (1957), decided the same day as the Roth case, the Court had found a procedure that met the requirements of the First Amendment. New York laws provide a municipality with a "limited injunctive remedy" under which the government requests in court an injunction against the sale of an allegedly obscene book until the matter of obscenity can be determined judicially. The bookseller against whom the injunction is sought is entitled to bring the issues before the court within one day and a decision shall be rendered by the court within two days of the conclusion of the trial. Only a person disobeying an injunction issued after such a trial would be subject to criminal penalty. The Court pointed out that the procedure had marked advantages over the simple criminal prosecution for selling obscene matter. It advances the public interest by preventing the sale of something already adjudged obscene, at the same time it enables a bookseller to avoid selling a book which may "without prior warning subject him to a criminal prosecution with the hazard of imprisonment." Moreover, since the act "studiously withholds restraint upon matters not already published and not yet found to be offensive," it avoids any limitation on the sale of nonobscene material. In Freedman v. Maryland (1965), the Court extended this doctrine of expiditious judicial review to the censorship of movies.

In the other First Amendment areas, the Court distinguishes between protected and unprotected speech on the basis of its potential for actual harm. In most areas this is articulated by the clear and present danger test. However, in the case of obscene matter, there is no apparent agreement that reading pornography increases sex crimes or has any other injurious effect. Such material is suppressed here, not because it produces injurious results, but because many people find it offensive, and especially do not want their children exposed to it. By deciding to judge obscenity by its distastefulness rather than by its potential for tangible harm, the Court has made it almost impossible to judge the validity of censorship in terms of the purpose to be served.

In the Roth case, five members of the Court agreed that obscene material was that "which deals with sex in a manner appealing to prurient interest." Such material, it was emphasized, does not enjoy constitutional protection because it is "utterly without social importance." The Court in Roth found that the jury had been properly instructed on the standard, so the conviction was valid.

In Jacobellis v. Ohio (1964) the Court again applied the Roth rule and reversed the Ohio court finding that the movie *The Lovers* was obscene. The Court divided badly on the reasoning for its decision, no more than two justices agreeing on the test to be applied. Justices Brennan and Goldberg reaffirmed the Roth test, but added that "community standards" meant national, not local, standards; and the question whether something was obscene could not be left solely to a jury, but must ultimately be decided by the Supreme Court itself. They also raised the "redeeming social importance" phrase to the level of an independent test, holding that any material having such importance, however slightly, could not be banned. Justices Black and Douglas joined in the judgment on the ground that punishing any publication was unconstitutional, and Justice Stewart held that the First Amendment forbids only hard core pornography "and the motion picture involved in this case is not that."

In Memoirs v. Massachusetts (1966), six members of the Court joined in overruling a Massachusetts court decision that the book *Fanny Hill,* was obscene—still without agreeing on a definition of obscenity. Justices Brennan, Warren, and Fortas reiterated the Roth rule that "(a) the dominant theme of the material taken as a whole appeals to a prurient interest in sex; (b) the material is patently offensive because it affronts contemporary community standards relating to the description or representation of sexual matters; and (c) the material is utterly without redeeming social value." They held the Massachusetts court had misapplied this test when they weighed the obscenity of *Fanny Hill* against its limited social value. "A book can not be proscribed unless it is found to be utterly without redeeming social value. This is so even though the book is found to possess the requisite prurient appeal and to be patently offensive."

In Miller v. California (1973), the Court reaffirmed that obscenity was outside the First Amendment, but abandoned the "redeeming social value" test and substituted another: "The basic guidelines for the trier of fact must be: (a) whether 'the average person, applying contemporary community standards' would find that the work, taken as a whole, appeals to the prurient interest. . . . (b) whether the work depicts or describes, in a patently offensive way, sexual conduct specifically defined by the applicable state law; and (c) whether the work, taken as a whole, lacks serious literary, artistic, political, or scientific value. We do not adopt as a constitutional standard the '*utterly* without redeeming social value' test of Memoirs v. Massachusetts; that concept has never commanded the adherence of more than three Justices at one time. . . .

"We emphasize that it is not our function to propose regulatory schemes for the States. That must await their concrete legislative efforts. It is possible, however, to give a few plain examples of what a state statute could define for regulation under the second part (b) of the standard announced in this opinion, supra: (a) Patently offensive representations or descriptions of ultimate sexual acts, normal or perverted, actual or simulated. (b) Patently offensive representations or descriptions of masturbation, excretory functions, and lewd exhibitions of the genitals."

Paris Adult Theater I v. Slaton (1973) raised the question whether the government could censor pornographic films shown in "adults only" theaters devoid of offensive advertizing. Using procedures which met the test of Freedman v. Maryland (1965), the city of Atlanta, Georgia had moved to enjoin the exhibition of two "adult" films in such theaters and the Court in a five-to-four decision held that such censorship was constitutionally permissable. While apparently recognizing an adult person's right to see and read what he chooses, the Court found that the " 'right of the nation and of the states to maintain a decent society' " may legitimately outweigh the individual's right to do what he will in private.

Writing for the majority, Chief Justice Burger stated, "we hold that there are legitimate state interests at stake in stemming the tide of commercialized obscenity, even assuming it is feasible to enforce effective safeguards against exposure to juveniles and to the passerby. . . . These [legitimate state interests] include the interest of the public in the quality of life and the total community environment, the tone of commerce in the great city centers, and possibly, the public safety itself."

The Court was not troubled by the lack of conclusive scientific data to show that obscene materials adversely affect individuals or society. "Although there is no conclusive proof of a connection between antisocial behavior and obscene material, the legislature of Georgia could quite reasonably determine that such a connection does or might exist."

Justice Brennan's dissent was based in large part on the Court's experience with obscenity cases since Roth. After reviewing those cases, Brennan concluded "that obscenity cannot be defined with sufficient specificity and clarity to provide fair notice to persons who create and distribute sexually oriented materials, to prevent substantial erosion of protected speech as a by-product of the attempt to suppress unprotected speech, and to avoid very costly institutional harms." For Brennan, the consequences of censoring obscenity were severe enough to make such censorship unconstitutional unless the state possessed a "very substantial interest" in suppressing such speech. Brennan contended that there was no very substantial state interest in censoring obscene material distributed only to consenting adults and, "would hold, therefore, that at least in the absence of distribution to juveniles or obtrusive exposure to unconsenting adults, the First and Fourteenth Amendments prohibit the State and Federal Governments from attempting wholly to suppress sexually oriented materials. . . ."

One of Brennan's major objections to the majority's approach in Paris and Miller was that the standards enunciated in those cases do nothing to alleviate the uncertainty about what is obscene, leaving it to judges and justices to decide this question subjectively on a case-by-case basis. As if to prove Brennan's point, one year after Paris and Miller a unanimous Court reversed the conviction of a theater operator for showing a movie which dealt with sex, but without showing "hard core" explicit sexual conduct. "Our own view of the film satisfies us that 'Carnal Knowledge' could not be found under the Miller standards to depict sexual conduct in a patently offensive way." See Jenkins v. Georgia (1974).

Mr. Chief Justice Hughes delivered the opinion of the Court, saying in part:

Chapter 285 of the Session Laws of Minnesota for the year 1925 provides for the abatement, as a public nuisance, of a "malicious, scandalous and defamatory newspaper, magazine or other periodical." Section one of the act is as follows:

"Section 1: Any person who, as an individual, or as a member or employee of a firm, or association or organization, or as an officer, director, member or employee of a corporation, shall be engaged in the business of regularly or customarily producing, publishing or circulating, having in possession, selling or giving away,

(a) an obscene, lewd and lascivious newspaper, magazine, or other periodical, or

(b) a malicious, scandalous and defamatory newspaper, magazine or other periodical, is guilty of a nuisance, and all persons guilty of such nuisance may be enjoined, as hereinafter provided.

"Participation in such business shall constitute a commission of such nuisance and render the participant liable and subject to the proceedings, orders and judgments provided for in this act. Ownership, in whole or in part, directly or indirectly, of any such periodical, or of any stock or interest in any corporation or organization which owns the same in whole or in part, or which publishes the same, shall constitute such participation. . . ."

Section two provides that whenever any such nuisance is committed or exists, the county attorney of any county where any such periodical is published or circulated, or, in case of his failure or refusal to proceed upon written request in good faith of a reputable citizen, the attorney general, or upon like failure or refusal of the latter, any citizen of the county, may maintain an action in the district court of the county in the name of the state to enjoin perpetually the persons committing or maintaining any such nuisance from further committing or maintaining it. Upon such evidence as the court shall deem sufficient, a temporary injunction may be granted. The defendants have the right to plead by demurrer or answer, and the plaintiff may demur or reply as in other cases.

The action, by section three, is to be "governed by the practice and procedure applicable to civil actions for injunctions," and after trial the court may enter judgment permanently enjoining the defendants found guilty of violating the act from continuing the violation and, "in and by such judgment, such nuisance may be wholly abated." The court is empowered, as in other cases of contempt, to punish disobedience to a temporary or permanent injunction by fine of not more than $1000 or by imprisonment in the county jail for not more than twelve months.

Under this statute, (section one, clause (b)), the county attorney of Hennepin county brought this action to enjoin the publication of what was described as a "malicious, scandalous and defamatory newspaper, magazine and periodical," known as "The Saturday Press," published by the defendants in the city of Minneapolis. . . .

Without attempting to summarize the contents of the voluminous exhibits attached to the complaint, we deem it sufficient to say that the articles charged in substance that a Jewish gangster was in control of gambling, bootlegging and racketeering in Minneapolis, and that law enforcing officers and agencies were not energetically performing their duties. Most of the charges were directed against the chief of police; he was charged with gross neglect of duty, illicit relations with gangsters, and with participation in graft. The county attorney was charged with knowing the existing conditions and with failure to take adequate measures to remedy them. The mayor was accused of inefficiency and dereliction. One member of the grand jury was stated to be in sympathy with the gangsters. A special grand jury and a special prosecutor were demanded to deal with the situation in general, and, in particular, to investigate an attempt to assassinate one Guilford, one of the original defendants, who, it appears from the articles, was shot by gangsters after the first issue of the periodical had been published. There is no question but that the articles made serious accusations against the public officers named and others in connection with the prevalence of crimes and the failure to expose and punish them. . . .

[Upon complaint the state court ordered Near to show cause why a temporary injunction should not be issued and forbade, meanwhile, further publication of the periodical. Near demurred on constitutional grounds. The district court certified the question of the constitutionality of the statute to the state supreme court, which held it valid. Near then answered the complaint but presented no evidence, and a permanent injunction was issued.]

From the judgment as thus affirmed, the defendant Near appeals to this court.

This statute, for the suppression as a public nuisance of a newspaper or periodical, is unusual, if not unique, and raises questions of grave importance transcending the local interests involved in the particular action. It is no longer open to doubt that the liberty of the press and of speech is within the liberty safeguarded by the due process clause of the 14th Amendment from invasion by state action. . . . In maintaining this guaranty, the authority of the State to enact laws to promote the health, safety, morals and general welfare of its people is necessarily admitted. The limits of this sovereign power must always be determined with appropriate regard to the particular subject of its exercise. . . . Liberty of speech and of the press is also not an absolute right, and the state may punish its abuse. . . . Liberty, in each of its phases, has its history and connotation and, in the present instance, the inquiry is as to the historic conception of the liberty of the press and whether the statute under review violates the essential attributes of that liberty. . . .

With respect to these contentions it is enough to say that in passing upon constitutional questions the court has regard to substance and not to mere matters of form, and that, in accordance with familiar principles, the statute must be tested by its operation and effect. . . . That operation and effect we think are clearly shown by the record in this case. We are not concerned with mere errors of the trial court, if there be such, in going beyond the direction of the statute as construed by the supreme court of the state. It is thus important to note precisely the purpose and effect of the statute as the state court has construed it.

First. The statute is not aimed at the redress of individual or private wrongs. Remedies for libel remain available and unaffected. The statute, said the state court, "is not directed at threatened libel but at an existing business which, generally speaking, involves more than libel." It is aimed at the distribution of scandalous matter as "detrimental to public morals and to the general welfare," tending "to disturb the peace of the community" and "to provoke assaults and the commission of crime." . . . Men who are victims of such assaults seldom resort to the courts. This is especially true of their sins are exposed and the only question relates to whether it was done with good motives and for justifiable ends. This law is not for the protection of the person attacked nor to punish the wrongdoer. It is for the protection of the public welfare."

Second. The statute is directed not simply at the circulation of scandalous and defamatory statements with regard to private citizens, but at the continued publication by newspapers and periodicals of charges against public officers of corruption, malfeasance in office, or serious neglect of duty. Such charges by their very nature create a public scandal. They are scandalous and defamatory within the meaning of the statute, which has its normal operation in relation to publications dealing prominently and chiefly with the alleged derelictions of public officers.

Third. The object of the statute is not punishment, in the ordinary sense, but suppression of the offending newspaper or periodical. The reason for the enactment, as the state court has said, is that prosecutions to enforce penal statutes for libel do not result in "efficient repression or suppression of the evils of scandal." . . . In the present instance, the proof was that nine editions of the newspaper or periodical in question were published on successive dates, and that they were chiefly devoted to charges against public officers and in relation to the prevalence and protection of crime. In such a case, these officers are not left to their ordinary remedy in a suit for libel, or the authorities to a prosecution for criminal libel. Under this statute, a publisher of a newspaper or periodical, undertaking to conduct a campaign to expose and to censure official derelictions, and devoting his publication principally to that purpose, must face not simply the possibility of a verdict against him in a suit or prosecution for libel, but a determination that his newspaper or periodical is a public nuisance to be abated, and that this abatement and suppression will follow unless he is prepared with legal evidence to prove the truth of the charges and also to satisfy the court that, in addition to being true, the matter was published with good motives and for justifiable ends.

This suppression is accomplished by enjoining publications and that restraint is the object and effect of the statute.

Fourth. The statute not only operates to suppress the offending newspaper or periodical but to put the publisher under an effective censorship. When a newspaper or periodical is found to be "malicious, scandalous and defamatory," and is suppressed as such, resumption of publication is punishable as a contempt of court by fine or imprisonment. Thus, where a newspaper or periodical has been suppressed because of the circulation of charges against public officers of official misconduct, it would seem to be clear that the renewal of the publication of such charges would constitute a contempt and that the judgment would lay a permanent restraint upon the publisher, to escape which he must satisfy the court as to the character of a new publication. Whether he would be permitted again to publish matter deemed to be derogatory to the same or other public officers would depend upon the court's ruling. In the present instance the judgment restrained the defendants from "publishing, circulating, having in their possession, selling or giving away any publication whatsoever which is a malicious, scandalous or defamatory newspaper, as defined by law." The law gives no definition except that covered by the words "scandalous and defamatory," and publications charging official misconduct are of that class. While the court, answering the objection that the judgment was too broad, saw no reason for construing it as restraining the defendants "from operating a newspaper in harmony with the public welfare to which all must yield," and said that the defendants had not indicated "any desire to conduct their business in the usual and legitimate manner," the manifest inference is that, at least with respect to a new publication directed against official misconduct, the defendant would be held, under penalty of punishment for contempt as provided in the statute, to a manner of publication which the court considered to be "usual and legitimate" and consistent with the public welfare.

If we cut through mere details of procedure, the operation and effect of the statute in substance is that public authorities may bring the owner or publisher of a newspaper or periodical before a judge upon a charge of conducting a business of publishing scandalous and defamatory matter—in particular that the matter consists of charges against public officers of official dereliction—and unless the owner or publisher is able and disposed to bring competent evidence to satisfy the judge that the charges are true and are published with good motives and for justifiable ends, his newspaper or periodical is suppressed and further publication is made punishable as a contempt. This is of the essence of censorship.

The question is whether a statute authorizing such proceedings in restraint of publication is consistent with the conception of the liberty of the press as historically conceived and guaranteed. In determining the extent of the constitutional protection, it has been generally, if not universally, considered that it is the chief purpose of the guaranty to prevent previous restraints upon publication. The struggle in England, directed against the legislative power of the licenser, resulted in renunciation of the censorship of the press. The liberty deemed to be established was thus described by Blackstone: "The liberty of the press is indeed essential to the nature of a free state; but this consists in laying no *previous* restraints upon publications, and not in freedom from censure for criminal matter when published. Every freeman has an undoubted right to lay what sentiments he pleases before the public; to forbid this, is to destroy the freedom of the press; but if he publishes what is improper, mischievous or illegal, he must take the consequence of his own temerity." 4 Bl. Com. 151, 152; see Story on the Constitution, §§ 1884, 1889. . . .

The criticism upon Blackstone's statement has not been because immunity from previous restraint upon publication has not been regarded as deserving of special emphasis, but chiefly because that immunity cannot be deemed to exhaust the conception of the liberty guaranteed by state and Federal constitutions. The point of criticism has been "that the mere exemption from previous restraints cannot be all that is secured by the constitutional provisions;" and that "the liberty of the press might be rendered a mockery and a delusion, and the phrase itself a by-word, if, while every man was at liberty to publish what he pleased, the public authorities might nevertheless punish him for harmless publications." 2 Cooley, Const. Lim. 8th ed., p. 885. But it is recognized that punishment for the abuse of the liberty accorded to the press is essential to the protection of the public, and that the common law rules that subject the libeler to responsibility for the public offense, as well as for the private injury, are not abolished by the protection extended in our constitutions. . . . In the present case, we have no occasion to inquire as to the permissible scope of subsequent punishment: For whatever wrong the appellant has committed or may commit, by his publications, the state appropriately affords both public and private redress by its libel laws. As has been noted, the statute in question does not deal with punishments; it provides for no punishment, except in case of contempt for violation of the court's order, but for suppression and injunction, that is, for restraint upon publication.

The objection has also been made that the principle as to immunity from previous restraint is stated too broadly, if every such restraint is deemed to be prohibited. That is undoubtedly true; the protection even as to previous restraint is not absolutely unlimited. But the limitation has been recognized only in exceptional cases. "When a nation is at war many things that might be said in time of peace are such a hindrance to its effort that their utterance will not be endured so long as men fight and that no court could regard them as protected by any constitutional right." Schenck v. United States. No one would question but that a government might prevent actual obstruction to its recruiting service or the publication of the sailing dates of transports or the number and location of troops. On similar grounds, the primary requirements of decency may be enforced against obscene publications. The security of the community life may be protected against incitements to acts of violence and the overthrow by force of orderly government. The constitutional guaranty of free speech does not "protect a man from an injunction against uttering words that may have all the effect of force. . . ."

The exceptional nature of its limitations places in a strong light the general conception that liberty of the press, historically considered and taken up by the Federal Constitution, has meant, principally, although not exclusively, immunity from previous restraints or censorship. The conception of the liberty of the press in this country had broadened with the exigencies of the colonial period and with the efforts to secure freedom from oppressive administration. That liberty was especially cherished for the immunity it afforded from previous restraint of the publication of censure of public officers and charges of official misconduct. . . .

The importance of this immunity has not lessened. While reckless assaults upon public men, and efforts to bring obloquy upon those who are endeavoring faithfully to discharge official duties, exert a baleful influence and deserve the severest condemnation in public opinion, it cannot be said that this abuse is greater, and it is believed to be less, than that which characterized the period in which our institutions took shape. Meanwhile, the administration of government has become more complex, the opportunities for malfeasance and corruption have multiplied, crime has grown to most serious proportions, and the danger of its protection by unfaithful officials and of the impairment of the fundamental security of life and property by criminal alliances and official neglect, emphasizes the primary need of a vigilant and courageous press, especially in great cities. The fact that the liberty of the press may be abused by miscreant purveyors of scandal does not make any the less necessary the immunity of the press from previous restraint in dealing with official misconduct. Subsequent punishment for such abuses as may exist is the appropriate remedy, consistent with constitutional privilege. . . .

The statute in question cannot be justified by reason of the fact that the publisher is permitted to show, before injunction issues, that the matter published is true and is published with good motives and for justifiable ends. If such a statute, authorizing suppression and injunction on such a basis, is constitutionally valid, it would be equally permissible for the legislature to provide that at any time the publisher of any newspaper could be brought before a court, or even an administrative officer (as the constitutional protection may not be regarded as resting on mere procedural details) and required to produce proof of the truth of his publication, or of what he intended to publish, and of his motives, or stand enjoined. If this can be done, the legislature may provide machinery for determining in the complete exercise of its discretion what are justifiable ends and restrain publication accordingly. And it would be but a step to a complete system of censorship. The recognition of authority to impose previous restraint upon publication in order to protect the community against the circulation of charges of misconduct, and especially of official misconduct, necessarily would carry with it the admission of the authority of the censor against which the constitutional barrier was erected. The preliminary freedom, by virtue of the very reason for its existence, does not depend, as this court has said, on proof of truth. . . .

Equally unavailing is the insistence that the statute is designed to prevent the circulation of scandal which tends to disturb the public peace and to provoke assaults and the commission of crime. Charges of reprehensible conduct, and in particular of official malfeasance, unquestionably create a public scandal, but the theory of the constitutional guaranty is that even a more serious public evil would be caused by authority to prevent publication. . . .

For these reasons we hold the statute, so far as it authorized the proceedings in this action under clause (b) of section one, to be an infringement of the liberty of the press guaranteed by the 14th Amendment. We should add that the decision rests upon the operation and effect of the statute, without regard to the question of the truth of the charges contained in the particular periodical. The fact that the public officers named in this case, and those associated with the charges of official dereliction, may be deemed to be impeccable, cannot affect the conclusion that the statute imposes an unconstitutional restraint upon publication.

Judgment reversed.

Mr. Justice Butler dissented in an opinion in which Justices Van Devanter, McReynolds, and Sutherland concurred.

RICHMOND NEWSPAPERS, INC. v. VIRGINIA

488 U. S. 555; 100 S. Ct. 2814; 65 L. Ed. 2d 973
(1980)

On Sunday morning, June 13, 1971, *The New York Times* ran on its front page a modest headline spanning columns five, six, and seven:

Vietnam Archive: Pentagon Study Traces
3 Decades of Growing U.S. Involvement

A small box underneath said, "Three pages of documentary material from the Pentagon study begin on page 35."

In this unobtrusive way, the reading public was introduced to what was to become one of the most dramatic and sensational cases ever to reach the Supreme Court. The study, tracing the deliberate involvement of the United States in Vietnam during the administrations of four presidents, was based on a 7000-word top secret study made by the Pentagon and was turned over to the *Times* by Daniel Ellsberg, a Pentagon employee, as an act of conscience.

The following Monday night, just as the third in the series was about to appear, the Justice Department called the *Times* and asked them to desist from further publication on the ground that publication violated the Espionage Act. The *Times* refused, and Tuesday afternoon the Attorney General filed a motion for an injunction in the district court in New York. That afternoon District Judge Gurfein, who just that day had started work as a federal judge, issued the first federal injunction against a newspaper publication in the history of the nation. He revoked the order a few days later, only to have the revocation set aside by the Court of Appeals on June 23. Three days later the Supreme Court heard oral argument and on June 30 it decided in New York Times Co. v. United States (1971) that the injunction could not stand. Nine opinions accompanied the short per curiam opinion for the Court, with Justices Burger, Harlan, and Blackmun dissenting, largely on the ground that no one, not even the government, had had time to learn the facts of the case. The orderly thing, they felt, was to delay publication until the impact of the release of the material could be assessed.

While it is perhaps true, as Justice Holmes said, that great cases make bad law, the importance of the Supreme Court's decision in the *Times* case would be hard to overstate. Over the past forty years, the growing complexity and pervasiveness of government have resulted in a steady increase in presidential power at the expense of congressional power. Nowhere is this more apparent than in the areas of foreign affairs and national defense, in which the President has special constitutional authority, and it is widely assumed that constitutional limitations on presidential prerogatives in these areas should bow to presidential determinations of what the national security requires. The Supreme Court has apparently agreed, and not since Ex parte Milligan (1866), except for the Steel Seizure Case in 1952, has the Supreme Court said "no" to the President on matters of this kind. It thus came as a shock to those who approve such presidential authority that the Court should refuse to prevent the publication of material which the government deemed harmful to the national interest despite the refusal of Congress to provide such a remedy.

While Justice Black was probably right in saying that the First Amendment was drafted to prevent just such assumptions of governmental power over the press, his contention that the Amendment should be applied absolutely literally was so at odds with its judicial development that it attracted few adherents. Far more impressive were the votes of Justices Stewart and White, who felt that the publication was certainly wrong and might even be a crime, but refused to enjoin it because the "heavy burden" borne by the government under the First Amendment had not been met.

In a far less spectacular case decided some six weeks before the Pentagon Papers case the Court also held void an injunction against publication—in this case the distribution of pamphlets in the home neighborhood of an Illinois realtor accused of "block-busting." The leaflets were designed to let "his neighbors know what he was doing to us" in the hope he would agree to stop such tactics. Rejecting the argument that the purpose of the leaflets was to force "rather than inform" and that the injunction was a valid protection for the realtor's right of privacy, the Court held it void as a previous restraint on speech and publication. "The claim that the expressions were intended to exercise a coercive impact on respondent does not remove them from the reach of the First Amendment. Petitioners plainly intended to influence respondent's conduct by their activities; this is not fundamentally different from the function of a newspaper. . . . But so long as the means are peaceful, the communication need not meet standards of acceptability." See Organization for a Better Austin v. Keefe (1971).

The cardinal value which we attach to freedom of speech and press in a democratic society sometimes tends to obscure the fact that the use of these freedoms may jeopardize other civil liberties of the individual. One of these is the right of a litigant in a court of law to have his case tried by an impartial judge or jury. The conflict arises when unrestrained newspaper comment on a pending or current trial threatens the impartiality of any jury which could be drawn, or brings pressure upon judge or jury to reach a particular decision. An essential phase of judicial power has always been the power of a judge to protect the administration of justice in his court by punishing for contempt those who would interfere with it. In England, this power has always been very sternly used, and as recently as 1949 the Lord Chief Justice fined the London *Daily Mirror* £ 10,000 and sentenced the editor to three months in jail for the paper's lurid comments on the crimes of the so-called "English Bluebeard" who was then on trial for murder.

In dealing with this conflict, courts in the United States have been far more lenient to questionable newspaper comment than have courts in England. In three cases decided in the 1940s, the Court struck down judicial efforts to curb the press. In Bridges v. California (1941), it set aside the contempt conviction of union leader Harry Bridges who had released to the press a threat that he would close down the West Coast ports if the court tried to enforce a decision against him. In Pennekamp v. Florida (1946), it quashed a contempt resulting from editorials and cartoons appearing in the *Miami*

Herald which accused the local judge of playing into the hands of criminal elements and thwarting the efforts of the district attorney to enforce the law. In Craig v. Harney (1947), it set aside a contempt conviction where the newspaper, by a bitter attack on a trial judge, had tried to alter his decision. In all three cases the Court stressed the importance of an unfettered press and added in Craig that "the law of contempt is not made for the protection of judges who may be sensitive to the winds of public opinion. Judges are supposed to be men of fortitude, able to thrive in a hardy climate. . . . Nor can we assume that the trial judge was not a man of fortitude."

While the Court has been unwilling to permit the punishment of newspapers for trying to influence the course of justice, it has not hesitated to reverse the conviction of persons whose trials were clearly so influenced. In Irvin v. Dowd (1961) the police issued a press release stating that Irvin had confessed to six murders. The one change of venue allowed by the state law merely took him into the next county—a county so blanketed by the adverse publicity that nearly 90 percent of the prospective jurors, and eight of the 12 members of the actual jury, believed the defendant was guilty before the trial even started. And in Rideau v. Louisiana (1963) police permitted the filming of a twenty-minute interview between Rideau and the sheriff, in which Rideau confessed to robbery, kidnapping, and murder. He was denied a change of venue despite the fact that three television broadcasts had carried the "interview," and three members of the jury had seen it. The Supreme Court reversed both convictions.

The cooperation between police and the news media following President Kennedy's assassination in 1963, which culminated in the murder two days later of Lee Harvey Oswald before a nationwide television audience, brought public demand for reform. In 1964 the New Jersey supreme court ordered a ban on pretrial statements to newsmen by prosecutors, police, and defense attorneys, while the Judicial Conference of the United States recommended to Congress the passage of a bill prohibiting the release of information to the press which had not previously been filed with the trial court. And in 1966 a committee of the American Bar Association recommended strong limits on pretrial reporting by both prosecutors and defense attorneys. While official moves of this kind met considerable opposition from the organized press, informal codes of conduct, such as those adopted in Nebraska in the case below, have been worked out in conference among the industry, the bar associations, and the courts.

Strong impetus was given the reform movement by the decision in Sheppard v. Maxwell (1966) overturning the conviction of Dr. Sam Sheppard for the murder of his wife. "Doctor Sam," a prominent Cleveland physician, was tried in a suburban court in what the Supreme Court described as a "carnival atmosphere." The press, convinced of his guilt, demanded his conviction and innundated the community with highly inflamatory, prejudicial statements which the judge, who refused to sequester the jury or grant a change of venue, was unable to keep from reaching the jury. The Court noted that "every court that has considered this case, save the court that tried it, has deplored the manner in which the news media inflamed and prejudiced the public." As for the trial itself, "the fact is that bedlam reigned at the courthouse during the trial, and newsmen took over practically the entire courtroom hounding most of the participants in the trial, especially Sheppard." After a careful review of the authority of a trial court to control the conduct of the trials before it, the Court concluded that they were adequate to protect the fairness of the trial. Strict rules of press behavior were enforced when Dr. Sheppard was retried by Ohio in 1966. An unspectacular trial resulted in his acquittal.

The result of the efforts at reform has been to shift the constitutional battle between the courts and the press to new ground as courts have tried to devise ways of preventing the publication of prejudicial news comments. In 1975, Erwin Simants was arrested and prosecuted for the brutal murder of six members of the Henry Kellie family in their home in Sutherland, Nebraska, a town of about 850 people. The crime attracted nationwide attention, and both Simant's attorney and the county attorney, fearing the "reasonable likelihood of prejudicial news which would make difficult, if not impossible, the impaneling of an impartial jury and tend to prevent a fair trial," obtained from the county court an order restricting press coverage. The news media asked the United States district court to vacate the order, but that court issued an order of its own prohibiting reporting on five subjects: "(1) the existence or contents of a confession Simants had made to law enforcement officers, which had been introduced in open court at arraignment; (2) the fact or nature of statements Simants had made to other persons; (3) the contents of a note he had written the night of the crime; (4) certain aspects of the medical testimony at the preliminary hearing; (5) the identity of the victims of the alleged sexual assault and the nature of the assault."

In Nebraska Press Asso. v. Stuart (1976), the Supreme Court unanimously held the court's order void. While conceding that the trial judge was justified in concluding there would be intense pretrial publicity, it found no evidence that the restraining order, on its face a serious limit on freedom of the press, was the only or even an effective way of guaranteeing an impartial jury. Not only did the trial court not explore other alternatives open to it, but in a town of 850 there was no reason to suppose the press accounts would be any more damaging than the rumors that were bound to circulate. As far as the material that had been introduced in open court, the Court reiterated its statement in Sheppard v. Maxwell (1966) that "there is nothing that proscribes the press from reporting events that transpire in the courtroom." In 1979, this latter point was reaffirmed and extended to information obtained by normal reporting techniques—in this case the name of a juvenile killer obtained by merely querying witnesses. The Court held the state's interest in protecting the privacy of juveniles insufficient to justify punishing the paper for publishing the name, especially since the law did not apply to either radio or television. See Smith v. Daily Mail Publishing Co. (1979).

To what extent does the news media, as the eyes and ears of a public that can rarely if ever witness events and conditions first hand, have a right of access to information not available to the public at large? In Branzburg v. Hayes (1972) the Supreme Court refused to create a constitutional privilege under the First Amendment for newsmen to withhold confidential sources of information from a grand jury investigating crime. The case involved newspaper reporters who had won the confidence of drug users and of the Black Panther Party and had written behind-the-scenes stories about them. Grand juries investigating these matters subpoenaed the reporters to testify and they refused on the ground that to do so would dry up their news sources and obstruct the free flow of news protected by the First Amendment. A five-man majority rejected their claim, holding that "the First Amendment does not guarantee the press a constitutional right of special access to information not available to the public generally."

In a series of cases the Supreme Court used this statement to justify forbidding the press access to prison facilities not available to the public at large. In Pell v. Procunier (1974), it upheld rules adopted by a California prison forbidding interviews with selected inmates on the ground that the inmates so selected became celebrities and posed a disciplinary problem. The Court noted that the rules reflected no intention to conceal conditions within the prison and that the press was free to visit the prison and speak with prisoners they happened to meet. In Saxbe v. Washington Post Co. (1974), the Court extended the same rule to federal prisons, and in Houchins v. KQED, Inc. (1978), in a four-to-three decision, it extended it to a California jail where it seemed apparent that the authorities were trying to conceal conditions within the jail from public scrutiny.

The first suggestion that the Court might be rethinking the question of access came in Gannett v. DePasquale (1979). Following the apparent murder of an upstate New

York man, three suspects were apprehended in Michigan with the victim's pickup truck and gun. They were returned to New York for trial, and following their arraignment asked for a pretrial hearing to argue the inadmissibility in evidence of the gun and certain statements made to the Michigan police that they claimed were involuntary. Arguing that the "unabated buildup of adverse publicity had jeopardized the ability of the defendants to receive a fair trial," they moved that the hearings be closed to the public and the press. Without objection from the press the hearing was closed but the trial judge later held a full hearing on whether or not the transcript of the hearing should be released. The trial judge presumed a constitutional right of access on the part of the press but after finding on the record that an open suppression hearing would pose a "reasonable probability of prejudice to these defendants," he refused to release the transcript.

In a five-to-four decision, the Court upheld the trial judge. Justice Stewart's opinion reviewed the commentaries and precedents and concluded that the Sixth Amendment guarantee of a public trial was for the benefit of the accused, not the public. While he conceded the importance of open trials to the public, he made clear that "recognition of an independent public interest in the enforcement of Sixth Amendment guarantees is a far cry . . . from the creation of a constitutional right on the part of the public." Furthermore, while "there is no question that the Sixth Amendment permits and even assumes open trials as a norm," historically the public had no right to attend *pretrial* proceedings. In addition, even assuming a constitutional right of access on the part of the press, it had not been violated in this case because the trial court had properly "balanced the 'constitutional rights of the press and public' against the 'defendants' right to a fair trial.'" In 1965 in Estes v. Texas the Court had held that televising a sensational trial had denied the defendant due process of law, noting that the "public trial" guaranteed by the Sixth Amendment was not the equivalent of a day in a "stadium . . . or nationwide arena." In 1981, however, the Court in Chandler v. Florida construed Estes as not banning all television coverage, although a defendant clearly had a right (which had not been exercised in this case) to try to show that media coverage had an adverse affect upon the fairness of his trial.

In the present case, the state's prosecution of the defendant for murder had resulted in three mistrials, at least one of which was apparently the result of a prospective juror reading about inadmissible evidence. At the start of the fourth trial, the defendant asked that the trial be closed. A hearing was held from which the press was excluded and the judge ruled that the press and public be excluded from the trial.

Mr. Chief Justice Burger announced the judgment of the Court and delivered an opinion in which Mr. Justice White and Mr. Justice Stevens joined, saying in part:

II.

We begin consideration of this case by noting that the precise issue presented here has not previously been before this Court for decision. In Gannett Co., Inc. v. DePasquale, (1979), the Court was not required to decide whether a right of access to *trials,* as distinguished from hearings on *pre*trial motions, was constitutionally guaranteed. The Court held that the

Sixth Amendment's guarantee to the accused of a public trial gave neither the public nor the press an enforceable right of access to a *pre*trial suppression hearing. One concurring opinion specifically emphasized that "a hearing on a motion before trial to suppress evidence is not a *trial*. . . ." (Burger, C. J., concurring). Moreover, the Court did not decide whether the First and Fourteenth Amendments guarantee a right of the public to attend trials: nor did the dissenting opinion reach this issue.

In prior cases the Court has treated questions involving conflicts between publicity and a defendant's right to a fair trial; as we observed in Nebraska Press Assn. v. Stuart (1976), "[t]he problems presented by this [conflict] are almost as old as the Republic." . . . But here for the first time the Court is asked to decide whether a criminal trial itself may be closed to the public upon the unopposed request of a defendant, without any demonstration that closure is required to protect the defendant's superior right to a fair trial, or that some other overriding consideration requires closure.

A.

The origins of the proceeding which has become the modern criminal trial in Anglo-American justice can be traced back beyond reliable historical records. We need not here review all details of its development, but a summary of that history is instructive. What is significant for present purposes is that throughout its evolution, the trial has been open to all who cared to observe. . . .

[The Court here traced the development of the English court system from the days before the Norman Conquest down to the sixteenth century, noting the uniform openness of the criminal trial.] Three centuries later, Sir Frederick Pollock was able to state of the "rule of publicity" that, "[h]ere we have one tradition, at any rate, which has persisted through all changes." . . . See also E. Jenks, The Book of English Law 73-74 (6th ed. 1967): "[O]ne of the most conspicuous features of English justice, that all judicial trials are held in open court, to which the public have free access, . . . appears to have been the rule in England from time immemorial."

We have found nothing to suggest that the presumptive openness of the trial, which English courts were later to call "one of the essential qualities of a court of justice," . . . was not also an attribute of the judicial systems of colonial America. In Virginia, for example, such records as there are of early criminal trials indicate that they were open, and nothing to the contrary has been cited. . . . Indeed, when in the mid-1600's the Virginia Assembly felt that the respect due the courts was "by the clamorous unmannerlyness of the people lost, and order, gravity and decoram which should manifest the authority of a court in the court it selfe neglicted," the response was not to restrict the openness of the trials to the public, but instead to prescribe rules for the conduct of those attending them. . . .

In some instances, the openness of trials was explicitly recognized as part of the fundamental law of the colony. . . .

B.

As we have shown, and as was shown in both the Court's opinion and the dissent in Gannett, the historical evidence demonstrates conclusively that at the time when our organic laws were adopted, criminal trials both here and in England had long been presumptively open. This is no quirk of history; rather, it has long been recognized as an indispensible attribute of an Anglo-American trial. Both Hale in the 17th century and Blackstone in the 18th saw the importance of openness to the proper functioning of a trial; it gave assurance that the proceedings were conducted fairly to all concerned, and it discouraged perjury, the misconduct of participants, and decisions based on secret bias or partiality. . . . The nexus between openness, fairness, and the perception of fairness was not lost on [foreign observers]: "[T]he judge, the counsel, and the jury, are constantly exposed to public animadversion; and this greatly tends to augment the extraordinary confidence, which the English repose in the administration of justice."

This observation raises the important point that "[t]he publicity of a judicial proceeding is a requirement of much broader bearing than its mere effect on the quality of testimony." . . . The early history of open trials in part reflects the widespread acknowledgement, long before there were behavioral scientists, that public trials had significant community therapeutic value. Even without such experts to frame the concept in words, people sensed from experience and observation that, especially in the administration of criminal justice, the means used to achieve justice must have the support derived from public acceptance of both the process and its results.

When a shocking crime occurs, a community reaction of outrage and public protest often follows. . . . Thereafter the open processes of justice serve an important prophylactic purpose, providing an outlet for community concern, hostility, and emotion. Without an awareness that society's responses to criminal conduct are underway, natural human reactions of outrage and protest are frustrated and may manifest themselves in some form of vengeful "self-help," as indeed they did regularly in the activities of vigilante "committees" on our frontiers. . . .

Civilized societies withdraw both from the victim and the vigilante the enforcement of criminal laws, but they cannot erase from people's consciousness the fundamental, natural yearning to see justice done—or even the urge for retribution. The crucial prophylactic aspects of the administration of justice cannot function in the dark; no community catharsis can occur if justice is "done in a corner [or] in any covert manner." It is not enough to say that results alone will satiate the natural community desire for "satisfaction." A result considered untoward may undermine public confidence, and where the trial has been concealed from public view an unexpected outcome can cause a reaction that the system at best has failed and at worst has been corrupted. To work effectively, it is important that society's criminal process "satisfy the appearance of justice," . . . and the appearance of justice can best be provided by allowing people to observe it.

Looking back, we see that when the ancient "town meeting" form of trial became too cumbersome, twelve members of the community were delegated to act as its surrogates, but the community did not surrender its right to observe the conduct of trials. The people retained a "right of visitation" which enabled them to satisfy themselves that justice was in fact being done. . . .

In earlier times, both in England and America, attendance at court was a common mode of "passing the time." . . . With the press, cinema, and electronic media now supplying the representations or reality of the real life drama once available only in the courtroom, attendance at court is no longer a widespread pastime. Yet "[i]t is not unrealistic even in this day to believe that public inclusion affords citizens a form of legal education and hopefully promotes confidence in the fair administration of justice." . . . Instead of acquiring information about trials by firsthand observation or by word of mouth from those who attended, people now acquire it chiefly through the print and electronic media. In a sense, this validates the media claim of functioning as surrogates for the public. While media representatives enjoy the same right of access as the public, they often are provided special seating and priority of entry so that they may report what people in attendance have seen and heard. This "contribute[s] to public understanding of the rule of law and to comprehension of the functioning of the entire criminal justice system. . . ." Nebraska Press Assn. v. Stuart (Brennan, J., concurring).

C.

From this unbroken, uncontradicted history, supported by reasons as valid today as in centuries past, we are bound to conclude that a presumption of openness inheres in the very nature of a criminal trial under our system of justice. This conclusion is hardly novel; without a direct holding on the issue, the Court has voiced its recognition of it in a variety of contexts over the years. . . . Recently in Gannett Co. Inc. v. DePasquale (1979), both the majority and dissenting opinions agreed that open trials were part of the common law tradition.

Despite the history of criminal trials being presumptively open since long before the Constitution, the State presses its contention that neither the Constitution nor the Bill of Rights contains any provision which by its terms guarantees to the public the right to attend criminal trials. Standing alone, this is correct, but there remains the question whether, absent an explicit provision, the Constitution affords protection against exclusion of the public from criminal trials.

III.

A.

The First Amendment, in conjunction with the Fourteenth, prohibits governments from "abridging the freedom of speech, or of the press; or the right of the people peaceably to assemble, and to petition the Government for a redress of grievances." These expressly guaranteed freedoms share a common core purpose of assuring freedom of communication on matters relating to the functioning of government. Plainly it would be difficult to single out any aspect of government of higher concern and importance to the people than the manner in which criminal trials are conducted; as we have shown, recognition of this pervades the centuries-old history of open trials and the opinions of this Court.

The Bill of Rights was enacted against the backdrop of the long history of trials being presumptively open. Public access to trials was then regarded as an important aspect of the process itself; the conduct of trials "before as many of the people as chuse to attend" was regarded as one of "the inestimable advantages of a free English constitution of government." . . . In guaranteeing freedoms such as those of speech and press, the First Amendment can be read as protecting the right of everyone to attend trials so as to give meaning to those explicit guarantees. "[T]he First Amendment goes beyond protection of the press and the self-expression of individuals to prohibit government from limiting the stock of information from which members of the public may draw." First National Bank of Boston v. Bellotti (1978). Free speech carries with it some freedom to listen. "In a variety of contexts this Court has referred to a First Amendment right to 'receive information and ideas.'" Kleindienst v. Mandel (1972). What this means in the context of trials is that the First Amendment guarantees of speech and press, standing alone, prohibit government from summarily closing courtroom doors which had long been open to the public at the time that amendment was adopted. "For the First Amendment does not speak equivocally. . . . It must be taken as a command of the broadest scope that explicit language, read in the context of a liberty-loving society, will allow." Bridges v. California (1941).

It is not crucial whether we describe this right to attend criminal trials to hear, see, and communicate observations concerning them as a "right of access," cf. Gannett (Powell, J., concurring); Saxbe v. Washington Post Co. (1974); Pell v. Procunier (1974),* or a "right to gather information," for we have recognized that "without some protection for seeking out the news, freedom of the press could be eviscerated." Branzburg v. Hayes (1972). The explicit, guaranteed rights to speak and to publish concerning what takes place at a trial would lose much meaning if access to observe the trial could, as it was here, be foreclosed arbitrarily.

B.

The right of access to places traditionally open to the public, as criminal trials have long been, may be seen as assured by the amalgam of the First Amendment guarantees of speech and press; and their affinity to the right of assembly is not without relevance. From the outset, the right of assembly

---

*Procunier and Saxbe, supra, are distinguishable in the sense that they were concerned with penal institutions which, by definition, are not "open" or public places. Penal institutions do not share the long tradition of openness. . . .

was regarded not only as an independent right but also as a catalyst to augment the free exercise of the other First Amendment rights with which it was deliberately linked by the draftsmen. "The right of peaceable assembly is a right cognate to those of free speech and free press and is equally fundamental." DeJonge v. Oregon (1937). People assemble in public places not only to speak or to take action, but also to listen, observe, and learn; indeed, they may "assembl[e] for any lawful purpose," Hague v. C.I.O. (1939) (opinion of Stone, J.). Subject to the traditional time, place, and manner restrictions, . . . streets, sidewalks, and parks are places traditionally open, where First Amendment rights may be exercised . . . ; a trial courtroom also is a public place where the people generally—and representatives of the media—have a right to be present, and where their presence historically has been thought to enhance the integrity and quality of what takes place.

C.

The State argues that the Constitution nowhere spells out a guarantee for the right of the public to attend trials, and that accordingly no such right is protected. The possibility that such a contention could be made did not escape the notice of the Constitution's draftsmen; they were concerned that some important rights might be thought disparaged because not specifically guaranteed. . . .

But arguments such as the State makes have not precluded recognition of important rights not enumerated. Notwithstanding the appropriate caution against reading into the Constitution rights not explicitly defined, the Court has acknowledged that certain unarticulated rights are implicit in enumerated guarantees. For example, the rights of association and of privacy, the right to be presumed innocent and the right to be judged by a standard of proof beyond a reasonable doubt in a criminal trial, as well as the right to travel, appear nowhere in the Constitution or Bill of Rights. Yet these important but unarticulated rights have nonetheless been found to share constitutional protection in common with explicit guarantees. The concerns expressed by Madison and others have thus been resolved; fundamental rights, even though not expressly guaranteed, have been recognized by the Court as indispensable to the enjoyment of rights explicitly defined.

We hold that the right to attend criminal trials is implicit in the guarantees of the First Amendment; without the freedom to attend such trials, which people have exercised for centuries, important aspects of freedom of speech and "of the press could be eviscerated." . . .

D.

. . . Despite the fact that this was the fourth trial of the accused, the trial judge made no findings to support closure; no inquiry was made as to whether alternative solutions would have met the need to ensure fairness;

there was no recognition of any right under the Constitution for the public or press to attend the trial. In contrast to the pretrial proceeding dealt with in Gannett there exist in the context of the trial itself various tested alternatives to satisfy the constitutional demands of fairness. See, e.g., Nebraska Press Association v. Stuart, Sheppard v. Maxwell. There was no suggestion that any problems with witnesses could not have been dealt with by their exclusion from the courtroom or their sequestration during the trial. Nor is there anything to indicate that sequestration of the jurors would not have guarded against their being subjected to any improper information. All of the alternatives admittedly present difficulties for trial courts, but none of the factors relied on here was beyond the realm of the manageable. Absent an overriding interest articulated in findings, the trial of a criminal case must be open to the public. Accordingly, the judgment under review is reversed.

Reversed.

Mr. Justice Powell took no part in the consideration or decision of this case.

Mr. Justice White wrote a short concurring opinion.

Mr. Justice Stevens, concurring, said in part:

This is a watershed case. Until today the Court has accorded virtually absolute protection to the dissemination of information or ideas, but never before has it squarely held that the acquisition of newsworthy matter is entitled to any constitutional protection whatsoever. An additional word of emphasis is therefore appropriate. . . .

. . . In Houchins v. KQED, Inc. [1978], I explained at length why Mr. Justice Brennan, Mr. Justice Powell, and I were convinced that "[a]n official prison policy of concealing . . . knowledge from the public by arbitrarily cutting off the flow of information at its source abridges the freedom of speech and of the press protected by the First and Fourteenth Amendments to the Constitution." . . .

It is somewhat ironic that the Court should find more reason to recognize a right of access today than it did in Houchins. For Houchins involved the plight of a segment of society least able to protect itself, an attack on a longstanding policy of concealment, and an absence of any legitimate justification for abridging public access to information about how government operates. In this case we are protecting the interests of the most powerful voices in the community, we are concerned with an almost unique exception to an established tradition of openness in the conduct of criminal trials, and it is likely that the closure order was motivated by the judge's desire to protect the individual defendant from the burden of a fourth criminal trial.

Mr. Justice Brennan, with whom Mr. Justice Marshall joins, concurring in the judgment, said in part:

Gannett Co. v. DePasquale (1979), held that the Sixth Amendment right to a public trial was personal to the accused, conferring no right of access to pretrial proceedings that is separately enforceable by the public or the press. The instant case raises the question whether the First Amendment, of its own force and as applied to the States through the Fourteenth Amendment, secures the public an independent right of access to trial proceedings. Because I believe that the First Amendment—of itself and as applied to the States through the Fourteenth Amendment—secures such a public right of access, I agree with those of my Brethren who hold that, without more agreement of the trial judge and the parties cannot constitutionally close a trial to the public.

Mr. Justice Blackmun, concurring in the judgment, said in part:

II.

The Court's ultimate ruling in Gannett, with such clarification as is provided by the opinions in this case today, apparently is now to the effect that there is no *Sixth* Amendment right on the part of the public—or the press—to an open hearing on a motion to suppress. I, of course, continue to believe that Gannett was in error, both in its interpretation of the Sixth Amendment generally, and in its application to the suppression hearing, for I remain convinced that the right to a public trial is to be found where the Constitution explicitly placed it—in the Sixth Amendment.

The Court, however, has eschewed the Sixth Amendment route. The plurality turns to other possible constitutional sources and invokes a veritable potpourri of them—the speech clause of the First Amendment, the press clause, the assembly clause, the Ninth Amendment, and a cluster of penumbral guarantees recognized in past decisions. This course is troublesome, but it is the route that has been selected and, at least for now, we must live with it. . . .

Having said all this, and with the Sixth Amendment set to one side in this case, I am driven to conclude, as a secondary position, that the First Amendment must provide some measure of protection for public access to the trial. The opinion in partial dissent in Gannett explained that the public has an intense need and a deserved right to know about the administration of justice in general; about the prosecution of local crimes in particular; about the conduct of the judge, the prosecutor, defense counsel, police officers, other public servants, and all the actors in the judicial arena; and about the trial itself. . . . It is clear and obvious to me, on the approach the Court has chosen to take, that, by closing this criminal trial, the trial judge abridged these First Amendment interests of the public.

I also would reverse, and I join the judgment of the Court.

Mr. Justice Rehnquist, dissenting, said in part:

For the reasons stated in my separate concurrence in Gannett Co., Inc. v. DePasquale, I do not believe that either the First or Sixth Amendments, as made applicable to the States by the Fourteenth, require that a State's reasons for denying public access to a trial, where both the prosecuting attorney and the defendant have consented to an order of closure approved by the judge, are subject to any additional constitutional review at our hands. And I most certainly do not believe that the Ninth Amendment confers upon us any such power to review orders of state trial judges closing trials in such situations. . . .

The proper administration of justice in any nation is bound to be a matter of the highest concern to all thinking citizens. But to gradually rein in, as this Court has done over the past generation, all of the ultimate decision-making power over how justice shall be administered, not merely in the federal system but in each of the 50 States, is a task that no Court consisting of nine persons, however gifted, is equal to. Nor is it desirable that such authority be exercised by such a tiny numerical fragment of the 220 million people who compose the population of this country.

WALKER v. BIRMINGHAM

388 U.S. 307; 87 S. Ct. 1824; 18 L. Ed. 2d 1210 (1967)

During the late 1950s and early 1960s Southern Negroes, led by such people as Martin Luther King, Jr., undertook to bring an end to segregation by nonviolent means. This was to be done by attracting public attention to segregation policies in the hope that the public conscience would be aroused and demand their abolition.

Against these efforts the Southern communities rolled out a battery of legal field pieces, some of them dating back to the early days of the common law. One of these was a prosecution for criminal trespass. Among the techniques employed to publicize segregation was the "sit-in" demonstration, in which Negroes, sometimes accompanied by sympathetic whites, would enter a restaurant or lunch counter with a *White Only* sign in the window and ask to be served. When service was denied, they refused to leave, and the police would be called to arrest them for trespass.

In five cases decided in 1964 the Supreme Court reversed on nonconstitutional grounds convictions for sit-in demonstrations. Although the Court carefully avoided the issue whether state enforcement of trespass laws to effect private discrimination made the state a party to the discrimination, six justices in separate opinions indicated their stand on this issue. Justices Black, Harlan, and White argued that in the absence of a statute forbidding such discrimination, the impartial enforcement of trespass statutes does not make the state a party to the discrimination and hence does not deny equal protection, while Justices Warren, Goldberg, and Douglas argued that the framers of the Fourteenth Amendment had assumed the continued existence of the right of all citizens to enter places of public accommodation, and the refusal of the state to enforce that right as to Negroes denies them the equal protection of the law. See Bell v. Maryland, Bouie v. Columbia, Griffin v. Maryland, Robinson v. Florida, and Barr v. Columbia.

The final chapter in the sit-in cases was written in Hamm v. Rock Hill (1964), decided the same day as Heart of Atlanta Motel v. United States. Again the Court failed to reach the constitutional issue but concluded that the Civil Rights Act of 1964, by making sit-ins no longer a crime, had abated sit-in prosecutions then in progress, since the states no longer had a policy to be served by such prosecutions. Federal statutes would decree this result as far as federal crimes were concerned, and the supremacy clause dictated the same result for state crimes. The effect of the decision was to stop the prosecution of some 3,000 sit-in demonstrators.

A second technique relied upon by the Southern communities was the well-established right of any organized community to protect itself from a breach of the peace. Such a breach is "a substantive evil which the state can prevent" through the exercise of its police power; therefore a speech which presents a "clear and present danger" of causing a breach of the peace is punishable. Although the use of such statutes against demonstrations and "marches" presented some novel features, the general rules regarding them had been laid down years before. The Supreme Court, in reviewing cases which allege a violation of freedom of speech on this ground must determine (1) that the statute, as interpreted by the state court or by the judge in his charge to the jury, really defines a breach of the peace, and (2) that a clear and present danger of such breach actually exists.

In Chaplinsky v. New Hampshire (1942) a Jehovah's Witness called a police officer "a God damned/racketeer" and "a damned Fascist," in violation of a state statute whose purpose, the state court said, was to forbid words "such as have a direct tendency to cause acts of violence by the persons to whom, individually, the remark is addressed." The Court agreed that such speech could constitutionally be punished: "There are certain well-defined and narrowly limited classes of speech, the prevention and punishment of which have never been thought to raise any constitutional problem. These include the lewd and obscene, the profane, the libelous, and the insulting or 'fighting' words—those which by their very utterance inflict injury or tend to incite an immediate breach of the peace. . . . 'Resort to epithets or personal abuse is not in any proper sense communication of information or opinion safeguarded by the Constitution. . . .' " There was, moreover, a clear and present danger: ". . . The appellations 'damned racketeer' and 'damned Fascist' are epithets likely to provoke the average person to retaliation, and thereby cause a breach of the peace."

Another case in which the making of a speech was punished by the city as a breach of the peace is Terminiello v. Chicago (1949), a case which remains bitterly controversial. Terminiello (who denied he was a Fascist) was introduced by Gerald L. K. Smith and spoke in an auditorium in Chicago to a crowd of about 800 persons, under the sponsorship of the Christian Veterans of America. Outside, a protesting crowd of over a thousand (who denied they were Communist-led) milled about, yelling and throwing stones at the windows. Inside Terminiello spoke despite the tumult, linking Democrats, Jews, and Communists together in a speech filled with race hatred. A cordon of policemen assigned to the meeting was unable to prevent several outbreaks of violence, including the smashing of doors and windows.

Terminiello was found guilty of inciting a breach of the peace and fined $100. The trial court charged the jury that " 'breach of the peace' consists of any 'misbehavior which violates the public peace and decorum'; and that the 'misbehavior may constitute a breach of the peace if it stirs the public to anger, invites dispute, brings about a condition of unrest, or creates a disturbance. . . .' " The Supreme Court never reached the question whether the speech itself might be punishable, because it found that the statute as interpreted by the trial judge permitted the punishment of speech that was protected by the Constitution: ". . . A function of free speech under our system of government is to invite dispute. It may indeed best serve its high purpose when it induces a condition of unrest, creates dissatisfaction with conditions as they are, or even stirs people to anger. Speech is often provocative and challenging. It may strike at prejudices and preconceptions and have profound unsettling effects as it presses for acceptance of an idea. . . . The ordinance as construed by the trial court seriously invaded this province."

In contrast to the Terminiello decision, the Court in Feiner v. New York (1951) upheld the disorderly conduct conviction of a Syracuse University student for a street-corner speech in which he was apparently "endeavoring to arouse the Negro people against the whites, urging that they rise up in arms and fight for equal rights." The two policemen present later testified that the mixed crowd of 75 to 80 persons "was restless and there was some pushing, shoving, and milling around." Fearful that they could not control the crowd if violence erupted, they asked Feiner to stop speaking and arrested him when he refused. The Court held the trial court justified in finding a clear and present danger of causing a riot.

In 1963 in Edwards v. South Carolina the Court upheld the right to demonstrate on public property. A group of Negro students had gathered on the statehouse lawn to protest state segregation policies. The pickets listened to a religious harangue, sang, stamped their feet, and clapped. They refused to disperse when ordered and were arrested for a breach of the peace. The Court held that "the Fourteenth Amendment does not permit a State to make criminal the peaceful expression of unpopular views . . ." and the breach of the peace statute was so vague as to "permit punishment of the fair use of this opportunity." In this case "there was no violence or threat of violence on their part, or on the part of any member of the crowd watching them. Police protection was ample. . . . And the record is barren of any evidence of 'fighting words.'"

The courageous efforts of the Southern Negro to achieve racial equality through nonviolent means won widespread admiration and support from the liberal white community and strong encouragement was given the National Association for the Advancement of Colored People (NAACP) in its efforts to win recognition for Negro rights in the courts. Since the average victim of race discrimination was ill-equipped to fight for legal rights, the NAACP shouldered the financial burden and provided legal assistance, with the result that a number of Southern states made serious efforts to oust or cripple the organization. The result was a series of Supreme Court holdings that the organization need not divulge its membership lists either as a condition of doing business in the state (NAACP v. Alabama, 1958), or to a legislative committee investigating Communism in civil rights organizations (Gibson v. Florida Investigation Committee, 1963). Nor was its bringing of test cases punishable as barratry (NAACP v. Button, 1963), and it could not be forbidden to do business in the state (NAACP v. Alabama, 1964). All of these decisions rested on a freedom of association held to be protected by the First Amendment and made applicable to the states by the Fourteenth.

With the outbreak of racial violence in Northern cities in the summer of 1965 and with the breach between the conservative, law-oriented NAACP on the one hand and the more militant Congress of Racial Equality (CORE) and Student Nonviolent Coordinating Committee (SNCC) on the other, Northern white support for the civil rights movement fell off sharply. In 1966 a civil rights bill with provisions against anticivil rights terrorism and an open housing provision failed to pass Congress, and in the fall elections of that year a number of congressional candidates and advocates of referendum measures exploited the fear of "black power" and looked, in some cases successfully, to a "white backlash" for support.

In 1966, in Adderley v. Florida, the Supreme Court for the first time held valid a state criminal trespass statute against Negro demonstrators. A group of some 200 students from Florida A&M had marched to the jail in Tallahassee to protest the arrest of some of their body for trying to integrate public theaters, as well as against segregation policies generally. Over 100 remained after being ordered to leave, and were arrested for trespass. In contrast to Edwards, the Court held the trespass statute was not too broad to be valid. "It is aimed at conduct of one limited kind, that is for one person or persons to trespass upon the property of another with a malicious and mischievous intent. There is no lack of notice in this law, nothing to entrap or fool the unwary." Moreover, the demonstration was found to be on "that part of the jail grounds reserved for jail uses," and "the State, no less than a private owner of property, has power to preserve the property under its control for the use to which it is lawfully dedicated. . . . The United States Constitution does not forbid a State to control the use of its own property for its own lawful nondiscriminatory purpose."

The difficulties that confront a state in imposing those "reasonable" limits on free speech which the Constitution allows are illustrated by cases involving the suppression of public nuisances. The Supreme Court held that a statute which forbade entirely the distribution of literature was unconstitutional. In Jamison v. Texas (1943) an ordinance forbade the distribution of handbills on the streets of Dallas. Mrs. Jamison, a member of Jehovah's Witnesses, was convicted of violating the ordinance and fined $5.00. The Court held that "one who is rightfully on a street which the state has left open to the public carries with him there as elsewhere the constitutional right to express his views in an orderly fashion. . . . The right to distribute handbills concerning religious subjects on the streets may not be prohibited at all times, at all places, and under all circumstances."

The state may, on the other hand, place freedom of speech under reasonable police regulations for the protection of the recognized social interests of the community. In Kovacs v. Cooper (1949) the Court upheld a Trenton, New Jersey, ordinance which forbade the use on the streets of a sound-truck which emitted "loud and raucous noises." The Court found that "loud and raucous" was a sufficiently clear definition of the crime, since it has "through daily use acquired a content that conveys to any interested person a sufficiently accurate concept of what is forbidden." Moreover, the restriction was a reasonable one, since "the unwilling listener is not like the passerby who may be offered a pamphlet in the street but cannot be made to take it." However, while a city may legitimately regulate the display of billboards within its jurisdiciton in the interest of traffic safety and the appearance of the city, it may not validly permit exceptions which favor commercial messages over non-commercial messages; see Metromedia, Inc., v. San Diego (1981).

What a state may not limit directly by statute, it may not permit a policeman or other officer to limit under a grant of administrative discretion which amounts to censorship. Many municipalities have used the device of requiring a license for all public modes of expression, and making it a crime to violate the license requirement. The Supreme Court has almost uniformly held these ordinances to be unconstitutional limitations on freedom of speech and press. If the licensing officer has authority to pass on the desirability of the intended speech, or has authority broad enough to forbid a speech protected by the First Amendment, the ordinance is void on its face because it establishes previous censorship, condemned by the Court in Near v. Minnesota (1931). Thus in Saia v. New York (1948) the Court held void an ordinance which forbade the use of a sound-truck on the streets without the permission of the chief of police: "There are no standards prescribed for the exercise of his discretion. The statute is not narrowly drawn to regulate the hours or places of use of loud-speakers, or the volume of sound. . . ."

What the state may do directly by statute it may also do through the device of administrative discretion provided the discretion is so narrow that the administrator may not censor speech or press. In Cox v. New Hampshire (1941) the Court sustained an ordinance that required a permit from a license board in order to parade in the streets. A group of Jehovah's Witnesses staged an "information march" without applying for a permit and were convicted of violating the ordinance; the state court held that any other form of expression was open to them, and "the defendants, separately, or collectively in groups not constituting a parade or procession" were "under no contemplation of the Act." Furthermore, the discretion of the license board had to be exercised with "uniformity of method of treatment upon the facts of each application, free from improper or inappropriate considerations and from unfair discrimination." The statutory mandate was held to be a "systematic, consistent and just order of treatment, with reference to the convenience of public use of the highways." This, the Supreme Court found, was a valid use of the authority to "control the use of its public streets for parades or processions."

But if a state may not deny a person a license to speak, may it, nevertheless, enjoin a person from speaking and then punish him when he violates the injunction? This problem first arose in the case of Thomas v. Collins (1945). A Texas statute required every labor union organizer operating in the state to secure from the secretary of state an organizer's card before soliciting any members for his union. In order to get the card he had to give his name and his union affiliations and show his credentials. The secretary of state had no discretion to refuse to register such an organizer if he met these requirements. When registered, he was given a card which he was required to carry with him and show to any person whom he solicited for membership. R. J. Thomas, president of the United Automobile Workers, went to Texas after the passage of this act for the express purpose of contesting its validity. He announced his intention to address a labor union meeting, and this plan was widely advertised in advance. He did not apply for registration as a labor organizer as required by the statute. He addressed a meeting of union men and he specifically invited any nonunion person present to join the union. Prior to the meeting, a restraining order was served on Thomas, forbidding him to address the meeting in the capacity of an organizer since he had not registered; and he was later cited for contempt for a deliberate and willful violation of the order.

The Court held the statute void on two grounds. First, the statute was so broad as to make possible the punishment of legitimate speech. It forbade soliciting members, and "how," the Court said, "one might 'laud unionism,' as the State and the State Supreme Court conceded Thomas was free to do, yet in these circumstances not imply an invitation, is hard to conceive. . . . The restriction's effect, as applied, in a very practical sense was to prohibit Thomas not only to solicit members and memberships, but also to speak in advocacy of the cause of trade unionism. . . ." In the second place, there was not a clear and present danger of bringing about a sufficiently substantial injury to the public to justify the restriction: "We cannot say that 'solicit' in this setting is such a dangerous word. So far as free speech alone is concerned, there can be no ban or restriction or burden placed on the use of such a word except on showing of exceptional circumstances where the public safety, morality or health is involved or some other substantial interest of the community is at stake. . . . A restriction so destructive of the right of public discussion, without greater or more imminent danger to the public interest than existed in this case, is incompatible with the freedoms secured by the First Amendment. . . . If the exercise of the rights of free speech and free assembly cannot be made a crime, we do not think this can be accomplished by the device of requiring previous registration as a condition for exercising them and making such a condition the foundation for restraining in advance their exercise and for imposing a penalty for violating such a restraining order."

A similar problem was presented in Poulos v. New Hampshire (1953), which arose under a different section of an ordinance like the one involved in the Cox case. Poulos, a Jehovah's Witness, applied for a permit to speak in Goodwin Park in Portsmouth on a particular Sunday and was refused; Poulos spoke without the permit and was arrested. The state court interpreted the statute as it had in the Cox case, as requiring uniformity and impartiality of treatment. It found that Poulos had not received such treatment, and that the denial of the license had been arbitrary and unreasonable. It held, however, that Poulos was properly convicted; he had no right to violate the ordinance, but should have brought a civil suit in the courts to compel the issuance of a license.

The Supreme Court sustained the conviction on the ground that the ordinance was valid and the state could validly require that arbitrary administrative action be corrected by orderly court procedure: "It must be admitted that judicial correction of arbitrary refusal by administrators to perform official duties under valid laws is exulcerating and costly. But to allow applicants to proceed without the required permits to run businesses, erect structures, purchase firearms, transport or store explosives or inflammatory products, hold public meetings without prior safety arrangements or take other unauthorized action is apt to cause breaches of the peace or create public dangers. The valid requirements of license are for the good of the applicants and the public. It would be unreal to say that such official failures to act in accordance with the state law, redressable by state judicial procedures, are state acts violative of the Federal Constitution. Delay is unfortunate, but the expense and annoyance of litigation is a price citizens must pay for life in an orderly society where the rights of the First Amendment have a real and abiding meaning. Nor can we say that a state's requirement that redress must be sought through appropriate judicial procedure violates due process." The Court distinguished this case from Thomas v. Collins, holding that there the statute was void on its face, while here the ordinance was valid.

While Thomas v. Collins suggests that a person is free to ignore a judicial restraining order if the statute under which it is issued is void on its face, recent decisions cast serious doubt upon the vitality of this holding. In April of 1963, Martin Luther King, Jr. and two other ministers announced plans for a "march" on Good Friday to protest alleged civil rights violations in the city of Birmingham. They requested, and were denied, a permit for the march under Section 1159 of the Birmingham city code which provided that the city commission "shall grant a written permit for such parade, procession or other public demonstration, prescribing the streets or other public ways which may be used therefor, unless in its judgment the public welfare, peace, safety, health, decency, good order, morals or convenience require that it be refused."

Apparently fearing the march would take place without a permit, city officials applied the Wednesday before Good Friday for an injuction against "participating in or encouraging mass street parades or mass processonsion without a permit." The injunction was served the following day, and that night a meeting was held at which one of the petitioners announced that "injunction or no injunction we are going to march tomorrow." No attempt was made to seek judicial review of the injunction, and the petitioners marchecd both on Good Friday and again on Easter Sunday, leading a group of 50 to 60 followers each time.

The petitioners were convicted both of disobeying the injunction and of marching without a license, receiving sentences of five days in jail and a $50 fine for the first and 90 days at hard labor (plus 48 days at hard labor in default of payment of a $75 fine and $24 costs) for the second. Because of their different rates of movement through the judicial labyrinth, the two cases reached the Supreme Court almost two years apart. It is interesting to speculate what the outcomes might have been had Shuttlesworth been decided before Walker, rather than the other way around.

Mr. Justice Stewart delivered the opinion of the Court, saying in part:

... On Easter Sunday, April 14, a crowd of between 1,500 and 2,000 people congregated in the midafternoon in the vicinity of Seventh Avenue and Eleventh Street North in Birmingham. One of the petitioners was seen organizing members of the crowd in formation. A group of about 50, headed by three other petitioners, started down the sidewalk two abreast. At least one other petitioner was among the marchers. Some 300 or 400 people from among the onlookers followed in a crowd that occupied the entire width of the street and overflowed onto the sidewalks. Violence occurred. Members of the crowd threw rocks that injured a newspaperman and damaged a police motorcycle.

The next day the city officials who had requested the injunction applied to the state circuit court for an order to show cause why the petitioners should not be held in contempt for violating it. At the ensuing hearing the petitioners sought to attack the constitutionality of the injunction on the ground that it was vague and overbroad, and restrained free speech. They also sought to attack the Birmingham parade ordinance upon similar grounds, and upon the further ground that the ordinance had previously been administered in an arbitrary and discriminatory manner.

The circuit judge refused to consider any of these contentions, pointing out that there had been neither a motion to dissolve the injunction, nor an effort to comply with it by applying for a permit from the city commission before engaging in the Good Friday and Easter Sunday parades. Consequently, the court held that the only issues before it were whether it had jurisdiction to issue the temporary injunction, and whether thereafter the petitioners had knowingly violated it. Upon these issues the court found against the petitioners, and imposed upon each of them a sentence of five days in jail and a $50 fine, in accord with an Alabama statute.

The Supreme Court of Alabama affirmed. . . .

Howat v. Kansas [1922] was decided by this Court almost 50 years ago. That was a case in which people had been punished by a Kansas trial court for refusing to obey an anti-strike injunction issued under the state industrial relations act. They had claimed a right to disobey the court's order upon the ground that the state statute and the injunction based upon it were invalid under the Federal Constitution. The Supreme Court of Kansas had affirmed the judgment, holding that the trial court "had general power to issue injunctions in equity and that, even if its exercise of the power was erroneous, the injunction was not void, and the defendants were precluded from attacking it in this collateral proceeding . . . that, if the injunction was erroneous, jurisdiction was not thereby forfeited, that the error was subject to correction only by the ordinary method of appeal, and disobedience to the order constituted contempt."

This Court, in dismissing the writ of error, not only unanimously accepted but fully approved the validity of the rule of state law upon which the judgment of the Kansas court was grounded:

"An injunction duly issuing out of a court of general jurisdiction with equity powers upon pleadings properly invoking its action, and served upon persons made parties therein and within the jurisdiction, must be obeyed by them however erroneous the action of the court may be, even if the error be in the assumption of the validity of a seeming but void law going to the merits of the case. It is for the court of first instance to determine the question of the validity of the law, and until its decision is reversed for error by orderly review, either by itself or by a higher court, its orders based on its decision are to be respected, and disobedience of them is contempt of its lawful authority, to be punished."

The rule of state law accepted and approved in Howat v. Kansas is consistent with the rule of law followed by the federal courts.

In the present case, however, we are asked to hold that this rule of law, upon which the Alabama courts relied, was constitutionally impermissible. We are asked to say that the Constitution compelled Alabama to allow the petitioners to violate this injunction, to organize and engage in these mass street parades and demonstrations, without any previous effort on their part to have the injunction dissolved or modified, or any attempt to secure a parade permit in accordance with its terms. Whatever the limits of Howat v. Kansas, we cannot accept the petitioners' contentions in the circumstances of this case.

Without question the state court that issued the injunction had, as a court of equity, jurisdiction over the petitioners and over the subject matter of the controversy. And this is not a case where the injunction was transparently invalid or had only a frivolous pretense to validity. We have consistently recognized the strong interest of state and local governments in regulating the use of their streets and other public places. Cox v. New Hampshire [1941]; Kovacs v. Cooper [1949]; Poulos v. New Hampshire [1953]; Adderley v. Florida [1966]. When protest takes the form of mass demonstrations, parades, or picketing on public streets and sidewalks, the free passage of traffic and the prevention of public disorder and violence become important objects of legitimate state concern. As the Court stated, in Cox v. Louisiana, "We emphatically reject the notion ... that the First and Fourteenth Amendments afford the same kind of freedom to those who would communicate ideas by conduct such as patrolling, marching, and picketing on streets and highways, as these amendments afford to those who communicate ideas by pure speech." ...

The generality of the language contained in the Birmingham parade ordinance upon which the injunction was based would unquestionably raise substantial constitutional issues concerning some of its provisions. . . . The petitioners, however, did not even attempt to apply to the Alabama courts for an authoritative construction of the ordinance. Had they done so, those courts might have given the licensing authority granted in the ordinance a narrow and precise scope, as did the New Hampshire courts in Cox v. New Hampshire and Poulos v. New Hampshire. . . . Here, just as in Cox and Poulos, it could not be assumed that this ordinance was void on its face.

The breadth and vagueness of the injunction itself would also unquestionably be subject to substantial constitutional question. But the way to raise that question was to apply to the Alabama courts to have the injunction modified or dissolved. The injunction in all events clearly prohibited mass parading without a permit, and the evidence shows that the petitioners fully understood that prohibition when they violated it.

The petitioners also claim that they were free to disobey the injunction because the parade ordinance on which it was based had been administered in the past in an arbitrary and discriminatory fashion. In support of this claim they sought to introduce evidence that, a few days before the injunction issued, requests for permits to picket had been made to a member of the city commission. One request had been rudely rebuffed, and this same official had later made clear that he was without power to grant the permit alone, since the issuance of such permits was the responsibility of the entire city commission. Assuming the truth of this proffered evidence, it does not follow that the parade ordinance was void on its face. The petitioners, moreover, did not apply for a permit either to the commission itself or to any commissioner after the injunction issued. Had they done so, and had the permit been refused, it is clear that their claim of arbitrary or discriminatory administration of the ordinance would have been considered by the state circuit court upon a motion to dissolve the injunction.

This case would arise in quite a different constitutional posture if the petitioners, before disobeying the injunction, had challenged it in the Alabama courts, and had been met with delay or frustration of their constitutional claims. But there is no showing that such would have been the fate of a timely motion to modify or dissolve the injunction. There was an interim of two days between the issuance of the injunction and the Good Friday march. The petitioners give absolutely no explanation of why they did not make some application to the state court during that period. The injunction had issued ex parte; if the court had been presented with the petitioners' contentions, it might well have dissolved or at least modified its order in some respects. If it had not done so, Alabama procedure would have provided for an expedited process of appellate review. It cannot be presumed that the Alabama courts would have ignored the petitioners' constitutional claims. Indeed, these contentions were accepted in another case by an Alabama appellate court that struck down on direct review the conviction under this very ordinance of one of these same petitioners. . . .

The rule of law that Alabama followed in this case reflects a belief that in the fair administration of justice no man can be judge in his own case, however exalted his station, however righteous his motives, and irrespective of his race, color, politics, or religion. This Court cannot hold that the petitioners were constitutionally free to ignore all the procedures of the law and carry their battle to the streets. One may sympathize with the petitioners' impatient commitment to their cause. But respect for judicial process is a small price to pay for the civilizing hand of law, which alone can give abiding meaning to constitutional freedom.

Affirmed.

Mr. Chief Justice Warren, whom Mr. Justice Brennan and Mr. Justice Fortas join, dissenting, said in part:

Petitioners in this case contend that they were convicted under an ordinance that is unconstitutional on its face because it submits their First and

Fourteenth Amendment rights to free speech and peaceful assembly to the unfettered discretion of local officials. They further contend that the ordinance was unconstitutionally applied to them because the local officials used their discretion to prohibit peaceful demonstrations by a group whose political viewpoint the officials opposed. The Court does not dispute these contentions, but holds that petitioners may nonetheless be convicted and sent to jail because the patently unconstitutional ordinance was copied into an injunction—issued ex parte without prior notice or hearing on the request of the Commissioner of Public Safety—forbidding all persons having notice of the injunction to violate the ordinance without any limitation of time. I dissent because I do not believe that the fundamental protections of the Constitution were meant to be so easily evaded, or that "the civilizing hand of law" would be hampered in the slightest by enforcing the First Amendment in this case.

The salient facts can be stated very briefly. Petitioners are Negro ministers who sought to express their concern about racial discrimination in Birmingham, Alabama, by holding peaceful protest demonstrations in that city on Good Friday and Easter Sunday, 1963. For obvious reasons, it was important for the significance of the demonstrations that they be held on those particular dates. A representative of petitioners' organization went to the City Hall and asked "to see the person or persons in charge to issue permits, permits for parading, picketing, and demonstrating." She was directed to Public Safety Commissioner Connor, who denied her request for a permit in terms that left no doubt that petitioners were not going to be issued a permit under any circumstances. "He said, 'No, you will not get a permit in Birmingham, Alabama to picket. I will picket you over to the City Jail,' and he repeated that twice." A second, telegraphic request was also summarily denied, in a telegram signed by "Eugene 'Bull' Connor," with the added information that permits could be issued only by the full City Commission, a three-man body consisting of Commissioner Connor and two others.* According to petitioners' offer of proof, the truth of which is assumed for purposes of this case, parade permits had uniformly been issued for all other groups by the city clerk on the request of the traffic bureau of the police department, which was under Comissioner Connor's direction. The requirement that the approval of the full Commission be obtained was applied only to this one group.

---

*. . . The attitude of the city administration in general and of its Public Safety Commissioner in particular are a matter of public record, of course, and are familiar to this Court from previous litigation. See Shuttlesworth v. City of Birmingham (1965); Shuttlesworth v. City of Birmingham (1964); Shuttlesworth v. City of Birmingham (1963); Gober v. City of Birmingham (1963); In Re Shuttlesworth (1962). The United States Commission on Civil Rights found continuing abuse of civil rights protestors by the Birmingham police, including use of dogs, clubs, and firehoses . . . Commissioner Eugene "Bull" Connor, a self-proclaimed white supremacist . . . made no secret of his personal attitude toward the rights of Negroes and the decisions of this Court. He vowed that racial integration would never come to Birmingham, and wore a button inscribed "Never" to advertise that vow. Yet the Court indulges in speculation that these civil rights protestors might have obtained a permit from this city and this man had they made enough repeated applications.

Understandably convinced that the City of Birmingham was not going to authorize their demonstrations under any circumstances, petitioners proceeded with their plans despite Commissioner Connor's orders. On Wednesday, April 10, at 9 in the evening, the city filed in a state circuit court a bill of complaint seeking an ex parte injunction. . . . The Circuit Court issued the injunction in the form requested, and in effect ordered petitioners and all other persons having notice of the order to refrain for an unlimited time from carrying on any demonstrations without a permit. A permit, of course, was clearly unobtainable; the city would not have sought this injunction if it had any intention of issuing one.

Petitioners were served with copies of the injunction at various times on Thursday and on Good Friday. Unable to believe that such a blatant and broadly drawn prior restraint on their First Amendment rights could be valid, they announced their intention to defy it and went ahead with the planned peaceful demonstrations on Easter weekend. On the following Monday, when they promptly filed a motion to dissolve the injunction, the court found them in contempt, holding that they had waived all their First Amendment rights by disobeying the court order.

These facts lend no support to the court's charges that petitioners were presuming to act as judges in their own case, or that they had a disregard for the judicial process. They did not flee the jurisdiction or refuse to appear in the Alabama courts. Having violated the injunction, they promptly submitted themselves to the courts to test the constitutionality of the injunction and the ordinance it parroted. They were in essentially the same positions as persons who challenge the constitutionality of a statute by violating it, and then defend the ensuing criminal prosecution on constitutional grounds. It has never been thought that violation of a statute indicated such a disrespect for the legislature that the violator always must be punished even if the statute was unconstitutional. . . .

I do not believe that giving this Court's seal of approval to such a gross misuse of the judicial process is likely to lead to greater respect for the law any more than it is likely to lead to greater protection for First Amendment freedoms. The ex parte temporary injunction has a long and odious history in this country, and its susceptibility to misuse is all too apparent from the facts of the case. As a weapon against strikes, it proved so effective in the hands of judges friendly to employers that Congress was forced to take the drastic step of removing from federal district courts the jurisdiction to issue injunctions in labor disputes. The labor injunction fell into disrepute largely because it was abused in precisely the same way that the injunctive power was abused in this case. Judges who were not sympathetic to the union cause commonly issued, without notice or hearing, broad restraining orders addressed to large numbers of persons and forbidding them to engage in acts that were either legally permissible or, if illegal, that could better have been left to the regular course of criminal prosecution. The injunctions might later be dissolved, but in the meantime strikes would be crippled because the occasion on which concerted activity might have been effective had passed. Such injunctions, so long discredited as weapons against concerted

Court as weapons against the exercise of First Amendment freedoms. Respect for the courts and for judicial process was not increased by the history of the labor injunction. . . .

. . . The majority opinion in this case rests essentially on a single precedent, and that a case the authority of which has clearly been undermined by subsequent decisions. Howat v. Kansas (1922), was decided in the days when the labor injunction was in fashion. . . .

It is not necessary to question the continuing validity of the holding in Howat v. Kansas, however, to demonstrate that neither it nor the Mine Workers [United States v. United Mine Workers (1947)] case supports the holding of the majority in this case. In Howat the subpoena and injunction were issued to enable the Kansas Court of Industrial Relations to determine an underlying labor dispute. In the Mine Workers case, the District Court issued a temporary anti-strike injunction to preserve existing conditions during the time it took to decide whether it had authority to grant the Government relief in a complex and difficult action of enormous importance to the national economy. In both cases the orders were of questionable legality, but in both cases they were reasonably necessary to enable the court or administrative tribunal to decide an underlying controversy of considerable importance before it at the time. This case involves an entirely different situation. The Alabama Circuit Court did not issue this temporary injunction to preserve existing conditions while it proceeded to decide some underlying dispute. There was no underlying dispute before it, and the court in practical effect merely added a judicial signature to a pre-existing criminal ordinance. Just as the court had no need to issue the injunction to preserve its ability to decide some underlying dispute, the city had no need of an injunction to impose a criminal penalty for demonstrating on the streets without a permit. The ordinance already accomplished that. In point of fact, there is only one apparent reason why the city sought this injunction and why the court issued it: to make it possible to punish petitioners for contempt rather than for violating the ordinance, and thus to immunize the unconstitutional statute and its unconstitutional application from any attack. I regret that this strategy has been so successful. . . .

Mr. Justice Douglas, with whom The Chief Justice, Mr. Justice Brennan, and Mr. Justice Fortas concur, dissenting, said in part:

The right to defy an unconstitutional statute is basic in our scheme. Even when an ordinance requires a permit to make a speech, to deliver a sermon, to picket, to parade, or to assemble, it need not be honored when it is invalid on its face. Lovell v. Griffin [1938] . . . Thomas v. Collins [1945] . . . .

Mr. Justice Brennan, with whom The Chief Justice, Mr. Justice Douglas, and Mr. Justice Fortas joined, wrote a dissenting opinion.

SHUTTLESWORTH v. BIRMINGHAM

394 U. S. 147; 89 S. Ct. 935; 22 L. Ed. 2d 162
(1969)

Mr. Justice Stewart delivered the opinion of the Court, saying in part:

The petitioner stands convicted for violating an ordinance of Birmingham, Alabama, making it an offense to participate in any "parade or procession or other public demonstration" without first obtaining a permit from the City Commission. The question before us is whether that conviction can be squared with the Constitution of the United States. . . .

The petitioner was convicted for violation of § 1159 and was sentenced to 90 days' imprisonment at hard labor and an additional 48 days at hard labor in default of payment of a $75 fine and $24 costs. The Alabama Court of Appeals reversed the judgment of conviction, holding the evidence was insufficient "to show a procession which would require, under the terms of § 1159, the getting of a permit," that the ordinance had been applied in a discriminatory fashion, and that it was unconstitutional in imposing an "invidious prior restraint" without ascertainable standards for the granting of permits. The Supreme Court of Alabama, however, giving the language of § 1159 an extraordinarily narrow construction, reversed the judgment of the Court of Appeals and reinstated the conviction. We granted certiorari to consider the petitioner's constitutional claims.

There can be no doubt that the Birmingham ordinance, as it was written, conferred upon the City Commission virtually unbridled and absolute power to prohibit any "parade," "procession," or "demonstration" on the city's streets or public ways. For in deciding whether or not to withhold a permit, the members of the Commission were to be guided only by their own ideas of "public welfare, peace, safety, health, decency, good order, morals or convenience." This ordinance as it was written, therefore, fell squarely within the ambit of the many decisions of this Court over the last 30 years, holding that a law subjecting the exercise of First Amendment freedoms to the prior restraint of a license, without narrow, objective, and definite standards to guide the licensing authority, is unconstitutional. "It is settled by a long line of recent decisions of this Court that an ordinance which, like this one, makes the peaceful enjoyment of freedoms which the Constitution guarantees contingent upon the uncontrolled will of an official —as by requiring a permit or license which may be granted or withheld in the discretion of such official—is an unconstitutional censorship or prior restraint upon the enjoyment of those freedoms." Staub v. Baxley [1958]. And our decisions have made clear that a person faced with such an unconstitutional licensing law may ignore it, and engage with impunity in the exercise of the right of free expression for which the law purports to require a license. "The Constitution can hardly be thought to deny to one subjected to the restraints of such an ordinance the right to attack its constitutionality, because he has not yielded to its demands." Jones v. Opelika [1942]. (Stone, C. J., dissenting).

It is argued, however, that what was involved here was not "pure speech," but the use of public streets and sidewalks, over which a municipality must rightfully exercise a great deal of control in the interest of traffic regulation and public safety. That, of course, is true. We have emphasized before this that "the First and Fourteenth Amendments [do not] afford the same kind of freedom to those who would communicate ideas by conduct such as patrolling, marching, and picketing on streets and highways, as these amendments afford to those who communicate ideas by pure speech." Cox v. Louisiana [1965]. "Governmental authorities have the duty and responsibility to keep their streets open and available for movement."

But our decisions have also made clear that picketing and parading may nonetheless constitute methods of expression, entitled to First Amendment protection. Cox v. Louisiana; Edwards v. South Carolina [1963]; Thornhill v. Alabama [1940]. "Wherever the title of streets and parks may rest, they have immemorially been held in trust for the use of the public and, time out of mind, have been used for purposes of assembly, communicating thoughts between citizens, and discussing public questions. Such use of the streets and public places has, from ancient times, been a part of the privileges, immunities, rights, and liberties of citizens. . . ." Hague v. C.I.O. [1939] (opinion of Mr. Justice Roberts, joined by Mr. Justice Black).

Accordingly, "[a]lthough this Court has recognized that a statute may be enacted which prevents serious interference with normal usage of streets and parks, . . . we have consistently condemned licensing systems which vest in an administrative official discretion to grant or withhold a permit upon broad criteria unrelated to proper regulation of public places." Kunz v. New York [1951] . . . . Even when the use of its public streets and sidewalks is involved, therefore, a municipality may not empower its licensing officials to roam essentially at will, dispensing or withholding permission to speak, assemble, picket, or parade, according to their own opinions regarding the potential effect of the activity in question on the "welfare," "decency," or "morals" of the community.

Understandably, under these settled principles, the Alabama Court of Appeals was unable to reach any conclusion other than that § 1159 was unconstitutional. The terms of the Birmingham ordinance clearly gave the City Commission extensive authority to issue or refuse to issue parade permits on the basis of broad criteria entirely unrelated to legitimate municipal regulation of the public streets and sidewalks.

It is said, however, that no matter how constitutionally invalid the Birmingham ordinance may have been as it was written, nonetheless the authoritative construction that has now been given it by the Supreme Court of Alabama has so modified and narrowed its terms as to render it constitutionally acceptable. It is true that in affirming the petitioner's conviction in the present case, the Supreme Court of Alabama performed a remarkable job of plastic surgery upon the face of the ordinance. The court stated that when § 1159 provided that the City Commission could withhold a permit whenever "in its judgment the public welfare, peace, safety, health, decency, good order, morals or convenience require," the ordinance really meant something quite different:

"[W]e do not construe this [language] as vesting in the Commission an unfettered discretion in granting or denying permits, but, in view of the purpose of the ordinance, one to be exercised in connection with the safety, comfort and convience in the use of the streets by the general public. . . . The members of the Commission may not act as censors of what is to be said or displayed in any parade. . . .

" . . .[We] do not construe § 1159 as conferring upon the 'commission' of the City of Birmingham the right to refuse an application for a permit to carry on a parade, procession or other public demonstration solely on the ground that such activities might tend to provoke disorderly conduct. . . .

"We also hold that under § 1159 the Commission is without authority to act in an arbitrary manner or with unfettered discretion in regard to the issuance of permits. Its discretion must be exercised with uniformity of method of treatment upon the facts of each application, free from improper or inappropriate considerations and from unfair discrimination. A systematic, consistent and just order of treatment with reference to the convenience of public use of the streets and sidewalks must be followed. Applications for permits to parade must be granted if, after an investigation it is found that the convenience of the public in the use of the streets or sidewalks would not thereby be unduly disturbed."

In transforming § 1159 into an ordinance authorizing no more than the objective and even-handed regulation of traffic on Birmingham's streets and public ways, the Supreme Court of Alabama made a commendable effort to give the legislation "a field of operation within constitutional limits." We may assume that this exercise was successful, and that the ordinance as now authoritatively construed would pass constitutional muster.* It does not follow, however, that the severely narrowing construction put upon the ordinance by the Alabama Supreme Court in November of 1967 necessarily serves to restore constitutional validity to a conviction that occurred in 1963 under the ordinance as it was written. . . .

. . . In April of 1963 the ordinance that was on the books in Birmingham contained language that affirmatively conferred upon the members of the Commission absolute power to refuse a parade permit whenever they thought "the public welfare, peace, safety, health, decency, good order, morals or convenience require that it be refused." It would have taken extraordinary clairvoyance for anyone to perceive that this language meant what the Supreme Court of Alabama was destined to find that it meant more than four years later; and, with First Amendment rights hanging in the balance, we would hesitate long before assuming that either the members of the Commission or the petitioner possessed any such clairvoyance at the time of the Good Friday march.

But we need not deal in assumptions. For, as the respondent in this case has reminded us, in assessing the constitutional claims of the petitioner, "[i]t

---

*The validity of this assumption would depend upon, among other things, the availability of expeditious judicial review of the Commission's refusal of a permit. Cf. Poulos v. New Hampshire [1953] (Frankfurter, J., concurring); Freedman v. Maryland [1965]. See also the concurring opinion of Mr. Justice Harlan, post.

is less than realistic to ignore the surrounding relevant circumstances. These include not only facts developed in the Record in this case, but also those shown in the opinions in the related case of Walker v. City of Birmingham (1967) . . . ."

Uncontradicted testimony was offered in Walker to show that over a week before the Good Friday march petitioner Shuttlesworth sent a representative to apply for a parade permit. She went to the City Hall and asked "to see the person or persons in charge to issue permits, permits for parading, picketing and demonstrating." She was directed to Commissioner Connor, who denied her request in no uncertain terms. "He said, 'No, you will not get a permit in Birmingham, Alabama to picket. I will picket you over to the City Jail,' and he repeated that twice."

Two days later petitioner Shuttlesworth himself sent a telegram to Commission Connor requesting, on behalf of his organization, a permit to picket "against the injustices of segregation and discrimination." His request specified the sidewalks where the picketing would take place, and stated that "the normal rules of picketing" would be obeyed. In reply, the Commissioner sent a wire stating that permits were the responsibility of the entire Commission rather than of a single Commissioner, and closing with the blunt admonition: "I insist that you and your people do not start any picketing on the streets in Birmingham, Alabama."*

These "surrounding relevant circumstances" make it indisputably clear, we think, that in April of 1963—at least with respect to this petitioner and his organization†—the city authorities thought the ordinance meant exactly what it said. The petitioner was clearly given to understand that under no circumstances would he and his group be permitted to demonstrate in Birmingham, not that a demonstration would be approved if a time and place were selected that would minimize traffic problems. There is no indication whatever that the authorities considered themselves obligated—as the Alabama Supreme Court more than four years later said that they were—to issue a permit "if, after an investigation [they] found that the convenience of the public in the use of the streets or sidewalks would not thereby be unduly disturbed."

This case, therefore, is a far cry from Cox v. New Hampshire [1941], where it could be said that there was nothing to show "that the statute has been administered otherwise than in the . . . manner which the state court has construed it to require." Here, by contrast, it is evident that the ordinance was administered so as, in the words of Chief Justice Hughes, "to deny or unwarrantedly abridge the right of assembly and the opportunities

---

*The legal and constitutional issues involved in the Walker case were quite different from those involved here. The Court recently summarized the Walker decision as follows:

"In that case, the Court held that demonstrators who had proceeded with their protest march in face of the prohibition of an injunctive order against such a march, could not defend contempt charges by asserting the unconstitutionality of the injunction. The proper procedure, it was held, was to seek judicial review of the injunction and not to disobey it, no matter how well-founded their doubts might be as to its validity." . . .

†In Walker the petitioner made an offer of proof that parade permits had been issued to other groups by the city clerk at the request of the traffic bureau of the police department.

for the communication of thought . . . immemorially associated with resort to public places." The judgment is
Reversed.

Mr. Justice Black concurs in the result.

Mr. Justice Marshall took no part in the consideration or decision of this case.

Mr. Justice Harlan, concurring.

The Alabama Supreme Court's opinion makes it clear that if petitioner Shuttlesworth had carried his efforts to obtain a parade permit to the highest state court, he could have required the city authorities to grant permission for his march, so long as his proposals were consistent with Birmingham's interest in traffic control. Thus, the difficult question this case presents is whether the Fourteenth Amendment ever bars a State from punishing a citizen for marching without a permit which could have been procured if all available remedies had been pursued.

The Court answers that a citizen is entitled to rely on the statutory construction adopted by the state officials who are on the frontline, administering the permit scheme. If these officials construe a vague statute unconstitutionally, the citizen may take them at their word, and act on the assumption that the statute is void. The Court's holding seems to me to carry seeds of mischief that may impair the conceded ability of the authorities to regulate the use of public thoroughfares in the interests of all. The right to ignore a permit requirement should, in my view, be made to turn on something more substantial than a minor official's view of his authority under the governing statute.

Simply because an inferior state official indicates his view as to a statute's scope, it does not follow that the State's judiciary will come to the same conclusion. Situations do exist, however, in which there can be no effective review of the decision of an inferior state official. In the present case, for example, the decision of Commissioner Connor had the practical effect of the decision of a court of last resort. One week before the Good Friday march, Shuttlesworth learned from Connor that he, as Commissioner of Public Safety, would not issue parade permits, and that the marchers would have to apply to the entire City Commission. But Birmingham's ordinances did not require a prompt decision by the City Commission.* Nor did the State of Alabama provide for a speedy court review of the denial of a parade permit.**

---

*Section 1159 does not require the City Commission to act on an application within any fixed amount of time. Indeed, by the time Connor definitively declared that he could not issue parade permits, it is not at all clear that petitioner could even have made a timely permit application to the City Commission at its only remaining regular session set before the scheduled Good Friday march. . . .

**Although Shuttlesworth could have petitioned for a writ of mandamus in the Alabama Circuit Court if the City Commission denied his application, that state court is not obliged to render a decision within any fixed period of time.

Given the absence of speedy procedures, the Reverend Shuttlesworth and his associates were faced with a serious dilemma when they received their notice from Mr. Connor. If they attempted to exhaust the administrative and judicial remedies provided by Alabama law, it was almost certain that no effective relief could be obtained by Good Friday. Since the right to engage in peaceful and orderly political demonstrations is, under appropriate conditions, a fundamental aspect of the "liberty" protected by the Fourteenth Amendment, . . . the petitioner was not obliged to invoke procedures which could not give him effective relief. With fundamental rights at stake, he was entitled to adopt the more probable meaning of the ordinance and act on his belief that the city's permit regulations were unconstitutional.

It may be suggested, however, that Shuttlesworth's dilemma was of his own making. He could have requested a permit months in advance of Good Friday, thereby allowing Alabama's administrative and judicial machinery the necessary time to operate fully before the date set for the march. But such a suggestion ignores the principle established in Freedman v. Maryland (1965), which prohibits the States from requiring persons to invoke unduly cumbersome and time-consuming procedures before they may exercise their constitutional right of expression. Freedman holds that if the State is to protect the public from obscene movies, it must afford exhibitors a speedy administrative or judicial right of review, lest "the victorious exhibitor might find the most propitious opportunity for exhibition [passed]." The Freedman principle is applicable here. . . .

I do not mean to suggest that a State or city may not reasonably require that parade permit applications be submitted early enough to allow the authorities and the judiciary to determine whether the parade proposal is consistent with the important interests respecting the use of the streets which local authority may legitimately protect. But such applications must be handled on an expedited basis so that rights of political expression will not be lost in a maze of cumbersome and slow-moving procedures.

WALZ v. TAX COMMISSION

397 U. S. 664; 90 S. Ct. 1409; 25 L. Ed. 2d 697 (1970)

In its first one hundred and fifty years the Supreme Court decided but one important case which dealt with freedom of religion. In 1879 the case of Reynolds v. United States reached the conclusion that the religious liberty protected by the First Amendment does not include the right to commit immoral or criminal acts even though these are sanctioned by religious doctrine. Thus Reynolds, a Mormon in the Territory of Utah, was held properly convicted of the crime of polygamy in spite of the fact that the Mormon religion held polygamy to be proper and desirable. Supreme Court cases involving religious liberty were rare because the First Amendment, which protects freedom of religion, applied only to Congress and not to the states. See Barron v. Baltimore (1833). Congress had little opportunity and less inclination to violate the First Amendment, and what the states did by way of dealing with religious matters was their own business so far as the federal Constitution was concerned.

By the 1930s this situation began to change, and the Supreme Court has long held that freedom of religion in the First Amendment, like freedom of speech and press, is part of the liberty which the due process clause of the Fourteenth Amendment forbids the states to abridge. The first case decided on this theory was Hamilton v. Regents of University of California (1934), which held that a student with religious scruples against bearing arms could be compelled, under penalty of expulsion from the university, to take military drill. The alleged invasion of his religious liberty did not deny him due process of law, since he was not compelled to attend the university and could assert no constitutional right to do so without complying with the state's requirement of military training.

In the early 1930s a religious group called Jehovah's Witnesses began a militant, nation-wide campaign to spread their religious tenets, which include virulent condemnation of all organized religions and churches, especially the Roman Catholic Church. They spread their teachings by personal appeals, by the sale or giving away of literature, and by going from house to house asking permission to play phonograph records, one of which, called "Enemies," is a bitter attack on religious organizations. Community resentment against the Witnesses and their methods was often intense; it expressed itself in a variety of legal measures designed to discourage the Witnesses and curb their more unpopular activities. With fanatical zeal the Witnesses fought every legal attempt to restrict their freedom of action. As a result they have brought to the Supreme Court many cases involving religious liberty issues. In a majority of these they were successful. These decisions have done much to clarify our constitutional law relating to freedom of religion.

The most spectacular issue of religious liberty to be raised by the Jehovah's Witnesses was that of the compulsory flag salute. The Witnesses refuse to salute the flag or permit their children to do so, because they believe that this violates the First Commandment. This refusal caused bitter resentment, and some seventeen states passed statutes requiring all school children to salute the flag and providing for the expulsion of those who refused. The question whether these acts unconstitutionally restricted freedom of religion came to the Court in Minersville School District v. Gobitis (1940). With one judge dissenting the Court held that it did not. In a opinion by Justice Frankfurter it was stated that freedom of religion is not absolute, and that some compromises may be necessary in order to secure the national unity which is the basis of national security. The flag salute contributes to that national unity, or at least the question whether it does or not is "an issue of educational policy for which the courtroom is not the proper arena." For the Court to hold the requirement void as abridging religious liberty "would amount to no less than the pronouncement of a pedagogical and psychological dogma in a field where courts possess no marked and certainly no controlling competence." The Court seemed content to assume that the Minersville school board was more competent to settle the flag salute issue than the Supreme Court, and it allowed the board's judgment to prevail. Justice Stone wrote a powerful dissenting opinion. The decision came as a shock and was widely and sharply criticized. Members of the Court who had participated in it began to have misgivings. When Jones v. Opelika was decided in 1942, Justices Black, Douglas, and Murphy dissented, and went further to state that they had become convinced that the Gobitis case was "wrongly decided." With Justice Stone, this made four members of the Court who no longer supported the Gobitis decision. When, in February, 1943, Justice Rutledge replaced Justice Byrnes on the bench, he joined with these four to overrule the Gobitis case by the decision in West Virginia State Board of Education v. Barnette (1943).

Although most of the Court's early cases involved the free exercise clause of the

First Amendment, a number of difficult problems have arisen in recent years under the provision that "Congress shall make no law respecting an establishment of religion." Perhaps the most challenging and controversial of these problems have been by-products of the tremendous expansion in public education, to which parents are abdicating an increasing share of the child's social development. One is the extent to which the state may aid religious schools. The other is the extent to which religion may be fostered by the public schools.

Early education in America was religious education, supported by the civil government in the Bible-commonwealth of Massachusetts, and by the various church groups in the middle and southern colonies. In the early nineteenth century the demand for free public education resulted in a system of public schools free from religious control and largely free from any sectarian influence, a situation wholly satisfactory to an overwhelmingly Protestant nation. Waves of Catholic immigration injected a new element into the picture. The Catholic Church regards the teaching of religion as a primary function of education. Unwilling to send their children to the public schools, which they regarded as either devoid of all religious influence or tainted with Protestantism, the Catholics felt obliged to build and maintain a system of parochial schools at their own expense. When these parochial schools met the state's educational standards they were accredited as schools in which the requirements of the compulsory education laws could be satisfied. In 1922 the state of Oregon passed a law requiring all parents to send their children to the public schools of the state. The Supreme Court, in Pierce v. Society of Sisters (1925), held that the statute denied due process of law by taking from parents their freedom to "direct the upbringing and education" of their children by sending them either to parochial or to private nonsectarian schools of approved educational standards. It is not surprising that Catholic citizens, who paid taxes to support public schools that they did not use, should try to secure some public aid for the parochial schools; and that they exerted a good deal of pressure to bring this about. Opposition to this was, however, bitter and widespread; and by the end of the nineteenth century practically every state had adopted some kind of prohibition against the use of state funds for the support of religious education. In numerous cases the state courts held void attempts to extend direct or indirect aid to parochial schools.

Since the 1930s new and varied services and benefits have been offered by the states to pupils in the public schools. These include free textbooks, free bus transportation, free lunches, and free medical service. Can the state, if it desires, also give these benefits to children attending parochial or private schools? It was argued on the one hand that to do so would not only violate the constitutional clauses which forbid the use of public money in aid of religion or religious education, but would violate also the clause of the First Amendment which forbids "an establishment of religion," a clause now carried over into the Fourteenth Amendment as a limitation on the states. It was argued on the other side that in providing these services and benefits the state was aiding the child and not the school which he attends. Most state courts accepted this latter reasoning, which came to be known as the "child benefit theory" and the Supreme Court applied it in Everson v. Board of Education (1947), discussed in the opinion below, to hold valid the provision of free bus transportation to children attending parochial schools.

Unfortunately, the child benefit theory, while giving a plausible explanation for the results reached, does not provide any real test for reaching those results in the first place. If the fact that a child is benefited makes an expenditure valid, it is hard to see why the state cannot build and support religious schools. On the other hand, if anything that aids religion is forbidden by the First Amendment, why are not fire and police protection for churches unconstitutional? What the Constitution demands is state neutrality toward religion, but what constitutes neutrality in a society where governmental aid and supervision are almost ubiquitous? How is the line to be drawn between neutrality and impermissible state aid to religion?

In Abington School Dist. v. Schempp (1963), a case holding void the required reading in school of "at least ten verses from the Holy Bible," the Court undertook to clarify this distinction: "The test may be stated as follows: what are the purpose and the primary effect of the enactment? If either is the advancement or inhibition of religion then the enactment exceeds the scope of legislative power as circumscribed by the Constitution. That is to say that to withstand the strictures of the Establishment Clause there must be a secular legislative purpose and a primary effect that neither advances nor inhibits religion." In 1980 the doctrine was applied to hold void a Kentucky law requiring the posting in every classroom of a copy of the Ten Commandments. The Court found the document had "no secular legislative purpose." See Stone v. Graham.

One of the main difficulties encountered in challenging alleged aid to religious schools has been a rule of the Supreme Court dating back to 1923 that a person could not contest in federal court the expenditure of tax money solely on the ground that he was a taxpayer and had an interest in how the money was spent. See Massachusetts v. Mellon (1923). Not only was the share of the interested taxpayer in the money too small to deserve judicial notice, but the Court clearly viewed with concern the spectre of millions of taxpayers in a position to challenge in the courts every expenditure of federal funds. The result of this ruling was to make virtually impregnable to judicial attack any distribution of federal funds to religious groups. With the passage of Titles I and II of the Elementary and Secondary Education Act of 1965, under which funds could be used to finance secular education in religious schools, the attack on the "no taxpayer suits" rule was reopened. In Flast v. Cohen, decided the same day as the Allen case, the Court eased the rule as applied to challenges brought under the establishment clause of the First Amendment. The Court held that "the taxpayer must show that the challenged enactment exceeds specific constitutional limitations imposed upon the exercise of the congressional taxing and spending power and not simply that the enactment is generally beyond the powers delegated to Congress by Art. I, Sec. 8." Since one of the reasons for adopting the establishment clause was to prevent using the tax power to aid religion, this clause was such a "specific limitation."

The free exercise and no establishment clauses of the First Amendment were the framers' answer to the place of religion in the highly pluralistic social structures of the time. Religion was to be a private affair; the heavy thumb of the government was to be used neither to aid nor hinder, lest man's freedom to worship as he chose and the right to support only the church of his choice be jeopardized. But even as the framers wrote, many of the practices of the time made clear that the "separation of church and state" would not entail the government ignoring the existence of religion. Both houses of the Congress employed a chaplain; "In God We Trust" was embossed on our coins; and the help and understanding of God were exhorted on all public occasions. In general the people thought of themselves as religious, mostly Christian, and a government recognition of that fact did not seem in any way inconsistent with the doctrines of the First Amendment.

With the gradual diversification of religious belief many well-accepted religious practices and manifestations were challenged in the courts, and with the application to the states of the religion clauses of the First Amendment, these challenges raised potential federal questions.

The Supreme Court has shown considerable reluctance to review many of these activities. In November 1964, it left untouched a New York decision upholding the words "under God" in the pledge of allegiance; in 1971 it let stand the rejection by a district court of an effort to stop the astronauts from praying over television on their way to the moon (O'Hair v. Paine, 1971) and as recently as 1966 (Murray v. Goldstein) it declined to review a Maryland case upholding the validity of tax exemption for church buildings.

The present case was brought by a reclusive New York attorney who is a Christian, but not a member of any religious organization. He owned a 22 X 29-foot plot of land on Staten Island which, with neither buildings nor street access, was assessed by the City of New York at $100. Walz refused to pay the $5.24 a year property tax on the ground he was being forced to support churches and synogogues, which pay no taxes.

Mr. Chief Justice Burger delivered the opinion of the Court, saying in part:

Appellant, owner of real estate in Richmond County, New York, sought an injunction in the New York courts to prevent the New York City Tax Commission from granting property tax exemptions to religious organizations for religious properties used solely for religious worship. The exemption from state taxes is authorized by Art. 16, § 1, of the New York Constitution, which provides in relevant part: "Exemptions from taxation may be granted only by general laws. Exemptions may be altered or repealed except those exempting real or personal property used exclusively for religious, educational or charitable purposes as defined by law and owned by any corporation or association organized or conducted exclusively for one or more of such purposes and not operating for profit."

The essence of appellant's contention was that the New York City Tax Commission's grant of an exemption to church property indirectly requires the appellant to make a contribution to religious bodies and thereby violates provisions prohibiting establishment of religion under the First Amendment which under the Fourteenth Amendment is binding on the States.

I. . . .

The Establishment and Free Exercise Clauses of the First Amendment are not the most precisely drawn portions of the Constitution. The sweep of the absolute prohibitions in the Religion Clauses may have been calculated; but the purpose was to state an objective, not to write a statute. In attempting to articulate the scope of the two Religion Clauses, the Court's opinions reflect the limitations inherent in formulating general principles on a case-by-case basis. The considerable internal inconsistency in the opinions of the Court derives from what, in retrospect, may have been too sweeping utterances on aspects of these clauses that seemed clear in retention to the particular cases but have limited meaning as general principles.

The Court has struggled to find a neutral course between the two Religion Clauses, both of which are cast in absolute terms, and either of which, if expanded to a logical extreme, would tend to clash with the other. . . .

The course of constitutional neutrality in this area cannot be an absolutely straight line; rigidity could well defeat the basic purpose of these provisions, which is to insure that no religion be sponsored or favored, none commanded, and none inhibited. The general principle deducible from the First Amendment and all that has been said by the Court is this: that we will not tolerate either governmentally established religion or governmental interference with religion. Short of those expressly proscribed governmental acts there is room for play in the joints productive of a benevolent neutrality which will permit religious exercise to exist without sponsorship and without interference.

Each value judgment under the Religion Clauses must therefore turn on whether particular acts in question are intended to establish or interfere with religious beliefs and practices or have the effect of doing so. Adherence to the policy of neutrality that derives from an accommodation of the Establishment and Free Exercise Clauses has prevented the kind of involvement that would tip the balance toward government control of churches or governmental restraint on religious practice.

Adherents of particular faiths and individual churches frequently take strong positions on public issues including, as this case reveals in the several briefs amici, vigorous advocacy of legal or constitutional positions. Of course, churches as much as secular bodies and private citizens have that right. No perfect or absolute separation is really possible; the very existence of the Religion Clauses is an involvement of sorts—one that seeks to mark boundaries to avoid excessive entanglement.

The hazards of placing too much weight on a few words or phrases of the Court is abundantly illustrated within the pages of the Court's opinion in Everson [1947]. Mr. Justice Black, writing for the Court's majority, said the First Amendment "means at least this: Neither a state nor the Federal Government can . . . pass laws which aid one religion, aid all religions, or prefer one religion over another," yet he had no difficulty in holding that "Measured by these standards, we cannot say that the First Amendment prohibits New Jersey from spending tax-raised funds to pay the bus fares of parochial school pupils as a part of a general program under which it pays the fares of pupils attending public and other schools. *It is undoubtedly true that children are helped to get to church schools. There is even a possibility that some of the children might not be sent to the church schools if the parents were compelled to pay their children's bus fares out of their own pockets. . . .*" (Emphasis added.)

The Court did not regard such "aid" to schools teaching a particular religious faith as any more a violation of the Establishment Clause than providing "state-paid policemen, detailed to protect children . . . [at the schools] from the very real hazards of traffic . . . ."

Mr. Justice Jackson, in perplexed dissent in Everson, noted that "the undertones of the opinion, advocating complete and uncompromising separation . . . seem utterly discordant with its conclusion . . . ." Perhaps so. One can sympathize with Mr. Justice Jackson's logical analysis but agree with the Court's eminently sensible and realistic application of the language of the Establishment Clause. In Everson the Court declined to construe the religion clauses with a literalness that would undermine the ultimate constitutional objective as illuminated by history. Surely, bus transportation and police protection to pupils who receive religious instruction "aid" that particular religion to maintain schools that plainly tend to assure future adherents to a particular faith by having control of their total education at an early age. No religious body that maintains schools would deny this as an affirmative if not dominant policy of church schools. But if as in Everson buses can be provided to carry and policemen to protect church school pupils, we fail to see how a broader range of police and fire protection given equally to all churches, along with nonprofit hospitals, art galleries, and libraries receiving the same tax exemption, is different for puposes of the Religion Clauses.

Similarly, making textbooks available to pupils in parochial schools in common with public schools was surely an "aid" to the sponsoring churches because it relieved those churches of an enormous aggregate cost for those books. Supplying of costly teaching materials was not seen either as manifesting a legislative purpose to aid or as having a primary effect of aid contravening the First Amendment. Board of Education v. Allen (1968). In so holding the Court was heeding both its own prior decisions and our religious tradition. Mr. Justice Douglas, in Zorach v. Clauson [1952] after recalling that we "are a religious people whose institutions presuppose a Supreme Being," went on to say: "We make room for as wide a variety of beliefs and creeds as the spiritual needs of man deem necessary. . . . *When the state encourages religious instruction . . . it follows the best of our traditions.* For it then respects the religious nature of our people and accommodates the public service to their spiritual needs." (Emphasis added.)

With all the risks inherent in programs that bring about administrative relationships between public education bodies and church-sponsored schools, we have been able to chart a course that preserved the autonomy and freedom of religious bodies while avoiding any semblance of established religion. This is a "tight rope" and one we have successfully traversed.

II.

The legislative purpose of a property tax exemption is neither the advancement nor the inhibition of religion; it is neither sponsorship nor hostility. New York, in common with the other States, has determined that certain entities that exist in a harmonious relationship to the community at large, and that foster its "moral or mental improvement," should not be inhibited in their activities by property taxation or the hazard of loss of those properties for nonpayment of taxes. It has not singled out one particular church or religious group or even churches as such; rather, it has granted exemption to all houses of religious worship within a broad class of property owned by nonprofit, quasi-public corporations which include hospitals, libraries, playgrounds, scientific, professional, historical, and patriotic groups. The State has an affirmative policy that considers these groups as beneficial and stabilizing influences in community life and finds this classification useful, desirable, and in the public interest. Qualification for tax exemption is not perpetual or immutable; some tax-exempt groups lose that status when their activities take them outside the classification and new entities can come into being and qualify for exemption.

Governments have not always been tolerant of religious activity, and hostility toward religion has taken many shapes and forms—economic, political, and sometimes harshly oppressive. Grants of exemption historically reflect the concern of authors of constitutions and statutes as to the latent dangers inherent in the imposition of property taxes; exemption constitutes a reasonable and balanced attempt to guard against those dangers. The limits of permissible state accommodation to religion are by no means co-extensive with the noninterference mandated by the Free Exercise Clause. To equate the two would be to deny a national heritage with roots in the Revolution itself. . . . We cannot read New York's statute as attempting to establish religion; it is simply sparing the exercise of religion from the burden of property taxation levied on private profit institutions. . . .

Determining that the legislative purpose of tax exemption is not aimed at establishing, sponsoring, or supporting religion does not end the inquiry, however. We must also be sure that the end result—the effect—is not an excessive government entanglement with religion. The test is inescapably one of degree. Either course, taxation of churches or exemption, occasions some degree of involvement with religion. Elimination of exemption would tend to expand the involvement of government by giving rise to tax valuation of church property, tax liens, tax foreclosures, and the direct confrontations and conflicts that follow in the train of those legal processes.

Granting tax exemptions to churches necessarily operates to afford an indirect economic benefit and also gives rise to some, but yet a lesser, involvement than taxing them. In analyzing either alternative the questions are whether the involvement is excessive, and whether it is a continuing one calling for official and continuing surveillance leading to an impermissible degree of entanglement. Obviously a direct money subsidy would be a relationship pregnant with involvement and, as the most governmental grant programs, could encompass sustained and detailed administrative relationships for enforcement of statutory or administrative standards, but that is not this case. The hazards of churches supporting government are hardly less in their potential than the hazards of governments supporting churches; each relationship carries some involvement rather than the desired insulation and separation. We cannot ignore the instances in history when church support of government led to the kind of involvement we seek to avoid.

The grant of a tax exemption is not sponsorship since the government does not transfer part of its revenue to churches but simply abstains from demanding that the church support the state. No one has ever suggested that tax exemption has converted libraries, art galleries, or hospitals into arms of the state or put employees "on the public payroll." There is no genuine nexus between tax exemption and establishment of religion. As Mr. Justice Holmes commented in a related context "a page of history is worth a volume of logic." New York Trust Co. v. Eisner (1921). The exemption creates only a minimal and remote involvement between church and state and far less than taxation of churches. It restricts the fiscal relationship between church and state, and tends to complement and reinforce the desired separation insulating each from the other. . . .

All of the 50 States provide for tax exemption of places of worship, most of them doing so by constitutional guarantees. For so long as federal income taxes have had any potential impact on churches—over 75 years—religious organizations have been expressly exempt from the tax. . . .

It is significant that Congress, from its earliest days, has viewed the Religion Clauses of the Constitution as authorizing statutory real estate tax exemption to religious bodies. . . .

It is obviously correct that no one acquires a vested or protected right in violation of the Constitution by long use, even when that span of time covers our entire national existence and indeed predates it. Yet an unbroken practice of according the exemption to churches, openly and by affirmative state action, not covertly or by state inaction, is not something to be lightly cast aside. . . .

Nothing in this national attitude toward religious tolerance and two centuries of uninterrupted freedom from taxation has given the remotest sign of leading to an established church or religion and on the contrary it has operated affirmatively to help guarantee the free exercise of all forms of religious beliefs. Thus, it is hardly useful to suggest that tax exemption is but the "foot in the door" or the "nose of the camel in the tent" leading to an established church. If tax exemption can be seen as this first step toward "establishment" of religion, as Mr. Justice Douglas fears, the second step has been long in coming. Any move that realistically "establishes" a church or tends to do so can be dealt with "while this Court sits." . . .

Affirmed.

Mr. Justice Brennan and Mr. Justice Harlan each wrote a concurring opinion.

Mr. Justice Douglas wrote a dissenting opinion.

ZORACH v. CLAUSON

343 U. S. 306; 72 S. Ct. 679; 96 L. Ed. 954 (1952)

"Well, in our country," said Alice, still panting a little, *"You'd generally get to somewhere else—if you ran very fast for a long time as we've been doing."*

"A slow sort of country!" said the Queen. *"Now,* here, *you see, it takes all the running* you *can do, to keep in the same place."*

Lewis Carroll *Through the Looking Glass,*

This sums up the plight of religious education in the United States. Born in an era when school teachers were poorly paid, school facilities simple and inexpensive, and extracurricular activities virtually nonexistent, the religious school had little difficulty keeping up with its public counterpart. But time has seen marked changes in the public schools. The curriculum, once limited to the three "Rs," now includes a wide and sophisticated group of "cultural" subjects; organized athletics has replaced the simple playground games; pupils are transported to school, fed lunch in school, and transported home again; expensive electronic teaching devices have replaced or supplemented the traditional classroom teacher, and even that teacher comes to the job more completely and expensively educated, asking and receiving more money. The religious school must compete with all of this if it is to "keep in the same place." An additional difficulty for the Roman Catholic Church, which operates most religious schools, is the falling enrollment in those religious orders whose members were called to teaching and who received no personal compensation.

Prolonged political efforts to obtain aid for parochial schools have not been wholly unsuccessful. More than 20 states provide bus transportation for nonpublic school pupils, while a handful provide textbooks, health services, school lunches, and the like. In Board of Education v. Allen (1968) the Court upheld lending textbooks to parochial school pupils and since then efforts have been made to obtain financial help for the non-religious side of the religious schools' curriculum. New York, Ohio, Pennsylvania, and Rhode Island undertook to pay from the state treasury part of the cost of the teachers' salaries, while Minnesota provided a tax credit for parents with children in nonpublic schools.

In Lemon v. Kurtzman (1971) the Pennsylvania and Rhode Island plans were held void. Conceding that it could "only dimly perceive the lines of demarcation in this extraordinarily sensitive area of constitutional law," the Court identified three tests to be applied. "First, the statute must have a secular legislative purpose; second, its principal or primary effect must be one that neither advances nor inhibits religion, Board of Education v. Allen (1968); finally, the statute must not foster 'an excessive government entanglement with religion.' Walz [1970]. . . ." It was the last of these tests which the Court found to be violated by the teacher payment plans. Since the money was to be used to pay only for secular teaching, "a comprehensive, discriminating, and continuing state surveillance will inevitably be required to ensure that these restrictions are obeyed and the First Amendment otherwise respected. Unlike a book, a teacher cannot be inspected once so as to determine the extent and intent of his or her personal beliefs and subjective acceptance of the limitations imposed by the First Amendment. These prophylactic contacts will involve excessive and enduring entanglement between state and church. . . ." In Pennsylvania the entanglement was increased by a system of post-audit of school records "to determine which expenditures are religious and which are secular."

The Court found an even "broader base of entanglement . . . presented by the divisive political potential of these state programs." "Political division along religious lines was one of the principal evils against which the First Amendment was intended to protect," and in this case the inevitable religious divisiveness would be aggravated by "the need for continuing annual appropriations and the likelihood of larger and larger demands as costs and populations grow."

Efforts to provide aid to religious schools which did not entail such entanglement have not been notably successful. An elaborate New York scheme for paying the cost of state-mandated functions, "maintenance and repair" costs, and tuition money for parents was held void in Levitt v. Committee for Public Education and Committee for Public Education v. Nyquist in 1973, and in Sloan v. Lemon (1973) a similar tuition plan passed by Pennsylvania was struck down. In Meek v. Pittenger (1975), while the Court upheld Pennsylvania's loan of textbooks to religious school pupils, it struck down the loan of other instructional equipment made to the school and not the pupil, and a provision for professional personnel was held bad because it involved both an "entangling" degree of supervision and a potential for political entanglement and divisiveness. In Committee for Public Education v. Regan (1980), the Court in a five-to-four decision held that a revised New York law providing for state reimbursement to cover the costs of administering standardized tests and keeping attendance and other required records did not "foster an excessive government entanglement with religion."

In 1963, in response to a demand for federal help for higher education, Congress passed the Higher Education Facilities Act, which provided building grants and loans to colleges and universities. The act expressly excluded "any facility used or to be used for sectarian instructions or as a place of worship . . ." or "any part of the program of a school or department of divinity," but did not otherwise rule out denominational schools. The interest of the government was to last only 20 years, after which the school was allowed to do what it pleased with the buildings.

In Tilton v. Richardson (1971), decided the same day as Lemon, the Court upheld the validity of the grants to religious colleges, except that the interest of the United States could not end at the end of 20 years. Chief Justice Burger, speaking for himself and Justices Harlan, Stewart, and Blackmun, found that the purpose of the act was to aid education, not religion; that the schools in this case had apparently quite separable secular and religious activities, and the buildings were devoted solely to the former. He refused to deal with the case in terms of a "composite profile" of sectarian institutions, which "imposes religious restrictions on admissions, requires attendance at religious activities, compels obedience to the doctrines and dogmas of the faith . . . and does everything it can to propagate a particular religion." He noted that a number of institutions had been denied aid, and at least one had had its funds withdrawn. "Individual projects can be properly evaluated if and when challenges arise with respect to particular recipients and some evidence is then presented to show that the institution does in fact possess these characteristics. We cannot, however, strike down an Act of Congress on the basis of a hypothetical profile." He agreed, however, that unless the restriction on the use of the buildings were maintained, the grant might become an aid to religion and hence violate the First Amendment.

The four justices found that the Tilton case did not violate the "excessive entanglement" test under which the aid in Lemon had been striken down. First, it was not the dominant purpose of these colleges, as it was the secondary schools, to inculcate religious values in their students "to assure future adherents to a particular faith." Not only were the courses taught with the normal internal self-discipline and academic freedom, but "the skepticism of the college student is not an inconsiderable barrier to any attempt or tendency to subvert the congressional objectives and limitations." In addition, both the one-shot nature of the aid and the fact it was in the form of buildings rather than teachers tended to reduce the entanglement.

Justice White, the fifth member of the majority, concurred with the Chief Justice on the theory that since the purpose of all the aid was secular, the fact it aided religion did not make it unconstitutional.

While the Everson case involving school buses for parochial schools had held valid certain kinds of aid to children attending religious schools, it did not answer the needs of parents whose children were getting what was viewed as a "Godless" education in the public schools. Churches, whose success in competing for the time and interest of children has never been outstanding, and parents who wanted their child to have religious training but could no longer get him to go to Sunday School finally devised a scheme of "released time," whereby the child could get such religious training during his "working day" rather than after school or on weekends. One such program was set up in Champaign, Illinois. Public school pupils whose parents signed "request cards" attended religious-instruction classes conducted during regular school hours in the school building, but taught by outside teachers (chosen by a religious council representing the various faiths) who were subject to the approval and supervision of the superintendent of schools. These teachers were not paid from public funds. Records of attendance at these classes were kept and reported to the school authorities, and pupils who did not attend them spent their time on their ordinary studies. The Supreme Court held the plan void in Illinois ex rel. McCollum v. Board of Education (1948). The facts stated, the Court said, "show the use of tax-supported property for religious instruction and the close cooperation between the school authorities and the religious council in promoting religious education. The operation of the State's compulsory education system thus assists and is integrated with the program of religious instruction carried on by separate religious sects. Pupils compelled by law to go to school for secular education are released in part from their legal duty upon the condition that they attend the religious classes. This is beyond all question a utilization of the tax-established and tax-supported public school system to aid religious groups to spread their faith."

Although the justices in both Everson and McCollum agreed unanimously that the First Amendment set up a complete separation of church and state, they differed sharply in each case on whether aid to religion was in fact shown. They did not question that if it had been, it would have been bad. Religious leaders, both Catholic and Protestant, together with some lay critics, have challenged the basic rule which the Court has announced. They urge that the framers did not intend by the First Amendment to forbid completely all government aid to religion, but only such aid as favors one religion over another.

They argue, first, that there is no really persuasive historical ground for holding that the framers had in mind an absolute separation of church and state; The "establishment" clause was intended merely to prevent the establishment of a state church, such as the Church of England. Second, the historical material mustered by Justice Black in the Everson case to show that what the framers intended was, in Jefferson's phrase, a wall of separation between church and state has been sharply criticized by a number of historical scholars as presenting an incomplete and distorted picture. Third, the Supreme Court had itself recognized some aid to religion. In Bradfield v. Roberts (1899) it had held valid federal aid to a Roman Catholic hospital, although on the technical ground that the hospital corporation was a secular body which served patients with regard to denomination. Also, weight has been attached to the fact that in 1844 in the Girard Will case, Vidal v. Girard's Executors, Justice Story had announced (though by way of dictum) that the "Christian religion is part of the common law."

Those who were arguing that state and national governments should be permitted to give impartial aid to religion were encouraged by the Court's decision in the Zorach case. There seemed little doubt that the Court, in holding that "the First Amendment . . . does not say that in every and all respects there shall be a separation of Church and State" and government need not show a "callous indifference" to religious groups, had backed away sharply from its position in the Everson and McCollum cases.

Mr. Justice Douglas delivered the opinion of the Court, saying in part:

New York City has a program which permits its public schools to release students during the school day so that they may leave the school buildings and school grounds and go to religious centers for religious instruction or devotional exercises. A student is released on written request of his parents. Those not released stay in the classrooms. The churches make weekly reports to the schools, sending a list of children who have been released from public school but who have not reported for religious instruction.

This "released time" program involves neither religious instruction in public school classrooms nor the expenditure of public funds. All costs, including the application blanks, are paid by the religious organizations. The case is therefore unlike McCollum v. Board of Education [1948] which involved a "released time" program from Illinois. In that case the classrooms were turned over to religious instructors. We accordingly held that the program violated the First Amendment which (by reason of the Fourteenth Amendment) prohibits the states from establishing religion or prohibiting its free exercise.

Appellants, who are taxpayers and residents of New York City and whose children attend its public schools, challenge the present law, contending it is in essence not different from the one involved in the McCollum Case. Their argument, stated elaborately in various ways, reduces itself to this: the weight and influence of the school is put behind a program for religious instruction; public school teachers police it, keeping tab on students who are released; the classroom activities come to a halt while the students who are released for religious instruction are on leave; the school is a crutch on which the churches are leaning for support in their religious training; without the cooperation of the schools this "released time" program, like the one in the McCollum Case, would be futile and ineffective. The New York Court of Appeals sustained the law against this claim of unconstitutionality. The case is here on appeal. . . .

It takes obtuse reasoning to inject any issue of the "free exercise" of religion into the present case. No one is forced to go to the religious classroom and no religious exercise or instruction is brought to the classrooms of the public schools. A student need not take religious instruction. He is left to his own desires as to the manner or time of his religious devotions, if any.

There is a suggestion that the system involves the use of coercion to get public school students into religious classrooms. There is no evidence in the record before us that supports that conclusion. The present record indeed tells us that the school authorities are neutral in this regard and do no more than release students whose parents so request. If in fact coercion were used, if it were established that any one or more teachers were using their office to persuade or force students to take the religious instruction, a wholly different case would be presented. Hence we put aside that claim of coercion both as respects the "free exercise" of religion and "an establishment of religion" within the meaning of the First Amendment.

Moreover, apart from that claim of coercion, we do not see how New York by this type of "released time" program has made a law respecting an establishment of religion within the meaning of the First Amendment. There is much talk of the separation of Church and State in the history of the Bill of Rights and in the decisions clustering around the First Amendment. See Everson v. Board of Education [1947]; McCollum v. Board of Education. There cannot be the slightest doubt that the First Amendment reflects the philosophy that Church and State should be separated. And so far as interference with the "free exercise" of religion and an "establishment" of religion are concerned, the separation must be complete and unequivocal. The First Amendment within the scope of its coverage permits no exception; the prohibition is absolute. The First Amendment, however, does not say that in every and all respects there shall be a separation of Church and State. Rather, it studiously defines the manner, the specific ways, in which there shall be no concert or union or dependency one on the other. That is the common sense of the matter. Otherwise, the state and religion would be aliens to each other—hostile, suspicious, and even unfriendly. Churches could not be required to pay even property taxes. Municipalities would not be permitted to render police or fire protection to religious groups. Policemen who helped parishioners into their places of worship would violate the Constitution. Prayers in our legislative halls; the appeals to the Almighty in the messages of the Chief Executive; the proclamations making Thanksgiving Day a holiday; "so help me God" in our courtroom oaths—these and all other references to the Almighty that run through our laws, our public rituals, our ceremonies would be flouting the First Amendment. A fastidious atheist or agnostic could even object to the supplication with which the Court opens each session: "God save the United States and this Honorable Court."

We would have to press the concept of separation of Church and State to these extremes to condemn the present law on constitutional grounds. The nullification of this law would have wide and profound effects. A Catholic student applies to his teacher for permission to leave the school during hours on a Holy Day of Obligation to attend a mass. A Jewish student asks his teacher for permission to be excused for Yom Kippur. A Protestant wants the afternoon off for a family baptismal ceremony. In each case the teacher requires parental consent in writing. In each case the teacher, in order to make sure the student is not a truant, goes further and requires a report from the priest, the rabbi, or the minister. The teacher in other words cooperates in a religious program to the extent of making it possible for her students to participate in it. Whether she does it occasionally for a few students, regularly for one, or pursuant to a systematized program designed to further the religious needs of all the students does not alter the character of the act.

We are a religious people whose institutions presuppose a Supreme Being. We guarantee the freedom to worship as one chooses. We make room for as wide a variety of beliefs and creeds as the spiritual needs of man deem necessary. We sponsor an attitude on the part of government that shows no partiality to any one group and that lets each flourish according to the zeal of its adherents and the appeal of its dogma. When the state encourages religious instruction or cooperates with religious authorities by adjusting the schedule of public events to sectarian needs, it follows the best of our traditions. For it then respects the religious nature of our people and accommodates the public service to their spiritual needs. To hold that it may not would be to find in the Constitution a requirement that the government show a callous indifference to religious groups. That would be preferring those who believe in no religion over those who do believe. Government may not finance religious groups nor undertake religious instruction nor blend secular and sectarian education nor use secular institutions to force one or some religion on any person. But we find no constitutional requirement which makes it necessary for government to be hostile to religion and to throw its weight against efforts to widen the effective scope of religious influence. The government must be neutral when it comes to competition between sects. It may not thrust any sect on any person. It may not make a religious observance compulsory. It may not coerce anyone to attend church, to observe a religious holiday, or to take religious instruction. But it can close its doors or suspend its operations as to those who want to repair to their religious sanctuary for worship or instruction. No more than that is undertaken here. . . .

In the McCollum Case the classrooms were used for religious instruction and the force of the public school was used to promote that instruction. Here, as we have said, the public schools do no more than accommodate their schedules to a program of outside religious instruction. We follow the McCollum Case. But we cannot expand it to cover the present released time program unless separation of Church and State means that public institutions can make no adjustments of their schedules to accommodate the religious needs of the people. We cannot read into the Bill of Rights such a philosophy of hostility to religion.

Affirmed.

Justices Black and Frankfurter wrote dissenting opinions.

Mr. Justice Jackson, dissenting, said in part:

This released time program is founded upon a use of the State's power of coercion, which, for me, determines its unconstitutionality. Stripped to its essentials, the plan has two stages, first, that the State compel each student to yield a large part of his time for public secular education and, second, that some of it be "released" to him on condition that he devote it to sectarian religious purposes.

No one suggests that the Constitution would permit the State directly to require this "released" time to be spent "under the control of a duly constituted religious body." This program accomplishes that forbidden result by indirection. If public education were taking so much of the pupils' time as to injure the public or the students' welfare by encroaching upon their religious opportunity, simply shortening everyone's school day would facilitate voluntary and optional attendance at Church classes. But that suggestion is rejected upon the ground that if they are made free many students will not go to the Church. Hence, they must be deprived of freedom for this period, with Church attendance put to them as one of the two permissible ways of using it.

The greater effectiveness of this system over voluntary attendance after school hours is due to the truant officer who, if the youngster fails to go to the Church school, dogs him back to the public schoolroom. Here schooling is more or less suspended during the "released time" so the nonreligious attendants will not forge ahead of the churchgoing absentees. But it serves as a temporary jail for a pupil who will not go to Church. It takes more subtlety of mind than I possess to deny that this is governmental constraint in support of religion. It is as unconstitutional, in my view, when exerted by indirection as when exercised forthrightly.

As one whose children, as a matter of free choice, have been sent to privately supported Church schools, I may challenge the Court's suggestion that opposition to this plan can only be antireligious, atheistic, or agnostic. My evangelistic brethren confuse an objection to compulsion with an objection to religion. It is possible to hold a faith with enough confidence to believe that what should be rendered to God does not need to be decided and collected by Caesar.

The day that this country ceases to be free for irreligion it will cease to be free for religion—except for the sect that can win political power. The same epithetical jurisprudence used by the Court today to beat down those who oppose pressuring children into some religion can devise as good epithets tomorrow against those who object to pressuring them into a favored religion. And, after all, if we concede to the State power and wisdom to single out "duly constituted religious" bodies as exclusive alternatives for compulsory secular instruction, it would be logical to also uphold the power and wisdom to choose the true faith among those "duly constituted." We start down a rough road when we begin to mix compulsory public education with compulsory godliness.

A number of Justices just short of a majority of the majority that promulgates today's passionate dialectics joined in answering them in Illinois ex rel. McCollum v. Board of Education. The distinction attempted between that case and this is trivial, almost to the point of cynicism, magnifying its nonessential details and disparaging compulsion which was the underlying reason for invalidity. A reading of the Court's opinion in that case along with its opinion in this case will show such difference of overtones and undertones as to make clear that the McCollum Case has passed like a storm in a teacup. The wall which the Court was professing to erect between Church and State has become even more warped and twisted than I expected. Today's judgment will be more interesting to students of psychology and of the judicial processes than to students of constitutional law.

7

Rights of Persons Accused of Crimes

UNITED STATES v. PELTIER

422 U. S. 531; 95 S. Ct. 2313; 45 L. Ed. 2d 374
(1975)

One of the areas in which the Supreme Court has had the most difficulty agreeing on a consistent philosophy is that of unreasonable searches and seizures. In part, this is merely a reflection of the conflicting values in the country as a whole, but it is also the result of the methods by which the guarantee is enforced. Individual rights can be divided into two types. Those like free speech and religion have intrinsic value to the individual and are thought of as "substantive" rights, while those like the right to counsel and a jury trial are termed "procedural" because their purpose is to insure that one will only be convicted of crime on the basis of true evidence fairly presented and impartially appraised. Appellate courts will normally enforce the substantive rights by ordering the government either to stop interfering with their exercise or to grant those which are being withheld. The procedural rights, on the otherhand, are usually policed by ordering a new, untainted trial to take the place of the unfair one.

The Fourth Amendment guarantee against unreasonable searches and seizures, like the protection against compulsory self-incrimination, is in the anomalous position of being a *substantive* right, of value to the individual for its own sake, but enforceable by the courts only through the procedural technique of ordering excluded at a new trial the evidence gotten by its violation. The result in those cases where the tainted evidence was essential to conviction is the release of a person who has been found guilty on the basis of probative evidence fairly appraised, not because he might be innocent, but because the police have violated his rights. In Justice Cardozo's famous phrase, "the criminal is to go free because the constable has blundered." People v. Defore, 242 N. Y. 13 (1926). While Supreme Court justices are not supposed to be influenced in constitutional judgments by the apparent guilt or innocence of a particular defendant, it is hard to escape the conclusion that a more consistent concern for the rights of the accused might emerge if the price were not the freeing of so many obviously guilty defendants.

It was in Weeks v. United States (1914) that the Supreme Court introduced into the federal court system the rule that evidence obtained as the result of an unconstitutional search was inadmissible in federal court. "If," said the Court, "letters and private documents can thus be seized and held and used in evidence against a citizen accused of an offense, the protection of the Fourth Amendment, declaring his right to be secure against such searches and seizures, is of no value, and, so far as those thus placed are concerned, might as well be stricken from the Constitution."

Whether this language meant that the "exclusionary rule" was required by the Constitution has been debated by the Court over the years. In Wolf v. Colorado (1949), the Court held that it was not, and found that while due process in the Fourteenth Amendment forbade a state to search and seize unreasonably, it did not forbid it to use the evidence obtained by such searches. Twelve years later the Court in Mapp v. Ohio (1961) abandoned this interpretation and extended the exclusionary rule to the states. While a plurality made clear that the "exclusionary rule is an essential part of both the Fourth and Fourteenth Amendments," Justice Black, the majority's fifth vote, held that it was not the Fourth alone, but the combination of the Fourth and Fifth that dictated exclusion.

In 1965, in a case holding that the Mapp rule was not retroactive, it avoided saying that it was a constitutional rule and found that Mapp, like all the cases since Wolf, was "based on the necessity for an effective deterrent to illegal police action." It found that the cause of deterrence would not be advanced by making the rule retroactive, since not only had the misconduct of the police prior to Mapp already occurred, but at the time it occurred it had been sanctioned by Wolf. See Linkletter v. Walker (1965).

In the years that followed there was no suggestion that the exclusionary rule was required by the Fourth Amendment, and the Court leaned increasingly on the deterrent purpose of the rule in deciding whether or not it should be applied. In United States v. Calandra (1974), referring to the rule as "a judicially created remedy designed to safeguard Fourth Amendment rights generally through its deterrent effect," the Court described its application as a "balancing process" in which the effectiveness of the deterrence was weighed against the loss to society of valuable probative evidence. There the Court found the deterrent effect of excluding unconstitutionally gotten evidence from a grand jury investigation was "uncertain at best," since it was unlikely that the police would search and seize evidence merely to obtain an indictment if they could not use it later at the trial.

Two years later, in United States v. Janis (1976), the Court relied on this balancing process to justify the admission of unconstitutionally seized evidence in a federal civil trial. In this case the state had seized bookmaking equipment and records pursuant to a search warrant later found to be invalid, and the Court held they could be introduced by the Internal Revenue Service in a suit for unpaid wagering taxes. Since they were inadmissible in the state criminal proceedings for which they had originally been sought, the Court felt that the state agents had been "punished" enough.

The Court has always been badly divided over the desirability of the exclusionary rule and over the years, as sympathetic majorities came and went, it has alternately construed the rule liberally to permit more protection for the accused or narrowly to permit the admission of more evidence. In Terry v. Ohio (1968), however, it introduced a new dimension into the controversy. Prior to Terry, the rule had been that before a person could be arrested and searched as incident to that arrest the police had to have probable cause to believe that person had committed a crime. Terry was apparently casing a jewelry store preparatory to a stick-up when he was stopped for suspicious conduct by a policeman and given a "pat-down" search. The search was made without sufficient evidence to constitute probable cause. However, given Terry's suspicious conduct the officer was found justified in questioning him, and was entitled "to conduct a carefully limited search of [his] outer clothing . . . in an attempt to discover weapons which might be used to assault him." In upholding this search, the Court noted with approval that the officer had "confined his search strictly to what was minimally necessary to learn whether [Terry was] armed."

On the other hand, where there was an actual arrest prior to the search, a full search was justified as incident to the arrest. In United States v. Robinson (1973) Robinson was arrested for a traffic violation. He was then fully searched and marijuana was found in his pocket. The Court rejected the argument that since there was no "evidence" to be protected in connection with a license violation, the search should have been limited to the self-defensive pat-down conducted in Terry. The Court has since made clear, however, that the police do not have carte blanche to stop passing motorists at random. "Except in those situations in which there is at least articulable and reasonable suspicion that a motorist is unlicensed or that an automobile is not registered, or that either the vehicle or an occupant is otherwise subject to seizure for violation of law, stopping an automobile and detaining the driver in order to check his driver's license and the registration of the automobile are unreasonable under the Fourth Amendment." See Delaware v. Prouse (1979).

The background of the present case lies in our laws restricting immigration of persons and the importation of goods into the United States. Since the United States has undoubted power as a nation to keep out both aliens and unwanted merchandise, it has authority to stop at the border and inspect those seeking entry to be sure their entrance is legal. This power clearly extends to the functional equivalent of such borders, such as the Chicago terminus of a nonstop flight from Paris. To ease the enforcement problem along the land borders, Congress has authorized the search without warrant of all vehicles "within a reasonable distance from any external boundary," and administrative regulations have interpreted this as "100 air miles," a distance which would include on the Mexican border such cities as San Diego and El Paso.

In Almeida-Sanches v. United States (1973), the Court held the Fourth Amendment violated by the stopping and searching of a vehicle 25 miles from the border without either a warrant or probable cause, but in United States v. Brignoni-Ponce (1975), the Court, while reaffirming Almeida-Sanchez, held that where the roving border patrol merely stopped a car to question its occupants for "usually no more than a minute" it needed only the kind of suspicion held adequate for the "pat-down" in Terry v. Ohio. As in Terry, the intrusion was "modest" and while in Terry the officers' need for self-protection justified a properly limited search, here it was "the importance of the governmental interest at stake, the minimal intrusion of a brief stop, and the absence of practical alternatives for policing the border.. . . Except at the border and its functional equivalents, officers on roving patrol may stop vehicles only if they are aware of specific articulable facts, together with rational inferences from those facts, that reasonably warrant suspicion that the vehicles contain aliens who may be illegally in the country." In this case the only ground for suspicion was the apparent Mexican ancestry of the defendants, and this, standing alone, was not enough. Justices White and Blackmun concurred in the two cases in part because of the almost total ineffectiveness of the border patrol approach while it is "lawful for business firms and others to employ aliens who are illegally in the country." In United States v. Cortez (1981) the Court, faced with a complex set of facts, noted that in judging a stop-and-frisk "the totality of the circomstances—the whole picture—must be taken into account."

The case below arises in the context of the retroactivity question mentioned above. The abrupt reversal of many long-standing constitutional rules in the years of the Warren Court brought to the fore a new kind of problem: To what extent were the new interpretations of the constitution to be made retroactive so as to free prisoners held under the old interpretations. The traditional rule had always been to apply any new interpretation retroactively, but faced with the spectre of thousands of retrials, the Court reexamined this doctrine and in Linkletter v. Walker (1965) set a precedent for limiting the retroactivity of certain rights. Whether a holding is to be applied retroactively depends on the nature of the right and the purposes it is designed to serve and in the case below both the majority and the dissent shed considerable light on how they view the rights protected by the exclusion of evidence.

In 1979, Michigan v. Defillippo, the Court extended the Peltier doctrine beyond the confines of the retroactivity question. Defillippo was stopped by the police in a Detroit alley under suspicious circumstances and asked to identify himself. When he refused he was arrested under a city ordinance that made it a crime to refuse such identification, was searched incident to the arrest, and marijuana was found in his pocket. He was charged with possession but the Michigan court, holding the ordinance void for vagueness and hence the arrest invalid, held the evidence inadmissible as the product of an invalid search. The Supreme Court reversed. Police officers, it held, have a duty to enforce laws until they are held void unless they are "so grossly and flagrantly unconstitutional that any person of reasonable prudence would be bound to see its flaws." Such was not the case here, and since the refusal to give his name was a crime being committed in the presence of the officer, the arrest and incident search were valid. The Court distinguished Admeida-Sanchez on the ground that the law there directly authorized an unconstitutional search, while here it did not.

The "good faith" of police officers is clearly assuming a role of major importance in Court decisions concerning the admissibility of evidence. Not only can it make invalidly obtained evidence admissible, but it can make otherwise inadmissible statements admissible. After giving a murder suspect Miranda warnings, three police officers were taking him to the police station for questioning. During the ride, two of them discussed the danger posed to the community by the fact that the murder gun was still missing. A school for handicapped children was nearby "and God forbid one of them might find a weapon with shells and might hurt themselves." The suspect interrupted and asked the officers to return to the scene of the crime. There he produced the hidden weapon because " 'he wanted to get the gun out of the way because of the kids in the area in the school.' " The Court upheld the admission of the gun and the defendant's statements pointing out that the officers had not intended their conversation as interrogation and they could not have known of the defendant's sensitivity where handicapped children were concerned. See Rhode Island v. Innis (1980).

At the same time that the Court has been moving gradually to reduce the scope of the exclusionary rule, three decisions have drastically reduced its availability. Voting six to three, the Court in Stone v. Powell (1976) held a federal writ of habeas corpus (a remedy traditionally available where a person is held by a state in violation of federal constitutional rights) should no longer be issued to review claims that evidence should have been excluded from a trial as unconstitutionally obtained where there had been adequate state consideration of the claims. The Court rejected the "judicial integrity" rationale discussed in the case below, noting that it "has limited force as a justification for the exclusion of highly probative evidence," and that it "becomes minimal where the federal habeas corpus relief is sought by a prisoner who previously has been afforded the opportunity for full and fair consideration of his search-and-seizure claim at trial and on direct review."

Nor did the Court find reason to believe "that the overall educative effect of the exclusionary rule would be appreciably diminished if search-and-seizure claims could not be raised in federal habeas corpus review of state convictions. . . . The view that the deterrence of the Fourth Amendment violations would be furthered rests on the dubious assumption that law enforcement authorities would fear that federal habeas review might reveal flaws in a search or seizure that went undetected at trial and on appeal." Chief Justice Burger, while concurring in the opinion, urged that the exclusionary rule be abandoned except in cases of "egregious, bad-faith conduct."

In United Stated v. Salvucci (1980), the Court overruled an earlier case and abolished the "automatic standing" rule under which a person caught with drugs was presumed to own them for purposes of standing to contest their admissibility in evidence, since having to prove ownership would almost surely result in that person's conviction on the merits. The Court held the rule was no longer needed, since an earlier case had held that evidence from a suppression hearing could not be used to convict. On the same day, the Court held that the mere fact that a person was the owner of illegal drugs did not give grounds to object to their admission in evidence against him where, as here, they were found in the possession of a third party; see Rawlings v. Kentucky (1980).

Mr. Justice Rehnquist delivered the opinion of the Court, saying in part:

Four months before this Court's decision in Almeida-Sanchez v. United States (1973), respondent was stopped in his automobile by a roving border patrol, and three plastic garbage bags containing 270 pounds of marijuana were found in the trunk of his car by Border Patrol agents. On the basis of this evidence an indictment was returned charging him with a violation of 21 USC § 841(a)(1). When respondent's motion to suppress the evidence was denied after a hearing, he stipulated in writing that he "did knowingly and intentionally possess, with intent to distribute, the marijuana concealed in the 1962 Chevrolet which he was driving on February 28, 1973." The District Court found respondent guilty and imposed sentence. On appeal from that judgment, the Court of Appeals for the Ninth Circuit, sitting en banc, reversed the judgment on the ground that the "rule announced by the Supreme Court in Almeida-Sanchez v. United States . . . should be applied to similar cases pending on appeal on the date the Supreme Court's decision was announced." We granted the Government's petition for certiorari.

In Almeida-Sanchez, this Court held that a warrantless automobile search, conducted approximately 25 air miles from the Mexican border by Border Patrol agents acting without probable cause, was unconstitutional under the Fourth Amendment. In this case the Government conceded in the Court of Appeals that the search of respondent's automobile approximately 70 air miles from the Mexican border and the seizure of the marijuana were unconstitutional under the standard announced in Almeida-Sanchez, but it contended that that standard should not be applied to searches conducted prior to June 21, 1973, the date of the decision in Almeida-Sanchez. In an inquiry preliminary to balancing the interests for and against retroactive application, see Stovall v. Denno (1967), the majority of the Court of Appeals first considered whether this Court had "articulated a new doctrine" in Almeida-Sanchez. . . . Concluding that Almeida-Sanchez overruled no prior decision of this Court and instead "reaffirmed well-established Fourth Amendment standards" that did not "disturb a long-accepted and relied-upon practice," the Court of Appeals held: "[Respondent] is entitled to the benefit of the rule announced in Almeida-Sanchez, not because of retroactivity but because of Fourth Amendment principles never deviated from by the Supreme Court." The judgment of conviction was reversed, and the case was remanded to the District Court to suppress the evidence seized from respondent's automobile.

. . . The dissenters concluded that Almeida-Sanchez had announced a new constitutional rule because the decision overruled a consistent line of Courts of Appeals precedent and disrupted a long accepted and widely relied upon administrative practice. Border Patrol agents had conducted roving searches pursuant to congressional authorization, and administrative regulation, which had been continuously upheld until this Court's decision in Almeida-Sanchez. Since Almeida-Sanchez stated a new rule, the dissenters concluded that the applicability of that decision to pre-June 21, 1973, roving patrol vehicle searches should be determined by reference to the standards summarized in Stovall v. Denno.* . . .

Despite the conceded illegality of the search under the Almeida-Sanchez standard, the Government contends that the exclusionary rule should not be mechanically applied in the case now before us because the policies underlying the rule do not justify its retroactive application to pre-Almeida-Sanchez searches. We agree.

I.

Since 1965 this Court has repeatedly struggled with the question of whether rulings in criminal cases should be given retroactive effect. In those cases "[w]here the major purpose of new constitutional doctrine is to overcome an aspect of the criminal trial that substantially impairs its truth-finding function and so raises serious questions about the accuracy of guilty verdicts in past trials," Williams v. United States (1971), the doctrine has quite often been applied retroactively. It is indisputable, however, that in every case in which the Court has addressed the retroactivity problem in the context of the exclusionary rule, whereby concededly relevant evidence is excluded in order to enforce a constitutional guarantee that does not relate to the integrity of the factfinding process, the Court has concluded that any such new constitutional principle would be accorded only prospective application. Linkletter v. Walker (1965) . . . .

We think that these cases tell us a great deal about the nature of the exclusionary rule, as well as something about the nature of retroactivity analysis. Decisions of this Court applying the exclusionary rule to unconsti-

---

*Stovall v. Denno: "The criteria guiding resolution of the question [of retroactivity] implicate (a)the purpose to be served by the new standards, (b)the extent of the reliance by law enforcement authorities on the old standards, and(c)the effect on the administration of justice of a retroactive application of the new standards."

tutionally seized evidence have referred to "the imperative of judicial integrity," Elkins v. United States (1960), although the Court has relied principally upon the deterrent purpose served by the exclusionary rule. See Mapp v. Ohio (1961) . . . .

When it came time to consider whether those decisions would be applied retroactively, however, the Court recognized that the introduction of evidence which had been seized by law enforcement officials in good-faith compliance with then-prevailing constitutional norms did not make the courts "accomplices in the willful disobedience of a Constitution they are sworn to uphold." Elkins v. United States. Thus, while the "imperative of judicial integrity" played a role in this Court's decision to overrule Wolf v. Colorado, the Mapp decision was not applied retroactively: "Rather than being abhorrent at the time of seizure in this case, the use in state trials of illegally seized evidence had been specifically authorized by this Court in Wolf." Linkletter v. Walker. . . .

The teaching of these retroactivity cases is that if the law enforcement officers reasonably believed in good faith that evidence they had seized was admissible at trial, the "imperative of judicial integrity" is not offended by the introduction into evidence of that material even if decisions subsequent to the search or seizure have broadened the exclusionary rule to encompass evidence seized in that manner. It would seem to follow a fortiori from the Linkletter . . . holding that the "imperative of judicial integrity" is also not offended if law enforcement officials reasonably believed in good faith that their *conduct* was in accordance with the law even if decisions subsequent to the search or seizure have held that conduct of the type engaged in by the law enforcement officials is not permitted by the Constitution. For, although the police in Linkletter . . . could not have been expected to foresee the application of the exclusionary rule to state criminal trials, they could reasonably have entertained no similar doubts as to the illegality of their conduct. . . .

This approach to the "imperative of judicial integrity" does not differ markedly from the analysis the Court has utilized in determining whether the deterrence rationale undergirding the exclusionary rule would be furthered by retroactive application of new constitutional doctrines. See Linkletter v. Walker . . . . In Desist [v. United States, 1969], the Court explicitly recognized the interrelation between retroactivity rulings and the exclusionary rule: "[W]e simply decline to extend the courtmade exclusionary rule to cases in which its deterrent purpose would not be served."

This focus in the retroactivity cases on the purposes served by the exclusionary rule is also quite in harmony with the approach taken generally to the exclusionary rule. In United states v. Calandra [1974] we said that the exclusionary rule "is a judicially created remedy designed to safeguard Fourth Amendment rights generally through its deterrent effect, rather than a personal constitutional right of the party aggrieved." It follows that "the application of the rule has been restricted to those areas where its remedial objectives are thought most efficaciously served." We likewise observed in Michigan v. Tucker [1974]:

"The deterrent purpose of the exclusionary rule necessarily assumes that the police have engaged in willful, or at the very least negligent, conduct which has deprived the defendant of some right. By refusing to admit evidence gained as a result of such conduct, the courts hope to instill in those particular investigating officers, or in their future counterparts, a greater degree of care toward the rights of an accused. Where the official action was pursued in complete good faith, however, the deterrence rationale loses much of its force."

The "reliability and relevancy" of the evidence found in the trunk of respondent's car is unquestioned. It was sufficiently damning on the issue of respondent's guilt or innocence that he stipulated in writing that in effect he had committed the offense charged. Whether or not the exclusionary rule should be applied to the Roving Border patrol search conducted in this case, then, depends on whether considerations of either judicial integrity or deterrence of Fourth Amendment violations are sufficiently weighty to require that the evidence obtained by the Border Patrol in this case be excluded.

II.

[The Court here finds that until the decision in Almeida-Sanchez, roving Border Patrol searches had been "upheld repeatedly against constitutional attack."]

. . . It was in reliance upon a validly enacted statute, supported by long-standing administrative regulations and continuous judicial approval, that Border Patrol agents stopped and searched respondent's automobile. Since the parties acknowledge that Almeida-Sanchez was the first roving border patrol case to be decided by this Court, unless we are to hold that parties may not reasonably rely upon any legal pronouncement emanating from sources other than this Court, we cannot regard as blameworthy those parties who conform their conduct to the prevailing statutory or constitutional norm. . . . If the purpose of the exclusionary rule is to deter unlawful police conduct, then evidence obtained from a search should be suppressed only if it can be said that the law enforcement officer had knowledge, or may properly be charged with knowledge, that the search was unconstitutional under the Fourth Amendment. Admittedly this uniform treatment of roving border patrols searches by the federal judiciary was overturned by this Court's decision in Almeida-Sanchez. But in light of this history and of what we perceive to be the purpose of the exclusionary rule, we conclude that nothing in the Fourth Amendment, or in the exclusionary rule fashioned to implement it, requires that the evidence here be suppressed, even if we assume that respondent's Fourth Amendment rights were violated by the search of his car.

The judgment of the Court of Appeals is therefore Reversed.

Mr. Justice Stewart dissents from the opinion and judgment of the Court for the reasons set out in Part I of the dissenting opinion of Mr. Justice Brennan.

Mr. Justice Douglas, dissenting.

I agree with my Brother Brennan that Almeida-Sanchez v. United States (1973) reaffirmed traditional Fourth Amendment principles and that the purposes of the exclusionary rule compel exclusion of the unconstitutionally seized evidence in this case. I adhere to my view that a constitutional rule made retroactive in one case must be applied retroactively in all. . . . It is largely a matter of chance that we held the Border Patrol to the command of the Fourth Amendment in Almeida-Sanchez rather than in the case of this defendant. Equal justice does not permit a defendant's fate to depend upon such a fortuity. The judgment below should be affirmed.

Mr. Justice Brennan with whom Mr. Justice Marshall joins, dissenting, said in part:

I.

[Justice Brennan here argues that Almeida-Sanchez did not suddenly announce a new rule, hence the question of retroactivity was not properly involved.]

III.

The Court's opinion depends upon an entirely new understanding of the exclusionary rule in Fourth Amendment cases, one which, if the vague contours outlined today are filled in as I fear they will be, forecasts the complete demise of the exclusionary rule as fashioned by this Court in over 61 years of Fourth Amendment jurisprudence. See Weeks v. United States (1914). An analysis of the Court's unsuccessfully veiled reformulation demonstrates that its apparent rush to discard 61 years of constitutional development has produced a formula difficult to comprehend and, on any understanding of its meaning, impossible to justify.

The Court signals its new approach in these words: "If the purpose of the exclusionary rule is to deter unlawful police conduct, then evidence obtained from a search should be suppressed only if it can be said that the law enforcement officer had knowledge, or may properly be charged with knowledge, that the search was unconstitutional under the Fourth Amendment." True, the court does not state in so many words that this formulation of the exclusionary rule is to be applied beyond the present retroactivity context. But the proposition is stated generally and, particularly in view of the concomitant expansion of prospectivity announced today, Part I, supra, I have no confidence that the new formulation is to be confined to putative retroactivity cases. Rather, I suspect that when a suitable opportunity arises, today's revision of the exclusionary rule will be pronounced applicable to all search-and-seizure cases. I therefore register my strong disagreement now.

The new formulation obviously removes the very foundation of the exclusionary rule as it has been expressed in countless decisions. Until now the rule in federal criminal cases decided on direct review has been that suppression is necessarily the sanction to be applied when it is determined that the evidence was in fact illegally acquired. The revision unveiled today suggests that instead of that single inquiry, district judges may also have to probe the subjective knowledge of the official who orders the search, and the inferences from existing law that official should have drawn. The decision whether or not to order suppression would then turn upon whether, based on that expanded inquiry, suppression would comport with either the deterrence rationale of the exclusionary rule or "the imperative of judicial integrity."

On this reasoning, Almeida-Sanchez itself was wrongly decided. For if the Border Patrolmen who searched Peltier could not have known that they were acting unconstitutionally, and thus could not have been deterred from the search by the possibility of the exclusion of the evidence from the trial, obviously the Border Patrolmen who searched Almeida-Sanchez several years earlier had no reason to be any more percipient. If application of the exclusionary rule depends upon a showing that the particular officials who conducted or authorized a particular search knew or should have known that they were violating a specific, established constitutional right, the reversal of Almeida-Sanchez' conviction was plainly error.

UNITED STATES v. UNITED STATES DISTRICT COURT

407 U. S. 297; 92 S. Ct. 2125; 32 L. Ed. 2d 752
(1972)

No area of Fourth Amendment rights stirs both political and constitutional disputes as does the question of electronic surveillance. Law enforcement and security agencies tend to view the technical advance in eavesdropping equipment as heaven-sent tools in their battle against organized crime and the foreign and domestic enemies of the country. What better way to catch criminals and subversives than to listen to their telephone conversations and "bug" a room in which their nefarious plans are laid. The difficulty lies in the necessarily clandestine nature of such work and the consequent inability of the public to judge how much and against whom the techniques are being used. The realization that everyone must be watched, if the evildoers are to be identified, and that many innocent conversations may rise up to haunt one disturbs many people who approve of the suppression of crime and subversion. Evidence that the military was collecting information on private citizens (see Laird v. Tatum, 1972), and the dramatic exposures of widespread eavesdropping by government security agencies do nothing to reassure a person who feels these powers may be misused.

Among the most challenging tasks faced by the Supreme Court in recent years has been the extension of the Fourth Amendment protection to cover the threat of privacy posed by electronic eavesdropping. The Fourth Amendment was drafted in an age when all one needed to do to communicate in private was to whisper, or go into the house and shut the door. The amendment does not speak of privacy. It speaks of the security of "persons, houses, papers and effects," and the warrant needed to search has to describe the "persons or things" to be seized. Thus it was a protection only against the physical invasion of a person or house and the seizure of tangible things belonging to that person. What could be heard by the eavesdropper under the window or seen by peeping at the keyhole was not being seized, and the search of a defendant's open field which resulted in the finding of a whiskey bottle was held to be neither a search nor a seizure. See Hester v. United States (1924). It was this interpretation that led the Court, in Olmstead v. United States (1928), to hold that tapping a telephone wire outside the premises of the defendant did not constitute an unreasonable search and seizure. The Court argued first that since the wire-tap itself had not been made on Olmstead's premises, there was no physical trespass. Second, Olmstead had not intended that his voice should reach only the ears of those present in the room—he had intended "to project his voice to those quite outside." And third, what had been seized from Olmstead was his spoken word. Nothing tangible had been taken that would make applicable the constitutional injunction requiring a warrant describing "things to be seized." Justice Brandeis's prophetic warning of the evils of electronic eavesdropping was considered irrelevant largely because the Fourth Amendment was not viewed by the Court as a general protection of the right of private communication.

The argument in Olmstead that the Fourth Amendment was limited to tangible items was the first to be abandoned by the Court. In Goldman v. United States (1942) the Court held that eavesdropping by means of a detectophone, a sensitive device which could pick up conversations in an adjoining room, was not an unreasonable search and seizure; and in 1952 the rule was reaffirmed in On Lee v. United States, in which an undercover narcotics agent with a hidden pocket transmitter engaged a shopkeeper in conversation and transmitted damaging admissions to an agent in a car outside. In both these cases the Court relied on the absence of trespass to sustain the use of the evidence rather than upon the fact that nothing tangible was being seized. Finally, in Silverman v. United States (1961) the Court held void a search for intangibles where there was trespass. A "spike-mike" had been driven into a hot-air duct in a building wall so that police could overhear conversations within the building. While probably not amounting to trespass under local law, it was considered by the Court to be a "physical intrusion into a constitutionally protected area." The Court emphasized that physical trespass distinguished the case from Olmstead, but simply ignored Olmstead's limitation of the amendment to "things" that were tangible.

While breaking into a home or office, or an obvious physical intrusion however slight (like a spike-mike), could clearly be viewed as trespass, what was the status of the traditional undercover agent who posed as a member of the "gang" in order to gain evidence of crime? In 1921 the Court in Gouled v. United States had held unanimously that "whether entrance to the home or office of a person suspected of crime be obtained by a representative of . . . the government . . . by stealth or through social acquaintance, or in the guise of a business call, and whether the owner be present or not when he enters, any search and seizure subsequently and secretly made in his absence falls within the scope of the Fourth Amendment." Does this mean that planting an informer in a criminal conspiracy violates the Fourth Amendment right of the conspirators? In Hoffa v. United States (1966), the Court held that it did not. Partin, a local teamster official, acted as a paid informer to bring federal officials reports on Hoffa's efforts to bribe the jury in a federal trial in which Hoffa was involved. The Court conceded that a hotel room can be an area protected by the Fourth Amendment, that the amendment can be violated by guile as well as by forceful entry, and that its protection is not limited to tangibles. But Hoffa had no protection in this instance because "what the Fourth Amendment protects is the security a man relies upon when he places himself or his property within a constitutionally protected area." In this case Hoffa "was not relying on the security of the hotel room; he was relying upon his misplaced confidence that Partin would not reveal his wrongdoing." A similar result was reached in Lewis v. United States (1966) where a narcotics pusher had invited a federal agent to his home and sold him narcotics, not knowing what he was. By converting his home into a "commercial center to which outsiders are invited for purposes of transacting unlawful business" the pusher forfeited its sanctity under the Fourth Amendment.

And if serving as an undercover agent to obtain evidence does not violate the Fourth Amendment, neither does carrying electronic equipment to insure that the evidence is accurately reported. On Lee v. United States (1952) had upheld the use of a pocket transmitter carried by an old friend of the accused who had turned informer, and in Lopez v. United States (1963) the Court sustained the use of a pocket tape recorder by an internal revenue agent whom Lopez had attempted to bribe. Without specifically reaffirming On Lee, the Court emphasized in this case that "the Government did not use an electronic device to listen in on conversations it could not otherwise have heard." Lopez had known he was addressing a federal officer, and the only result of excluding the tape would have been to permit Lopez "to rely on flaws in the agent's memory, or to challenge the agent's credibility without being beset by corroborating evidence that is not susceptible of impeachment." Chief Justice Warren concurred, but argued that On Lee should be overruled. Justices Brennan, Douglas, and Goldberg, citing the evils of uncontrolled eavesdropping attacked the decision on the broad ground that electronic eavesdropping posed a threat to privacy and free communication—both essential to our type of society. "If a person must always be on his guard against his auditor's having authorized a secret recording of their conversation, he will be no less reluctant to speak freely than if his risk is that a third party is doing the recording. . . . I believe that there is a grave danger of chilling all private, free, and unconstrained communication if secret recordings, turned over to law enforcement officers by one party to a conversation, are competent evidence of any self-incriminating statements the speaker may have made. In a free society, people ought not have to watch their every word so carefully."

In Osborn v. United States (1966), decided the same day as Hoffa, the Court reaffirmed the validity of such "participant surveillance," in which a participant in a conversation carries an electronic device. Here Osborn, a lawyer for Hoffa, learned that one Vick, a local policeman who had been hired to investigate the backgrounds of potential jurors in the Hoffa trial, was related to one of the potential jurors. He allegedly told Vick to approach his relative about voting to acquit Hoffa if he got on the jury, and Vick went to the federal agents with the story. On the strength of Vick's sworn statements, two federal district judges authorized the FBI to conceal a tape recorder on Vick's person, and a record of the attempt to tamper with the jury was introduced in court against Osborn. The Court, while upholding the use of the recorded evidence, declined to do so on the broad grounds of the Lopez case. Bowing, in part at least, to the dissenters in Lopez, it emphasized that "the issue here . . . is not the permissibility of 'indiscriminate use of such devices in law enforcement,' but the permissibility of using such a device under the most precise and discriminate circumstances, circumstances which fully met the 'requirement of particularity' which the dissenting opinion in Lopez found necessary." The Court noted that only "in response to a detailed factual affidavit alleging the commission of a specific criminal offense directly and immediately affecting the administration of justice in the federal court, the judges of that court jointly authorized the use of a recording device for the narrow and particularized purpose of ascertaining the truth of the affidavit's allegations. . . . There could hardly be a clearer example of the procedure of antecedent justification before a magistrate that is central to the Fourth Amendment as 'a precondition of lawful electronic surveillance.' ''

The traditional method of protecting the right of privacy in a simple society was through the use of a search warrant, but the nature of the information to be gotten and the techniques involved in getting it make the ordinary search warrant inapplicable to electronic eavesdropping. In Berger v. New York (1967) the Court indicated that at least prior judicial approval was necessary for wire tapping. There the Court held void the use of electronic eavesdrop evidence obtained by the police under a warrant issued by a New York court. The New York statute authorized the issue of an eavesdrop warrant if the police officer swore that there was reasonable ground to believe "that evidence of crime may thus be obtained" and particularly describing the persons whose communications were sought and why, and the telephone to be tapped. The tapping could take place for up to two months, with a two-month renewal at the request of the police. This, the Court held, did not meet the "requirement of particularity" required by the Fourth Amendment which had been met in Osborn v. United States (1966). There the orders sought had "described the type of conversation sought with particularity," had "authorized one limited intrusion rather than a series or a continuous surveillance," and "probable cause was shown for the succeeding one," and the officer was required to make a return to the court showing how the order had been executed and what had been seized.

In Katz v. United States (1969), such prior authorization was held necessary for the electronic bugging of a telephone booth. Abandoning both the trespass requirement of Olmstead and the "constitutionally protected area" concept of Silverman, the Court announced that "what a person knowingly exposes to the public, even in his own home or office, is not a subject of Fourth Amendment protection. . . . But what he seeks to preserve as private, even in an area accessible to the public, may be constitutionally protected."

Did these new rules apply to the kind of participant surveillance involved in On Lee v. United States (1952) and Lopez v. United States (1963)? In deciding Osborn, the Court had carefully refrained from reaffirming Lopez and had approved the use of the transmitted evidence only because the agents had gotten prior approval and the eavesdropping had been carried out under the vigilant surveillance of the court. This fact, plus the approval of Osborn expressed in both Berger and Katz, suggested that the answer might be "yes."

In United States V. White (1971) this apparent trend of the cases was reversed. The case involved an informer who transmitted conversations to which he was a party (concerning narcotics) to a federal agent outside with a radio receiver. Justice White, joined by Chief Justice Burger and Justices Stewart and Blackmun, reaffirmed On Lee and Lopez, noting that the Katz rule had been held not to be retroactive (see Desist v. United States, 1969), and in any event did not deal with the problem of participant surveillance. Although Katz had extended Fourth Amendment protection to "justifiable" expectations of privacy, Hoffa v. United States (1966), "which was left undisturbed by Katz," had made it clear that the "amendment affords no protection to 'a wrongdoer's misplaced belief that a person to whom he voluntarily confides his wrongdoing will not reveal it.' '' Since White's expectation of privacy was based upon just such a belief, it was not "justifiable."

With the passage of the Omnibus Crime Control and Safe Streets Act of 1968, Congress for the first time permitted both stated and federal officers to tap telephone wires and intercept "oral communications" under court order in cases involving any in a long list of state and federal crimes, including those dealing with gambling and narcotics. The procedures set out in the statute for authorizing such interception conform closely to those required by Berger, and where an "emergency" requires interception before an order can "with due diligence" be obtained, and "there are grounds upon which an order could be entered," the police may tap or bug for 48 hours before applying for an order. If the order is subsequently denied, or never asked for, neither the contents of the communication "nor evidence derived therefrom" may be used in any trial court or other hearing. If the President, however, in exercising constitutional powers to protect the national security, intercepts wire or oral communications, their contents "may be received in evidence in any trial hearing, or other proceeding only where such interception was reasonable, and shall not be otherwise used or disclosed except as is necessary to implement that power."

The present case arose out of the efforts of one Plamondon to find out whether wire-tap evidence that would be used against him on a charge of bombing a CIA office in Ann Arbor, Michigan, had been obtained illegally and should be made available to him. The government conceded it had not obtained a warrant, but argued that the surveillance was lawful under the President's power to protect the national security. The district court held the evidence illegally gotten, and the government filed for a writ of mandamus to set aside the court's order.

Mr. Justice Powell delivered the opinion of the Court, saying in part:

I.

Title III of the Omnibus Crime Control and Safe Streets Act authorizes the use of electronic surveillance for classes of crimes carefully specified in 18 U.S.C. § 2516. Such surveillance is subject to prior court order. Section 2518 sets forth the detailed and particularized application necessary to obtain such an order as well as carefully circumscribed conditions for its use. The Act represents a comprehensive attempt by Congress to promote more effective control of crime while protecting the privacy of individual thought and expression. Much of Title III was drawn to meet the constitutional requirements for electronic surveillance enunciated by this Court in Berger v. New York (1967) and Katz v. United Stated (1967).

Together with the elaborate surveillance requirements in Title III, there is the following proviso, 18 U.S.C. § 2511 (3):

"Nothing contained in this chapter or in section 605 of the Communications Act of 1934 shall limit the constitutional power of the President to take such measures as he deems necessary to protect the Nation against actual or potential attack or other hostile acts of a foreign power, to obtain foreign intelligence information deemed essential to the security of the United States, or to protect national security information against foreign intelligence activities. *Nor shall anything contained in this chapter be deemed to limit the constitutional power of the President to take such measures as he deems necessary to protect the United States against the overthrow of the Government by force or other unlawful means, or against any other clear and present danger to the structure or existence of the Government.* The contents of any wire or oral communication intercepted by authority of the President in the exercise of the foregoing powers may be received in evidence in any trial, hearing, or other proceeding only where such interception was reasonable, and shall not be otherwise used or disclosed except as is necessary to implement that power." (Emphasis supplied.)

The Government relies on §2511 (3). It argues that "in excepting national security surveillances from the Act's warrant requirement Congress recognized the President's authority to conduct such surveillances without prior judicial approval." The section thus is viewed as a recognition or affirmance of a constitutional authority in the President to conduct warrantless domestic security surveillance such as that involved in this case.

We think the language of §2511 (3), as well as the legislative history of the statute, refutes this interpretation. The relevant language is that: "Nothing contained in this chapter . . . shall limit the constitutional power of the President to take such measures as he deems necessary to protect . . ." against the dangers specified. At most, this is an implicit recognition that the President does have certain powers in the specified areas. Few would doubt this, as the section refers—among other things—to protection "against actual or potential attack or other hostile acts of a foreign power." But so far as the use of the President's electronic surveillance power is concerned, the language is essentially neutral.

Section 2511 (3) certainly confers no power, as the language is wholly inappropriate for such a purpose. It merely provides that the Act shall not be interpreted to limit or disturb such power as the President may have under the Constitution. In short, Congress simply left presidential powers where it found them. This view is reinforced by the general context of Title III. Section 2511 (1) broadly prohibits the use of electronic surveillance "[ex]cept as otherwise specifically provided in this chapter." Subsection (2) thereof contains four specific exceptions. In each of the specified exceptions, the statutory language is as follows: "It shall not be unlawful . . . to intercept" the particular type of communication described.

The language of subsection (3), here involved, is to be contrasted with the language of the exceptions set forth in the preceding subsection. Rather than stating that warrantless presidential uses of electronic surveillance "shall not be unlawful" and thus employing the standard language of exception, subsection (3) merely disclaims any intention to "limit the constitutional power of the President." . . .

The legislative history of §2511 (3) supports this interpretation. . . .

. . . If we could accept the Government's characterization of §2511 (3) as a congressionally prescribed exception to the general requirement of a warrant, it would be necessary to consider the question of whether the surveillance in this case came within the exception and, if so, whether the statutory exception was itself constitutionally valid. But viewing § 2511 (3) as a congressional disclaimer and expression of neutrality, we hold that the statute is not the measure of the executive authority asserted in this case. Rather, we must look to the constitutional powers of the President.

II.

It is important at the outset to emphasize the limited nature of the question before the Court. This case raises no constitutional challenge to electronic surveillance as specifically authorized by Title III of the Omnibus Crime Control and Safe Streets Act of 1968. Nor is there any question or doubt as to the necessity of obtaining a warrant in the surveillance of crimes unrelated to the national security interest. Katz v. United States (1967); Berger v. New York (1967). Further, the instant case requires no judgment on the scope of the President's surveillance power with respect to the activities of foreign powers, within or without this country. The Attorney General's affidavit in this case states that the surveillances were "deemed necessary to protect the nation from attempts of *domestic organizations* to attack and subvert the existing structure of Government" (emphasis supplied). There is no evidence of any involvement, directly or indirectly, of a foreign power.

Our present inquiry, though important, is therefore a narrow one. It addresses a question left open by Katz: "Whether safeguards other than prior authorization by a magistrate would satisfy the Fourth Amendment in a situation involving the national security . . . ." The determination of this question requires the essential Fourth Amendment inquiry into the "reasonableness" of the search and seizure in question, and the way in which that "reasonableness" derives content and meaning through reference to the warrant clause. Coolidge v. New Hampshire (1971).

We begin the inquiry by noting that the President of the United States has the fundamental duty, under Art. II, § 1, of the Constitution, "to preserve, protect, and defend the Constitution of the United States." Implicit in that duty is the power to protect our Government against those who would subvert or overthrow it by unlawful means. In the discharge of this duty, the President—through the Attorney General—may find it necessary to employ electronic surveillance to obtain intelligence information on the plans of those who plot unlawful acts against the Government. The use of such surveillance in internal security cases has been sanctioned more or less continuously by various Presidents and Attorneys General since July 1946. Herbert Brownell, Attorney General under President Eisenhower, urged the use of electronic surveillance both in internal and international security matters on the grounds that those acting against the Government "turn to the telephone to carry on their intrigue. The success of their plans frequently rests upon piecing together shreds of information received from many sources and many nests. The participants in the conspiracy are often dispersed and stationed in various strategic positions in government and industry throughout the country."

Though the Government and respondents debate their seriousness and magnitude, threats and acts of sabotage against the Government exist in sufficient number to justify investigative powers with respect to them. The covertness and complexity of potential unlawful conduct against the Government and the necessary dependency of many conspirators upon the telephone make electronic surveillance an effective investigatory instrument in certain circumstances. The marked acceleration in technological developments and sophistication in their use have resulted in new techniques for the planning, commission and concealment of criminal activities. It would be contrary to the public interest for Government to deny to itself the prudent and lawful employment of those very techniques which are employed against the Government and its law-abiding citizens.

It has been said that "[t]he most basic function of any government is to provide for the security of the individual and of his property." Miranda v. Arizona, (1966) (White, J., dissenting). And unless Government safeguards its own capacity to function and to preserve the security of its people, society itself could become so disordered that all rights and liberties would be endangered. . . .

But a recognition of these elementary truths does not make the employment by Government of electronic surveillance a welcome development—even when employed with restraint and under judicial supervision. There is, understandably, a deep-seated uneasiness and apprehension that this capability will be used to intrude upon cherished privacy of law-abiding citizens. We look to the Bill of Rights to safeguard this privacy. Though physical entry of the home is the chief evil against which the wording of the Fourth Amendment is directed, its broader spirit now shields private speech from unreasonable surveillance. . . . Our decision in Katz refused to lock the Fourth Amendment into instances of actual physical trespass. Rather, the Amendment governs "not only the seizure of tangible items, but extends as well to the recording of oral statements . . . without any 'technical trespass under . . . local property law.' " That decision implicitly recognized that the broad and unsuspected governmental incursions into conversational privacy which electronic surveillance entails necessitate the application of Fourth Amendment safeguards.

National security cases, moreover, often reflect a convergence of First and Fourth Amendment values not present in cases of "ordinary" crime. Though the investigative duty of the executive may be stronger in such cases, so also is there greater jeopardy to constitutionally protected speech. "Historically the struggle for freedom of speech and press in England was bound up with the issue of the scope of the search and seizure power," Marcus v. Search Warrant (1961). History abundantly documents the tendency of Government—however benevolent and benign its motives—to view with suspicion those who most fervently dispute its policies. Fourth Amendment protections become the more necessary when the targets of official surveillance may be those suspected of unorthodoxy in their political beliefs. The danger to political dissent is acute where the Government attempts to act under so vague a concept as the power to protect "domestic security." Given the difficulty of defining the domestic security interest, the danger of abuse in acting to protect that interest becomes apparent. Senator Hart addressed this dilemma in the floor debate on § 2511 (3): "As I read it—and this is my fear—we are saying that the President, on his motion, could declare—name your favorite poison—draft dodgers, Black Muslims, the Ku Klux Klan, or civil rights activists to be a clear and present danger to the structure or existence of the Government." The price of lawful public dissent must not be a dread of subjection to an unchecked surveillance power. Nor must the fear of unauthorized official eavesdropping deter vigorous citizen dissent and discussion of Government action in private conversation. For private dissent, no less than open public discourse, is essential to our free society.

III.

As the Fourth Amendment is not absolute in its terms, our task is to examine and balance the basic values at stake in this case: the duty of Government to protect the domestic security, and the potential danger posed by unreasonable surveillance to individual privacy and free expression. If the legitimate need of Government to safeguard domestic security requires the use of electronic surveillance, the question is whether the needs of citizens for privacy and free expression may not be better protected by requiring a warrant before such surveillance is undertaken. We must also ask whether a warrant requirement would unduly frustrate the efforts of Government to protect itself from acts of subversion and overthrow directed against it.

Though the Fourth Amendment speaks broadly of "unreasonable searches and seizures," the definition of "reasonableness" turns, at least in part, on the more specific commands of the warrant clause. Some have argued that "[t]he relevant test is not whether it was reasonable to procure a search warrant, but whether the search was reasonable," United States v. Rabinowitz (1950).* This view, however, overlooks the second clause of the Amendment. The warrant clause of the Fourth Amendment is not dead language. Rather it has been "a valued part of our constitutional law for decades, and it has determined the result in scores and scores of cases in the courts all over this country. It is not an inconvenience to be somehow 'weighed' against the claims of police efficiency. It is, or should be, an important working part of our machinery of government, operating as a matter of course to check the 'well-intentioned but mistakenly overzealous executive officers' who are a part of any system of law enforcement." Coolidge v. New Hampshire. . . .

Over two centuries ago, Lord Mansfield held that common-law principles prohibited warrants that ordered the arrest of unnamed individuals whom the *officer* might conclude were guilty of seditious libel. "It is not fit," said Mansfield, "that the receiving or judging of the information should be left to the discretion of the officer. The magistrate ought to judge; and should give certain directions to the officer." Leach v. Three of the King's Messengers (1765).

---

*This view has not been accepted. In Chimel v. California (1969) the Court considered the Government's contention that the search be judged on a general "reasonableness" standard without reference to the warrant clause. The Court concluded that argument was "founded on little more than a subjective view regarding the acceptability of certain sorts of police conduct, and not on considerations relevant to Fourth Amendment interests. Under such an unconfined analysis, Fourth Amendment protection in this area would approach the evaporation point."

Lord Mansfield's formulation touches the very heart of the Fourth Amendment directive: that, where practical, a governmental search and seizure should represent both the efforts of the officer to gather evidence of wrongful acts and the judgment of the magistrate that the collected evidence is sufficient to justify invasion of a citizen's private premises or conversation. Inherent in the concept of a warrant is its issuance by a "neutral and detached magistrate." . . . The further requirement of "probable cause" instructs the magistrate that baseless searches shall not proceed.

These Fourth Amendment freedoms cannot properly be guaranteed if domestic security surveillances may be conducted solely within the discretion of the executive branch. The Fourth Amendment does not contemplate the executive officers of Government as neutral and disinterested magistrates. Their duty and responsibility is to enforce the laws, to investigate and to prosecute. . . . But those charged with this investigative and prosecutorial duty should not be the sole judges of when to utilize constitutionally sensitive means in pursuing their tasks. The historical judgment, which the Fourth Amendment accepts, is that unreviewed executive discretion may yield too readily to pressures to obtain incriminating evidence and overlook potential invasions of privacy and protected speech.

It may well be that, in the instant case, the Government's surveillance of Plamondon's conversation was a reasonable one which readily would have gained prior judicial approval. But this Court "has never sustained a search upon the sole ground that officers reasonably expected to find evidence of a particular crime and voluntarily confined their activities to the least intrusive means consistent with that end." Katz. The Fourth Amendment contemplates a prior judicial judgment,* not the risk that executive discretion may be reasonably exercised. This judicial role accords with our basic constitutional doctrine that individual freedoms will best be preserved through a separation of powers and division of functions among the different branches and levels of Government. . . . The independent check upon executive discretion is not satisfied, as the Government argues, by "extremely limited" post-surveillance judicial review.† Indeed, post-surveillance review would never reach the surveillances which failed to result in prosecutions. Prior review by a neutral and detached magistrate is the time tested means of effectuating Fourth Amendment rights. . . .

It is true that there have been some exceptions to the warrant requirement. . . . But those exceptions are few in number and carefully delineated; in general they serve the legitimate needs of law enforcement officers to protect their own well-being and preserve evidence from destruction. Even

---

*We use the word "judicial" to connote the traditional Fourth Amendment requirement of a neutral and detached magistrate.

†The Government argues that domestic security wiretaps should be upheld by courts in post-surveillance review "[u]nless it appears that the Attorney General's determination that the proposed surveillance relates to a national security matter is arbitrary and capricious, i.e., that it constitutes a clear abuse of the broad discretion that the Attorney General has to obtain all information that will be helpful to the President in protecting the Government . . ." against the various unlawful acts in § 2511 (3).

while carving out those exceptions, the Court has reaffirmed the principle that the "police must, whenever practicable, obtain advance judicial approval of searches and seizures through the warrant procedure," Terry v. Ohio . . . .

The Government argues that the special circumstances applicable to domestic security surveillances necessitate a further exception to the warrant requirement. It is urged that the requirement of prior judicial review would obstruct the President in the discharge of his constitutional duty to protect domestic security. We are told further that these surveillances are directed primarily to the collecting and maintaining of intelligence with respect to subversive forces, and are not an attempt to gather evidence for specific criminal prosecutions. It is said that this type of surveillance should not be subject to traditional warrant requirements which were established to govern investigation of criminal activity, not ongoing intelligence gathering.

The Government further insists that courts "as a practical matter would have neither the knowledge nor the techniques necessary to determine whether there was probable cause to believe that surveillance was necessary to protect national security." These security problems, the Government contends, involve "a large number of complex and subtle factors" beyond the competence of courts to evaluate.

As a final reason for exemption from a warrant requirement, the Government believes that disclosure to a magistrate of all or even a significant portion of the information involved in domestic security surveillances "would create serious potential dangers to the national security and to the lives of informants and agents. . . . Secrecy is the essential ingredient in intelligence gathering; requiring prior judicial authorization would create a greater 'danger of leaks . . . , because in addition to the judge, you have the clerk, the stenographer and some other official like a law assistant or bailiff who may be apprised of the nature' of the surveillance."

These contentions in behalf of a complete exemption from the warrant requirement, when urged on behalf of the President and the national security in its domestic implications, merit the most careful consideration. We certainly do not reject them lightly, especially at a time of worldwide ferment and when civil disorders in this country are more prevalent than in the less turbulent periods of our history. There is, no doubt, pragmatic force to the Government's position.

But we do not think a case has been made for the requested departure from Fourth Amendment standards. The circumstances described do not justify complete exemption of domestic security surveillance from prior judicial scrutiny. Official surveillance, whether its purpose be criminal investigation or ongoing intelligence gathering, risks infringement of constitutionally protected privacy of speech. Security surveillances are especially sensitive because of the inherent vagueness of the domestic security concept, the necessarily broad and continuing nature of intelligence gathering, and the temptation to utilize such surveillances to oversee political dissent. We recognize, as we have before, the constitutional basis of the President's domestic security role, but we think it must be exercised in a manner compatible with the Fourth Amendment. In this case we hold that this requires an appropriate prior warrant procedure.

We cannot accept the Government's argument that internal security matters are too subtle and complex for judicial evaluation. Courts regularly deal with the most difficult issues of our society. There is no reason to believe that federal judges will be insensitive to or uncomprehending of the issues involved in domestic security cases. Certainly courts can recognize that domestic security surveillance involves different considerations from the surveillance of "ordinary crime." If the threat is too subtle or complex for our senior law enforcement officers to convey its significance to a court, one may question whether there is probable cause for surveillance.

Nor do we believe prior judicial approval will fracture the secrecy essential to official intelligence gathering. The investigation of criminal activity has long involved imparting sensitive information to judicial officers who have respected the confidentialities involved. Judges may be counted upon to be especially conscious of security requirements in national security cases. . . . Whatever security dangers clerical and secretarial personnel may pose can be minimized by proper administrative measures, possibly to the point of allowing the Government itself to provide the necessary clerical assistance.

Thus, we conclude that the Government's concerns do not justify departure in this case from the customary Fourth Amendment requirement of judicial approval prior to initiation of a search or surveillance. Although some added burden will be imposed upon the Attorney General, this inconvenience is justified in a free society to protect constitutional values. Nor do we think the Government's domestic surveillance powers will be impaired to any significant degree. A prior warrant establishes presumptive validity of the surveillance and will minimize the burden of justification in post-surveillance judicial review. By no means of least importance will be the reassurance of the public generally that indiscriminate wiretapping and bugging of law-abiding citizens cannot occur.

IV.

We emphasize, before concluding this opinion, the scope of our decision. As stated at the outset, this case involves only the domestic aspects of national security. We have not addressed, and express no opinion as to, the issues which may be involved with respect to activities of foreign powers or their agents. . . .

V.

As the surveillance of Plamondon's conversations was unlawful, because conducted without prior judicial approval, the courts below correctly held that Alderman v. United States (1969) is controlling and that it requires disclosure to the accused of his own impermissibly intercepted conversations. As stated in Alderman, "the trial court can and should, where appropriate, place a defendant and his counsel under enforceable orders against unwarranted disclosure of the materials which they may be entitled to inspect."

The judgment of the Court of Appeals is hereby
Affirmed.

The Chief Justice concurs in the result.

Mr. Justice Rehnquist took no part in the consideration or decision of this case.

Mr. Justice Douglas wrote a concurring opinion.

Mr. Justice White, concurring in the judgment, said in part:

... Because I conclude that on the record before us the surveillance undertaken by the Government in this case was illegal under the statute itself, I find it unnecessary, and therefore improper, to consider or decide the constitutional questions which the courts below improvidently reached.

MIRANDA v. ARIZONA

384 U. S. 436; 86 S. Ct. 1602; 16 L. Ed. 2d 694 (1966)

In 1963, in the celebrated case of Gideon v. Wainwright, the Supreme Court held applicable to trials in state courts the Sixth Amendment right to counsel; in the years since, the Court has decided a series of cases, some of them highly controversial, extending that right to points both earlier and later in the criminal process. In Hamilton v. Alabama (1961) it held that an accused was entitled to counsel (at state expense, if necessary) at the time of arraignment, since certain defenses such as insanity had to be plead at that time or completely forfeited. In White v. Maryland (1963) it was pushed back to the preliminary hearing stage, because a guilty plea made at that stage became a permanent part of the record; and in Douglas v. California (1963) it was moved forward to cover the first appeal from a criminal conviction which is normally given by the state as a matter of right. The rationale behind all of these cases was that these were "critical stages" in the criminal process. It was at these points that a person might do or fail to do, or say or fail to say, something that could irrevocably prejudice his chances of acquittal. It was at these points that the "guiding hand of counsel" was vital if his rights were to receive full protection. In United States v. Wade and Gilbert v. California (1967) the Court extended the right of counsel to include that point where an accused is identified as a wanted suspect by being picked out of a police line-up by an eye witness, although it did hold in Gilbert that taking a handwriting sample from a suspect before he saw his lawyer did not violate his rights. Here, too, the suspect's right to an unprejudiced identification may easily be jeopardized by an excess of police enthusiasm.

While these changes were going on the Court was also struggling with the somewhat unrelated problem of coerced confessions. Although it had held in Brown v. Mississippi (1936) that a confession based on coercion—in this case physical torture —was void, it was continually plagued by the problem of what constituted coercion. While physical violence clearly amounts to coercion, it is apparent that certain types of psychological pressure may do so, too. In Chambers v. Florida (1940) the Court held a denial of due process the "sunrise confessions" of four Negroes which followed five days of interrogation in the absence of "friends, advisors or counselors, and under circumstances calculated to break the strongest nerves and the stoutest resistance." The same result was reached in Ashcraft v. Tennessee (1944), where the prisoner confessed to a murder after 36 hours of continuous questioning under powerful electric lights, though without any physical abuse.

In Lisenba v. California (1941), however, the Court upheld the use of a confession despite the fact that the defendant had been subject to two sleepless days and nights of almost continuous questioning by relays of police officers. The confession took place ten days after this questioning, and the Court concluded that he had not "so lost his freedom of action that the statements made were not his but were the result of the deprivation of his free choice to admit, to deny, or to refuse to answer." A similar result was reached in Stein v. New York (1953), the *Reader's Digest* murder case. The Court held the confessions were " 'voluntary,' in the only sense in which confessions to the police by one under arrest and suspicion ever are" and hence were admissible. After prolonged questioning one defendant had confessed after receiving assurances that his father and brother would not be molested by the police; the second had confessed when confronted with the confession of the first. "Of course, these confessions were not voluntary in the sense that petitioners wanted to make them or that they were completely spontaneous, like a confession to a priest, a lawyer, or a psychiatrist. But in this sense no criminal confession is voluntary." The Court made it clear that "the limits in any case depend upon a weighing of the circumstances of pressure against the power of resistance of the person confessing." Neither man, the Court noted, was "young, soft, ignorant or timid." Their will to resist had not been broken by psychological coercion.

It is interesting to note that the Court is not entirely consistent in its reasons for excluding evidence obtained by coercion. The common-law rule against the admission of forced confessions was not based on any theory of fairness, but was a practical one designed to prevent the admission in court of untrustworthy evidence. A confession was rejected if sufficient force was applied in getting it to cast doubt upon its reliability. In Lisenba v. California, however, the Court made clear what was implied in previous cases, that "the aim of the requirement of due process is not to exclude presumptively false evidence, but to prevent fundamental unfairness in the use of evidence whether true or false. . . . Such unfairness exists when a coerced confession is used as a means of obtaining a verdict of guilt." Without mentioning either the Lisenba or Rochin cases, the Court in the Stein case suggested a return to the common-law rationale, noting that forced confessions constitute "illusory and deceptive evidence," while stolen or wiretap evidence "often is of the utmost verity." In Spano v. New York (1959) it was made clear that only where the Court has found a confession to be voluntary may a jury convict on the basis of other evidence; a forced confession always voids the conviction. And in Rogers v. Richmond (1961) the Court reaffirmed the rule that the truth or falsity of a confession does not determine its admissibility.

A definition of "voluntary" that meant some pressure could be used, but not too much, raised endless difficulties for the Court. Since most confessions are secured before a person is formally charged with crime, the Court had managed to solve much of the problem in the federal courts by requiring that an accused be taken immediately before a committing magistrate. But this ruling rested on the supervisory authority of the Court over the administration of federal justice and so could not be extended to the states. Consequently the Court had to trace a guideline for the states as cases came before it, and as the Court noted in Spano v. New York, as "the methods used to extract confessions become more sophisticated, our duty . . . only becomes more difficult because of the more delicate judgments to be made." In the Spano case the defendant was persuaded to confess by fatigue and the false sympathy aroused by a boyhood friend on the police force, while in subsequent cases the techniques used included threatening to bring the defendant's wife in for questioning (Rogers v. Richmond, 1961), threatening to take her infant children from her and give them to strangers (Lynumn v. Illinois, 1963), injecting "truth serum" into his veins (Townsend v. Sain, 1963), and refusing to let him call his wife or lawyer until he had confessed (Haynes v. Washington, 1963). While in some of these cases the police disputed the defendant's version, in all of them the defendants were denied access to counsel who might have given them moral support and perhaps furnished a dispassionate version of the proceedings. Claims that the right to counsel was being denied were noted by the Court but not reached because the confessions were held to be coerced. Clearly the amount of "pressure" a state could use to invoke a confession was getting less and less.

Then in 1964 the Court moved sharply to merge these two lines of development, extending the right to counsel, but in such a way that would serve also as a protection against forced confessions. In Massiah v. United States the government was forbidden to question an accused, who was under indictment, in the absence of his lawyer, and in Escobedo v. Illinois (1964) it held that where "the investigation is no longer a general enquiry into an unsolved crime but has begun to focus on a particular suspect, the suspect has been taken into police custody, the police carry out a process of interrogations that lends itself to eliciting incriminating statements, the suspect has requested and been denied an opportunity to consult with his lawyer, and the police have not effectively warned him of his absolute constitutional right to remain silent, the accused has been denied 'the Assistance of Counsel' in violation of the Sixth Amendment to the Constitution as 'made obligatory upon the States by the Fourteenth Amendment.' "

The two years following the Escobedo decision (1964) witnessed a nationwide debate on the implications and wisdom of what the Court had done. The case itself had involved only the denial of Danny Escobedo's request to see his attorney and reaffirmed his absolute right to remain silent. But did it imply, in effect, an adoption of the English "Judge's Rule" that a suspect must be warned of his right to silence and cautioned that anything he said could be used abainst him? Did it require that he be told of his right to counsel? That he be furnished counsel at state expense? Did it, perhaps, outlaw all confessions? All police interrogation?

The Court itself was bitterly attacked for what was considered a gratuitous hamstringing of the police in their efforts to protect society against criminals. It was asserted that between 75 percent and 80 percent of the convictions in major crimes were dependent upon confessions; and police officers and prosecutors across the country, together with some courts, echoed the sentiments of New York City's police commissioner, Michael J. Murphy, that "if suspects are told of their rights they will not confess." Certainly a competent lawyer would tell them not to confess, and then this effective method of solving crimes would come to an end.

Meanwhile, public confidence in the reliability of confessions as a substitute for investigatory evidence was badly shaken in early 1965 when George Whitmore, Jr., was conceded to be innocent of the sensational murder of career girls Janice Wylie and Emily Hoffert in their New York apartment. Whitmore had been arrested a year and a half after the murders and during 28 hours of questioning had given a 61-page confession filled with details "which only he, as the killer, could have known." Although

Whitmore repudiated his confession to this and two other major crimes, the police contended it had been freely given, and his indictment was not dismissed until eight months later when incontrovertible evidence of his innocence was presented—evidence which the police could have obtained at once had they checked into the truth of his alibi.

Not until 1971 in Harris v. New York did the Court move to reduce the impact of Miranda. In Harris the Court allowed evidence obtained in violation of the Miranda rule to be used in court, not to prove the defendant's guilt, but to attack his credibility as a witness. Harris, on trial for a narcotics violation, took the stand and testified that a bag of powder he had sold to an undercover agent was baking powder rather than heroin. He was asked on cross-examination if this did not contradict statements made to the police at the time of his arrest and without the Miranda warnings. The statements were then read to him. The jury was instructed that they could not be used to determine his guilt, but only his credibility. In a five-to-four decision the Court held this use of the statements valid. Conceding that "some comments in the Miranda opinion can indeed be read as indicating a bar to use of any uncounseled statement for any purpose," they were only dicta and "it does not follow from Miranda that evidence inadmissible against an accused in the prosecution's case in chief is barred for all purposes, provided of course that the trustworthiness of the evidence satisfies legal standards." The Court reaffirmed Walder v. United States (1954) in which a similar decision had been reached with regard to illegally seized evidence and added, "the shield provided by Miranda cannot be perverted into a license to use perjury by way of a defense, free from the risk of confrontation with prior inconsistent utterances."

In Oregon v. Hass (1975), the Court not only reaffirmed Harris but extended it to a defendant who had been given the Miranda warnings and had his request for an attorney ignored. "One might concede that when proper Miranda warnings have been given, and the officer then continues his interrogation after the suspect asks for an attorney, the officer may be said to have little to lose and perhaps something to gain by way of possibly uncovering impeachment material. . . . In any event, the balance was struck in Harris, and we are not disposed to change it now." Where the testimony is used to convict, however, the Court has adhered firmly to Miranda. In Edwards v. Arizona (1981) Edwards' request for a lawyer was ignored and a resumption of questioning produced a confession. The Court held he had not waived his right to counsel.

While the Miranda case seems to rest on the ground that the right to "Miranda warnings" stems from a right not to incriminate one's self, the Court made clear in New Jersey v. Portash (1979) that there is a difference between statements obtained in violation of the Miranda rule and those obtained from direct compulsion. Here the defendant was faced with having his testimony in a criminal trial impeached by the use of testimony he had given before the grand jury under a grant of immunity. "Testimony given in response to a grant of legislative immunity is the essence of coerced testimony. In such cases there is no question whether physical or psychological pressures overrode the defendant's will; the witness is told to talk or face the government's coercive sanctions, notably a conviction for contempt. . . . Balancing of interests was thought to be necessary in Harris and Hass when the attempt to deter unlawful police conduct collided with the need to prevent perjury. Here, by contrast, we deal with the constitutional privilege against compulsory self-incrimination in its most pristine form. Balancing, therefore, is not simply unnecessary, it is impermissible."

The purpose of the Miranda warnings is to inform an accused that he need not aid the police in making a case against him and that he is entitled to legal counsel as to what he should say and not say. But suppose a person is arrested without probable cause, given the Miranda warnings, and voluntarily confesses. Does the invalidity of the arrest make the confession inadmissible even though it was voluntarily made? In

Brown v. Illinois (1975), Justice Blackmun, speaking for six members of a unanimous court, held that it was. Here Brown had been illegally seized by the police (a Fourth Amendment violation) and voluntarily confessed after Miranda warnings which assured there was no Fifth Amendment violation. The Court pointed out that despite the intimate relationship between the two amendments the exclusionary rule did not serve the same purpose with regard to each. When used with the Fourth Amendment it excluded all statements or evidence—not just those which were self-incriminating. Not only do the Miranda warnings not inform the accused about the right not to be illegally detained, but the exclusion of only non-Miranda confessions would not deter other Fourth Amendment violations. "If Miranda warnings, by themselves, were held to attenuate the taint of an unconstitutional arrest, regardless of how wanton and purposeful the Fourth Amendment violation, the effect of the exclusionary rule would be substantially diluted. . . . Arrests made without warrant or without probable cause, for questioning or 'investigation,' would be encouraged by the knowledge that evidence derived there-from hopefully could well be made admissible at trial by the simple expedient of giving Miranda warnings. Any incentive to avoid the Fourth Amendment violations would be eviscerated by making the warnings, in effect, a 'cure-all' and the constitutional guarantee against unlawful searches and seizures could be said to be reduced to 'a form of words.'" Of course it is possible for a person to confess voluntarily even though subjected to an unreasonable search and seizure, but the Court made clear that in passing on the validity of such confessions "the temporal proximity of the arrest and the confession, the presence of intervening circumstances, . . . and, particularly, the purpose and flagrancy of the official misconduct are all relevant." The decision was reaffirmed in 1979 in Dunaway v. New York.

The case below is a combination of four cases, all raising questions of the admissibility of confessions. Miranda was convicted of kidnapping and rape on the basis of a confession obtained after two hours of questioning in which he was not told of his right to counsel or silence.

Mr. Chief Justice Warren delivered the opinion of the Court, saying in part:

The cases before us raise questions which go to the roots of our concepts of American criminal jurisprudence: the restraints society must observe consistent with the Federal Constitution in prosecuting individuals for crime. More specifically, we deal with the admissibility of statements obtained from an individual who is subjected to custodial police interrogation and the necessity for procedures which assure that the individual is accorded his privilege under the Fifth Amendment to the Constitution not to be compelled to incriminate himself. . . .

Our holding will be spelled out with some specificity in the pages which follow but briefly stated it is this: the prosecution may not use statements, whether exculpatory or inculpatory, stemming from custodial interrogation of the defendant unless it demonstrates the use of procedural safeguards effective to secure the privilege against self-incrimination. By custodial interrogation, we mean questioning initiated by law enforcement officers after a person has been taken into custody or otherwise deprived of his freedom of action in any significant way. As for the procedural safeguards to be employed, unless other fully effective means are devised to inform accused persons of their right of silence and to assure a continuous opportunity to exercise it, the following measures are required. Prior to any questioning, the person must be warned that he has a right to remain silent, that any statement he does make may be used as evidence against him, and that he has a right to the presence of an attorney, either retained or appointed. The defendant may waive effectuation of these rights, provided the waiver is made voluntarily, knowingly and intelligently. If, however, he indicates in any manner and at any stage of the process that he wishes to consult with an attorney before speaking there can be no questioning. Likewise, if the individual is alone and indicates in any manner that he does not wish to be interrogated, the police may not question him. The mere fact that he may have answered some questions or volunteered some statements on his own does not deprive him of the right to refrain from answering any further inquiries until he has consulted with an attorney and thereafter consents to be questioned.

I.

The constitutional issue we decide in each of these cases is the admissibility of statements obtained from a defendant questioned while in custody or otherwise deprived of his freedom of action in any significant way. In each, the defendant was questioned by police officers, detectives, or a prosecuting attorney in a room in which he was cut off from the outside world. In none of these cases was the defendant given a full and effective warning of his rights at the outset of the interrogation process. In all the cases, the questioning elicited oral admissions, and in three of them, signed statements as well which were admitted at their trials. They all thus share salient features —incommunicado interrogation of individuals in a police-dominated atmosphere, resulting in self-incriminating statements without full warnings of constitutional rights.

. . . The use of physical brutality and violence is not, unfortunately, relegated to the past . . . . Unless a proper limitation upon custodial interrogation is achieved—such as these decisions will advance—there can be no assurance that practices of this nature will be eradicated in the foreseeable future. . . .

Again we stress that the modern practice of in-custody interrogation is psychologically rather than physically oriented. As we have stated before, "Since Chambers v. Florida [1940], this Court has recognized that coercion can be mental as well as physical, and that the blood of the accused is not the only hallmark of an unconstitutional inquisition." Blackburn v. Alabama (1960). Interrogation still takes place in privacy. Privacy results in secrecy and this in turn results in a gap in our knowledge as to what in fact goes on in the interrogation rooms. A valuable source of information about present police practices, however, may be found in various police manuals and texts which document procedures employed with success in the past, and which recommend various other effective tactics. These texts are used by law enforcement agencies themselves as guides. It should be noted that these texts professedly present the most enlightened and effective means presently used to obtain statements through custodial interrogation. By considering these texts and other data, it is possible to describe procedures observed and noted around the country.... [The Court here quotes at length from a number of books on criminal investigation.]

From these representative samples of interrogation techniques, the setting prescribed by the manuals and observed in practice becomes clear. In essence, it is this: To be alone with the subject is essential to prevent distraction and to deprive him of any outside support. The aura of confidence in his guilt undermines his will to resist. He merely confirms the preconceived story the police seek to have him describe. Patience and persistence, at times relentless questioning are employed. To obtain a confession, the interrogator must "patiently maneuver himself or his quarry into a position from which the desired objective may be obtained." When normal procedures fail to produce the needed result, the police may resort to deceptive stratagems such as giving false legal advice. It is important to keep the subject off balance, for example, by trading on his insecurity about himself or his surroundings. The police then persuade, trick, or cajole him out of exercising his constitutional rights.

Even without employing brutality, the "third degree" or the specific stratagems described above, the very fact of custodial interrogation exacts a heavy toll on individual liberty and trades on the weakness of individuals. This fact may be illustrated simply by referring to three confession cases decided by this Court in the Term immediately preceding our Escobedo decision. In Townsend v. Sain (1963), the defendant was a 19-year-old heroin addict, described as a "near mental defective." The defendant in Lynumn v. Illinois (1963), was a woman who confessed to the arresting officer after being importuned to "cooperate" in order to prevent her children from being taken by relief authorities. This Court as in those cases reversed the conviction of a defendant in Haynes v. Washington (1963), whose persistent request during his interrogation was to phone his wife or attorney. In other settings, these individuals might have exercised their constitutional rights. In the incommunicado police-dominated atmosphere, they succumbed.... [The Court here discusses the facts of the cases before it, noting that in each the questioning in an "incommunicado police dominated atmosphere" had resulted in a confession.]

In these cases, we might not find the defendants' statements to have been involuntary in traditional terms. Our concern for adequate safeguards to protect precious Fifth Amendment rights is, of course, not lessened in the slightest. In each of the cases, the defendant was thrust into an unfamiliar atmosphere and run through menacing police interrogation procedures. The potentiality for compulsion is forcefully apparent, for example, in Miranda, where the indigent Mexican defendant was a seriously disturbed individual with pronounced sexual fantasies, and in Stewart, in which the defendant was an indigent Los Angeles Negro who had dropped out of school in the sixth grade. To be sure, the records do not evince overt physical coercion or patented psychological ploys. The fact remains that in none of these cases did the officers undertake to afford appropriate safeguards at the outset of the interrogation to insure that the statements were truly the product of free choice.

It is obvious that such an interrogation environment is created for no purpose other than to subjugate the individual to the will of his examiner. This atmosphere carries its own badge of intimidation. To be sure, this is not physical intimidation, but it is equally destructive of human dignity. The current practice of incommunicado interrogation is at odds with one of our Nation's most cherished principles—that the individual may not be compelled to incriminate himself. Unless adequate protective devices are employed to dispell the compulsion inherent in custodial surroundings, no statement obtained from the defendant can truly be the product of his free choice.

From the foregoing, we can readily perceive an intimate connection between the privilege against self-incrimination and police custodial questioning. . . .

II. . . .

. . . We have recently noted that the privilege against self-incrimination —the essential mainstay of our adversary system—is founded on a complex of values . . . . All these point to one overriding thought: the constitutional foundation underlying the privilege is the respect a government—state or federal—must accord to the dignity and integrity of its citizens. To maintain a "fair state-individual balance," to require the government "to shoulder the entire load," . . . to respect the inviolability of the human personality, our accusatory system of criminal justice demands that the government seeking to punish an individual produce the evidence against him by its own independent labors, rather than by the cruel, simple expedient of compelling it from his own mouth. . . . In sum, the privilege is fulfilled only when the person is guaranteed the right "to remain silent unless he chooses to speak in the unfettered exercise of his own will." . . .

The question in these cases is whether the privilege is fully applicable during a period of custodial interrogation. . . . We are satisfied that all the principles embodied in the privilege apply to informal compulsion exerted by law-enforcement officers during in-custody questioning. An individual swept from familiar surroundings into police custody, surrounded by antagonistic forces, and subjected to the techniques of persuasion described above cannot be otherwise than under compulsion to speak. As a practical matter, the compulsion to speak in the isolated setting of the police station may well be greater than in courts or other official investigations, where there are often impartial observers to guard against intimidation or trickery.

This question, in fact, could have been taken as settled in federal courts almost 70 years ago, when in Bram v. United States (1897), this Court held: "In criminal trials, in the courts of the United States, wherever a question arises whether a confession is incompetent because not voluntary, the issue is controlled by that portion of the Fifth Amendment . . . commanding that no person 'shall be compelled in any criminal case to be a witness against himself.' " . . .

III. . . .

It is impossible for us to foresee the potential alternatives for protecting the privilege which might be devised by Congress or the States in the exercise of their creative rule-making capacities. Therefore we cannot say that the Constitution necessarily requires adherence to any particular solution for the inherent compulsions of the interrogation process as it is presently conducted. Our decision in no way creates a constitutional straitjacket which will handicap sound efforts at reform, nor is it intended to have this effect. We encourage Congress and the States to continue their laudable search for increasingly effective ways of protecting the rights of the individual while promoting efficient enforcement of our criminal laws. However, unless we are shown other procedures which are at least as effective in apprising accused persons of their right of silence and in assuring a continuous opportunity to exercise it, the following safeguards must be observed. . . .

[The Court here elaborates on and justifies the requirements summarized at the beginning of the opinion.]

If the interrogation continues without the presence of an attorney and a statement is taken, a heavy burden rests on the government to demonstrate that the defendant knowingly and intelligently waived his privilege against self-incrimination and his right to retained or appointed counsel. . . . This Court has always set high standards of proof for the waiver of constitutional rights, Johnson v. Zerbst (1938), and we re-assert these standards as applied to in-custody interrogation. Since the State is responsible for establishing the isolated circumstances under which the interrogation takes place and has the only means of making available corroborated evidence of warnings given during incommunicado interrogation, the burden is rightly on its shoulders. . . .

The warnings required and the waiver necessary in accordance with our opinion today are, in the absence of a fully effective equivalent, prerequisites to the admissibility of any statement made by a defendant. No distinction can be drawn between statements which are direct confessions and statements which amount to "admissions" of part or all of an offense. The privilege against self-incrimination protects the individual from being compelled to incriminate himself in any manner; it does not distinguish degrees of incrimination. Similarly, for precisely the same reason, no distinction may be drawn between inculpatory statements and statements alleged to be merely "exculpatory." If a statement made were in fact truly exculpatory it would, of course, never be used by the prosecution. In fact, statements merely intended to be exculpatory by the defendant are often used to impeach his testimony at trial or to demonstrate untruths in the statement given under interrogation and thus to prove guilt by implication. These statements are incriminating in any meaningful sense of the word and may not be used without the full warnings and effective waiver required for any other statement. In Escobedo itself, the defendant fully intended his accusation of another as the slayer to be exculpatory as to himself.

The principles announced today deal with the protection which must be given to the privilege against self-incrimination when the individual is first subjected to police interrogation while in custody at the station or otherwise deprived of his freedom of action in any significant way. It is at this point that our adversary system of criminal proceedings commences, distinguishing itself at the outset from the inquisitorial system recognized in some countries. Under the system of warnings we delineate today or under any other system which may be devised and found effective, the safeguards to be erected about the privilege must come into play at this point. . . .

In dealing with statements obtained through interrogation, we do not purport to find all confessions inadmissible. Confessions remain a proper element in law inforcement. Any statement given freely and voluntarily without any compelling influences is, of course, admissible in evidence. The fundamental import of the privilege while an individual is in custody is not whether he is allowed to talk to the police without the benefit of warnings and counsel, but whether he can be interrogated. There is no requirement that police stop a person who enters a police station and states that he wishes to confess to a crime, or a person who calls the police to offer a confession or any other statement he desires to make. Volunteered statements of any kind are not barred by the Fifth Amendment and their admissibility is not affected by our holding today. . . .

IV.

A recurrent argument made in these cases is that society's need for interrogation outweighs the privilege. This argument is not unfamiliar to this Court. . . . The whole thrust of our foregoing discussion demonstrates that the Constitution has prescribed the rights of the individual when confronted with the power of government when it provided in the Fifth Amendment that an individual cannot be compelled to be a witness against himself. That right cannot be abridged. As Mr. Justice Brandeis once observed:

"Decency, security and liberty alike demand that government officials shall be subjected to the same rules of conduct that are commands to the citizen. In a government of laws, existence of the government will be imperilled if it fails to observe the laws scrupulously. Our Government is the potent, the omnipresent teacher. For good or for ill, it teaches the whole people by its example. Crime is contagious. If the Government becomes a lawbreaker, it breeds contempt for law; it invites every man to become a law unto himself; it invites anarchy. To declare that in the administration of the criminal law the end justifies the means . . . would bring terrible retribution. Against that pernicious doctrine this Court should resolutely set its face." Olmstead v. United States (1928) (dissenting opinion). . . .

V.

Because of the nature of the problem and because of its recurrent significance in numerous cases, we have to this point discussed the relationship
of the Fifth Amendment privilege to police interrogation without specific
concentration on the facts of the cases before us. We turn now to these facts
to consider the application to these cases of the constitutional principles
discussed above. In each instance, we have concluded that statements were
obtained from the defendant under circumstances that did not meet constitutional standards for protection of the privilege.

[The Court here reviews in detail the facts of the four cases and concludes
either that the defendant did not waive his right to silence, or was not
informed that he had a right to silence or to counsel.]

Mr. Justice Clark dissented in part.

Mr. Justice Harlan, whom Mr. Justice Stewart and Mr. Justice White
joined, dissented, saying in part:

I believe the decision of the Court represents poor constitutional law and
entails harmful consequences for the country at large. How serious these
consequences may prove to be only time can tell. But the basic flaws in the
Court's justification seem to me readily apparent now once all sides of the
problem are considered. . . .

While the fine points of this scheme are far less clear than the Court
admits, the tenor is quite apparent. The new rules are not designed to guard
against police brutality or other unmistakable banned forms of coercion.
Those who use third-degree tactics and deny them in court are equally able
and destined to lie as skillfully about warnings and waivers. Rather, the
thrust of the new rules is to negate all pressures, to reinforce the nervous
or ignorant suspect, and ultimately to discourage any confession at all. The
aim in short is toward "voluntariness" in a utopian sense, or to view it from
a different angle, voluntariness with a vengeance. . . .

What the Court largely ignores is that its rules impair, if they will not
eventually serve wholly to frustrate, an instrument of law enforcement that
has long and quite reasonably been thought worth the price paid for it.
There can be little doubt that the Court's new code would markedly de-
crease the number of confessions. To warn the suspect that he may remain
silent and remind him that his confession may be used in court are minor
obstructions. To require also an express waiver by the suspect and an end
to questioning whenever he demurs must heavily handicap questioning.
And to suggest or provide counsel for the suspect simply invites the end of
the interrogation.

How much harm this decision will inflict on law enforcement cannot fairly
be predicted with accuracy. Evidence on the role of confessions is notori-
ously incomplete, . . . and little is added by the Court's reference to the FBI
experience and the resources believed wasted in interrogation. . . . We do

know that some crimes cannot be solved without confessions, that ample expert testimony attests to their importance in crime control, and that the Court is taking a real risk with society's welfare in imposing its new regime on the country. The social costs of crime are too great to call the new rules anything but a hazardous experimentation.

While passing over the costs and risks of its experiment, the Court portrays the evils of normal police questioning in terms which I think are exaggerated. Albeit stringently confined by the due process standards interrogation is no doubt often inconvenient and unpleasant for the suspect. However, it is no less so for a man to be arrested and jailed, to have his house searched, or to stand trial in court, yet all this may properly happen to the most innocent given probable cause, a warrant, or an indictment. Society has always paid a stiff price for law and order, and peaceful interrogation is not one of the dark moments of the law. . . .

Mr Justice White, with whom Mr. Justice Harlan and Mr. Justice Stewart joined, dissented, saying in part:

The proposition that the privilege against self-incrimination forbids in-custody interrogation without the warnings specified in the majority opinion and without a clear waiver of counsel has no significant support in the history of the privilege or in the language of the Fifth Amendment. As for the English authorities and the common-law history, the privilege, firmly established in the second half of the seventeenth century, was never applied except to prohibit compelled judicial interrogations. The rule excluding coerced confessions matured about 100 years later, "[b]ut there is nothing in the reports to suggest that the theory has its roots in the privilege against self-incrimination. And so far as the cases reveal, the privilege, as such, seems to have been given effect only in judicial proceedings, including the preliminary examinations by authorized magistrates."

GREGG v. GEORGIA

428 U. S. 153; 96 St. Ct. 2909; 49 L. Ed. 2d 859
(1976)

The Eighth Amendment prohibits the infliction of cruel and unusual punishment, but makes no effort to define such punishment. In early England most felonies were punished by hanging, and for certain serious crimes, such as treason, a person could be drawn and quartered. In colonial America the pillory and stocks were a feature of nearly every town square, and flogging was common for many offenses. Many, if not all, of these forms of punishment would be considered uncivilized today, and have long since been abolished. In 1963 the supreme court of Delaware, the last state to permit flogging (except for infraction of prison rules), upheld the sentence of 20 lashes for breaking parole in a car theft case; but the state pardons board freed the man and the sentence was not carried out. In Louisiana ex. rel. Francis v. Resweber (1947) the Supreme Court, assuming capital punishment to be valid, rejected the contention that the state's failure to electrocute the defendant on the first try made subsequent tries cruel and unusual. In Wilkerson v. Utah (1879) the Court had held shooting was not cruel and unusual, but suggested the ban would include both drawing and quartering and burning alive.

The idea that punishment could be cruel and unusual, not in the abstract, but because it did not "fit the crime" to which it was attached, was argued as early as 1892 by Justice Field in his dissent in O'Neil v. Vermont, a case in which a New Yorker selling liquor illegally in Vermont stood to serve 19,914 days in jail for 307 separate illegal sales. The Court found that since the Eighth Amendment did not limit the states, no federal question was involved. In reviewing a case arising under the Philippine constitution, whose cruel and unusual punishment clause was identical to the Eighth Amendment's, the Court struck down as cruel and unusual a fifteen-year sentence for knowingly making a false statement in a public document; see Weems v. United States (1910).

It is also cruel to punish a person for being sick or having some affliction over which that person has no control. In Robinson v. California (1962) the Court struck down a state statute making it a misdemeanor "to be addicted to the use of narcotics." While the state was free to punish the use of narcotics or prescribe a mandatory program of treatment for addicts, such addiction was an "illness which may be contracted innocently or involuntarily. We hold that a state law which imprisons a person thus afflicted as a criminal, even though he has never touched any narcotic drug within the State or been guilty of any irregular behavior there, inflicts a cruel and unusual punishment in violation of the Fourteenth Amendment. To be sure, imprisonment for ninety days is not, in the abstract, a punishment which is either cruel or unusual. But the question cannot be considered in the abstract. Even one day in prison would be a cruel and unusual punishment for the 'crime' of having a common cold."

Following the Robinson case, a sixty-year-old bootblack with over one hundred convictions for public drunkenness argued that alcoholism, like drug addiction, was a disease and could not be punished. Five members of the Court agreed that his conviction for public drunkenness was not a cruel and unusual punishment. While they were unable to agree on an opinion regarding alcoholism, they did agree that Powell was not being punished for alcoholism, but for being in public while drunk. Four members of the Court dissented on the ground that his affliction was such that he could not resist being drunk in public. See Powell v. Texas (1968).

Unlike most constitutional developments, which take place gradually with the Court hinting broadly at the path it plans to follow, the inclusion of the death penalty in the Eighth Amendment came with startling suddenness. In nearly every case involving cruel and unusual punishment, the Court had discussed the death penalty, and while none of these cases had raised the Eighth Amendment question directly, in each of them the Court had left no doubt that the penalty, as such, was valid. As late as 1958, four members of the majority (Justice Brennan concurred on other grounds) said in Trop v. Dulles that while expatriation was cruel and unusual punishment, the death penalty "cannot be said to violate the constitutional concept of cruelty."

Then in the 1960s an all-out legal attack was launched against the penalty, underwritten largely by the American Civil Liberties Union and the NAACP Legal Defense Fund, which had evidence that most of those executed since 1930 were black. The penalty was challenged on a variety of grounds, and on June 3, 1967, the execution of more than 500 condemned prisoners throughout the country came to a halt while courts and governors waited to see what the Supreme Court would do.

The first of these challenges reached the Supreme Court in Witherspoon v. Illinois (1968), and for the first time the Court gave an indication that the death penalty was in trouble. Illinois permitted a verdict of guilty and a sentence of death to be handed down by a jury from which the state had deliberately excluded all persons with scruples against capital punishment. The Court declined to reverse the verdict of guilty, since the jury would not be necessarily prone to convict, but it held that no jury so constituted could hand down a sentence of death since such a jury "fell woefully short of that impartiality to which the petitioner was entitled under the Sixth and Fourteenth Amendments." "A jury that must choose between life imprisonment and capital punishment can do little more—and must do nothing less—than express the conscience of the community on the ultimate question of life or death. Yet, in a nation less than half of whose people believe in the death penalty, a jury composed exclusively of such people cannot speak for the community. Culled of all who harbor doubts about the wisdom of capital punishment—of all who would be reluctant to pronounce the extreme penalty —such a jury can speak only for a distinct and dwindling minority." Justice Black, dissenting with Justices Harlan and White, pointed up the majority's underlying motives. "If this Court is to hold capital punishment unconstitutional, I think it should do so forthrightly, not by making it impossible for States to get juries that will enforce the death penalty."

The hopes of opponents of the death penalty that it had been abolished by the Witherspoon case proved unduly optimistic, but the moratorium on executions remained in effect while other challenges were readied for Supreme Court review. One such challenge involved the question of whether a jury could constitutionally impose the death penalty without any governing standards, and in McGautha v. California (1971) the Court held that it could. Justice Harlan, writing for a six-man majority, traced the efforts of the states to reduce the rigors of mandatory death sentences, first by introducing "degrees" of murder, and, when juries still took the law into their own hands, finally giving way to reality and providing for complete jury discretion to hang or not to hang.

On the basis of this history the Court concluded that "to identify before the fact those characteristics of criminal homicides and their perpetrators which call for the death penalty, and to express these characteristics in language which can be fairly understood and applied by the sentencing authority, appear to be tasks which are beyond present human ability." It cited the efforts of a British Royal Commission to solve the same problem and its conclusion that "no simple formula can take account of the innumerable degrees of culpability, and no formula which fails to do so can claim to satisfy public opinion." The list of "aggravating and mitigating circumstances" provided in the Model Penal Code for jury consideration, the Court said, "bear witness to the intractable nature of the problem of 'standards' . . . [and] caution against this Court's undertaking to establish such standards itself. ". . .

The Court concluded that "in the light of history, experience, and the present limitations of human knowledge, we find it quite impossible to say that committing to the untrammelled discretion of the jury the power to pronounce life or death in capital cases is offensive to anything in the Constitution." At the same time it held that the Ohio system of having the jury decide both guilt and punishment together did not deny due process merely because a defendant who wanted to argue for clemency could hardly do so without incriminating himself. "The criminal process, like the rest of the legal system, is replete with situations requiring 'the making of difficult judgments' as to which course to follow."

In a long and carefully reasoned dissent Justice Brennan, joined by Justices Douglas and Marshall, attacked the discretion of the sentencing jury to kill or not to kill as it wished as amounting to "nothing more than government by whim"—a form totally at odds with the "government of laws" protected by the due process clause. "We are not presented with the slightest attempt to bring the power of reason to bear on the considerations relevant to capital sentencing. We are faced with nothing more than stark legislative abdication. Not once in the history of this Court, until today, have we sustained against a due process challenge such an unguided, unbridled, unreviewable exercise of naked power. Almost a century ago, we found an almost identical California procedure constitutionally inadequate to license a laundry. Yick Wo v. Hopkins (1886). Today we hold it adequate to license a life."

The decision in McGautha was widely viewed as the Supreme Court's final word on the death penalty. No more cases involving it were pending before the Court, and with the right of juries to act arbitrarily firmly guaranteed, there seemed little likelihood that an Eighth Amendment argument would prevail. As states made preparations to start executing the now almost 700 prisoners on death row, the Court suddenly announced it would hear a group of cases involving the Eighth Amendment. In June 1972, in Furman v. Georgia, it held the death penalty void.

None of the five members of the majority could agree on an opinion. Justices Marshall and Brennan agreed that all capital punishment was cruel and unusual, with the latter reasoning that "a punishment may not be so severe as to be degrading to the dignity of human beings," and no punishment met this test which was inflicted arbitrarily, which was unacceptable to contemporary society, and which was excessive in view of the purpose to be achieved. In view of its waning popularity and erratic application, the death penalty failed on all counts. Justice Douglas argued that since it was applied disproportionately to the underprivileged, it was therefore "not compatible with the idea of equal protection of the laws that is implicit in the ban on 'cruel and unusual' punishments." Justice Marshall agreed about the discrimination, but stressed that it was ineffective as a deterrent of the crimes for which it was inflicted and would be rejected by a public that was truly "informed" about its operation and impact. Justices Stewart and White, without arguing that the death penalty was cruel per se, noted that the cruelty of the provisions currently in use lay in the results they produced —that the infliction of the penalty was so infrequent and unpredictable that it served neither the goal of deterrence nor of retribution.

The dissenting justices argued that since the Fifth Amendment alluded to capital offenses, it was clear that the framers of the Eighth did not consider death cruel and unusual; that the Court had said uniformly over the years and as recently as Trop v. Dulles in 1958 that it was not cruel; and that the evidence did not show "that capital punishment offends the conscience of society to such a degree that our traditional deference to legislative judgment just be abandoned."

The effect of Furman was to invalidate every death penalty statute in the country, and legislatures studied the case in the hope of discerning from the multitude of opinions what sort of statute might pass constitutional muster. Since the fault of previous statutes seemed to lie in the erratic use of the penalty, two answers suggested themselves. Either the discretion of the sentencing authority could be carefully guided to produce more consistent results, or it could be taken away altogether in an effort to have the penalty inflicted in all cases.

The first of these approaches came to the Court in the case below and two companion cases. In Proffit v. Florida, the law required that a trial judge set the final sentence after a consideration of certain listed aggravating and mitigating factors, while in Jurek v. Texas, the state was required by law to convince a sentencing jury beyond a reasonable doubt of the existence of a number of aggravating factors. Here the swing votes of Justices Stewart, Powell, and Stevens were joined by those of Justices Burger, White, Blackman, and Rehnquist to uphold the penalty.

The validity of mandatory death penalties came to the Court in Stanislaus Roberts

v. Louisiana and Woodson v. North Carolina. Here, the three swing justices joined Justices Brennan and Marshall to hold the statutes void. Insistence that the death penalty *always* be applied, the Court found, would merely perpetuate the pre-Furman pattern in which juries would simply refuse to convict if they felt the death penalty inappropriate for a particular case.

A year after the decision in the present case, the Court in Coker v. Georgia (1977) held the same statute invalid as applied to the crime of rape of an adult woman. Here the Court, with only Justices Burger and Rehnquist dissenting, found that in the absence of gross brutality in the act itself, death "is a disproportionate punishment for rape." Not only was Georgia the only state to punish the rape of an adult woman by death, but in 90 percent of the rape convictions under the new law the jury had not imposed the death sentence. And in Godfrey v. Georgia (1980), the Court held the limiting aggravating circumstance that the murder be "outrageously and wantonly vile" to be unconstitutionally vague and without force as a standard where it was clear a jury could find *every* murder outrageously and wantonly vile. Here the defendant had simply shot his wife and mother-in-law instantly to death.

Mr. Justice Stewart, Mr. Justice Powell, and Mr. Justice Stevens announced the judgment of the Court and filed an opinion delivered by Mr. Justice Stewart, saying in part:

The issue in this case is whether the imposition of the sentence of death for the crime of murder under the law of Georgia violates the Eighth and Fourteenth Amendments.

I.

The petitioner, Troy Gregg, was charged with committing armed robbery and murder. In accordance with Georgia procedure in capital cases, the trial was in two stages, a guilt stage and a sentencing stage. The evidence at the guilt trial established that on November 21, 1973, the petitioner and a traveling companion, Floyd Allen, while hitchhiking north in Florida were picked up by Fred Simmons and Bob Moore. Their car broke down, but they continued north after Simmons purchased another vehicle with some of the cash he was carrying. While still in Florida, they picked up another hitchhiker, Dennis Weaver, who rode with them to Atlanta, where he was let out about 11 p.m. A short time later the four men interrupted their journey for a rest stop along the highway. The next morning the bodies of Simmons and Moore were discovered in a ditch nearby. . . .

. . . The next afternoon, the petitioner and Allen, while in Simmons' car, were arrested in Asheville, N.C. In the search incident to the arrest a .25-caliber pistol, later shown to be that used to kill Simmons and Moore, was found in the petitioner's pocket. After receiving the warnings required by Miranda v. Arizona (1966), and signing a written waiver of his rights, the petitioner signed a statement in which he admitted shooting, then robbing Simmons and Moore. . . . His version of these events was as follows: After

Simmons and Moore left the car, the petitioner stated that he intended to rob them. The petitioner then took his pistol in hand and positioned himself on the car to improve his aim. As Simmons and Moore came up an embankment toward the car, the petitioner fired three shots and the two men fell near a ditch. The petitioner, at close range, then fired a shot into the head of each. He robbed them of valuables and drove away with Allen. . . .

. . . The jury found the petitioner guilty of two counts of armed robbery and two counts of murder.

At the penalty stage, which took place before the same jury, neither the prosecutor nor the petitioner's lawyer offered any additional evidence. . . . The trial judge instructed the jury that it could recommend either a death sentence or a life prison sentence on each count. . . .

Finally, the judge instructed the jury that it "would not be authorized to consider [imposing] the penalty of death" unless it first found beyond a reasonable doubt one of these aggravating circumstances:

"One—That the offense of murder was committed while the offender was engaged in the commission of two other capital felonies, to-wit the armed robbery of [Simmons and Moore].

"Two—That the offender committed the offense of murder for the purpose of receiving money and the automobile described in the indictment.

"Three—The offense of murder was outrageously and wantonly vile, horrible and inhuman, in that they [sic] involved the depravity of [the] mind of the defendant."

Finding the first and second of these circumstances, the jury returned verdicts of death on each count.

The Supreme court of Georgia affirmed the convictions and the imposition of the death sentences for murder. After reviewing the trial transcript and the record, including the evidence, and comparing the evidence and sentence in similar cases in accordance with the requirements of Georgia law, the court concluded that, considering the nature of the crime and the defendant, the sentences of death had not resulted from prejudice or any other arbitrary factor and were not excessive or disproportionate to the penalty applied in similar cases. The death sentences imposed for armed robbery, however, were vacated on the grounds that the death penalty had rarely been imposed in Georgia for that offense and that the jury improperly considered the murders as aggravating circumstances for the robberies after having considered the armed robberies as aggravating circumstances for the murders. . . .

II.

Before considering the issues presented it is necessary to understand the Georgia statutory scheme for the imposition of the death penalty. The Georgia statute, as amended after our decision in Furman v. Georgia (1972), retains the death penalty for six categories of crime: murder, kidnapping for ransom or where the victim is harmed, armed robbery, rape, treason, and aircraft hijacking. The capital defendant's guilt or innocence is determined in the traditional manner, either by a trial judge or a jury, in the first stage of a bifurcated trial.

If trial is by jury, the trial judge is required to charge lesser included offenses when they are supported by any view of the evidence.... After a verdict, finding, or plea of guilty to a capital crime, a presentence hearing is conducted before whoever made the determination of guilt. The sentencing procedures are essentially the same in both bench and jury trials. At the hearing: "[T]he judge [or jury] shall hear additional evidence in extenuation, mitigation, and aggravation of punishment, including the record of any prior criminal convictions and pleas of guilty or pleas of nolo contendere of the defendant, or the absence of any prior conviction and pleas: Provided, however, that only such evidence in aggravation as the State has made known to the defendant prior to his trial shall be admissible. The judge [or jury] shall also hear argument by the defendant or his counsel and the prosecuting attorney ... regarding the punishment to be imposed. "...

III.

C.

... We now consider specifically whether the sentence of death for the crime of murder is a per se violation of the Eighth and Fourteenth Amendments to the Constitution. We note first that history and precedent strongly support a negative answer to this question.

The imposition of the death penalty for the crime of murder has a long history of acceptance both in the United States and in England. The common-law rule imposed a mandatory death sentence on all convicted murderers. McGautha v. California (1971)....

It is apparent from the text of the Constitution itself that the existence of capital punishment was accepted by the Framers. At the time the Eighth Amendment was ratified, capital punishment was a common sanction in every State. Indeed, the First Congress of the United States enacted legislation providing death as the penalty for specified crimes. The Fifth Amendment, adopted at the same time as the Eighth, contemplated the continued existence of the capital sanction by imposing certain limits on the prosecution of capital cases .... And the Fourteenth Amendment, adopted over three-quarters of a century later, similarly contemplates the existence of the capital sanction in providing that no State shall deprive any person of "life, liberty, or property" without due process of law.

For nearly two centuries, this Court, repeatedly and often expressly, has recognized that capital punishment is not invalid per se....

Four years ago, the petitioners in Furman and its companion cases predicated their argument primarily upon the asserted proposition that standards of decency had evolved to the point where capital punishment no longer could be tolerated....

The petitioners in the capital cases before the Court today renew the "standards of decency" argument, but developments during the four years since Furman have undercut substantially the assumptions upon which their argument rested. Despite the continuing debate, dating back to the 19th century, over the morality and utility of capital punishment, it is now evident that a large proportion of American society continues to regard it as an appropriate and necessary criminal sanction.

The most marked indication of society's endorsement of the death penalty for murder is the legislative response to Furman. The legislatures of at least 35 States have enacted new statutes that provide for the death penalty for at least some crimes that result in the death of another person. And the Congress of the United States, in 1974, enacted a statute providing the death penalty for aircraft piracy that results in death. . . .

. . . The Court has said that "one of the most important functions any jury can perform in making . . . a selection [between life imprisonment and death for a defendant convicted in a capital case] is to maintain a link between contemporary community values and the penal system." Witherspoon v. Illinois (1968). It may be true that evolving standards have influenced juries in recent decades to be more discriminating in imposing the sentence of death. But the relative infrequency of jury verdicts imposing the death sentence does not indicate rejection of capital punishment per se. Rather, the reluctance of juries in many cases to impose the sentence may well reflect the humane feeling that this most irrevocable of sanctions should be reserved for a small number of extreme cases. . . . Indeed, the actions of juries in many States since Furman is fully compatible with the legislative judgments, reflected in the new statutes, as to the continued utility and necessity of capital punishment in appropriate cases. At the close of 1974 at least 254 persons had been sentenced to death since Furman, and by the end of March 1976, more than 460 persons were subject to death sentences. . . .

The death penalty is said to serve two principal social purposes: retribution and deterrence of capital crimes by prospective offenders.

In part, capital punishment is an expression of society's moral outrage at particularly offensive conduct. This function may be unappealing to many, but it is essential in an ordered society that asks its citizens to rely on legal processes rather than self-help to vindicate their wrongs. "The instinct for retribution is part of the nature of man, and channeling that instinct in the administration of criminal justice serves an important purpose in promoting the stability of a society governed by law. When people begin to believe that organized society is unwilling or unable to impose upon criminal offenders the punishment they 'deserve,' then there are sown the seeds of anarchy— of self-help, vigilante justice, and lynch law." Furman v. Georgia (Stewart, J., concurring). "Retribution is no longer the dominant objective of the criminal law," . . . but neither is it a forbidden objective nor one inconsistent with our respect for the dignity of men. Furman v. Georgia (Burger, C. J., dissenting) . . . . Indeed, the decision that capital punishment may be the appropriate sanction in extreme cases is an expression of the community's belief that certain crimes are themselves so grievous an affront to humanity that the only adequate response may be the penalty of death.

Statistical attempts to evaluate the worth of the death penalty as a deterrent to crimes by potential offenders have occasioned a great deal of debate. The results simply have been inconclusive. As one opponent of capital punishment has said: "[A]fter all possible inquiry, including the probing of all possible methods of inquiry, we do not know, and for systematic and easily visible reasons cannot know, what the truth about this 'deterrent' effect may be . . . ." . . .

In sum, we cannot say that the judgment of the Georgia legislature that capital punishment may be necessary in some cases is clearly wrong. . . .

Finally, we must consider whether the punishment of death is disproportionate in relation to the crime for which it is imposed. There is no question that death as a punishment is unique in its severity and irrevocability. . . . But we are concerned here only with the imposition of capital punishment for the crime of murder, and when a life has been taken deliberately by the offender, we cannot say that the punishment is invariably disproportionate to the crime. It is an extreme sanction, suitable to the most extreme of crimes.

We hold that the death penalty is not a form of punishment that may never be imposed, regardless of the circumstances of the offense, regardless of the character of the offender, and regardless of the procedure followed in reaching the decision to impose it.

IV.

We now consider whether Georgia may impose the death penalty on the petitioner in this case.

A. . . .

Furman mandates that where discretion is afforded a sentencing body on a matter so grave as the determination of whether a human life should be taken or spared, that discretion must be suitably directed and limited so as to minimize the risk of wholly arbitrary and capricious action.

It is certainly not a novel proposition that discretion in the area of sentencing be exercised in an informed manner. We have long recognized that "[f]or the determination of sentences, justice generally requires . . . that there be taken into account the circumstances of the offense together with the character and propensities of the offender. ". . .

Jury sentencing has been considered desirable in capital cases in order "to maintain a link between contemporary community values and the penal system—a link without which the determination of punishment could hardly reflect 'the evolving standards of decency that mark the progress of a maturing society.' But it creates special problems. Much of the information that is relevant to the sentencing decision may have no relevance to the question of guilt, or may even be extremely prejudicial to a fair determination of that question. This problem, however, is scarcely insurmountable. Those who have studied the question suggest that a bifurcated procedure—one in which the question of sentence is not considered until the determination of guilt has been made—is the best answer. . . .

. . . When a human life is at stake and when the jury must have information prejudicial to the question of guilt but relevant to the question of penalty in order to impose a rational sentence, a bifurcated system is more likely to ensure elimination of the constitutional deficiencies identified in Furman. . . .

The idea that a jury should be given guidance in its decision making is also hardly a novel proposition. Juries are invariably given careful instructions on the law and how to apply it before they are authorized to decide the merits of a lawsuit. It would be virtually unthinkable to follow any other course in a legal system that has traditionally operated by following prior precedents and fixed rules of law. . . .

While some have suggested that standards to guide a capital jury's sentencing deliberations are impossible to formulate, the fact is that such standards have been developed. When the drafters of the Model Penal Code faced this problem, they concluded "that it is within the realm of possibility to point to the main circumstances of aggravation and of mitigation that should be weighed, *and weighed against each other*, when they are presented in a concrete case. ". . .

B.

We now turn to consideration of the constitutionality of Georgia's capital-sentencing procedures. In the wake of Furman, Georgia amended its capital punishment statute, but chose not to narrow the scope of its murder provisions. Thus, now as before Furman, in Georgia "[a] person commits murder when he unlawfully and with malice aforethought, either express or implied, causes the death of another human being." All persons convicted of murder "shall be punished by death or by imprisonment for life."

Georgia did act, however, to narrow the class of murderers subject to capital punishment by specifying 10 statutory aggravating circumstances, one of which must be found by the jury to exist beyond a reasonable doubt before a death sentence can ever be imposed. In addition, the jury is authorized to consider any other appropriate aggravating or mitigating circumstances. The jury is not required to find any mitigating circumstance in order to make a recommendation of mercy that is binding on the trial court, but it must find a *statutory* aggravating circumstance before recommending a sentence of death.

These procedures require the jury to consider the circumstances of the crime and the criminal before it recommends sentence. No longer can a Georgia jury do as Furman's jury did: reach a finding of the defendant's guilt and then, without guidance or direction, decide whether he should live or die. Instead, the jury's attention is directed to the specific circumstances of the crime: Was it committed in the course of another capital felony? Was it committed for money? Was it committed upon a peace officer or judicial officer? Was it committed in a particularly heinous way or in a manner that endangered the lives of many persons? In addition, the jury's attention is focused on the characteristics of the person who committed the crime: Does he have a record of prior convictions for capital offenses? Are there any special facts about this defendant that mitigate against imposing capital punishment (e.g., his youth, the extent of his cooperation with the police, his emotional state at the time of the crime). As a result, while some jury discretion still exists, "the discretion to be exercised is controlled by clear and objective standards so as to produce non-discriminatory application." . . .

As an important additional safeguard against arbitrariness and caprice, the Georgia statutory scheme provides for automatic appeal of all death sentences to the State's Supreme Court. That court is required by statute to review each sentence of death and determine whether it was imposed under the influence of passion or prejudice, whether the evidence supports the jury's finding of a statutory aggravating circumstance, and whether the sentence is disproportionate compared to those sentences imposed in similar cases. . . .

1.

First, the petitioner focuses on the opportunities for discretionary action that are inherent in the processing of any murder case under Georgia law. He notes that the state prosecutor has unfettered authority to select those persons whom he wishes to prosecute for a capital offense and to plea bargain with them. Further, at the trial the jury may choose to convict a defendant of a lesser included offense rather than find him guilty of a crime punishable by death, even if the evidence would support a capital verdict. And finally, a defendant who is convicted and sentenced to die may have his sentence commuted by the Governor of the State and the Georgia Board of Pardons and Paroles. . . .

. . . Nothing in any of our cases suggests that the decision to afford an individual defendant mercy violates the Constitution. Furman held only that, in order to minimize the risk that the death penalty would be imposed on a capriciously selected group of offenders, the decision to impose it had to be guided by standards so that the sentencing authority would focus on the particularized circumstances of the crime and the defendant. . . .

3.

Finally, the Georgia statute has an additional provision designed to assure that the death penalty will not be imposed on a capriciously selected group of convicted defendants. The new sentencing procedures require that the state supreme court review every death sentence to determine whether it was imposed under the influence of passion, prejudice, or any other arbitrary factor, whether the evidence supports the findings of a statutory aggravating circumstance, and "[w]hether the sentence of death is excessive or disproportionate to the penalty imposed in similar cases, considering both the crime and the defendant." In performing its sentence-review function, the Georgia court has held that "if the death penalty is only rarely imposed for an act or it is substantially out of line with sentences imposed for other acts it will be set aside as excessive. "... The court on another occasion stated that "we view it to be our duty under the similarity standard to assure that no death sentence is affirmed unless in similar cases throughout the state the death penalty has been imposed generally...." ...

It is apparent that the Supreme Court of Georgia has taken its review responsibilities seriously. . . .

. . . If a time comes when juries generally do not impose the death sentence in a certain kind of murder case, the appellate review procedures assures that no defendant convicted under such circumstances will suffer a sentence of death.

V. . . .

For the reasons expressed in this opinion, we hold that the statutory system under which Gregg was sentenced to death does not violate the Constitution. Accordingly, the judgment of the Georgia Supreme Court is affirmed.

It is so ordered.

Mr. Justice White, with whom The Chief Justice and Mr. Justice Rehnquist join, concurring in the judgment, said in part:

III. . . .

. . . The Georgia Legislature has plainly made an effort to guide the jury in the exercise of its discretion, while at the same time permitting the jury to dispense mercy on the basis of factors too intangible to write into a statute, and I cannot accept the naked assertion that the effort is bound to fail. As the types of murders for which the death penalty may be imposed become more narrowly defined and are limited to those which are particularly serious or for which the death penalty is peculiarly appropriate as they are in Georgia by reason of the aggravating-circumstance requirement, it becomes reasonable to expect that juries—even given discretion *not* to impose the death penalty—will impose the death penalty in a substantial portion of the cases so defined. If they do, it can no longer be said that the penalty is being imposed wantonly and freakishly or so infrequently that it loses its usefulness as a sentencing device. There is, therefore, reason to expect that Georgia's current system would escape the infirmities which invalidated its previous system under Furman. However, the Georgia Legislature was not satisfied with a system which might, but also might not turn out in practice to result in death sentences being imposed with reasonable consistency for certain serious murders. Instead, it gave the Georgia Supreme Court the power and the obilgation to perform precisely the task which three Justices of this Court, whose opinions were necessary to the result, performed in Furman: namely, the task of deciding whether *in fact* the death penalty was being administered for any given class of crime in a discriminatory, standardless, or rare fashion. . . .

Mr. Justice White, with whom The Chief Justice, Mr. Justice Blackmun, and Mr. Justice Rehnquist join, dissenting in Roberts v. Louisiana [which held void a mandatory death penalty], said in part:

III.

I also cannot agree with the petitioner's other basic argument that the death penalty, however imposed and for whatever crime, is cruel and unusual punishment. The opposing positions on this issue, as well as the history of the death penalty, were fully canvassed by various Justices in their separate opinions in Furman v. Georgia, and these able and lucid presentations need not be repeated here. It is plain enough that the Constitution drafted by the Framers expressly made room for the death penalty. . . .

. . . In Furman, it was concluded by at least two Justices that the death penalty had become unacceptable to the great majority of the people of this country and for that reason, alone or combined with other reasons, was invalid under the Eighth Amendment, which must be construed and applied to reflect the evolving moral standards of the country. . . . That argument, whether or not accurate at that time, when measured by the manner in which the death penalty was being administered under the then prevailing statutory schemes, is no longer descriptive of the country's attitude. Since the judgment in Furman, Congress and 35 state legislatures re-enacted the death penalty for one or more crimes. All of these States authorize the death penalty for murder of one kind or another. With these profound developments in mind, I cannot say that capital punishment has been rejected by or is offensive to the prevailing attitudes and moral presuppositions in the United States . . . .

The widespread re-enactment of the death penalty, it seems to me, answers any claims that life imprisonment is adequate punishment to satisfy the need for reprobation or retribution. It also seems clear enough that death finally forecloses the possibility that a prisoner will commit further crimes, whereas life imprisonment does not. This leaves the question of general deterrence as the principal battleground: does the death penalty more effectively deter others from crime than does the threat of life imprisonment? . . .

. . . In this posture of the case, it would be neither a proper or wise exercise of the power of judicial review to refuse to accept the reasonable conclusions of Congress and 35 state legislatures that there are indeed certain circumstances in which the death penalty is the more efficacious deterrent of crime.

It will not do to denigrate these legislative judgments as some form of vestigial savagery or as purely retributive in motivation; for they are solemn judgments, reasonably based, that imposition of the death penalty will save the lives of innocent persons. . . .

IV.

The plurality offers two additional reasons for invalidating the Louisiana statute, neither of which had been raised by the parties and with both of which I disagree.

The plurality holds the Louisiana statute unconstitutional for want of a separate sentencing proceeding in which the sentencing authority may focus on the sentence and consider some or all of the aggravating and mitigating circumstances. In McGautha v. California (1971), after having heard the same issues argued twice before . . . we specifically rejected the claims . . . . For myself, I see no reason to reconsider McGautha and would not invalidate the Louisiana statute for its failure to provide what McGautha held it need not provide. . . .

Implicit in the plurality's holding that a separate proceeding must be held at which the sentencer may consider the character and record of the accused is the proposition that States are constitutionally prohibited from considering any crime, no matter how defined, so serious that every person who commits it should be put to death regardless of extraneous factors related to his character. Quite apart from McGautha v. California, supra, I cannot agree. It is axiomatic that the major justification for concluding that a given defendant deserves to be punished is that he committed a crime. . . . Moreover, quite apart from the character of a criminal, a State should constitutionally be able to conclude that the need to deter some crimes and that the likelihood that the death penalty will succeed in deterring these crimes is such that the death penalty may be made mandatory for all people who commit them. Nothing resembling a reasoned basis for the rejection of these propositions is to be found in the plurality opinion.

Statement of the Chief Justice and Mr. Justice Rehnquist [in Gregg]:

We concur in the judgment and join the opinion of Mr. Justice White, agreeing with its analysis that Georgia's system of capital punishment comports with the Court's holding in Furman v. Georgia (1972).

Mr. Justice Blackmun, concurred in the judgment.

Mr. Justice Brennan, dissenting, said in part:

This Court inescapably has the duty, as the ultimate arbiter of the meaning of our Constitution, to say whether, when individuals condemned to death stand before our Bar, "moral concepts" require us to hold that the law has progressed to the point where we should declare that the punishment of death, like punishments on the rack, the screw, and the wheel, is no longer morally tolerable in our civilized society. My opinion in Furman v. Georgia concluded that our civilization and the law had progressed to this point and that therefore the punishment of death, for whatever crime and under all circumstances, is "cruel and unusual" in violation of the Eighth and Fourteenth Amendments of the Constitution. . . .

The fatal constitutional infirmity in the punishment of death is that it treats "members of the human race as nonhumans, as objects to be toyed with and discarded. [It is] thus inconsistent with the fundamental premise of the Clause that even the vilest criminal remains a human being possessed of common human dignity." As such it is a penalty that "subjects the individual to a fate forbidden by the principle of civilized treatment guaranteed by the [Clause]." I therefore would hold, on that ground alone, that death is today a cruel and unusual punishment prohibited by the Clause. "Justice of this kind is obviously no less shocking than the crime itself, and the new 'official' murder, far from offering redress for the offense committed against society, adds instead a second defilement to the first."

Mr. Justice Marshall, dissenting, said in part:

In Furman I concluded that the death penalty is constitutionally invalid for two reasons. First, the death penalty is excessive. And second, the American people, fully informed as to the purposes of the death penalty and its liabilities, would in my view reject it as morally unacceptable. . . .

. . . But if the constitutionality of the death penalty turns, as I have urged, on the opinion of an *informed* citizenry, then even the enactment of new death statutes cannot be viewed as conclusive. In Furman, I observed that the American people are largely unaware of the information critical to a judgment on the morality of the death penalty, and concluded that if they were better informed they would consider it shocking, unjust, and unacceptable. A recent study, conducted after the enactment of the post-Furman statutes, has confirmed that the American people know little about the death penalty, and that the opinions of an informed public would differ significantly from those of a public unaware of the consequences and effects of the death penalty.

8

Right to Equal Protection of the Laws

PLESSY v. FERGUSON

163 U. S. 537; 16 S. Ct. 1138; 41 L. Ed. 256
(1896)

With the passing of the Reconstruction era and the return of "white man's government" to the Southern states, state laws were again adopted reminiscent of the "Black Codes" which had been passed right after the Civil War to "keep the Negro in his place." These laws established, and enforced by criminal penalties, a system of racial segregation under which members of the Negro and white races were required to be separated in the enjoyment of public and semi-public facilities. Separate schools, parks, waiting rooms, bus, and railroad accommodations were required by law to be furnished each race; and where completely separate facilities proved to be not feasible, as in a dining car, a curtained partition served to separate the races.

Where racial segregation was effected by private action, as in the case of stores or clubs, no constitutional issue could be raised after the decision in the Civil Rights Cases in 1883. Where the segregation was required by law, however, the question arose whether it violated the rights guaranteed to the newly freed Negro by the Fourteenth Amendment. This problem came to the Court for the first time in the present case, 28 years after the Amendment had been adopted. The legislature of Louisiana had passed in 1890 a statute providing "that all railway companies carrying passengers in their coaches in this state shall provide equal but separate accommodations for the white and colored races, by providing two or more passenger coaches for each passenger train, or by dividing the passenger coaches by a partition so as to secure separate accommodations. . . ." A fine of $25 or 20 days in jail was the penalty for sitting in the wrong compartment. Plessy, a person with one-eighth Negro blood, refused to vacate a seat in the white compartment of a railway car and was arrested for violating the statute.

The Plessy case made lawful for nearly 60 years the doctrine that the Negro is not denied the equal protection of the laws by compelling him to accept "equal but separate" accommodations. There is a bit of irony in the fact that the majority opinion in the Plessy case was written by Justice Brown, a Yale man from the state of Michigan, while the eloquent protest against racial discrimination is found in the dissenting opinion of Justice Harlan, a Southerner from Kentucky.

Mr. Justice Brown delivered the opinion of the Court, saying in part:

The object of the [Fourteenth] amendment was undoubtedly to enforce the absolute equality of the two races before the law, but in the nature of things it could not have been intended to abolish distinctions based upon color, or to enforce social, as distinguished from political, equality, or a commingling of the two races upon terms unsatisfactory to either. Laws permitting, and even requiring their separation in places where they are liable to be brought into contact do not necessarily imply the inferiority of either race to the other, and have been generally, if not universally, recognized as within the competency of the state legislatures in the exercise of their police power. The most common instance of this is connected with the establishment of separate schools for white and colored children, which [has] been held to be a valid exercise of the legislative power even by courts of states where the political rights of the colored race have been longest and most earnestly enforced.

One of the earliest of these cases is that of Roberts v. Boston [1849] in which the supreme judicial court of Massachusetts held that the general school committee of Boston had power to make provision for the instruction of colored children in separate schools established exclusively for them, and to prohibit their attendance upon the other schools. . . . Similar laws have been enacted by Congress under its general power of legislation over the District of Columbia as well as by the legislatures of many of the states, and have been generally, if not uniformly, sustained by the courts. . . .

Laws forbidding the intermarriage of the two races may be said in a technical sense to interfere with the freedom of contract, and yet have been universally recognized as within the police power of the state. . . .

The distinction between laws interfering with the political equality of the negro and those requiring the separation of the two races in schools, theatres, and railway carriages, has been frequently drawn by this court. . . .

In this connection, it is also suggested by the learned counsel for the plaintiff in error that the same argument that will justify the state legislature in requiring railways to provide separate accommodations for the two races will also authorize them to require separate cars to be provided for people whose hair is of a certain color, or who are aliens, or who belong to certain nationalities, or to enact laws requiring colored people to walk upon one side of the street, and white people upon the other, or requiring white men's houses to be painted white, and colored men's black, or their vehicles or business signs to be of different colors, upon the theory that one side of the street is as good as the other, or that a house or vehicle of one color is as good as one of another color. The reply to all this is that every exercise of the police power must be reasonable, and extend only to such laws as are enacted in good faith for the promotion of the public good, and not for the annoyance or oppression of a particular class. . . .

So far, then, as a conflict with the 14th Amendment is concerned, the case reduces itself to the question whether the statute of Louisiana is a reasonable regulation, and with respect to this there must necessarily be a large discretion on the part of the legislature. In determining the question of reasonableness it is at liberty to act with reference to the established usages, customs, and traditions of the people, and with a view to the promotion of their comfort, and the preservation of the public peace and good order. Gauged by this standard, we cannot say that a law which authorizes or even requires the separation of the two races in public conveyances is unreasonable or more obnoxious to the 14th Amendment than the acts of Congress requiring separate schools for colored children in the District of Columbia, the constitutionality of which does not seem to have been questioned, or the corresponding acts of state legislatures.

We consider the underlying fallacy of the plaintiff's argument to consist in the assumption that the enforced separation of the two races stamps the colored race with a badge of inferiority. If this be so, it is not by reason of anything found in the act, but solely because the colored race chooses to put that construction upon it. The argument necessarily assumes that if, as has been more than once the case, and is not unlikely to be so again, the colored race should become the dominant power in the state legislature, and should enact a law in precisely similar terms, it would thereby relegate the white race to an inferior position. We imagine that the white race, at least, would not acquiesce in this assumption. The argument also assumes that social prejudices may be overcome by legislation, and that equal rights cannot be secured to the negro except by an enforced commingling of the two races. We cannot accept this proposition. If the two races are to meet on terms of social equality, it must be the result of natural affinities, a mutual appreciation of each other's merits and a voluntary consent of individuals. . . . Legislation is powerless to eradicate racial instincts or to abolish distinctions based upon physical differences, and the attempt to do so can only result in accentuating the difficulties of the present situation. If the civil and political rights of both races be equal, one cannot be inferior to the other civilly or politically. If one race be inferior to the other socially, the Constitution of the United States cannot put them upon the same plane. . . .

The judgment of the court below is therefore affirmed.

Mr. Justice Brewer took no part in the decision of this case.

Mr. Justice Harlan wrote a dissenting opinion, saying in part:

While there may be in Louisiana persons of different races who are not citizens of the United States, the words in the act, "white and colored races" necessarily include all citizens of the United States of both races residing in that state. So that we have before us a state enactment that compels, under penalties, the separation of the two races in railroad passenger coaches, and makes it a crime for a citizen of either race to enter a coach that has been assigned to citizens of the other race.

Thus the state regulates the use of a public highway by citizens of the United States solely upon the basis of race.

However apparent the injustice of such legislation may be, we have only to consider whether it is consistent with the Constitution of the United States. . . .

In respect of civil rights, common to all citizens, the Constitution of the United States does not, I think, permit any public authority to know the race of those entitled to be protected in the enjoyment of such rights. Every true man has pride of race, and under appropriate circumstances, when the rights of others, his equals before the law, are not to be affected, it is his privilege to express such pride and to take such action based upon it as to him seems proper. But I deny that any legislative body or judicial tribunal may have regard to the race of citizens when the civil rights of those citizens are involved. Indeed such legislation as that here in question is inconsistent, not only with that equality of rights which pertains to citizenship, national and state, but with the personal liberty enjoyed by everyone within the United States. . . .

The white race deems itself to be the dominant race in this country. And so it is, in prestige, in achievements, in education, in wealth, and in power. So, I doubt not that it will continue to be for all time, if it remains true to its great heritage and holds fast to the principles of constitutional liberty. But in view of the Constitution, in the eye of the law, there is in this country no superior, dominant, ruling class of citizens. There is no caste here. Our Constitution is color-blind, and neither knows nor tolerates classes among citizens. In respect of civil rights, all citizens are equal before the law. The humblest is the peer of the most powerful. The law regards man as man, and takes no account of his surroundings or of his color when his civil rights as guaranteed by the supreme law of the land are involved. It is therefore to be regretted that this high tribunal, the final expositor of the fundamental law of the land, has reached the conclusion that it is competent for a state to regulate the enjoyment by citizens of their civil rights solely upon the basis of race.

In my opinion, the judgment this day rendered will, in time, prove to be quite as pernicious as the decision made by this tribunal in the Dred Scott Case. It was adjudged in that case that the descendants of Africans who were imported into this country and sold as slaves were not included nor intended to be included under the word "citizens" in the Constitution, and could not claim any of the rights and privileges which that instrument provided for and secured to citizens of the United States; that at the time of the adoption of the Constitution they were "considered as a subordinate and inferior class of beings, who had been subjugated by the dominant race, and, whether emancipated or not, yet remained subject to their authority, and had no rights or privileges but such as those who held the power and the government might choose to grant them." The recent amendments of the Constitution, it was supposed, had eradicated these principles from our institutions. But it seems that we have yet, in some of the states, a dominant race, a superior class of citizens, which assumes to regulate the enjoyment of civil rights, common to all citizens, upon the basis of race. The present decision, it may well be apprehended, will not [only] stimulate aggressions, more or less brutal and irritating, upon the admitted rights of colored citizens, but will encourage the belief that it is possible, by means of state enactments, to defeat the beneficent purposes which the people of the United States had in view when they adopted the recent amendments of the Constitution, by one of which the blacks of this country were made citizens of the United States and of the states in which they respectively reside and whose privileges and immunities, as citizens, the states are forbidden to abridge. Sixty millions of whites are in no danger from the presence here of eight millions of blacks. The destinies of the two races in this country are indissolubly linked together, and the interests of both require that the common government of all shall not permit the seeds of race hate to be planted under the sanction of law. What can more certainly arouse race hate, what more certainly create and perpetuate a feeling of distrust between these races, than state enactments which in fact proceed on the ground that colored citizens are so inferior and degraded that they cannot be allowed to sit in public coaches occupied by white citizens? That, as all will admit, is the real meaning of such legislation as was enacted in Louisiana.

The sure guarantee of the peace and security of each race is the clear, distinct, unconditional recognition by our governments, national and state, of every right that inheres in civil freedom, and of the equality before the law of all citizens of the United States without regard to race. State enactments, regulating the enjoyment of civil rights, upon the basis of race, and cunningly devised to defeat legitimate results of the war, under the pretense of recognizing equality of rights, can have no other result than to render permanent peace impossible and to keep alive a conflict of races, the continuance of which must do harm to all concerned. This question is not met by the suggestion that social equality cannot exist between the white and black races in this country. That argument, if it can be properly regarded as one, is scarcely worthy of consideration, for social equality no more exists between two races when traveling in a passenger coach or a public highway than when members of the same races sit by each other in a street car or in the jury box, or stand or sit with each other in a political assembly, or when they use in common the streets of a city or town, or when they are in the same room for the purpose of having their names placed on the registry of voters, or when they approach the ballot-box in order to exercise the high privilege of voting. . . .

The arbitrary separation of citizens, on the basis of race, while they are on a public highway, is a badge of servitude wholly inconsistent with the civil freedom and the equality before the law established by the Constitution. It cannot be justified upon any legal grounds.

If evils will result from the commingling of the two races upon public highways established for the benefit of all, they will be infinitely less than those that will surely come from state legislation regulating the enjoyment of civil rights upon the basis of race. We boast of the freedom enjoyed by our people above all other peoples. But it is difficult to reconcile that boast with a state of the law which, practically, puts the brand of servitude and degradation upon a large class of our fellow citizens, our equals before the law. The thin disguise of "equal" accommodations for passengers in railroad coaches will not mislead any one, or atone for the wrong this day done. . . .

I am of opinion that the statute of Louisiana is inconsistent with the personal liberty of citizens, white and black, in that state, and hostile to both the spirit and letter of the Constitution of the United States. If laws of like character should be enacted in the several states of the Union, the effect would be in the highest degree mischievous. Slavery as an institution tolerated by law would, it is true, have disappeared from our country, but there would remain a power in the states, by sinister legislation, to interfere with the full enjoyment of the blessings of freedom; to regulate civil rights, common to all citizens, upon the basis of race; and to place in a condition of legal inferiority a large body of American citizens, now constituting a part of the political community called the people of the United States, for whom and by whom, through representatives, our government is administered. Such a system is inconsistent with the guarantee given by the Constitution to each state of a republican form of government, and may be stricken down by congressional action, or by the courts in the discharge of their solemn duty to maintain the supreme law of the land, anything in the Constitution or laws of any state to the contrary notwithstanding.

For the reasons stated, I am constrained to withhold my assent from the opinion and judgment of the majority.

BROWN v. BOARD OF EDUCATION OF TOPEKA

347 U. S. 483; 74 S. Ct. 686; 98 L. Ed. 873 (1954).

Although Plessy v. Ferguson (1896) involved segregation only in the use of railroad facilities, there was no reason to doubt that the Court would uphold segregation in other areas as well, especially education. This became clear when the Court, in Berea College v. Kentucky (1908), held that the state could validly forbid a college, even though a private institution, to teach whites and blacks at the same time and place. This left no doubt of the validity of the Southern laws requiring the education of white and black children in separate tax-supported schools.

While the segregation of whites and blacks was valid, it was valid only on the theory that the facilities offered were equal, since it is the "equal" protection of the laws that is guaranteed by the Fourteenth Amendment. At first, however, the Supreme Court was extremely lenient in construing what this "equality" required. It held that the term meant, not exact or mathematical equality, but only "substantial" equality. In Cumming v. County Board of Education (1899), it found no denial of "equal" protection of the laws in the failure of a Southern county to provide a high school for sixty black children, although it maintained a high school for white children. The Court seemed satisfied with the county's defense that it could not afford to build a high school for black children. In Gong Lum v. Rice (1927), the Court held that a Chinese girl could validly be required to attend a school for black children in a neighboring school district, rather than be allowed to attend the nearby school for white children. It looked as though the black was not only to be segregated, but must also be content with very inferior accommodations and services under that segregation.

In 1914 the Supreme Court began to show signs of requiring a much closer approach to equality under segregation. In McCabe v. Atchison, T. & S. F. Ry. Co. (1914), an Oklahoma law was held not to accord equal accommodations to blacks and whites when it allowed railroads to haul sleeping, dining, and chair cars for the exclusive use of whites without providing them on demand for the use of blacks.

The tougher attitude of the Court toward what equality under segregation means was made abundantly clear in 1938 in the leading case of Missouri ex rel. Gaines v. Canada. Gaines, a black graduate of Lincoln University and a citizen of Missouri, applied for admission to the University of Missouri law school. Blacks were barred from the law school at the state university; but in order to give them "equal" treatment, the state would pay their tuition in any out-of-state law school (Illinois, Indiana, etc.) which would admit them. Gaines, a black, refused to accept this compromise, and Chief Justice Hughes, in a strong opinion, held that Gaines was "entitled to be admitted to the law school of the state university in the absence of other and proper provision for his legal training within the state . . . ."

In Sweatt v. Painter (1950), the state of Texas claimed that its new law school for Negroes afforded educational opportunities essentially equal to those at the University of Texas Law School. The Court rejected this claim of equality on very significant grounds. The law school for white students, it said, "possesses to a far greater degree those qualities which are incapable of objective measurement but which make for greatness in a law school. . . . The law school, the proving ground for legal learning and practice, cannot be effective in isolation from the individuals and institutions with which the law interacts. . . . The [Negro] law school . . . excludes from its student body members of racial groups which number 85% of the population of the State and include most of the lawyers, judges and other officials with whom petitioner will inevitably be dealing when he becomes a member of the Texas bar. With such a substantial and significant segment of society excluded, we cannot conclude that the education offered petitioner is substantially equal to that which he would receive if admitted to the University of Texas Law School." This strongly suggests that no Negro law school could ever be "equal" under segregation.

In the cases dealing with Negro segregation which reached the Supreme Court after Plessy v. Ferguson (1896) the doctrine of that case was followed and never reexamined. The Court seemed content with the "separate but equal" rule of that case, which, as someone aptly put it, guaranteed to the Negro "the equal, but different, protection of the laws." During the 40-year period beginning with the McCabe case in 1914, the Court, applying ever more rigid standards of equality under segregation, found that Negro plaintiffs in each case had in fact been denied equality of treatment; and so the Court, following the rule that it will not decide constitutional issues if it can avoid doing so, continued to grant relief to Negroes not because they were segregated but because they were unequally treated under segregation. While in the Texas Law School case and the dining car case the Court virtually stated that there were circumstances in which segregation in itself resulted in inequality of treatment, the rule of Plessy v. Ferguson remained intact.

In the fall of 1952, however, the Supreme Court had on its docket cases from four states (Kansas, South Carolina, Virginia, and Delaware), and from the District of Columbia, challenging the constitutionality of racial segregation in public schools. In all of these cases the facts showed that "the Negro and white schools involved have been equalized, or are being equalized, with respect to buildings, curricula, qualifications and salaries of teachers, and other 'tangible' factors." After nearly 60 years the Court again had squarely before it the question of the constitutionality of segregation per se —the question whether the doctrine of Plessy v. Ferguson should be affirmed or reversed.

The five cases were argued together in December, 1952, and the country waited with tense interest for the Court's decision. On June 8, 1953, the Court restored the cases to the docket for reargument in the fall and issued a list of questions upon which it wished that argument to turn. The Court asked for enlightenment on two main points. First, is there historical evidence which shows the intentions of those who framed and ratified the Fourteenth Amendment with respect to the impact of that amendment upon racial segregation in the public schools? Second, if the Court finds racial segregation violates the Fourteenth Amendment, what kind of decree could and should be issued to bring about an end of segregation?

The cases were reargued in December, 1953. Elaborate briefs set forth in great detail the background of the Fourteenth Amendment and the intentions of its framers and ratifiers. The negative result of this historical research is commented on in the opinion below. Some of the briefs, including the one filed by the Attorney General, presented suggestions on the form of the court decree by which segregation might best be ended should the Court hold it to be invalid. Counsel for the National Association for the Advancement of Colored People, who had played a major part in the instigation of these cases, declined to deal with this point. In their view segregation, if held invalid, should be abolshed completely and without delay.

Following the rehearing ordered in the opinion below, the Court handed down its decision remanding the cases back to the lower courts, which were directed to fashion decrees in accordance with "equitable principles." While recognizing that to abolish segregation "may call for the elimination of a variety of obstacles in making the transition," the Court declared that the district "courts will require that the defendants make a prompt and reasonable start toward full compliance with our May 17, 1954, ruling. Once such a start has been made, the courts may find that additional time is necessary to carry out the ruling in an effective manner. The burden rests upon the defendants to establish that such time is necessary in the public interest and is consistent with good faith compliance at the earliest practicable date. . . . The cases are remanded to the District Courts to take such proceedings and enter such orders and decrees consistent with this opinion as are necessary and proper to admit to public schools on a racially nondiscriminatory basis with all deliberate speed the parties to these cases."

The only persons directly bound by the decision in Brown v. Topeka were the five school boards actually parties to the suit, and the only laws specifically held unconstitutional were those involved in those cases. Normally, and in less controversial cases, a rule of constitutional law announced by the Court in a particular case will be accepted and complied with by all those across the country to whom the rule clearly applies. But this compliance is technically voluntary, since only the parties to the case are immediately bound by the Court's decree. It follows, therefore, that obstinate school boards can be compelled to desegregate their schools only as cases are brought against them in the courts and those courts apply to them the rule of the Brown case. In the years following Brown v. Board of Education of Topeka (1954), little or no actual desegregation was done voluntarily. Although they knew segregated schooling was unconstitutional, most school boards insisted on being brought into court and forced to take the first reluctant steps. Unlimited ingenuity was expended in devising techniques for thwarting the Court's ruling, and each technique was defended as long as possible in the courts in an effort to gain time, and in the hope that either Congress would come to the rescue or the Supreme Court would relent. For example, one of the five districts ordered to desegregate its public schools "with all deliberate speed" was Prince Edward County, Virginia. The response of the Virginia legislature was a program of "massive resistance," which included closing integrated schools, cutting off their funds, paying tuition grants to students in private, nonsectarian schools, and providing state and local financial aid (including teacher retirement benefits) for such schools. In 1959 the supreme court of Virginia held the program void under the Virginia constitution, so the legislature repealed it and enacted instead a program under which school attendance was a matter of local option.

Faced with the desegregation order, Prince Edward County closed its public schools and provided various kinds of financial support for privately operated segregated schools. In Griffin v. School Board of Prince Edward County (1964), the Court held the plan denied equal protection of the law. Noting that "the case has been delayed since 1951 by resistance at the state and county level, by legislation, and by law suits," it emphasized that "there has been entirely too much deliberation and not enough speed." The Court conceded to the state a "wide discretion" in deciding whether state laws should operate statewide or only in some counties, "but the record in the present case could not be clearer that Prince Edward's public schools were closed and private schools operated in their place with state and county assistance, for one reason, and one reason only: to ensure, through measures taken by the county and the State, that white and black children in Prince Edward County would not, under any circumstances, go to the same school. Whatever nonracial grounds might support a State's allowing a county to abandon public schools, the object must be a constitutional one, and grounds of race and opposition to desegregation do not qualify as constitutional." The district court was told to "enter a decree which will guarantee that these petitioners will get the kind of education that is given in the State's public schools" even if it had to order the Board of Supervisors to levy taxes to do it. After trying in vain to discover what the penalties for refusal would be, the supervisors finally decided to obey, and in the fall of 1964 Prince Edward County reopened its schools on an integrated basis.

Meanwhile the political branches of government had taken a hand in speeding integration, and threats to withhold federal aid to segregated schools under the Civil Rights Act of 1964 resulted in widespread token compliance, largely by offering blacks "freedom of choice" among schools. Yet with the start of the 1965–66 school year fewer than ten percent of the South's blacks were attending desegregated schools. In March of 1966 the Office of Education announced new guidelines designed to desegregate all 12 grades by the fall of 1967. Protracted litigation, complicated by disputes over the effectiveness of the toughened "freedom of choice" plan, culminated in an announcement by the court of appeals in a Georgia case in December, 1968, that all schools in the states of the fifth circuit—Alabama, Florida, Louisiana, Mississippi, and Texas—be integrated by the fall of 1969 or abandoned.

In July, 1969, it became apparent that some 30 schools in Mississippi would not be ready for integration with the opening of the fall term, and the government suddenly announced that it would no longer try to hold the South to "arbitrary" deadlines for desegregation. At the same time the United States Court of Appeals for the Fifth Circuit reaffirmed its policy and ordered full integration, by September, and the justice department replied by asking for a delay until December 1.

The announced change in policy came as a shock to the lawyers of the NAACP Legal Defense Fund who, after working for many years in partnership with government attorneys for full integration, suddenly found themselves carrying on the fight alone. Even the government attorneys themselves had trouble accepting the sudden switch, and a large number of them signed a statement of protest against the new policy. In spite of this the court of appeals granted the requested delay, and the Legal Defense Fund appealed to the Supreme Court. In a brief per curiam opinion, one of the first in which Chief Justice Berger participated, the Court rejected the government's request for a delay. The "continued operation of segregated schools under a standard of allowing 'all deliberate speed' for desegregation" said the Court, "is no longer constitutionally permissible. Under explicit holdings of this Court the obligation of every school district is to terminate dual school systems at once and to operate now and hereafter only unitary schools." See Alexander v. Holmes County Board of Education (1969).

With this rebuff by the Supreme Court, the Justice Department promptly announced that it would no longer push for more rapid desegregation in over 100 schools in the Deep South. It did not matter much because the Department of Health, Education, and Welfare (HEW) with its authority to withhold funds from schools that were not desegregating effectively had become the principal administrative support for the Courts' orders. The Mississippi school districts did integrate, but many whites in heavily black areas transferred to hastily created all-white "private academies." HEW promptly urged the Internal Revenue Service (IRS) to withhold tax exemption from such schools, and in July 1970 the IRS complied.

While apparently most rural and small town school districts moved rapidly and peacefully toward integration in 1970, in big cities a new cry was heard. To desegregate urban schools located in the center of black or white neighborhoods, it was necessary to transport students out of their home neighborhoods by school bus. As district courts prepared plans calling for busing between pairs of black and white schools, community voices rose in defense of their "neighborhood schools." In Florida, Governor Claude Kirk seized physically the Bradenton schools to prevent busing and relinquished them only when faced with a $10,000-a-day fine. In both the House and Senate, amendments passed to prevent HEW guidelines from requiring busing, only to have them fail when the act finally passed.

And in Charlotte-Mecklenburg, the country's 43rd largest school district, an "antibusing" school board was elected. The district court rejected a plan devised by the Board as not producing sufficient integration at the elementary level and accepted in its place a plan prepared by an outside expert which called for the pairing and grouping of elementary schools and the busing of pupils between them. In Swann v. Charlotte-Mecklenburg Board of Education and Davis v. Board of Commissioners in 1971, the Supreme Court upheld the district court's plan. It approved busing, pairing, and the limited use of mathematical ratios as tools to achieve desegregation and noted that while one-race schools were not outlawed, "the burden upon the school authorities will be to satisfy the court that their racial composition is not the result of present or past discriminatory action on their part." In Nyquist v. Lee (1971), the Court held void without opinion New York's 1969 antibusing statute upon which most of the Southern antibusing statutes had been patterned.

As the long fight to integrate Southern schools achieved increasing success, attention was turned to Northern cities in which segregation was as complete in many cases as it had ever been in the South. While segregation in the South had its genesis in laws providing separate facilities for the two races (de jure), in the big cities of the North an equally effective segregation (de facto) came about as a by-product of the development of single-race neighborhoods. The creation of these neighborhoods, while in part probably the result of personal preferences, has been fostered by both a tacit unwillingness of whites to sell to blacks and a system of economic zoning that puts the cost of homes in middle-class white communities beyond the financial reach of blacks whose economic opportunities are in turn restricted by both the inferior "ghetto" education afforded them and the hiring policies of business which reserves the best-paid jobs for whites. Thus, while in Charlotte-Mecklenburg only two-thirds of the black pupils were in schools that were 99 percent black and a quarter of them attended schools more than half white, in Chicago three-quarters of the black children went to all-black schools and only three percent went to schools that were mostly white.

Even systematic desegregation, however, does not always provide a permanent solution to the segregation problem. Experience has shown that the migration that tends to follow desegregation orders in big cities merely converts de jure patterns into de facto ones. The most striking illustration is the District of Columbia school system, which integrated in 1956; in subsequent years so many whites with school-age children left the District that only five percent of the pupils in the system are white.

This situation faced the cities of Detroit, Michigan and Richmond, Virginia. The school districts in those cities had such a high concentration of blacks that no amount of line-drawing or busing could change their racial composition. In contrast, the school districts in the surrounding suburban counties were almost entirely white. Where, as in Pontiac, Michigan and in Denver, Colorado school board action in locating schools and in drawing attendance lines had encouraged segregation in part of the school system, the Court viewed this as de jure segregative action which created a presumption that the entire system was unlawfully segregated; see Keyes v. School District (1973).

On the other hand, where only the city school district was found guilty of segregation, the remedy could not validly involve the surrounding white suburban school districts which had not acted unconstitutionally. In Milliken v. Bradley (1974), the district court and court of appeals had found that Detroit, with the aid of the state itself, had engaged in deliberate segregation within Detroit and that the only remedy, since Detroit was so largely black, was to bus students between Detroit and the nearby white suburbs. The Supreme Court, voting five to four, struck down the district court's "inter-district" plan and ordered a plan which involved "Detroit only." "Before the boundaries of separate and autonomous school districts may be set aside by consolidating the separate units for remedial purposes or by imposing a cross-district remedy, it must first be shown that there has been a constitutional violation within one district that produces a significant segregative effect in another district. . . . The constitutional right of the Negro respondents residing in Detroit is to attend a unitary school system in that district. Unless petitioners drew the district lines in a discriminatory fashion, or arranged for white students residing in the Detroit district to attend schools in Oakland and Macomb Counties, they were under no constitutional duty to make provisions for Negro students to do so."

Justices White, Douglas, Brennan and Marshall dissented, arguing that it was the constitutional obligation of the *state,* not the school district, to provide equal protection, and since the state had engaged in segregation it had an obligation to desegregate—an obligation it could not avoid by pleading the sanctity of its school district lines or the administrative inconvenience of inter-district cooperation.

The extension of the Brown doctrine to other areas of segregation has so far been done by the Court largely through the technique of affirming lower court decisions without opinion. In Baltimore v. Dawson (1955), the desegregation ruling was held applicable to public beaches, and in Holmes v. Atlanta (1955), to public golf courses. In 1963, in deciding Watson v. Memphis, the Court held that recreation facilities, like universities, must be desegregated at once. On the strength of this rule, the city of Jackson, Mississippi desegregated its parks and golf links but decided instead to close its five swimming pools. In Palmer v. Thompson (1971) the Court upheld the move, noting that a statute could not be held void because of the motivations of the legislature which adopted it, and there was no evidence that the city was "now covertly aiding the maintenance and operation of pools which are private in name only. It shows no state action affecting blacks differently from whites." Three of the four dissenting justices argued that the city action was a public stand against desegregating public facilities and the forbidding of Negroes to swim because of their color—both denials of equal protection.

A separate opinion was necessary to invalidate segregation in the schools of the District of Columbia, which is under congressional authority. In Bolling v. Sharpe, the Court holds that the due process clause of the Fifth Amendment forbids racial segregation by the federal government.

Mr. Chief Justice Warren, delivering the opinion of the Court in the Brown case, said in part:

These cases came to us from the States of Kansas, South Carolina, Virginia, and Delaware. They are premised on different facts and different local conditions, but a common legal question justifies their consideration together in this consolidated opinion.

In each of the cases, minors of the Negro race, through their legal representatives, seek the aid of the courts in obtaining admission to the public schools of their community on a nonsegregated basis. In each instance, they had been denied admission to schools attended by white children under laws requiring or permitting segregation according to race. This segregation was alleged to deprive the plaintiffs of the equal protection of the laws under the Fourteenth Amendment. . . .

The plaintiffs contend that segregated public schools are not "equal" and cannot be made "equal," and that hence they are deprived of the equal protection of the laws. Because of the obvious importance of the question presented, the Court took jurisdiction. Argument was heard in the 1952 Term, and reargument was heard this Term on certain questions propounded by the Court.

Reargument was largely devoted to the circumstances surrounding the adoption of the Fourteenth Amendment in 1868. It covered exhaustively consideration of the Amendment in Congress, ratification by the states, then existing practices in racial segregation, and the views of proponents and opponents of the Amendment. This discussion and our own investigation convince us that, although these sources cast some light, it is not enough to resolve the problem with which we are faced. At best, they are inconclusive. The most avid proponents of the post-War Amendments undoubtedly intended them to remove all legal distinctions among "all persons born or naturalized in the United States." Their opponents, just as certainly, were antagonistic to both the letter and the spirit of the Amendments and wished them to have the most limited effect. What others in Congress and the state legislatures had in mind cannot be determined with any degree of certainty.

An additional reason for the inconclusive nature of the Amendment's history, with respect to segregated schools, is the status of public education at that time. In the South, the movement toward free common schools, supported by general taxation, had not yet taken hold. Education of white children was largely in the hands of private groups. Education of Negroes was almost nonexistent, and practically all of the race were illiterate. In fact, any education of Negroes was forbidden by law in some states. Today, in contrast, many Negroes have achieved outstanding success in the arts and sciences as well as in the business and professional world. It is true that public school education at the time of the Amendment had advanced further in the North, but the effect of the Amendment on Northern States was generally ignored in the congressional debates. Even in the North, the conditions of public education did not approximate those existing today. The curriculum was usually rudimentary; ungraded schools were common in rural areas; the school term was but three months a year in many states; and compulsory school attendance was virtually unknown. As a consequence, it is not surprising that there should be so little in the history of the Fourteenth Amendment relating to its intended effect on public education.

In the first cases in this Court construing the Fourteenth Amendment, decided shortly after its adoption, the Court interpreted it as proscribing all state-imposed discriminations against the Negro race. The doctrine of "separate but equal" did not make its appearance in this Court until 1896 in the case of Plessy v. Ferguson involving not education but transportation. American courts have since labored with the doctrine for over half a century. In this Court, there have been six cases involving the "separate but equal" doctrine in the field of public education. In Cumming v. County Board of Education [1899], and Gong Lum v. Rice [1927], the validity of the doctrine itself was not challenged. In more recent cases, all on the graduate school level, inequality was found in that specific benefits enjoyed by white students were denied to Negro students of the same educational qualifications. State of Missouri ex rel. Gaines v. Canada [1938]; Sipuel v. Board of Regents of University of Oklahoma [1948]; Sweatt v. Painter [1950]; McLaurin v. Oklahoma State Regents [1950]. In none of these cases was it necessary to reexamine the doctrine to grant relief to the Negro plaintiff. And in Sweatt v. Painter the Court expressly reserved decision on the question whether Plessy v. Ferguson should be held inapplicable to public education.

In the instant cases, that question is directly presented. Here, unlike Sweatt v. Painter, there are findings below that the Negro and white schools involved have been equalized, or are being equalized, with respect to buildings, curricula, qualifications and salaries of teachers, and other "tangible" factors. Our decision, therefore, cannot turn on merely a comparison of these tangible factors in the Negro and white schools involved in each of the cases. We must look instead to the effect of segregation itself on public education.

In approaching this problem, we cannot turn the clock back to 1868 when the Amendment was adopted, or even to 1896 when Plessy v. Ferguson was written. We must consider public education in the light of its full development and its present place in American life throughout the Nation. Only in this way can it be determined if segregation in public schools deprives these plaintiffs of the equal protection of the laws.

Today, education is perhaps the most important function of state and local governments. Compulsory school attendance laws and the great expenditures for education both demonstrate our recognition of the importance of education to our democratic society. It is required in the performance of our most basic public responsibilities, even service in the armed forces. It is the very foundation of good citizenship. Today it is a principal instrument in awakening the child to cultural values, in preparing him for later professional training, and in helping him to adjust normally to his environment. In these days, it is doubtful that any child may reasonably be expected to succeed in life if he is denied the opportunity of an education. Such an opportunity, where the state has undertaken to provide it, is a right which must be made available to all on equal terms.

We come then to the question presented: Does segregation of children in public schools solely on the basis of race, even though the physical facilities and other "tangible" factors may be equal, deprive the children of the minority group of equal educational opportunities? We believe that it does.

In Sweatt v. Painter, in finding that a segregated law school for Negroes could not provide them equal educational opportunities, this Court relied in large part on "those qualities which are incapable of objective measurement but which make for greatness in a law school." In McLaurin v. Oklahoma State Regents, the Court, in requiring that a Negro admitted to a white graduate school be treated like all other students, again resorted to intangible considerations: ". . . his ability to study, to engage in discussions and exchange views with other students, and, in general, to learn his profession." Such considerations apply with added force to children in grade and high schools. To separate them from others of similar age and qualifications solely because of their race generates a feeling of inferiority as to their status in the community that may affect their hearts and minds in a way unlikely ever to be undone. The effect of this separation on their educational opportunities was well stated by a finding in the Kansas case by a court which nevertheless felt compelled to rule against the Negro plaintiffs:

"Segregation of white and colored children in public schools has a detrimental effect upon the colored children. The impact is greater when it has the sanction of the law; for the policy of separating the races is usually interpreted as denoting the inferiority of the Negro group. A sense of inferiority affects the motivation of a child to learn. Segregation with the sanction of law, therefore, has a tendency to [retard] the educational and mental development of Negro children and to deprive them of some of the benefits they would receive in a racial[ly] integrated school system." Whatever may have been the extent of psychological knowledge at the time of Plessy v. Ferguson, this finding is amply supported by modern authority.* Any language in Plessy v. Ferguson contrary to this finding is rejected.

We conclude that in the field of public education the doctrine of "separate but equal" has no place. Separate educational facilities are inherently

---

*K. B. Clark, Effect of Prejudice and Discrimination on Personality Development (Midcentury White House Conference on Children and Youth, 1950); Witmer and Kotinsky, Personality in the Making (1952), ch VI; Deutscher and Chein, The Psychological Effects of Enforced Segregation: A Survey of Social Science Opinion, 26 J Psychol 259 (1948); Chein, What are the Psychological Effects of Segregation Under Conditions of Equal Facilities? 3 Int J Opinion and Attitude Res 229 (1949); Brameld, Educational Costs, in Discrimination and National Welfare (MacIver, ed, 1949), 44–48; Frazier, The Negro in the United States (1949), 674–681. And see generally Myrdal, An American Dilemma (1944).

unequal. Therefore, we hold that the plaintiffs and others similarly situated for whom the actions have been brought are, by reason of the segregation complained of, deprived of the equal protection of the laws guaranteed by the Fourteenth Amendment. This disposition makes unnecessary any discussion whether such segregation also violates the Due Process Clause of the Fourteenth Amendment.

Because these are class actions, because of the wide applicability of this decision, and because of the great variety of local conditions the formulation of decrees in these cases presents problems of considerable complexity. On reargument, the consideration of appropriate relief was necessarily subordinated to the primary question—the constitutionality of segregation in public education. We have now announced that such segregation is a denial of the equal protection of the laws. In order that we may have the full assistance of the parties in formulating decrees, the cases will be restored to the docket, and the parties are requested to present further argument on Questions 4 and 5 previously propounded by the Court for the reargument this Term.* The Attorney General of the United States is again invited to participate. The Attorneys General of the states requiring or permitting segregation in public education will also be permitted to appear as amici curiae upon request to do so by September 15, 1954, and submission of briefs by October 1, 1954.

It is so ordered.

UNIVERSITY OF CALIFORNIA v. BAKKE

438 U. S. 265; 98 S. Ct. 2733; 57 L. Ed. 2d 750
(1978)

A major factor in maintaining the intellectual and cultural disadvantage of blacks has been an almost universal discrimination against them economically. White small-business and professional men simply did not hire blacks, however well qualified. Large

---

*"4. Assuming it is decided that segregation in public schools violates the Fourteenth Amendment

"(a) would a decree necessarily follow providing that, within the limits set by normal geographic school districting, Negro children should forthwith be admitted to schools of their choice, or

"(b) may this Court, in the exercise of its equity powers, permit an effective gradual adjustment to be brought about from existing segregated systems to a system not based on color distinctions?

"5. On the assumption on which questions 4(a) and (b) are based, and assuming further that this Court will exercise its equity powers to the end described in question 4(b),

"(a) should this Court formulate detailed decrees in these cases;

"(b) if so, what specific issues should the decrees reach;

"(c) should this Court appoint a special master to hear evidence with a view to recommending specific terms for such decrees;

"(d) should this Court remand to the courts of first instance with directions to frame decrees in these cases, and if so what general directions should the decrees of this Court include and what procedures should the courts of first instance follow in arriving at the specific terms of more detailed decrees?"

employers hired some, but they were systematically left in the servile or menial positions represented by Pullman porters in the railroad industry and the janitorial staff of industry generally. Labor unions of skilled workers ordinarily discriminated against blacks. Even where whites and blacks could compete for the same jobs, whites were better paid for the same work and their chances for promotion were better. And when technological advances displaced workers, it was the unskilled black workers who most often were out of jobs.

During most of our constitutional history this has been a state problem, and only a handful of states forbade discrimination in private employment. During World War II the President's Fair Employment Practices Committee achieved significant results, but with the return to a peace-time economy and the abolition of the Committee, much of the progress was lost. It was not until the Civil Rights Act of 1964, held valid in Heart of Atlanta Motel v. United States (1964), that a systematic national attack on the problem was made. Title VII of the act forbade race discrimination in hiring and the classification of employees in such a way as to "adversely affect" their status because of their race, color, sex, religion, or national origin.

Although the act permitted the use of professionally constructed ability tests provided they were not used to discriminate, in Griggs v. Duke Power Co. (1971) the Court found that the company had violated the act by using a high school diploma and an intelligence test to qualify workers for all but manual laborer jobs. The Court noted that the tests bore no demonstrable relationship to the jobs for which they were required, and since blacks had long received an inferior education, the tests could be presumed to, and did in fact, discriminate against them. Speaking for a unanimous Court, Chief Justice Burger emphasized that "Congress has not commanded that the less qualified be preferred over the better qualified simply because of minority origins. Far from disparaging job qualifications as such, Congress has made such qualifications the controlling factor, so that race, religion, nationality and sex become irrelevant."

In Washington v. Davis (1976), however, the Court made clear "that the constitutional standards for adjudicating claims of invidious racial discrimination is [not] identical to the standards applicable under Title VII." The case involved two blacks who had failed to pass a verbal ability test required as a condition of admission to the Washington, D. C., police department. There was neither evidence nor claim of purposeful discrimination, and the Court declined to hold the test void because four times as many blacks as whites failed it. Noting that in both jury and de jure school segregation cases there had been purposeful discrimination, the Court said: "As an initial matter, we have difficulty understanding how a law establishing a racially neutral qualification for employment is nevertheless racially discriminatory and denies 'any person . . . equal protection of the laws' simply because a greater proportion of Negroes fail to qualify than members of other racial or ethnic groups. Had respondents, along with all others who had failed Test 21, whether white or black, brought an action claiming that the test denied each of them equal protection of the laws as compared with those who had passed with high enough scores to qualify them as police recruits, it is most unlikely that their challenge would have been sustained. Test 21, which is administered generally to prospective Government employees, concededly seeks to ascertain whether those who take it have acquired a particular level of verbal skill; and it is untenable that the Constitution prevents the Government from seeking modestly to upgrade the communicative abilities of its employees rather than to be satisfied with some lower level of competence, particularly where the job requires special ability to communicate orally and in writing. Respondents, as Negroes, could no more successfully claim that the test denied them equal protection than could white applicants who also failed."

Where both the Constitution and the law look to a policy of nondiscrimination and desegregation, what steps may be taken to bring about the desired result? Can blacks be identified and considered as blacks? And if so, for what purposes? May an employer who has always hired whites now consider only black applicants until the balance is redressed? If he may not, and due to educational background white applicants are better qualified, how is the balance ever to be redressed? If he may, is he not illegally discriminating in favor of blacks over whites? The question is the difficult one of defining equality of racial treatment in the context of a society in which nearly every institution is structured to favor whites.

The problem came to the Court in dramatic form in 1974 in DeFunis v. Odegard. DeFunis was denied admission to the University of Washington Law School despite the fact that a number of concededly less qualified minority applicants were admitted. The trial court ordered the law school to admit DeFunis, but by the time the appeal reached the Supreme Court he was already in his third year and when the case was argued orally the school conceded that DeFunis would be allowed to finish, whichever way the decision went. The Court, in a five-to-four per curiam opinion, dismissed the case as moot. Four dissenting justices pointed out that the issue was a real one, ripe for decision, and the 26 amicus briefs filed in the case amply testified to a public interest that would surely bring the case before them again.

Only Justice Douglas discussed the merits of the case. He condemned the use of the Law School Admissions Test (LSAT) as discriminating against minorities on cultural grounds and argued that students be selected "in a racially neutral way." But, he said, "there is no constitutional right for any race to be preferred. . . . If discrimination based on race is constitutionally permissible when those who hold the reins can come up with 'compelling' reasons to justify it, then constitutional guarantees acquire an accordion-like quality. . . . It may well be that racial strains, racial susceptibility to certain diseases, racial sensitiveness to environmental conditions that other races do not experience may in an extreme situation justify differences in racial treatment that no fairminded person would call 'invidious' discrimination. Mental ability is not in the category. All races can compete fairly at all professional levels. As far as race is concerned, any state sponsored preference to one race over another in that competition is in my view 'invidious' and violative of the Equal Protection Clause."

The present case raised again the questions left unanswered in DeFunis. The University of California Medical School at Davis, created in 1968 and with no history of race discrimination, set aside 16 of its 100 entering seats for minority and disadvantaged applicants. Allan Bakke, a 37-year-old white engineer was denied admission and brought suit against the University claiming he was better qualified than some of the 16 minority students and was being discriminated against because of his race. The California Supreme Court, noting that the University could not show that Bakke would not have been admitted had there been no quota, found the program denied him equal protection of the laws and ordered him admitted. The University appealed to the Supreme Court.

In Fullilove v. Klutznick (1980) a badly divided Court held valid a Congressional statute requiring that ten percent of money granted to the states for public works be set aside for minority contractors. Rejecting the Bakke reasoning, Justices White, Berger, and Powell agreed that the law's purpose was to prevent the perpetuation of discriminatory practices, and that Congress could act both under its spending power and under Section 5 of the Fourteenth Amendment. Justice Powell, speaking for himself, argued that because an appropriate governmental authority had identified the need for such affirmative action the law met the strict scrutiny test he had relied on in Bakke. Justices Marshall, Brennan, and Blackmun concurred on the basis of their opinion in the Bakke case. Justices Stewart and Rehnquist dissented, arguing that the Constitution is color-blind and that this decision, like in Plessy v. Ferguson, approved the creation of a government privilege based upon birth. Dissenting separately, Justice

Stevens conceded that classification based on race could be valid, but insisted that this law did not meet the strict scrutiny test since there was no assurance that those actually injured by discrimination would be its beneficiaries.

Mr. Justice Powell announced the judgment of the Court and wrote an opinion, saying in part:

For the reasons stated in the following opinion, I believe that so much of the judgment of the California court as holds petitioner's special admissions program unlawful and directs that respondent be admitted to the Medical School must be affirmed. For the reasons expressed in a separate opinion, my Brothers The Chief Justice, Mr. Justice Stewart, Mr. Justice Rehnquist, and Mr. Justice Stevens concur in this judgment.

I also conclude for the reasons stated in the following opinion that the portion of the court's judgment enjoining petitioner from according any consideration to race in its admissions process must be reversed. For reasons expressed in separate opinions, my Brothers Mr. Justice Brennan, Mr. Justice White, Mr. Justice Marshall, and Mr. Justice Blackmun concur in this judgment. Affirmed in part and reversed in part.

III.

A.

Petitioner does not deny that decisions based on race or ethnic origin by faculties and administrations of state universities are reviewable under the Fourteenth Amendment. . . . For his part, respondent does not argue that all racial or ethnic classifications are per se invalid. . . . The parties do disagree as to the level of judicial scrutiny to be applied to the special admissions program. Petitioner argues that the court below erred in applying strict scrutiny, as this inexact term has been applied in our cases. . . .

En route to this crucial battle over the scope of judicial review, the parties fight a sharp preliminary action over the proper characterization of the special admissions program. Petitioner prefers to view it as establishing a "goal" of minority representation in the Medical School. Respondent, echoing the courts below, labels it a racial quota.

This semantic distinction is beside the point: The special admissions program is undeniably a classification based on race and ethnic background. To the extent that there existed a pool of at least minimally qualified minority applicants to fill the 16 special admissions seats, white applicants could compete only for 84 seats in the entering class, rather than the 100 open to minority applicants. Whether this limitation is described as a quota or a goal, it is a line drawn on the basis of race and ethnic status.

The guarantees of the Fourteenth Amendment extend to all persons. Its language is explicit: "No State shall . . . deny to any person within its jurisdiction the equal protection of the laws." It is settled beyond question that the "rights created by the first section of the Fourteenth Amendment are, by its terms, guaranteed to the individual. The rights established are personal rights," Shelley v. Kraemer [1948]. . . . The guarantee of equal protection cannot mean one thing when applied to one individual and something else when applied to a person of another color. If both are not accorded the same protection, then it is not equal.

Nevertheless, petitioner argues that the court below erred in applying strict scrutiny to the special admissions program because white males, such as respondent, are not a "discrete and insular minority" requiring extraordinary protection from the majoritarian political process. . . . This rationale, however, has never been invoked in our decisions as a prerequisite to subjecting racial or ethnic distinctions to strict scrunity. Nor has this Court held that discreteness and insularity constitute necessary preconditions to a holding that a particular classification is invidious. . . . These characteristics may be relevant in deciding whether or not to add new types of classifications to the list of "suspect" categories or whether a particular classification survives close examination. . . . Racial and ethnic classifications, however, are subject to stringent examination without regard to these additional characteristics. We declared as much in the first cases explicitly to recognize racial distinctions as suspect:

"Distinctions between citizens solely because of their ancestry are by their very nature odious to a free people whose institutions are founded upon the doctrine of equality." Hirabayashi [1943]. "[A]ll legal restrictions which curtail the civil rights of a single racial group are immediately suspect. That is not to say that all such restrictions are unconstitutional. It is to say that courts must subject them to the most rigid scrutiny." Korematsu [1944]. The Court has never questioned the validity of those pronouncements. Racial and ethnic distinctions of any sort are inherently suspect and thus call for the most exacting judicial examination.

B. . . .

Although many of the Framers of the Fourteenth Amendment conceived of its primary function as bridging the vast distance between members of the Negro race and the white "majority," Slaughter-House Cases [1873], the Amendment itself was framed in universal terms, without reference to color, ethnic origin, or condition of prior servitude. As this Court recently remarked in interpreting the 1866 Civil Rights Act to extend to claims of racial discrimination against white persons, "the 39th Congress was intent upon establishing in the federal law a broader principle than would have been necessary to meet the particular and immediate plight of the newly freed Negro slaves." . . .

Over the past 30 years, this Court has embarked upon the crucial mission of interpreting the Equal Protection Clause with the view of assuring to all persons "the protection of equal laws" . . . in a Nation confronting a legacy of slavery and racial discrimination. . . . Because the landmark decisions in this area arose in response to the continued exclusion of Negroes from the mainstream of American society, they could be characterized as involving discrimination by the "majority" white race against the Negro minority. But they need not be read as depending upon that characterization for their results. It suffices to say that "[o]ver the years, this Court has consistently repudiated '[d]istinctions between citizens solely because of their ancestry' as being 'odious to a free people whose institutions are founded upon the doctrine of equality.' " . . .

Petitioner urges us to adopt for the first time a more restrictive view of the Equal Protection Clause and hold that discrimination against members of the white "majority" cannot be suspect if its purpose can be characterized as "benign."* The clock of our liberties, however, cannot be turned back to 1868. . . . It is far too late to argue that the guarantee of equal protection to *all* persons permits the recognition of special wards entitled to a degree of protection greater than that accorded others. "The Fourteenth Amendment is not directed solely against discrimination due to a 'two-class theory' —that is, based upon differences between 'white' and Negro." . . .

Once the artificial line of a "two-class theory" of the Fourteenth Amendment is put aside, the difficulties entailed in varying the level of judicial review according to a perceived "preferred" status of a particular racial or ethnic minority are intractable. The concepts of "majority" and "minority" necessarily reflect temporary arrangements and political judgments. As observed above, the white "majority" itself is composed of various minority groups, most of which can lay claim to a history of prior discrimination at the hands of the state and private individuals. Not all of these groups can receive preferential treatment and corresponding judicial tolerance of distinctions drawn in terms of race and nationality, for then the only "majority" left would be a new minority of White Anglo-Saxon Protestants. There is no principled basis for deciding which groups would merit "heightened

---

*In the view of Mr. Justice Brenan, Mr. Justice White, Mr. Justice Marshall, and Mr. Justice Blackmun, the pliable notion of "stigma" is the crucial element in analyzing racial classifications. The Equal Protection Clause is not framed in terms of "stigma." Certainly the word has no clearly defined constitutional meaning. It reflects a subjective judgment that is standardless. *All* state-imposed classifications that rearrange burdens and benefits on the basis of race are likely to be viewed with deep resentment by the individuals burdened. The denial to innocent persons of equal rights and opportunities may outrage those so deprived and therefore may be perceived as invidious. These individuals are likely to find little comfort in the notion that the deprivation they are asked to endure is merely the price of membership in the dominant majority and that its imposition is inspired by the supposedly benign purpose of aiding others. One should not lightly dismiss the inherent unfairness of, and the perception of mistreatment that acompanies, a system of allocating benefits and privileges on the basis of skin color and ethnic origin. Moreover, Mr. Justice Brennan, Mr. Justice White, Mr. Justice Marshall, and Mr. Justice Blackmun offer no principle for deciding whether preferential classifications reflect a benign remedial purpose or a malevolent stigmatic classification, since they are willing in this case to accept mere post hoc declarations by an isolated state entity—a medical school faculty —unadorned by particularized findings of past discrimination, to establish such a remedial purpose.

judicial solicitude" and which would not.* Courts would be asked to evaluate the extent of the prejudice and consequent harm suffered by various minority groups. Those whose societal injury is thought to exceed some arbitrary level of tolerability then would be entitled to preferential classifications at the expense of individuals belonging to other groups. Those classifications would be free from exacting judicial scrutiny. As these preferences began to have their desired effect, and the consequences of past discrimination were undone, new judicial rankings would be necessary. The kind of variable sociological and political analysis necessary to produce such rankings simply does not lie within the judicial competence—even if they otherwise were politically feasible and socially desirable.

Moreover, there are serious problems of justice connected with the idea of preference itself. First, it may not always be clear that a so-called preference is in fact benign. . . . Second, preferential programs may only reinforce common stereotypes holding that certain groups are unable to achieve success without special protection based on a factor having no relationship to individual worth. . . . Third, there is a measure of inequity in forcing innocent persons in respondent's position to bear the burdens of redressing grievances not of their making. . . .

. . . In expounding the Constitution, the Court's role is to discern "principles sufficiently absolute to give them roots throughout the community and continuity over significant periods of time, and to lift them above the level of the pragmatic political judgments of a particular time and place." A. Cox, The Role of the Supreme Court in American Government 114 (1976).

---

*As I am in agreement with the view that race may be taken into account as a factor in an admissions program, I agree with my Brothers Brennan, White, Marshall, and Blackmun that the portion of the judgment that would proscribe all consideration of race must be reversed. But I disagree with much that is said in their opinion.

They would require as a justification for a program such as petitioner's, only two findings: (i) that there has been some form of discrimination against the preferred minority groups "by society at large," (it being conceded that petitioner had no history of discrimination), and (ii) that "there is reason to believe" that the disparate impact sought to be rectified by the program is the "product" of such discrimination:

"If it was reasonable to conclude—as we hold that it was—that the failure of minorities to qualify for admission at Davis under regular procedures was due principally to the effects of past discrimination, then there is a reasonable likelihood that, but for pervasive racial discrimination, respondent would have failed to qualify for admission even in the absence of Davis' special admission program."

The breadth of this hypothesis is unprecedented in our constitutional system. The first step is easily taken. No one denies the regrettable fact that there has been societal discrimination in this country against various racial and ethnic groups. The second step, however, involves a speculative leap; but for this discrimination by society at large, Bakke "would have failed to qualify for admission" because Negro applicants—nothing is said about Asians—would have made better scores. Not one word in the record supports this conclusion, and the authors of the opinion offer no standard for courts to use in applying such a presumption of causation to other racial or ethnic classifications. This failure is a grave one, since if it may be concluded *on this record* that each of the minority groups preferred by the petitioner's special program is entitled to the benefit of the presumption, it would seem difficult to determine that any of the dozens of minority groups that have suffered "societal discrimination" cannot also claim it, in any area of social intercourse.

If it is the individual who is entitled to judicial protection against classifications based upon his racial or ethnic background because such distinctions impinge upon personal rights, rather than the individual only because of his membership in a particular group, then constitutional standards may be applied consistently. Political judgments regarding the necessity for the particular classification may be weighed in the constitutional balance, Korematsu v. United States (1944), but the standard of justification will remain constant. This is as it should be, since those political judgments are the product of rough compromise struck by contending groups within the democratic process. When they touch upon an individual's race or ethnic background, he is entitled to a judicial determination that the burden he is asked to bear on that basis is precisely tailored to serve a compelling governmental interest. The Constitution guarantees that right to every person regardless of his background. Shelly v. Kraemer [1948] . . . .

C.

Petitioner contends that on several occasions this Court has approved preferential classifications without applying the most exacting scrutiny. Most of the cases upon which petitioner relies are drawn from three areas: school desegregation, employment discrimination, and sex discrimination. Each of the cases cited presented a situation materially different from the facts of this case.

The school desegregation cases are inapposite. Each involved remedies for clearly determined constitutional violations. . . . Racial classifications thus were designed as remedies for the vindication of constitutional entitlement. Moreover, the scope of the remedies was not permitted to exceed the extent of the violations. . . . Here, there was no judicial determination of constitutional violation as a predicate for the formulation of a remedial classification.

The employment discrimination cases also do not advance petitioner's cause. . . . Such preferences . . . have been upheld where a legislative or administrative body charged with the responsibility made determinations of past discrimination by the industries affected, and fashioned remedies deemed appropriate to rectify the discrimination. . . . But we have never approved preferential classifications in the absence of proved constitutional or statutory violations. . . .

IV.

We have held that in "order to justify the use of a suspect classification, a State must show that its purpose or interest is both constitutionally permissible and substantial, and that its use of the classification is 'necessary . . . to the accomplishment' of its purpose or the safeguarding of its interest." . . . The special admissions program purports to serve the purposes of: (i) "reducing the historic deficit of traditionally disfavored minorities in medical schools and the medical profession,"; (ii) countering the effects of societal discrimination; (iii) increasing the number of physicians who will practice in communities currently underserved; and (iv) obtaining the educational benefits that flow from an ethnically diverse student body. It is necessary to decide which, if any, of these purposes is substantial enough to support the use of a suspect classification.

A.

If petitioner's purpose is to assure within its student body some specified percentage of a particular group merely because of its race or ethnic origin, such a preferential purpose must be rejected not as insubstantial but as facially invalid. Preferring members of any one group for no reason other than race or ethnic origin is discrimination for its own sake. This the Constitution forbids. . . .

B.

The State certainly has a legitimate and substantial interest in ameliorating, or eliminating where feasible, the disabling effects of identified discrimination. The line of school desegregation cases, commencing with Brown, attests to the importance of this state goal and the commitment of the judiciary to affirm all lawful means towards its attainment. In the school cases, the States were required by court order to redress the wrongs worked by specific instances of racial discrimination. That goal was far more focused than the remedying of the effects of "societal discrimination," an amorphous concept of injury that may be ageless in its reach into the past.

We have never approved a classification that aids persons perceived as members of relatively victimized groups at the expense of other innocent individuals in the absence of judicial, legislative, or administrative findings of constitutional or statutory violations. . . . After such findings have been made, the governmental interest in preferring members of the injured groups at the expense of others is substantial, since the legal rights of the victims must be vindicated. In such a case, the extent of the injury and the consequent remedy will have been judicially, legislatively, or administratively defined. Also, the remedial action usually remains subject to continuing oversight to assure that it will work the least harm possible to other innocent persons competing for the benefit. Without such findings of constitutional or statutory violations, it cannot be said that the government has any greater interest in helping one individual than in refraining from harming another. Thus, the government has no compelling justification for inflicting such harm.

Petitioner does not purport to have made, and is in no position to make, such findings. Its broad mission is education, not the formulation of any legislative policy or the adjudication of particular claims of illegality. . . .

Hence, the purpose of helping certain groups whom the faculty of the Davis Medical School perceived as victims of "societal discrimination" does not justify a classification that imposes disadvantages upon persons like respondent, who bear no responsibility for whatever harm the beneficiaries of the special admissions program are thought to have suffered. To hold otherwise would be to convert a remedy heretofore reserved for violations of legal rights into a privilege that all institutions throughout the Nation could grant at their pleasure to whatever groups are perceived as victims of societal discrimination. That is a step we have never approved. . . .

C.

Petitioner identifies, as another purpose of its program, improving the delivery of health-care services to communities currently underserved. It may be assumed that in some situations a State's interest in facilitating the health care of its citizens is sufficiently compelling to support the use of a suspect classification. But there is virtually no evidence in the record indicating that petitioner's special admissions program is either needed or geared to promote that goal. The court below addressed this failure of proof: "The University concedes it cannot assure that minority doctors who entered under the program, all of whom express an 'interest' in practicing in a disadvantaged community, will actually do so. It may be correct to assume that some of them will carry out this intention, and that it is more likely they will practice in minority communities than the average white doctor. . . . Nevertheless, there are more precise and reliable ways to identify applicants who are genuinely interested in the medical problems of minorities than by race. An applicant of whatever race who has demonstrated his concern for disadvantaged minorities in the past and who declares that practice in such a community is his primary professional goal would be more likely to contribute to alleviation of the medical shortage than one who is chosen entirely on the basis of race and disadvantage. In short, there is [sic] no empirical data to demonstrate that any one race is more selflessly socially oriented or by contrast that another is more selfishly acquisitive."

Petitioner simply has not carried its burden of demonstrating that it must prefer members of particular ethnic groups over all other individuals in order to promote better health-care delivery to deprived citizens. Indeed, petitioner has not shown that its preferential classification is likely to have any significant effect on the problem.

D.

The fourth goal asserted by petitioner is the attainment of a diverse student body. This clearly is a constitutionally permissible goal for an institution of higher education. Academic freedom, though not a specifically enumerated constitutional right, long has been viewed as a special concern of the First Amendment. . . . The atmosphere of "speculation, experiment and creation"—so essential to the quality of higher education—is widely believed to be promoted by a diverse student body. As the Court noted in Keyishian [v. Board of Regents (1967)], it is not too much to say that the "nation's future depends upon leaders trained through wide exposure" to the ideas and mores of students as diverse as this Nation of many peoples.

Thus, in arguing that its universities must be accorded the right to select those students who will contribute the most to the "robust exchange of ideas," petitioner invokes a countervailing constitutional interest, that of the First Amendment. In this light, petitioner must be viewed as seeking to achieve a goal that is of paramount importance in the fulfillment of its mission.

It may be argued that there is greater force to these views at the undergraduate level than in a medical school where the training is centered primarily on professional competency. But even at the graduate level, our tradition and experience lend support to the view that the contribution of diversity is substantial. . . . Physicians serve a heterogenous population. An otherwise qualified medical student with a particular background—whether it be ethnic, geographic, culturally advantaged or disadvantaged—may bring to a professional school of medicine experiences, outlooks and ideas that enrich the training of its student body and better equip its graduates to render with understanding their vital service to humanity. . . .

. . .As the interest of diversity is compelling in the context of a university's admissions program, the question remains whether the program's racial classification is necessary to promote this interest. . . .

V.

A.

It may be assumed that the reservation of a specified number of seats in each class for individuals from the preferred ethnic groups would contribute to the attainment of considerable ethnic diversity in the student body. But petitioner's argument that this is the only effective means of serving the interest of diversity is seriously flawed. In a most fundamental sense the argument misconceives the nature of the state interest that would justify consideration of race or ethnic background. It is not an interest in simple ethnic diversity, in which a specified percentage of the student body is in effect guaranteed to be members of selected ethnic groups, with the remaining percentage an undifferentiated aggregation of students. The diversity that furthers a compelling state interest encompasses a far broader array of qualifications and characteristics of which racial or ethnic origin is but a single though important element. Petitioner's special admissions program, focused *solely* on ethnic diversity, would hinder rather than further attainment of genuine diversity.

Nor would the state interest in genuine diversity be served by expanding petitioner's two-track system into a multitrack program with a prescribed number of seats set aside for each identifiable category of applicants. Indeed, it is inconceivable that a university would thus pursue the logic of petitioner's two-track program to the illogical end of insulating each category of applicants with certain desired qualifications from competition with all other applicants.

The experience of other university admissions programs, which take race into account in achieving the educational diversity valued by the First Amendment, demonstrates that the assignment of a fixed number of places to a minority group is not a necessary means toward that end. An illuminating example is found in the Harvard College program:

"In recent years Harvard College has expanded the concept of diversity to include students from disadvantaged economic, racial and ethnic groups. Harvard College now recruits not only Californians or Louisianans but also blacks and Chicanos and other minority students. . . .

"In practice, this new definition of diversity has meant that race has been a factor in some admission decisions. When the Committee on Admissions reviews the large middle group of applicants who are 'admissible' and deemed capable of doing good work in their courses, the race of an applicant may tip the balance in his favor just as geographic origin or a life spent on a farm may tip the balance in other candidates' cases. A farm boy from Idaho can bring something to Harvard College that a Bostonian cannot offer. Similarly, a black student can usually bring something that a white person cannot offer. . . ."

In such an admissions program, race or ethnic background may be deemed a "plus" in a particular applicant's file, yet it does not insulate the individual from comparison with all other candidates for the available seats. The file of a particular black applicant may be examined for his potential contribution to diversity without the factor of race being decisive when compared, for example, with that of an applicant identified as an Italian-American if the later is thought to exhibit qualities more likely to promote beneficial educational pluralism. Such qualities could include exceptional personal talents, unique work or service experience, leadership potential, maturity, demonstrated compassion, a history of overcoming disadvantage, ability to communicate with the poor, or other qualifications deemed important. . . .

This kind of program treats each applicant as an individual in the admissions process. The applicant who loses out on the last available seat to another candidate receiving a "plus" on the basis of ethnic background will not have been foreclosed from all consideration for that seat simply because he was not the right color or had the wrong surname. It would mean only that his combined qualifications, which may have included similar nonobjective factors, did not outweigh those of the other applicant. His qualifications would have been weighed fairly and competitively, and he would have no basis to complain of unequal treatment under the Fourteenth Amendment.

It has been suggested that an admissions program which considers race only as one factor is simply a subtle and more sophisticated—but no less effective—means of according racial preference than the Davis program. A facial intent to discriminate, however, is evident in petitioner's preference program and not denied in this case. No such facial infirmity exists in an admissions program where race or ethnic background is simply one element —to be weighed fairly against other elements—in the selection process. "A boundary line," as Mr. Justice Frankfurter remarked in another connection, "is none the worse for being narrow." . . . And a court would not assume that a university, professing to employ a facially nondiscriminatory admissions policy, would operate it as a cover for the functional equivalent of a quota system. In short, good faith would be presumed in the absence of a showing to the contrary in the manner permitted by our cases. . . .

B.

In summary, it is evident that the Davis special admission program involves the use of an explicit racial classification never before countenanced by this Court. It tells applicants who are not Negro, Asian, or Chicano that they are totally excluded from a specific percentage of the seats in an entering class. No matter how strong their qualifications, quantitative and extracurricular, including their own potential for contribution to educational diversity, they are never afforded the chance to compete with applicants from the preferred groups for the special admissions seats. At the same time, the preferred applicants have the opportunity to compete for every seat in the class.

The fatal flaw in petitioner's preferential program is its disregard of individual rights as guaranteed by the Fourteenth Amendment. . . . Such rights are not absolute. But when a State's distribution of benefits or imposition of burdens hinges on the color of a person's skin or ancestry, that individual is entitled to a demonstration that the challenged classification is necessary to promote a substantial state interest. Petitioner has failed to carry this burden. For this reason, that portion of the California court's judgment holding petitioner's special admissions program invalid under the Fourteenth Amendment must be affirmed.

C.

In enjoining petitioner from ever considering the race of any applicant, however, the courts below failed to recognize that the State has a substantial interest that legitimately may be served by a properly devised admissions program involving the competitive consideration of race and ethnic origin. For this reason, so much of the California court's judgment as enjoins petitioner from any consideration of the race of any applicant must be reversed. . . .

Opinion of Mr. Justice Brennan, Mr. Justice White, Mr. Justice Marshall, and Mr. Justice Blackmun, concurring in the judgment in part and dissenting in part, saying in part:

The Court today, in reversing in part the judgment of the Supreme Court of California, affirms the constitutional power of Federal and State Government to act affirmatively to achieve equal opportunity for all. The difficulty of the issue presented—whether Government may use race-conscious programs to redress the continuing effects of past discrimination—and the mature consideration which each of our Brethren has brought to it have resulted in many opinions, no single one speaking for the Court. But this should not and must not mask the central meaning of today's opinions: Government may take race into account when it acts not to demean or insult any racial group, but to remedy disadvantages cast on minorities by past racial prejudice, at least when appropriate findings have been made by judicial, legislative, or administrative bodies with competence to act in this area.

The Chief Justice and our Brothers Stewart, Rehnquist, and Stevens, have concluded that Title VI of the Civil Rights Act of 1964, as amended, prohibits programs such as that at the Davis Medical School. On this statutory theory alone, they would hold that respondent Allan Bakke's rights have been violated and that he must, therefore, be admitted to the Medical School. Our Brother Powell, reaching the Constitution, concludes that, although race may be taken into account in univerity admissions, the particular special admissions program used by petitioner, which resulted in the exclusion of respondent Bakke, was not shown to be necessary to achieve petitioner's stated goals. Accordingly, these Members of the Court form a majority of five affirming the judgment of the Supreme Court of California insofar as it holds that respondent Bakke "is entitled to an order that he be admitted to the University."

We agree with Mr. Justice Powell that, as applied to the case before us, Title VI goes no further in prohibiting the use of race than the Equal Protection Clause of the Fourteenth Amendment itself. We also agree that the effect of the California Supreme Court's affirmance of the judgment of the Superior Court of California would be to prohibit the University from establishing in the future affirmative action programs that take race into account. Since we conclude that the affirmative admissions program at the Davis Medical School is constitutional, we would reverse the judgment below in all respects. Mr. Justice Powell agrees that some uses of race in university admissions are permissible and, therefore, he joins with us to make five votes reversing the judgment below insofar as it prohibits the University from establishing race-conscious programs in the future. . . .

III.

A.

The assertion of human equality is closely associated with the proposition that differences in color or creed, birth or status, are neither significant nor relevant to the way in which persons should be treated. Nonetheless, the position that such factors must be "constitutionally an irrelevance," Edwards v. California (1941) (Jackson, J., concurring), summed up by the shorthand phrase "[o]ur Constitution is color-blind," Plessy v. Ferguson (1896) (Harlan, J., dissenting), has never been adopted by this Court as the proper meaning of the Equal Protection Clause. Indeed, we have expressly rejected this proposition on a number of occasions.

Our cases have always implied that an "overriding statutory purpose," . . . could be found that would justify racial classifications. See, e.g., . . . Korematsu v. United States (1944); Hirabayashi v. United States (1943). More recently, in McDaniel v. Barresi (1971), this Court unanimously reversed the Georgia Supreme Court which had held that a desegregation plan voluntarily adopted by a local school board, which assigned students on the basis of race, was per se invalid because it was not colorblind. . . .

We conclude, therefore, that racial classifications are not per se invalid under the Fourteenth Amendment. Accordingly, we turn to the problem of articulating what our role should be in reviewing state action that expressly classifies by race.

B.

Respondent argues that racial classifications are always suspect and, consequently, that this Court should weigh the importance of the objectives served by Davis' special admissions program to see if they are compelling. . . .

Unquestionably we have held that a government practice or statute which restricts "fundamental rights" or which contains "suspect classifications" is to be subjected to "strict scrutiny" and can be justified only if it furthers a compelling government purpose and, even then, only if no less restrictive alternative is available. . . . But no fundamental right is involved here. . . . Nor do whites as a class have any of the "traditional indicia of suspectness: the class is not saddled with such disabilities, or subjected to such a history of purposeful unequal treatment, or relegated to such a position of political powerlessness as to command extraordinary protection from the majoritarian political process." . . .

On the other hand, the fact that this case does not fit neatly into our prior analytic framework for race cases does not mean that it should be analyzed by applying the very loose rational-basis standard of review that is the very least that is always applied in equal protection cases. " '[T]he mere recitation of a benign, compensatory purpose is not an automatic shield which protects against any inquiry into the actual purposes underlying a statutory scheme.' " . . . Instead, a number of considerations—developed in gender-discrimination cases but which carry even more force when applied to racial classifications—lead us to conclude that racial classifications designed to further remedial purposes " 'must serve important governmental objectives and must be substantially related to achievement of those objectives.' " . . .

First, race, like "gender-based classifications too often [has] been inexcusably utilized to sterotype and stigmatize politically powerless segments of society." . . . State programs designed ostensibly to ameliorate the effects of past racial discrimination obviously create the same hazard of stigma, since they may promote racial separatism and reinforce the views of those who believe that members of racial minorities are inherently incapable of succeeding on their own. . . .

Second, race, like gender and illegitimacy, . . . is an immutable characteristic which its possessors are powerless to escape or set aside. While a classification is not per se invalid because it divides classes on the basis of an immutable characteristic, it is nevertheless true that such divisions are contrary to our deep belief that "legal burdens should bear some relationship to individual responsibility or wrongdoing," . . . and that advancement sanctioned, sponsored, or approved by the State should ideally be based on individual merit or achievement, or at the least on factors within the control of an individual. . . .

In sum, because of the significant risk that racial classifications established for ostensibly benign purposes can be misused, causing effects not unlike those created by invidious classifications, it is inappropriate to inquire only whether there is any conceivable basis that might sustain such a classification. Instead, to justify such a classification an important and articulated purpose for its use must be shown. In addition, any statute must be stricken that stigmatizes any group or that singles out those least well represented in the political process to bear the brunt of a benign program. Thus, our review under the Fourteenth Amendment should be strict—not " 'strict' in theory and fatal in fact," because it is stigma that causes fatality —but strict and searching nonetheless.

IV.

Davis' articulated purpose of remedying the effects of past societal discrimination is, under our cases, sufficiently important to justify the use of race-conscious admissions programs where there is a sound basis for concluding that minority underrepresentation is substantial and chronic, and that the handicap of past discrimination is impeding access of minorities to the Medical School.

A.

At least since Green v. County School Board (1968), it has been clear that a public body which has itself been adjudged to have engaged in racial discrimination cannot bring itself into compliance with the Equal Protection Clause simply by ending its unlawful acts and adopting a neutral stance. . . . The creation of unitary school systems, in which the effects of past discrimination had been "eliminated root and branch," was recognized as a compelling social goal justifying the overt use of race.

Finally, the conclusion that state educational institutions may constitutionally adopt admissions programs designed to avoid exclusion of historically disadvantaged minorities, even when such programs explicitly take race into account, finds direct support in our cases construing congressional legislation designed to overcome the present effects of past discrimination. Congress can and has outlawed actions which have a disproportionately adverse and unjustified impact upon members of racial minorities and has required or authorized race-conscious action to put individuals disadvantaged by such impact in the position they otherwise might have enjoyed. . . . Such relief does not require as a predicate proof that recipients of preferential advancement have been individually discriminated against; it is enough that each recipient is within a general class of persons likely to have been the victims of discrimination. . . .

These cases cannot be distinguished simply by the presence of judicial findings of discrimination, for race-conscious remedies have been approved where such findings have not been made. McDaniel v. Barresi [1971]. . . . Indeed, the requirement of a judicial determination of a constitutional or statutory violation as a predicate for race-conscious remedial actions would be self-defeating. Such a requirement would severely undermine efforts to achieve voluntary compliance with the requirements of law. And, our society and jurisprudence have always stressed the value of voluntary efforts to further the objectives of the law. Judicial intervention is a last resort to achieve cessation of illegal conduct or the remedying of its effects rather than a prerequisite to action.

Nor can our cases be distinguished on the ground that the entity using explicit racial classifications itself had violated § 1 of the Fourteenth Amendment or an antidiscrimination regulation, for again race-conscious remedies have been approved where this is not the case. . . . Moreover, the presence or absence of past discrimination by universities or employers is largely irrelevant to resolving respondent's constitutional claims. . . . If it was reasonable to conclude—as we hold that it was—that the failure of minorities to qualify for admission at Davis under regular procedures was due principally to the effects of past discrimination, then there is a reasonable likelihood that, but for pervasive racial discrimination, respondent would have failed to qualify for admission even in the absence of Davis' special admissions program.

Thus, our cases under Title VII of the Civil Rights Act have held that, in order to achieve minority participation in previously segregated areas of public life, Congress may require or authorize preferential treatment for those likely disadvantaged by societal racial discrimination. Such legislation has been sustained even without a requirement of findings of intentional racial discrimination by those required or authorized to accord preferential treatment, or a case-by-case determination that those to be benefited suffered from racial discrimination. These decisions compel the conclusion that States also may adopt race-conscious programs designed to overcome substantial, chronic minority underrepresentation where there is reason to believe that the evil addressed is a product of past racial discrimination. . . . We therefore conclude that Davis' goal of admitting minority students disadvantaged by the effects of past discrimination is sufficiently important to justify use of race-conscious admissions criteria.

B.

Properly construed, therefore, our prior cases unequivocally show that a state government may adopt race-conscious programs if the purpose of such programs is to remove the disparate racial impact its actions might otherwise have and if there is reason to believe that the disparate impact is itself the product of past discrimination, whether its own or that of society at large. There is no question that Davis' program is valid under this test.

Certainly, on the basis of the undisputed factual submissions before this Court, Davis had a sound basis for believing that the problem of underrepresentation of minorities was substantial and chronic and that the problem was attributable to handicaps imposed on minority applicants by past and present racial discrimination. Until at least 1973, the practice of medicine in this country was, in fact, if not in law, largely the perogative of whites. In 1950, for example, while Negroes constituted 10% of the total population, Negro physicians constituted only 2.2% of the total number of physicians. The overwhelming majority of these, moreover, were educated in two predominantly Negro medical schools, Howard and Meharry. By 1970, the gap between the proportion of Negroes in medicine and their proportion in the population had widened: The number of Negroes employed in medicine remained frozen at 2.2% while the Negro population had increased to 11.1%. The number of Negro admittees to predominantly white medical schools, moreover, had declined in absolute numbers during the years 1955 to 1964.

Moreover, Davis had very good reason to believe that the national pattern of underrepresentation of minorities in medicine would be perpetuated if it retained a single admissions standard. For example, the entering classes in 1968 and 1969, the years in which such a standard was used, included only 1 Chicano and 2 Negroes out of 50 admittees for each year. Nor is there any relief from this pattern of underrepresentation in the statistics for the regular admissions program in later years.

Davis clearly could conclude that the serious and persistent underrepresentation of minorities in medicine depicted by these statistics is the result of handicaps under which minority applicants labor as a consequence of a background of deliberate, purposeful discrimination against minorities in education and in society generally, as well as in the medical profession. . . .

. . . The generation of minority students applying to Davis Medical School since it opened in 1968—most of whom were born before or about the time Brown I was decided—clearly have been victims of this discrimination. Judicial decrees recognizing discrimination in public education in California testify to the fact of widespread discrimination suffered by California-born minority applicants; many minority group members living in California, moreover, were born and reared in school districts in southern States segregated by law. Since separation of school children by race "generates a feeling of inferiority as to their status in the community that may affect their hearts and minds in a way unlikely ever to be undone," Brown I, the conclusion is inescapable that applicants to medical school must be few indeed who endured the effects of de jure segregation, the resistance to Brown I, or the equally debilitating pervasive private discrimination fostered by our long history of official discrimination, and yet come to the starting line with an education equal to whites. . . .

C.

The second prong of our test—whether the Davis program stigmatizes any discrete group or individual and whether race is reasonably used in light of the program's objectives—is clearly satisfied by the Davis program.

It is not even claimed that Davis' program in any way operates to stigmatize or single out any discrete and insular, or even any identifiable, non-minority group. Nor will harm comparable to that imposed upon racial minorities by exclusion or separation on grounds of race be the likely result of the program. It does not, for example, establish an exclusive preserve for minority students apart from and exclusive of whites. Rather, its purpose is to overcome the effects of segregation by bringing the races together. True, whites are excluded from participation in the special admissions program, but this fact only operates to reduce the number of whites to be admitted in the regular admissions program in order to permit admission of a reasonable percentage—less than their proportion of the California population—of otherwise underrepresented qualified minority applicants.

Nor was Bakke in any sense stamped as inferior by the Medical School's rejection of him. Indeed, it is conceded by all that he satisfied those criteria regarded by the school as generally relevant to academic performance better than most of the minority members who were admitted. Moreover, there is absolutely no basis for concluding that Bakke's rejection as a result of Davis' use of racial preference will affect him throughout his life in the same way as the segregation of the Negro school children in Brown I would have affected them. Unlike discrimination against racial minorities, the use of racial preferences for remedial purposes does not inflict a pervasive injury upon individual whites in the sense that wherever they go or whatever they do there is a significant likelihood that they will be treated as second-class citizens because of their color. This distinction does not mean that the exclusion of a white resulting from the preferential use of race is not sufficiently serious to require justification; but it does mean that the injury inflicted by such a policy is not distinguishable from disadvantages caused by a wide range of government actions, none of which has ever been thought impermissible for that reason alone.

In addition, there is simply no evidence that the Davis program discriminates intentionally or unintentionally against any minority group which it purports to benefit. . . . The Davis program does not simply advance less qualified applicants; rather, it compensates applicants, who it is uncontested are fully qualified to study medicine, for educational disadvantages which it was reasonable to conclude were a product of state-fostered discrimination. Once admitted, these students must satisfy the same degree requirements as regularly admitted students; they are taught by the same faculty in the same classes; and their performance is evaluated by the same standards by which regularly admitted students are judged. Under these circumstances, their performance and degrees must be regarded equally with the regularly admitted students with whom they compete for standing. Since minority graduates cannot justifiably be regarded as less well qualified than non-minority graduates by virtue of the special admissions program, there is no reasonable basis to conclude that minority graduates at schools using such programs would be stigmatized as inferior by the existence of such programs.

D.

We disagree with the lower courts' conclusion that the Davis program's use of race was unreasonable in light of its objectives. First, as petitioner argues, there are no practical means by which it could achieve its ends in the foreseeable future without the use of race-conscious measures. With respect to any factor (such as poverty or family educational background) that may be used as a substitute for race as an indicator of past discrimination, whites greatly outnumber racial minorities simply because whites make up a far larger percentage of the total population and therefore far outnumber minorities in absolute terms at every socioeconomic level. . . . Moreover, while race is positively correlated with differences in GPA and MCAT scores, economic disadvantage is not. Thus, it appears that economically disadvantaged whites do not score less well than economically advantaged whites, while economically advantaged blacks score less well than do disadvantaged whites. These statistics graphically illustrate that the University's purpose to integrate its classes by compensating for past discrimination could not be achieved by a general preference for the economically disadvantaged or the children of parents of limited education unless such groups were to make up the entire class.

Second, the Davis admissions program does not simply equate minority status with disadvantage. Rather, Davis considers on an individual basis each applicant's personal history to determine whether he or she has likely been disadvantaged by racial discrimination. The record makes clear that only minority applicants likely to have been isolated from the mainstream of American life are considered in the special program; other minority applicants are eligible only through the regular admissions program. True, the procedure by which disadvantage is detected is informal, but we have never insisted that educators conduct their affairs through adjudicatory proceedings, and such insistence here is misplaced. . . . And it is clear from our cases that specific proof that a person has been victimized by discrimination is not a necessary predicate to offering him relief where the probability of victimization is great. . . .

E.

Finally, Davis' special admissions program cannot be said to violate the Constitution simply because it has set aside a predetermined number of places for qualified minority applicants rather than using minority status as a positive factor to be considered in evaluating the applications of disadvantaged minority applicants. For purposes of constitutional adjudication, there is no difference between the two approaches. In any admissions program which accords special consideration to disadvantaged racial minorities, a determination of the degree of preference to be given is unavoidable, and any given preference that results in the exclusion of a white candidate is no more or less constitutionally acceptable than a program such as that at Davis. . . .

The "Harvard" program as those employing it readily concede, openly and successfully employs a racial criterion for the purpose of ensuring that some of the scarce places in institutions of higher education are allocated to disadvantaged minority students. That the Harvard approach does not also make public the extent of the preference and the precise workings of the system while the Davis program employs a specific, openly stated number, does not condemn the latter plan for purposes of Fourteenth Amendment adjudication. It may be that the Harvard plan is more acceptable to the public than is the Davis "quota." If it is, any State, including California, is free to adopt it in preference to a less acceptable alternative, just as it is generally free, as far as the Constitution is concerned, to abjure granting any racial preferences in its admissions program. But there is no basis for preferring a particular preference program simply because in achieving the same goals that the Davis Medical School is pursuing, it proceeds in a manner that is not immediately apparent to the public.

V.

Accordingly, we would reverse the judgment of the Supreme Court of California holding the Medical School's special admissions program unconstitutional and directing respondent's admission, as well as that portion of the judgment enjoining the Medical School from according any consideration to race in the admissions process.

[Mr. Justice White filed a separate opinion in which he argued that Title VI did not authorize a private cause of action by an aggrieved applicant. His views regarding the merits of the Title VI issue and the equal protection issue were included in the opinion of Justices Brennan, White, Marshall and Blackmun. He also joined in Parts I, III-A, and V-C of Mr. Justice Powell's opinion.]

Mr. Justice Marshall. [Mr. Justice Marshall traces the history of the Negro in American society from slavery to the present.]

II.

The position of the Negro today in America is the tragic but inevitable consequence of centuries of unequal treatment. Measured by any benchmark of comfort or achievement, meaningful equality remains a distant dream for the Negro.

A Negro child today has a life expectancy which is shorter by more than five years than that of a white child. The Negro child's mother is over three times more likely to die of complications in childbirth, and the infant mortality rate for Negroes is nearly twice that for whites. The median income of the Negro family is only 60% that of the median of a white family, and the percentage of Negroes who live in families with incomes below the poverty line is nearly four times greater than that of whites.

When the Negro child reaches working age, he finds that America offers him significantly less than it offers his white counterpart. For Negro adults, the unemployment rate is twice that of whites, and the unemployment rate for Negro teenagers is nearly three times that of white teenagers. A Negro male who completes four years of college can expect a median annual income of merely $110 more than a white male who has only a high school diploma. Although Negroes represent 11.5% of the population, they are only 1.2% of the lawyers and judges, 2% of the physicians, 2.3% of the dentists, 1.1% of the engineers and 2.6% of the college and university professors.

The relationship between those figures and the history of unequal treatment afforded to the Negro cannot be denied. At every point from birth to death the impact of the past is reflected in the still disfavored position of the Negro.

In light of the sorry history of discrimination and its devastating impact on the lives of Negroes, bringing the Negro into the mainstream of American life should be a state interest of the highest order. To fail to do so is to ensure that America will forever remain a divided society.

III.

I do not believe that the Fourteenth Amendment requires us to accept that fate. Neither its history nor our past cases lend any support to the conclusion that a university may not remedy the cumulative effects of society's discrimination by giving consideration to race in an effort to increase the number and percentage of Negro doctors. . . .

IV.

While I applaud the judgment of the Court that a university may consider race in its admissions process, it is more than a little ironic that, after several hundred years of class-based discrimination against Negroes, the Court is unwilling to hold that a class-based remedy for that discrimination is permissible. In declining to so hold, today's judgment ignores the fact that for several hundred years Negroes have been discriminated against, not as individuals, but rather solely because of the color of their skins. It is unnecessary in 20th century America to have individual Negroes demonstrate that they have been victims of racial discrimination; the racism of our society has been so pervasive that none, regardless of wealth or position, has managed to escape its impact. The experience of Negroes in America has been different in kind, not just in degree, from that of other ethnic groups. It is not merely the history of slavery alone but also that a whole people were marked as inferior by the law. And that mark has endured. The dream of America as the great melting pot has not been realized for the Negro; because of his skin color he never even made it into the pot. . . .

It is because of a legacy of unequal treatment that we now must permit the institutions of this society to give consideration to race in making decisions about who will hold the positions of influence, affluence, and prestige in America. For far too long, the doors to those positions have been shut to Negroes. If we are ever to become a fully integrated society, one in which the color of a person's skin will not determine the opportunities available to him or her, we must be willing to take steps to open those doors. I do not believe that anyone can truly look into America's past and still find that a remedy for the effects of that past is impermissible. . . .

I fear that we have come full circle. After the Civil War our Government started several "affirmative action" programs. This Court in the Civil Rights Cases and Plessy v. Ferguson destroyed the movement toward complete equality. For almost a century no action was taken, and this nonaction was with the tacit approval of the courts. Then we had Brown v. Board of Education and the Civil Rights Acts of Congress, followed by numerous affirmative action programs. *Now,* we have this Court again stepping in, this time to stop affirmative action programs of the type used by the University of California.

Mr. Justice Blackmun, said in part:

I am not convinced, as Mr. Justice Powell seems to be, that the difference between the Davis program and the one employed by Harvard is very profound or constitutionally significant. The line between the two is a thin and indistinct one. In each, subjective application is at work. . . .

I suspect that it would be impossible to arrange an affirmative action program in a racially neutral way and have it successful. To ask that this be so is to demand the impossible. In order to get beyond racism, we must first take account of race. There is no other way. And in order to treat some persons equally, we must treat them differently. We cannot—we dare not—let the Equal Protection Clause perpetrate racial supremacy.

Mr. Justice Stevens, with whom The Chief Justice, Mr. Justice Stewart, and Mr. Justice Rehnquist join, concurring in the judgment in part and dissenting in part, said in part:

II.

Both petitioner and respondent have asked us to determine the legality of the University's special admissions program by reference to the Constitution. Our settled practice, however, is to avoid the decision of a constitutional issue if a case can be fairly decided on a statutory ground. "If there is one doctrine more deeply rooted than any other in the process of constitutional adjudication, it is that we ought not to pass on questions of constitutionality . . . unless such adjudication is unavoidable." . . .

III.

. . . In unmistakable terms the [Civil Rights Act of 1964] prohibits the exclusion of individuals from federally funded programs because of their race. As succinctly phrased during the Senate debate, under Title VI it is not "permissible to say 'yes' to one person; but to say 'no' to another person, only because of the color of his skin." . . .

The University's special admissions program violated Title VI of the Civil Rights Act of 1964 by excluding Bakke from the Medical School because of his race. It is therefore our duty to affirm the judgment ordering Bakke admitted to the University.

Accordingly, I concur in the Court's judgment insofar as it affirms the judgment of the Supreme Court of California. To the extent that it purports to do anything else, I respectfully dissent.

GEDULDIG v. AIELLO

417 U. S. 484; 94 S. Ct. 2485; 41 L. Ed. 2d 256
(1974)

Probably no group in the country is subject to a more pervasive, firmly established and staunchly defended system of discrimination than are women. Relying on such varied arguments as biblical authority, the woman's lack of muscular strength, her child-bearing function with its attendant incapacities, and the natural capacity for motherhood, male members of society have undertaken to protect "their women" from having to compete against men by assuring them, insofar as possible, a role of their own in society. Some states forbid women to work at certain jobs, to engage publicly in certain sports, to work while pregnant or to collect unemployment benefits when on maternity leave. Until 1968, a Connecticut statute provided that a woman serve a three-year indeterminant sentence at the "State Farm" for a crime for which a man could be sentenced to only eighteen months in jail, and a state may still establish a one-*sex* school, while one-*race* schools are held to deny equal protection. Even greater is the private discrimination against women. As with blacks, some employers simply refuse to hire women, hire them only for secretarial or clerical jobs, or pay them only about 60 percent of what they would pay a man for comparable work. Section 703 (a) of the Civil Rights Act of 1964 provides the first nationwide prohibition against discriminatory hiring practices affecting women and in Phillips v. Marietta Corp. (1971) the Supreme Court held that the act forbade the corporation to refuse to hire a woman with pre-school-age children when it hired men with such children.

On the few occasions when the Court dealt with the rights of women under the equal protection clause, it treated sex as a legitimate basis of classification. As early as 1904 it held, in Cronin v. Adams, that a state could by law not only prevent women from working in saloons, but could even prevent their entering as customers. In 1948, in Goessaert v. Cleary, the Court held that Michigan could validly forbid women to work as barmaids, while making an exception for the wife or daughter of a male owner. Speaking for six members of the Court, Justice Frankfurter noted that "Michigan could, beyond question, forbid all women from working behind a bar," and added that "the fact that women may now have achieved the virtues that men have long claimed as their prerogatives and now indulge in vices that men have long practiced, does not preclude the States from drawing a sharp line between the sexes, certainly in such matters as the regulation of the liquor traffic."

Nor was there any constitutional objection to treating men and women differently in regard to jury service. In Strauder v. West Virginia (1880) the Court suggested that a state could "confine the selection to males," and in Hoyt v. Florida (1961) it refused to review the "continuing validity of this dictum . . . which has gone unquestioned for more than eighty years in the decisions of this Court." The Court upheld a state law exempting women from jury service, noting that "despite the enlightened emancipation of women from the restrictions and protections of bygone years, and their entry into many parts of community life formerly considered to be reserved to men, woman is still regarded as the center of home and family life."

With the woman's rights amendment (ERA) a few votes short of ratification, the attitude of the Supreme Court began to reflect the changed status of women in society. When, in Taylor v. Louisiana (1975), it effectively overruled the Hoyt case, it acknowledged that "if at one time it could be held that Sixth Amendment juries must be drawn from a fair cross section of the community but that this requirement permitted the almost total exclusion of women, this is not the case today. Communities differ at different times and places. What is a fair cross section at one time or place is not necessarily a fair cross section at another time or a different place." The Court noted that 53 percent of the community were women, and added that the fact that 54 percent of all women between 18 and 64 were part of the labor force "certainly put to rest the suggestion that all women should be exempt from jury service based solely on their sex and the presumed role in the home."

But while the Court seemed prepared to accept the new role of women and viewed state laws treating them differently from men more critically than equal protection standards traditionally required, it was apparently not so convinced of their equality as to consider sex, like race, a "suspect" or "invidious" classification which can be used by the state only to achieve some compelling state interest which it cannot achieve in any other way.

In deciding Reed v. Reed in 1971, the first case ever to hold void a state classification based on sex, the Court held that women were as entitled as men to serve as administrators of estates. While it conceded that "the objective of reducing the work load on probate courts by elminating one class of contests is not without some legitimacy," it found that preferring one sex over another "merely to accomplish the elimination of hearings on the merits, is to make the very kind of arbitrary legislative choice forbidden by the Equal Protection Clause."

Although Reed was unanimous, it gave no clue as to the philosophy of the justices, and it was not until 1973 with the decision in Frontiero v. Richardson that their attitudes began to emerge. A divided Court held that a female member of the armed forces could claim her spouse as a dependent in the same way a male member could claim his, without having to prove actual dependency. In a plurality opinion, Justices Brennan, Douglas, White, and Marshall reasoned that "classifications based on sex, like classifications based upon race, alienage, or national origin, are inherently suspect, and must therefore be subjected to strict judicial scrutiny." Applying these standards, the four justices, quoting from Reed, found that "any statutory scheme which draws a sharp line between the sexes, *solely* for the purpose of achieving administrative convenience, necessarily commands 'dissimilar treatment for men and women who are . . . similarly situated,' and therefore involves the 'very kind of arbitrary legislative choice forbidden by the [Constitution].' " While Justice Stewart, citing Reed v. Reed, argued that the statutes "work an invidious discrimination in violation of the Constitution," Justices Powell, Burger, and Blackmun expressly rejected the idea "that all classifications based upon sex" are inherently suspect. Justice Rhenquist dissented, apparently on the ground that Congress could validly assume that the man was the "breadwinner" and it would be more economical to make married female members show actual dependency.

Despite this division on the nature of woman's equality, where the Court has been able to view a law favoring women as an affirmative action program to offset the economic disadvantages to which women are subjected, it has found there was no denial of equal protection or due process of law. Thus, in 1974 in Kahn v. Shevin, the Court upheld a Florida property tax exemption for widows but not widowers on the ground that "the financial difficulties confronting the lone woman in Florida or in another State exceed those facing the man. Whether from overt discrimination or from the socialization process or a male-dominated culture, the job market is inhospitable to the woman seeking any but the lowest paid jobs." Noting that this was a tax statute, Justice Douglas for a six-man majority applied the traditional rules regarding classification. "A state tax law is not arbitrary although it 'discriminates in favor of a certain class . . . if the discrimination is founded upon a reasonable distinction, or difference in state policy,' not in conflict with the Federal Constitution." And in Schlesinger v. Ballard (1975) a regulation allowing women to stay 13 years in the Navy although twice passed over for promotion did not discriminate against men who could only stay nine years since the opportunity for promotion among men was greater than among women.

In contrast, in Weinberger v. Wiesenfeld (1975) the Court struck down a provision of the Social Security Act providing that a widow with minor children was entitled to benefit from the earnings of her husband, while a widower with minor children was not entitled to benefit from the earnings of his wife. The government argued that, like Kahn v. Shevin, the scheme was designed to "offset the adverse economic situation of women," but the Court found the legislative purpose was to enable the surviving parent to stay home with the child and, as in Reed, this was not a purpose which justified discrimination on the basis of sex.

While a majority of the Court refused to hold that classifications based on sex were "invidious" in the same way as those based on race, it was clearly tightening the reins on the "rational basis" test where the challenged classification was sex. In Stanton v. Stanton (1975), it held void a Utah law setting different ages at which males and females became legal adults, and in Craig v. Boren (1976) it struck down an Oklahoma law setting the age for drinking 3.2 beer at 18 for females and 21 for males. In neither case was the Court willing to accept the state's argument that a legitimate state interest was being advanced, and in the latter case it rejected as unpersuasive the state's statistical evidence purporting to justify the law.

In General Electric v. Gilbert (1976), the Court extended the reasoning of the present case to cases arising under Title VII of the Civil Rights Act of 1964 forbidding sex discrimination by private employers. Noting the similarity of language used in the act with that appearing in equal protection decisions, the Court concluded that its decision in Geduldig was "quite relevant in determining whether or not the pregnancy exclusion did discriminate on the basis of sex." And in Washington County v. Gunther (1981) the

Court held that where the county had systematically set lower wage scales for women than for men, Title VII authorized the women to sue for lost wages resulting from such sex discrimination, despite the fact that none of them had performed work equal to that performed by the men.

Mr. Justice Stewart delivered the opinion of the Court, saying in part:

For almost 30 years California has administered a disability insurance system that pays benefits to persons in private employment who are temporarily unable to work because of disability not covered by workmen's compensation. The appellees brought this action to challenge the constitutionality of a provision of the California program that, in defining "disability," excludes from coverage certain disabilities resulting from pregnancy. Because the appellees sought to enjoin the enforcement of this state statute, a three-judge court was convened. . . . On the appellees' motion for summary judgment, the District Court, by a divided vote, held that this provision of the disability insurance program violates the Equal Protection Clause of the Fourteenth Amendment, and therefore enjoined its continued enforcement. . . .

I.

California's disability insurance system is funded entirely from contributions deducted from the wages of participating employees. Participation in the program is mandatory unless the employees are protected by a voluntary private plan approved by the State. Each employee is required to contribute one percent of his salary, up to an annual maximum of $85. These contributions are placed in the Unemployment Compensation Disability Fund, which is established and administered as a special trust fund within the state treasury.

. . . Benefits are not paid until the eighth day of disability, unless the employee is hospitalized, in which case benefits commence on the first day of hospitalization. . . .

In return for his one-percent contribution to the Disability Fund, the individual employee is insured against the risk of disability stemming from a substantial number of "mental or physical illness[es] and mental or physical injur[ies]." It is not every disabling condition, however, that triggers the obligation to pay benefits under the program. . . .

At all times relevant to this case, § 2626 of the Unemployment Insurance Code provided:

" 'Disability' or 'disabled' includes both mental or physical illness and mental or physical injury. An individual shall be deemed disabled in any day in which, because of physical or mental condition, he is unable to perform his regular or customary work. *In no case shall the term 'disability' or 'disabled' include any injury or illness caused by or arising in connection with pregnancy up to the termination of such pregnancy and for a period of 28 days thereafter.* " (Emphasis added.) . . .

. . . The state court construed the statute to preclude only the payment of benefits for disability accompanying normal pregnancy. The appellant acquiesced in this construction and issued administrative guidelines that exclude only the payment of "maternity benefits"—i.e., hospitalization and disability benefits for normal delivery and recuperation.

. . . Thus, the issue before the Court on this appeal is whether the California disability insurance program invidiously discriminates against [Aiello] and others similarly situated by not paying insurance benefits for disability that accompanies normal pregnancy and childbirth.

II.

It is clear that California intended to establish this benefit system as an insurance program that was to function essentially in accordance with insurance concepts. Since the program was instituted in 1946, it has been totally self-supporting, never drawing on general state revenues to finance disability or hospital benefits. The Disability Fund is wholly supported by the one percent of wages annually contributed by participating employees. At oral argument, counsel for the appellant informed us that in recent years between 90% and 103% of the revenue to the Disability Fund has been paid out in disability and hospital benefits. This history strongly suggests that the one-percent contribution rate, in addition to being easily computable, bears a close and substantial relationship to the level of benefits payable and to the disability risks insured under the program.

Over the years California has demonstrated a strong commitment not to increase the contribution rate above the one-percent level. The State has sought to provide the broadest possible disability protection that would be affordable by all employees, including those with very low incomes. Because any larger percentage or any flat dollar-amount rate of contribution would impose an increasingly regressive levy bearing most heavily upon those with the lowest incomes, the State has resisted any attempt to change the required contribution from the one-percent level. The program is thus structured, in terms of the level of benefits and the risks insured, to maintain the solvency of the Disability Fund at a one-percent annual level of contribution.

In ordering the State to pay benefits for disability accompanying normal pregnancy and delivery, the District Court acknowledged the State's contention "that coverage of these disabilities is so extraordinarily expensive that it would be impossible to maintain a program supported by employee contributions if these disabilities are included." There is considerable disagreement between the parties with respect to how great the increased costs would actually be, but they would clearly be substantial. For purposes of analysis the District Court accepted the State's estimate, which was in excess of $100 million annually, and stated that "it is clear that including these disabilities would not destroy the program. The increased costs could be accommodated quite easily by making reasonable changes in the contribution rate, the maximum benefits allowable, and the other variables affecting the solvency of the program."

Each of these "variables"—the benefit level deemed appropriate to compensate employee disability, the risks selected to be insured under the program, and the contribution rate chosen to maintain the solvency of the program and at the same time to permit low-income employees to participate with minimal personal sacrifice—represents a policy determination by the State. The essential issue in this case is whether the Equal Protection Clause requires such policies to be sacrificed or compromised in order to finance the payment of benefits to those whose disability is attributable to normal pregnancy and delivery.

We cannot agree that the exclusion of this disability from coverage amounts to invidious discrimination under the Equal Protection Clause. California does not discriminate with respect to the persons or groups which are eligible for disability insurance protection under the program. The classification challenged in this case relates to the asserted underinclusiveness of the set of risks that the State has selected to insure. Although California has created a program to insure most risks of employment disability, it has not chosen to insure all such risks, and this decision is reflected in the level of annual contribution exacted from participating employees. This Court has held that, consistently with the Equal Protection Clause, a State "may take one step at a time, addressing itself to the phase of the problem which seems most acute to the legislative mind. . . . The legislature may select one phase of one field and apply a remedy there, neglecting the others. . . ." . . . Particularly with respect to social welfare programs, so long as the line drawn by the State is rationally supportable, the courts will not interpose their judgment as to the appropriate stopping point. "[T]he Equal Protection Clause does not require that a State must choose between attacking every aspect of a problem or not attacking the problem at all." . . .

The District Court suggested that moderate alterations in what it regarded as "variables" of the disability insurance program could be made to accommodate the substantial expense required to include normal pregnancy within the program's protection. The same can be said, however, with respect to the other expensive class of disabilities that are excluded from coverage—short-term disabilities. If the Equal Protection Clause were thought to compel disability payments for normal pregnancy, it is hard to perceive why it would not also compel payments for short-term disabilities suffered by participating employees.

It is evident that a totally comprehensive program would be substantially more costly than the present program and would inevitably require state subsidy, a higher rate of employee contribution, a lower scale of benefits for those suffering insured disabilities, or some combination of these measures. There is nothing in the Constitution, however, that requires the State to subordinate or compromise its legitimate interests solely to create a more comprehensive social insurance program than it already has.

The State has a legitimate interest in maintaining the self-supporting nature of its insurance program. Similarly, it has an interest in distributing the available resources in such a way as to keep benefit payments at an adequate level for disabilities that are covered, rather than to cover all disabilities inadequately. Finally, California has a legitimate concern in maintaining the contribution rate at a level that will not unduly burden participating employees, particularly low-income employees who may be most in need of the disability insurance.

These policies provide an objective and wholly noninvidious basis for the State's decision not to create a more comprehensive insurance program than it has. There is no evidence in the record that the selection of the risks insured by the program worked to discriminate against any definable group or class in terms of the aggregate risk protection derived by that group or class from the program.* There is no risk from which men are protected and women are not. Likewise, there is no risk from which women are protected and men are not.

The appellee simply contends that, although she has received insurance protection equivalent to that provided all other participating employees, she has suffered discrimination because she encountered a risk that was outside the program's protection. For the reasons we have stated, we hold that this contention is not a valid one under the Equal Protection Clause of the Fourteenth Amendment.

Mr. Justice Brennan, with whom Mr. Justice Douglas and Mr. Justice Marshall join, dissenting, said in part:

. . . The Court today rejects appellees' equal protection claim and upholds the exclusion of normal pregnancy-related disabilities from coverage under California's disability insurance program on the ground that the legislative classification rationally promotes the State's legitimate cost-saving interests in "maintaining the self-supporting nature of its insurance program[,] . . . distributing the available resources in such a way as to keep benefit payments at an adequate level for disabilities that are covered, . . .

---

*The dissenting opinion to the contrary, this case is thus a far cry from cases like Reed v. Reed, (1971) and Frontiero v. Richardson (1973) involving discrimination based upon gender as such. The California insurance program does not exclude anyone from benefit eligibility because of gender but merely removes one physical condition—pregnancy—from the list of compensable disabilities. While it is true that only women can become pregnant, it does not follow that every legislative classification concerning pregnancy is a sex-based classification like those considered in Reed, supra, and Frontiero, supra. Normal pregnancy is an objectively identifiable physical condition with unique characteristics. Absent a showing that distinctions involving pregnancy are mere pretexts designed to effect an invidious discrimination against the members of one sex or the other, lawmakers are constitutionally free to include or exclude pregnancy from the coverage of legislation such as this on any reasonable basis, just as with respect to any other physical condition.

The lack of identity between the excluded disability and gender as such under this insurance program becomes clear upon the most cursory analysis. The program divides potential recipients into two groups—pregnant women and non-pregnant persons. While the first group is exclusively female, the second includes members of both sexes. The fiscal and actuarial benefits of the program thus accrue to members of both sexes.

[and] maintaining the contribution rate at a level that will not unduly burden participating employees . . . ." Because I believe that Reed v. Reed (1971), and Frontiero v. Richardson (1973), mandate a stricter standard of scrutiny which the State's classification fails to satisfy, I respectfully dissent. . . .

Despite the Act's broad goals and scope of coverage, compensation is denied for disabilities suffered in connection with a "normal" pregnancy— disabilities suffered only by women. Disabilities caused by pregnancy, however, like other physically disabling conditions covered by the Act, require medical care, often include hospitalization, anesthesia and surgical procedures, and may involve genuine risk to life. Moreover, the economic effects caused by pregnancy-related disabilities are functionally indistinguishable from the effects caused by any other disability: wages are lost due to a physical inability to work, and medical expenses are incurred for the delivery of the child and for postpartum care. In my view, by singling out for less favorable treatment a gender-linked disability peculiar to women, the State has created a double standard for disability compensation: a limitation is imposed upon the disabilities for which women workers may recover, while men receive full compensation for all disabilities suffered, including those that effect only or primarily their sex, such as prostatectomies, circumcision, hemophilia, and gout. In effect, one set of rules is applied to females and another to males. Such dissimilar treatment of men and women, on the basis of physical characteristics inextricably linked to one sex, inevitably constitutes sex discrimination. . . .

In the past, when a legislative classification has turned on gender, the Court has justifiably applied a standard of judicial scrutiny more strict than that generally accorded economic or social welfare programs. . . . Yet, by its decision today, the Court appears willing to abandon that higher standard of review without satisfactorily explaining what differentiates the gender-based classification employed in this case from those found unconstitutional in Reed and Frontiero. The Court's decision threatens to return men and women to a time when "traditional" equal protection analysis sustained legislative classifications that treated differently members of a particular sex solely because of their sex. See, e.g., Muller v. Oregon (1908); Goesaert v. Cleary (1948); Hoyt v. Florida (1961).

I cannot join the Court's apparent retreat. I continue to adhere to my view that "classifications based upon sex, like classifications based upon race, alienage, or national origin, are inherently suspect, and must therefore be subjected to strict judicial scrutiny." Frontiero v. Richardson. When, as in this case, the State employs a legislative classification that distinguishes between beneficiaries solely by reference to gender-linked disability risks, "[t]he Court is not . . . free to sustain the statute on the ground that it rationally promotes legitimate governmental interests; rather, such suspect classifications can be sustained only when the State bears the burden of demonstrating that the challenged legislation serves overriding or compelling interests that cannot be achieved either by a more carefully tailored legislative classification or by the use of feasible, less drastic means." Kahn v. Shevin (1974) (Brennan, J., dissenting).

ROSTKER V. GOLDBERG

June 25, 1981

The Supreme Court has devised two basic tests to resolve equal protection cases; the strict scrutiny test and the rational basis test. The strict scrutiny test is used when the law being challenged treats people differently based on what the Court calls a "suspect classification." Race, religion, and national origin are the prime examples of suspect classification because historically they have been used to discriminate invidiously against groups of people. A classification is more apt to be suspect if its characteristics are immutable, so that a person born into it can never escape. If a law's classification is not suspect, the Court usually employs the rational basis test and the underlying ingredient of both tests seems to be a question of who bears the burden of proof. The rational basis test assumes that the legislature had a valid, nondiscriminatory reason for passing the law and anyone challenging its validity bears the burden of proving the legislature's irrationality. The strict scrutiny test, on the other hand, assumes that the legislature passed the law to favor one group over another for reasons having nothing to do with legitimate governmental objectives. Those defending the law then bear the burden of proving that a neutral law would not serve those objectives equally well. These two tests are functional opposites: Laws usually pass the rational basis test while they almost always fail the strict scrutiny test.

For those classifications that the Court considers not quite suspect, yet something less than innocent, no one particular test has emerged. In this gray area which includes classifications based on sex and wealth, the Court sometimes appears to rely on one test and sometimes on the other. At still other times the Court appears to embrace a new intermediate test. In Craig v. Boren (1976) (holding void a discriminatory drinking-age law) a majority of the Court applied what was described as a midlevel test, under which "classification by gender must serve some important governmental objective and must be substantially related to the achievement of these objectives."

Despite its efforts to formulate an intermediate test, the members of the Court have not, in fact, balanced the burden of proof between those attacking and those defending the law, but are in reality placing the burden on one party or the other much as they did before. In Michael M. v. Sonoma County (1981) five members of the Court upheld a state statutory rape law against the challenge that it punished the male participant in a consensual sex act (in this case a minor) but not his minor female partner. The Court gave "great deference" to California's assertion that the purpose of the law was to prevent teenage pregnancies and agreed that this was certainly a legitimate state purpose. Moreover, punishing just the male was sufficiently related to the purpose of the law because the female was already sufficiently deterred from the act by the fear of pregnancy, and were she to become pregnant and have to deal with the consequences she would be further punished while the male would not.

Justices Brennan, White, and Marshall dissented, arguing that while ostensibly applying the same test, the majority had failed to carry the burden of showing that a sex-neutral law punishing both parties to the act would not be as effective a deterrent in preventing pregnancy as one punishing only the male. Justice Stevens dissented separately, pointing out that it was "totally irrational" to exempt from punishment the one most likely to be injured by the dangerous act. In contrast to the Michael M. case, the Court in Kirchberg v. Feenstra (1981) found no important governmental interest was served by a Louisiana law allowing a husband to mortgage without his wife's consent their jointly owned home.

The strict scrutiny test is an exception to the rule of constitutional interpretation that presumes that laws and acts of government are constitutional and in this sense the

II

Whenever called upon to judge the constitutionality of an Act of Congress—"the gravest and most delicate duty that this Court is called upon to perform," Blodgett v. Holden (1927) (Holmes, J.)—the Court accords "great weight to the decisions of Congress." CBS, Inc. v. Democratic National Committee (1973). The Congress is a coequal branch of government whose members take the same oath we do to uphold the Constitution of the United States. As Justice Frankfurter noted in Joint Anti-Fascist Refugee Committee v. McGrath (1951) (concurring opinion), we must have "due regard to the fact that this Court is not exercising a primary judgment but is sitting in judgment upon those who also have taken the oath to observe the Constitution and who have the responsibility for carrying on government." The customary deference accorded the judgments of Congress is certainly appropriate when, as here, Congress specifically considered the question of the Act's constitutionality.

This is not, however, merely a case involving the customary deference accorded congressional decisions. The case arises in the context of Congress' authority over national defense and military affairs, and perhaps in no other area has the Court accorded Congress greater deference. In rejecting the registration of women, Congress explicitly relied upon its constitutional powers under Art. I, § 8, cls. 12–14. The "specific findings" section of the Report of the Senate Armed Services Committee, later adopted by both Houses of Congress, began by stating: "Article I, section 8 of the Constitution commits exclusively to the Congress the powers to raise and support armies, provide and maintain a Navy, and make rules for Government and regulation of the land and naval forces, and pursuant to these powers it lies within the discretion of the Congress to determine the occasions for expansion of our Armed Forces, and the means best suited to such expansion should it prove necessary."

The operation of a healthy deference to legislative and executive judgments in the area of military affairs is evident in several recent decisions of this Court. The Court here reviews a number of cases in which the Court has permitted the reduction of the First Amendment rights of military personnel and of civilians wishing to make political speeches on military property.

None of this is to say that Congress is free to disregard the Constitution when it acts in the area of military affairs. In that area as any other Congress remains subject to the limitations of the Due Process Clause, see Ex parte Milligan (1866), but the tests and limitations to be applied may differ because of the military context. We of course do not abdicate our ultimate responsibility to decide the constitutional question, but simply recognize that the Constitution itself requires such deference to congressional choice. In deciding the question before us we must be particularly careful not to substitute our judgment of what is desirable for that of Congress, or our own evaluation of evidence for a reasonable evaluation by the Legislative Branch.

The District Court purported to recognize the appropriateness of deference to Congress when that body was exercising its constitutionally delegated authority over military affairs but it stressed that "[w]e are not here concerned with military operations or day-to-day conduct of the military into which we have no desire to intrude." Appellees also stress that this case involves civilians, not the military, and that "the impact of registration on the military is only indirect and attenuated." We find these efforts to divorce registration from the military and national defense context, with all the deference called for in that context, singularly unpersuasive. United States v. O'Brien (1968) recognized the broad deference due Congress in the selective service area before us in this case. Registration is not an end in itself in the civilian world but rather the first step in the induction process into the military one, and Congress specifically linked its consideration of registration to induction. Congressional judgments concerning registration and the draft are based on judgments concerning military operations and needs ("the starting point for any discussion of the appropriateness of registering women for the draft is the question of the proper role of women in combat"), and the deference unquestionably due the latter judgments is necessarily required in assessing the former as well. Although the District Court stressed that it was not intruding on military questions, its opinion was based on assessments of military need and flexibility in a time of mobilization. It would be blinking reality to say that our precedents requiring deference to Congress in military affairs are not implicated by the present case.* . . .

No one could deny that under the test of Craig v. Boren the Government's interest in raising and supporting armies is an "important governmental interest." Congress and its committees carefully considered and debated two alternative means of furthering that interest: the first was to register only males for potential conscription, and the other was to register both sexes. Congress chose the former alternative. When that decision is challenged on equal protection grounds, the question a court must decide is not which alternative it would have chosen, had it been the primary decisionmaker, but whether that chosen by Congress denies equal protection of the laws.

Nor can it be denied that the imposing number of cases from this Court previously cited suggest that judicial deference to such congressional exercise of authority is at its apogee when legislative action under the congressional authority to raise and support armies and make rules and regulations for their governance is challenged. As previously noted, *ante,* at 9, deference

---

*Congress recognized that its decision on registration involved judgments on military needs and operations, and that its decisions were entitled to particular deference: "The Supreme Court's most recent teachings in the field of equal protection cannot be read in isolation from its opinions giving great deference to the judgment of Congress and military commanders in dealing with the management of military forces and the requirements of military discipline. The Court has made it unmistakably clear that even our most fundamental constitutional rights must in some circumstances be modified in the light of military needs, and that Congress' judgment as to what is necessary to preserve our national security is entitled to great deference."

does not mean abdication. The reconciliation between the deference due Congress and our own constitutional responsibility is perhaps best instanced in Schlesinger v. Ballard (1975). . . .

Schlesinger v. Ballard did not purport to apply a different equal protection test because of the military context, but did stress the deference due congressional choices among alternatives in exercising the congressional authority to raise and support armies and make rules for their governance. In light of the floor debate and the report of the Senate Armed Services Committee hereinafter discussed, it is apparent that Congress was fully aware not merely of the many facts and figures presented to it by witnesses who testified before its committees, but of the current thinking as to the place of women in the Armed Services. In such a case, we cannot ignore Congress' broad authority conferred by the Constitution to raise and support armies when we are urged to declare unconstitutional its studied choice of one alternative in preference to another for furthering that goal.

III.

This case is quite different from several of the gender-based discrimination cases we have considered in that, despite appellees' assertions, Congress did not act "unthinkingly" or "reflexively and not for any considered reason." The question of registering women for the draft not only received considerable national attention and was the subject of wide-ranging public debate, but also was extensively considered by Congress in hearings, floor debate, and in committee. . . . The Court here reviews the legislative history of the Act.

The foregoing clearly establishes that the decision to exempt women from registration was not the "accidental byproduct of a traditional way of thinking about women." . . . The cause for rejecting the argument is considerably stronger here. The issue was considered at great length, and Congress clearly expressed its purpose and intent. Contrast Califano v. Westcott (1979) ("The gender qualification . . . escaped virtually unnoticed in the hearings and floor debate"). . . .

The MSSA established a plan for maintaining "adequate armed strength . . . to ensure the security of [the] nation." Registration is the first step "in a united and continuous process designed to raise an army speedily and efficiently," and Congress provided for the reactivation of registration in order to "provide the means for the early delivery of inductees in an emergency." Although the three-judge District Court often tried to sever its consideration of registration from the particulars of induction. Congress rather clearly linked the need for renewed registration with its views on the character of a subsequent draft. . . . Any assessment of the congressional purpose and its chosen means must therefore consider the registration scheme as a prelude to a draft in a time of national emergency. Any other approach would not be testing the Act in light of the purposes Congress sought to achieve.

Congress determined that any future draft, which would be facilitated by the registration scheme, would be characterized by a need for combat troops. The Senate Report explained, in a specific finding later adopted by both Houses, that "if mobilization were to be ordered in a wartime scenario, the primary manpower need would be for combat replacements." . . . Congress' determination that the need would be for combat troops if a draft took place was sufficiently supported by testimony adduced at the hearings so that the courts are not free to make their own judgment on the question. The purpose of registration, therefore, was to prepare for a draft *of combat troops.*

Women as a group, however, unlike men as a group, are not eligible for combat. The restrictions on the participation of women in combat in the Navy and Air Force are statutory. . . . The Army and Marine Corps preclude the use of women in combat as a matter of established policy. Congress specifically recognized and endorsed the exclusion of women from combat in exempting women from registration. . . .

The existence of the combat restrictions clearly indicates the basis for Congress' decision to exempt women from registration. The purpose of registration was to prepare for a draft of combat troops. Since women are excluded from combat, Congress concluded that they would not be needed in the event of a draft, and therefore decided not to register them. . . .

The District Court stressed that the military need for women was irrelevant to the issue of their registration. As that court put it: "Congress could not constitutionally require registration under MSSA of only black citizens or only white citizens, or single out any political or religious group simply because those groups contained sufficient persons to fill the needs of the Selective Service System." This reasoning is beside the point. The reason women are exempt from registration is not because military needs can be met by drafting men. This is not a case of Congress arbitrarily choosing to burden one of two similarly situated groups, such as would be the case with an all-black or all-white, or an all-Catholic or all-Lutheran, or an all-Republican or all-Democratic registration. Men and women, because of the combat restrictions on women, are simply not similarly situated for purposes of a draft or registration for a draft.

Congress' decision to authorize the registration of only men, therefore, does not violate the Due Process Clause. The exemption of women from registration is not only sufficiently but closely related to Congress' purpose in authorizing registration. The fact that Congress and the Executive have decided that women should not serve in combat fully justifies Congress in not authorizing their registration, since the purpose of registration is to develop a pool of potential combat troops. . . . The Constitution requires that Congress treat similarly situated persons similarly, not that it engage in gestures of superficial equality.

In holding the MSSA constitutionally invalid the District Court relied heavily on the President's decision to seek authority to register women and the testimony of members of the Executive Branch and the military in support of that decision. As stated by the Administration's witnesses before Congress, however, the President's "decision to ask for authority to register women is based on equity." . . . This was also the basis for the testimony by military officials. The Senate Report, evaluating the testimony before the Committee, recognized that "the argument for registration and induction of women . . . is not based on military necessity, but on considerations of equity." Congress was certainly entitled, in the exercise of its constitutional powers to raise and regulate armies and navies, to focus on the question of military need rather than "equity." . . .

Although the military experts who testified in favor of registering women uniformly opposed the actual drafting of women, there was testimony that in the event of a draft of 650,000 the military could absorb some 80,000 female inductees. The 80,000 would be used to fill noncombat positions, freeing men to go to the front. In relying on this testimony in striking down the MSSA, the District Court palpably exceeded its authority when it ignored Congress' considered response to this line of reasoning.

In the first place, assuming that a small number of women could be drafted for noncombat roles, Congress simply did not consider it worth the added burdens of including women in draft and registration plans. . . . As the Senate Committee recognized a year before, "training would be needlessly burdened by women recruits who could not be used in combat." . . . It is not for this Court to dismiss such problems as insignificant in the context of military preparedness and the exigencies of a future mobilization.

Congress also concluded that whatever the need for women for noncombat roles during mobilization, whether 80,000 or less, it could be met by volunteers. . . .

Most significantly, Congress determined that staffing noncombat positions with women during a mobilization would be positively detrimental to the important goal of military flexibility. "There are other military reasons that preclude very large numbers of women from serving. Military flexibility requires that a commander be able to move units or ships quickly. Units or ships not located at the front or not previously scheduled for the front nevertheless must be able to move into action if necessary. In peace and war, significant rotation of personnel is necessary. We should not divide the military into two groups—one in permanent combat and one in permanent support. Large numbers of non-combat positions must be available to which combat troops can return for duty before being redeployed."

In sum, Congress carefully evaluated the testimony that 80,000 women conscripts could be usefully employed in the event of a draft and rejected it in the permissible exercise of its constitutional responsibility. . . . The District Court was quite wrong in undertaking an independent evaluation of this evidence, rather than adopting an appropriately deferential examination of Congress' evaluation of that evidence.

In light of the foregoing, we conclude that Congress acted well within it constitutional authority when it authorized the registration of men, and not women, under the Military Selective Service Act. The decision of the District Court holding otherwise is accordingly

Reversed.

Justice White, with whom *Justice Brennan* joins, dissenting, said in part:

I assume what has not been challenged in this case—that excluding women from combat positions does not offend the Constitution. Granting that, it is self evident that if during mobilization for war, all noncombat military positions must be filled by combat-qualified personnel available to be moved into combat positions, there would be no occasion whatsoever to have any women in the Army, whether as volunteers or inductees. The Court appears to say that Congress concluded as much and that we should accept that judgment even though the serious view of the Executive Branch, including the responsible military services, is to the contrary. The Court's position in this regard is most unpersuasive. I perceive little, if any, indication that Congress itself concluded that every position in the military, no matter how far removed from combat, must be filled with combat-ready men. Common sense and experience in recent wars, where women volunteers were employed in substantial numbers, belie this view of reality. It should not be ascribed to Congress, particularly in the face of the testimony of military authorities, hereafter referred to, that there would be a substantial number of positions in the services that could be filled by women both in peacetime and during mobilization, even though they are ineligible for combat.

I would also have little difficulty agreeing to a reversal if all the women who could serve in wartime without adversely affecting combat readiness could predictably be obtained through volunteers. In that event, the equal protection component of the Fifth Amendment would not require the United States to go through, and a large segment of the population to be burdened with, the expensive and essentially useless procedure of registering women. But again I cannot agree with the Court that Congress concluded or that the legislative record indicates that each of the services could rely on women volunteers to fill all the positions for which they might be eligible in the event of mobilization. On the contrary, the record as I understand it, supports the District Court's finding that the services would have to conscript at least 80,000 persons to fill positions for which combat-ready men would not be required. The consistent position of the Defense Department representatives was that their best estimate of the number of women draftees who could be used productively by the Services in the event of a major mobilization would be approximately 80,000 over the first six months. . . . Except for a single, unsupported, and ambiguous statement in the Senate Report to the effect that "women volunteers would fill the requirements for women," there is no indication that Congress rejected the Defense Department's figures or relied upon an alternative set of figures. . . .

The Court also submits that because the primary purpose of registration and conscription is to supply combat troops and because the great majority of noncombat positions must be filled by combat-trained men ready to be rotated into combat, the absolute number of positions for which women would be eligible is so small as to be *de minimus* and of no moment for equal protection purposes, especially in light of the administrative burdens involved in registering all women of suitable age. There is some sense to this; but at least on the record before us, the number of women who could be used in the military without sacrificing combat-readiness is not at all small or insubstantial, and administrative convenience has not been sufficient justification for the kind of outright gender-based discrimination involved in registering and conscripting men but no women at all.

As I understand the record, then, in order to secure the personnel it needs during mobilization; the Government cannot rely on volunteers and must register and draft not only to fill combat positions and those noncombat positions that must be filled by combat-trained men, but also to secure the personnel needed for jobs that can be performed by persons ineligible for combat without diminishing military effectiveness. The claim is that in providing for the latter category of positions, Congress is free to register and draft only men. I discern no adequate justification for this kind of discrimination between men and women. Accordingly, with all due respect, I dissent.

Justice Marshall, with whom *Justice Brennan* joins, dissenting, said in part:

I.

A.

The background to this litigation is set out in the opinion of the Court and I will not repeat that discussion here. It bears emphasis, however, that the only question presented by this case is whether the exclusion of women from registration under the Military Selective Service Act (MSSA) contravenes the equal protection component of the Due Process Clause of the Fifth Amendment. Although the purpose of registration is to assist preparations for drafting civilians into the military, *we are not asked to rule on the constitutionality of a statute governing conscription.* * With the advent of the All-Volunteer Armed Forces, The MSSA was specifically amended to preclude conscription as of July 1, 1973, and reactivation of the draft would therefore require a legislative amendment. Consequently, we are not called upon to decide whether either men or women can be drafted at all, whether they must be drafted in equal numbers, in what order they should be drafted, or once inducted, how they are to be trained for their respective functions. In addition, this case does not involve a challenge to the statutes or policies that prohibit female members of the Armed Forces from serving in combat. It is with this understanding that I turn to the task at hand.

B.

By now it should be clear that statutes like the MSSA, which discriminate on the basis of gender, must be examined under the "heightened" scrutiny

---

*Given the Court's lengthy discourse on the background to this litigation, it is interesting that the Court chooses to bury its sole reference to this fact in a footnote. See *ante,* at 2, n. 1.

mandated by Craig v. Boren (1976). Under this test, a gender-based classification cannot withstand constitutional challenge unless the classification is substantially related to the achievement of an important governmental objective. . . . This test applies whether the classification discriminates against males or females. . . . The party defending the challenged classification carries the burden of demonstrating both the importance of the governmental objective it serves and the substantial relationship between the discriminatory means and the asserted end. . . . Consequently, before we can sustain the MSSA, the Government must demonstrate that the gender-based classification it employs bears "a close and substantial relationship to [the achievement of] important governmental objectives." . . .

C.

The MSSA states that "an adequate armed strength must be achieved and maintained to insure the security of this Nation." I agree with the majority, *ante,* at 12, that "none could deny that . . . the Government's interest in raising and supporting armies is an 'important governmental interest.' " Consequently, the first part of the Craig v. Boren, test is satisfied. But the question remains whether the discriminatory means employed itself substantially serves the statutory end.

. . . When, as here, a federal law that classifies on the basis of gender is challenged as violating this constitutional guarantee, it is ultimately for this Court, not Congress, to decide whether there exists the constitutionally required "close and substantial relationship" between the discriminatory means employed and the asserted governmental objective. In my judgment, there simply is no basis for concluding in this case that excluding women from registration is substantially related to the achievement of a concededly important governmental interest in maintaining an effective defense. The Court reaches a contrary conclusion only by using an "[a]nnounced degre[e] of 'deference' to legislative judgmen[t]" as "facile abstractio[n] . . . to justify a particular result."

II.

A.

The Government does not defend the exclusion of women from registration on the ground that preventing women from serving in the military is substantially related to the effectiveness of the Armed Forces. Indeed, the successful experience of women serving in all branches of the Armed Services would belie any such claim. Some 150,000 women volunteers are presently on active service in the military, and their number is expected to increase to over 250,000 by 1985. Congress has never disagreed with the judgment of the military experts that women have made significant contributions to the effectiveness of the military. On the contrary, Congress has repeatedly praised the performance of female members of the Armed Forces, and has approved efforts by the Armed Services to expand their role. . . . Thus, Congress' decision to exclude women from registration— and therefore from a draft drawing on the pool of registrants—cannot rest on a supposed need to prevent women from serving in the Armed Forces. The justification for the MSSA's gender-based discrimination must therefore be found in considerations that are peculiar to the objectives of registration.

The most authoritative discussion of Congress' reasons for declining to require registration of women is contained in the report prepared by the Senate Armed Services Committee on the Fiscal Year 1981 Defense Authorization Bill. . . . The Senate Report sets out the objectives Congress sought to accomplish by excluding women from registration and this Court may appropriately look to the Report in evaluating the justification for the discrimination.

B.

According to the Senate Report, "[t]he policy precluding the use of women in combat is . . . the most important reason for not including women in a registration system." . . . Had appellees raised a constitutional challenge to the prohibition against assignment of women to combat, this discussion in the Senate Report might well provide persuasive reasons for upholding the restrictions. But the validity of the combat restrictions is not an issue we need decide in this case. Moreover, since the combat restrictions on women have already been accomplished through statutes and policies that remain in force whether or not women are required to register or drafted, including women in registration and draft plans will not result in their being assigned to combat roles. Thus, even assuming that precluding the use of women in combat is an important governmental interest in its own right, there can be no suggestion that the exclusion of women from registration and a draft is substantially related to the achievement of this goal.

The Court's opinion offers a different though related explanation of the relationship between the combat restrictions and Congress' decision not to require registration of women. The majority states that "Congress . . . clearly linked the need for renewed registration with its views of the character of a subsequent draft." The Court also states that "Congress determined that any future draft, which would be facilitated by the registration scheme, would be characterized by a need for combat troops." The Court then reasons that since women are not eligible for assignment to combat, Congress' decision to exclude them from registration is not unconstitutional discrimination inasmuch as "[m]en and women, because of the combat restrictions on women, are simply not similarly situated for purposes of a draft or registration for a draft." There is a certain logic to this reasoning, but the Court's approach is fundamentally flawed.

In the first place, although the Court purports to apply the Craig v. Boren test, the "similarly situated" analysis the Court employs is in fact significantly different from the Craig v. Boren approach. . . . The Court essentially reasons that the gender classification employed by the MSSA is constitutionally permissible because nondiscrimination is not necessary to achieve the purpose of registration to prepare for a draft of combat troops. In other words, the majority concludes that women may be excluded from registration because they will not be needed in the event of a draft.

This analysis, however, focuses on the wrong question. The relevant inquiry under the Craig v. Boren test is not whether a *gender-neutral* classification would substantially advance important governmental interests. Rather, the question is whether the gender-based classification is itself substantially related to the achievement of the asserted governmental interest. Thus, the Government's task in this case is to demonstrate that excluding women from registration substantially furthers the goal of preparing for a draft of combat troops. Or to put it another way, the Government must show that registering women would substantially impede its efforts to prepare for such a draft. Under our precedents, the Government cannot meet this burden without showing that a gender-neutral statute would be a less effective means of attaining this end. . . . In this case, the Government makes no claim that preparing for a draft of combat troops cannot be accomplished just as effectively by *registering* both men and women but *drafting* only men if only men turn out to be needed.* Nor can the Government argue that this alternative entails the additional cost and administrative inconvenience of registering women. This Court has repeatedly stated that the administrative convenience of employing a gender classification is not an adequate constitutional justification under the Craig v. Boren test. See, e.g., Craig v. Boren; Frontiero v. Richardson (1973).

The fact that registering women in no way obstructs the governmental interest in preparing for a draft of combat troops points up a second flaw in the Court's analysis. The Court essentially reduces the question of the constitutionality of male-only *registration* to the validity of a hypothetical program for *conscripting* only men. The Court posits a draft in which *all* conscripts are either assigned to those specific combat posts presently closed to women or must be available for rotation into such positions. By so doing, the Court is able to conclude that registering women would be no more than a "gestur[e] of superficial equality," since women are necessarily ineligible for every position to be filled in its hypothetical draft. If it could indeed be guaranteed in advance that conscription would be reimposed by Congress only in circumstances where, and in a form under which, all conscripts would have to be trained for and assigned to combat or combat rotation positions from which women are categorically excluded, then it could be argued that registration of women would be pointless.

. . . As noted, the majority simply assumes that registration prepares for

---

*Alternatively, the Government could employ a classification that is related to the statutory objective but is not based on gender, for example, combat eligibility. Under the current scheme, large subgroups of the male population who are ineligible for combat because of physical handicaps or conscientious objector status are nonetheless required to register.

a draft in which *every* draftee must be available for assignment to combat. But the majority's draft scenario finds no support in either the testimony before Congress, or more importantly, in the findings of the Senate Report. Indeed, the scenario appears to exist only in the Court's imagination, for even the Government represents only that "in the event of mobilization, *approximately two-thirds* of the demand on the induction system would be for *combat skills.*" . . .

C.

Nothing in the Senate Report supports the Court's intimation that women must be excluded from registration because combat eligibility is a prerequisite for *all* the positions that would need to be filled in the event of a draft. . . . In testifying about the Defense Department's reasons for concluding that women should be included in registration plans, [Assistant Secretary of Defense] Pirie stated: "It is in the interest of national security that, in an emergency requiring the conscription for military service of the nation's youth, the best qualified people for a wide variety of tasks in our Armed Forces be available. The performance of women in our Armed Forces today strongly supports the conclusion that many of the best qualified people for some military jobs in the 18–26 age category will be women." The Defense Department also concluded that there are no military reasons that would justify excluding women from registration. . . . All four Service Chiefs agreed that there are no military reasons for refusing to register women and uniformly advocated requiring registration of women. . . .

Against this background, the testimony at the congressional hearings focused on projections of manpower needs in the event of an emergency requiring reinstitution of the draft, and, in particular, on the role of women in such a draft. . . . Since the classification precludes women from being drafted to fill positions for which they would be qualified and useful, the Government must demonstrate that excluding women from those positions is substantially related to the achievement of an important governmental objective.

III.

The Government argues, however, that the "consistent testimony before Congress was to the effect that there is *no military need* to draft women." And the Government points to a statement in the Senate Report that "[b]oth the civilian and military leadership agreed that there was no military need to draft women. . . . The argument for registration and induction of women . . . is not based on military necessity, but on considerations of equity." In accepting the Government's contention, the Court asserts that the President's decision to seek authority to register women was based on "equity," and concludes that "Congress was certainly entitled, in the exercise of its constitutional powers to raise and regulate armies and navies, to focus on the question of military need rather than 'equity.' " In my view, a more careful examination of the concepts of "equity" and "military need" is required. . . .

. . . By "considerations of equity," the military experts acknowledged that female conscripts can perform as well as male conscripts in certain positions, and that there is therefore no reason why one group should be totally excluded from registration and a draft. Thus, what the majority so blithely dismisses as "equity" is nothing less than the Fifth Amendment's guarantee of equal protection of the laws which "requires that Congress treat similarly situated persons similarly."

. . . To be sure, there is no "military need" to draft women in the sense that a war could be waged without their participation. This fact is, however, irrelevant to resolving the constitutional issue. As previously noted, it is not appellees' burden to prove that registration of women substantially furthers the objectives of the MSSA. Rather, because eligibility for combat is not a requirement for some of the positions to be filled in the event of a draft, it is incumbent on the Government to show that excluding women from a draft to fill those positions substantially furthers an important governmental objective.

It may be, however, that the Senate Report's allusion to "military need" is meant to convey Congress' expectation that women volunteers will make it unnecessary to draft any women. . . . But since the purpose of registration is to protect against unanticipated shortages of volunteers, it is difficult to see how excluding women from registration can be justified by conjectures about the expected number of female volunteers. I fail to see why the exclusion of a pool of persons who would be conscripted only *if needed* can be justified by reference to the current supply of volunteers. In any event, the Defense Department's best estimate is that in the event of a mobilization requiring reinstitution of the draft, there will not be enough women volunteers to fill the positions for which women would be eligible. . . . Thus, however the "military need" statement in the Senate Report is understood, it does not provide the constitutionally required justification for the total exclusion of women from registration and draft plans.

Constitution of
the United States

WE THE PEOPLE of the United States, in order to form a more perfect union, establish justice, insure domestic tranquility, provide for the common defense, promote the general welfare, and secure the blessings of liberty to ourselves and our posterity, do ordain and establish this Constitution for the United States of America.

Article I

SECTION 1.   All legislative powers herein granted shall be vested in a Congress of the United States, which shall consist of a Senate and House of Representatives.

SECTION 2.   (1) The House of Representatives shall be composed of members chosen every second year by the people of the several States, and the electors in each State shall have the qualifications requisite for electors of the most numerous branch of the State legislature.

(2) No person shall be a Representative who shall not have attained to the age of twenty-five years, and been seven years a citizen of the United States and who shall not, when elected, be an inhabitant of that State in which he shall be chosen.

(3) Representatives and direct taxes* shall be apportioned among the several States which may be included within this Union, according to their

---

*Modified as to income taxes by the 16th Amendment.

respective numbers, which shall be determined by adding to the whole number of free persons, including those bound to service for a term of years, and excluding Indians not taxed, three fifths of all other persons.* The actual enumeration shall be made within three years after the first meeting of the Congress of the United States, and within every subsequent term of ten years, in such manner as they shall by law direct. The number of Representatives shall not excede one for every thirty thousand, but each State shall have at least one Representative; and until such enumeration shall be made, the State of New Hampshire shall be entitled to choose three, Massachusetts eight, Rhode Island and Providence Plantations one, Connecticut five, New York six, New Jersey four, Pennsylvania eight, Delaware one, Maryland six, Virginia ten, North Carolina five, South Carolina five, and Georgia three.

(4) When vacancies happen in the representation from any State, the executive authority thereof shall issue writs of election to fill such vacancies.

(5) The House of Representatives shall choose their Speaker and other officers; and shall have the sole power of impeachment.

SECTION 3 (1) The Senate of the United States shall be composed of two Senators from each State, chosen by the legislature thereof,** for six years; and each Senator shall have one vote.

(2) Immediately after they shall be assembled in consequence of the first election, they shall be divided as equally as may be into three classes. The seats of the Senators of the first class shall be vacated at the expiration of the second year, of the second class at the expiration of the fourth year, and of the third class at the expiration of the sixth year, so that one third may be chosen every second year; and if vacancies happen by resignation, or otherwise, during the recess of the legislature of any State, the executive thereof may make temporary appointments until the next meeting of the legislature, which† shall then fill such vacancies.

(3) No person shall be a Senator who shall not have attained to the age of thirty years, and been nine years a citizen of the United States, and who shall not, when elected, be an inhabitant of that State for which he shall be chosen.

(4) The Vice President of the United States shall be president of the Senate, but shall have no vote, unless they be equally divided.

(5) The Senate shall choose their other officers, and also a president pro tempore, in the absence of the Vice President, or when he shall exercise the office of President of the United States.

(6) The Senate shall have the sole power to try all impeachments. When sitting for that purpose, they shall be on oath or affirmation. When the President of the United States is tried, the Chief Justice shall preside: and no person shall be convicted without the concurrence of two thirds of the members present.

---

*Replaced by the 14th Amendment.
**Modified by the 17th Amendment.
†Modified by the 17th Amendment.

(7) Judgment in cases of impeachment shall not extend further than to removal from office, and disqualification to hold and enjoy any office of honor, trust or profit under the United States: but the party convicted shall nevertheless be liable and subject to indictment, trial, judgment and punishment, according to law.

SECTION 4 (1) The times, places and manner of holding elections for Senators and Representatives, shall be prescribed in each State by the legislature thereof; but the Congress may at any time by law make or alter such regulations, except as to the places of choosing Senators.

(2) The Congress shall assemble at least once in every year, and such meeting shall be on the first Monday in December, unless they shall by law appoint a different day.

SECTION 5 (1) Each House shall be the judge of the elections, returns and qualifications of its own members, and a majority of each shall constitute a quorum to do business; but a smaller number may adjourn from day to day, and may be authorized to compel the attendance of absent members, in such manner, and under such penalties as each House may provide.

(2) Each House may determine the rules of its proceedings, punish its members for disorderly behavior, and, with the concurrence of two thirds, expel a member.

(3) Each House shall keep a journal of its proceedings, and from time to time publish the same, excepting such parts as may in their judgment require secrecy; and the yeas and nays of the members of either House on any question shall, at the desire of one fifth of those present, be entered on the journal.

(4) Neither House, during the session of Congress, shall, without the consent of the other, adjourn for more than three days, nor to any other place than that in which the two Houses shall be sitting.

SECTION 6 (1) The Senators and Representatives shall receive a compensation for their services, to be ascertained by law, and paid out of the Treasury of the United States. They shall in all cases, except treason, felony and breach of the peace, be privileged from arrest during their attendance at the session of their respective Houses, and in going to and returning from the same; and for any speech or debate in either House, they shall not be questioned in any other place.

(2) No Senator or Representative shall, during the time for which he was elected, be appointed to any civil office under the authority of the United States, which shall have been created, or the emoluments whereof shall have been increased during such time; and no person holding any office under the United States, shall be a member of either House during his continuance in office.

SECTION 7 (1) All bills for raising revenue shall originate in the House of Representatives; but the Senate may propose or concur with amendments as on other bills.

(2) Every bill which shall have passed the House of Representatives and the Senate, shall, before it become a law, be presented to the President of the United States; if he approve he shall sign it, but if not he shall return it, with his objections to that House in which it shall have originated, who shall enter the objections at large on their journal, and proceed to reconsider it. If after such reconsideration two thirds of that House shall agree to pass the bill, it shall be sent, together with the objections, to the other House, by which it shall likewise be reconsidered, and if approved by two thirds of that House, it shall become a law. But in all such cases the votes of both Houses shall be determined by yeas and nays, and the names of the persons voting for and against the bill shall be entered on the journal of each House respectively. If any bill shall not be returned by the President within ten days (Sundays excepted) after it shall have been presented to him, the same shall be a law, in like manner as if he had signed it, unless the Congress by their adjournment prevent its return, in which case it shall not be a law.

(3) Every order, resolution, or vote to which the concurrence of the Senate and House of Representatives may be necessary (except on a question of adjournment) shall be presented to the President of the United States; and before the same shall take effect, shall be approved by him, or being disapproved by him, shall be repassed by two thirds of the Senate and House of Representatives, according to the rules and limitations prescribed in the case of a bill.

SECTION 8 (1) The Congress shall have power to lay and collect taxes, duties, imposts and excises, to pay the debts and provide for the common defense and general welfare of the United States; but all duties, imposts and excises shall be uniform throughout the United States;

(2) To borrow money on the credit of the United States;

(3) To regulate commerce with foreign nations, and among the several States, and with the Indian tribes;

(4) To establish an uniform rule of naturalization, and uniform laws on the subject of bankruptcies throughout the United States;

(5) To coin money, regulate the value thereof, and of foreign coin, and fix the standard of weights and measures;

(6) To provide for the punishment of counterfeiting the securities and current coin of the United States;

(7) To establish post offices and post roads;

(8) To promote the progress of science and useful arts, by securing for limited times to authors and inventors the exclusive right to their respective writings and discoveries;

(9) To constitute tribunals inferior to the Supreme Court;

(10) To define and punish piracies and felonies committed on the high seas, and offenses against the law of nations;

(11) To declare war, grant letters of marque and reprisal, and make rules concerning captures on land and water;

(12) To raise and support armies, but no appropriation of money to that use shall be for a longer term than two years;

(13) To provide and maintain a navy;

(14) To make rules for the government and regulation of the land and naval forces;

(15) To provide for calling forth the militia to execute the laws of the Union, suppress insurrections and repel invasions;

(16) To provide for organizing, arming, and disciplining the militia, and for governing such part of them as may be employed in the service of the United States, reserving to the States respectively, the appointment of the officers, and the authority of training the militia according to the discipline prescribed by Congress;

(17) To exercise exclusive legislation in all cases whatsoever, over such district (not exceeding ten miles square) as may, by cession of particular States, and the acceptance of Congress, become the seat of the government of the United States, and to exercise like authority over all places purchased by the consent of the legislature of the State in which the same shall be, for the erection of forts, magazines, dockyards, and other needful buildings; and

(18) To make all laws which shall be necessary and proper for carrying into execution the foregoing powers, and all other powers vested by this Constitution in the government of the United States, or in any department or officer thereof.

SECTION 9 (1) The migration or importation of such persons as any of the States now existing shall think proper to admit, shall not be prohibited by the Congress prior to the year one thousand eight hundred and eight, but a tax or duty may be imposed on such importation, not exceeding ten dollars for each person.

(2) The privilege of the writ of habeas corpus shall not be suspended, unless when in cases of rebellion or invasion the public safety may require it.

(3) No bill of attainder or ex post facto law shall be passed.

(4) No capitation, or other direct, tax shall be laid, unless in proportion to the census or enumeration herein before directed to be taken.*

(5) No tax or duty shall be laid on articles exported from any State.

(6) No preference shall be given by any regulation of commerce or revenue to the ports of one State over those of another: nor shall vessels bound to, or from, one State, be obliged to enter, clear, or pay duties in another.

(7) No money shall be drawn from the Treasury, but in consequence of appropriations made by law; and a regular statement and account of the receipts and expenditures of all public money shall be published from time to time.

(8) No title of nobility shall be granted by the United States: and no person holding any office of profit or trust under them, shall, without the consent of the Congress, accept of any present, emolument, office, or title, of any kind whatever, from any king, prince, or foreign State.

---

*Modified by the 16th Amendment.

SECTION 10 (1) No State shall enter into any treaty, alliance, or confederation; grant letters of marque and reprisal; coin money; emit bills of credit; make anything but gold and silver coin a tender in payment of debts; pass any bill of attainder, ex post facto law, or law impairing the obligation of contracts, or grant any title of nobility.

(2) No State shall, without the consent of Congress, lay any imposts or duties on imports or exports, except what may be absolutely necessary for executing its inspection laws; and the net produce of all duties and imposts, laid by any State on imports or exports, shall be for the use of the Treasury of the United States; and all such laws shall be subject to the revision and control of the Congress.

(3) No State shall, without the consent of Congress, lay any duty of tonnage, keep troops, or ships of war in time of peace, enter into any agreement or compact with another State, or with a foreign power, or engage in war, unless actually invaded, or in such imminent danger as will not admit of delay.

Article II

SECTION 1 (1) The executive power shall be vested in a President of the United States of America. He shall hold his office during the term of four years, and, together with the Vice President, chosen for the same term, be elected, as follows:

(2) Each State shall appoint, in such manner as the legislature thereof may direct, a number of electors, equal to the whole number of Senators and Representatives to which the State may be entitled in the Congress: but no Senator or Representative, or person holding an office of trust or profit under the United States, shall be appointed an elector.

The electors* shall meet in their respective States, and vote by ballot for two persons, of whom one at least shall not be an inhabitant of the same State with themselves. And they shall make a list of all the persons voted for, and of the number of votes for each; which list they shall sign and certify, and transmit sealed to the seat of the government of the United States, directed to the president of the Senate. The president of the Senate shall, in the presence of the Senate and House of Representatives, open all the certificates, and the votes shall then be counted. The person having the greatest number of votes shall be the President, if such number be a majority of the whole number of electors appointed; and if there be more than one who have such majority, and have an equal number of votes, then the House of Representatives shall immediately choose by ballot one of them for President; and if no person have a majority, then from the five highest on the list the said House shall in like manner choose the President. But in choosing the President, the votes shall be taken by States, the representation from each State having one vote; a quorum for this purpose shall consist of a member or members from two thirds of the States, and a majority of all the

---

*This paragraph was replaced in 1804 by the 12th Amendment.

States shall be necessary to a choice. In every case, after the choice of the President, the person having the greatest number of votes of the electors shall be the Vice President. But if there should remain two or more who have equal votes, the Senate shall choose from them by ballot the Vice President.

(3) The Congress may determine the time of choosing the electors, and the day on which they shall give their votes; which day shall be the same throughout the United States.

(4) No person except a natural born citizen, or a citizen of the United States, at the time of the adoption of this Constitution, shall be eligible to the office of President; neither shall any person be eligible to that office who shall not have attained to the age of thirty five years, and been fourteen years a resident within the United States.

(5) In the case of the removal of the President from office, or of his death, resignation, or inability to discharge the powers and duties of the said office,* the same shall devolve on the Vice President, and the Congress may by law provide for the case of removal, death, resignation, or inability, both of the President and Vice President, declaring what officer shall then act as president, and such officer shall act accordingly, until the disability be removed, or a President shall be elected.

(6) The President shall, at stated times, receive for his services, a compensation, which shall neither be increased nor diminished during the period for which he shall have been elected, and he shall not receive within that period any other emolument from the United States, or any of them.

(7) Before he enter on the execution of his office, he shall take the following oath or affirmation:—"I do solemnly swear (or affirm) that I will faithfully execute the office of the President of the United States, and will to the best of my ability, preserve, protect and defend the Constitution of the United States."

SECTION 2 (1) The President shall be commander in chief of the army and navy of the United States, and of the militia of the several States, when called into the actual service of the United States; he may require the opinion, in writing, of the principal officer in each of the executive departments, upon any subject relating to the duties of their respective offices, and he shall have power to grant reprieves and pardons for offenses against the United States, except in cases of impeachment.

(2) He shall have power, by and with the advice and consent of the Senate, to make treaties, provided two thirds of the Senators present concur; and he shall nominate, and by and with the advice and consent of the Senate, shall appoint ambassadors, other public ministers and consuls, judges of the Supreme Court, and all other officers of the United States, whose appointments are not herein otherwise provided for, and which shall be established by law: but the Congress may by law vest the appointment of such inferior officers, as they think proper, in the President alone, in the courts of law, or in the heads of departments.

---

*Modified in 1967 by the 25th Amendment.

(3) The President shall have power to fill up all vacancies that may happen during the recess of the Senate, by granting commissions which shall expire at the end of their next session.

SECTION 3   He shall from time to time give to the Congress information of the state of the Union, and recommend to their consideration such measures as he shall judge necessary and expedient; he may, on extraordinary occasions, convene both Houses, or either of them, and in case of disagreement between them, with respect to the time of adjournment, he may adjourn them to such time as he shall think proper; he shall receive ambassadors and other public ministers; he shall take care that the laws be faithfully executed, and shall commission all the officers of the United States.

SECTION 4   The President, Vice President and all civil officers of the United States, shall be removed from office on impeachment for, and conviction of, treason, bribery, or other high crimes and misdemeanors.

Article III

SECTION 1   The judicial power of the United States, shall be vested in one Supreme Court, and in such inferior courts as the Congress may from time to time ordain and establish. The judges, both of the Supreme and inferior courts, shall hold their offices during good behavior, and shall, at stated times, receive for their services, a compensation, which shall not be diminished during their continuance in office.

SECTION 2   (1) The judicial power shall extend to all cases, in law and equity, arising under this Constitution, the laws of the United States, and treaties made, or which shall be made, under their authority;—to all cases affecting ambassadors, other public ministers and consuls;—to all cases of admiralty and maritime jurisdiction;—to controversies to which the United states shall be a party;—to controversies between two or more States;—between a State and citizens of another State;* —between citizens of different States;—between citizens of the same State claiming lands under grants of different States, and between a State, or the citizens thereof, and foreign States, citizens or subjects.

(2) In all cases affecting ambassadors, other public ministers and consuls, and those in which a State shall be party, the Supreme Court shall have original jurisdiction. In all the other cases before mentioned, the Supreme Court shall have appellate jurisdiction, both as to law and fact, with such exceptions, and under such regulations as the Congress shall make.

---

*Restricted by the 11th Amendment.

(3) The trial of all crimes, except in cases of impeachment, shall be by jury; and such trial shall be held in the State where the said crimes shall have been committed; but when not committed within any State, the trial shall be at such place or places as the Congress may by law have directed.

SECTION 3 (1) Treason against the United States, shall consist only in levying war against them, or in adhering to their enemies, giving them aid and comfort. No person shall be convicted of treason unless on the testimony of two witnesses to the same overt act, or on confession in open court.

(2) The Congress shall have power to declare the punishment of treason, but no attainder of treason shall work corruption of blood, or forfeiture except during the life of the person attainted.

Article IV

SECTION 1 Full faith and credit shall be given in each State to the public acts, records, and judicial proceedings of every other State. And the Congress may by general laws prescribe the manner in which such acts, records and proceedings shall be proved, and the effect thereof.

SECTION 2 (1) The citizens of each State shall be entitled to all privileges and immunities of citizens in the several States.

(2) A person charged in any State with treason, felony, or other crime, who shall flee from justice, and be found in another State, shall on demand of the executive authority of the State from which he fled, be delivered up, to be removed to the State having jurisdiction of the crime.

(3) No person held to service or labor in one State, under the laws thereof, escaping into another, shall, in consequence of any law or regulation therein, be discharged from such service or labor, but shall be delivered up on claim of the party to whom such service or labor may be due.

SECTION 3 (1) New States may be admitted by the Congress into this Union; but no new State shall be formed or erected within the jurisdiction of any other State; nor any State be formed by the junction of two or more States, or parts of States, without the consent of the legislatures of the States concerned as well as of the Congress.

(2) The Congress shall have power to dispose of and make all needful rules and regulations respecting the territory or other property belonging to the United States; and nothing in this Constitution shall be so construed as to prejudice any claims of the United States, or of any particular State.

SECTION 4 The United States shall guarantee to every State in this Union a republican form of government, and shall protect each of them against invasion; and on application of the legislature, or of the executive (when the legislature cannot be convened) against domestic violence.

Article V

The Congress, whenever two thirds of both Houses shall deem it necessary, shall propose amendments to this Constitution, or, on the application of the legislatures of two thirds of the several States, shall call a convention for proposing amendments, which, in either case, shall be valid to all intents and purposes, as part of this Constitution, when ratified by the legislatures of three fourths of the several States, or by conventions in three fourths thereof, as the one or the other mode of ratification may be proposed by the Congress; Provided that no amendment which may be made prior to the year one thousand eight hundred and eight shall in any manner affect the first and fourth clauses in the ninth section of the first article; and that no State, without its consent, shall be deprived of its equal suffrage in the Senate.

Article VI

SECTION 1 All debts contracted and engagements entered into, before the adoption of this Constitution, shall be as valid against the United States under this Constitution, as under the Confederation.

SECTION 2 This Constitution, and the laws of the United States which shall be made in pursuance thereof; and all treaties made, or which shall be made, under the authority of the United States, shall be the supreme law of the land; and the judges in every State shall be bound thereby, anything in the constitution or laws of any State to the contrary notwithstanding.

SECTION 3 The Senators and Representatives before mentioned, and the members of the several State legislatures, and all executive and judicial officers, both of the United States and of the several States, shall be bound by oath or affirmation to support this Constitution; but no religious test shall ever be required as a qualification to any office or public trust under the United States.

Article VII

The ratification of the conventions of nine States, shall be sufficient for the establishment of this Constitution between the States so ratifying the same.

DONE in Convention by the unanimous consent of the States present the seventeenth day of September in the year of our Lord one thousand seven hundred and eighty-seven, and of the independence of the United States of America the twelfth. In witness whereof we have hereunto subscribed our names.

GO. WASHINGTON—
President and Deputy from Virginia

ARTICLES in addition to and AMENDMENTS of the Constitution of the United States of America, proposed by Congress, and ratified by the legislatures of the several States, pursuant to the fifth article of the original Constitution.

Article I*

Congress shall make no law respecting an establishment of religion, or prohibiting the free exercise thereof; or abridging the freedom of speech, or of the press; or the right of the people peaceably to assemble, and to petition the government for a redress of grievances.

Article II

A well regulated militia, being necessary to the security of a free State, the right of the people to keep and bear arms, shall not be infringed.

Article III

No soldier shall, in time of peace be quartered in any house, without the consent of the owner, nor in time of war, but in a manner to be prescribed by law.

Article IV

The right of the people to be secure in their persons, houses, papers, and effects, against unreasonable searches and seizures, shall not be violated, and no warrants shall issue, but upon probable cause, supported by oath or affirmation,and particularly describing the place to be searched, and the persons or things to be seized.

Article V

No person shall be held to answer for a capital, or otherwise infamous crime, unless on a presentment or indictment of a grand jury, except in cases arising in the land or naval forces, or in the militia, when in actual service in time of war or public danger; nor shall any person be subject for the same offense to be twice put in jeopardy of life or limb; nor shall be compelled in any criminal case to be a witness against himself, nor be deprived of life, liberty, or property, without due process of law; nor shall private property be taken for public use, without just compensation.

---

*The first ten Amendments were adopted in 1791.

Article VI

In all criminal prosecutions the accused shall enjoy the right to a speedy and public trial, by an impartial jury of the State and district wherein the crime shall have been committed, which district shall have been previously ascertained by law, and to be informed of the nature and cause of the accusation; to be confronted with the witnesses against him; to have compulsory process for obtaining witnesses in his favor, and to have the assistance of counsel for his defense.

Article VII

In suits at common law, where the value in controversy shall exceed twenty dollars, the right of trial by jury shall be preserved, and no fact tried by a jury shall be otherwise reexamined in any court of the United States, than according to the rules of the common law.

Article VIII

Excessive bail shall not be required, nor excessive fines imposed, nor cruel and unusual punishments inflicted.

Article IX

The enumeration in the Constitution, of certain rights, shall not be construed to deny or disparage others retained by the people.

Article X

The powers not delegated to the United States by the Constitution, nor prohibited by it to the States, are reserved to the States respectively, or to the people.

Article XI*

The judicial power of the United States shall not be construed to extend to any suit in law or equity, commenced or prosecuted against one of the United States by citizens of another State, or by citizens or subjects of any foreign State.

---

*Ratified in 1795; proclaimed in 1798.

Article XII*

The electors shall meet in their respective States and vote by ballot for President and Vice-President, one of whom, at least, shall not be an inhabitant of the same State with themselves; they shall name in their ballots the person voted for as President, and in distinct ballots the person voted for as Vice-President, and they shall make distinct lists of all persons voted for as President, and of all persons voted for as Vice-President, and of the number of votes for each, which lists they shall sign and certify, and transmit sealed to the seat of the government of the United States, directed to the president of the Senate;—The president of the Senate shall, in the presence of the Senate and House of Representatives, open all the certificates and the votes shall then be counted;—The person having the greatest number of votes for President, shall be the President, if such number be a majority of the whole number of electors appointed; and if no person have such majority, then from the persons having the highest numbers not exceeding three on the list of those voted for as President, the House of Representatives shall choose immediately, by ballot, the President. But in choosing the President, the votes shall be taken by States, the representation from each State having one vote; a quorum for this purpose shall consist of a member or members from two thirds of the States, and a majority of all the States shall be necessary to a choice. And if the House of Representatives shall not choose a President whenever the right of choice shall devolve upon them, before the fourth day of March next following, then the Vice-President shall act as President, as in the case of the death or other constitutional disability of the President.—The person having the greatest number of votes as Vice-President, shall be the Vice-President, if such number be a majority of the whole number of electors appointed, and if no person have a majority, then from the two highest numbers on the list, the Senate shall choose the Vice-President; a quorum for the purpose shall consist of two thirds of the whole number of Senators, and a majority of the whole number shall be necessary to a choice. But no person constitutionally ineligible to the office of President shall be eligible to that of Vice-President of the United States.

Article XIII**

SECTION 1 Neither slavery nor involuntary servitude, except as a punishment for crime whereof the party shall have been duly convicted, shall exist within the United States, or any place subject to their jurisdiction.

SECTION 2 Congress shall have power to enforce this article by appropriate legislation.

---

*Adopted in 1804.
**Adopted in 1865.

Article XIV*

SECTION 1   All persons born or naturalized in the United States, and subject to the jurisdiction thereof, are citizens of the United States and of the State wherein they reside. No State shall make or enforce any law which shall abridge the privileges or immunities of citizens of the United States; nor shall any State deprive any person of life, liberty, or property, without due process of law; nor deny any person within its jurisdiction the equal protection of the laws.

SECTION 2   Representatives shall be apportioned among the several States according to their respective numbers, counting the whole number of persons in each State, excluding Indians not taxed. But when the right to vote at any election for the choice of electors for President and Vice President of the United States, Representatives in Congress, the executive and judicial offices of a State, or the members of the legislature thereof, is denied to any of the male inhabitants of such State, being twenty-one years of age, and citizens of the United States, or in any way abridged, except for participation in rebellion, or other crime, the basis of representation therein shall be reduced in the proportion which the number of such male citizens shall bear to the whole number of male citizens twenty-one years of age in such State.

SECTION 3   No person shall be a Senator or Representative in Congress, or elector of President and Vice President, or hold any office, civil or military, under the United States, or under any State, who, having previously taken an oath, as a member of Congress, or as an officer of the United States, or as a member of any State legislature, or as an executive or judicial officer of any State, to support the Constitution of the United States, shall have engaged in insurrection or rebellion against the same, or given aid or comfort to the enemies thereof. But Congress may by a vote of two thirds of each House, remove such disability.

SECTION 4   The validity of the public debt of the United States, authorized by law, including debts incurred for payment of pensions and bounties for services in suppressing insurrection or rebellion, shall not be questioned. But neither the United States nor any State shall assume or pay any debt or obligation incurred in aid of insurrection or rebellion against the United States, or any claim for the loss or emancipation of any slave; but all such debts, obligations and claims shall be held illegal and void.

SECTION 5   The Congress shall have power to enforce, by appropriate legislation, the provision of this article.

---

*Adopted in 1868.

Article XV*

SECTION 1   The right of citizens of the United States to vote shall not be denied or abridged by the United States or by any State on account of race, color, or previous condition of servitude.

SECTION 2   The Congress shall have the power to enforce this article by appropriate legislation.

Article XVI**

The Congress shall have the power to lay and collect taxes on incomes, from whatever sourced derived, without apportionment among the several States, and without regard to any census or enumeration.

Article XVII†

The Senate of the United States shall be composed of two Senators from each State, elected by the people thereof, for six years; and each Senator shall have one vote. The electors in each State shall have the qualifications requisite for electors of the most numerous branch of the State legislatures.

When vacancies happen in the representation of any State in the Senate, the executive authority of such State shall issue writs of election to fill such vacancies: *Provided,* That the legislature of any State may empower the executive thereof to make temporary appointments until the people fill the vacancies by election as the legislature may direct.

This amendment shall not be so construed as to affect the election or term of any Senator chosen before it becomes valid as part of the Constitution.

Article XVIII††

SECTION 1   After one year from the ratification of this article the manufacture, sale, or transportation of intoxicating liquors within, the importation thereof into, or the exportation thereof from the United States and all territory subject to the jurisdiction thereof for beverage purposes is hereby prohibited.

SECTION 2   The Congress and the several States shall have concurrent power to enforce this article by appropriate legislation.

---

*Adopted in 1870.
**Adopted in 1913.
†Adopted in 1913.
††Adopted in 1919. Repealed by the 21st Amendment.

SECTION 3 This article shall be inoperative unless it shall have been ratified as an amendment to the Constitution by the legislatures of the several States, as provided in the Constitution, within seven years from the date of the submission hereof to the States by the Congress.

Article XIX*

The right of citizens of the United States to vote shall not be denied or abridged by the United States or by any State on account of sex.

The Congress shall have power to enforce this article by appropriate legislation.

Article XX†

SECTION 1 The terms of the President and Vice President shall end at noon on the 20th day of January, and the terms of Senators and Representatives at noon on the 3rd day of January, of the years in which such terms would have ended if this article had not been ratified; and the terms of their successors shall then begin.

SECTION 2 The Congress shall assemble at least once in every year, and such meeting shall begin at noon on the 3rd day of January, unless they shall by law appoint a different day.

SECTION 3 If, at the time fixed for the beginning of the term of the President, the President elect shall have died, the Vice President elect shall become President. If a President shall not have been chosen before the time fixed for the beginning of his term, or if the President elect shall have failed to qualify, then the Vice President elect shall act as President until a President shall have qualified; and the Congress may by law provide for the case wherein neither a President elect nor a Vice President elect shall have qualified, declaring who shall then act as President, or the manner in which one who is to act shall be selected, and such person shall act accordingly until a President or Vice President shall have qualified.

SECTION 4 The Congress may by law provide for the case of the death of any of the persons from whom the House of Representatives may choose a President whenever the right of choice shall have devolved upon them, and for the case of the death of any of the persons from whom the Senate may choose a Vice President whenever the right of choice shall have devolved upon them.

---

*Adopted in 1920.
†Adopted in 1933.

SECTION 5   Sections 1 and 2 shall take effect on the 15th day of October following the ratification of this article.

SECTION 6   This article shall be inoperative unless it shall have been ratified as an amendment to the Constitution by the legislatures of three fourths of the several States within seven years from the date of its submission.

Article XXI*

SECTION 1   The Eighteenth Article of Amendment to the Constitution of the United States is hereby repealed.

SECTION 2   The transportation or importation into any State, Territory or Possession of the United States for delivery or use therein of intoxicating liquors in violation of the laws thereof is hereby prohibited.

SECTION 3   This article shall be inoperative unless it shall have been ratified as an amendment to the Constitution by conventions in the several States, as provided in the Constitution, within seven years from the date of submission hereof to the States by the Congress.

Article XXII†

SECTION 1   No person shall be elected to the office of the President more than twice, and no person who has held the office of President, or acted as President, for more than two years of a term to which some other person was elected President shall be elected to the office of the President more than once. But this Article shall not apply to any person holding the office of President when this Article was proposed by the Congress, and shall not prevent any person who may be holding the office of President, or acting as President, during the term within which the Article becomes operative from holding the office of President or acting as President during the remainder of such term.

SECTION 2   This article shall be inoperative unless it shall have been ratified as an amendment to the Constitution by the legislatures of three-fourths of the several States within seven years from the date of its submission to the States by the Congress.

---

*Adopted in 1933.
†Adopted in 1951.

Article XXIII*

SECTION 1   The District constituting the seat of Government of the United States shall appoint in such manner as the Congress may direct:

A number of electors of President and Vice President equal to the whole number of Senators and Representatives in Congress to which the District would be entitled if it were a State, but in no event more than the least populous State; they shall be in addition to those appointed by the States, but they shall be considered, for the purpose of the election of President and Vice President, to be electors appointed by a State; and they shall meet in the District and perform such duties as provided by the twelfth article of amendment.

SECTION 2   The Congress shall have power to enforce this article by appropriate legislation.

Article XXIV**

SECTION 1   The right of citizens of the United States to vote in any primary or other election for President or Vice President, for electors for President or Vice President, or for Senator or Representative in Congress, shall not be denied or abridged by the United States or any State by reason of failure to pay any poll tax or other tax.

SECTION 2   The Congress shall have power to enforce this article by appropriate legislation.

Article XXV†

SECTION 1   In case of the removal of the President from office or his death or resignation, the Vice President shall become President.

SECTION 2   Whenever there is a vacancy in the office of the Vice President, the President shall nominate a Vice President who shall take the Office upon confirmation by a majority vote of both houses of Congress.

SECTION 3   Whenever the President transmits to the President pro tempore of the Senate and the Speaker of the House of Representatives his written declaration that he is unable to discharge the powers and duties of his office, and until he transmits to them a written declaration to the contrary, such powers and duties shall be discharged by the Vice President as Acting President.

---

*Adopted in 1961.
**Adopted in 1964.
†Adopted in 1967.

SECTION 4   Whenever the Vice President and a majority of either the principal officers of the executive departments, or of such other body as Congress may by law provide, transmit to the President pro tempore of the Senate and the Speaker of the House of Representatives their written declaration that the President is unable to discharge the powers and duties of his office, the Vice President shall immediately assume the powers and duties of the office as Acting President.

Thereafter, when the President transmits to the President pro tempore of the Senate and the Speaker of the House of Representatives his written declaration that no inability exists, he shall resume the powers and duties of his office unless the Vice President and a majority of either the principal officers of the executive department, or of such other body as Congress may by law provide, transmit within four days to the President pro tempore of the Senate and the Speaker of the House of Representatives their written declaration that the President is unable to discharge the powers and duties of his office. Thereupon Congress shall decide the issue, assembling within 48 hours for that purpose if not in session. If the Congress, within 21 days after receipt of the latter written declaration, or, if Congress is not in session, within 21 days after Congress is required to assemble, determines by two-thirds vote of both houses that the President is unable to discharge the powers and duties of his office, the Vice President shall continue to discharge the same as Acting President; otherwise, the President shall resume the powers and duties of his office.

Article XXVI*

SECTION 1   The right of citizens of the United States, who are eighteen years of age, or older, to vote shall not be denied or abridged by the United States or by any state on account of age.

SECTION 2   The Congress shall have the power to enforce this article by appropriate legislation.

Article XXVII†

SECTION 1   Equality of rights under the law shall not be denied or abridged by the United States or by any state on account of sex.

SECTION 2   The Congress shall have the power to enforce, by appropriate legislation, the provisions of this article.

SECTION 3   This amendment shall take effect two years after the date of ratification.

---

*Adopted in 1971.
†Proposed to states for ratification March 22, 1972.